W9-BLD-090

Romania &
Moldova

Robert Reid

Leif Pettersen

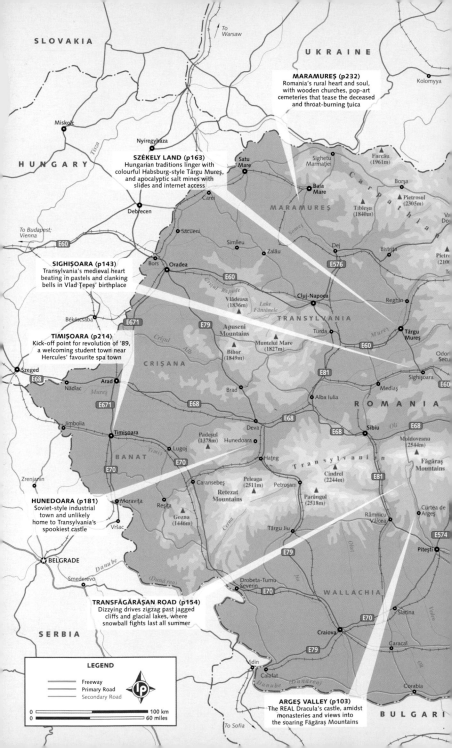

SLOVAKIA

UKRAINE

To Warsaw

MARAMUREŞ (p232)
Romania's rural heart and soul,
with wooden churches, pop-art
cemeteries that tease the deceased
and throat-burning ţuica

Miskolc

Nyíregyháza

Satu Mare

Sighetu
Marmaţiei

Farcău
(1961m)

Borşa

HUNGARY

SZÉKELY LAND (p163)
Hungarian traditions linger with
colourful Habsburg-style Târgu Mureş,
and apocalyptic salt mines with
slides and internet access

Debrecen

Săcueni

Carei

Baia
Mare

MARAMUREŞ

Tibleşu
(1840m)

Pietrosul
(2305m)

To Budapest;
Vienna

E60

Simleu

Zalău

Dej

Bistriţa

Pietro
(210

SIGHIŞOARA (p143)
Transylvania's medieval heart
beating in pastels and clanking
bells in Vlad Ţepeş' birthplace

Bors

Oradea

Vlădeasa
(1836m)

Lake
Fântânele

Cluj-Napoca

Reghin

TRANSYLVANIA

Vă
Do

Békéscsaba

E671

E60

Crişul Repede

Apuseni
Mountains

Muntelui Mare
(1827m)

Turda

Mureş

Târgu
Mureş

TIMIŞOARA (p214)
Kick-off point for revolution of '89,
a welcoming student town near
Hercules' favourite spa town

Szeged

E68

Nădlac

Arad

E671

Crişul
Alb

Mureş

CRIŞANA

Bibor
(1849m)

Brad

E79

E81

Mediaş

Alba Iulia

Sighişoara

Odor
Secu

E60

E68

ROMANIA

Jimbolia

E68

Deva

Sibiu

E68

Moldoveanu
(2544m)

Zrenjanin

BANAT

Timişoara

Lugoj

Padeşul
(1378m)

Hunedoara

Hateg

Transylvanian

Cindrel
(2244m)

E81

Făgăraş
Mountains

HUNEDOARA (p181)
Soviet-style industrial
town and unlikely
home to Transylvania's
spookiest castle

Moraviţa

E70

Caransebeş

Reşiţa

Peleaga
(2511m)

Petroşani

Parângul
(2518m)

Curtea de
Argeş

Vršac

Gozna
(1446m)

Retezat
Mountains

Râmnicu
Vâlcea

E574

BELGRADE

Corna

Târgu Jiu

Piteşti

Smederevo

Danube

(Dunărea)

Drobeta-Turnu
Severin

E79

E70

Olt

WALLACHIA

Slatina

TRANSFĂGĂRĂŞAN ROAD (p154)
Dizzying drives zigzag past jagged
cliffs and glacial lakes, where
snowball fights last all summer

E70

Jiu

Craiova

Caracal

SERBIA

Vidin

E79

Corabia

LEGEND

Freeway
Primary Road
Secondary Road

0   100 km
0   60 miles

Calafat

Danube (Dunărea)

To Sofia

ARGEŞ VALLEY (p103)
The REAL Dracula's castle, amidst
monasteries and views into
the soaring Făgăraş Mountains

BULGARI

Kolomyya

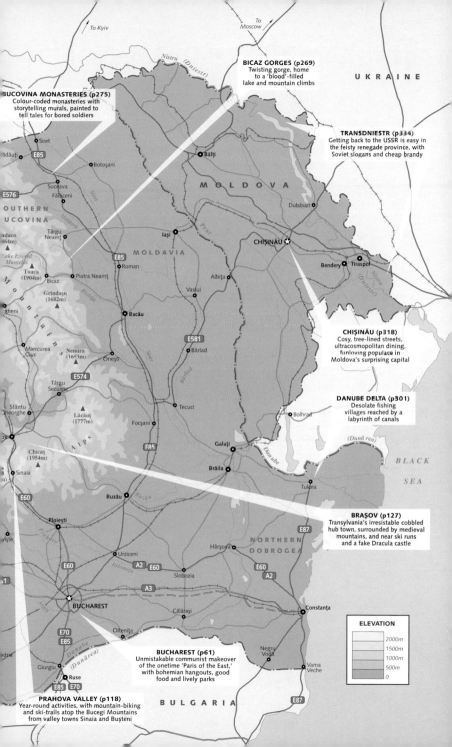

BICAZ GORGES (p269)
Twisting gorge, home to a 'blood'-filled lake and mountain climbs

BUCOVINA MONASTERIES (p275)
Colour-coded monasteries with storytelling murals, painted to tell tales for bored soldiers

TRANSDNIESTR (p334)
Getting back to the USSR is easy in the feisty renegade province, with Soviet slogans and cheap brandy

CHIȘINĂU (p318)
Cosy, tree-lined streets, ultracosmopolitan dining, funloving populace in Moldova's surprising capital

DANUBE DELTA (p301)
Desolate fishing villages reached by a labyrinth of canals

BRAȘOV (p127)
Transylvania's irresistible cobbled hub town, surrounded by medieval mountains, and near ski runs and a fake Dracula castle

BUCHAREST (p61)
Unmistakable communist makeover of the onetime 'Paris of the East,' with bohemian hangouts, good food and lively parks

PRAHOVA VALLEY (p118)
Year-round activities, with mountain-biking and ski-trails atop the Bucegi Mountains from valley towns Sinaia and Bușteni

ELEVATION

2000m
1500m
1000m
500m
0

Destination Romania & Moldova

Travelling in Romania, the EU's newest member, is like being somewhere between an eternal Halloween and the *Led Zeppelin IV* cover that features a twig-carrying farmer. Even in cities where Audis zoom across highways under video-camera speed traps, Romanian life is defined by its sweet country heart. Most anywhere, you'll spot horse-drawn buggies crossing the (often cratered) paved roads – up green mountains, past cone-shaped haystacks and herds of sheep – which bounce along as if the roads themselves are aliens to the land.

And then there's that Dracula thing. Many visitors, lured by bloodcurdling tales, make full trips out of Transylvania's castles and lovely medieval Saxon towns like Sighişoara, where the 'real Dracula' (Vlad Ţepeş) first grew his teeth.

But travellers limiting themselves to chasing vampires will miss so much. The capital, Bucharest, has its critics, but the blend of grotesque communist monuments and purposefully hidden-away cathedrals makes for fascinating exploring. Excellent hiking, biking and skiing are found all over the Transylvanian Alps (aka the Carpathian Mountains), which curl across central Romania. Farmhouse B&Bs allow guests to soak up some village life, particularly in the bucolic paradises of Maramureş and Southern Bucovina, where cemeteries and monasteries are painted as boldly as pop-art paintings.

Romania's neighbour Moldova – a trickier place to visit, but equally as fascinating – is no closer to EU consideration than when the Soviet Union collapsed, largely because it lives on as if this had never happened. Russian is spoken commonly here and its renegade province, Transdniestr, still supports a communist government. Adding a few days in this Cold War timewarp on a trip to Romania's vampire trails and Alp-like ski runs easily makes up one of Europe's most interesting, and least understood, destinations. Go now, before it changes.

CRAIG P

Highlights

Stony figure surveying medieval
Braşov (p127), Transylvania

Step into Sighişoara (p143) – the original home town of
Vlad Ţepeş (aka Dracula), Transylvania

The sun setting over the Bega Canal,
Timişoara (p214), Banat

University student from Chişinău p
a *cobză* (p38)

CRAIG PERSHOUSE

Glass ceiling encasing the Vulturul Negru Complex (p224), Oradea, Crişana

Triumphal Arch (p76) lights up at dusk, Bucharest

RICHARD I'ANSON

Fisherman checking nets at dawn on the Danube Delta (p301), Northern Dobrogea

Chilling out on the Black Sea coast in Constanţa (p287), Northern Dobrogea

Contents

Regional Map Contents

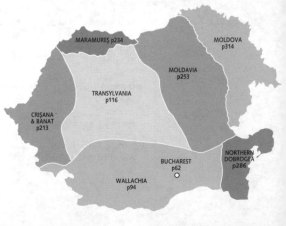

MARAMUREŞ p234

MOLDOVA
p314

MOLDAVIA
p253

CRIŞANA
& BANAT
p213

TRANSYLVANIA
p116

NORTHERN
DOBROGEA
p286

BUCHAREST
p62

WALLACHIA
p94

The Authors

ROBERT REID Coordinating Author, Bucharest & Transylvania

Raised in Oklahoma, Robert skipped *Rambo* films and looked to the Soviet bloc for a source of rebellion and inspiration. After spending a summer studying in Russia and travelling across Eastern Europe, Robert has returned with LP business cards to update Bulgaria for the *Eastern Europe* guide, and then the Russian Far East for *Russia & Belarus* and the *Trans-Siberian Railway*. Romania's mountains, villages, Latin way and friendly locals have always been a European highlight for him. His dream? Driving an East German Trabant from Bulgaria, across Romania's Carpathians into Moldova, maybe up through Minsk en route to the former East Germany. Meanwhile he lives quietly in Brooklyn, New York.

My Favourite Trip

A lot of travellers miss the area entirely, but I found Transylvania's Székely Land (p163), home to many ethnic Hungarians, something like going to Eastern Europe shortly after the area 'opened' to the West. Locals are poised for conversation and seem particularly happy that you've taken the trouble to visit their home. Plus the food's a little better here. In Târgu Mureş (p171) I sat in on a raucous high-school talent show in the Habsburg-era Culture Palace. To the south is Praid (p171), a weird salt mine that feels like a post-apocalyptic world. My favourite, though, is Odorheiu Secuiesc (p169), an almost purely Hungarian town where there's little to get in the way of hanging in bars or cafés and talking with some of Romania's friendliest people.

LONELY PLANET AUTHORS

Why is our travel information the best in the world? It's simple: our authors are independent, dedicated travellers. They don't research using just the internet or phone, and they don't take freebies in exchange for positive coverage. They travel widely, to all the popular spots and off the beaten track. They personally visit thousands of hotels, restaurants, cafés, bars, galleries, palaces, museums and more – and they take pride in getting all the details right, and telling it how it is. For more, see the authors section on www.lonelyplanet.com.

LEIF PETTERSEN   Wallachia, Crişana & Banat, Maramureş, Moldavia, Northern Dobrogea & Moldova

In 2003, Leif Pettersen's 'unhinged contempt for reality' spurred him to abandon an idiot-proof career with the US Federal Reserve and embark on an odyssey of homeless travel writing. Despite no leads or training – and a dubious grasp of grammar – he somehow managed modest success by deluging hapless editors with material so raw and protracted that a trilingual international support group was formed to cope with the situation. Leif's weakness for pretty girls first brought him to Romania in 2004, where the low cost of living compelled him to stay. Speaking the language, having an apartment and owning a 1990 Dacia 1310, it's said Leif needs only to learn *ţuică* distilling to gain honorary Romanian citizenship. You can read more on Leif's travels at www.killingbatteries.com.

My Favourite Trip

Vexingly, there are must-see destinations scattered around Romania and Moldova, but with the great distances and slow transport between them, my favourite trip can only comprise a compact area – until the introduction of rocket buses.

Start in Suceava (p271) and take a guided tour of the wondrous Painted Monasteries (p275). Then head south and spend a few days tramping though the Ceahlău (p267) or Rarău (p280) mountains. Take a swing through the mindbending Bicaz Gorge and the mysterious Lacu Roşu (p269) on your way to Iaşi (p254). After wandering through Iaşi's deluge of attractions, zip over the border to Chişinău (p318) to drink in excellent wine tours (p329) by day and party by night (p327). Break up the carousing by spending a day at the fantastic cave monastery at Orheiul Vechi (p331).

MOLDOVA

Rarău Massif ▲   ○ Suceava   Orheiul ○ Vechi

Ceahlău Massif ▲   ○ Iaşi   ○ CHIŞINĂU

Lacu ○ Roşu   ● Bicaz Gorge

MOLDAVIA

TRANSYLVANIA

Getting Started

Half the fun is planning a trip – and Romania and Moldova offer a range of diverse possibilities. See our suggested itineraries (p17) for more.

Local travel agents offer some excellent trips (or advice) – see p363 for a recommended list.

WHEN TO GO

Its winters are quite cold and summers quite hot, but Romania is a year-round destination. There is much variation in its climate: the average annual temperature in the south is 11°C, 7°C in the north and only 2°C in the mountains. In recent summer months, temperatures have risen to above 40°C in Bucharest and along the Black Sea coast, while winter chills of below -35°C are not unknown in the Braşov depression and around Miercurea Ciuc in Transylvania.

In general, Romania's climate is transitional between temperate regions (the southeast can feel positively Mediterranean) and the more extreme weather characteristics of the continental interior. The average annual rainfall is 675mm; this figure is doubled in the mountains and in the Danube Delta it's often half that.

See Climate Charts (p346) for more information.

Summer (June to August) is an obvious time to visit for beach fun on the coast and for hiking and mountain biking in the Carpathians; all tourist facilities are open then and the weather is usually great, but you will have to share the sites with more tourists. Best times for bird-watching in the Danube Delta are mid-April to mid-May, and in October. Spring in Romania is a pastiche of wildflowers, melting snow and melodious bird song.

At higher elevations, snow lingers as late as mid-May (the Transfăgărăşan road doesn't open until June!) and the hiking season doesn't begin in earnest until mid-June. The best months for skiing are December to March, though the season extends either way some winters.

Moldova is best to visit from spring to autumn, as skiing is almost non-existent and winter sports are not well-developed there. October's Wine Festival is an especially tempting time to visit, though spring and summer are best for city strolling and hiking in remote areas.

COSTS & MONEY

Cheaper than much of Europe, Romania and Moldova have nevertheless graduated from the dirt-cheap-trip category in recent years, with basic, modern hotel rooms edging into the €40-per-night level, and a sit-down meal with a beer, some meat and soup costing between €7 and €10 (and higher in Bucharest or Chişinău). Car-hire rates tend to be high too – up to €40 per day – but bus and train tickets are quite cheap (about €3.50 to €7 per 100km by train).

Those looking to save can relish the abundant fast-food stands selling burgers, kebabs and pizza slices (about €1.50 to €2.50), and the abundance of *cazare* (private rooms) available from entrepreneurs loitering at train stations or the more organised *agroturism* B&B network, which run about €10 to €15 per person, including breakfast. These can provide lunch and dinner upon request.

For a couple wishing to stay in mid-priced hotels, dine out once or twice a day and perhaps hire the occasional guide or go on guided tours, expect to pay €60 to €100 per day total, excluding travel. Backpackers staying in private rooms, eating only one meal in a restaurant and excluding guides or travel expenses can expect to pay more like €20 to €30 per day.

HOW MUCH?

In Romania/Moldova

Bottle of Mufatlar/Cricova table wine €3-5/US$2-4

Museum admission (adult) €0.60-2/US$0.40-1.15

One-hour internet access €0.60-1.50/US$0.50

Phonecards €3/US$2.25-3

Local map €2.50-4/US$1.50

Some remote areas – such as Maramureş, Transylvania's Saxon churches, Moldavia's painted churches, much of Moldova – are far easier to see with a guide or a hired car. Those wanting to go on long-term hikes should consider going with a guide too; see p48.

TRAVEL LITERATURE

Much of the travel literature about Romania deals with historical or topical social issues. Olivia Manning's *Balkan Trilogy* (1987, reprinted 1998) is a colourful portrait of Bucharest at the outbreak of WWII that has long been considered the classic work on Romania. Serialised on British TV as *The Fortunes of War*, it has reached a large audience with its details about life in the capital in the late 1930s.

Norman Manea's *The Hooligan's Return: A Memoir* (2003) details this accomplished author's return to his homeland in the late 1990s, unleashing not only a search for identity and a flood of memories (of having lived in a Transdniestrian transit camp), but also many memorable observations on contemporary life in Romania.

More of a history book, Lucian Boia's interesting *Romania* (2001), published in the UK, is the rare Romanian-written overview, with a rather philosophical perspective on its complex history. Boia, now living in France, nobly tries to show all sides to continually debated questions like nationalism, Romania's Slavic/Roman background – while adding an unexpected Bucharest 'walking tour'.

Dominique Fernandez' political *Romanian Rhapsody: An Overlooked Corner of Europe* (2000) is a good bet. This French author made four trips through Romania and Moldova and nicely interweaves history, culture and art with everyday people's stories, and in the process shakes up some distorted notions the West has of Romania and Eastern Europe in general.

Isabel Fonseca's *Bury Me Standing – the Gypsies and their Journey* (1996) offers one of the best insights into the Roma and their culture that you can find. The author spent several months travelling with the Roma in Eastern

---

DON'T LEAVE HOME WITHOUT...

'Western-style' shops sell just about anything you need, but it can be more expensive than back home. Camping supplies aren't always readily available but outdoors equipment shops generally have pretty good stock on offer. Remember these few things:

- Extra tissues or toilet paper
- First-aid kit
- Swiss army knife
- Three-prong European adaptor
- Torch (flashlight)
- Universal sink plug
- Sun block lotion
- Insect repellent
- Ear plugs
- Extra video tapes or memory cards
- Contact lens solution
- Souvenir flag pins or postcards of your home country (to give as gifts!)
- Checking the latest visa regulations (p354) – especially for Moldova

Europe between 1991 and 1995. The chapter covering Romania looks at racial attacks against Roma in Transylvania.

Bruce Benderson's unusual *The Romanian: Story of an Obsession* is an account of nine months spent in the hay with a Romanian hustler who maintains his heterosexuality – Benderson weirdly compares his exploits with kings, writers and artists from Romania's past.

One of the more intriguing titles is Alan Ogden's 2000 book *Romania Revisited: On the Trail of English Travellers 1602-1941*. The author travelled the country in 1998, following in the footsteps of historical travellers, from the first motorists to romantics like Leigh Fermor. Dacian, Byzantine and Saxon Romania are beautifully evoked in this gripping series of tales. Ogden's *Winds of Sorrow: Travels in and Around Transylvania* is an ensemble of essays written following travels there between 1998 and 2002.

Compare Transylvania today with its 1930s state in Patrick Leigh Fermor's classic *Between the Woods and the Water*, based on the author's shoestring romp across Europe on foot.

Princes Among Men: Journeys with Gypsy Musicians describes Garth Cartwright's fascinating, if on occasion annoying, travels with Roma musicians across the Balkans.

Highly recommended is Stephen Henighan's *Lost Province: Adventures in a Moldovan Family* (2003). One of the best travelogues about Moldova, it follows a Canadian's experiences teaching English in this forgotten country and is humorous and touching while bringing up astute, even disturbing points about Soviet cultural colonisation and the inter-ethnic tension he finds there.

There are very few English-language accounts of travelling through Moldova, but Tony Hawks' *Playing the Moldovans at Tennis* provides a witty but respectful travelogue account of the author's exploits pursuing members of the Moldovan football team for a game of tennis – all to win a bet.

INTERNET RESOURCES

Lonely Planet (www.lonelyplanet.com) Go to Thorn Tree to talk with travellers in or just back from Romania. Lots of news items and features too.

Moldovan Ministry of Tourism (www.turism.md) This state site is extremely helpful with news bulletins, the latest visa regulations, festival information and travel advice.

Nine O'Clock News (www.nineoclock.com) Website of English-language paper in Bucharest.

Romania National Tourism Office (www.romaniatourism.com) In lieu of tourist information centres in much of Romania, there's at least this: a detailed site listing special events and overviews of regions.

Romania.org (www.romania.org) Includes many links to sites on Romania.

Rural Tourism (www.ruralturism.ro) Lists rural B&Bs across Romania; also see p343 for more sites dedicated to accommodation.

Sapte Seri (www.sapteseri.ro) Lists up-to-date restaurants, clubs, events (films, concerts) around Romania.

TOP TENS

Top Festivals

Festivals dot Romania all year long (less so in Moldova), running the gamut from film festivals, and DJ contests to shepherd shindigs welcoming the sheep home. Here are our favourites:

- Rooster Shooting, April, Apata (p136)
- Snow Festival, April, Păltiniş (p162)
- Juni Pageant, May, Braşov (p132)
- Sibiu Jazz Festival, May, Sibiu (p159)
- Transylvania International Film Festival, June, Cluj-Napoca (p191)
- Hora de la Prislop, August, Maramureş (p239)
- Mountain Festival, August, Fundata (p141)
- Wine Festival, October, Chişinău (p318)
- National Theatre Festival, December, Bucharest (p80)
- Winter Festival, December, Maramureş (p136)

Top Communist Sites

No, really. Some of Romania's communist achievements may be grisly or ugly or just dreadful seas of concrete, but at least a couple are pretty awe-inspiring. Either way, these 10 sites are such that when you see one it's impossible not to look.

- Palace of Parliament & B-dul Unirii, Bucharest (p68)
- Transfăgărăşan road (p154)
- Soviet tanks, living-and-breathing communism in Tiraspol, Transdniestr (p337)
- National Archaeology and History Museum, Chişinău, Moldova (p323)
- Iron Gates hydroelectric power station (p110)
- Gherla Prison (p199)
- Danube Canal (p301)
- Former Communist party Black Sea resorts, Neptun-Olimp (p297)
- Blackened factory shells at Copşa Mică (p151)
- Ceauşescu's apartment, Villa International, Timişoara (p218)

Top Movies

Both local and international films are finding Romania the perfect back-drop. Here are 10 to whet the appetite: the first two are Romanian stand-outs, the rest are foreign films shot on location in Romania and one is a wacky movie about a guy who hates mirrors:

- *Filantropica* (Nae Caranfil, 2005)
- *The Death of Mr Lazarescu* (Cristi Pulu, 2005)
- *Cold Mountain* (Anthony Minghella, 2003)
- *Vlad* (Michael Sellers, 2004)
- *Elvira's Haunted Hills* (Sam Irvin, 2002)
- *Pulse* (Jim Sonzero, 2006)
- *Beowulf* (Graham Baker, 1999)
- *Wild Dogs* (Thom Fitzgerald, 2003)
- *Bloodrayne* (Uwe Boll, 2006)
- *Bram Stoker's Dracula* (Francis Ford Coppola, 1992)

Itineraries

CLASSIC ROUTE

CASTLES, MOUNTAINS & FANGS   10 Days / Bucharest to Sibiu

The classic route for travellers wanting a taste of Transylvania starts outside it at **Bucharest** (p61), where most flights come in. With only 10 days, don't linger. Hire a car from the Bucharest airport (p87) or hop in a train north toward the hills, stopping in **Sinaia** (p118) for a couple nights and checking out Peleş Castle. From there, cable-car up into the **Bucegi Mountains** (p122) for hiking or biking. Drive or bus north for a couple nights in **Braşov** (p127), a surprisingly unjaded hub with a cobbled centre. Take day trips to the infamous 'Dracula Castle' at **Bran** (p138) and the better one at **Râşnov** (p137), with the options of skiing and hiking at **Poiana Braşov** (p136).

If you have a car, spend a night in the timeless Saxon town **Viscri** (p151), before continuing on for a night in **Sighişoara** (p143), where the cute citadel offers B&Bs, espresso and Dracula's birthplace. Head southwest for a night or two in **Sibiu** (p153), Transylvania's most culturally rich town.

If you have a car (and it's summer), drive south along the winding, stunning **Transfăgărașan road** (p154) that tackles the biggest of the Carpathians. South of the pass, stop in the 'real Dracula castle' at Poienari outside **Curtea de Argeş** (p103) before returning to Bucharest.

This 800km route takes in the 'big three' of Transylvania's Saxon country: Braşov, Sighişoara and Sibiu. On the way are many opportunities to poke into rural life, and up into the mighty Carpathian mountains. Those with a couple extra days should consider spending some time in underrated (and over-criticised) Bucharest.

ROADS LESS TRAVELLED

DRACULA? SCHMACULA!   21-28 Days / Bucharest to Timişoara

This whirlwind month-long trip around Romania and Moldova skips the heart of Transylvania. Start with a couple days in **Bucharest** (p61), before heading east to hit the beach at **Mamaia** (p294) and visit the **Eforie Nord** mud baths (p295). Go north to **Tulcea** (p303), the springboard for bird-rich boat trips through the **Danube Delta** (p301).

Bus or drive north to **Iaşi** (p254), a youthful gateway to Moldova, where you spend three or four days in the more Soviet, but surprisingly modern **Chişinău** (p318), with winner day trips to the **Orheiul Vechi Monastery** (p331) and the **Cojuşna Winery** (p330).

Return to Iaşi then head northwest to **Suceava** (p271) for a couple of days' touring the nearby cartoon-esque, colour-coded **Bucovina Monasteries** (p275). Cross into Transylvania's Hungarian-rich Székely Land via the stunning **Bicaz Gorges** (p269), taking in a hike if time allows. Stop in at Székely Land's biggest town, Habsburg-influenced **Târgu Mureş** (p171), then head to **Cluj-Napoca** (p184), home to a lively student base, clubs, quirky museums and a Hungarian/Romanian population. Head west for hiking and caving in the **Apuseni Mountains** (p43); otherwise head southwest to another great under-appreciated city, **Timişoara**, (p214), home to the 1989 revolution and now a popular alternative air hub for Romania.

No castles, no fangs, no blood-red steaks served with a wink. This roughly 2000km trip ventures through some of the region's most diverse and stunning territory. Those going by train and maxitaxi may need to allow more time for transfers. Those saving time with a car could add a few days in Maramureş (p232).

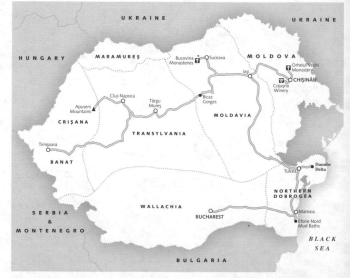

TAILORED TRIPS

THE COUNTRY LIFE

'Peasant' isn't a bad word but a proud one in these parts, and no visitor really can get a sense of Romania or Moldova without spending some time in the sticks – where family-run *pensiunes* (pensions) open their doors as one-stop, kick-back bases. In Transylvania, and within half an hour of Brasov, you can wake to the sound of chickens in **Râşnov** (p137); a bit more rugged is **Vama Buzăului** (p143), in the lesser-visited mountains northeast.

Down from the Bârgău Valley, home to Dracula in Bram Stoker's novel, is remote **Lunca Ilvei** (p211), with horse-riding options.

Outside Sibiu, just a couple kilometres off the highway, are traditional villages that feel worlds away, such as **Sibiel** (p163), with its glass-icon museum and its hillbound paths. For more Hungarian flavour, get to villages outside Cluj-Napoca, including **Rimitea** (p196), and **Sâncraiu** (p197) or **Gârda de Sus** (p198), both on the foothills to the Apuseni Mountains.

The king of rural life is Maramureş, where you can stay in thatched-hut villages. Good options abound in the Izei Valley, such as **Botiza** (p245) or **Săpânţa** (p243), home to a 'merry cemetery' of Pop Art–styled headstones.

In Moldavia, a good base to see the cartoon-like murals of the Bucovina Monasteries is the High Hostel outside **Suceava** (p273). In Moldova, you can hire an island for US$12 near a cliffside monastery at **Orheiul Vechi** (p331).

TAKE THE KIDS ALONG

So much of Romania evokes past worlds and eerie myths that it's sure to capture the imagination of any child – or adult. The Dracula thing may be overblown, but the castles are not. Tourists squeeze through the narrow passageways of the so-called 'Dracula castle' – 15th-century **Bran Castle** (p159) – but **Poienari** (p105) is home to the 'real' Dracula's castle and Hunedoara's **Corvin Castle** (p181) looks more the part, with a drawbridge and walkways over deep dungeon-like corridors.

The country route can offer horse-cart rides, walks to meet shepherds' herds of sheep in the hills, or tours of local craftsfolk at work. You can sleep in a fun, drawer-style 'Saxon bed' in traditional homes in **Viscri** (p151).

Underground worlds beg for kids, particularly the **Apuseni Mountain caves** (p197) and the swing sets and sculptures in the bizarre **Praid salt mine** (p171).

For all its noise, **Bucharest** (p80) teems with child-friendly fun, like The Dracula Show and puppet theatre.

Half a million birds, including pelicans, flap some wing in the **Danube Delta** (p301), which can only be seen by ferry or hiring a fisher's boat. Just south of the beach resorts are Eforie Nord's **mud baths** (p296), where you can encourage kids to get slimy. If that's not enough mud, Moldavia is home to **muddy volcanoes** (p283) that burp and gurgle out all shades of brown. Cool.

Snapshot

The biggest thing on the minds of Romanians is the EU and whether the last-minute granting of membership in 2006 can propel one of Eastern Europe's slowest-to-start economies. Even before the official word came in, the EU optimistically appointed Sibiu, along with Luxembourg, as European City of Culture for 2007. For much of the midpart of this decade, the EU pressed Romania to address a number of concerns – pollution, corruption, poor conditions for orphans, destitute farmers – that threatened to delay membership indefinitely.

In 2004, Romania voted against a former communist as president for the first time since 1989 and elected ex-Mayor of Bucharest Traian Basescu. While many here were worried about changes the EU may bring (such as disallowing the free-range roaming of sheep or cow herds, and unpasteurised cheese stalls on roadside stands), Romania seems ready for a change. One local said, 'We deserve a better future…we deserve a better present!'

Many Romanian youth can't wait for change though and record numbers are leaving for summer or long-term jobs in the USA, Greece, Italy, Spain or the UK. The latter sees over 75,000 Romanians come annually and has increased civil services in anticipation of many coming after EU membership. The numbers of Romanians in Spain are even higher. Unfortunately many Romanians leave to pursue false dreams and become ensnared in the tragic world of human trafficking. Lured by 'paying jobs' as wait-staff and the like, thousands of boys, girls and young women are sold for as little as €3000 into forced prostitution in Western Europe, the Middle East and North America. The numbers are even worse in Moldova. Both countries have increased investigations and Romania convicted over 200 traffickers in 2005.

In recent years, Romania has made international headlines, when the Danube rose to its highest level in over a century and birds found with the Avian flu led to a short-lived panic (but no human cases). It's also increasingly been used by international filmmakers as a cheap place to shoot big-budget films such as *Cold Mountain* and more, ahem, lowbrow efforts such as *The Seed of Chucky*. Sacha Baron Cohen filmed the 'Kazakh village' scenes from *Borat: Cultural Learnings of America for Make Benefit Glorious Nation of Kazakhstan* in Romania, with villagers unapologetically speaking Romanian – close enough to Kazakh for the film apparently.

In 2005 Romania passed a property restitution law allowing former owners of communist-held property – often buildings in town centres – to reclaim their buildings. Most famously, Bran Castle returned to Habsburg hands in 2006. A fund of US$4 billion was set up for property owners not able to recover former property.

In Moldova, EU integration remains a far-off dream. Currently there are too many problems to be resolved, especially Moldova's unsettled internal integration, namely with the breakaway region of Transdniestr, which erupted onto worldwide newspapers following a bomb explosion on a bus in summer 2006. The contentious possibility of Moldova becoming a federation of several autonomous regions has not been completely abandoned. Until these issues are cleared up, it will be hard to deal with other major issues of a backwards economy: lack of foreign investment, corruption and unemployment, to name just a few.

QUICK FACTS

Romania/Moldova

Population (millions): 22.3/4.5

Area (sq km): 238,391/33,700

GDP growth (2005): 4.5%/7.1%

Inflation rate (2005): 9%/11.9%

Official unemployment rate: 5.9%/8%

Average monthly salary: €320/80

Life expectancy (male-female): 68-75/62-70

Number of people bitten by stray dogs in Bucharest (2005): 15,000

Percentage of working-age Moldovans living abroad: 25%

Price of nice house in wine-rich Prahova Valley: €70,000

History

The name 'Romania' didn't refer to Wallachia or Moldavia until 1859, and Transylvania remained part of the Astro-Hungarian empire until 1918 – even 'Dracula' was actually a Magyar – so what is 'Romania'? It's a fair question, and one that frequently yields long, philosophical answers when travelling around the country – often without much of a clear answer at the end of it. Romania is a product of many incarnations – sometimes tied with Slavic neighbours, Greece, Turkey, Saxon Germany, the USSR or Hungary. But more often Romanians link their past with the Dacians or (more fashionably, at times) with the century the Romans hung out in the area. As one local said, 'We're a mix of both. The Romans mingled with Dacians – they didn't kill them all off, because the Dacian women were too beautiful.' Understanding the past is the best way to get a grip on this fascinatingly complex country.

The name 'Romania' supposedly comes from Romanus (Latin for 'Roman') but others argue it's also from *rumân* (dependent peasant).

ANTIQUITY

Ancient Romania was inhabited by Thracian tribes. The Greeks called them the Getae, the Romans called them Dacians, but they were actually a single Geto-Dacian people. Their principal religion was the cult of Zalmoxis; when people died, they went to him. The Geto-Dacians communicated with their god through meditation, ritual sacrifice and shunning bodily desires.

From the 7th century BC the Greeks established trading colonies along the Black Sea at Callatis (Mangalia, p298), Tomis (Constanța, p287) and Histria (p300). In the 1st century BC, a strong Dacian state was established by King Burebista to counter the Roman threat. The last Dacian king, Decebal (r AD 87–106), consolidated this state but was unable to stave off attacks led by the Roman emperor Trajan in 101–2. Further attacks ensued in 105–6, leading to the Roman victory at the Dacian capital of Sarmizegetusa and the final Roman conquest of the region. Dacia thus became a province of the Roman Empire.

The Romans recorded their expansion north of the Danube (most of present Romania, including the Transylvanian plateau, came under their rule) on two famous monuments: Trajan's Column in Rome, and the 'Tropaeum Trajani' at Adamclisi, on the site of their victory in Dobrogea. The slave-owning Romans brought with them a superior civilisation and mixed with the conquered tribes to form a Daco-Roman people speaking Latin.

Burebista ignited tension with Rome by meddling with internal rivalry between Pompey and Julius Caesar, who died the same year as Burebista (48 BC) – both by assassination.

Faced with Goth attacks in AD 271, Emperor Aurelian (r 270–75) decided to withdraw the Roman legions south of the Danube, meaning that Rome governed the region for under 175 years. Romanised peasants remained in Dacia and mixed with the locals; hence the Roman heritage of contemporary Romanians.

THE MIDDLE AGES

Waves of migrating peoples, including the Goths, Huns, Avars, Slavs, Bulgars and Magyars (Hungarians), swept across this territory from the 4th to the 10th centuries, each leaving their mark on the local culture, language and gene pool. Romanians survived in village communities and gradually assimilated the Slavs and other peoples who settled there. By the 10th century a fragmented feudal system ruled by a military class appeared.

From the 10th century the Magyars expanded into Transylvania, north and west of the Carpathian Mountains, and by the 13th century all of Transylvania was an autonomous principality under the Hungarian crown.

Following devastating Tartar raids on Transylvania in 1241 and 1242, King Bela IV of Hungary persuaded German Saxons to settle in Transylvania with free land and tax incentives. He wanted to defend the crown's southeastern flank. He also granted the Székelys (p163) – a Hungarian ethnic group who had earlier migrated to the region with the Magyars – autonomy in return for their military support.

In the 14th century, Prince Basarab I (r 1310–52) united various political formations in the region south of the Carpathians to create the first Romanian principality – Wallachia, dubbed Ţara Românească (Romanian Land). Its indigenous peasantry became known as Vlachs.

Peasants dominated the populations of these medieval principalities. In Wallachia and Moldavia peasants were subjugated as serfs to the landed aristocracy *(boyars)*, a hereditary class. There were some free, land-owning peasants *(moşneni)* too. The two principalities were ruled by a prince who was also the military leader. Most noblemen were Hungarian; the peasants were Romanians. After a 1437 peasant uprising in Transylvania, Magyar nobles formed a political alliance with the Székely and Saxon leaders. This Union of the Three Nations became the constitutional basis for government in Transylvania in the 16th century.

> Let the debates begin: when the Magyars expanded into Transylvania in the 10th century, it's argued (by Hungarians) that the Daco-Romanians were gone, having migrated south of the Danube; while some (ie the Romanians) say that Daco-Romanians never left the area.

OTTOMAN EXPANSION

Throughout the 14th and 15th centuries Wallachia and Moldavia offered strong resistance to the Ottoman's northward expansion. Mircea cel Bătrân (Mircea the Old; r 1386–1418), Vlad Ţepeş ('The Impaler'; r 1448, 1456–62, 1476), and Ştefan cel Mare (Stephen the Great; r 1457–1504) were legendary figures in this struggle.

When the Turks conquered Hungary in the 16th century, Transylvania became a vassal of the Ottoman Empire, retaining its autonomy by paying tribute to the sultan. Catholicism and Protestantism were recognised as official state religions; the Orthodox faith of many Romanians remained an unofficial religion. Later, attempts were made to force them to convert to Catholicism.

After the Ottoman victory in Transylvania, Wallachia and Moldavia also paid tribute to the Turks but maintained their autonomy (this indirect control explains why the only Ottoman buildings seen in Romania today are in Northern Dobrogea).

In 1600 Wallachia and Moldavia were briefly united with Transylvania under Mihai Viteazul (Michael the Brave; r 1593–1601) at Alba Iulia. In order to fight Ottoman rule, he joined forces in 1594 with the ruling princes of Moldavia and Transylvania against the Turks, attacking strongholds and massacring Turks. In 1595 the Turks called a truce with Viteazul.

The Transylvanian prince, Andrew Báthory, subsequently turned against the Wallachian prince and, on 28 October 1599, Mihai Viteazul defeated and killed Báthory's troops near Sibiu. Viteazul declared himself the new prince of Transylvania, then in spring 1600 invaded Moldavia, where he

> For a Hungarian perspective on Transylvanian history, check http://members.fortunecity.com/magyarhun/magyar/id3.html.

The Magyars settle in the Carpathian Basin; a century later Stephen I, their king, integrates Transylvania into his Hungarian kingdom.

The Mongols invade Transylvania and go on a year-long rampage, plundering the region and slaying much of the local populace.

THE DRACULA MYTH

Fifteenth-century Wallachian prince Vlad Ţepeş is all too often credited with being Dracula, the vampire-count featured in the classic Gothic horror story *Dracula* (1897) written by Anglo-Irish novelist Bram Stoker.

The madcap association of these two diabolical figures – one historical, the other fictitious – is nothing more than a product of the popular imagination. But while Romanians increasingly reap the tourist reward of this confusion, many are concerned that the identity of a significant figure in their history has been overshadowed by that of an immortal literary vampire.

The 'real' Dracula, Vlad Ţepeş, a Wallachian born in 1431 in Sighişoara (p143), ruled Wallachia in 1448, 1456–1462 and 1476. He was outrageously bloodthirsty and killed heaps of people but he did not eat people or drink blood. His princely father, Vlad III, was called Vlad Dracul (from the Latin 'draco', meaning 'dragon') after the chivalric Order of the Dragon accredited to him by Sigismund of Luxembourg in 1431. The Romanian name Drăculea – literally 'son of Dracul' – was bestowed on Vlad Ţepeş by his father, and was used as a term of honour. Another meaning of 'draco', however, was 'devil' and this was the meaning that Stoker's novel popularised.

Little Vlad had an unhappy childhood. He spent many of his youthful years in a Turkish prison, where he was allegedly raped by members of the Turkish court.

While Vlad Ţepeş was undoubtedly a strong ruler and is seen by some Romanians as a national hero and brave defender of his principality, his practices were ruthless and cruel. Notorious for his brutal punishment methods, ranging from decapitation to boiling and burying alive, he gained the name 'Ţepeş' ('impaler') after his favourite form of punishing his enemies. A wooden stake was carefully driven through the victim's anus, to emerge from the body just below the shoulder in such a way as to not pierce any vital organs. This ensured at least 48 hours of unimaginable suffering before death. Ţepeş had a habit of eating a full meal (rare, one presumes) while outside watching his Turkish and Greek prisoners writhing on stakes in front of him.

Vlad was truly a man of his time; this torture was not unusual in medieval Europe. Ţepeş' first cousin, Ştefan cel Mare, is said to have 'impaled by the navel, diagonally, one on top of each other' 2300 Turkish prisoners in 1473. That Vlad was likely raped repeatedly as a boy and teen in his captive years in a Turkish prison adds another dimension to his favoured method of torture.

Bram Stoker's literary Dracula, by contrast, was a bloodsucking vampire – an undead corpse reliant on the blood of the living to sustain his own immortality. And also a Magyar. Until 1824 in Stoker's adopted England a wooden stake was commonly driven through the heart of suicide victims to ensure the ill-fated corpse did not turn into a vampire in its grave. In Romania, vampires form an integral part of traditional folklore. The seventh-born child is particularly susceptible to this evil affliction, identifiable by a hoof as a foot or a tail at the end of its spine.

Stoker set *Dracula* in Transylvania, a region the novelist never set foot in. The novel, originally set in Austria, was first entitled *The Undead*. But following critics' comments that it was too close to a pastiche of Sheridan le Fanu's *Camilla* (1820) – a vampire novel set in southern France – Stoker switched titles and geographical settings. Count Dracula's fictitious castle on the Borga Pass was inspired by Cruden Bay castle in Aberdeenshire, where Stoker drafted much of the novel. The historical facts were uncovered at the British Museum in London.

While Vlad Ţepeş died in 1476, and Stoker in 1912, Count Dracula lives on, sustaining an extraordinary subculture of fiction and film. The novel itself has never been out of print (it was first translated into Romanian in 1990), while film-makers have remade the film countless times, kicking off with FW Murnau's silent *Nosferatu* (1922) and multiplying it into dozens of spin-offs. Tom Cruise, for example, would never have added fangs to his repertoire if it weren't for Stoker's original hero, who started a lineage leading to Anne Rice's Lestat.

Dracula fan clubs have been set up around the globe, many of whom meet up with fellow fans at the annual Dracula World Congress. Closer to 'home', the Transylvanian Dracula Society continues the tradition and offers Dracula-themed tours (p200).

1431	1437
Vlad Ţepeş (Vlad the Impaler) is born. He grows the handlebar moustache much later.	The Union of the Three Nations is formed in Transylvania.

was also crowned prince. This first political union of the three Romanian principalities lasted for slightly more than a year: Viteazul was defeated by a joint Habsburg-Transylvanian noble army just months later and in August 1601 he was captured and beheaded.

In 1683 the Turks were defeated at the gates of Vienna and in 1687 Transylvania came under Habsburg rule.

The 18th century marked the start of Transylvanian Romanians' fight for political emancipation. Romanian peasants constituted 60% of the population, yet continued to be excluded from political life. In 1784 three serfs called Horea, Cloşca and Crişan led a major uprising. It was quashed, and its leaders were crushed to death on what is today a favoured tourist site (p176). But on 22 August 1785 the Habsburg emperor, Joseph II, abolished serfdom in Transylvania.

The 17th century in Wallachia was marked by the lengthy reign of Constantin Brâncoveanu (r 1688-1714), a period of relative peace and prosperity characterised by a great cultural and artistic renaissance. In 1775 part of Moldavia's northern territory – Bucovina – was annexed by Austria-Hungary. This was followed in 1812 by the loss of its eastern territory – Bessarabia (most of which is in present-day Moldova) – to Russia. After the Russo-Turkish War of 1828-9, Wallachia and Moldavia became Russian protectorates while remaining in the Ottoman Empire.

ONE STATE

In Transylvania the revolutionary spirit that gripped much of Europe in the years leading up to 1848 was entangled with the Hungarian revolution, which in Transylvania was led by Hungarian poet Sándor Petőfi. Hungarian revolutionaries sought an end to Habsburg domination of Hungary. Concurrently, Romanian revolutionaries demanded their political emancipation, equality and the abolition of serfdom.

The Austrian authorities struck a deal with Transylvania's Romanians, promising them national recognition in return for joining forces with them against the Hungarian revolutionaries in Transylvania. Thus Transylvanian Romanians fought against and enacted revenge upon Transylvanian Hungarians for what was seen as centuries of mistreatment. Russian intervention finally quashed the Hungarian revolutionaries, ending a revolution that had shocked all sides by its escalation to civil war.

In its aftermath, the region fell under direct rule of Austria-Hungary from Budapest. Ruthless 'Magyarisation' followed: Hungarian was established as the official language and any Romanians who dared oppose the regime – such as the Memorandumists of 1892, a group of intellectual and political figures who voiced their opposition to Austro-Hungarian rule in a memorandum – were severely punished.

By contrast Wallachia and Moldavia prospered. In 1859, with French support, Alexandru Ioan Cuza was elected to the thrones of Moldavia and Wallachia, creating a national state known as the United Romanian Principalities on 11 December 1861. This was renamed Romania in 1862.

The reform-minded Cuza was forced to abdicate in 1866 by mutinous army officers, and his place was taken by the Prussian prince Carol I. With Russian assistance, Romania declared independence from the Ottoman Empire in 1877. After the 1877–8 War of Independence, Dobrogea became

Romanians are proud, proud, proud that the Turks never completely conquered their land, but – in quiet tones – some admit that Bucharest wasn't on the way between Constantinople and the Ottomans' main goal, Vienna.

1453	1467
The fall of Constantinople. The Ottomans block trade on the Black Sea and Romania's isolation deepens.	Stephen the Great defeats the Hungarian army at Baia; it is Hungary's last attempt to conquer Moldova.

THE WARRIOR QUEEN

'There is only one man in Romania and that is the queen.' That is how a French diplomat described Queen Marie of Romania whose diplomatic experience at the Paris Peace Conference in 1919 bolstered Romania's flagging image abroad, raised its political profile and assured her legendary status.

Queen Marie (1875–1938), the granddaughter of Britain's Queen Victoria, married Ferdinand I (1865–1927), heir to the Romanian throne, in 1892 when she was 17. Despite widespread horror in Britain at her mismatch to a prince of a 'semibarbaric' country, Marie developed a strong kinship with Romania, declaring, 'My love for my country Romania is my religion'.

Following an alleged love affair with American aristocrat Waldorf Astor, she knuckled down to twisting her tongue around the Romanian language and acquainting herself with Romanian politics.

During the second Balkan War (1913) the princess ran a cholera hospital for Romanian soldiers on the Bulgarian side of the Danube. In 1914 Ferdinand I was crowned king and Marie became queen.

Despite proving herself to be a 'viable political force', Queen Marie remained the 'people's princess' throughout her reign. She dressed in peasant attire – an eyebrow-raising gesture for royalty. At the outbreak of WWI she wrote her first book, *My Country*, to raise funds for the British Red Cross in Romania.

Prior to her evacuation to Iaşi in 1916, she worked in hospitals in Bucharest, distributing food and cigarettes to wounded soldiers. In Iaşi she set about reorganising the appallingly makeshift hospitals.

After she represented Romania at the peace conference in Paris, the French press dubbed her the 'business queen'. A mother of six, she wrote over 100 diaries from 1914 until her death in 1938. During her lifetime 15 of her books were published. Her autobiography, *The Story of My Life*, appeared in two volumes in 1934–5.

Queen Marie is buried in Curtea de Argeş (p103). Her heart, originally encased in a gold casket and buried in Balcic (in today's Bulgaria) is safeguarded in Bucharest's National History Museum.

part of Romania. Under the consequent Treaty of San Stefano and the Congress of Berlin in 1878, Romanian independence was recognised. In 1881 it was declared a kingdom and on 22 May 1881 Carol I was crowned the first king of Romania.

WWI & GREATER ROMANIA

Through shrewd political manoeuvring, Romania greatly benefited from WWI. Despite Romania having formed a secret alliance with Austria-Hungary in 1883, it began WWI with neutrality. In 1916, the government under Ion Brătianu declared war on Austria-Hungary. Its objective was to seize Transylvania from Austria-Hungary.

The defeat of Austria-Hungary in 1918 paved the way for the formation of modern Romania. Bessarabia, the area east of the Prut River which had been part of Moldavia until 1812 when it was taken by the Russians, was joined to Romania. Likewise, Bucovina, which had been in Austro-Hungarian hands since 1775, was also reunited with Romania. Part of the Austrian-Hungarian Banat, which had been incorporated in Romania, was also handed over. Furthermore, Transylvania was finally united with Romania. Hence, at the end

1600	1812
Wallachia, Transylvania and Moldavia are united for 15 months under Mihai Viteazul.	Treaty of Bucharest grants Russia control of eastern Moldavia and the Ottoman Empire gains control of western Moldavia.

of WWI, Romania – now known as Greater Romania – more than doubled its territory (from 120,000 to 295,000 sq km) and its population (from 7.5 to 16 million). The acquisition of this new territory was ratified by the Triple Entente powers in 1920 under the Treaty of Trianon.

WWII

In the years leading up to WWII, Romania, under the able guidance of foreign minister Nicolae Titulescu, sought security in an alliance with France and Britain, and joined Yugoslavia and Czechoslovakia in the Little Entente. Romania also signed a Balkan Pact with Yugoslavia, Turkey and Greece, and later established diplomatic relations with the USSR. These efforts were weakened by the Western powers' appeasement of Hitler and by Romania's own King Carol II.

See p352 for a rundown on all those blokes on Romanian lei notes.

Carol II succeeded his father Ferdinand I to the throne. Extreme right-wing parties opposed to a democratic regime emerged, notably the anti-Semitic League of the National Christian Defence, which consequently gave birth to the Legion of the Archangel Michael in 1927. This notorious breakaway faction, better known as the fascist Iron Guard, was led by Corneliu Codreanu and by 1935 dominated the political scene.

Finding himself unable to manipulate the political parties, Carol II declared a royal dictatorship in February 1938. All political parties were dissolved and laws were passed to halve the size of the electorate. Between 1939 and 1940 alone, Romania had no less than nine different governments.

In 1939 Carol II clamped down on the anti-Semitic Iron Guard, which until 1937 he had supported. Codreanu and 13 other legionaries were arrested, sentenced to 10 years' imprisonment, and then assassinated. In revenge for their leader's death, Iron Guard members murdered Carol II's prime minister, Armand Călinescu, leading to the butchering of 252 Iron Guard members by Carol II's forces. In accordance with the king's wishes, the corpses were strung up in public squares. Only with the collapse of the Axis powers at the end of WWII did the Iron Guard disintegrate (in 1999, Codreanu's nephew Nicador Zelea Codreanu tried unsuccessfully to revive the reviled group).

Fifty years after his death, Carol II's remains were transferred back to Romania from Portugal, where he died. He was interred in Curtea de Argeş.

Romania was isolated after the fall of France in May 1940, and in June 1940 Greater Romania collapsed in accordance with the Molotov-Ribbentrop Pact. The USSR re-occupied Bessarabia. On 30 August 1940 Romania was forced to cede northern Transylvania to Hungary by order of Nazi Germany and fascist Italy. In September 1940, Southern Dobrogea was given to Bulgaria.

Not surprisingly, the loss of territories sparked widespread popular demonstrations. Even Carol II realised he could not quash the increasing mass hysteria and on the advice of one of his councillors, the king called in General Marshall Ion Antonescu. To defend the interests of the ruling classes, Antonescu forced King Carol II to abdicate in favour of the king's 19-year-old son Michael. Antonescu then imposed a fascist dictatorship, with himself as *conducător* (supreme leader).

German troops were allowed to enter Romania in October 1940, and in June 1941 Antonescu joined Hitler's anti-Soviet war. One of Antonescu's aims in joining forces with Hitler was to recover Bessarabia and this was achieved in August 1941. The results of this Romanian-Nazi alliance were gruesome, with over 200,000 Romanian Jews – mainly from newly regained Bessarabia – and 40,000 Roma deported to transit camps in Transdniestr and murdered

1819 – 34	1864
Wallachia and Moldavia were occupied by Russia. Between 1835 and 1856, the two principalities were Russian protectorates.	Romanian Jews forbidden to practice law.

in Auschwitz. After the war, Antonescu was turned over to the Soviet authorities who condemned him to death in a show trial. Bessarabia fell back into Soviet hands.

As the war went badly and the Soviet army approached Romania's borders, a rare national consensus was achieved. On 23 August 1944 an opportunistic Romania suddenly changed sides again, capturing the 53,159 German soldiers who were stationed in Romania at the time, and declared war on Nazi Germany. By this dramatic act, Romania salvaged its independence and shortened the war. By 25 October the Romanian and Soviet armies had driven the Hungarian and German forces from Transylvania, replacing the valued territory back under Romanian control. The costs, however, were appalling: 500,000 Romanian soldiers died fighting for the Axis powers, and another 170,000 died after Romania joined the Allies.

Radu Ioanid's *The Holocaust in Romania* (2000) chronicles how Romania used other brutal methods aside from organised murder to try and rid itself of Roma and Jews during WWII.

THE COMMUNIST ERA

Of all the countries that burst forward into the mass-industrialised, communist experiment in the 20th century, Romania and Russia were the most ill-prepared, both being overwhelmingly rural, agricultural countries. Prior to 1945, Romania's Communist Party had no more than 1000 members. Its postwar ascendancy, which saw membership soar to 710,000 by 1947, was a consequence of backing from Moscow. The Soviet-engineered return of Transylvania greatly enhanced the prestige of the left-wing parties, which won the parliamentary elections in November 1946. A year later Prime Minister Petru Groza forced King Michael to abdicate (allegedly by holding the queen mother at gunpoint), the monarchy was abolished, and a Romanian People's Republic proclaimed.

A period of terror ensued in which all the prewar leaders, prominent intellectuals and suspected dissidents were imprisoned or interned in hard-labour camps. The most notorious prisons were in Pitești, Gherla, Sighetu Marmației and Aiud. Factories and businesses were nationalised, and in 1953 a new Slavicised orthography was introduced to obliterate all Latin roots of the Romanian language, while street and town names were changed to honour Soviet figures. Brașov was renamed Orașul Stalin.

Romania's loyalty to Moscow continued only until the late 1950s. Soviet troops were withdrawn from Romania in 1958, and street and town names were changed once more to emphasise the country's Roman heritage. After 1960 Romania adopted an independent foreign policy under two 'national' communist leaders, Gheorghe Gheorghiu-Dej (leader from 1952 to 1965) and his protégé Nicolae Ceaușescu (from 1965 to 1989), both of whom had been imprisoned during WWII. Under these figures the concept of a great Romanian socialist state was flaunted.

Romania never broke completely with the USSR, but Ceaușescu refused to assist the Soviets in their 1968 'intervention' in Czechoslovakia. His public condemnation of it earned him praise and economic aid from the West. In 1975 Romania was granted 'most favoured nation' status by the USA, which yielded more than US$1 billion in US-backed credits in the decade that followed. And when Romania condemned the Soviet invasion in Afghanistan and participated in the 1984 Los Angeles Olympic Games despite a Soviet-bloc boycott, Ceaușescu was officially decorated by Great Britain's Queen Elizabeth II.

On Clowns (1993) is a cutting rant on Romanian dictatorship by Norman Manea, who was deported to a Transdniestr concentration camp when he was five years old.

1881	1897
Carol I is crowned the first king of Romania.	Vlad Țepeș is reborn when Bram Stoker's *Dracula* is published.

Meanwhile, Romanians suffered painfully during the 25-year dictatorship of Nicolae Ceauşescu and his family. Thousands were imprisoned or repressed by the much-feared secret police (Securitate), huge amounts of money were squandered on megalomaniacal, grandiose projects and the population lived in abject poverty.

Of course Moldova's communist era continues.

See p16 for a list of communist-related sights.

Stanciu Stroia's *My Second University: Memories from Romanian Communist Prisons* (2005) retells the days a doctor spent behind bars.

THE 1989 REVOLUTION

In late 1989, as the world watched the collapse of one communist regime after another, it seemed only a matter of time before Romania's turn would come. The Romanian revolution was carried out with Latin passion and intensity. Of all the Soviet Bloc countries, only Romania's government transfer ended with a dead leader.

The spark that ignited Romania came on 15 December 1989, when Father László Tökés publicly condemned the dictator from his Hungarian church in Timişoara, prompting the Reformed Church of Romania to remove him from his post. Police attempts to arrest demonstrating parishioners failed and within days the unrest had spread across the city, leading to some 115 deaths. Ceauşescu proclaimed martial law in Timiş County and dispatched trainloads of troops to crush the rebellion. The turning point came on 19 December, when the army in Timişoara went over to the side of the demonstrators.

On 21 December in Bucharest, an address made by Ceauşescu during a mass rally was interrupted by anti-Ceauşescu demonstrators in the 100,000-strong crowd who booed the dictator and shouted 'murderer', 'Timişoara' and other provocations. The demonstrators retreated to the wide boulevard between Piaţa Universităţii and Piaţa Romană – only to be brutally crushed a couple of hours later by police gunfire and armoured cars. Drenched by ice-cold water from fire hoses, the demonstrators refused to submit and instead began erecting barricades, under the eyes of Western journalists in the adjacent Hotel Inter-Continental. At 11pm the police began their assault on Piaţa Universităţii, using a tank to smash through the barricades. By dawn the square had been cleared of the debris and the bodies of those killed removed from the site. Estimates vary, but at least 1033 were killed.

Conspiracy? Not a few people wonder if the communist bystanders turned 'National Salvation Front (NSF)' who jolted to power following Ceauşescu's fall had actually engineered the revolution – ie that it was more in fact a 'coup d'état'. Only in 2004 did Romania have a president other than a former communist.

The following morning thousands more demonstrators took to the streets, and a state of emergency was announced. At noon Ceauşescu reappeared on the balcony of the Central Committee building to try to speak again, only to be forced to flee by helicopter from the roof of the building. Ceauşescu and his wife, Elena, were arrested in Târgovişte, taken to a military base and, on 25 December, condemned by an anonymous court and executed by a firing squad. Footage of the Ceauşescu family's luxury apartments broadcast on TV showed pure gold food scales in the kitchen and rows of diamond-studded shoes in Elena's bedroom.

While these events had all the earmarks of a people's revolution, many scholars have advanced the notion that they were just as much the result of a coup d'état as well: the Communist Party, tired of having to bow down to Ceauşescu as royalty, had been planning an overthrow for months before the events of December 1989.

1945	1976
Following secret talks between Stalin, Churchill and Roosevelt, Romania falls under the Soviet 'sphere of influence'.	Nadia Comaneci scores a perfect 10 at the Montreal Summer Olympics.

THE DICTATOR'S BRIGHT IDEAS

In the 1980s, in his attempts to eliminate foreign debt and look good in front of the world, Nicolae Ceauşescu exported Romania's food while his own people were forced to ration even staple goods (meat was all but unattainable by the mid-1980s) and instituted power cuts to save money. His opponents were at best harassed, at worst killed by experimental methods of torture. One such method, known as *radu*, was used by Ceauşescu on his political opponents, especially Hungarian nationalists, whom he despised. It consisted of bombarding the body with low-level radiation and allowing cancer to settle. Many of those he had arrested eventually died of strange forms of cancer.

In March 1987, Ceauşescu embarked on a rural urbanisation program that would see the total destruction of 8000 villages (mainly in Transylvania) and the resettlement of their (mainly Hungarian) inhabitants. After having bulldozed a neighbourhood in Bucharest to build his Palace of the People (p68), no one doubted he'd proceed with his plans. Several dozen villages were razed, but thankfully the project went uncompleted. However, one result was stray dogs – the number now hovers at 200,000 by some estimates – most of whom are ancestors of guard dogs that couldn't make the move into compact apartments.

Part of Ceauşescu's Securitate were child spies, forced into ratting on friends and family. It's estimated as many as 15% of the Securitate were children.

ATTEMPTS AT DEMOCRACY

The National Salvation Front (FSN) took immediate control of the country. In May 1990, it won the country's first democratic elections since 1946, placing Ion Iliescu, a Communist Party member since the age of 14, at the helm as president. Protests ensued, but Iliescu graciously sent in 20,000 coal miners to violently quash them. Iliescu was nonetheless re-elected in 1992 as the head of a coalition government under the banner of the Party of Social Democracy. New name, same policies. Market reforms remained nowhere in sight. In 1993 subsidies on food, transportation and energy were scrapped, prompting prices to fly sky-high and employment to plummet to an all-time low. Iliescu, meanwhile, personally benefited from shady dealmaking, including a pyramid scheme that rocked Cluj-Napoca in the early 1990s.

Iliescu was finally ousted in the 1996 presidential elections by an even more embittered, impoverished and desperate populace who ushered in Emil Constantinescu, leader of the right-of-centre election alliance Democratic Convention of Romania (CDR), as president.

Constantinescu's reform-minded government made entry into NATO and the European Union (EU) its top priorities, together with fast-paced structural economic reform, the fight against corruption and improved relations with Romania's neighbours, especially Hungary.

Scandal and corruption surrounded the November 2000 electoral race. In May of that year, the National Fund for Investment (NFI) collapsed. Thousands of investors – mainly pensioners who'd deposited their life savings into the government fund – took to the streets to demand their cash back (US$47.4 million, long squandered by the NFI). Police used tear gas to dispel rioters in Bucharest.

After Constantinescu refused to run in the 2000 'Mafia-style' elections, Iliescu retook the helm as the country's president and his Social Democrat Party (PSD) formed a minority government, with Adrian Nastase as prime

Lucian Boia's *Romania* (2001) is a rare overview of Romania written by a local; the philosophical, even playful (it includes a walking tour of Bucharest) overview covers various viewpoints of sometimes debated truths behind the origin of Romania.

For an in-depth look at Romania since communism, check out Tom Gallagher's *Modern Romania* (2005).

1989	1991
Nicolae Ceauşescu and money-squandering wife Elena are found guilty of genocide by a makeshift tribunal and executed.	Moldova declares its full independence, establishing the Dniestr Moldovan Republic.

minister. The 2004 elections were marred by accusations of electoral fraud, and there were two rounds of voting before Traian Băsescu was announced the winner, with 51% of the votes. The PNL (National Liberal Party) leader, Călin Popescu Tăriceanu, became prime minister and swore in a new coalition that excluded the PSD.

Romania's 1991 constitution provides for a parliamentary system of government. Its two-chamber parliament – comprising the Chamber of Deputies (lower house) and Senate (upper house) – is elected every four years. The next general elections are scheduled for 2009.

The government's main goal, aside from their many domestic issues, was integration with international bodies, most notably the EU. In 2002, Romania was invited to join NATO. During the American war against Iraq in 2003, Romania was one of the first countries to guarantee access to airfields and allowed Americans to set up military bases on their soil. In 2006 it was reported that Romania allegedly provided the CIA with a secret detention centre for suspected terrorists – one of a few scattered 'Guatanamos' of Eastern Europe. Exact locations have been kept quiet, but some reports say that the US has used the Mihail-Kogalniceanu military airport on the Black Sea coast.

Romania (and Bulgaria) finally received approval for EU membership in 2007 just a few months before the year began. Romania's record of organised crime, corruption and food safety had delayed the membership previously, and the EU noted that progress checks would continue following membership. The EU has been a big supporter of Romania's EU cause, with Brussels granting billions of euro to infrastructure, business development, environmental protection and social services. Yet by mid 2006, only 10% to 20% of the aid in some cases had been used due to various bureaucratic hurdles.

> Only half of Romanians have access to running water, and slightly fewer than half of Romania's roads are paved.

MOLDOVA SINCE 2000

For details on Moldova's earlier history, see p315.

Visitors are surprised to hear that there is a communist government in power in Moldova – after all the tiny country has suffered through after declaring independence from the USSR. Vladimir Voronin is president of the republic, and also the president of the parliamentary Communist Party. He has strong Russian sympathies and has taken steps to dissociate Moldova from its Romanian roots, focusing instead on the separateness of the Moldovan identity and language, but ones fashioned very much under its Soviet and Russian history of dominance. In his inaugural address in April 2001, he described Moldova as a European Cuba which needed to guard itself against 'imperialist predators' in Europe, just as Cuba had against the USA. The president is elected by parliamentary assembly. The current prime minister is Vasile Tarlev.

These officials have become highly unpopular. In 2002 several thousands took to the streets in Chişinău to protest a government plan to force school children to learn Russian. The government backed down but refused to step down, as the crowds were demanding. In November 2003, up to 50,000 took to the capital's streets in a peaceful protest demanding the government's resignation; they were incensed that Russian troops remain on Moldovan soil (in the breakaway region of Transdniestr) and about a Russian plan to change Moldova to a federation, giving self-rule to Transdniestr. Placards read: Down with Communists! and We Want to Join NATO!

> Moldova ranks second in the world for the percentage of its population living under the official poverty line: 80% (2002).

1992	1997
Civil war breaks out between Moldovan authorities and the region of Transdniestr.	The number of stray dogs (PC term 'community dogs') in Bucharest reaches between 150,000 and 200,000.

In 2003, Russian troops started to honour their years-old agreement of pulling out of Transdniestr; by the end of the year, they had removed some 20,000 tons of weapons, ammunition and equipment – about half of all that had remained on the territory since the communist era.

Run by former Red Army guards, with all its Soviet statues standing, a communist government firmly in place, and the reputation for corruption and illegal arms trade, Transdniestr has a hard sell to make its case for independence to be recognised internationally. Presently it's not, other than in Russia. In 2005, Ukraine closed its border to Transdniestr imports unless Moldovan customs had been processed. Transdniestr returned the favour by closing all train routes in/out of the country, meaning certain routes from Mo ldova east were no longer running.

The government under Voronin has been both trying to buddy up to the EU and international bodies (they joined the WTO in 2001), signing a Partnership and Cooperation Agreement with the EU in 1999. But it's made no clear advances towards EU membership this decade.

Nicholas Dima's *Moldova and the Transdneistr Republic* (2001) offers the most complete analysis of Moldova's odd political positioning, and explores Russia's interest in the area.

2004	2007
Romania joins NATO.	Lonely Planet releases its 4th edition of *Romania & Moldova*, and Romania joins EU (listed in order of achievement).

The Culture

THE NATIONAL PSYCHE

No one can settle on what it means to be 'Romanian', but the perceived Latin link – from the lone century Romans lived here 2000 years ago – seems to affect daily life to a degree (notably the Latin roots of the Romanian language). Although Romanians can be formal in business and when meeting strangers, couples of all ages are more openly affectionate than you see in some of Romania's neighbouring countries. If you say you like local delicacies like *mămăligă* (cornmeal) or are just enjoying someone's village, it's taken as a personal compliment – sometimes returned with a warm, deeply felt 'thank you'.

The struggling economy and hopes of a rejuvenating EU membership dominate the feeling of the day. Some older workers in bureaucratic jobs hold onto a 'can't do' style linked with socialism; a thoughtful 45-year-old train worker told us without bitterness that Romania has 'no hope', and dreamed his son could get a job out of the country. Many younger Romanians hightail it to summer (or lifelong) jobs abroad – in Spain, Italy, Greece, the UK or the USA – thus creating a 'brain drain'. A 25-year-old hotel clerk/clarinettist lamented, 'I get paid US$100 a month. I can never have a family at this salary. I'd rather clean toilets in America.' But those who return see new options. Returning to Braşov from a year in Switzerland, a 25-year-old entrepreneur said, 'I wish I had been born 10 years earlier so I could have capitalised on things sooner!'

Romanians are hypersensitive of the reputation the country has abroad, with reports of corruption, rip-off taxi drivers, human trafficking, street crime, stray dogs, pollution, poverty and terrible roads. No doubt they were not happy with the 2006 *South Park* spoof where Colorado rallied against Romanians bureaucrats, shown in black-and-grey Bucharest and speaking with Russian accents, who rallied to keep orphans in Romania. The animated Colorado signs read: 'Romania sucks'.

Pro-Romanian nationalism has reared its ugly head in some places, with right-wing groups such as Nouă Dreapta (New Right) organising anti-gay banners during GayFest in Bucharest, Pro-TV talk shows discussing anti-Semitic views, groups denying the Holocaust, anti-Roma chants and banners enveloping crowds at Steaua football games, and frequent commentary complaining about the Hungarians, the nation's second largest ethnic minority.

Through it all, however, Romanians remain open and friendly to visitors. Even if you haven't had a few rounds of *ţuică* (plum brandy), friendliness abounds, like the old lady in a Saxon town who came up to us with the gift of an apple from her garden: 'It's so hot today. Wouldn't you like an apple?'

Moldovans, though they are ethnically related to Romanians, have less of the reserve, shyness or formality of their cousins, thanks to generations of Slavic influence under Soviet and Russian rule. Highly approachable people, they will happily enter into conversation, extend genuine offers of help and show unbounded curiosity about you. Moldovans like to mix being productive with having a good time and will easily find time to spend with newfound friends. With a keen intelligence leaning towards the philosophical, they have no illusions about where their country stands in relation to the world but aren't self-pitying about it. The Russian language is alive and well in Moldova, whereas in Romania it's a rare occasion to find someone speaking the *russki*.

Donald Leroy Dyer has written seminal books about Moldovan culture and language issues. Try *Studies in Moldovan* (1996) and *The Romanian Dialect of Moldova* (1999).

LIFESTYLE

Romania and Moldova are jigsaws of economics and attitude as much as of ethnicity. This has given rise to tension between minority groups, but most people today are united in their struggle to make a decent living. While pensioners are often the ones to have had the hardest time adapting to recent social changes, the younger generation is full of beans. In the cities, a sizable chunk of it drives fast cars and sports mobile phones; another chunk is driven by the dream of doing the same. Still others have embarked on a more difficult route: questioning where their country is headed and defining values and priorities. Sometimes it's easier to just head off into the mountains where no social issue matters much!

In 2006 the travel sector gave Romania 485,000 jobs, nearly 6% of total employment.

During the 1990s, Romania stumbled through ineffectual economic reforms and it has only recently found its footing and a sense of direction. This has led to a feeling of optimism, but the country is left with a host of lingering social issues to contend with. The problem of its high number of orphanages was complicated by a ban on foreign adoptions in 2001 in an effort to stem a system of auctioning babies to the highest bidder and to comply with EU directives. Only in the last days of 2001 did Romania finally repeal the criminalisation of homosexuality, becoming one of the last European countries to do so, and any women's or feminist movement is barely nascent.

Moldova remains off the EU radar, while Romania seems to be holding out for positive changes the EU membership may bring. But as one Romanian told us, 'The EU won't be the saviour some hope for and it won't be the end-all others fear.'

Romania hopes to be the 'next India' in terms of IT. Software developers earn about US$6000 annually (about double the average income) and number 45,000, with 8000 graduates entering the field annually.

POPULATION

Along with Russia, Romania was the most rural country of the former Soviet Bloc to enter the communist experiment of mass urbanisation. Modernisation, industrialisation and Ceauşescu's attempts to urbanise and centralise Romania saw the urban population rise from 23.4% in 1948 to 53% today – still low by European standards. Moldova's figure of 46% makes it the second-least urbanised country in Europe (Liechtenstein gets gold in that one). Romania's overall population is decreasing by 0.12% a year, while Moldova's is increasing at a snail-paced 0.2%.

Romanians make up 89.5% of their population of 22.3 million; Hungarians are the next largest ethnic group (6.6%), followed by Roma (2.5%), Ukrainians and Germans (each 0.3%). Russians and Turks each take up but 0.2%. Germans and Hungarians live almost exclusively in Transylvania, while

---

LOVE OUR TOILETS!

Toilets created a bit of a stir in EU-hopeful Romania in 2005, when WaterAid's World Toilet Day exposed Romania as lacking adequate sanitation on their Bogroll of Dishonour list, revealing that at least 10 million people were without hygienic lavatories.

It's a serious issue: a couple of million people die from diarrhoea annually, often due to unhygienic bathrooms. The problem is more serious for locals in rural areas than for foreigner visitors and the conditions in most restaurants and hotels are improving and toilet paper availability is on the upswing.

Some visitors, however, do grumble over some toilets – we heard of the Duke of Luxembourg getting uppity over a pit toilet in a Saxon village in 2006 (royal bowel movements require certain standards apparently – go take a dump back in Lux, pal).

One hilarious Romanian blog we stumbled upon had a fiery debate over the issue, with one local poster lashing out that Romanians need to stick up for the 'home-team' toilets. 'Tinkle with pride' would make a great bumper sticker.

IN EMINESCU WE TRUST

Set up to save much of Romania's traditional heritage from the merciless Ceauşescu bulldozers during communism, the Mihai Eminescu Trust (MET; www.mihaieminescutrust.org) has continued working to preserve Romanian heritage. In recent years, Prince Charles has got in on the act as a patron of the cause, making several trips around Saxon villages outside Sighişoara and in Maramureş.

Highlight achievements include the churches in Biertan (p149) and traditional homes providing accommodation in Viscri (p151).

Ukrainians and Russians live mainly near the Danube Delta, and Turks are found along the Black Sea coast.

Moldovans comprise but 76% of their population of 4.5 million, followed by Ukrainians (8.4%), Russians (6%), Gagauz (4.4%) and Bulgarians (2%).

MULTICULTURALISM
Germans

The German population in Romania peaked in the 1930s when there were 800,000 Saxons in Transylvania. Numbers have dwindled to no more than 65,000 today. During WWII, 175,000 Romanian Germans were killed or left the country. After Romania switched sides to join the Allies against Hitler's Nazi Germany, 70,000 Germans were accused of Nazi collaboration and sentenced to five years' hard labour. Survivors returned to find their land and property confiscated by the newly installed communist regime.

Under Ceauşescu, Germans, like all other inhabitants, were not allowed to freely leave Romania. Instead Ceauşescu charged West Germany about US$8000 for each exit permit it issued. In the 1980s, some 70,000 exit permits were 'bought'. Unsurprisingly, between 1989 and 1995 an estimated 100,000 Germans left the country. Today's remaining Saxon community in Transylvania is served by state-run German schools and represented politically by the German Democratic Forum (Demokratisches Forum der Deutschen).

Roma

Official statistics estimate the number of Roma, Romania's third-largest ethnic group, at only 550,000 within Romania. However, according to a 2004 European Commission report, the Budapest-based European Roma Rights Centre (http://errc.org) and the community itself, the number is somewhere between 1.8 and 3 million, making it the largest such community in the world. The remaining nomadic Roma number anywhere from 2500 to 10,000. They are split between 40 different clans comprising 21 castes, each of which has its own traditional costume, superstitions and taboos.

The Mongols and Tartars brought the first enslaved Roma (ţigan in Romanian) to Romania in 1242. Nomadic Roma (corturari) from India settled in Romania from the 15th century onwards. Around 50% of the world's Roma population was wiped out by the Holocaust.

Marxist theories in Romania and across Eastern Europe led to forced assimilation policies that forbade nomadism, set up 'Roma' communities and denied the existence of the group. Since the fall of communism, the Roma have fallen harder into extreme poverty than any other group in the country (something like four in five are 'impoverished', earning something like US$2.15 per day). Those who were uprooted and relocated into 'gypsy districts' (particularly in Bucharest) have fared the worst. In 2005, the US State Department's Human Rights report on Romania noted dozens of forced evictions of Roma (including 250 in Zalaǔǎ and 140 in Miercurea Ciuc, and relocations from historic neighbourhoods in Bucharest). Public racism is on the rise – including anti-Roma banners at football matches – and there have been reports of police harassment of NGOs working to help the Roma. Divisional politicians badmouth the Roma to win local elections. Roma children attend school less regularly than Romanians; many of those who do go find some schools segregating classes.

During the 2002 census, however, the Roma found themselves highly sought after, as Romanians, Hungarians and Roma organisations courted them to declare themselves as part of their respective ethnic group (the census oddly didn't allow double ethnicity).

Though the legal wedding age in Romania is 16, many Roma marry earlier. Romanian authorities intervened when a 15-year-old groom and his (allegedly) 12-year-old bride (the daughter of a self-proclaimed 'gypsy king') were wed in Sibiu, stating the couple would have to live apart.

In 2005, the World Bank initiated the EU-funded Decade of Roma Inclusion, a ten-year plan across Eastern Europe aimed to aid education, housing and health for the Roma.

Not all Roma are hurting. Some 'Gypsy palaces' (rather garish, Disney-esque homes) have been built by more affluent figures.

Politically, Roma are represented by several groups, including the Roma Party (Partida Romilor), which is guaranteed a seat in Romania's national legislature (Romania is the only Eastern European country to provide this).

Hungarians

Under Ceauşescu, all Hungarian-language newspapers and magazines in Romania were closed down, and very few Hungarian schools and cultural centres existed. Since 1989, however, the rights of Romania's 1.5 million Hungarians have been recognised. They are represented politically in parliament and have their own publications, schools and cultural centres.

Though relations have calmed between Romanians and Hungarians (and their respective countries), there is still a palpable level of distrust and tension, fuelled by historical injustices on both sides. Despite attempts to assimilate the Hungarians into local culture, they have retained a distinct identity; in Székely Land, it sometimes feels as if the population has no idea they're actually living in Romania!

Moldova

In 1992 tension between the Ukrainian- and Russian-dominated Transdniestr region and the rest of Moldova sparked a brutal civil war. The great disagreement between the Moldovan government and the Transdniestrian

Because public discrimination, racism and violence have erupted since 1989 across Eastern Europe, many Roma actually lament the days of communism. In her insightful book on the Roma population in Eastern Europe, *Bury Me Standing* (1995), Isabel Fonseca wrote that some Roma here actually mourned Ceauşescu, whom some call 'Papa.'

LAND OF CONFUSION

- **Bucharest/Budapest?** Famously during Michael Jackson's visit to Bucharest, he called out that he was 'happy to be in Budapest' – a common slip, white glove or no.

- **Compass Points of Confusion?** Northern Dobrogea is a region in extreme southeastern Romania and 'Southern Bucovina' is in northeastern Romania.

- **Moldova/Moldavia?** Moldova is the neighbouring republic in the former USSR; Moldavia comprises the eastern region of Romania.

- **Roma-nia?** Romania is not named for the Roma; recently officials controversially changed the spelling to Rroma to stress the distinction.

- **Roman-ia?** Many westward-thinking leaders have stressed the link with Rome, but the truth is that Romans spent more time in present-day England than here.

administration erupted again on the streets of Tiraspol in 2006, with Transdniestr closing off all train service to/from its region. Despite this, very little inter-ethnic tension is felt between Moldovans and any of their minority groups.

WOMEN IN ROMANIA & MOLDOVA

Romania is still a 'man's country', as writer Lucian Boia states. This was typified by the Romanian head delegate to the world's women's congress in recent years: a man. Memory of Romania's Queen Marie, the leader once called 'the only man in Romania' due to her selfless acts during WWI, has faded considerably.

Despite some laws of equality between men and women, some things remain off-balance in both Romania and Moldova. Domestic violence is a problem and 'spousal abuse' is not necessarily covered by any laws. In 2002, the UN estimated that nearly half of Romanian women had been verbally abused and 7% sexually abused, yet only 380 convictions were recorded.

> 'Romania is still a 'man's country', as writer Lucian Boia states.'

Rapes are hard to convict in Romania because a witness and medical certificate are required. In neither Romania nor Moldova is spousal rape a crime. Several dozen NGOs have set up rape crisis centres in Romania and aim to educate the public about sexual harassment. Most public awareness about domestic violence is handled by NGOs in Moldova too.

The fight against human trafficking – particularly of females– remains a work in progress and is a big problem in both countries. In July 2005, the Romanian government increased the penalty, though prison sentences remain a light five to 15 years' imprisonment. In Moldova sentences range from 10 years to life imprisonment. A 2005 study found that the majority of women sold into forced marriages or prostitution, following false ads for employment abroad, were recommended by someone they knew. Police corruption at borders, particularly in Transdniestr and Moldova, adds to the problem.

MEDIA

After an initial explosion in print media after the fall of communism, the situation has stabilised in Romania, despite reports of journalist harassment and a continued tendency towards sensationalism in its news reporting. Among today's most influential papers are *Evenimentual zilei* (www.expres .ro), *Adevarul* (www.adevarulonline.ro), *Ziua* (www.ziua.ro) and *Cronica Româna* (www.cronicaromana.ro).

Moldova maintains a troubled relationship between the media and the government. Most papers are under some form of state control, and restriction of journalists' access to information runs high – harassment is common. The Chişinău-based Independent Journalism Centre (http://ijc.md) monitors the situation. The government suspended the popular Romanian TV1 channel (replacing it with a Ukrainian station).

Useful media sources in English include the following:

www.azi.md English-language site devoted to Moldovan news.

www.jurnalul.ro Romanian-language paper *Jurnalul Naţional* has English version online.

www.mediafax.ro English-language site with Romanian news.

www.nineoclock.ro English-language Bucharest-based paper.

RELIGION

The majority of Romania's population (87%) is Eastern Orthodox Christian. The rest is split between Protestant (7.5%), Catholic (4.7%) and Muslim (0.4%), plus there are some 39,000 Jehovah's Witnesses and 14,000 Jews.

In Moldova, 98% of the population is Eastern Orthodox, 1.5% are Jewish, and there are some 18,000 Jehovah's Witnesses.

SPIES ARE US

In 2006, former BBC reporter Carol Sebastian admitted to working as informant (ie 'spy') for the Securitate under Ceauşescu's rule, but claimed he was blackmailed by the government. Carol apparently reported on the doings of a writer (who was a friend), who later forgave him.

SPORT

Football has a huge following in both Romania and Moldova. Romania's national team impressed in the World Cups throughout the 1990s, when their biggest star was Gheorghe Hagi. Two popular teams are Dinamo (www .fcdinamo.ro) and Steaua Bucureşti (www.steauafc.com), the latter forging a formidable international reputation by winning the European Champions' Cup in 1986. Steaua Bucharesti's home ground is **Ghencea Stadium** (aka Steaua Stadium; ☎ 21-410 7710; B-dul Ghencea 35). Tickets are sold at the stadium gates.

One of the most famous Romanians is Oneşti-born gymnast Nadia Comaneci. In 1976, at the age of 15, she stunned the world by receiving the first perfect 10 in Olympic history (plus five medals) for her feats on the compulsory bars at the Montreal Olympics. She later caused a stir by moving to Oklahoma, USA, where she lives with her husband, US gymnast Bart Conner, and their baby.

Moldova is still reeling with joy from a silver medal in the 500m doubles canoe race at the 2000 Sydney Olympics. See p316 for an amusing account of Moldova's infamous underwater hockey team.

Number of medals Romania has won in all the Summer Olympics: 283 (world ranking: 15th).

Number of medals Romania has won in all the Winter Olympics: one bronze (world ranking: tied with Latvia for last place).

ARTS

In 15th-century medieval society, when writings were still scripted in Slavonic, an oral epic folk literature called *miorița* emerged. Writings in Romanian, initially religious, took shape around 1420. Modern literature emerged in the mid-19th century with two great figures: Mihai Eminescu and Ion Luca Caragiale, two writers who couldn't have been less alike. A member of the influential Junimea literary society, the face of the 500-lei bill and considered to be Romania's 'national poet', Eminescu (1850–89) studied abroad but never betrayed his Romanian roots. His brooding, romantic poems sprung from folk myths and Romanian history. In recent years, some ultraconservative politicians have misused his work to rally support around xenophobic causes.

The other great 19th-century writer, Caragiale, is something of a Mark Twain or Anton Chekhov of Romania, innocently poking fun at an absurd, lightliving urban version of Romanian life at a time when Romania toyed with Western forms – something Eminescu loathed.

Romanian literature became a tool of the Communist Party from 1947 onwards, with few works of note emerging and much repression of dissident voices. Andrei Codrescu was exiled to the USA in 1966 and went on to write numerous books about Romanian-related issues.

A couple of relatively rare books show off post-communist poets: *Young Poets of a New Romania* (1996) and *An Anthology of Contemporary Romanian Poetry* (1984) translated by Andrea Deletant.

Feminist poet Nina Cassian (whose Cheerleader for a Funeral and Call Yourself Alive? are available in English) sought asylum in the USA in 1985 after her poems were discovered by the Securitate.

Music

CLASSICAL & OPERA

The Romanian classical music world is nearly synonymous with George Enescu (1881–1955), whose *Romanian Rhapsodies Nos 1 & 2* and opera *Odeipe* are considered classics. He was as accomplished a violinist as composer, studied under Fauré in Paris and was also a conductor, cellist and pianist. Other figures of note include composer Ciprian Porumbescu (1853–83) and Paul Constantinescu (1909–63).

Transylvania was an important European centre of classical music from the 16th century. Most of the activity centred in Sibiu, the base for Romanian composer Ion Caianu and frequent stop-off for musicians such as Liszt, Johann and Richard Strauss and Johannes Brahms.

In Moldova, two of the most prolific modern composers are Arkady Luxemburg and Evgeny Doga, who have both scored films and multimedia projects, and written songs, concertos, suites and symphonies. For over three decades, Dimitrie Gagauz has been the foremost composer of songs reflecting the folklore of the Turkic-influenced Gagauz population of southern Moldova.

Despite the cheesy name, Romantic Walk Through Romanian Music *is the best introduction to Romanian classical music, with works by Enescu, Dimitrescu, Porumbescu and others.*

FOLK & ROMA MUSIC

Traditional Romanian folk instruments include the *bucium* (alphorn), the *cimpoi* (bagpipes), the *cobză* (a pear-shaped lute) and the *nai* (a panpipe of about 20 cane tubes). Many kinds of flute are used, including the *ocarina* (a ceramic flute) and the *tilinca* (a flute without finger holes). Today, the violin is the most common folk instrument.

The *doină* is a solo, improvised love song, a sort of Romanian blues with a social or romantic theme. The *baladă* (ballad) is a collective narrative song steeped with feeling. Couples may dance in a circle, a semicircle or a line. In the *sârbă*, males and females dance quickly in a closed circle with their hands on each other's shoulders. The *hora* is another fast circle dance. In the *brâu* (belt dance), dancers form a chain by grasping their neighbour's belt.

When they perform, Roma musicians circulate through their village, inviting neighbours to join in weddings, births, baptisms, funerals and harvest festivals. Improvised songs are often directed at a specific individual and are designed to elicit an emotional response (and a tip).

To appeal to older people, the musicians sing traditional *baladă* or epic songs in verse, often recounting the exploits of Robin Hood–style outlaws who apply justice through their actions. *Muzică lătărească* is the term to describe the music you're likely to see performed with violin and accordion in restaurants.

Modern Roma or Tzigane (Gypsy) music rode a buzz in 2006, with the band Fanfare Ciocarlia winning the World Music Awards for Europe and the band Mahala Rai Banda playing UK festivals.

POP, ROCK & HIP-HOP

Pop music in Romania is alive and well, pumped out on the nation's radios and distorting old speakers from maxitaxi cassette players. Radio stations have a tendency to play the same few songs repeatedly through the day; you may think the stations only have five CDs to choose from. Other than the Cheeky Girls (p193), Gheorghe Zamfir is Romania's other regrettable music export – a successfully self-promoting pan-flute player who inspires groans and, enigmatically, gets big sales abroad.

Rock pioneers Iris have had fervent fans since 1977, continuing to win local MTV awards in 2006. Another rock pioneer is Compact, whose bass player was killed in a road accident when a (allegedly drunk) US marine hit him in Bucharest. Two popular, guitar-oriented pop groups from Moldova are Zdob si Zdup and Gândul Mâței. Boy band O-Zone has lit up discos with its bouncy electronica.

Hip-hop is fast gaining in popularity and is well represented by local bands like Paraziți, Morometi, The Family, and Bustaflex. The R&B queen of Romania is Nico. Pashaman is a mildly popular singer doing something akin to reggae.

BEST FOLK CDS

■ **Band of Gypsies by Taraf de Haidouks** – Romania's' most famous 13-piece band once played Johnny Depp's Viper Room in LA

■ **Art of the Bratsch by Anatol Ştefăneţ** – frenzied viola playing from Moldavia

■ **Baro Biao by Fanfare Ciocarlia** – intoxicatingly fast and furious Roma horn section romping through tango-tinged songs at punk speed

■ **World Library of Folk & Primitive Music, Vol XVII** – 35 Alan Lomax–collected recordings of traditional folk and dance songs

---

A pop style termed *manele* has overtaken the airwaves recently; it's a suspicious mix of dance, hip-hop, reggae and home-made techno with wild flourishes of pseudo-Turkish and Middle Eastern–influenced wailings to boot.

Architecture

Travelling through Romania, you're likely to notice a variety of styles: arched Byzantine porches and windows in Northern Dobrogea; ornamental, wooden gates in Székely Land; lavish villas in areas peopled with rich Roma; gothic and baroque structural masterpieces in Transylvania; traditional folk-styled homes in small villages; and endless stretches of functionalist concrete block apartment buildings in and around most city centres. This is aside from the unique Saxon fortified churches in Transylvania, and Moldavia's fortified and painted monasteries. Bucharest is a fascinating blend of grand, florid buildings, French eclecticism, rococo and grey Soviet-style experiments. The Brancovan style, incorporating Oriental and baroque elements, was developed under Wallachian Constantin Brâncoveanu.

Visual Arts

PAINTING

Medieval painting was marked by a strong Byzantine influence. Devised to educate illiterate peasants, paintings took the form of frescoes depicting scenes from the Bible on the outside walls of churches; they also appeared on iconostases inside churches and in miniature form as a decorative frame for religious manuscripts. Bucovina's monasteries (p275) – with almost pop art–like scenes, painted to instruct and entertain soldiers waiting for battles with the Turks – are home to Romania's loveliest and most colourful frescoes.

As art entered its 'modern' phase, Romania often trailed behind Western Europe. One young art historian told us, 'Our masters were merely the first to see works in France that they'd mimic and bring back. They weren't expressing a Romanian need.' A key exception, the historian agreed, were the paintings of Nicolae Grigorescu (1838–1907), big with international collectors. Grigorescu absorbed French impressionism, but brought it home with scenes celebrating Romanian peasantry. He broke the prevailing strict academic mould, heralding the emergence of modern Romanian painting. His straight-on portraits included unexpected subjects, like Roma women and Jewish Romanians. There are many of his works at Bucharest's National Art Museum (p73).

Modernism was further embraced b73y Gheorghe Petraşcu (1872–1949), whose paintings also drew on the world around him. The symbolist movement was represented by Ion Ţuculescu (1910–62), who incorporated elements of decorative motifs of Moldavian carpets in his work.

Since 1989, Romanian painting has undergone an explosion of exploration; artists are experimenting with a variety of styles and themes which beforehand were either discouraged or repressed.

The biggest name in Moldovan painting is Mihai Grecu (1916–98), who co-founded the National School of Painting and was also a poet and 'free love' advocate.

GLASS ICONS

Painting on glass and wood remains a popular folk art today. Considered to be of Byzantine origin, this traditional peasant art was widespread in Romania from the 17th century onwards. Superstition and strong religious beliefs surrounded these icons, painted to protect the household from evil spirits. Well-known 19th-century icon painters include Dionisie Iuga, Maria Chifor and Tudor Tocariu. The glass icons of contemporary artist Georgeta Maria Uiga (from Baia Mare) are exhibited worldwide.

SCULPTURE

Romania's most famous sculptor is Constantin Brâncuşi (1876–1957), whose polished bronze and wood works display a refined subtlety which belie the great passion and depth of thought which has gone into them. His work is held at the Pompidou Centre in Paris (across the street from which is a replica of his Paris studio), the Guggenheim, New York's MOMA, the Philadelphia Museum of Art, the Australian National Gallery in Canberra and in Romania at Craiova's Museum of Art and Bucharest's National Museum of Art.

Moldovan sculptor and designer Anatol Coseac today produces some highly original woodworks.

In 2005, one of Brâncuşi's *Bird in Space pieces sold* *for US$27.5 million at a* *Christie's Auction*

Theatre

The first theatre on Romanian soil was reputedly in the ancient city of Histria. The first Romanian-language theatre opened in 1817 and the literary cultural boom of the following decade gave rise to talented playwrights and stage actors. Today, there are theatres in every major city and town, and several respected theatre schools.

A Jewish theatre was established in Bucharest in 1948 and the first-ever Jewish professional theatre in the world was formed in Iaşi in 1876. The Hungarian minority have established theatres in Cluj-Napoca, Timişoara and Târgu Mures.

Cinema

The so-called 'Romanian New Wave' exploded in the 1990s and is gaining steam this decade, with increased attention at international film festivals such as Cannes. The biggest success of recent years is Cristi Puiu's *The Death of Mr Lazarus* (2005), a black comedy that follows an unlikable sick man's journey from hospital to hospital, as he attempts to get treatment. Puiu apparently based it on his tense dealings with the National Centre of Cinematography (CNC; www.cncinema.abt.ro in Romanian), who finance most Romanian films, and a 1997 incident where a hospital left a patient to die on the Bucharest streets.

A couple of other recent hits include: Nae Caranfil's *Filantropica* (2002), a comedy about corruption and greed and how to get a free meal in fancy restaurants; and Corneliu Porumboiu's 2006 debut *East of Bucharest*, where three people argue on a local talk show about whether the revolution happened in their town.

Much of the international film world is heading to Romania too, as the Transylvania Film Festival (held in Cluj-Napoca) brings in dozens of movies annually. Anthony Minghella's *Cold Mountain* (2003, starring Nicole Kidman) and *An American Haunting* (2005) both shot southern USA scenes on location in Transylvania. Director Francis Ford Coppola shot a low-budget flick in Romania in 2005; the film *Youth Without Youth* is based on Romanian Mircea Eliade's novella. Sacha Baron Cohen shot his 'Kazakhstan' scenes for *Borat: Cultural Learnings of America for Make Benefit Glorious Nation of Kazakhstan* (2006) in the village of Glod, which was not without its repercussions; see p100.

During the communist years, the government controlled much of cinema's content. One big director, Lucian Pintilie, gained awareness in the west with the political *Reconstituirea* (1969), which the government promptly banned. His film *Unforgettable Summer* made a splash at Cannes in 1994 and is seen as a key film to igniting the last decade of action.

In Moldova, a separate film industry came into being with Khrushchev's thaw, when emerging works combined unabashed romance with Soviet realism (known as 'Moldovan poetic film') and became popular throughout the USSR. Moldova's films are generally more lyrical and nostalgic than Romania's, which have tended to prefer realistic depictions of life. One of the most famous 'Soviet films' ever was a Moldovan masterpiece from 1976: Emil Loteanu's *The Gypsy Camp Vanishes into Heaven*, which blends hauntingly beautiful music with sweeping landscapes and impassioned love between a Gypsy horse thief and a young girl. Very few films are made in Moldova today and Moldovans are far less rabid about going to the cinema than Romanians are.

Environment

THE LAND

See the difference!
Highest elevation in
Romania: 2543m (Mt
Moldoveanu); highest
elevation in Moldova:
430m (Mt Balaneşti).

Covering 237,500 sq km, oval-shaped Romania is made up of three main geographical regions, each with its particular features. The mighty Carpathian Mountains form the shape of a scythe swooping down into the country's centre from Serbia and curling up northwards towards Ukraine. West of this are large plateaus where bucolic villages and towns lie among the hills and valleys. South and southeast of the mountains are the low-lying plains (where most of the country's agricultural output comes from) which end at the Black Sea and Europe's second-largest delta region where the Danube spills into the sea.

Moldova couldn't look more different. Tiny (33,843 sq km) and landlocked, it's a flat country of gently rolling steppes, with a gradual sloping towards the Black Sea. With one of the highest percentages of arable land in the world, Moldova is blessed with rich soil. Fields of grains, fruits and sunflowers are characteristic of the countryside. Mineral and rock deposits are typically lignite, gypsum and limestone. A great effort has been made by environmental groups to protect Moldova's wetland regions along the lower Prut and Dniestr rivers.

WILDLIFE
Animals

Proportion of forested
land in Romania/
Moldova: 26.3%/9.9%.

Proportion of agricultural
land in Romania/Moldova:
up to 60%/64%.

The highest concentration of large carnivores anywhere in Europe is found in the Romanian Carpathians (about half of Europe's bear population and a third of its wolves live here).

Romania's splendid nature teems with enough life to keep enthusiasts busy for quite a while: there are 33,802 species of animals here (32 of these are endangered) as well as 3700 species of plants (39 of which are endangered).

Birdlife in the Danube Delta is a never-ending treat, as the delta provides a major transit hub for birds migrating from as far off as the Russian arctic to the Nile Delta. About 60% of the world's small pygmy cormorant population tweets in Romania.

Moldova counts some 16,500 species of animals (460 of which are vertebrates) as its citizens.

TRAVEL WIDELY, TREAD LIGHTLY, GIVE SUSTAINABLY – THE LONELY PLANET FOUNDATION

The Lonely Planet Foundation proudly supports nimble nonprofit institutions working for change in the world. Each year the foundation donates 5% of Lonely Planet company profits to projects selected by staff and authors. Our partners range from Kabissa, which provides small nonprofits across Africa with access to technology, to the Foundation for Developing Cambodian Orphans, which supports girls at risk of falling victim to sex traffickers.

Our nonprofit partners are linked by a grass-roots approach to the areas of health, education or sustainable tourism. Many – such as Louis Sarno who works with BaAka (Pygmy) children in the forested areas of Central African Republic – choose to focus on women and children as one of the most effective ways to support the whole community. Louis is determined to give options to children who are discriminated against by the majority Bantu population.

Sometimes foundation assistance is as simple as restoring a local ruin like the Minaret of Jam in Afghanistan; this incredible monument now draws intrepid tourists to the area and its restoration has greatly improved options for local people.

Just as travel is often about learning to see with new eyes, so many of the groups we work with aim to change the way people see themselves and the future for their children and communities.

Plants

Both Romania and Moldova are home to 6600 plant species. About 1350 floral species have been recorded.Typical Alpine flora species include the yellow poppy, Transylvanian columbine, saxifrage and, in the southern Carpathians, the protected edelweiss.

The Carpathian Mountains are among the least-spoilt mountains in Europe, with Alpine pastures above and thick beech, fir, spruce and oak forests below.

NATIONAL PARKS

Romania has more than 500 protected areas, including a dozen national parks, three biosphere reserves and one World Heritage site (the Danube Delta), totalling over 12,000 sq km. Most of these areas are located in the Carpathians.

Except for the Danube Delta Biosphere Reserve (DDBR), none of the reserves or national parks have organised visitor facilities. Some reserves and national parks are accessible by public transport; others are not. More information on many reserves and parks is included in the relevant regional chapters.

Moldova has five scientific reserves and 30 protected areas, but has only recently designated one area as a national park; the 500-sq-km Lower Dniestr National Park (p333).

Following is a rundown of Romania's major parks and reserves.

Apuseni Mountains

Running across the Transylvania/Crişana border, the Apuseni Mountains were recognised as a geological reserve in 1938. At their centre is a karst plateau with an extensive cave system lying beneath and rich wildlife above (eg boars, deer, stags, bears). See p197 for access from the north, or p226 from the south.

Frank Carter and David Turnock's Environmental Problems in East-Central Europe *(2002) is the place to turn for the specific ecological problems – and solutions – for this area.*

Bucegi Nature Reserve

The Bucegi Nature Reserve protects the entire 300 sq km of the Bucegi Mountain Range (p122). The reserve contains a variety of forests and abundant botanic species including edelweiss.

Ceahlău Massif

The 52-sq-km area of the Ceahlău Massif (p267) in Moldavia has been protected since 1941 as the Ceahlău Massif National Park (Parcul Naţionale Muntele Ceahlău). Among its many treasures are countless flower species and rare fauna.

Danube Delta Biosphere Reserve

One of the world's biggest wetlands (and Europe's biggest), the Danube Delta Biosphere Reserve (www.ddrba.ro), a UNESCO World Heritage site, is home to over 5000 plant and animal species. About 2700 sq km are protected lands, maintaining the migratory hub for the 300 bird species that pass through. See above.

Iron Gates Natural Park

Wallachia's phenomenal park (Porţile de Fier; www.portiledefier.ro; p110) takes up a staggering 115,655 sq km of spectacular scenery at the area where the Danube first enters Romania at the most impressive stretch of the great river's entire course. The park contains a series of stunning gorges 134km long.

Piatra Craiului

The Transylvanian range Piatra Craiului (p142), a staggering wall of mountains 25km long, stretches from Zărneşti in the north to Podu Dâmboviţei in the south. Since 1939 the area has been protected but it was only declared a national park in 1990. Its treasures include wolves, stags and unusual hazel-coloured bears.

It's not been counted, but by the naked eye, it would appear that Romania, and in particular Bucharest, may have more public trash cans than anywhere else on the planet. Walk through Çismiu Gardens and you'll see one between each of the hundreds of benches. Next up is getting people to use them…

Retezat National Park

Transylvania's Retezat Mountains (p183) encompass Romania's first national park, established in 1935 on 130 sq km. Today it has been declared a Unesco Biosphere Reserve and expanded to 544 sq km. It has some 300 plant species and its wilds are roamed by black mountain goats, bears, foxes and stags. Come migration season, the monk eagle is known to pass by.

Todirescu Flower Reservation

The crowning glory of the Rarău Massif (p280) is the glorious Todirescu Flower Reservation (Fâneţele Montane de la Plaiul Todirescu; 1933), which sprawls for 44 hectares across Todirescu Mountain on the southern edge of the Slătioara Reservation. In July its meadows are ablaze with colour. Tulips, bluebells, chrysanthemums and the poisonous omagul (*Aconitum anthora*) are just some of the many floral delights found here.

ENVIRONMENTAL ISSUES

It's a sad and distressing scenario that repeats itself throughout Romania: you'll be in the middle of nearly incomprehensible beauty when you suddenly stumble upon a dozen crushed beer cans or spot a pile of garbage floating in a creek. Two key EU criticisms of Romania included waste management and water pollution. For NGOs like Pro Natura (www.pronatura.ro) and the Transylvania Ecological Club (p187; www.greenagenda.org), in Cluj-Napoca, sensitising an apathetic public about how to diminish the impact of tourism on the environment is a main priority.

In spring 2006, the Danube River water level rose to its highest level in over a century. Various engineering projects have resulted in up to 20,000 sq km of floodplains being cut off from the river, which has endangered many species in this area. Romania's neighbours to the north haven't helped either. The controversial Bystroye Canal, which Ukraine began building in 2004 to allow ships to reach the Black Sea from the Danube in their territory, is currently on hiatus, but at research time Moldova was going ahead on a new oil terminus that could affect the delta.

In 2005 and 2006, birds with the Avian flu virus were found in the Danube Delta, and through spring several towns became quarantined – as far inland as Făgăraş – for safe measure. No people were afflicted.

The Romanian government issued an ambitious plan to cut energy used by at least 30% by 2015, partly by introducing renewable energy sources.

Cleanup since 1990

Much has been done since 1990, including cleaning up a chemical and nuclear waste-pit at Sulina; building new smoke stacks at Baia Mare, Romania's largest nonferrous metal centre; closing industrial plants in Giurgiu and Copşa Mică (p151) and outfitting others with special filters.

Though the pollution bellowing out of Romania's factories has been halved, air pollution still exceeds acceptable levels in some areas, and the Danube Delta has a long way to go before it can be pronounced a healthy environment (particularly with an increase in fertilisers being used in farms).

In 2006 tension built up over the mining of Roşia Montana (p180). This followed a disaster in 2000 at a gold mine in Baia Mare, when 100,000 cubic metres of cyanide-contaminated water spilled into the Tisa and Danube

ROMANIA'S UNESCO WORLD HERITAGE SITES

- Danube Delta
- Villages with fortified churches in Transylvania
- Monastery of Horezu
- Churches of Moldavia
- Historic Centre of Sighişoara
- Dacian fortresses of the Orastie Mountains
- Wooden churches of Maramureş

Rivers; half a decade later, the UN reported that previous risks still hadn't been properly curbed. In 2006, Romania took a €55 million loan to modernise its water supply to meet EU standards.

Change in Moldova has been even slower. Never heavily industrial, it faces more issues of protection and conservation than pollution. A majority of its 3600 rivers and rivulets are drained, diverted or dammed, threatening ecosystems.

Activities

Considering the beauty of Romania's diverse landscape, it's a shame to visit and not get your boots dirty or adrenaline tapped. This alphabetised chapter is a teaser for all you can do in the region. Detailed listings of activities, including where to find guides and maps, are found in the relevant destination chapters throughout this book.

Moldova trails behind Romania in terms of organised activities; it's possible the still largely undeveloped Lower Dneistr National Park (p333) will gear itself to activities in the future.

BIKING

Given Romania's ideal mountain-biking terrain, it is not surprising that the sport has taken off in a big way in recent years.

The best place to mountain-bike, and it's no secret, is the plateau atop the Bucegi Mountains, up from Buşteni (p124) in the Prahova Valley south of Braşov. From here, or from Sinaia (p118), you can hire bikes, pay for an extra ticket on the gondola lift and go up for the day on top of the world, so to speak. There are also many organised 'marathon' races (see below).

Hire

Bike-hire places aren't found everywhere, and not all main tourist hubs have easy-to-find bikes for hire. Aside from Sinaia and Buşteni, other bike-hire options are in Sibiu (p159), Sighişoara (p147), Sovata (p171) and, up in Maramureş, Botiza (p245) in the Izei Valley from €5 per day, or in Bucharest (p78) for €12 per day. Ask staff at a hostel or pension, who sometimes can track down a bike for you to ride on country roads.

Clubs & Events

Based in Cluj-Napoca, Clubul de Cicloturism Napoca (p190) is one of Romania's leading bicycle clubs. They don't offer tours or hire out equipment, but are happy to offer advice on cycling in the region and can point you to tours.

TOP 10 ACTIVITIES

- Hiking, biking or skiing atop the **Bucegi Mountains plateau** (p122)
- Skiing **Poiana Braşov** (p136), or kicking back with herbal tea and mountain-top cabana and looking over snowy Bucegi
- Biking on trails through the off-the-radar **Cindrel Mountains** (p162), south of Sibiu
- Hiking to Padiş Plateau's campsites and cabins in the **Apuseni Mountains** (p197), then day-tripping to glacial caves
- Horse riding on week-long trips through Dracula's land at **Bârgău Valley** (p210)
- Boating through the bird-rich **Danube Delta** (p301) from Tulcea
- Climbing up 1480 steps to – at last! – Dracula's real castle, **Poienari** (p105), outside Curtea de Argeş
- Soothing your ills in Roman baths in Hercules' former spa, **Băile Herculane** (p220)
- Rock-climbing Romania's most challenging walls at **Piatra Craiului National Park** (p142), near Zârneşti
- Arranging hikes from traditional villages to meet mountain shepherds in places such as **Maramureş' Izei Valley** (p244)

MOUNTAIN RESCUE

Emergency rescue is provided by Salvamont (www.salvamont.org, in Romanian), a voluntary mountain rescue organisation with 20 stations countrywide (listed throughout the book). Its members are skilled climbers, skiers and medics. They are also an invaluable source of weather warnings and practical advice.

Contact Salvamont via the local hospital or the mayor's office *(primăria)* or through Salvamont's headquarters in Braşov. However, in an emergency dial ☎ 112.

Some of Salvamont's major contact points:

Braşov (☎ 268-471 517, 0725-826 449; Str Michael Weiss 26)
Buşteni (☎ 244-320 048; Primărie, B-dul Libertăţii 91)
Sibiu (☎ 0745-140 144, 269-216 477; Str Nicolae Bălcescu 9)
Sinaia (☎ 244-313 131; Primărie, B-dul Carol I)
Vatra Dornei (☎ 230-372 767; Str Garii)
Zărneşti (☎ 0722-553 121; Str Metropolit Ion Meţianu 17)

Other biking clubs that sponsor *maraton* (marathon) racing events:

Bike Attack (☎ 0726-187 399; www.bikeattack.ro; Reşita, Banat) Organises events in September in the Banat mountains.
Ciclomed (☎ 0742-149 685; maraton_medieval@birotec.ro; Mediaş) Organises a July marathon.
IntersportSE (☎ 0745-594 030; botond@csik.ro; Miercurea Ciuc) Organises events in May.

Tours

Green Mountain Holidays (www.greenmountainholidays.ro) runs a 10-night biking trip through Transylvania's greatest hits for €600 including guides, transfers, accommodation and food – bikes are €75 extra. For something more adventurous and off-road, contact Apuseni Experience (www.apuseniexperience.ro).

Transylvania Adventure (www.adventuretransylvania.com), located in Satu Mare, also offers biking tours over the Făgăraş Mountains – a seven-night inclusive trip is €800.

BIRD-WATCHING

Europe's greatest wetland, the Danube Delta, is the obvious destination for bird-watching travellers to Romania. Here you can hire boats or take tours or ferries on one of three channels through Romania's 3446-sq-km wetland. Almost the entire world's population of red-breasted geese (up to 70,000) winter here and, in the summer, thousands of pygmy cormorants and white pelicans, along with birds from up to 300 other species, can be seen.

Though you are guaranteed to see some birds on any of the boat excursions you take, Tulcea's Ibis Tours (p304) can organise specialised tours guided by ornithologists from €30 per day. Otherwise, the Information & Ecological Education Centre (p304) can suggest other ways to spot the flying beauties.

There are also bird-watching excursions in Transylvania's mountains. Roving Romania (p130) in Braşov runs well-regarded bird trips.

Migration season in spring runs from March to May, in autumn August to October. It's particularly good in mid-April and October.

CAVING

Romania has more than 12,000 caves *(peştera)* but only a few are open to tourism. Two of Romania's best caves are reached from south of the Apuseni Mountains: the spectacular Scărişoara Ice Cave (p227), which is one of Romania's five glacier caves, and the Bear Cave (Peştera Urşilor; p227).

More accessible, but a bit less remarkable, is the 3566m-long Peștera Muierii (Women's Cave, p107).

Romania is a serious contender in the world of caves and speleology (study of caves), thanks to Emil Racoviţa, who set up the world's first speleology institute and studied over 1000 caves in his lifetime (see p189).

Check with the Apuseni Experience (www.apuseniexperience.re), based in Oradea, for caving tours. Green Mountain Holidays (www.greenmountain holidays.ro) offers a seven-day, all-inclusive caving tour for €450.

Romania's main speleological organisations are other good sources of information. They can give practical details, help and advice and let you know the best way to visit the best caves. They sometimes organise trips of their own. The **Emil Racoviţa Institute of Speleology** (☎ 264-595 954; www.speleological-institute -cluj.org), based in Cluj-Napoca, can offer a guided tour to the otherwise-closed 45km Wind Cave, Romania's largest.

The Romanian Speleological Foundation (www.frspeo.ro/prezentare) has offices with Apuseni Experience in Oradea, plus a **Bucharest office** (☎ 21-212 8863; iser@rol.ro) and a **Cluj-Napoca office** (☎ 264-195 954). GESS (p287) is an ecological group in Northern Dobrogea involved in marine and cave biology. A great bunch, they occasionally organise exploratory and diving trips to the famous Movile cave near Mangalia.

In 2002, cavers found a 35,000-year-old human jawbone while digging around in the Peștera cu Oase (Cave with Bones) in the south-western Carpathians, which turned out to be the oldest known human fossil in Europe.

HEALTH SPAS

The curative properties of minerals from Romania's mountains have been known since the Romans set up baths here 2000 years ago. These days many 'spa vacations' get booked in Black Sea resorts in places like Mangalia – mostly by domestic tourists. Those with aches in their bones can find relief across the country; check the map provided by National Organisation of Spas (www.spas.ro), a national organisation that represents many of the 70-plus spas nationwide. Many are geared for illnesses including kidney, liver and heart diseases as well as metabolism, gynaecological and nutrition disorders.

Treatment goes underground at popular salt mines at Turda (p195) outside Cluj-Napoca, and Praid (p171).

Some stand-out spas include the following:

Băile Felix (p225) Famous for its large mineral-water pool.

Băile Herculane (p220) If it's good enough for Hercules, then mere mortals like us can't complain. The Hercules statue's genitals have been broken off by men seeking sexual potency.

Băile Tușnad (p165) A pension-filled valley in Transylvania's Székely Land, with mineral baths and pools in the volcano-made Harghita Mountains.

Covasna spa resort (p165) Also in Székely Land. Feels like an untouched, communism-ho! resort with an elder set roaming the halls in pink and sky-blue robes.

Eforie Nord's mud baths (p296) Bathers (some nude) slop mud on their dirty selves and bake under the Black Sea sun.

Sovata (p171) Between Târgu Mureș and Sighișoara in Transylvania. Famed for a curative dip in a bear-shaped lake.

Vatra Dornei (p281) Moldavia's most popular spa resort.

HIKING & CLIMBING

Hiking is Romania's most popular pastime in summer, and the action is mostly around the mountains, particularly in Transylvania, Moldavia and Crișana.

Trails are generally well marked, and a system of cabanas, huts, and even hotels along the trails on the mountain tops and plateaus makes even a several-day trek more than comfortable. Generally it's not possible or necessary to reserve rooms in a hut.

SAFE & RESPONSIBLE HIKING

The popularity of hiking and camping is placing great pressure on the natural environment. Please consider the following tips:

- Carry out all your rubbish. If you've carried it in, you can carry it out. Especially don't forget plastic bottles, sanitary napkins and condoms!

- Never bury your rubbish. This disturbs soil and ground cover, encourages erosion, may injure animals that dig it up and may take years to decompose.

- Minimise the waste you must carry out by taking minimal packaging and no more food than you will need.

- Don't use detergents or toothpaste in or near watercourses, even if they are biodegradable.

- Stick to existing tracks   if you blaze a new trail, it will turn into a watercourse with the next heavy rainfall and eventually cause soil loss and scarring.

- If you light a fire, use an existing fireplace rather than creating a new one. Don't surround fires with rocks as this creates a visual scar. Use only dead, fallen wood. Remember the adage 'the bigger the fool, the bigger the fire'. Use minimal wood, just what you need for cooking.

Where to Hike

The Carpathians (aka Transylvanian Alps) offer endless opportunities for hikers, the most popular areas being the Bucegi (p122) and Făgăraș (p151) ranges, south and west of Brașov. The Bucegi has a flat-top plateau that can be reached by cable cars from Sinaia or Bușteni, but not all the hikes are cake walks. It's possible for the strong-kneed to walk down the steep range into Bran, then bus to Brașov.

Growing in popularity are the Apuseni Mountains, southwest of Cluj-Napoca. This area, rich with hikes, karst and glacier caves, is reached from the south (p226), southeast of Oradea, or from the north (p197), west of Cluj.

Other zones include the Retezat National Park (p183), Romania's first national park, which lies northwest of Târgu Jiu and south of Deva in Transylvania; around Păltiniș, (p162) south of Sibiu; and, in Romania's Moldavian region, the less-frequented Rarău Mountains (p280) and the Ceahlău Massif (p267) near the Bicaz Gorge.

Moldova's 50,000-hectare Lower Dneistr National Park (p333) has yet to create hiking trails, but this may change.

SHORT HIKES

Maramureș is potentially good hiking turf, though information on hikes is scarce. A good day hike is up Prislop Pass (p248).

For other shorter treks, there are dozens of options: take the cable car up from Sinaia or Bușteni and make your way to the Ialomiceora monastery; hike from Poiana Brașov to Râșnov castle (p137); take a two-hour ramble up to the Rodna Mountains from Borșa (p248) in Maramureș; or trek from one colour-coded monastery to another in Moldavia's Southern Bucovina (p275). Even Prince Charles managed the 20km hike from Putna to the Sucevița monasteries here.

Rock-climbers (who speak Romanian) can get the best info on the Carpathians' rocky climbs at www.roclimbing.net.

Where to Climb

Rock-climbers take to the walls at the Piatra Craiului National Park (p142), not far from Bran. The Bicaz Gorges (p269) offers spectacular challenges too. There's some climbing near Băile Herculane (p220).

Finding Guides

If you prefer booking a hiking trip from home (and you live in the UK), check Sheffield-based www.highplaces.co.uk, which runs 14-day Transylvanian hikes from £790 (not including flight).

Though individual hiking is more than possible, we also recommend going on organised treks in small groups or hiring a guide familiar with the area you choose to explore – this is partly a safety issue but also local guides' familiarity with the land can help you get the most out of the experience.

Throughout the text, we offer suggestions for guided tours. There are good guides and guided tours available from Brașov (p129) and Cluj-Napoca (p190). Some youth hostels (like the Retro Hostel in Cluj-Napoca, p191) offer fun, guided excursions. Another good source of guides can be found at www .alpineguide.ro. In some more out-of-the-way places, like Retezat, it's hard to just show up and assume you can find a guide – but ask around.

Maps

Detailed hiking maps are available but are of varying quality. You'll more easily find maps in big city bookstores and outdoor activities shops. Most tourist information centres don't carry them. You might also stumble upon old maps in shops and cable car stations; some are surprisingly helpful – some. Cartografica produces excellent maps and, to a lesser degree, some of Amco Press' publications might be of use.

Your best bet, however, are maps by Bel Alpin, which also publishes excellent books on hiking in the Făgăraș Mountains.

HORSE RIDING

Horses are everywhere in Romania – ploughing fields, pulling logs, roaming mountains, pulling carts from town to town on the same highways that new sports cars zoom along. It's tempting to join the fracas. There are some tourist-oriented outfitters that offer remarkable long-term trips.

Throughout the Carpathians a network of trails leading to some of the country's most beautiful and remote areas can be explored on horseback. The best on offer is Lunca Ilvei's Riding Centre (p211) near Bistrița in the heart of Dracula country. Fully inclusive five-day trips cost about €780, including guides and food. Another good bet is Daksa (p190) located just outside Cluj-Napoca, which offers three- to seven-week trips from €80 or €90 per person.

Cross-Country Farm (p147), outside Sighișoara, offers day rides from €35 per person.

It's hard to beat the rural terrain around the villages of Maramureș. You can arrange horse trips from Baia Mare (p234).

PARAGLIDING

It's not exactly the real thing, but the Moldovan capital, Chișinău, has a parachuting club (p324) with a 40m 'parachute machine' – only US$2 per jump.

Paragliding is far from widespread in Romania, despite the fantastic choices of jagged cliffs from which to throw yourself. Many groups are geared for more experienced locals, but you can arrange 10-day classes from ECO-S in Brașov (p132) for €180, or through Timișoara's Latura Extremă (p218), a good place for beginners; it offers day trips from €35 per person for a group of three.

Eagle Air Sport (www.paragliding.ro) is a national network of paraglider pilots and groups – check the site for locations in and around Romania. One English-speaking pilot that can help hook you up with travel agencies or gliding clubs is **Alexandru Balmus** (☎ 0722-520 123; alexandru_b@mccann.ro).

SKIING & SNOWBOARDING

With all its mountains, skiing and snowboarding in Romania is a big draw for locals and visitors seeking long runs and cheaper lift tickets than in Western Europe. The mountains don't have the numbers of runs that are available in Bulgaria, just south, but there are full-service resorts and ski runs for all levels. Beginner, intermediate and expert slopes are marked as blue, red and black, respectively.

The ski season runs generally from December to March, with some slopes opening by mid-November and staying open into April.

Many mountains see cross-country skiers take to hiking trails in winter. Cross-country gear is not easy to hire, but some places might let out personal gear. Wild skiing is popular atop the Bucegi.

Tickets & Gear

Some lifts have credit passes based on type of lift – gondola, chairlift, pull lines. Prices have gone up a bit in recent years, unfortunately: it's €2 to €2.50 per ride. Hiring skis or widely available snowboards costs about €10 per day.

The equipment and services are not at Western European levels, but that doesn't stop skiers from having a great time. For proof, check out the forum at www.ski-in-romania.com, which also posts snowfall information and other listings.

Where to Ski

Transylvania dominates Romania's ski world. By far the most popular places to ski or snowboard are daytrips from Braşov, for those who like to finish a day on the mountain with juicy steaks amid cobbled Saxon sidewalks. In the Prahova Valley is the resort Sinaia (p118), and Poiana Braşov (p136) is a 20-minute bus ride west. Also nearby is the ski resort Predeal (p126), which is the focus of a lot of youth ski trips.

South of Sibiu, you can find smaller lifts at Păltiniş (p162).

Outside Transylvania, there are some fun smaller ski hills in Maramureş, at Izvoare (p238) and Borsa (p248), though the latter has no rentals. The south side of the Apuseni Mountains has a couple of ski hills at Stâna de Vale (p226) and Gârda de Sus (p227). In Moldavia, you can ski at Vatra Dornei (p281).

Check www.surmont.ro (in Romanian only) for listings of snowboarding, skiing and mountain-biking events in the Bucegi Mountains.

To get information on great skiing expeditions outside the main resorts, check out www.mountain guide.ro/en/ski.htm. You'll find some excellent options in some of Romania's most scenic spots.

Food & Drink

Let's leave the debate as to whether or not something called Romanian cuisine actually exists and plunge, mouth wide open, into a world of hearty, simple (if a little repetitious) food. Incorporating the fertile land's fresh, organic produce into uncomplicated recipes, Romanian dishes have a homemade character to them. Relying heavily upon pork (at least half their traditional meals feature this meat in some form), staples like potatoes and cabbage, and liberal borrowings from the cultures which have traversed and occupied the land (Turks, Germans, Romans, Hungarians, Roma), Romanian and Moldovan cooking is not for those seeking to diet. Oh, and there's pizza too.

If you want to make your own *mămăligă*, a couple of good books include Galia Sperber's *The Art of Romanian Cooking* and Nicolae Klepper's *Taste of Romania*.

STAPLES & SPECIALITIES

Mămăligă is a word you'd better familiarise yourself with, and quick. You'll find it on every menu, and you're likely to be served it in guesthouses morning, noon or night. In short, it is a cornmeal mush similar to polenta and can be boiled, baked or fried. Traditionally it is served with nothing more than a sprinkling of *brânză*, a salty sheep cheese. *Mămăligă* can be frightfully bland (and very filling), especially the kind served in diners and bistros, but when homemade, warm and served with fresh *smântână* (sour cream), it's excellent comfort food.

Ciorbă (soup) is the other mainstay of the Romanian diet and is consistently a highlight of meals. Derived from Turkish *çorba*, it is tart, deliciously warming on cold winter days and usually served with a dollop of *smântână*. By far the local favourite, and worth trying despite its name, is *ciorbă de burtă* (a light, garlicky tripe soup – made from cow's innards if you don't know).

Five things you must try in Romania: *ciorbă de burtă* (tripe soup), *mămăligă* (polenta), *sarmale* (vine leaves stuffed with meat and rice), *mici* (meatballs) and *ţuică* (plum brandy).

Other popular soups include *ciorbă de perişoare* (spicy soup with meatballs and vegetables) and *ciorbă de legume* (vegetable soup cooked with meat stock). Often, *bors* (a fermented liquid mixture of bran and water) with lemon or sauerkraut juice is added to give a sour taste.

Tochitură is likely to be found on most menus across both countries. There are regional variances (see Regional & Seasonal Cooking, opposite), but it's usually comprised of pan-fried pork, sometimes mixed with other meats, in a spicy pepper sauce served with *mămăligă* and topped with a fried egg. In cheaper restaurants, this can be horribly salty and the meat rubbery, but when done well, it's delicious.

Sarmale (cabbage or vine leaves stuffed with spiced meat and rice), an inheritance from the days of Ottoman rule, is another popular dish. Restaurants and beer gardens typically offer *mititei* or *mici* (spicy grilled meatballs).

Typical desserts include *plăcintă* (turnovers), *clătite* (crepes) and *cozonac* (a brioche) – not to mention *îngheţată* (ice cream). *Saraillie* is a yummy almond cake soaked in syrup. *Papanaşi* are cheese-filled pastries covered with jam and sour cream. *Kuros kalacs* are enormous round donuts with candied sprinkles or chocolate coating; arteries alert! For a Romanian snack attack while on the move, munch on *covrigi*, rings of hard bread speckled with salt crystals.

Since communism, a new national dish has emerged, sneaking its way into all but the most fervently 'traditional' of Romanian menus: pizza. Quality varies from crispy pies with fresh ingredients (a real veggie-a-rama), to baloney bits o'er smeared ketchup.

Romanian and Moldovan cuisines are very similar. In Moldova, some Russian influences have made pickled fruits and vegetables more popular there, as are Russian meals like *pelmeni* (similar to ravioli). A Turkic influence has arguably been stronger in Moldova; in the south you may find the delicious *gagauz sorpa*, a spicy ram soup.

REGIONAL & SEASONAL COOKING

You'll be surprised at how different the same dishes can taste depending on where you eat them; each historical region of Romania has its own culinary influences, which you as a traveller can benefit from.

Moldavia is the place to try *tochitură* (where it's known as its original name *tochitură moldovenească*). Here it's made with pig's livers and kidneys, wine, pepper and garlic, and it's served without *mămăligă*. In Rădăuți, 30km north of Suceava, a worthy local specialty is *ciorbă Rădăuți*, a chicken soup with mashed garlic and vinegar, doused with sour cream.

Moldavia is also famous for other meals likely to make a vegetarian lose their cookies: *racituri* is a jelly made from pig's hooves, used primarily in winter folk celebrations, and their *ciorbă de potroace*, a soup made with chicken entrails, rice and vegetables is said to be a guaranteed cure for hangovers. Some may prefer aspirin.

Transylvania boasts a variety of flavours, plus German and Hungarian dishes. For those who find traditional Romanian dishes bland and devoid of spices, flavourful and hot Hungarian dishes like *gulash*, paprikas and *panierte* will be welcome. When in Cluj-Napoca, look out for *varză de la Cluj* (cabbage à la Cluj), a scrumptious mix of cabbage, minced meat and light spices baked and served with sour cream.

In Wallachia, you'll find lots of prunes *(prună uscată)* on the menu, often mixed with meat in a stew *(tocană)*. In the Banat region, you'll find food spicier than in the rest of Romania, as it's influenced by Serbian cuisine. *Coajă* is a unique type of cheese found only in the villages around Bran, which comes wrapped in (and tasting of) tree bark.

In and around the Danube Delta region, fish and game figure largely on the menu; a local specialty is soup made from up to 10 kinds of fish and vegetables (pieces of garlic are thrown in later), usually slowly simmered in a cast-iron kettle. Carp kebab is another goodie. In Dobrogea, mutton is cooked in sunflower oil, giving it a unique flavour, and plates like pickled fish, fillets, rolls, mincemeat balls, croquettes of zander, Danube herring, shoat fish, carp, pike and sturgeon are also very tasteful.

On All Saints Day (9 March), little *mucenici* (martyrs) are baked, in most of Romania they are pieces of unleavened dough in the form of the figure '8'. However, in Moldavia they're brushed with honey and sprinkled with walnuts, and in Wallachia they're boiled in water with sugar then covered with crushed walnuts and cinnamon.

Easter meals revolve around lamb; especially tasty is lamb *stufat*, a stew made with green onions and garlic. Traditional Christmas cakes, to coincide with carolling, are *cozonac* (a pound cake), walnut cake and pumpkin pie.

DRINKS

Romanian wine hasn't reached its big-league potential in the world yet, but the promise is there. The reds and whites, many slightly sweet and delicious, come from five main regions: Transylvania's Târnave plateau (outside Alba Iulia), Cotnari (outside Iași in Moldavia), Murfatlar (near the Black Sea coast), Dealu Mare (south of the Carpathians, east of Prahova Valley) and Odobești (in southern Moldavia). Crafty 'Dracula'-label wines often get exported, but the best you'll find are homemade local varieties or ones such as Cotnari's Feteasca Negra (slightly sweet red wine), Grasa de Cotnari (a sweet white), Feteasca Regalas (sparkling wine from outside Alba Iulia), and distinctive Chardonnay, Cabernet Sauvignon and Pinot Gris from Murfatlar.

In Moldova, the big names are Cricova, Ialoveni, Cojușna, Milești Mici and Strășeni.

At Christmas in Transylvania, you will find *singeretta* – sausages made with pig's blood, liver, kidneys and fat. How perfect in Dracula country. They're a German inheritance.

What might run through your mind while watching locals feast on things like blood sausage: *gustul disputa n-are* (there's no accounting for taste).

It's said that Dionysus, the God of wine, was born on present-day Romanian lands and when the Romans marched there in AD 106, they found the local wines superior to their own.

Wine production took a hit during communism – things revived with privatisation after 1989, but problems remain. In 2006, lack of funding for grape cultivation resulted in wine imports exceeding exports for the first time.

Red wines are called *negru* and *roşu*, white wine is *vin alb*, while *sec* means 'dry', *dulce* is 'sweet' and *spumos* translates as 'sparkling'. You'll find that Romanian semisweet is most people's idea of sweet and dry is closer to semisweet.

Bucharest, Cluj-Napoca, Constanța and Iași get tipsy all May as part of the Festivinum Wine Festival.

A common practice is to mix the sweeter wines with mineral water; this idea makes connoisseurs' skin crawl – until they taste how sweet it would be otherwise. Prices for a bottle of wine in a restaurant have risen in recent years, and range from €5 to €20 or more. It's less from a *crama* (wine cellar) where you can fill empty litre bottles with local wines for a couple of euros.

Watch for *must* (pronounced 'moost'), a sweet, fermented, not-quite-wine brew, available for a few weeks after grape harvest in October.

In Northern Dobrogea, you're likely to find cafés which make a mean Turkish coffee, with a thick sludge at the bottom and a generous spoonful of sugar. Unless you specifically ask, coffee and *ceai* (tea) are served black and with sugar. If you want it white ask for it *cu lapte* (with milk); without sugar, *fără zahăr*.

The harder stuff is worth trying as well – if you're a male, you're bound to be offered this on social occasions, but beware of the gigantic wallop it packs. *Țuică* is a once-filtered clear brandy made from fermented fruit (the tastiest and most popular is plum *țuică*), usually 30 proof. *Palincă* (called *Horinca* in Maramureș and *Jinars* in the Cluj-Napoca region) is similar, only it's filtered twice and is usually around 60 proof; the stuff can knock your socks off. Both of these are often made at home, where the resulting moonshine can either be much tastier than the store-bought versions or much stronger and wince-inducing. In northern Moldavia, moonshine is called *samahonca*, similar to the Russian word for it.

The maverick republic of Transdniestr has delighted communist bellies (not livers), from Warsaw to Vladivostok for decades, with its cognac from the century-old Kvint factory in Tiraspol (p 338).

WHERE TO EAT & DRINK

There are two types of main eateries: restaurants and fast-food stands. After communism fell, the restaurant scene exploded, but in many places locals go only on splurge outings or special occasions. Hence, many restaurants feel a little more formal, and more pricey, than in more developed food nations.

Many restaurants follow the same template – decked out in traditional Romanian style, with loads of grilled meats and usually pizza on the menu. That said, fast-food stands (often for pizza or kebabs) are everywhere, though not all are that cheap. A kebab in Bucharest runs about €3 – street food in New York is cheaper!

Something you might be offered as you stagger out of your Romanian or Moldovan friends' house: *la botul calului* (literally 'horse's mouth'). It means 'one for the road'!

Most bars or cafés have limited food – maybe a pastry or sandwich – and in farther flung places, particularly Moldova, options may be limited to a hotel restaurant. Few restaurants cater to children (it's rare to find a children's menu or booster chair), but staff are usually accommodating.

Self-catering is relatively simple in these countries. Every town has a central market (*piață centrală*), piled high with fresh fruits and vegetables, and sometimes fish and dried products. Pastries and cakes are sold everywhere in kiosks or shops for €0.20 to €0.40 a piece, a loaf of bread is about €0.40. In most cities and towns there are 24-hour shops and/or Western-style supermarkets. If you're in small towns, you'll probably be limited to getting fresh, filled pastries from kiosks.

Restaurant prices are remarkably consistent, with broad ranges. Mains (often a grilled meat) without sides or a salad start at €2 and go up to €5 or more. Salads and entrees are often the same, making a quick meal sometimes reach €10 per person – Bucharest and Chișinău tend to be more expensive.

Beer is about the same price as bottled water – about €1 or €1.50 – in most restaurants. Wine usually can only be ordered by the bottle (ranging from €5 to €20 or more in finer restaurants).

A 10% tip is considered decent. Always check your bill; some restaurants conveniently add in a tip (or items not ordered – particularly in Bucharest). Do your own maths and ask if something's amiss.

VEGETARIANS & VEGANS

Romanian restaurants really aren't looking out for this group, but thanks to the Orthodox diet, vegetarians can always find some veggie dishes (unexciting and repetitious, yes, but veggie all the same). If you're in the area don't miss Oradea's vegetarian restaurant (p225), the only one in Romania.

Most restaurants have expansive salad lists, not all of which are veggie. The *salată roşii* (tomato salad) is bowl of tomato slices doused in olive oil, vinegar and covered in chopped parsley and onion. Another popular one is *salată castraveţi* (cucumber salad), or tomatoes and cucumbers combined in a *salată asortată* (mixed salad).

On appetiser lists, look for *murături* (pickled vegetables, such as cucumbers or cauliflower), *ciuperci umplute* (stuffed mushrooms), and various sorts of potatoes, including the popular *cartofi ţărăneşti* (country-style potatoes), which is often served alongside meats.

Some menus, if you're lucky, offer vegetable soup or stew, or an eggplant dish, such as *vinete au gratin*, a heavily buttered and cheese-sprinkled stewed or sauteed eggplant.

Otherwise, fresh fruits are easy to find (including huge watermelons), and whatever's grown locally is bound to have had less chemicals involved in its growth than the ones in your home country.

In this guide, care was taken to note which restaurants serve substantial vegetarian meals and go beyond the bare minimum.

EAT YOUR WORDS

To avoid having to mime the animal or vegetable of your choice, here are a few phrases and words to help you get by. See our Language chapter (p368) for more information.

Useful Phrases

Please, bring me the ...
Vă rog să-mi aduceti ... — va rawg, sa-mee a-doo-che-tee ...

Where can I get a quick snack?
Unde aş putea găsi un bar expres? — oon-de ash poo-te-a ga-see oon bar eks-pres?

Do you know a cheap/good restaurant nearby?
Cunoaşteti prin apropiere un restaurant ieftin/bun? — koo-naw-ash-te-ti preen a-praw-pee-e-re oon re-staw-ron ee-ef-tin/boon?

Can you tell me what this is?
Spuneţi-mi, vă rog, ce bucate sunt acesta? — spoo-ne-tsi-mee va-rog che boo-ka-te soont a-ches-ta?

Keep the change.
Fără rest. — fa-ra rest

Is this a vegetarian meal?
Aceste bucate sunt din legume? — a-che-ste boo-ka-te soont deen le-goo-me?

I don't want ketchup.
Nu vreau ketchup. — noo vre-a-oo ke-chup

I don't eat ...
Eu nu mănânc ... — e-oo noo ma-nink ...

Romanians expect that every 'real' meal must have meat in it. There's even a proverb: *Cel mai bun peşte este porcul* (The best fish is pork).

The notion of 'organic' food doesn't exist in Romania as the vast bulk of the locally grown produce is already chemical-free to begin with! The catch though – and it's a big one – is that many restaurants don't add them to menus, as some consider 'vegetables' to be merely peasant fare.

Romanian-English Menu Decoder

VEGETABLES

anchinară	artichoke
ardei	peppers
cartofi	potatoes
castravete	cucumber
ceap	onion
ciuperci	mushrooms
conopidă	cauliflower
dovlecei	zucchini
fasole	bean
legume	vegetable
marcov	carrot
măsline	olive
roşie	tomato
sfecl	beet
spanac	spinach
varz	cabbage
vinete	eggplant

When in Székely Land, you might need to know that *vendeglo* and *etterem* mean 'restaurant' in Hungarian.

FRUIT

caisă	apricot
căpşun	strawberry
fruct	fruit
lămâie	lemon
măr	apple
pepene galben	melon
pepene verde	watermelon
portocală	orange
prun	plum
smochina	fig
struguri	grapes
vişin	cherry

SPECIALITIES

ciorbă	soup
ciorbă de burtă	tripe soup
mămăligă	polenta-like cornmeal
sarmale	vine leaves stuffed with meat and rice
ţuică	plum brandy

STAPLES

ardei umpluti	stuffed peppers
brânză	cheese
caşcaval	yellow cheese
găluşcă	dumpling
iaurt	yogurt
lapte	milk
orez	rice
ou	egg
pâine	bread
smântână	sour cream

SOUPS

ciorbă	mixed soup with sour creme
ciorbă de burtă	tripe soup
ciorbă de legume	vegetable soup
ciorbă de perişoare	meatball soup
ciorbă ţăranească	meat-and-vegetable soup
supă de fasole	bean soup
supă de roşii	tomato soup

CONDIMENTS

busuioc	basil
ceapă de apă	shallot
ghimber	ginger
mărar	dill
mujdei	garlic sauce
pătrunjel	parsley
piper	pepper
sare	salt
sovârf	oregano
unt	butter
untdelemn	olive oil
usturoi	garlic
zahăr	sugar

MEATS & PREPARATION

berbec	mutton
bine prăjit	well done
capră	female goat
creier	brains
cu puţin sânge	rare
curcan	turkey
în sânge	very rare
miel	lamb
mititei/mici	spicy grilled meatballs
muşchi	sirloin
pâine	bread
pe grătar	grilled
porc	pork
potrivit	medium
prăjit la cuptor	roasted
pui	chicken
pulpă de miel	leg of lamb
rasol	poached meat
rinichi	kidneys
slănină	bacon
şniţel	schnitzel
stufat	braised meat
şunca	ham
ţap	male goat
vacă	beef

FISH

crap	carp
crevete	shrimp
homar	lobster
morun	sturgeon
păstrăv	trout
pete	fish
raci	crayfish
sardele	sardine
scrumbrie	herring
somon	salmon
ştuică	pike
ton	tuna
ţipar	eel

DRINKS

ap rece	cold water
apă cald	hot water
apă mineral	mineral water
bere	beer
cafea	coffee
ceai	tea
lapte	milk
suc de mere	apple juice
suc de portocale	orange juice
ţuică	plum brandy
vin alb	white wine
vin roşu	red wine

OTHER

barărie	bar/beer hall
brutărie	bakery
cafenea	cafeteria
cofetărie	confectionery
copti	baked
crama	wine cellar
fiert	boiled
gogoşerie	place selling donuts
list	menu
not de plat	bill
patiserie	patisserie
prjit/pai	fried
restaurant	restaurant
tavernă	tavern
terasă	terrace

Romania

DIANA MAYFIELD

Bucharest

Much of Romania slags it and Europe in general doesn't always speak favourably of Romania's capital. They're all wrong. Its perplexing mismatch of eras – grey housing blocks from Ceauşescu's brutal rebuilding phase, deliberately French palaces with baroque clam-shaped canopies, (limited) remains of medieval churches and courts, 21st-century office buildings – means that even a short walk around blurs time. Bucharest is home to Romania's best museums – lots of them – some of which defy limited budgets by illustrating the rural side of Romanian life. Others, like the communist bon voyage Palace of Parliament (the world's second-biggest building), show off another era.

More importantly, like any great city, Bucharest believes in itself: a lively student base takes over the historic centre's open-air bar scene, all-age couples attend theatre or opera or foreign-language films kept in their original tongue, and families seeking weekend quiet lounge all day in Bucharest's (often) well-kept parks. Not what one might expect, considering revolution tore the city apart less than two decades ago.

Alas, Bucharest has its problems – taxi scams, glue-sniffing beggars, packs of stray dogs, loud traffic – but it has a heart too. Stick around more than a day – as some visitors flee at first sight – and you start to get it. Bucharest has something going on.

HIGHLIGHTS

- Learn why you don't appreciate granny enough at the heartbreakingly sweet **Museum of the Romanian Peasant** (p75)
- Visit Ceauşescu's madhouse, the **Palace of Parliament** (p68), on a 40-minute tour that ends at the National Museum of Contemporary Art's rooftop cafe
- Pay tribute to Holocaust victims and Romania's diminished Jewish population at the **Jewish History Museum** (p75)
- Kick back in one of Bucharest's two most beloved parks: **Cişmigiu Garden** (p76) and **Herăstrău Park** (p76)
- Explore the eerie backlots off **B-dul Unirii** (p70), where Ceauşescu had churches and monasteries demolished and hemmed in by towering, grey housing blocks

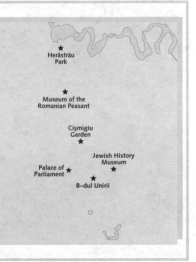

★ Herăstrău Park

★ Museum of the Romanian Peasant

Cişmigiu Garden ★

★ Jewish History Museum

Palace of ★ Parliament

★ B-dul Unirii

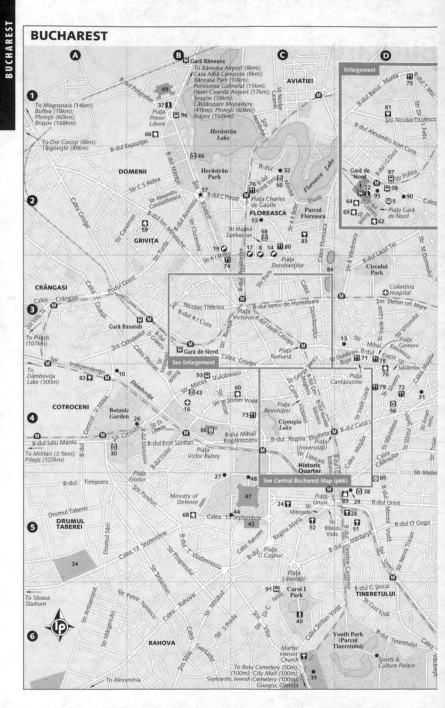

BUCHAREST

Gară Băneasa

To Băneasa Airport (8km);
Casa Albă Campsite (8km);
Băneasa Park (10km);
Pensiunea Gabrielal (15km);
Henri Coanda Airport (17km);
Snagov (38km);
Căldărușani Monastery
(41km); Ploiești (60km);
Brașov (168km)

To Mogoșoaia (14km);
Buftea (18km);
Ploiești (60km);
Brașov (168km)

To Doi Cocoși (6km);
Târgoviște (49km)

Herăstrău Lake

Herăstrău Park

DOMENII

Piața Presei Libere

B-dul Expoziției

B-dul Mărăști

B-dul Poligrafiei

AVIATIEI

Enlargement

Str Barbu Văcărescu

B-dul 1 Mai

Șos Nicolae Titulescu

B-dul Alexandru Ioan Cuza

Gară de Nord

Piața Gară de Nord

Calea

Piața Charles de Gaulle

FLOREASCA

Floreasca Lake

Parcul Floreasca

Str Muzeul Zambaccian

Piața Dorobanților

Str C.S. Aldea

Str Caraiman

Str Alexandru Constantinescu

GRIVIȚA

CRÂNGAȘI

Calea Griviței

Gară Basarab

Podul Grant

Șos Virtuți

To Pitești (107km)

To Dâmbovița Lake (300m)

COTROCENI

Botanic Garden

Dâmbovița

Splai Independenței

Str Mircea Vulcănescu

Piața Victoriei

Piața Nicolae Titulescu

B-dul A I Cuza

Gară de Nord

See Enlargement

B-dul Iancu de Hunedoara

Piața Romană

Piața Revoluției

Cișmigiu Lake

Piața Universității

Str Lipscani

Historic Quarter

See Central Bucharest Map (p66)

Piața Unirii

B-dul Regina Elisabeta

B-dul Mihail Kogălniceanu

Piața Victor Babeș

Piața Eroilor

B-dul Iuliu Maniu

To Militari (3.5km);
Pitești (107km)

B-dul Timișoara

Ministry of Defence

Calea 13 Septembrie

DRUMUL TABEREI

Str Progresului

Calea 13 Septembrie

To Steaua Stadium

RAHOVA

Calea Rahovei

Piața G. Coșbuc

Piața Libertății

Carol I Park

Martyr Heroes' Church

To Belu Cemetery (50m);
City Mall (100m);
Sephardic Jewish Cemetery (100m);
Giurgiu; Olenița

TINERETULUI

Youth Park (Parcul Tineretului)

Sports & Culture Palace

Colentina Hospital

Circului Park

Șos Ștefan cel Mare

Piața Gemeni

Piața Cantacuzino

Str Dacia

Str Silvestru

Str Matei

B-dul Carol I

B-dul Unirii

B-dul Dimitrie Cantemir

B-dul G Șincai

B-dul O Goga

B-dul Mărășești

Str Mitropolei

Str Bibescu Vodă

Splai Nerva Traian

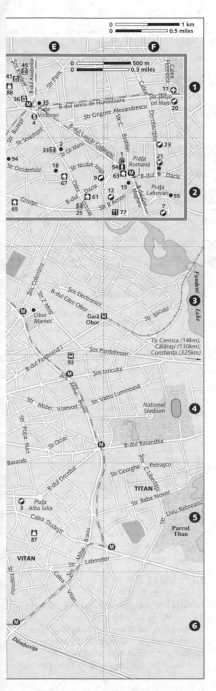

HISTORY

Legend has it that Bucharest was founded by a shepherd named Bucur (*bucurie*; literally 'joy') who built a church on the right bank of the Dâmboviţa River.

The city, which lies on the Wallachian plains between the Carpathian foothills and the Danube River, was settled by Geto-Dacians as early as 70 BC. By 1459 a princely residence and military citadel had been established under the chancellery of infamous Prince Vlad Ţepeş. By the end of the 17th century, the city was the capital of Wallachia and ranked among southeastern Europe's wealthiest cities. Bucharest became the national capital in 1862, as it lay on the main trade route between east and west.

The early 20th century was Bucharest's golden age. Large neoclassical buildings sprang up, fashionable parks were laid out and landscaped on Parisian models and, by the end of the 1930s, Bucharest was known throughout Europe as 'Little Paris'.

Bombing by the Allies during WWII, coupled with a 1940 earthquake measuring 7.4 on the Richter scale, destroyed much of Bucharest's prewar beauty. In March 1977 a second major earthquake claimed 1391 lives and flattened countless buildings. Ceauşescu's criminal redevelopment of the city marked the final death knell of Romania's elegant past.

The revolution of 1989 ripped the city to shreds. Although still haunted by its bloody history, Bucharest is recovering from its painful rebirth with contemporary building projects, the cull of snarling street dogs, care of street children who once roamed the city, crime prevention measures and an optimism born of hard-won freedom. Yet there's still much to do and Bucharest's future is as uncertain as it is exciting.

These days, as Bucharest finally assumes its status as a new EU capital, abandoned cranes remain next to abandoned projects from Ceauşescu buildings, while new ones tower over glittering new hotels or office buildings. A lot of people bump elbows in the tight space – Bucharest is Europe's most crowded capital, with over 8000 people per sq kilometre, about 10 times more packed than Paris.

ORIENTATION

Bucharest's international airport, Henri Coandă, is 17km north of the centre. Şoseaua

BUCHAREST

Kiseleff runs south past Băneasa domestic airport (8km from the city) and Herăstrău Park to Piaţa Victoriei. Calea Victorei cuts through the heart of the historic centre, connecting to the Romanian Athenaeum on Piaţa Revoluţiei (south).

The main train station, Gară de Nord, is 2km northwest of central Bucharest. B-dul General Magheru, the southern foot of which is called B-dul Nicolae Bălcescu, links Piaţa Romană (north) with Piaţa Universităţii (south)– a central focal point close to the Ion Luca Caragiale National Theatre and Hotel Inter-Continental. Forming the eastern edge of the historic centre, B-dul IC Brătianu runs south from Piaţa Universităţii to Piaţa Unirii, the Civic Centre and the Palace of Parliament.

Maps

By far the best Bucharest map, available at bus ticket stands, is the so-called *100% Planul Oraşului Bucureşti Map*, with all transportation routes and an index for all streets.

Relatively disappointing is Amco Press' bilingual *Bucharest City Plan*, available at many bookshops.

INFORMATION
Bookshops

Libraria Noi (Map p66; ☎ 311 0700; B-dul Nicolae Balcescu 18; 🕙 9.30am-8.30pm Mon-Sat, 11am-7pm Sun) Best bookshop in Bucharest by a kilometre. It stocks the only decent range of English-language novels, has Lonely Planet guides, lots of maps, and a fab antiques section with old maps, sketches and photos of Bucharest's glory days.

Salingers (Map pp62-3; ☎ 403 3534; www.salingers.ro; Calea 13 Septembrie 90, Marriott Grand Hotel; ☽ 10am-9pm) Stocks some English language fiction and nonfiction and Lonely Planet guides.

Cultural Centres

British Council Library (Map pp62-3; ☎ 307 9600; www.britishcouncil.ro; Calea Dorobanţilor 14; ☽ 10am-5pm Mon-Fri, to noon Sat) English-language newspapers and internet.
French Institute (Map pp62-3; ☎ 316 0224; www .culture-france.ro; B-dul Dacia 77; ☽ 9am-6.30pm Mon-Thu, 9am-4.30pm Fri, 10am-2.30pm Sat) Film screenings, plus an excellent bistro (open noon to midnight Monday to Saturday).

Emergency

Emergency numbers are Romanian-speaking only. The catch-all general emergency number is ☎ 112. Otherwise you can call:
Ambulance (☎ 973)
Central Police Station (Map p66; ☎ 311 2021; Calea Victoriei 17)
Fire (☎ 981)
Police (☎ 955)

Internet Access

Acces Internet (Map pp62-3; ☎ 650 7879; B-dul Lascar Catargiu 6; per hr €0.75-0.90; ☽ 24hr) International calls are US$0.04 per min.
Access Internet (Map p66; B-dul Nicolae Bălcescu 24; per 20min €0.30; ☽ 7am-2am)
Internet & Games (Map p66; ☎ 0721-877-866; B-dul Regina Elisabeta 25; per hr €0.30; ☽ 24hr)

Laundry

Welcome to Romania: getting your laundry isn't as easy as it would seem. Travellers at some hostels, including Butterfly Villa (p82), get free laundry service. Most hotels will do it for you (sometimes for high prices). Most laundry services in town are actually dry cleaners, although one place where you can drop off laundry is the huge department store **Carrefour** (Map pp62-3; ☎ 317 7646; Spl Independentei 210-210B; ☽ 8am-10pm), near the Grozaveşti metro station in western Bucharest.

Left Luggage

Gară de Nord (Map pp62-3; Piaţa Gară de Nord 1; per day €1.75; ☽ 24hr) Left luggage is on the right side of the long hallway if heading from the tracks to the exit.

Media

International press is found in the newsagents at the Hotel Inter-Continental, Marriott Grand Hoel and Athénée Palace Hilton.
Bucharest Daily News (www.daily-news.ro) The better of Bucharest's English-language dailies (€0.85), with entertainment listings and original content.
Bucharest In Your Pocket (www.inyourpocket.com) Bi-monthly, comprehensive guide to Bucharest (€2.30) with opinionated (if occasionally dated) entertainment, hotel and restaurant listings.
Expat Life Bizarre fanzine brimming with blokey wisecracks. Free for the taking at pubs and the like.
Nine O'Clock (www.nineoclock.ro) English-language daily (€0.75); includes minimal TV coverage, restaurant reviews and movie listings.

BUCHAREST IN...

One Day
What makes Bucharest so interesting is its unruly Parisian/communist/medieval overlaps. Start with the **walking tour** (p78) of Ceauşescu's Bucharest, making sure to take a tour of the **Palace of Parliament** (p68), and save time to peek into the **Art Museum** (p73). Afterwards sit for a beer at **Cişmiu Garden** (p76) then take a bus or metro north to the **National Museum of the Romanian Peasant** (p75).

Three Days
After day one, spend a second visiting **Herăstrău Park** (p76) allowing time to see the open-air **National Village Museum** (p76) on its western bank. Walk down Şos Kiseleff, stopping at the Triumphal Arch (p76) and take the metro to Piaţa Universităţii to see where many died during the 1989 revolution. For your last day, consider taking a tour to **Snagov** (p89) to see Dracula's, er, Vlad Ţepeş', final resting place. Those not on the Drac trail can enjoy the fascinating **Jewish History Museum** (p75) and then a walk from the **Belu Cemetery** (p78) back to the centre via **Carol I Park** (p77).

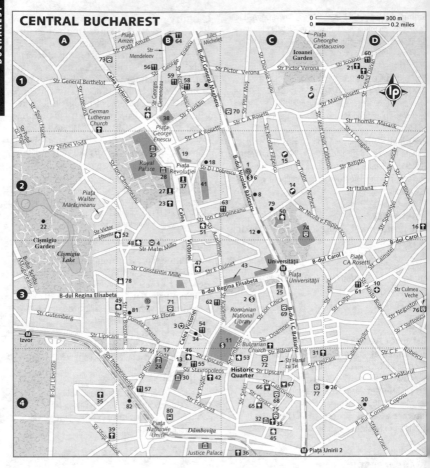

CENTRAL BUCHAREST

Şapte Seri (www.sapteseri.ro) Widespread, complimentary entertainment listing in Romanian only; the useful website is also in English.

Vivid (www.vivid.ro) Colourful, free English-language magazine published nine times a year. Articles cover Romanian politics and business, tapping into expat life here. Found at stationers in the Athenée Palace Hilton and Marriott Grand Hotel.

24-Fun Another Romanian-language weekly with entertainment listings.

Medical Services

Emergency Clinic Hospital (Map pp62-3; ☎ 230 0106; Calea Floreasca 8; ☼ 24hr) Bucharest's best state hospital.

Medicover (Map pp62-3; ☎ 310 4410, emergency ☎ 310 4040; www.medicover.ro; Calea Plevnei 96;

☼ 8am-8pm Mon-Fri, to 1pm Sat) Good private clinic.

Pro-Dental Care (Map p66; ☎ 313 4781; Str Hristo Botev 7; ☼ 10am-8pm Mon-Fri, to 4pm Sat)

Puls (☎ 224 0187; ☼ 7.30am-7.30pm, to 1.30pm Sun) Private ambulance company with English-speaking medics. Not for emergencies.

Sensi-Blu (www.sensiblu.com) B-dul Nicolae Bălcescu (Map p66; ☎ 305 7314; B-dul Nicolae Bălescu 7; ☼ 24hr); Calea Victoriei (☎ 315 3160; Calea Victoriei 12A; ☼ 8am-10pm Mon-Fri, 9am-9pm Sat & Sun) Excellent pharmacy chain with 18 locations in Bucharest.

Money

Currency exchanges are everywhere. Don't use the exchanges in the baggage claim hall of Henri Coanda airport as they offer the worst rates in the city. There is an ATM in the arrivals hall.

ATMs are around every corner. If you're looking for an indoor ATM, **ING** (Map p66; B-dul Nicolae Bălcescu 20) has one.

Exchange booths, open 24 hours, along B-dul Nicolae Bălcescu are good places to change money. Be sure to count your lei notes before handing over US dollars, euro or British pounds.

For cash transfers, travellers cheques and banking services, try the following:
Banca Comercială Română B-dul Regina Elisabeta (Map p66; B-dul Regina Elisabeta 5; 8.30am-5.30pm Mon-Fri, to 12.30pm Sat); Calea Victoriei (Map pp62-3; Calea Victoriei 155; 8.30am-6pm Mon-Fri, to 12.30pm Sat) Most services run weekdays only.

Post
Central post office (Poşta Română Oficiul Bucureşti 1; Map p66; ☎ 315 9030; www.post-romana.ro; Str Matei Millo 10; 7.30am- 8pm Mon-Fri, 8am-2pm Sat) Collect poste restante mail here.

Branch post office Str Gării de Nord (Map pp62-3; Str Gării de Nord 6-8; 7.30am-8pm Mon-Fri, 8am-2pm Sat) See website for other locations.

Telephone
A testimony of its times: Romania's telephone centres – where long-distance calls could be made – have pretty much all shut their services, and started selling mobile phones. RomTelecom cards (from €3), available from kiosks, can be used in neglected phone booths to make national and international calls.

If you're wanting a Romanian number on your mobile phone, SIM cards for Orange or Vodafone are available everywhere.

Access Internet (p65) can make calls as well.

Tourist Information & Travel Agencies
Sometimes you have to wonder if the Bucharest government just doesn't care about itself, because the nation's capital is woefully unrepresented in the world of information.

And the many travel agencies seem focused on getting you *out* of the country.

Hostels tend to be excellent sources of info, helping with hire cars or day trips to Snagov or even Bran Castle.

The following agencies at least won't look confused if you ask for travel information for around Romania.

Atlantic Tours (Map pp62-3; ☎ 311 0235; www .atlantic.ro; Calea Victoriei 202; ☼ 9am-6pm Mon-Fri, to 1pm Sat) Can arrange trips based on budget and hire cars, although it's more geared to digital visits than actual ones; email ahead via office@atlantic.ro.

Marshal Turism (Map pp62-3; ☎ 319 4457; www .marshal.ro; B-dul General Magheru 43; ☼ 9am-6pm Mon-Fri, to 1pm Sat) Upstairs office can try to help with domestic travel; can hire cars or find apartments in Bucharest (€65 to €70).

ONT Carpaţi (Map p66; ☎ 314 1922; www.ont.ro; B-dul General Magheru 7; ☼ 9am-6.30pm Mon-Fri, to 2pm Sat) Lots of outbound business, but helpful staff are happy to talk you through a Romania trip, arrange daily guides (€30) and offer city tours (from €40 with driver).

RoCultours/CTI (Map pp62-3; ☎ 650 8145; www .rotravel.com/cti; Str Sfinţii Voievozi 49-51; ☼ 9am-7pm) Reliable agent with many cultural tours, and personalised itineraries listed on the website. It also has a couple of rooms for €45 for two people. It's best to contact them in advance.

Wasteels (Map pp62-3; ☎ 317 0370; www.wasteels travel.ro; Gară de Nord; ☼ 8am-7pm Mon-Fri, to 2pm Sat) Conveniently located on the left side of the exit hallway of the train station, Wasteels can hire cars, help with train reservations (it's €4 for a seat, €15 for a couchette – same as at station), and may be able to call you a reliable taxi.

DANGERS & ANNOYANCES

Bucharest gets a bad rap sometimes and we think it's exaggerated. Still, like any big European city, there are risks to be aware of.

It's said that Bucharest's stray dogs (politically correct term of late: 'community dogs') number 100,000 – some say 200,000. Though it's rarely a problem, travellers are occasionally bitten, and in 2006 a Japanese businessmen bled to death following a freak bite, which resulted in a severed artery. If bitten, go to a hospital for antirabic injections within 36 hours. Avoid any packs of dogs, who occasionally occupy empty lots behind buildings.

Another 'danger' is the taxi drivers who charge extortionately high prices. Worst are those outside Gară de Nord. Avoid using these

(we've heard of travellers paying US$150 for a US$5 ride!). Wasteels can usually call for a taxi from the train station, if you don't have a phone to call the reliable companies listed on p89.

In the past, the fake-taxi scam tricked some new arrivals. These English-speaking drivers approached travellers at the train station and claimed to be from a hostel, then charged skyscraper-high rates for the ride. Unless you have arranged transport from your accommodation, don't take a ride with someone claiming to be from there. Glue-sniffing homeless people sometimes approach new arrivals outside the train station, asking for handouts.

Pick-pocket incidents are most likely on the sometimes very packed public buses or metro. Groups of begging kids can get touchy-feely around Piaţa Revoluţiei. In our many weeks in Bucharest, we heard of no travellers getting robbed, but it can happen. Never produce your wallet to a stranger – we've heard of a friendly looking local asking to see a 100-lei note, then taking the whole wallet and running.

Watch for the fake 'tourist police,' where a man in an official-looking uniform demands to see your passport. Never hand one over on the street. If they persist, ask to go to the nearest police station. We've *never* had to show a passport to any real official other than at a random highway check for all cars and trucks.

SIGHTS

Bucharest teems with museums and attractions, all relatively dirt cheap and many among the nation's best. The historic thoroughfare Calea Victoriei makes a nice walk, as it connects the two main squares of the city: Piaţa Victoriei in the north, and Piaţa Revoluţiei in the centre; then one could follow the river east to where it goes under the sprawling Piaţa Unirii, the heart of 'Ceauşescu's Bucharest' (p78).

Palace of Parliament & Around

Facing B-dul Unirii is the impossible-to-miss **Palace of Parliament** (Palatul Parlamentului; Map pp62-3; ☎ 311 3611; B-dul Naţiunile Unite; adult/student €6/3; ☼ 10am-4pm), the world's second-largest building (after the US Pentagon) and Ceauşescu's most infamous creation. Built in 1984 (and still 10% unfinished), the building's 12 storeys and 3100 rooms cover 330,000 sq m – an estimated €3.3 billion project. Rushed, but interesting, 45-minute tours go every half hour or so and lead into a handful of marble rooms – still hired out for conferences – finishing at the balcony Nicolae didn't live long enough to speak from. The whopping €8.60 photography or video fee is widely ignored. Facing from B-dul Unirii, the entrance is around to the right (a 12-minute walk).

Back on the building's west side, walk back past B-dul Unirii to the building's south side, noting the half-finished **National Institute for Science & Technology** (Map pp62-3; cnr B-dul Libertăţii & Calea 13 Septembrie), of which Elena Ceauşescu was

president; half-done or abandoned buildings like this litter Bucharest.

In the back of the Palace of Parliament is the superb **National Museum of Contemporary Art** (Muzeul Naţionalde Arta Contemporana; ☎ 318 9137; www.mnac.ro; Calea 13 Septembrie; adult/student €1.50/free; ☑ 10am-6pm Wed-Sun), which opened in 2004. A fully changing four-floor space, with double all-glass elevators built onto the outside of the building, features eclectic European artists' installation and video art, and is easily one of Eastern Europe's most provocative spaces

---

PALACE OF PARLIAMENT: FACTS & FICTION

Controversy still rages around this massive edifice. More than a symbol of Ceauşescu's communist vision, it stands today as a reminder of the price Romania paid to satisfy the egotistical whims of Nicolae and Elena. While people starved, hospitals suffered medicine shortages and industry ground to a halt, Ceauşescu embarked on building the world's second-largest building at an estimated cost of €3.3 billion. The monument has even attracted its own myths which, added to the facts, make this Bucharest's most fascinating architectural wonder.

FACTS:

- It was built in 1984 to house the Central Committee, presidential office and state ministries. Today it houses the chamber of deputies, constitutional court and an international conference centre.
- One sixth of Bucharest was bulldozed to accommodate the monstrous building and its surroundings. It stands 85m tall and has a surface area of 330,000 sq m.
- It is the world's second-largest building in surface area (after the US Pentagon) and the third-largest in volume.
- More than 700 architects and three shifts of 20,000 workers laboured on it 24 hours a day for five years.
- It has 12 storeys and 3100 furnished rooms. Two of its 60-plus galleries are 150m long and 18m wide. Forty of its 64 reception halls are 600 sq m. Union Hall is 3000 sq m in size.
- Beneath it is a vast nuclear bunker, plummeting 20m deep.
- In the 1980s, when lit, the building consumed a day's electricity supply for the whole of Bucharest in four hours.
- The carpet once covering the floor of Union Hall weighed 14 tonnes; it's rolled up today.
- The crystal chandelier in the Human Rights Hall weighs 2½ tonnes.
- It is still known locally by its former name, the House of the People (Casa Poporului).
- In 2000 the halls of the palace were plastered with religious icons during the making of the movie *Amen*.

FICTION:

- The glass ceiling of the ballroom can open to allow a helicopter to land!
- Michael Jackson stood on the balcony and said 'Hello Budapest, I'm so glad to be here' – he actually made the legendary error at the national stadium (though palace guides encourage the irresistible tale when leading groups to the balcony).
- The entire palace is decorated with pure gold.

Past exhibits included collapsed walls lined with large claustrophobic images of Ceauşescu and the communist era. There's a top-floor open-air cafe. The entry is from the southwestern side of the building – a 20-minute walk from the palace-tour entry!

The best way to the palace is walking from Piaţa Unirii (and its metro station) along B-dul Unirii.

Piaţa Unirii & Around

In the blocks around Piaţa Unirii – that commie-built wonder of cement – are a number of religious sites that miraculously survived the 1980s demolition. (Also see p78 for a walking tour that begins here.)

On the northeastern side of Piaţa Unirii – up from the metro station – is the **Unirea Department Store** (Map pp62–3), and the main **city market** is a long block behind it – shop here for fresh fruit and vegetables. Just behind the Unirea is the **Jewish History Museum** (p75). The **Dâmboviţa River** snakes up to the northeastern corner before disappearing underground, beneath the square, on its journey to the southwest of the city. The natural twists and turns of the river were canalised between 1880 and 1883 and later enhanced with concrete.

Romanian Patriarchal Cathedral (Catedrala Patriahală Română; Map pp62–3; Str Dealul Mitropoliei; admission free; 7am-8pm) sits south of Piaţa Unirii, atop Patriarchy Hill. It's the majestic centre of the Romanian Orthodox faith. During the 15th century a small wooden church surrounded by vineyards stood on the hill. The cathedral consecrated the metropolitan centre of Wallachia in 1868, and was built in 1656–8 by Wallachian prince Şerban Basarab. None of the original interior paintings or icons remains, bar a single icon (1665) depicting Constantin and Helen, the cathedral's patron saints. The present-day frescoes were painted by Dimitrie Belizarie in 1923. To the west is a small **chapel**, linked by a balcony to the **Patriarchal Palace**, the south wings of which date to 1932. Three beautifully carved 16th- and 17th-century **stone crosses** flank the northern wall of the cathedral. Alongside is a belfry (1698) and a former parliament building dating from 1907.

Other surviving churches include the 16th-century **Prince Radu Monastery** (Mânăstirea Radu Vodă; Map pp62–3; Str Radu Vodă 24), southeast of Piaţa Unirii, and the nearby **Church of Bucur the Shepherd** (Biserica Bucur Ciobanul; Map pp62–3; Str Radu Vodă), dating from 1743 and dedicated to the city's legendary founder.

Tiny **St Apostles' Church** (Map p66; Biserica Sfintii Apostoli; Str Apostoli 33a), north of B-dul Unirii (west of the square), survived systemisation to a degree. The church, built in 1636, was not moved but the surrounding parkland was ripped up and replaced with blocks of flats. It's overgrown with trees and near abandoned buildings inhabited by squatters, with packs of stray dogs sometimes walking by. It's hard to believe it's only 100m from the 'Parliament of the People'!

Across B-dul Unirii is the surviving **Antim Monastery** (Mânăstirea Antim; Map pp62–3; Str Antim), a beautiful walled complex built in 1715 by the metropolitan bishop Antim Ivireanu.

Another impressive church that survives is the candy-striped **Princess Bălaşa Church** (Map p66; Biserica Domniţa Bălaşa). The church, just northwest of Piaţa Unirii (behind the riverside Justice Palace), is named after Brâncoveanu's sixth daughter, who had a small wooden church built here in 1744. Widowed from 1745, the princess replaced the church with a stone

---

PROPS TO THE STINKY D

All great cities have their rivers, and Bucharest slips in its quest for greatness thanks to the way it's treated the miserly Dâmboviţa River. Centuries ago, when Bucharest first took its steps, the river rushed through woods on this relatively hilly part of the plain. Mosquitoes loved the river though, and brought malaria to a growing population; sewage seemed drawn to it too, and the flood-prone river grew more and more contaminated.

In the 1970s, Ceauşescu's destructive gaze fell on the river – perhaps the USSR's canal-building history steered it – and he displaced villages west of the centre to build the Dâmboviţa Lake (aka Lake Morii), a concrete-floored lake that accumulates a healthy collection of trash on its eastern rim (though some locals dare to swim in or wind-board on it).

All in all, it's not pretty. In fact, it's trashy and murky and stinky. But – don't slag it – the Dâmboviţa just won't quit. Got to respect that in a river.

structure in 1751 and set up a school and asylum. Damaged by an earthquake, the second church was replaced by a third church in 1838–42, which was subsequently damaged by floods and replaced by a fourth church in 1881–5.

A block northwest is the nearly lost former symbol of the city: the 16th-century **Prince Mihai Monastery** (Mânăstirea Mihai Vodă; Map p66; Str Sapienţei), built in 1589–91 under the orders of Mihai Viteazul (r 1593–1601). Ceauşescu moved it 279m east in 1985 to this patch of wasteland between apartment blocks.

Piaţa Universităţii

Some of the fiercest fighting during the 1989 revolution took place here. Journalists watched tanks roll over Romanian freedom fighters and soldiers shoot into crowds of protestors from their viewpoint inside Hotel Inter-Continental. Scour the area and you'll find bullet marks in buildings and 10 stone crosses commemorating those killed. A black **memorial cross** (Map p66; B-dul Nicolae Bălescu 18), a couple of blocks north of the square, marks the spot where the first protestor, Mihai Gătlan, died at 5.30pm on 21 December 1989.

Piaţa Universităţii (sometimes called 'Piaţa Tiananmen') is the hub of Bucharest's intellectual and political life. The main **university building** (Map p66) built in 1856–68 and inaugurated in 1869 is on the northwestern corner.

Housed in a neo-Gothic palace built in the 1830s to host fancy balls, the **History & Art Museum** (Map p66; ☎ 315 6858; B-dul IC Brătianu 2; admission €0.60; ⊗ 10am-6pm Wed-Sun), facing the square, is a lovely spot with an interesting collection of old artefacts, photos and costumes. A few pieces pre-date the Bronze Era, and some documents hail from the days when Romanians wrote in Cyrillic. Designed by two Austrian architects, the neo-Gothic palace was built in 1832–4 for the Şuţu family, notorious for their high-society parties. One document upstairs is the first known chronicle of the city (1459), and was issued by the moustached Vlad Ţepeş. A giant Venetian mirror on the stairway reflects a mirrored clock (eternally reading 2.15 these days). Changing art exhibitions are held downstairs.

A few blocks south of the square is the 1699 **New St George's Church** (Map p66; Biserica Sfântul Gheorghe-Nou; cnr Str Lipscani & B-dul Brătianu), burial place of Wallachian prince Constan-

---

DIY WALKING TOURS

If you had time to walk only four streets, these highlight different sides of Bucharest – all equally fascinating.

- **Calea Victoriei** Bucharest's historic road goes by many belle époque buildings; designed to connect the centre with Mogoşoia (p91).

- **Şos Kiseleff** This is a tree-lined boulevard leading from Piaţa Victoriei to the Triumphal Arch and the Stalinesque Press House.

- **Calea Griviţei** From glue-sniffers outside scrappy Gară de Nord, past quiet blocks and French-style buildings (some abandoned) to Calea Victoriei.

- **B-dul Unirii** It's not inspiring, but Ceauşescu's B-dul Unirii is a 3.5km statement – in concrete.

---

tin Brâncoveanu (r 1688–1714). Brâncoveanu was captured by the Turks in 1714, following his refusal to take part in the Russo-Turkish War (1711). He and his four sons were taken to Istanbul where they were tortured, then decapitated. His wife smuggled his mutilated body back to Romania.

Historic Centre

Bucharest's historic heart – on and off historic Calea Victoriei – sprang up around the **Old Princely Court** (Curtea Veche; Map p66; ☎ 314 0375, Str Franceza 21-23; admission €0.60; ⊗ 10am-5pm) in the 15th century. The battered remains of this court reveal little; you can peer through the fence to the statues of Vlad Ţepeş. Artisans and traders whose occupations are still reflected in street names like Str Covaci (trough-makers street) and Str Şelari (saddle-makers street) settled in this area in the 14th century, but it was not until the reigning prince of Wallachia, Vlad Ţepeş, fortified the settlement and built a **Prince's Palace** (Palatul Voievodal) that it flourished as a commercial centre. At the end of the 18th century, heavily damaged by earthquakes, it was auctioned off to local merchants.

The **Old Princely Court Church** (Biserica Curtea Veche; Map p66; Str Franceza), built in 1546–59 during the reign of Mircea Ciobanul (Mircea the Shepherd), is Bucharest's oldest church. The faded 16th-century frescoes next to the altar are originals. The carved stone portal was added in 1715. Southeast of the church stands **Hanul lui Manuc** (see p81), built to shelter travelling merchants.

A couple of short cobbled blocks north, **Str Lipscani** is the centre of bohemian nightlife with small streets crowded with bars and clubs. The area particularly comes alive in summer.

At its western end, Str Lipscani crosses **Calea Victoriei**, Bucharest's most historic street. It was built under Brâncoveanu's orders in 1692 to link his summer palace in Mogoşoaia, 14km north-west of Bucharest, with the heart of his capital city.

On the road, the **National History Museum** (Map p66; ☎ 311 3356; Calea Victoriei 12; adult/student €0.90/0.45; ☒ 9am-5pm), housed in the neoclassical ex-Post Office Palace (1894), is smaller than it looks, thank to a long-running renovation ('maybe finished by 2010', we heard from an employee) that has closed all but a couple of exhibits. Still it's worth it to see a dismantled replica of the 2nd-century AD Trajan's Column; its 2500 characters retell the Dacian Wars against Rome (the location of the original column). Go to panel 18 to see decapitated heads, panel 35 to see Dacian women torture Romans, or panel 116 for Dacian King Decebal's suicide. There's also a gold-crammed treasury with a gold-studded helmet from the 4th century BC.

A block east of the museum, the **Stavropoleos Church** (Map p66; Str Stavropoleos), on a street meaning 'town of the cross', dates from 1724 and is Bucharest's nicest church, with a court-yard filled with old tombstones and an ornate wooden interior. Prominent Romanian architect Ion Mincu designed the courtyard and restored this little gem in 1899.

Bucharest's financial houses moved to the historic heart in the 19th century after the princely residence was moved to the north of the city. Just north of the museum is the **Economic Consortium Palace** (Casa de Economii ş Consemnaţiuni, CEC; Map p66), designed by French architect Paul Gottereau in 1894–1900 Next door stands the **Bucharest Financial Plaza** (Map p66), a mirrored building.

A couple of blocks north is the **Pasajul Vilacrosse** (Map p66), a U-shaped lane under sepia-toned skylights, with cafes and bars spilling onto the sidewalks. East of the passageway is the **Romanian National Bank**, which dates from 1880.

Just across B-dul Regina Elisabeta, **Hotel Capşa** (p81), at Calea Victoria 36, once housed **Casa Capşa**, an historic cafe dating from 1852 that was the meeting place of Romania's eminent artists, literary figures and politicians of the 1930s. It's now a swanky hotel – far removed from its bohemian roots.

Piaţa Revoluţiei

The scene of Ceauşescu's infamous last speech was on the balcony of the former **Central Committee of the Communist Party** (Map p66) building on 21 December 1989. Amid cries of 'Down with Ceauşescu!' he escaped (briefly) by helicopter from the roof. Meanwhile, the crowds were riddled with bullets and many died.

'PARIS OF THE EAST' OR 'BALKAN MOSCOW'?

From Saigon to Prague, it seems that every second city wants to be Paris. But Bucharest's architecture has drawn inspiration from the East too. In the early 20th century, a French accent got you society points, while half a century later everything leaned towards the Stalinesque. Going around the city, it's easy to spot one building from the 'Paris of the East' days rubbing shoulders with a building from the 'Balkan Moscow' era. Here are some stand-outs:

Paris of the East	Balkan Moscow
George Enescu Museum	Press House
Pasajul Vilacrosse	Palace of the Parliament
Triumphal Arch (c'mon!)	National Theatre
Economic Consortium	Romanian TV Headquarters
Romanian Athenaeum	Carol I Park & Unknown Soldier Mausoleum
Hotel Capşa & Around	Government Building, Piaţa Victoriei

On the front façade next to the entrance is a plaque dedicated to the 'young and courageous people' who 'drove out the dictator', thus 'giving the Romanian people back their freedom and dignity'. A statue of a man, broken but put back together again, dominates the small green area in front. The building now houses the Senate. In an island in Calea Victoriei is a new, controversial (due to its ugliness and lack of symbolism) **Rebirth Memorial** (Memorialul Renaşterii; Map p66) – a white obelisk piercing a basket-like crown (some have called it the 'potato of the revolution' because of its crown shape).

Creţulescu Church (Map p66) stands just south of the square. The 1722 red-brick structure was damaged in the 1989 Revolution. To the side stands a **memorial bust of Corneliu Coposu**, who spent 17 years in prison for his anticommunist activities and, prior to his death in 1995, was awarded the Légion d'Honneur by the French government. Behind the church is a statue of a headless torso, a memorial to fallen revolutionaries.

The 1895 **Central University Library** (Map p66) houses the European Union Information Centre, HVB bank and the university library. The **building shell** (Map p66), on the corner of Str Dobrescu and Str Boteanu, housed the hated Securitate and was destroyed by protestors. In 2003 the Romanian Architecture Union built a contemporary glass structure inside it to house their headquarters.

NATIONAL ART MUSEUM
Housed in the **Royal Palace**, this massive, three-part **museum** (Muzeul Naţional de Artă; Map p66; ☎ 313 3030; http://art.museum.ro; Calea Victoriei 49-53; combined ticket adult/student €3.40/1.70, Romanian & European collections €2.30/1.15, free 1st Wed of month; ☽ 10am-6pm Wed-Sun) – all signed in English – could take, along with Piaţa Revoluţii and lunch, the bulk of a day. Start at the north door with the **Gallery of Romanian Art** (adult/student €2/0.70), a three-floor survey of Romania's art with several hundred icons and jaw-dropping carved wood altars saved from communist-destroyed churches – all laid out on funky purple and crimson walls. The country's oil masters – from the impasto strokes of Gheorghe Petrascu to Nicolae Grigorescu's arrestingly frank portraits of Roma and peasant folk – are on the top floor. Walking through the chronological collection, note the phase out/in of 'Eastern' Turk-style/'Western' French-style dress on the painting subjects by the mid-19th century. Also in the building is the small **Treasures of Roman Art** (€1.40/0.60), which is less impressive than the collection at the Grigore Antipa National History Museum (p75).

Save time and energy for the absorbing **Gallery of European Art** (€1.20/0.60), a 12,000-piece collection, largely assembled from Tsar Carol I's collection and laid out according to nationality. The Italian collection includes the earliest-known painting by Bartolomeo (c 1430). The Dutch collection includes a few Rembrandts and Rubens, but we like the dramatic hand gesturing of Van Hemessen's *The Calling of St Matthew* (1556) the most. Naturally France gets the final spot – and the nicest part of the palace, with marble stairways and wood-carved ceilings – to house a few works by Rodin and Monet. Guides (€6) must be booked in advance; call ☎ 314 8119.

The Royal Palace itself is a treat to see. Built in 1812–15 by Prince Dinicu Golescu, the Palace became the official royal residence in 1834 during the reign of Prince Alexandru Ghica (r 1834–42). The current facade dates from the 1930s. Until 1989 it was the seat of the State Council and was called the Palace of the Republic.

ROMANIAN ATHENAEUM
This exquisite circular building is the majestic heart of Romania's classical music tradition. The **Romanian Athenaeum** (Ateneul Român; Map p66; ☎ 315 6875; admission €1.40; visits ☽ noon-6pm, box office ☽ noon-7pm Mon-Fri, 9am-5pm Sat) hosts prestigious concerts and should not be missed. Scenes from Romanian history are featured on the interior fresco inside the Big Hall on the first floor and the dome is 41m high. A huge appeal dubbed 'Give a Penny for the Athenaeum' saved it from disaster after the original patron's funds dried up. The peristyle is adorned with mosaics of five Romanian rulers, including Moldavian prince Vasile Lupu (r 1512–21), Wallachian Matei Basarab (r 1632–54) and King Carol I (r 1881–1914). Built in 1888, George Enescu made his debut here in 1898, followed five years later by the first performance of his masterpiece *Romanian Rhapsody*. Today it's home to the George Enescu Philharmonic Orchestra.

ATHÉNÉE PALACE HILTON
Now home to the Hilton hotel (p81), the **Athénée Palace** (Map p66) is the grand dame

---

REVOLUTION: WITNESSING HISTORY

Ceauşescu stepped onto the balcony. He started talking about Timişoara, about stamping down the first wave of protest against him. He told us it would get better; 10,000 lei more for studying; crazy lies. First people were murmuring; the voices from the crowd around me started saying 'Down with Ceauşescu!' Then the voices got louder. I heard myself shout. The sounds of bullets shattered the air. We heard shooting and I ran, I didn't know where to. They had killed people. Troops were loading bodies into trucks. I escaped but later heard that they'd barricaded people into University Square. Students sat down in front of the tanks but the tanks just rolled over them. They were hemmed in like animals, with no escape and gunned down. One thousand people perished in that square that night. It was our darkest hour.

Cornelui, eyewitness on the night of 21 December 1989

On the outskirts of Bucharest the tanks rolled towards the city centre, the crunch of their tracks and the heavy labouring of heavy outdated machinery adding to the menace that had filled the grey skies for days. When the gun turrets lay still, the soldiers who defected over to their people stood out of the tanks and smiled. People threw flowers at the tanks and gave crews meagre offerings of food. The elation at having overthrown decades of oppression was hitting home – it was a humbling experience. People walked around wearing Romanian flags draped over their heads, the centre circle which bore an Imperial crest cut out. Over the next few days I struck out from the journalists' enclave of the Hotel Inter-Continental to see the Paris of the East. But fear took a long time to subside. The TV station – perhaps unprepared for the first moments of liberty – played Charlie Chaplin's film *The Great Dictator*, followed by a Lisa Stansfield concert. It only added to the surreal feel of Bucharest.

Journalist Danny Buckland, who covered the revolution in Romania for London's Daily Star

---

of Bucharest, holding a particular place in the city's history. Built by French architect Téophile Bradeau in 1914, it's had a bumpy life. Sitting on the northern side of Piaţa Revoluţiei, it hosted political intrigue, scandals and high living when German *and* Allied officers used it as their base during the WWII. Under communism it became notorious for being a den of iniquity, with high-class prostitutes (most of who worked, along with the hotel staff, for the KGB-like Securitate). Its façade got pockmarked by bullets and fire during the 1989 Revolution but has since been cleaned up, and its patio bar is now quite the expat hang-out in good weather.

Piaţa Victoriei & Around

The huge plaza in northern Bucharest, dominated by the 1938 **Government Building** (Map pp62–3), has little to detain you, but its metro station is a good access point for walks north along Şoseaua Kiseleff or south into the centre.

Walk southeast down B-dul Lascăr Catargiu to Piaţa Romană, where you can see the **Romulus and Remus statue** (Map pp62–3), which depicts Lupoaica Romei (the wolf of Rome) and the abandoned children Romulus and Remus, whom the wolf fed and cared for, enabling them to found the city of Rome. The statue was a gift from Italy.

Calea Victoriei leads south of Piaţa Victoriei, where you can visit a couple of interesting museums that most visitors miss.

National composer George Enescu (1881–1955) lived for a short time in the former Cantacuzino Palace, a few blocks south of Piaţa Victoriei. The lovely building, built in the early 1900s in a seriously French baroque style, features a fantastic clam-shaped portecochere above the main entrance. Now called the **George Enescu Museum** (Muzeul George Enescu; Map pp62-3; ☎ 318 1450; Calea Victoriei 141; adult/student €0.60/0.30; ☼ 10am-5pm Tue-Sun), the palace is home to various manuscripts and belongings from George (Romanian-language only); be sure to see George's little home-studio, with original furnishings, behind the palace.

The grab-bag of 15 private collections at the well-named **Art Collection Museum** (Muzeul Colecţiilor de Artă; Map pp62-3; ☎ 211 1749; Calea Victoriei 111; adult/student €2/0.85; ☼ 10am-6pm Sat-Wed Oct-Apr, 11am-7pm Sat-Wed May-Sep), a couple more blocks south, is now part of the National Art Museum. A lot of the late 19th- to mid–20th century Romanian works take on French landscapes or styles. But there are also paintings of Balchik before it went to Bulgaria, a re-creation of a 19th-century Arab room on the 2nd floor, plenty of Ottoman weaponry, and fine Japanese woodblock prints.

Şoseaua Kiseleff

Home to some of Bucharest's finest villas, Şoseaua Kiseleff stretches from Piaţa Victoriei to Herăstrău Park in northern Bucharest; tree-lined sidewalks lead from communist monuments to French-inspired ones and past a couple of must-see museums. During the communist era Şoseaua Kiseleff was the most prestigious residential area in the city, reserved strictly for Communist Party officials *(nomenklatura)*.

GRIGORE ANTIPA NATURAL HISTORY MUSEUM

At the start of the boulevard, on the north-western side of Piaţa Victoriei, is this interesting **natural history museum** (Muzeul de Istorie Naturală

Grigore Antipa; Map pp62-3; ☎ 312 8826; Sos Kiseleff 1; adult/child €1.70/0.85; 🕒 10am-6pm Wed-Sun). Children get a kick out of it, despite the dated exhibits. In one room, a display of crude earth suddenly clanks when you walk by and 'lava' flows out. There are lots of ethnographic displays, including eerie decapitated mummy heads and Sioux head-dresses, plus test tubes of various invertebrates and stuffed (smiling) pythons.

MUSEUM OF THE ROMANIAN PEASANT

About 200m north, this **museum** (Muzeul Ţăranului Român; Map pp62-3; ☎ 212 9661; Şos Kiseleff 3; adult/student €1.80/0.60; 🕒 10am-6pm Tue-Sun) is so good you may want to hug it. Chosen as Europe's best museum in 1996, the museum makes the best of little money. Hand-made cards (in English) personalise exhibits, such as a full 19th-century home upstairs, a heartbreakingly sweet room devoted to grandmas, and 'hidden' rooms that you're ushered to via hand-scrawled directions. Don't miss the (rare) communism exhibit downstairs, with Lenin busts, portraits of Romanian leader Gheorghiu-Dej, and

---

JEWISH BUCHAREST

Once a thriving part of Romania, the Jewish community in the capital dates from the 16th century, when merchants and traders settled here. In 1941 800,000 Jews lived in Romania; today the number is less than 10,000. In Lucian Boia's book *Romania* he lamented the Jewish exodus from Romania after WWII as losing 'part of the Romanian soul'. There was reason to leave – as many as 400,000 Jews were killed in Romania during the war.

Several sites keep this part of Romanian history in the public memory.

Housed in the beautiful former Tailor's synagogue, the well-arranged **Jewish History Museum** (Muzeul de Istorie al Comunitaţilor Evreieşti din România; Map pp62-3; ☎ 311 0870; Str Mămulari 3; admission by donation; 🕒 9am-1pm Mon-Sat) bears testimony to the city's once-thriving Jewish life. Exhibits – in English and Romanian – highlight Jewish contributions to Romania (culturally, politically and militarily), while the Holocaust Room shows horrific photographs and a sculpture of a shrouded man, in memory of the 150,000 Jews who were deported to hard-labour camps in Transdniestr, Moldova, and the 200,000 from Transylvania who died at Auschwitz, Poland. The synagogue dates from 1850 and is one of three pre-WWII synagogues to survive in the city. You must bring your passport to visit. It's on a small lane behind the Unirea Shopping Centre.

Little remains of the old **Jewish quarter** of Văcăreşti, northeast of Piaţa Unirii in Bucharest's historic heart; nearly all of what wasn't destroyed during the Iron Guard's fascist pogrom in 1941 was levelled by Ceauşescu in the mid-1980s.

The **Choral Temple** (Map p66; ☎ 315 5090; Str Vineri 9; 🕒 9am-2pm Mon-Fri), built in 1857, is the city's main working synagogue and is visually stunning inside. You'll need your passport to enter. A **memorial** to the victims of the Holocaust (including 400,000 Romanian Jews), erected in 1991, fronts the temple.

The **Sephardic Jewish Cemetery** (Cimitirul Evreiesc de rit Sefard; Calea Şerban Vodă) lies opposite Belu Cemetery in the south of the city (metro Eroii Revoluţiei). Two rows of graves dated 21–23 January 1941 mark the Iron Guard's pogrom against the Jewish community in Bucharest, during which at least 170 Jews were murdered. From the metro walk 100m towards the modern City Hall; it's to the right.

heart-rending accounts of those who objected to collectivisation (in Romanian only). An 18th-century Transylvanian church is in the backlot, as is its gift shop.

Across the street is the **National Museum of Geology** (Muzeul Naţional de Geologie; Map pp62-3; ☎ 212 8952; Şos Kiseleff; adult/child €0.85/0.60; ☾ 10am-4pm), where you can while away an hour or two among Romania's finest rocks.

TRIUMPHAL ARCH
About half way up Şos Kiseleff, the 11m **Triumphal Arch** (Arcul de Triumf; Map pp62-3), based on Paris' namesake monument, was built in 1935 to commemorate the reunification of Romania in 1918. Sites of WWI battles are inscribed inside the arch, while King Ferdinand and Queen Marie feature on its southern façade. Previously a shoddy makeshift monument had been made in 1922 (just before King Ferdinand's triumphant entry into the city). The arch was so ludicrous that composer George Enescu wrote to the city mayor, demanding to know when a 'real' triumphal arch would be erected. Its viewing platform is now closed to the public.

NATIONAL VILLAGE MUSEUM
On the shores of Herăstră Lake, this **museum** (Muzeul Naţional al Satului; Map pp62-3; ☎ 317 9110; Şos Kiseleff 28-30; adult/student €1.50/0.60; ☾ 9am-7pm Tue-Sun, to 4pm Mon May-Sept, to 5pm Tue-Fri, to 4pm Mon Oct-Apr) is a terrific open-air collection of several dozen homesteads, churches, mills and windmills relocated from rural Romania. At times in July and August artisans in traditional garb show off various rural trades. Built in 1936 by Royal Decree, it is one of Europe's oldest open-air museums and a must for children. Get here from the centre by taking bus 131

or 331 from B-dul General Magheru or Piaţa Romană to the 'Muzeul Satului' stop.

PRESS HOUSE
At its northern end, Şos Kiseleff splays out into Piaţa Presei Libere, which is dominated by the giant **Press House** (Casa Presei Libere; Map pp62-3), a 1956 Stalinist wedding-cake of a structure. It gave a clear message to the citizens of Bucharest – Big Brother is watching you! A potent symbol of the powerful communist regime, until 1990 the house was called the 'House of the Sparks' (Casa Scânteii); behind closed doors it was known as the 'House of Lies'. It's still home to the city's hacks.

You can see the imprint on the tower where the hammer and sickle once were. In front of the building is an artful **Intersection of Europe sculpture** (Interşectie cu Europe), showing two rods entering a cone from different directions – something for the pedestal's previous resident, a **statue of Lenin**, to ponder at his new resting place in the weeds at Mogoşoaia (p91).

Herăstrău Park & Around
A couple of blocks east of the Triumphal Arch in northern Bucharest, **Piaţa Charles de Gaulle** (metro Piaţa Aviatorilor) is in the heart of some of Bucharest's most well-to-do areas.

Facing the square from the north is the 200-hectare **Herăstrău Park**, which stretches along the wide namesake lake. It's Bucharest's nicest park, with plenty of shaded strolls and open-air cafés, plus boats to hire.

Just east of the square is the **former main residence of Ceauşescu** (Map pp62-3; B-dul Primăverii 50), also known as the Primăverii Palace. It's heavily guarded now, and off-limits to everyone but state guests, but it is easy to look over the

---

BUCHAREST PARKS

Escape the heat or honks at some of Bucharest's urban oases. They tend to be best during the week when fewer people are enjoying the outdoors. All have nice areas to sit and drink beer or espresso, and many have swings or small rides for children.

- **Băneasa Park** (Parcul Băneasa) Nice respite from the city. 10km north of Piaţa Romana – take bus 301
- **Carol I Park** (opposite)
- **Cişmigiu Garden** (Grădina Cişmigiu; Map p66) Central and peaceful; open-air cafés look over the pond and plenty of benches (and flirters – it's known as 'lovers' park' locally)
- **Herăstrău Park** (above) 2 sq km and lots of water
- **Youth Park** (opposite) Scrappier park with lots of events

wall at the lush and leafy pad. Just across is the **former residence of Gheorghe Gheorghiu-Dej**, Romania's communist ruler until 1965.

A block south of Piaţa Charles de Gaulle is the long aqua-blue **Romanian TV Headquarters** (Calea Dorobanţilor; Map pp62–3), which was reduced to two hours' air-time a day in the late 1980s, one devoted to presidential activities. On 22 December 1989 revolutionaries broke into the television building and announced on air the collapse of the government. At the northern gate of the building is a small **memorial** to those killed here.

Tricky to find, the little **Zambaccian Museum** (Muzeul Zambaccian; Map pp62–3; ☎ 230 1920; Str Muzeul Zambaccian 21a; adult/student €0.85/0.30; ۞ 11am-7pm Wed-Sun May-Sep, 10am-6pm Wed-Sun Oct-Apr) is in a nicely restored villa between B-dul Aviatorilor and Calea Dorobanţilor (just north of Piaţa Dorobanţilor). The small collection boasts mostly Romanian works from the early 20th century, plus a Matisse, a Cezanne and a couple of Renoirs – all collected by Armenian businessman Krikor Zambaccian (1889–1962).

East Bucharest

The 'historic centre' gets the fabled glory, but many of the cobbled blocks east of Piaţa Romană and Piaţa Universităţii are some of Bucharest's most evocative.

East of Piaţa Romană, via Str Pictor Verona or Str Jules Michelet, past the slightly scrappy **Icoanei Garden** (Map p66), are a couple of religious sites. The **Church of the Icon** (Biserica Icoanei; Map p66; Str Icoanei 12) was built by monk and former privy secretary Mihail Băbeanu in 1745–50. Around the corner at Str Schitul Darvari 3 is pretty **St Slujbă's Monastery** (Mănăstirea Sfânta Slujbă; Map p66; Str Schitul Darvari 3), surrounded by a lush walled garden.

Along B-dul Carol I, east of Piaţa Universităţii, is the alabaster **Armenian Church** (Map pp62–3; ☎ 313 9070; B-dul Carol I 43; ۞ 9am-6pm, 8am-1pm Sun), which originally dates from 1781 (though this church was built in 1915).

Two blocks east, and north on Str Latina, you reach the **Theodor Pallady Museum** (Muzeul Theodor Pallady; Map pp62–3; ☎ 211 4979; Str Spătarului 22; adult/student €0.60/0.15; ۞ 11am-7pm Wed-Sun May-Sep, 10am-6pm Wed-Sun Oct-Apr), housed inside the exquisite early 18th-century Casa Melik, a former merchant's house. It contains the private art collection of the Raut family (part of the National Art Museum today).

West Bucharest

Only ten minutes by foot from the train station, the interesting pinky-peach **National Military Museum** (Muzeul Militar Naţional; Map pp62–3; ☎ 319 6015; Str Mircea Vulcănescu 125-7; adult/student €1.40/0.70; ۞ 9am-5pm Tue-Sun) doubles nicely as a Romanian history museum, with its chronological rundown of how the country defended itself. Out front are heroic busts (including Vlad Ţepeş), while in the museum entry note the 1988 communist mural that eerily celebrates the Palace of Parliament (a year before the revolution). In back is a superb hangar with Aurel Vlaicu's historic 1911 plane and cosmonaut uniforms. The army's backlash in the 1989 revolution (unsurprisingly) gets little play.

About 10 minutes south is the rather let-it-be **Botanic Garden** (Map pp62–3; Str Kogaulniceanu 36-46; adult/student & child €0.60/0.40; ۞ 9am-dusk), on the former grounds of the nearby **Cotroceni Palace** (which can be visited by prior arrangement; call ☎ 430 6171). The 17-hectare garden is home to some 20,000 plant species from around Romania.

Farther west, **Dâmboviţa Lake** (aka Morii Lake; off Map pp62–3) is a murky, mossy concrete-bedded lake created from a dam built to control the Dâmboviţa River (see p70). Couples stroll down the wind-swept sidewalk facing a fairly edgy neighbourhood of towering housing blocks. Some dare to swim; others cross to Şoseaua Virtuţii, where there's a water park. To reach it walk 300m through the park to the elevated rim from the Crângaşi metro station.

Southern Bucharest

About 1km southwest from Piaţa Unirii, **Carol I Park** (Map pp62–3) may have been inaugurated in 1906, but the eternal flame burning for an unknown soldier, and 20m black-granite **mausoleum** – and a heavy military presence who ask you not to photograph it – make it feel more of the communist era. The mausoleum, topped with five arches made of red Swedish granite, was put up in memory of the 'Heroes for the Struggle for the People's and the Homeland's Liberty for Socialism'. That's pretty communist. Enter the park from the north at Piaţa Libertăţii or from the south along Calea Şerban Vodă.

A couple of blocks east along Calea Şerban Vodă (near metro Tineretului) is the bigger **Youth Park** (Parcul Tineretului; Map pp62–3), where various sporting events and open-air

PAUPERS' GRAVES

About 3km west of the Palace of Parliament, **Ghencea Civil Cemetery** (Cimitirul Civil Ghencea; Map pp62–3; ☎ 413 8590; Calea 13 Septembrie; ☉ 8am-8pm) has two infamous inhabitants: Nicolae Ceauşescu and his wife Elena (dubbed the 'Romanian Eva Perón').

The pair were secretly buried here – and notably not at Belu Cemetery, the city's most reputable resting place – on 30 December 1989, in hastily prepared graves. Both lie before the small chapel that faces the entry.

Nicolae lies in row I-35, to the left of the path. No stone tomb adorns his earth grave, dug into a pathway, but two crosses mark it. One is a stone cross with a red star; the other is a black steel cross which is inscribed with his name, date of birth and death (26 January 1918–24 December 1989). Surprisingly, there's no graffiti here, just a lit candle and a motley collection of fresh flowers.

Hated Elena was buried separately from him, in row H-25, directly across the cemetery to the right (just behind the modern marble tomb). They weren't buried together, as it was said they did too many bad things together and should stay apart. Her name is daubed with white paint across a black metal cross. The body of their playboy son Nicu, who died from liver cirrhosis in 1996, lies nearby.

Get there on bus 385 from Piaţa Unirii or outside the Palace of Parliament's northern entrance, from which it's a dusty 40-minute walk here.

concerts take place in the Sports & Culture Palace.

Going west from the southern end of Carol I Park (near metro Eroii Revoluţiei), the road curves past the **Martyr-Heroes of the December 1989 Revolution Cemetery** (Cimitirul Eroii Martiri ai Revoluţei din Decembrie 1989; Map pp62–3; Calea Şerban Vodă), where many of the 1033 victims are buried.

Just south is **Belu Cemetery** (Cimitirul Belu; off Map pp62–3; Calea Şerban Vodă; ☉ 9am-7pm), the city's most prestigious cemetery, which houses the tombs of many notable Romanian writers. Space has become so tight, people are recycling spots from past family members; in other areas, sidewalks are filling with new grave sites! A map inside the gate points out locations. Many Romanians pay respects to national poet Mihai Eminescu (1850–89) and comic playwright and humorist Ion Luca Caragiale (1852–1912), who only have a bloke named Traian Savalescu between them; go to Figura 9 (to the right after you enter).

The **Sephardic Jewish Cemetery** is across the street (p75).

ACTIVITIES

Row boats (€1.50-1.70 per hour) are available for hire at Cişmigiu Garden's lake, Carol I Park's pond, or in Herăstrău Lake's western bank. Also on the western shores of Herăstrău Lake, there's a fairly frequent **ferry service** (adult/child €1.20/0.60; ☉ noon-8pm Mon, roughly 10am-8pm Tue-Sun May-Oct) to the other side of the lake.

In winter there's often **ice skating** on Cişmigiu Garden's frozen lake.

You can hire bikes at **Magellan Bikes** (Map p66; ☎ 0724-296 487; Calea Moşilor 46; ☉ 10am-7pm Mon-Fri, 10am-4pm Sat). It's about €12 per day, cheaper if hiring for long term.

High-end hotels, like the Hotel Inter-Continental, Marriott Grand Hotel and Crowne Plaza Bucharest will let you use their **fitness centres** or **pools** for €15 or so a day.

If you're looking for mountains, Sinaia is two hours' north (p118).

WALKING TOUR
Ceauşescu's Bucharest

Locals roll their eyes, or get outright angry about it (or call something like the following as the 'walk to hell'), but an unmistakable draw for the city is the fascinatingly gruesome and ill-conceived changes Ceauşescu's threw upon it. Following a 1977 earthquake that damaged many city buildings, and a fateful visit to Pyongyang that inspired him, Ceauşescu finished the Bucharest wreck-job in the early 1980s, levelling neighbourhoods with priceless ancient buildings. All done to make room for a grandiose world of housing blocks and government buildings that all but dominate the lowly pedestrian in a mostly car-free city (at the time). If you have only one day in Bucharest, you'll want to see this.

Traffic roaring by, ugly **Piaţa Unirii** (**1**; Union Square) was built as the communist dream. To

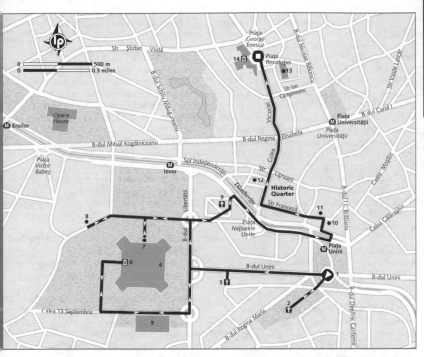

Start/Finish Piaţa Unirii/Piaţa Revoluţiei
Distance 3.5km
Duration about 3–6 hours

---

the northwest, the crippled Dâmboviţa River gets sucked under the square's concrete – reappearing on the other side of B-dul Unirii. This 3.5km boulevard – previously known as the 'Boulevard of the Victory of Socialism' – was intentionally built a half-metre wider than Paris' Champs-Élysées. Fountains dot the expanse of cars and grey buildings, one fountain for each of the counties in Romania. Looking southwest, and up a bit, you can spot the **Romanian Patriarchal Cathedral** (**2**; p70), a rare view of the action from a place of worship.

Heading east on B-dul Unirii, with the world's second-largest building looming, we can see some religious buildings not so lucky. Take the last left down the boulevard – lined with (half-abandoned) storefronts and towering housing – to reach the **Antim Monastery** (**3**; p70). In some alleys you'll find dilapidated homes, left for squatters to take over –

not exactly the 'Victory' Ceauşescu probably imagined.

Ahead is the monstrous **Palace of Parliament** (**4**; p68) – locally called still the Palace of the People. If not in a hurry, go around to the left (south) past the **National Institute for Science & Technology** (**5**; p69) to visit the surprisingly good **National Museum of Contemporary Art** (**6**; p69). Afterwards, it's a 20-minute walk to the north side, where you can take a **palace tour (7)**.

If keen, you can take a bus outside to **Ghencea Cemetery** (**8**; opposite), the humble resting grounds for Nicolae Ceauşescu and his wife Elena. Otherwise, head north on B-dul Libertăţii a block, then veer right behind the blocks, to reach the **Prince Mihai Monastery** (**9**; p71) – the last surviving piece of the one-time symbol of the city (Ceauşescu moved it 279m behind the buildings).

To get some sense of what this grey civic centre replaced, cross the river into the scrappy heart of Bucharest's historic centre. Built in 1808 by an Armenian merchant, the **Hanul lui Manuc** (**10**; p81), a rare unrazed old-timer, is now a hotel with a courtyard drinking area. Walk past the statue of **Vlad Ţepeş (11)** on Str Franceza to Calea Victoriei, Bucharest's historic main thoroughfare. A couple of blocks north you can see **Economic Consortium Palace (12)**, built in a rah-rah Parisian fervour in 1900.

About eight blocks north is Piaţa Revoluţiei. To the right, past the statue of the pieced-together seated man, is the former **Central Committee of the Communist Party (13)**, where Ceauşescu made his last public appearance from the balcony. The crowd yelled 'Down with Ceauşescu!' and the 1989 Revolution was born.

If time allows, the National Gallery of Art's **Gallery of Romanian Art (14; p73)** includes many religious icons saved from churches Ceauşescu had demolished.

COURSES

Echo (Map pp62-3; ☎ 252 0115; www.theecho.ro; Str Dimitrie Onciul 33) offers private Romanian courses for €12 per hour.

BUCHAREST FOR CHILDREN

Parks, particularly **Cişmigiu Garden** (p76) and **Herăstrău Park** (p76), set up play areas for kids.

Tăndărică Puppet Theatre (Teatrul de Marionete şi Păpuşi Tăndărică; Map pp62-3; ☎ 315 2377; Str Eremia Grigorescu 24; box office ⏰ 9am-5pm Mon-Sat) is a favourite but shows are mostly in Romanian.

City Mall and **Bucureşti Mall** (see p86) have play areas and some kids events planned.

It's hard to beat the **Dracula show** at the Count Dracula Club (p83) held on Tuesday and Friday nights.

Many kids will get a kick out of the **plane hangar** at the National Military Museum (p77), with parachute displays, a host of planes and all sorts of tanks outside.

TOURS

Most travel agents offer various forms of city tours.

Jolly Tours (Map p66; ☎ 303 3796; www.jollytours.ro; ⏰ 9am-6pm Mon-Sat, 10am-3pm Sun), at the Athénée Palace Hilton offers three-hour city tours from €60 for two people.

Cultural Travel & Tours (☎ 336 3163; www.cttours.ro) offers several half/full day city tours from €29/49 per person.

One local guide, **Corneliu Serban** (☎ 0723-356 096), offers personalised city tours for €100 for two people; he witnessed the 1989

Revolution and can give plenty of insider's observations.

FESTIVALS & EVENTS

Annual events worth the wait include:

Bucharest Carnival (late May-early Jun) Week-long carnival with street dancers, street theatre, folk dancers and live bands performing in Bucharest's historic heart.

Dreher Beer Festival (mid-Jun) Four-day beer festival with live bands and drinking contests in Herăstrău Park.

Open Air Concerts (mid-Jun) Showcase for young classical musicians held yearly in Izvorani Village (40km north of Bucharest).

Fête de la Musique (21 Jun) Annual French music festival organised by the French Institute.

Hora Festival (1 Aug) Three-day dance festival attracting traditional folk dance troupes from all over the country; held in the Village Museum.

Craftsman's Fair (15 Aug) Local craft fair hosted by the Village Museum with guest craftspeople from all over Romania.

George Enescu Music Festival (4-24 Sep) Held every odd-numbered year, attracting musicians from all over the world.

National Theatre Festival (Oct) Week-long theatre festival held in the National Theatre.

St Dumitru Day (late Oct) Two-day carnival celebrating Bucharest's patron saint, Dumitru.

SLEEPING

Prices in Bucharest are higher than in most of Romania. Budget accommodation here is below €50 for a double, midrange goes up to €130 and top end soars above. All prices include breakfast unless otherwise noted.

Central Bucharest
BUDGET

Hotel Muntenia (Map p66; ☎ 314 6010; Str Academiei 19-21; s/d with shared bathroom €14/20, d with private bathroom €49) If you're looking to slumber like it's pre-1989, check out the Muntenia. It's pretty meagre: inside the grey chipped façade are yellowing walls, an antique glass elevator, a spent bulb or two, and red-and-black floral carpets. No breakfast.

our pick **Hotel Carpaţi** (Map p66; ☎ 315 0140; carpati@compace.ro; Str Matei Millo 16; s/d €25/42, d with private bathroom €55-68) If you're looking to save and be central, it's hard to beat this place, which has 40 recently renovated rooms – some are tiny, with little light – and a fun, rather scary, two-door lift that clanks up to the floors. Breakfast comes with a little pomp in the Paris-style lobby lounge, and all rooms have TV and sink.

MIDRANGE

Hostel Mioriţa (Map p66; ☎ 312 0361; www.hostel -miorita.ro; Str Lipscani 12; r €50; ✗ 🖳) Reached from a nice block in the historic centre by a maze of doors and steps in a rather clinical building, this six-room inn (not a hostel) has pleasant if plain rooms, and has TV, free wi-fi and tiger (grrr!) bedspreads.

Hanul lui Manuc (Map p66; ☎ 313 1415; hmanuc@rnc .ro; Str Franceză 62-64; s/d €35/56) Originally a 19th century merchants' inn (*caravanserai*), this hotel has a colourful guest list, including prostitutes, criminals, rogues, merchants and Lonely Planet authors. Sculpted wooden balconies overlook the courtyard (filled with some open-air seats for the wine cellar, plus a few Coke machines and parked cars). Considering its location it's a steal, but the 22 rooms (wood-beam ceilings, brown carpets, TV, old bathroom tile) could be better maintained.

Rembrandt Hotel (Map p66; ☎ 313 9315; www .rembrandt.ro; Str Smârdan 11; s €63, d weekday/weekend €91-113/81-93; ✗ 🖳) This wonderful, relatively new 15-room, Dutch-owned hotel faces the landmark National Bank in the historic centre. Breakfast is tight, on the lobby's mezzanine, but rooms win serious points for polished wood floors, wall-size wooden headboards and DVD players. 'Business' rooms face the front, but the top-floor 'standard' gets the lone balcony. The lone single and 'tourist' double are quite small.

Hotel Central (Map p66; ☎ 315 5636; www.central hotel.ro; Str Brezoianu 13; s/d €90/105; ✗ 🖳) Above a McDonald's, half of the 61 rooms overlook busy B-dul Regina Elisabeta. Rooms are run by the book to the 'modern hotel' template.

TOP END

Hotel Capşa (Map p66; ☎ 313 4038; www.capsa.ro; Calea Victoriei 36; s/d €135 & 170/200; ✗ 🖳) Behind the charming 1852 façade, this central hotel served as a bohemian hang-out through the 1930s, and its cake shop (still running) is a lone survivor of the 'cake craze' of the times. Rooms benefit from old practices – high ceilings – and new touches like fleur-de-lys designs, dark-wood panelling, and a fitness centre.

Hotel Opera (Map p66; ☎ 312 4857; www.hotelopera .ro; Str Ion Brezoianu 37; s/d €120/140; ✗ 🖳) Set on a back-street triangular corner, this 33-room, faintly Art Deco hotel goes for an all-out music theme inside (lobby nooks for violins, occasional hip-hop through the speakers). The rooms are small, but nicely arranged.

Hotel Inter-Continental (Map p66; ☎ 310 2020; www.intercontinental.com; B-dul Nicolae Bălcescu 4; s/d from €290/320; ✗ 🖳 ☎) Its 283 rooms brag of a 21st-century makeover (cranberry carpets, padded walls, wi-fi), and the 1971 tower playfully shows its period at times (dig the bubbly skylights in the top-floor fitness centre – but there's no joking about the pool's panoramic views). During the 1989 Revolution, journos shot fighting footage from the balconies here. Nonguests can use the fitness centre for €15 to €25. Room rates often drop by half.

Athénée Palace Hilton (Map p66; ☎ 303 3777; hilton@hilton.ro; Str Episcopiei 1-3, s/d from €340/360; ✗ 🖳 ☎) The queen of Bucharest's hotels is a testament to the century-past infatuation with Paris. These days, the 272 rooms' makeovers nearly live up to the glory you'd expect from the marble-pillar entry. Rooms in the older wing mix layouts – some with steps up from an entry to blue fleur-de-lys-patterned carpets. For €35 more, the 'king deluxe' rooms grant you an adjoining TV room. In summer the terrace serves as a hotspot for the cocktail crowd. There's an indoor pool in the fitness centre.

Gară de Nord & Around

Those really not wanting to deal with the con-artist taxi drivers lingering at the train station can walk their bags to nearby choices.

Vila 11 (Map pp62-3; ☎ 0722-495 900; vila11bb@ hotmail.com; Str Institutul Medico Miliitar 11; dm/s/d €10/18/28) Run by a Canadian family, this homy *pensiune* is on a back street, and rates usually include breakfast. Call ahead; sometimes no one's around.

Hotel Astoria (Map pp62-3; ☎ 318 9989; B-dul Dinica Golescu 27; s/d €30/45) Your mother might not like it, but the nine-floor Astoria, run by the railroad, carries some yesteryear grace in its weathered halls, with stone-tile entries and wooden armoires in rooms.

Hotel Elizeu (Map pp62-3; ☎ 319 1734; rezervari@ hotelelizeu.ro; Str Elizeu 11-13; s/d €46/57; ✗) A nice hotel, this 54-room option is rather standard, but it's in a quiet pocket of residential buildings a few blocks north of the station.

Outside the Centre

Don't be put off that these choices aren't near the historic core of Bucharest. Many of the city's best options – including hostels – are just outside the centre, some (like Helios or Funky Chicken) just a few blocks' walk away.

BUDGET

Casa Albă (☎ 230 4525; Alea Privighetorilor 1-3; camp site €6, bungalows €21.50) If you insist, camping is possible at these fine grounds northeast of Băneasa airport in north Bucharest. Take bus 301 north from Piaţa Romană; get off a few stops past the airport and walk 500m east along Alea Privighetorilor. Bus 783 to the main airport also goes by here. There is a restaurant at the site. Breakfast is not included.

our pick **Butterfly Villa Hostel** (Map pp62-3; ☎ 0747-032 644; www.villa-butterfly.com; Str Dumitru Zosima 82; dm/s/d €9/14/26; ⌘ ▣) Bucharest's best hostel, run by a German/Romanian couple, is not the best located. The clean, two-floor hostel has three dorms and three bathrooms, plus two private bathrooms. There's a small courtyard and terrace to kick back on, darts to throw, video games and DVDs to play with. Wi-fi is free throughout, as is laundry, and breakfast sprawls all day. Staff is quite helpful (if not 100% laid-back at times). Bus 282 leads from the train station, bus 300 from Piaţa Romana.

Funky Chicken (Map pp62-3; ☎ 312 1425; funkychickenhostel@hotmail.com; Str Gen Berthelot 63; dm €8) Just a couple of blocks from lovely Cişmigiu Gardens, this hostel occupies a historic home on a shaded street, with three dorm rooms that sleep 18. There's a kitchen to use and free cigs to smoke on courtyard benches, but no breakfast. It has less travel information than other hostels.

Youth Hostel Villa Helga (Map pp62-3; ☎ 610 2214; www.rotravel.com/hotels/helga; Str Salcâmilor 2; dm/s/d €11/16/28; ▣) A converted old villa in the evocative back lanes east of the centre, this place has nice, clean rooms, with a new kitchen to use, two private rooms, and patio seats under the vine shade. Stay six days and get an additional night free. The laundry will hopefully be repaired by the time you read this.

Pensiunea Gabriela (☎ 352 2053; Str Margaritarului 18, Vila A-104, Otopeni village; dm/s/d/tr €12/18/25/35) Run by lovely English- and French-speaking retirees in an unlikely village base 2km from the airport, this five-room, one-dorm home has welcoming rooms and a garden outside. Staff can offer rides to/from the airport, plus there's internet, restaurants and banks nearby. All but the triple have shared bathrooms. Take bus 783 towards the airport – get off at the first stop after the McDonald's, 15km from the centre.

MIDRANGE

Hotel Helios (Map pp62-3; ☎ 310 7083; www.hotelhelios.ro; Str Iulia Haşden 16; s/d €66/77; ⌘ ▣) This 15-room hotel is only a few blocks from the train station, but feels far away – facing a quaint Orthodox church, with stylish rooms and floor-to-ceiling wardrobes. Prices drop 20% Saturday and Sunday.

TOP END

Le Boutique Hotel Moxa (Map pp62-3; ☎ 650 5555; www.hotelmoxa.com; Str Mihail Moxa 4; s/d €130/145 & 165; ⌘ ▣) The 24 rooms are small but stylish at this new 24-room boutique hotel, a few steps from Calea Victoriei. Padded headboards face the flat-screen TVs and there's free wi-fi throughout, plus a small gym and sauna to use. Prices drop by €20 Friday to Sunday.

Hotel Duke (Map p66; ☎ 317 4186; www.hotelduke.ro; B-dul Dacia 33; s/d €130/150; ⌘ ▣) At Piaţa Romana, the 38-room Duke is a pleasant business-style hotel with mint-and-caramel rooms, attentive staff, internet in the lobby, and a casual bar where suits chat.

Golden Tulip (Map pp62-3; ☎ 212 5558; www.goldentulipbucharest.com; Calea Victoriei 166; r €160 & 180; ⌘ ▣) This very stylish 82-room hotel opened close to the centre of town in 2005, giving Bucharest a much-needed modern boost. Stark rooms feature plush red chairs set before full-wall glass windows, and the lobby bar goes curbside in good weather. Rates drop 20% Friday to Sunday.

Hotel Sofitel (Map pp62-3; ☎ 318 3000; www.sofitel.com; B-dul Expoziţiei 2; s/d from €230/245; ⌘ ▣) Adjoining the World Trade Centre, the 12-floor Sofitel has 202 classy rooms – geometric shapes, purple carpets in the hallways – with incredible views over the city, four distinctive eating/drinking areas in the luxe lobby, plus a small fitness centre and use of a nearby pool.

APARTMENTS

■ **IMOB-Shop** (☎ 335 7686; www.imobshop.ro) Apartments around Piaţa Victoriei in slightly dated buildings from €30 per night.

■ **RomVision Travel** (☎ 322 6533; www.romvision.ro) A bit more stylish; apartments range from €60 to €80 per night.

EATING
European
Burebista (Map pp62-3; ☎ 210 9704; Calea Moşilor 195; mains €1.50-4.50; ☯ noon-midnight) Dark-shaded patio seats outside, with tree-trunk tables and furs inside, rustic Burebista is a popular spot for excellent quality grilled meats. Salads start at €1.50.

Casa Veche (Map p66; ☎ 0724-232 631; Str Enescu 15; pizzas €4-6; ☯ noon-1am) Some of Bucharest's finest clay-oven pies – thin, crispy versions with fresh ingredients – are served in this nice trellised courtyard and upstairs woodbeam dining room. Make sure extras aren't added to your bill though.

Red Lion (Map p66; ☎ 315 1526; Str Academiei 1a; pizza €5; ☯ 9am-midnight Mon-Fri, 3pm-midnight Sat & Sun) This popular pizza/pasta place near the university fills two rooms – one a dark-wood pub, the other a trellised Roman 'garden' of sorts – with locals looking for €0.60 draught beer, crispy pizza or pasta.

ourpick Bistro Vilacrosse (Map p66; ☎ 315 4562; Pasajul Macca/Vilacrosse; meal €3.30-8; ☯ lunch & dinner;) This bistro borrows its style heavily from Parisian side-streets, with sepia photos of Bucharest's most Parisian-influenced buildings, wooden floors and gingham table-cloths. Settle into a seat and escape the city heat and/or crowds in this glass-domed passage while sipping fresh coffee and eating a wine-splattered Transylvania pork filet on a bed of (French!) fries and roasted cabbage. Of all things, the toilet entrance is a red (English!) telephone booth. It has a few vegetarian options and a bottle of wine costs €7.30.

Trattoria Il Calcio (Map p66; ☎ 0722-134 299; Str Mendeleev 14; mains €4-7; ☯ noon-midnight or 1am) Run by 'Romania's George Best' (football legend Gino Lorgucescu), this pasta/pizza place looks Tuscan, if not for the framed *Futbol* journals from the 1960s on the walls. The food's great, with hearty meals and good salads. It gets busy at lunch.

Balthazar (Map pp62-3; ☎ 212 1460; www.balthazar .ro; Str Dumbrava Rosie 2; mains €10-15; ☯ noon-12.30am) On a strip of embassies (US and Austrian included – so no Schwarzenegger jokes), Balthazar is among Bucharest's classiest restaurants, filling the ground floor and front courtyard of a superbly maintained old villa. Snazzy locals and business lunchers come for Thai/French fusion, lots of seafood and filet mignon.

Casa Doina (Map pp62-3; ☎ 222 6717; Şos Kiseleff 4; mains €7-20; ☯ noon-3am) Off the grand avenue, this casa was an ornate 1892 villa, with al-most Raj-style rooms complementing its high-quality Romanian fare. The best option is to sit outside near the fountains in the inviting courtyard (too bad about the Carlsberg ban-ners). Try the beef carpaccio with olive oil and lemon juice.

Romanian
Caru cu Bere (Map p66; Str Stavropoleos 3-5) Bucharest's oldest beer hall plays home to serious Gothic style and an irresistible atmosphere, although it was closed for renovation when we visited. Check to see its new state – it's likely they'll bring back the Roma bands, but revive the sour service.

La Mama (Map p66; ☎ 312 9797; Str Epislopiei 9; mains €3-4.80; ☯ 10am-2am Sun-Thu, to 4am Fri & Sat) Mama knows what she's doing. This converted villa, with a sprawling covered deck that's filled to all hours, dates from the late 19th century, and deserves its many fans, thanks to the very tasty, meat-heavy options. Sheep pastrami with po lenta is a winner, but the roasted pork neck with country-style potatoes is unbeatable.

G City Grill (Map pp62-3; ☎ 233 9818; B-dul Primăverii; mains €3.50-10; ☯ 10am-2am) Outside tables at this appealing villa, just east of Piaţa Charles de Gaulle, draw a stylin' biz crowd seeking typical Romanian fare in a modern setting.

Count Dracula Club (Map p66; ☎ 312 1353; Splaiul Independenţei 8a; mains €8; ☯ 3pm-1am Mon-Sat) Don't pretend you don't want this. A spooky home with blood-dripping walls and cosy rooms themed as hunting, medieval, Transylvanian style, plus a chapel/coffin room with impaled heads, hands reaching through walls and blood-red lights. In addition, Drac himself shows up 'for a show' at 9.30pm Tuesday and Friday. The food's fine – mostly bloody meats. ('Um, we have vegetarian soup', said a ghoul-ishly goateed waiter, perplexed at the very thought of vegetarians.)

Smart's (Map pp62-3; ☎ 211 9035; Str Alex Donici 14; mains 15-30; ☯ 11am-late) On a shaded lane, this great pub serves (rather Romanian) pub fare, with a selection of salads (€3.25 to €4.15) and pastas (€4.45 to €5.90). It's popular, and a fine spot to sit over a bottle of Leffe.

Other Cuisines
Paradis (Map p66; ☎ 315 2601; Str. Hristo Botev 10; dishes €1.80; ☯ 8am-10.30pm) Come for a brilliant value

buffet lunch at this Lebanese joint, with spicy aubergine stew, spinach over rice, spinach stews, meatballs in tomato sauce and mounds of flat bread.

Mediterraneo (Map p66; ☎ 211 5308; Str Icoanei 20; €3.60-5.90; ☺ 10am-midnight or later) This great little corner restaurant on the cobbled back lanes draws expats and locals for Turkified Mediterranean fare. Sunday brunch (€10) is a big deal – with sausage, eggs, olives, French toast and fresh OJ. Fresh fish fillets join a posse of kebabs (€6) and pastas (€5.50).

Don Taco (Map pp62-3; ☎ 316 9452; cnr Str Dr Felix & B-dul Banal Manta; mains €3.75-5.90; ☺ 10am-1 or 2am) Romania's only 'Mexican' restaurant (um, half the menu sticks with Romanian fare) does an inventive, but pretty good take on burritos, enchiladas and *carnitas* (stewed pork).

Cafés

Café & Latte (Map p62-3; ☎ 314 3834; B-dul Schitu Măgureanu 35; ☺ 8am-10pm) Facing the Cişmigiu Garden, this spot offers pastries and coffees to a jovial crowd.

IO Coffee Bar (Map p66; ☎ 315 6098; Str Demetrie Dobrescu 5) On a chic spot looking from a blown-out ruin of the 1989 clash at nearby Piaţa Revoluţiei, this two-floor cafe has back-lit wall-length B&W prints of the 1989 scene and candles on the table.

Quick Eats

Snack Attack! (www.snackattack.ro) Str Ion Câmpineanu (Map p66; ☎ 312 7664; Str Ion Câmpineau 10; ☺ 8am-8pm Mon-Fri, to 2pm Sat) Piaţa Dorobanţilor (Map pp62-3; Piaţa Dorobanţilor 28; ☺ 8am-8pm Mon-Fri, to 2pm Sat) You haven't been in Romania long enough if the idea of a cheap, fresh sandwich (€1.50) or salad (including hummus and tabouli with tortillas; €2) doesn't tempt you. Listed above are two of eight locations in Bucharest.

Grand Cafe Galleron (Map p66; ☎ 313 4565; Str Golescu 18a; sandwiches €3-4.50; ☺ 9am-midnight) A block east of Piaţa Revoluţiei, this stylish cafe has indoor nooks and outdoor seats for ice cream, sandwiches, drinks and all-day breakfast (€4).

Self-Catering

Piaţa Amzei (Amzei Market; Map pp62-3; ☺ sunrise-sunset) Just off Calea Victoriei on Piaţa Amzei, this market opens daily from sunrise to sunset and has the juiciest selection of fresh fruit and veg in Bucharest. Another open-air market, Piaţa Gemeni (Map pp62-3) is off B-dul Dacia.

DRINKING

Bucharest's two liveliest scenes are around Lipscani in the historic centre (with pedestrianised roads and trendy pubs) and in the student dorms area near Grozăveşti metro station. Fancier hotels have slicker drinking scenes.

Amsterdam Grand Cafe (Map p66; ☎ 313 7580; Str Covaci 6; ☺ 10am-2am) This rustic, two-floor bar with great seating areas has big windows to look onto the cobblestone lane. There's live jazz some afternoons. Food's available, but it's better for drinks.

Dubliner (Map pp62-3; Şos Titulescu 18; ☺ 9am-2am) This is a long-time expat hangout, with draught Guinness and football games attracting a grab-bag of fans. Locals tend to stick with the sidewalk tables, while jaded sports fans linger by the TVs or dartboard inside. The Dubliner's steak sandwich (€6.60) is super, but priced for foreign budgets.

Fire Club (Map p66; ☎ 0722-390 946; Str Gabroveni 12) A big red-brick room with student groups crouched on stools around small tables, bottles of Tuborg in hand. Rock and punk shows are staged in the basement.

La Butoaie (Map p66; B-dul Nicolae Bălcescu 2) Huge with uni students, this lively open-deck bar on the 5th floor of the Ion Luca Caragiale National Theatre fits hundreds, with benches and big pillows in the seating areas. It fills early on nice days.

Mes Amis (Map p66; Str Zarafi; ☺ 9pm-2am) More Marais than its glitz-job neighbours on Gabroveni, this alley bar has wood-beam ceilings, grapefruit-pink walls and alt rock coming through the speakers.

White Horse (Map pp62-3; Str George Călinescu 4; ☺ noon-3am) This British-style pub caters to a more professional, but still boozey, crowd in this smoky, busy two-floor place in northern Bucharest.

ourpick Piranha Club (Map pp62-3; ☎ 315 9129; www.clubpiranha.ro; Spl Independenţei 313; ☺ 10am-late) About 2.5km west of the town centre, this student-dorm area teems with Bucharest's merriest drinking/eating life. Action's found on either side of the Dâmboviţa River. Best is this, a jungle-lodge-type place with piranhas in aquariums, low-lit gazebos decked out like country homes, cosy seating inside for when it's cold and pretty good food. There are frequent live shows too. It's south of the river, a couple of hundred metres west of the Grozăveşti metro station.

ENTERTAINMENT

Check **Şapte Seri** (www.sapteseri.ro, in English on website only) for entertainment listings. Posters advertising DJ events, live bands and new hot nightclubs plaster the city.

Cinemas

Most films are shown in their original language. Check www.sapteseri.ro or www.cinema .ro for film information.

Cinematica Eforie (Map p66; ☎ 313 0483; Str Eforie 2; tickets €3) Plays Bergman and arthouse films, and some Romanian films.

Cinema Pro (☎ 824 1360; Str IC Brătianu 6; tickets €2.30-3)

Cinema Scala (Map p66; ☎ 316 6708; B-dul General Magheru 2-4; tickets €2, free Tue)

Hollywood Multiplex (Map pp62-3; ☎ 327 7020; Bucureşti Mall, Calea Vitan 55-59; tickets €2.50-4.25) Multiscreen jobbie.

The French Institute (p65) also screens films (in French).

Classical Music

It's a very good idea to dress up for a night out, at least once. For information on seeing the philharmonic at the **Romanian Athenaeum** see p73. Most shows are scheduled September through June (usually Thursday and Friday nights).

Opera House (Opera Română; Map pp62-3; ☎ 313 1857; B-dul Mihail Kogălniceanu 70) Enjoy a full-scale opera in a lovely building for €1 to €4.

Gay & Lesbian Venues

Accept (www.accept-romania.ro) is a gay-, lesbian- and transgender-rights Romanian group that organises the annual six-day **GayFest** (ends 1st Sun in Jun), with events, films and disco nights around Bucharest.

The most popular gay venue in Bucharest is **Queen's** (Map pp62-3; ☎ 0722-988 541; Str Juliu Barach 13; ☽ noon-3am).

Nightclubs & Live Music

Backstage (Map p66; ☎ 312 3943; www.backstage.ro; Str Gabroveni 14; ☽ 9pm-5am) Behind the cursive neon sign is this ground-floor bar, with a basement disco (€1.50) that hosts Thursday rock concerts (€0.60).

Club A (Map p66; ☎ 315 6853; Str Blănari 14; ☽ 10am-5 or 6am Mon-Fri, 9pm-5 or 6am Sat & Sun) Run by students, this club is a classic and beloved by all who go there. Indie pop/rock tunes play until very late Friday and Saturday nights.

Green Hours 22 Jazz Club (Map p66; ☎ 314 5751; Calea Victoriei 120; ☽ 24hr) This cosy basement jazz hall has stools and artfully patched books in arched nooks. A gin-and-tonic is €3.70.

Jukebox (Map p66; ☎ 314 8314; Str Sepcari 22; ☽ noon-5am) Laid-back basement venue with lively karaoke on Tuesday, Thursday and Saturday nights, plus live music Wednesday.

Twice (Map p66; ☎ 313 5593; Str Sfânta VIneri 4, Sect 3; ☽ 9pm-5am) DJs and amateur stripping are part of the hip-to-hip youth dancing to two beats in two rooms. Prepare to sweat.

Sport

Of the four Bucharest football teams, Steaua Bucureşti dominate local sports fans' imaginations. They play at **Steaua Stadium**. Red-gold-and-blue paraphernalia can be picked up at the **club shop** (Map p66; ☎ 094 299 037; cnr Str Jon Zalomit & Str Ion Brezioanu; ☽ 10am-6pm Mon-Fri, to 2pm Sat).

One rival, **Dinamo Bucureşti** (www.fcdinamo.ro), plays at **Dinamo Stadium** (Map pp62-3; Şos Ştefan cel Mare 7-9).

Theatre

Bucharest's many theatres offer a lively mix of comedy, farce, satire and straight contemporary plays in a variety of languages. Tickets cost no more than €3. Theatres close in July and August.

Ion Luca Caragiale National Theatre (Teatrul Naţional Ion Luca Caragiale; Map p66; ☎ 314 7171; B-dul Nicolae Bălcescu 2; box office ☽ 10am-7pm) Named after the 20th-century playwright who kicked off his career here as a prompter, this place was built in the 1970s. The box office is on the southern side of the building.

Jewish State Theatre (Teatrul Evreiesc de Stat; Map pp62-3; ☎ 323 4530; Str Iuliu Barasch 15; box office ☽ 9am-2pm) Plays in Romanian and Yiddish are held here.

SHOPPING

For beautifully made woven rugs, table runners, national Romanian costumes, ceramics and other local crafts, don't miss the excellent folk-art shop at the **Museum of the Romanian Peasant shop** (Map pp62-3; ☎ 317 9661; Şos Kiseleff 3; ☽ 10am-6pm Tue-Sun); access is from the back side of the museum.

Librăria Noi (p64) has a great collection of antique books and maps.

In the historic centre, wrought iron gates lead to cobblestoned pedestrian lane **Str Hanul** cu Tei (Map p66), a well-kept passageway with galleries, art supplies and antiques.

A couple of shopping malls include **City Mall** (Map pp62-3; ☎ 311 4260; Şos Olteniţei 2; ☼ 10am-10pm Mon-Thu, to midnight Fri & Sat) and **Bucureşti Mall** (Map pp62-3; ☎ 327 6100; Calea Vitan 55-59; ☼ 10am-10pm), both with children's activities and movie theatres. You can purchase some souvenir shirts at **Unirea Department Store** (Map pp62-3; Piaţa Unirii 3; ☼ 9am-10pm Mon-Sat, 11am-8pm Sun).

See Sport (p85) for the famed local football team Steaua's club shop.

GETTING THERE & AWAY
Air
Most international flights use the **Henri Coanda Airport** (formerly Otopeni; ☎ 201 4788; Şos Bucureşti-Ploieşti), 16km north of Bucharest on the road to Braşov.

Arrivals and departures use marked side-by-side terminals (arrivals is to the north). The **information desks** (☎ 204 1220; www.otp-airport .ro; ☼ 24hr) are in both terminals.

Romania's national airline is **Tarom** (Transporturile Aeriene Române; www.tarom.ro) Airport (☎ 201 400) Centre (Map p66; ☎ 337 0400; Spl Independenţei 17; ☼ 8.30am-7.30pm Mon-Fri, 9am-2pm Sat). Daily service includes a couple of daily flights to Cluj-Napoca and Timişoara (about €55 one way including tax); one daily flight to Iaşi (€52); three weekly to Târgu Mures (€45); four weekly to Suceava (€60); and a Friday flight to Oradea (€50) and Baia Mare (€50). Note that, enigmatically, a return flight booked online costs more than two one-way tickets – by as much as 30% extra!

Air Moldova (Map p66; ☎ 312 1258; www.airmoldova .md) also serves Henri Coanda.

Băneasa Airport (☎ 232 0020; Şos Bucureşti-Ploieşti 40), 8km north of the centre, is used for some internal flights, charter flights, and – as of January 2007 – irresistible discount flights from London via **Wizz Air** (www.wizzair.com).

Bus
DOMESTIC DESTINATIONS
Bucharest's bus system is, frankly, a mess – scarred by ever-changing departure locations, companies and schedules. Try checking websites such as www.cdy.ro and www.autogara .ro, or asking your hotel to help with the latest before you show up in a dusty lot with your bags, bent on a ticket for Iaşi. The most popular routes are the maxitaxis to Braşov, which

stop in Sinaia, Buşteni and Predeal on the way. When in doubt, take the train.

Chief 'stations' – some are lots, or spaces by a curb – include the following:

Autogară Diego (Map p66; ☎ 311 1283; Spl Independentei 2K)

Autogară Filaret (Map pp62-3; ☎ 336 0692; Piaţa Garii Filaret 1) Three kilometres south of Piaţa Universitaţii; take bus 7 and 232 from Piaţa Unirii.

Autogară Militari (☎ 434 1084; B-dul Iuliu Maniu 141) Eight kilometres west of the centre; metro station Păcii.

Central Bus Station (aka Autogară Gară de Nord; Map pp62-3) 350m east of the train station.

C&I (Map pp62-3; ☎ 256 8039; Str Ritmului 35) 3¼km east of Piaţa Romana; four blocks north of metro station Piaţa Iancului; bus 69 or 85 goes from Gară de Nord.

The following table gives a rough idea of how often and from where a bus, or microbus, or maxitaxi, goes to various destinations. Things will likely change.

Destination	Price	Duration	Frequency	Station
Arad	€14.70-15.90	6hr	5 daily	Alegro (4), Filaret (1)
Baia Mare	€15.90	12hr	1 daily	Filaret
Braşov	€5.10	2½hr	half-hourly	C&I
Calafat	€8.70	8hr	2 daily	Filaret, Rahova
Costanţa	€6.60	3¼hr	hourly	Central
Craiova	€9	4½hr	half-hourly	C&I
Curtea de Argeş	€4.50	2½hr	4 daily	Militari
Giurgiu	€2.70-3.90	1¼hr	half-hourly	Filaret
Iaşi	€10-12	7½hr	7 daily	Alegro (5), Diego (2)
Piteşti	€2.70-3	1½hr	hourly	Diego, Militari
Ploieşti	€2.70	1½hr	hourly	C&I
Sibiu	€9.90	5½hr	5 daily	Militari
Sighişoara	€8.10	6hr	6 daily	C&I
Snagov	€1.50	1hr	every 45 min	Piaţa Presei Libre
Suceava	€12	9hr	2 daily	Filaret
Târgovişte	€3.30-3.90	1½hr	hourly	Filaret
Târgu Jiu	€10.50-11.10	5½hr	10 daily	Militari
Timişoara	€15.90	11½hr	4 daily	Militari (2), Alegro (2)

INTERNATIONAL BUSES

Bulgaria

Maxitaxi services depart three times daily from Autogară Diego for Ruse, Bulgaria (€12 one way, 3 to 4 hours) – the only bus service between Romania and its neighbour to the south.

Moldova

A regular bus service leaves for Chişinau (€11, 12 hours) from Filaret bus station.

Turkey

The Turkey-bound have several options around Gară de Nord, including **Ortadoğu Tur** (Map pp62-3; ☎ 318 7538; Str Gară de Nord 6-8), **Troy** (Map pp62-3; ☎ 318 7920; Piaţa Gară de Nord 2); and **Toros** (Map pp62-3; ☎ 233 1898; Calea Griviţei 134-136). Each sends one or more buses daily. The 12-hour trip is about €37.50 one way.

Western Europe

The biggest name in international buses is **Eurolines** (☎ 316 3661; www.eurolines.ro; Str Buzeşti 44; ۞ 24hr), which links many Western European destinations with Bucharest. One-way fares for sample routes include two weekly buses to Athens (€80, 22 hours) and Berlin (€115), a daily service to Rome (€115) and Vienna (€64), and three weekly buses to Paris (€125). Working with Eurolines, Atlassib handles Italian destinations. Buses pick up passengers at various Romanian cities, but there's no domestic service.

    Double T (Map p66; ☎ 313 3642; www.doublet.ro; Calea Victoriei 2) has frequent buses to Germany, Switzerland, Austria, Italy and Spain. A ticket to Munich is €77.

Car & Motorcycle

Bucharest offers some of the country's cheapest car-hire rates. Major car-hire agencies can be found at the Henri Coanda Airport arrivals hall, as well as offices around town.

Absolut Rent-a-Car (Map p66; ☎ 319 5473; www.rentacar.com.ro; Spl Unirii 160) Rates start with Daewoo Ticos at €22 per day.

Avis (www.avis.ro) Hilton (Map p66; ☎ 312 2043); Henri Coanda Airport (☎ 201 1957); Hotel Inter-Continental (Map p66; ☎ 314 1837) Typical rates of the international big boys: from €52 per day at airport, from €64 in town.

Budget (☎ 204 1667; www.budgetro.ro; Henri Coanda Airport) Other locations around town.

C&V (☎ 201 4611, 0788-998 877; www.dvtouring.ro; Henri Coanda Airport) Cheaper than the big names. Offers Dacia Solenzas for €42 per day (including unlimited mile-age and insurance), or €27 per day if you hire for more than a week.

Europcar (☎ 201 4937; www.europcar.com; Henri Coanda Airport)

Hertz (☎ 201 4954; www.hertz.com; Henri Coanda Airport)

Parking a car in the centre, particularly off Piaţa Victoriei and Piaţa Universităţii, costs €0.30; look for the wardens in yellow-and-blue uniforms. In many places you can just pull up to the sidewalk. Petrol costs about €1 per litre.

Train

Gară de Nord (Map pp62-3; ☎ 223 2060; Piaţa Gară de Nord 1) is the central station for national and international trains. Call ☎ 9521 or ☎ 9522 for telephone reservations. It has two halls, where same-day tickets can be purchased. Facing the station, the one to the right sells 1st- and 2nd-class domestic tickets; the one to the left sells international (marked 'casa internaţionale') and 1st-class domestic tickets. If you don't have a ticket, you have to pay €0.15 to get on the platform. Some train station workers push for tips for doing their job, such as pointing out the correct window.

    For all advance tickets (more than 24 hours before departure), go to the central **Agenţie de Voiaj CFR office** (Map p66; ☎ 313 2643; www.cfr.ro; Str Domnita Anastasia 10-14; ۞ 7.30am-7.30pm Mon-Fri, 9am-1.30pm Sat). A seat reservation is compulsory if you are travelling with an Inter-Rail or Eurail pass. There's also a nearby **CFR office** (Map pp62-3; ☎ 319 0306; Calea Griviţei; ۞ 7.30am-7.30pm Mon-Fri, 9am-1.30pm Sat).

    The Wasteels agency on the platform (see p67) can help out too. International tickets must be bought in advance.

    Some local trains to/from Constanţa use **Gară Obor station** (Map pp62–3) to the east of the centre. Bus 85 operates between the two stations.

    Check the latest schedules on www.cfr.ro or the reliable German site www.bahn.de.

    Sample direct daily service includes:

Destination	Price	Duration	Daily Departures
Braşov	€7.60	2½hr	hourly
Cluj-Napoca	€11-16	7½hr	six
Constanţa	€8.75	2½-4hr	almost hourly
Iaşi	€14.50	7hr	five

Destination	Price	Duration	Daily Departures
Sibiu	€14	5hr	three
Sighişoara	€8-12	4½hr	nine
Suceava	€15.50	8hr	one
Timişoara	€22.50	8hr	eight
Tulcea	€9.80	6hr	one

Daily international services include six trains to Budapest (13 to 15 hours); two trains to Sofia (11 hours) and Gorna Oryakhovitsa (near Veliko Târnovo, Bulgaria; 6½ hours); and one train to Belgrade (12 hours), Chişinău (13 hours), Istanbul (19 hours), Kyiv (27 hours) and Moscow (39 hours).

GETTING AROUND
To/From the Airport
BUS

To get to Henri Coanda (Otopeni) or Băneasa airport take bus 783 from the city centre, which departs every 15 minutes between 5.37am and 11.23pm (every half-hour at weekends) from Piaţa Unirii and goes via Piaţa Victoriei.

Buy a ticket, valid for two trips, for €1 at any RATB (Régie Autonome de Transport de Bucureşti) bus-ticket booth near a bus stop. Once inside the bus remember to feed the ticket into the machine.

Băneasa is 20 minutes from the centre; get off at the 'aeroportul Băneasa' stop.

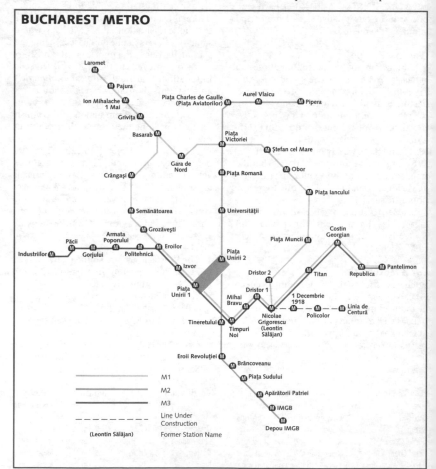

BUCHAREST METRO

Henri Coanda is about 40 minutes from the city centre. The bus stops outside the departures hall before continuing to arrivals.

To get to the centre from Henri Coanda, catch bus 783 from the downstairs ramp outside the arrivals hall; you'll need to buy a ticket from the stand at the north end of the waiting platform (to right as you exit).

TAXI
Taking a reputable taxi from the centre to Henri Coanda should cost no more than €6 or €7.

Fly Taxi monopolises airport transfers and charges about €15 to the centre – go for a flat rate; don't rely on the meter.

Public Transport
For buses, trams and trolleybuses buy tickets (€0.35) at any RATB street kiosk, marked 'casa de bilete' or simply 'bilete'. Punch your ticket on board or risk a €10 on-the-spot fine.

Public transport runs from 5am to approximately 11pm (reduced service on Sunday). There's some info online at www.ratb.ro. See Maps (p64) for a good one with routes.

Bucharest's metro dates from 1979 and has four lines and 46 stations. Trains run every five to seven minutes during peak periods and about every 20 minutes off-peak between 5.30am and 11.30pm.

To use the metro buy a magnetic-strip ticket at the subterranean kiosks inside the main entrance to the metro station. Tickets valid for two/10 journeys cost €0.60/1.90. A one-month unlimited travel ticket costs C5.75.

Taxi
Opt for a cab with a meter, and avoid the guys outside Gară de Nord. It's best to call one – or have a restaurant or hotel call one for you. Reputable companies include **Cobalcescu** (☎ 9451), **CrisTaxi** (☎ 9461) and **Taxi Sprint** (☎ 9495).

Check to see the meter is on. Rates are posted on the door. Better (and common) rates are about €0.30 per kilometre.

AROUND BUCHAREST

Most visitors looking for a break from Bucharest keep going through this broad plain to the mountains north. But there are some nice day trips nearby, peaking with the blood-curling Dracula's tomb in Snagov, 'Lenin's graveyard' outside Mogoşoaia Palace, and a monastery pretty enough to host a Swedish tennis star's wedding. The nearest and best slopes and hiking trails are in Sinaia (p118), two hours north.

SNAGOV
☎ 21 / pop 7040

Most visitors to this serpent-shaped lake 30km north of Bucharest couldn't care less about its main draw for foreign visitors – the wee island in the middle, home to a 16th-century monastery and the remains of Vlad Ţepeş. Bucharestians love this place for the water and sun and fresh air, coming in droves on weekends (aim for a weekday) in good weather, picnicking at places like Complex Astoria.

The rather unexciting village runs south of the 18km (and out of sight from town) Snagov Lake.

Sights
The headless torso of Vlad Ţepeş – Romania's favourite impaling tyrant of yester-century – lies in a grave on the tiny island. A simple wooden church was built on the island in the 11th century by Mircea cel Bătrân. A monastery was added in the late 14th century during the reign of King Dan I (r 1383–86), and in 1453 the wooden church was replaced by a stone edifice, which later sank in the lake.

In 1456 Vlad Ţepeş (the Impaler) built fortifications around the monastery. He also built a bridge from the lake to the mainland, a bell tower, a new church, an escape tunnel, and a prison and torture chamber. Nicolae Bălcescu, leader of the 1848 revolution in Wallachia, and other 1848 revolutionaries were imprisoned in Snagov prison for a short time. A mass grave for those who died in the prison was dug in the grounds. The remains of the prison behind the present-day church can still be seen today.

The present stone church, listed as a Unesco World Heritage building and under renovation for several years, dates from 1521. Some paintings date from 1563. The body of Vlad Ţepeş was reputedly buried below the dome, just in front of the church's wooden iconostasis, but when the grave was opened in 1931 it was reported to be empty. Nevertheless, there is mounting credibility given to the presence of a headless torso, evidence that the unfortunate owner was killed by the Turks. The humble grave inside the church, marked by a simple portrait of Vlad, is simply known as 'Dracula's tomb' today.

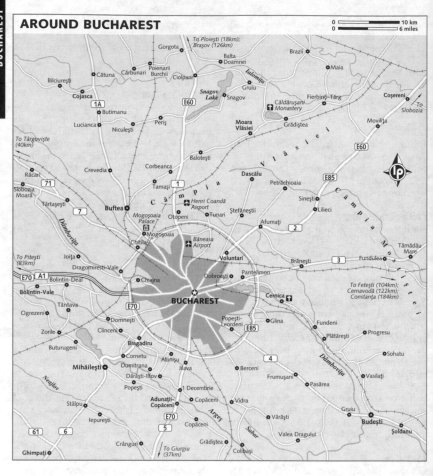

AROUND BUCHAREST

The early-20th-century **Snagov Palace**, just across the lake from the island, was built by Prince Nicolae, brother of King Carol II, in the Italian Renaissance style. During the Ceauşescu era the palace was used for meetings of high-level government officials, and today it houses a restaurant, conference centre and hotel reserved exclusively for state guests. Ceauşescu had a summer home on Snagov Lake, **Villa No 10**, now occasionally hired to rich and famous tourists.

The bulk of visitors come by tour – and it isn't a brcczc to get here on your own – but it's possible to hire a rowboat from Complex Astoria (€3 per hour) and visit by yourself. You can also hire a rowboat from the northern shore at the village Silestru. To get to Sile-

stru, continue north along the E60 past the 'Snagav Sat. 11km' turn-off and turn right in Ciolpani.

Some winters, in December and January, it is often possible to walk or ice skate across the frozen lake to the monastery.

Sleeping & Eating

Most people visit Snagov on a day trip.

Complex Astoria (☎ 316 7550; r €28-45) A few kilometres east of Snagov on the southern side of the lake, this 22-acre wooded complex has plenty of space to pitch your tent or stay in one of the pleasant hotel rooms. On weekends it's the number-one spot for Bucharest locals (who can number in the hundreds); weekdays are quiet. There is a pool (€4.25), tennis (€5.75 per hour), boats to hire, and ping pong, plus a couple of restaurants. Entrance to the complex costs €2.80 Saturday and Sunday, and is free Monday to Friday.

To get to there by car, turn east off the E60 (signposted 'Snagov Sat. 11km') and follow the road for 11km to Snagov village. Continue past the village, ignoring the sign 'centru', for a further 2km to the complex (signposted 'Baza Turistică Snagov').

Getting There & Away

The best way is to get here is to grab a maxitaxi, which go every hour from the Press House in Bucharest (€1.30 each way; 45 minutes).

Otherwise there are several local trains which run between May and September to and from Gară de Nord and Snagov Plajă, a stop in the middle of an oak forest which is 10 minutes' walk from Complex Astoria.

Some hotels, as well as the Butterfly Villa Hostel (p82) and the Villa Helga Youth Hostel (p82), offer guided tours to Snagov. A hostel tour is around €10 per person, including a stop at the monastery. An agent like Jolly Tours (p80) charges about €40 per person for a group of two, including Mogoşoaia Palace.

CĂLDĂRUŞANI MONASTERY

Filled with icons painted by Romanian master Nicolae Grigorescu at 16 years old, this idyllic monastery, 6km southeast of Snagov, is often included in tours of Dracula's tomb. Eight exquisite icons line the walls of the former monks' dining hall.

It was built in 1638, under the guidance of Wallachian prince Matei Basarab (r 1632–54), and was forced into the international spotlight when Swedish tennis champion Björn Borg married Romanian player Mariana Simionescu here.

In 1945 a fire destroyed the building – and it took eight years to rebuild between 1950 and 1958. It's generally possible to sleep here for a donation.

Bus 452 leaves twice a day for the monastery from the Press House in Bucharest. Most people go by car, but note that some road maps incorrectly mark its location. By car, take the E60 highway north to Ploieşti for 16km and turn right onto the 101C road to Fierbinţi. Go for another 16km and do a left at the sign for the monastery.

Some Bucharest–Galaţi trains, departing from Gară de Nord, stop at Greci (50 minutes), 2km south of the monastery.

MOGOŞOAIA PALACE

Easily combined with a day trip to Snagov, the **Mogoşoaia Palace** (☎ 350 6618; admission €0.45; ☼ 10am-6pm Tue-Fri, to 7pm Sat & Sun), 14km northwest of Bucharest, gives an inside look at one of Romania's best examples of Brânoveanu architecture, plus the scrappy 'graveyard' of a few knocked-down communist statues.

Located in Mogoşoaia (literally, Mogoş' wife), the palace was built by Wallachian prince Constantin Brâncoveanu between 1698 and 1702 as a summer residence. After he and his four sons were killed in Istanbul in 1714, the palace became an inn and was all but demolished by Russian forces in 1853. At the end of the 19th century, the estate was handed down to the Bibescu family, descendants of the Brâncoveanus through the female line. A large guesthouse was built and, in 1912, Prince George Valentin Bibescu (1880–1941) relinquished Mogoşoaia to his wife, Martha (1886–1973). Under her guidance, Italian architect Domenico Rupolo restored the estate. State-owned since 1956, the palace served as a museum until the 1970s, when Ceauşescu closed it and took the furniture for his own use. It's again a museum, albeit a bit of a bare one, with a collection of tapestries and old photos.

Prince George Valentin Bibescu is buried in the small, white 1688 church on the estate. A path from the main entrance to the palace leads to the **Bibescu family tomb** where Elizabeth Asquith (1898–1945), the daughter of former British prime minister Henry Herbert Asquith, lies.

The **grave of 'Lenin'** is just north of the palace walls, where statues of Lenin and 1940s communist prime minister Petru Groza lie head-to-head in the weeds. The Lenin statue previously stood outside Bucharest's Press House, and was dumped here after the downfall of Romanian communism.

Getting There & Away

The palace entrance is 750m north of the start of the lake, on its east side. To get here take tram 20 from Gară de Nord to the last stop on the line (in the Laromet district), from where bus 460 trundles to/from Mogoşoaia.

By car, take national road DN 1A.

CERNICA

Often missed, but home to some breathtaking interior paintings, Cernica (Sfânta Mănăstire Cernica) is on a small island in the middle of Cernica Lake, 14km east of Bucharest. Two churches, some chapels, a cemetery, seminary and a small **museum** are contained within the intensely beautiful fortified complex, founded on the site of a 17th-century church in 1781.

An earthquake destroyed much of the complex in 1842 but it was successfully restored in the 1990s. A smaller church, **St Nicolae's Church** (Biserica Sfântul Nicolae din Ostrov) was built in 1815, but it was not until the mid–19th century, under the guidance of St Calinic of Cernica, that the monastery really flourished.

Between 1831 and 1838 **St Gheorghe's Church** (Biserica Sfântul Gheorghe) was built, a library and seminary was opened and a school for religious painting set up. After WWII the monastery was closed, not reopening until 1995. Some 50 monks live on the island complex – joined by a causeway to the mainland.

Getting There & Away

From Bucharest's Pantelimon metro station in east Bucharest, take bus 410 or 459 for about 20 minutes, where it stops outside the monastery gates.

By car, take road 3 past Pantelimon; once across the lake turn right on Şos Cernica towards Budreşti.

Wallachia

With competition like the rural idyll of Maramureş, the elegant Habsburgs cities of Crişana and Banat and the deluge of tempting offerings just north in Transylvania, Wallachia (Ţara Românească) is shamefully underrated, thus ignored by most travellers. All the better for you.

This geographically flat southern swipe of Romania has a culturally mountainous landscape that offers increasing rewards the further one ventures from Bucharest. Snuggled into the seams of the Carpathians are Horezu, Cozia and Turnul, some of Romania's most beautiful and peaceful monasteries. Off-the-beaten-track attractions such as Câmpina's spooky Haşdeu Castle or Târgu Jiu's open-air museum of sculptor Brâncuşi's work, are refreshingly free of tour buses. The heart of the Roma community can be found here, tearing through villages on horse-drawn carts and tending to their unusual houses. During summer months, fearless drivers will want to navigate the heart-stopping Transfăgărăşan road – said to be one of the highest roads in Europe – cutting across the Făgăraş Mountains and passing the *real* 'Dracula's castle'.

The Danube River flows along the southern edge of Wallachia and is best seen between Moldova Veche and Drobeta-Turnu Severin in the west where it breaks through the Carpathians at the legendary Iron Gates (Porţile de Fier), a gorge on the Romanian–Yugoslav border. Equally scenic is the drive east along the Danube from Ostrov into northern Dobrogea.

Wallachia has charming treasures and enough elbow room to make it special. Sidle down here for a few days, but don't tell the others where you'll be!

HIGHLIGHTS

- Know the misery of captured Turks as you gasp up 1480 steps to Vlad Ţepeş' **Poienari Citadel** (p105), the 'real' Dracula's castle

- Visit the region's exquisite monasteries – **Horezu** (p106), **Curtea de Argeş** (p104) and **Bistriţa** (p106)

- Submit to total immersion (read inebriation) while eating, drinking *ţuică* (fruit brandy), singing and dancing around a campfire in the rural village of **Arefu** (p105)

- Judiciously cruise the **Transfăgărăşan road** (p105), stopping to ogle **Lake Vidraru** (p105)

- Enjoy Brâncuşi's ornamental contributions to **Târgu Jiu** (p107), including his 'Endless Column'

HISTORY

Before the formation of Romania in the 19th century, the Romanians were known as Vlachs, hence Wallachia. Romanians call Wallachia 'Țara Românească' (Land of the Romanians).

Founded by Radu Negru in 1290, this principality was subject to Hungarian rule until 1330 when Basarab I (r 1310–52) defeated the Hungarian king Charles I and declared Wallachia independent, the first of the Romanian lands to achieve independence. The Wallachian princes (voievozi) built their first capital cities – Câmpulung Muscel, Curtea de Argeş and Târgovişte – close to the protective mountains, but in the 15th century Bucharest gained ascendancy.

After the fall of Bulgaria to the Turks in 1396 Wallachia faced a new threat, and in 1415 Mircea cel Bătrân (Mircea the Old; r 1386–1418) was forced to acknowledge Turkish suzerainty. Other Wallachian princes such as Vlad Țepeş (r 1448, 1456–62, 1476) and Mihai Viteazul (r 1593–1601) became national heroes by defying the Turks and refusing to pay tribute. Indeed, Vlad Țepeş' legendary disposition and gruesome tactics against the Turks – and the old and the crippled and anyone else he didn't much care for – directly inspired Bram Stoker's *Dracula*, four centuries later, curiously relocating the 'Prince of Darkness' to Transylvania.

In 1859 Wallachia was united with Moldavia, paving the way for the modern Romanian state.

PLOIEŞTI

☎ 244 / pop 234,929

Ploieşti, the main city in the Prahova region, ranks as Romania's second-most important industrial city. Dubbed the city of 'black gold', Ploieşti has had an oil refining industry since 1857 and this is a source of enormous pride for its inhabitants.

Glamorous it may not be, but Ploieşti has a nice little centre and several interesting museums.

Orientation

Ploieşti has four train stations, but most travellers will only use the southern station (Gară Sud) and the western station (Gară Vest).

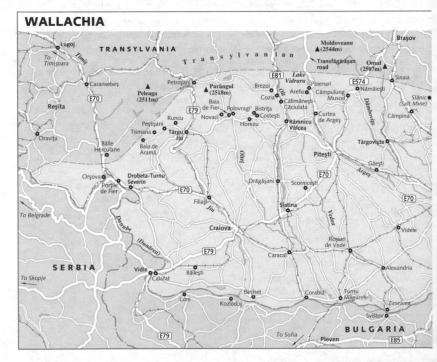

WALLACHIA

If you are arriving from Moldavia you will stop at the southern train station. Exit the station and head north up B-dul Independenței for 15 minutes to Piaţa Victoriei. All hotels, museums and restaurants are centred on this square.

From Transylvania, you will arrive at the western train station. From here, take bus 1 or 2 to Piaţa Victoriei in the centre. If you are coming from Bucharest or Târgovişte you could arrive at either station; get off at the southern station, as it's closer to the centre.

Information

There is an ATM and exchange office next to McDonald's on Piaţa Victoriei.

Agenţia de Turism Passion (☎ 514 507, 515 118; Piaţa Victoriei 3; ⏱ 8.30am-6pm Mon-Fri) This is the best choice in Ploieşti as there's no official tourist information office. Friendly staff offer maps, information, hotel bookings and wine tours of the Prahova Valley.

Eurom Bank (☎ 540 351; Piaţa Victoriei 6) Offers the usual services.

Post & telephone office (Piaţa Victoriei 10; ⏱ 7am-8pm Mon-Fri, 8am-noon Sat) The central office is south of Piaţa Victoriei on B-dul Republicii.

Transivania Travel (⏱ 9am-5pm Mon-Fri, to 1pm Sat) Inside Hotel Central (p96).

Sights

The **Museum of Oil** (Muzeul Naţional al Petrolului; ☎ 523 564; Dr Bagdasar 8; admission €0.50; ⏱ 10am-5pm Tue-Sun) charts Ploieşti's place as Romania's *Dallas*.

Nearby is the **History & Archaeology Museum** (Muzeul de Istorie şi Arheologie; ☎ 514 437; Str Toma Caragiu 10; admission adult/student €0.85/0.45; ⏱ 9am-5pm Tue-Sun). Housed in a former girls' school dating from 1865, it has a room devoted to Romanian sporting achievements (ie gymnastics). At the same location is the **Museum of Popular Art** (Muzeul de Artă Populară).

The **Clock Museum** (Muzeul Ceasului; ☎ 542 861; Str Nicolae Simachei 1; ⏱ 9am-5pm Tue-Sun; admission adult/student €1/0.45) boasts clocks owned by several famous Romanians including Carol I, King Mihei and an 18th-century rococo Austrian clock that belonged to Wallachian prince Alexandru Ioan Cuza.

In the centre of the park on Piaţa Victoriei, there is a **memorial** to the victims of the 1989 revolution, as well as a **Liberty Statue**. The **Culture Palace** (Palatul Culturii), at the northern end of the square, is home to the **Museum of Natural Science** (Muzeul de Ştiinţe ale Naturii Prahova; admission €0.60; ⏱ 9am-5pm). Opposite the Culture Palace is the impressive **St John's Cathedral**, dating from 1810. To its east lies the **Central Market**, housed in two large, domed buildings.

A 19th-century white Empire-style building houses the **Art Museum** (Muzeul de Artă; ☎ 511 375; B-dul Independenţei 1; admission adult/student €0.70/0.40, Sun free; ⏱ 10am-4pm Sun-Fri) displaying engravings, Romanian paintings and ongoing temporary exhibitions.

Sleeping

our pick **Hotel Forum** (☎ 595 628; hf_ploiesti@yahoo .com; Str Gheorghe Doja 215a; s/d/ste €25/28/43; 🖵) No doubt, you're a little frustrated with the dubious price-versus-quality quotient of many Romanian hotels and *pensiunes*. Enter this budget traveller's dream. New beds, sparkling bathrooms, public internet station, wi-fi, minibars, room service and a bar-restaurant (mains €2 to €4) are all on site. The youthful staff tear through the English language and the lobby's plasma TV area is within lurching distance of the bar, making it the perfect night-out staging point. Breakfast not included.

WALLACHIA

WALLACHIA

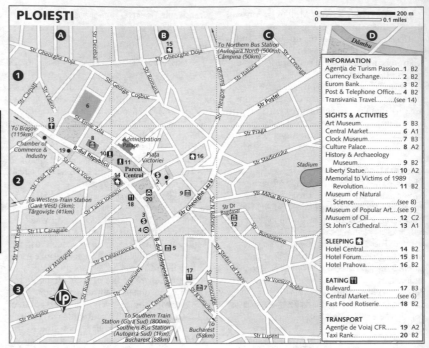

PLOIEŞTI

Hotel Central (☎ 526 641; paul_palas@yahoo.com; B-dul Republicii 9; s/d 2-star €35/43, 3-star €51/69, 4-star €85/130; ☐) Reborn after the last earthquake destroyed it, only the four-star rooms have been significantly beautified and have internet access. The two-star rooms are looking worn.

Hotel Prahova Plazza (☎ 526 850; hotelprahova@ yahoo.com; Str Dobrogeanu Gherea 11; s/d/ste €81/81/115; ☒ ☐) This Soviet architect's delight is starting to crumble outside, but has been newly renovated inside, with the ambitious prices to prove it.

Eating

Ploieşti is shamefully devoid of decent eateries. Hotel restaurants are your best bet for a simple, filling meal.

Fast Food Rotiserie (Piaţa Victoriei; mains €2; ☼ 9am-11pm) This place is next to Cinema Patria, facing Piaţa Victoriei. Good for refuelling rather than savouring.

Bulevard (☎ 517 549; Str Goleşti 25; mains €6-17) This is hands down the best dining experience in Ploieşti, with a large menu (English available), heavy on Romanian cuisine, a classy dining room and the best summer garden in town.

Get your fresh veggies and fish from the monster-sized **central market** (B-dul Unirii).

Getting There & Away

BUS

There are two bus stations: long-distance buses arrive at and depart from the **northern bus station** (Autogară Nord; Str Griviţei 25), and buses to nearby villages use the **southern bus station** (Autogară Sud; Str Depoului), a two-minute walk from the southern train station.

The southern bus station has services to Bucharest (€2.10, 1½ hours, one daily), Câmpina (€1.10, 30 minutes, eight daily) and Târgovişte (€1.40, one hour, two daily).

TRAIN

You can purchase train tickets in advance from the **Agenţie de Voiaj CFR** (☎ 542 080; B-dul Republicii 17; ☼ 7am-8pm Mon-Fri).

Fast trains to/from Bucharest, Constanţa, Timişoara, Craiova and Moldavia use the southern train station (Gară Sud). Local trains use the western train station (Gară Vest).

From the southern train station, services include those to Bucharest (€4.20, 10 daily), Braşov (€7, 10 daily), Cluj-Napoca (€19.60, two daily), Baia Mare (€21, two daily) and, in summer, Constanţa (two daily).

Trains to Budapest from Bucharest stop at the southern train station, as does the daily Warsaw train.

Getting Around

Bus 1 and 2 travel from the southern train station to Piaţa Victoriei in the city centre and then on to the western train station. From here, bus 2 continues to the university. A taxi rank is adjacent to Parcul Central (Central Park). Avoid taxis that don't list their price per kilometre on their doors.

CÂMPINA & AROUND
☎ 244

Travelling out of Ploieşti is a surreal experience. Romania's Texas has miles of flat, bleak landscape pitted by constantly moving oil drills.

Heading 32km north of Ploieşti into the Prahova Valley you come to Câmpina. Approaching this small town, you pass a memorial to pioneering pilot Aurel Vlaicu. Vlaicu, who built three planes and a glider – and designed a dirigible that was never built due to lack of funding – won several international aviation contests, flying his own planes. He met his death in 1913 after his arrow-shaped plane, the *Vlaicu-II*, crashed near Baneşti as he rushed to beat a foreign aviator to be the first to cross the Carpathians by plane.

Sights

HAŞDEU CASTLE

Get spooked in this creepy tribute to fatherly love. Construction on the **castle** (☎ 335 599; B-dul Carol I 197; admission adult/student €1.20/0.60; ☀ 9am-5pm Tue-Sun Sep-Apr, 10am-6pm May-Aug) began in 1893, built by history professor Bogdan Petriceicu Haşdeu in memory of his academically brilliant daughter, Iulia, who died of tuberculosis at the age of 19 – just before she was to have been the first woman to enter the Sorbonne in Paris.

Although Iulia was buried in the Belu Cemetery in Bucharest it was here that her father held seances to communicate with her and composed the eerie funeral music said to be communicated from daughter to father via the spirit world.

NICOLAE GRIGORESCU MUSEUM

Romania's signature **museum** (Muzeul Nicolae Grigorescu; ☎ 333 598; B-dul Carol I 166; admission adult/student €0.65/0.30), dedicated to its most famous artist, is the pride of Câmpina. It charts the life and works of Grigorescu (1838–1907) who started his career painting icons to support his family. Soon he was getting commissioned for private work, most notably the murals at Agapia Monastery (p264) in Moldavia. He studied in Paris with Pierre Auguste Renoir. Much of his mature work revolved around landscapes and peasant life, though his depictions of battles and prisoners produced while volunteering at the front during the Romanian Independence War are also renowned. His works attracted the attention of the Barbizon group and Napoleon III, who bought two of his paintings in 1867.

SLANIC

Forty kilometres north of Ploieşti lies a Disneyland of salt. The **Unirea Salt Mine Complex** (admission €3.50; ☀ 9am-3pm Tue-Sun), the largest salt mine in Europe, is the result of three decades (1943–70) of furious mining and now serves as a tourist attraction, as well as offering health and sport facilities. Salt pools and lakes notwithstanding, the very air in the mine's microclimate 220m below the surface is reputed to work wonders on the respiratory system. Additionally visitors can admire the salt statues and giant halls, dump the kids at the playground, play some football or tennis, or race through the run field. Ground-level attractions include the **Museum of Salt** (☀ 9am-7pm), depicting miner life, and the notably diminished **Salt Mountain**.

From Ploieşti's southern train station, maxitaxis run to Slanic every 45 minutes (or when full), and a daily local train leaves from Ploieşti's western train station.

Sleeping

The only choice in the area, **Hotel Muntenia** (☎ 333 091; B-dul Carol I 61; s/d €23/47), is OK for a one-night stopover.

Getting There & Away

From Ploieşti's southern bus station there are several daily buses to Câmpina (32km). There are also five daily trains from Ploieşti's western station to Câmpina.

Maxitaxi services run between Sinai and Câmpina.

WALLACHIA

TÂRGOVIŞTE
☎ 245 / pop 92,320

All eyes were on Târgovişte, 49km northwest of Bucharest, following the dramatic arrest here of dictator Nicolae Ceauşescu and his wife Elena on 22 December 1989.

The Ceauşescus hijacked a car in Titu, 44km northwest of Târgovişte, where they were spotted by two soldiers who finally caught up with them in the town. Four days later, the first bloody images of the hastily arranged court session and execution by firing squad inside the military garrison flashed across the world's TV screens, 'proving' the hated pair was dead.

Aside from its spotlight in history, Târgovişte is a charming market town dating from 1396. It was the capital of Wallachia from 1418 until 1659, when the capital was moved to Bucharest. During the 15th century, Vlad Ţepeş, the notorious impaler with whom the fictitious Dracula is associated, held princely court here.

Orientation

The town centre is a 20-minute walk from the train station. Exit the station and head east, past the military barracks, up B-dul Castanilor, then turn right into B-dul Mircea cel Bătrân (previously Str Victoriei). All eastbound buses along this street stop in the centre. The bus station and central market are 3km northwest of town; turn right as you leave the bus station, then cross the large roundabout and take any eastbound bus down Calea Câmpulung.

The main shops, banks and hotels are in the modern centre clustered around Central Park (Parcul Central), which is straddled by B-dul Libertăţii to the north and B-dul Mircea cel Bătrân to the south. The Princely Court and key museums are in the older part of town, along Calea Domnească.

Information

Surprise! There's no tourist office! Instead head straight for the Princely Court or the nearby History Museum where you can buy tourist brochures in English or French (€0.75) covering all the main sights. Hotel Dâmboviţa (p100) offers a currency exchange service.

Banca Comercială Română (B-dul Independenţiei; ☺ 8am-5pm Mon-Fri) Does it all.

Central post office (Str Dr Marinoiu; ☺ 7.30am-8pm Mon-Fri, 8am-1pm Sat) Dates from 1906.

Internet (Str C A Rosetti; per hr €0.60; ☺ 8am-11pm)

Telephone office (Str Ion Rădulescu; ☺ 7am-8.30pm)

Sights

The **military barracks**, where the Ceauşescus were executed, are immediately on the right as you leave the train station. At the hasty trial the pair faced joint charges of being accomplices to the murder of some 60,000 people, of genocide, and of attempting to flee Romania with state money, totalling US$1 billion, stashed away in foreign bank accounts. None of the charges were proven. It's forbidden to enter or to take photographs of the garrison at the western end of B-dul Castanilor.

During the 15th century, the bloodthirsty prince Vlad Ţepeş resided at **Princely Court** (Curtea Domnească; Calea Domnească 181; admission adult/student €0.85/0.40; ☺ 9am-9pm Tue-Sun). The court was built in the 14th century for Mircea cel Bătrân (Mircea the Old) and remained a residence for Wallachia's princes until the reign of Constantin Brâncoveanu (r 1688–1714). The court was gradually fortified by most princes. Matei Basarab (1632–1654) was the most prolific court developer, and also raised many of the town's churches. Mircea cel Bătrân added defensive towers and Vlad Ţepeş the 27m-high **Sunset Tower** (Turnul Chindiei), from where guards would announce the closing of the city gates as the sun went down (the current tower is a replica). It houses an exhibition – in Romanian – recounting the stories of Vlad Ţepeş' life: one display freely describes how he made sure impaled Turkish soldiers had their eyes cut out so they couldn't see the heavenly maidens they believed awaited them after death. Also on site are ruins of two princes' houses, aqueducts, and a church, as well as two surviving churches from the 16th century – one a museum with 18th-century frescoes, the other a functioning house of worship.

The local **History Museum** (Muzeul de Istorie Dâmboviţa; cnr Calea Domnească & Str Justiţei; admission adult/student €0.85/0.40; ☺ 10am-6pm Tue-Sun) has local artefacts from the Stone Age to the Middle Ages. An English tour is available upon request. Nearby is Romania's only **Museum of Romanian Police** (Muzeul Poliţiei Române; admission €0.60; ☺ 9am-5pm Tue-Sun), with a number of exhibitions from the 19th and 20th centuries, including an overfilled cloakroom-style display of uniforms, verily inviting one to don and model the inventory. In the same courtyard is an **Art Museum**, under construction at the time of writing.

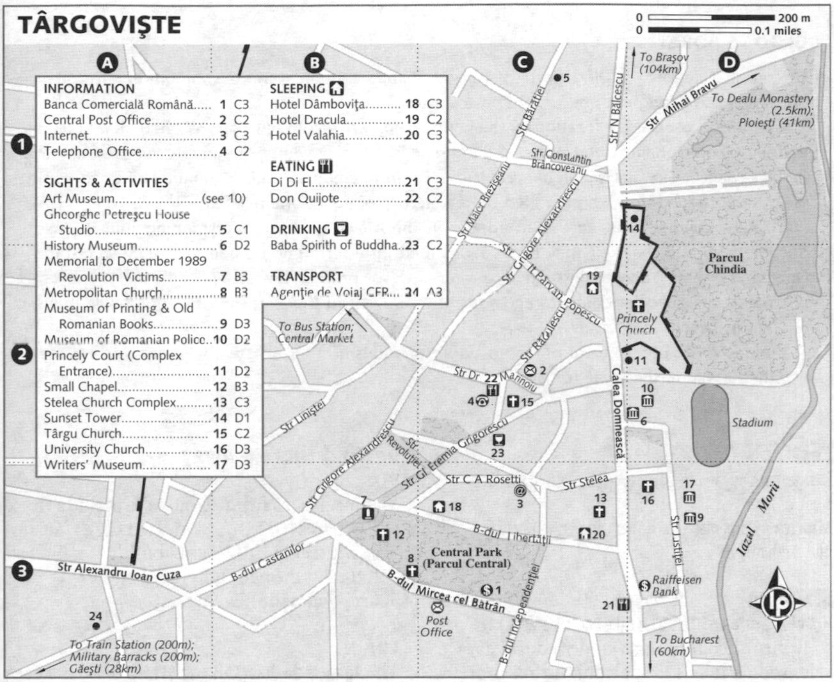

The **Museum of Printing & Old Romanian Books** (Muzeul Tiparului şi al Cărţii Româneşti Vechi; ☎ 612 877; Str Justiţei 3-5; admission €0.60) is housed inside a 17th-century palace built by Constantin Brâncoveanu for his daughter Safta. It is bejewelled with original books from the beginning of Romania's printing age and manuscripts by 17th- and 18th-century Romanian writers, including poet Ion Alexandru Bratescu. All exhibits are in Romanian, but a brochure is available in English. A **Writers' Museum** (Muzeul Scriitorilor Dâmboviţeni) adjoins the book museum.

Opposite is the **University Church** (Biserica Universităţii), dating from the 19th century. In front of it are busts of local academic Ienăchiţă Văcărescu (1740–97) and Radu de la Afumaţi, ruler of Wallachia from 1522 to 1529.

Across from the University Church is the **Stelea Church Complex** (Complexul Biserica Stelea), founded as a monastery by Moldavian prince Vasile Lupu (r 1634–53) in 1645 as a peace offering to Wallachian ruler Matei Basarab.

In Central Park the marble cross **Memorial to December 1989** stands outside a small chapel. Also in the park is the 18th-century **Metropolitan Church**. At its monks' quarters, the 16th-century **Dealu Monastery** on a hill 3km northeast of the centre, the head of the great Wallachian prince Mihai Viteazul (Michael the Brave) is buried. Beheaded on the orders of the Habsburg general George Basta on 3 August 1601, Viteazul is still hailed as the crusader of Romanian nationalism. It was at this monastery that he swore his allegiance to the Hungarian emperor Rudolph II in 1598.

A few blocks north of the park is the partially frescoed **Târgu Church** (Biserica Târgului; Str Ion Rădulescu). The 1654 church was painted during the 17th and 18th centuries but destroyed during an earthquake in 1940. Extensive renovations followed in 1941 and in the 1970s. Inside is a **memorial plaque** to local priest and teacher Professor Georgescu, who was among the thousands to die while toiling under communist forced labour to build the Danube–Black Sea Canal in Dobrogea (p301).

Gheorghe Petreşcu House Studio (Casa Atelier Gheorghe Petreşcu; Str Bărăţiei; admission €0.60; 🕒 9am-5pm) was where the Romanian painter (1872–1949) spent the last 20 years of his life, capturing most of the town's major sights on canvas, several of which are on display.

WALLACHIA

GLOD VS BORAT

The ramshackle town of Glod, north of Târgovişte, had a moment in the spotlight in late 2006… but for all the wrong reasons, according to locals.

Glod was chosen as the location for the fictional hometown of Sacha Baron Cohen's Kazakhstani journalist, Borat, and featured in the opening scenes of the film *Borat: Cultural Learnings of America for Make Benefit Glorious Nation of Kazakhstan*. Far from enjoying their 15 minutes of fame, some of those portrayed in the film argued they were exploited and humiliated.

Villagers claimed they agreed to appear in the movie on the understanding that it was a documentary and they felt they had been duped into performing crude and demeaning acts. One armless man, who was persuaded to wear a sex-toy prosthesis while allegedly being unaware of what it was, sued for damages and sought to prevent further screenings of the movie unless offending scenes were removed.

Curiously, the Borat movie proved a boon for tourism in Kazakhstan. It remains to be seen whether it will do the same for Glod.

Festivals

Dragaica A pagan pre-harvest celebration in the last week of June.

Miorița A Romanian folk-singer competition held in mid-September.

Sleeping

Hotel Dracula (☎ 620 013; Calle Domnească; r €17) Possibly furnished through a student dorm garage sale, rooms here are spartan, but reasonably clean. Music is audible from the restaurant until 11pm.

Hotel Valahia (☎ 634 491; B-dul Libertăţii 7; s/d €30.50/40.50) This place has a strange, slightly spooky air due to the contrast of being quite grand but a bit dark and dingy. Rooms are reasonable and spacious. Reception is deficient in both English and the ambition to provide timely service.

Hotel Dâmbovița (☎ 213 370; www.hoteldambovita.ro; B-dul Libertăţii 1; s/d €37/49; 🛇) This comfortable hotel has helpful multilingual staff, and rooms with balconies overlooking Central Park.

Eating & Drinking

Di Di El (☎ 212 916; Calea Domenască; mains €3) Excellent pizzas (17 types!) and spaghetti are served on the pavement terrace.

Don Quijote (Str Dr Marinoiu 9; mains €4; 🕑 9am-midnight) This popular place has a small outside terrace and stone fireplace. Large portions of Romanian fodder are served.

Baba Spirith of Buddha (Str GI Eremia Grigorescu; 🕑 10am-midnight) Persian couches, tobaccoless hookahs and nightly 'Buddha music' await in this identity-crisis chillout bar.

Getting There & Away

BUS

Major services from Târgovişte include those to Bucharest (€2.10, 78km, 10 daily), Câmpulung Muscel (€2.10, 73km, four daily), Ploieşti (€1.40, 52km, two daily) and Braşov (€2.80, 90km, two daily).

TRAIN

The **Agenţie de Voiaj CFR** (☎ 611 554; B-dul Castanilor 2; 🕑 7am-7pm Mon-Fri), just north of the train station, sells advance tickets.

From Târgovişte there are local trains to Ploieşti's western train station (1¾ hours, five daily). To get to Târgovişte from other cities, you have to change trains at Ploieşti.

PITEŞTI

☎ 248 / pop 173,298

The infamously delicate and altogether Romanian Dacia cars have been produced here since 1966, giving Piteşti an important place in Bucharest's industrial heritage. Dacias may be the butt of endless jokes but they've kept Romania on the move (eventually) in the face of the worst roads in Europe. In mid-1999, French car manufacturer Renault acquired a majority stake in Dacia and followed through with a €500 million investment that has brought new esteem to the name, rolling out the affordable, frill-free, attractive and fast-selling Dacia Logan.

Piteşti boasts one of the country's few stretches of pristine motorway, linking it to Bucharest (114km east), and has a lovely pedestrianised centre lined with trendy new bars.

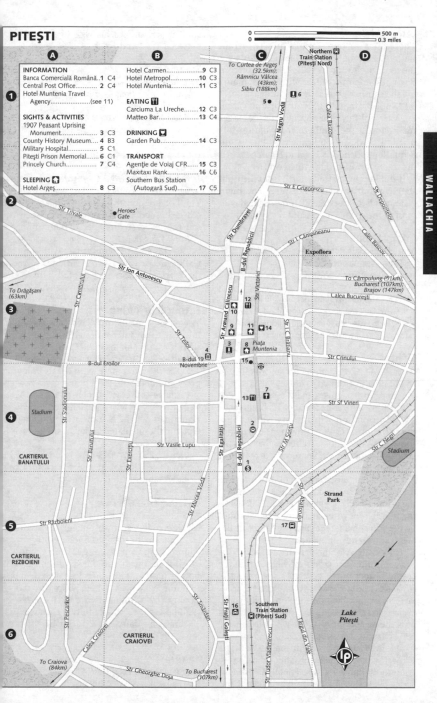

PITEŞTI

0	500 m
0	0.3 miles

INFORMATION
Banca Comercială Română..**1** C4
Central Post Office............ **2** C4
Hotel Muntenia Travel
    Agency.....................(see 11)

SIGHTS & ACTIVITIES
1907 Peasant Uprising
    Monument.................... **3** C3
County History Museum.... **4** B3
Military Hospital................ **5** C1
Piteşti Prison Memorial...... **6** C1
Princely Church................. **7** C4

SLEEPING
Hotel Argeş.................... **8** C3

Hotel Carmen...................**9** C3
Hotel Metropol.............**10** C3
Hotel Muntenia.............**11** C3

EATING
Carciuma La Ureche........**12** C3
Matteo Bar.....................**13** C4

DRINKING
Garden Pub.....................**14** C3

TRANSPORT
Agenţie de Voiaj CFR......**15** C3
Maxitaxi Rank.................**16** C6
Southern Bus Station
    (Autogară Sud)...........**17** C5

WALLACHIA

To Curtea de Argeş
(32.5km);
Râmnicu Vâlcea
(43km);
Sibiu (188km)

Northern
Train Station
(Piteşti Nord)

Expoflora

To Câmpulung (51km);
Bucharest (107km);
Braşov (147km)
Calea Bucureşti

To Drăgăşani
(63km)

To Craiova
(84km)

CARTIERUL
BANATULUI

CARTIERUL
RĂZBOIENI

CARTIERUL
CRAIOVEI

Heroes'
Gate

Stadium

Piaţa
Muntenia

Strand
Park

Stadium

Lake
Piteşti

Southern
Train Station
(Piteşti Sud)

To Bucharest
(107km)

WALLACHIA

Orientation

There are two bus stations and two train stations, although the southern stations are the most useful for travellers. Buses to/from Bucharest and other major cities in Romania use the southern bus station (Autogară Sud), off B-dul Brătianu on Str Abatorului Târgul din Vale. All Bucharest and Curtea de Argeş trains stop at the southern train station (officially Piteşti Sud but known as Piteşti) on B-dul Republicii. Bus 2, 4 and 8 run between the train station and the town centre.

B-dul Republicii leads north from the train station towards the town centre. The main pedestrianised street, Str Victoriei, is lined with most of the town's hotels and restaurants.

Information

Banca Comercială Română (B-dul Republicii 83; 8.30am-5pm Mon-Fri)

Central Post Office (Str Victoriei; 9am-7pm Mon-Fri, to noon Sat)

Hotel Muntenia Travel Agency (210 880; entrance on Str Victoriei; 8am-6pm Mon-Fri, 9am-1pm Sat) Arranges excursions to anywhere in Romania, including day trips to Curtea de Argeş, and organises car hire.

Sights

After WWII **Piteşti prison** (Str Negru Vodă), just to the north of the city centre, was a site of the communist government's 'Student Re-education Centre' because of its high security and isolation. Operational since 1900, it was not until 1949, following the arrest of some anti-communist students, that psychiatric abuse became a favoured correctional technique.

Today a tall, mosaic-tiled column in memory of those who died marks the spot where the prison stood. The **memorial** stands between the first two of three apartment blocks built on the site. A **military hospital** (Spitalul Militar; 1881) still stands opposite.

The existence of the prison and the atrocities committed are completely ignored in the **County History Museum** (Muzeul Judeţean de Istorie; Str Armand Călinescu 4; admission €0.60; 9am-5pm Tue-Sun) in favour of exhibitions on biology and archaeology. Crossing the park nearby you pass the **monument** to those who died in the 1907 peasant uprising.

On Str Victoriei, the unusual St George's Church (Biserica Sfântul Gheorghe), more commonly known as the **Princely Church** (Biserica Domnească), was built by Prince Constantin Şerban and his wife Princess Bălasa between 1654 and 1658.

Sleeping

Hotel Argeş (625 450; Piaţa Muntenia; s/d €18/30) This is the town's cheapest option; it's worn and noisy, but clean.

Hotel Metropol (222 407; Str Panselelor 1; s/d €23/28.50) There are large, passably clean rooms here, though the assumed nature of the 'transit rooms' – 'to rent for three or four hours' – may give one pause.

Hotel Muntenia (210 880; www.turism-muntenia .ro; B-dul Republicii; s/d 2-star €23/32, 3-star €41/58;) This hotel is monstrously ugly and fantastically old-fashioned, but it's dead centre. The two-star rooms are in dire need of renovation.

Hotel Carmen (215 297; B-dul Republicii 84; s/d €32/36) This small, friendly place with contemporary décor offers three varieties of room (and price); midrange, quoted here, is the best value.

Eating & Drinking

The restaurant at Hotel Carmen is the best in town, with an international menu in stylish surroundings (mains €5 to €10).

Matteo Bar (Str Victoriei 2; mains €4; 9am-10pm) Take in the buzz here with locals enjoying pizza and beer.

Carciuma 'La Ureche' (0723-281 110; B-dul Republicii 39; mains €5; noon-11pm) The long menu of Romanian cuisine is translated into English. Opt for the insulated cellar as the terrace is just off a noisy street.

Garden Pub (0723-201 254; Str Victoriei 20; 10am-11pm) Relax at the lovely terrace's wooden tables with large jugs of beer.

Getting There & Away

BUS

Maxitaxis depart from outside the southern train station, heading to Bucharest (€3, every 15 minutes), Constanţa (€12) and Craiova.

All state buses use the southern bus station (Autogară Sud). Services include buses to Râmnicu Vâlcea (€1.75, 75km, two daily), Braşov (€2, 136km, two daily), Bucharest (€2.50, 108km, three daily), Craiova (€2, 142km, one daily) and Târgu Jiu (174km, one daily).

TRAIN

The **Agenţie de Voiaj CFR** (630 565; Str Domniţa Bălaşa 13) sells advance tickets.

FROM VICTIM TO TORTURER

From 1949 to 1952 a unique and experimental 'student re-education program' was introduced in Piteşti, Gherla and Aiud prisons as a means of torturing political prisoners. The program was implemented by Eugen Ţurcanu, an inmate at Piteşti prison, acting on the orders of the Securitate. Ţurcanu rounded up a core team of torturers from among his fellow inmates.

'Re-education' induced tortured prisoners to become torturers themselves. The first stage of this grotesque process involved the prisoner confessing all his crimes and 'anti-state' thoughts that he'd failed to reveal earlier to Securitate interrogators. He then signed a declaration in which he consented to his re-education. Scrubbing floors with a rag between the teeth, eating soup with both hands tied behind the back, licking toilets clean and being beaten to unconsciousness were just some of the persuasive methods used.

Religiously inclined prisoners, dubbed 'Catholics', were baptised each morning with a bucket of urine. Others were forced to don a white sheet in imitation of Christ and wear a penis carved from soap around their necks. Fellow prisoners kissed the soap pendant and the prisoner was flogged by other inmates in imitation of Christ's ordeal on the road to Golgotha.

Next, the victim was forced to disclose the names of fellow inmates who'd shown him kindness or sympathy. He then had to renounce his own family, 'reviling them in such foul and hideous terms that it would be next to impossible ever to return to natural feelings towards them', according to former political prisoner Dimitru Bacu in his novel *The Anti-Humans*.

In the final stage of the program, victims had to prove their successful 'regeneration' – by inflicting the same mental and physical abuse on new prison recruits. If they refused they were driven through the program again. Those who slackened in their new role as re-educators spent time in the prison's incarceration cell, black room or isolation cell.

The incarceration cells were 1.8m-tall upright coffins with a small hole for ventilation. One or two prisoners had to stand in these cells for eight to 15 days. The black room was 2.7 sq metres and windowless. Up to 30 prisoners were detained here for a maximum of three weeks without water. Isolation cells were reserved for sentences of three months or more, and many prisoners kept in these cells died of tuberculosis.

In 1954 Eugen Ţurcanu and 21 other prisoners were secretly tried and sentenced to death for the murder of 30 prisoners and the abuse of 780. The Securitate denied all knowledge of the program.

Trains to/from the **southern train station** (Piteşti Sud; ☎ 627 908; B-dul Republicii) include InterCity (IC) services to/from Bucharest (€5.50, three daily) and Craiova (three daily), and *rapid* trains to Constanţa (€12.50, one daily).

CURTEA DE ARGEŞ
☎ 248 / pop 33,365

Curtea de Argeş was a princely seat in the 14th century after the capital of Wallachia was moved here from Câmpulung Muscel. The town's church is considered to be the oldest monument preserved in its original form in Wallachia, while the monastery (or Episcopal cathedral), sculpted from white stone, is unique for its chocolate-box architecture and the royal tombs it hides.

The historic town is a gateway to the Făgăraş Mountains.

Orientation

The train station, a 19th-century architectural monument, is 100m north of the bus station on Str Albeşti. The centre is a 10-minute walk along Str Albeşti then up the cobbled Str Castanilor and along Str Negru Vodă. Continue on until you reach a statue of Basarab I, from where all the major sights, camping ground and hotels (signposted) are a short walk.

Information

Post office (B-dul Basarabilor 17-19; ⏱ 7am-8pm Mon-Fri) The telephone office is in the same building.
Raiffeisen Bank (B-dul Basarabilor; ⏱ 8.30am-6.30pm Mon-Fri) Next to Hotel Posada.
Tourist office (☎ 721 451; B-dul Basarabilor 27-29; ⏱ 9am-5pm Mon-Fri) Within Hotel Posada.

Sights
PRINCELY COURT

The ruins of the **Princely Court** (Curtea Domnească; admission €0.60; ⏱ 9am-6pm), which originally comprised a church and palace, are in the city centre. The church was built in the 14th century by Basarab I, whose statue stands in the square outside the entrance to the court.

WALLACHIA

Basarab died in Târgovişte in 1352. His burial place near the altar in the princely church at Curtea de Argeş was discovered in 1939. The princely court was rebuilt by Basarab's son, Nicolae Alexandru Basarab (r 1352–68), and completed by Vlaicu Vodă (r 1361–77). While little remains of the palace today, the 14th-century church (built on the ruins of a 13th-century church) is almost perfectly intact.

HISTORIC CENTRE

The **County Museum** (Muzeul Orăşenesc; ☎ 711 446; Str Negru Vodă 2; ☒ 9am-4pm Tue-Sun) charts the history of the region. Rising on a hill are the ruins of the 14th-century **Sân Nicoară Church** (Biserica Sân Nicoară).

CURTEA DE ARGEŞ MONASTERY

This fantastical **Episcopal cathedral** (Mănăstirea Curtea de Argeş; admission €0.60; ☒ 8am-7pm) was built between 1514 and 1526 by Neagoe Basarab (r 1512–21) with marble and mosaic tiles from Constantinople. Legend has it that the wife of the master stonemason, Manole, was embedded in the stone walls of the church, in accordance with a local custom that obliged the mason to bury a loved one alive within the church to ensure the success of his work. The story goes that Manole told his workers that the first of the wives to bring their food the next day would be the one entombed alive. The workers duly went home and warned their women – it was hence Manole's wife who made the fateful visit.

The current edifice dates from 1875 when French architect André Lecomte du Nouy was brought in to save the monastery, which was in near ruins.

The white marble tombstones of Carol I (1839–1914) and his poet wife Elizabeth (1853–1916) lie on the right in the monastery's *pronaos* (entrance hall). On the left of the entrance are the tombstones of King Ferdinand I (1865–1927) and the British-born Queen Marie (1875–1938), whose heart, upon her request, was placed in a gold casket and buried in her favourite palace in Balcic in southern Dobrogea. Following the ceding of southern Dobrogea to Bulgaria in 1940, however, her heart was moved to a marble tomb in Bran. Neagoe Basarab and his wife Stâna are also buried in the *pronaos*.

In the park opposite lies **Manole's Well** (Fântâna lui Manole). Legend has it that the now widowed Manole tried – and failed – to fly from the monastery roof when his master Neagoe, removed the scaffolding to prevent him building a more beautiful structure for anyone else. The natural spring marks the hapless stonemason's supposed landing pad.

Sleeping

our pick **Pensiunea Ruxi** (☎ 0727-827 675; www.pensiunea-ruxi.ro; Str Negru Voda 104; r €19) Truly you can't go wrong with accommodation in Curtea de Argeş, but family-run Pensiunea Ruxi, directly across from Hotel Confarg, is exceptional. While the rooms are new and comfortable, the real treat is the homely atmosphere, where the family will go to heartbreaking lengths to take care of you. Sweet-talking the daughter, Ruxandra, who speaks passable English, will likely win you access to her computer for a quick, gratis email session. Breakfast (€2) is served in front of the TV, with remote control at the ready.

Hotel Posada (☎ 721 451; www.posada.ro; B-dul Basarabilor 27-29; s 1-star €19, s/d 2-star €23/30, 3-star €30/40; ☒) The front-facing rooms here enjoy mountain sunsets. Internet extra.

Montana Pizzerie (B-dul Basarabilor; s/d/ste €23/29/40) This place has simple but surprisingly comfortable rooms for rent.

Hotel Confarg (☎ 728 020; Str Negru Vodă 5; s/d/ste €26/34/46) Possibly the best-value hotel in Romania! Rooms are large, clean and modern. Doubles have huge baths and the suites are admirably swanky for the price. Breakfast is served in a top-floor glassed dining room. A sauna and well-stocked fitness centre are available, but that would require leaving your suite.

Eating & Drinking

Montana Pizzerie (B-dul Basarabilor; pizzas €2) This place serves up fresh pizzas and beer. Most nights there is live music.

Restaurant Capra Neagră (☎ 721 619; Str Alexandru Lahovary; mains €2) Sit on the terrace and enjoy the Romanian dishes here.

Hotel Confarg (☎ 728 020; Str Negru Vodă 5; mains €4) The hotel's restaurant has an excellent, reasonably priced menu of Romanian fare.

Be Happy Cafe (B-dul Basarabilor; ☒ to 5am) This is a café during the week, a thumping club on the weekends.

Disco Castel (Str Negru Vodă; ☒ 10pm-4am) The city's newest club, 50m down the road from Restaurant Capra Neagră. Be there or be mocked.

Getting There & Away

There are six daily local trains running to/from Piteşti; change at Piteşti for all train routes.

State buses run from the **bus station** (Str Albeşti) to/from Arefu, Câmpulung Muscel, Braşov and Bucharest. Check the station boards, as some buses travel only on weekdays and some only on weekends.

A daily maxitaxi to Bucharest via Piteşti leaves at 8am from outside Hotel Posada. Other maxitaxis go to/from Arefu and Piteşti from an unofficial **maxitaxi stop** (cnr Str Mai 1 & Str Lascăr Catargiu).

POIENARI & AREFU

☎ 248

From Curtea de Argeş, Draculaophiles head north up the spectacular Argeş Valley to **Poienari Citadel** (Cetatea Poienari). In 1459 Turks captured by Vlad Ţepeş in revenge for killing his father and brother marched along this route. At the end of the march, the Turks built the defensive fortress for the bloodthirsty prince. The result: a castle strategically positioned to guard the entrance from Transylvania into the Argeş Valley. It's considered by Dracula buffs to be Romania's 'real' Dracula's castle.

Some 1480 steps lead up from the side of a hydroelectric power plant to the ruins. A substantial amount of the castle, which towers on a crag above a village, fell down the side of the mountain in 1888. The head-high ruins exemplify the astounding setting and scale of the former structure. Tickets (€0.60) are sold by the castle-keeper at the top of the steps.

Six kilometres south of Poienari Citadel is **Arefu**, a tiny village inhabited solely by descendants of the minions who served Vlad Ţepeş – allegedly! The village has an *agroturism* scheme, so visitors can sit around campfires, sing folk songs and listen to tales told by villagers whose forebears mingled with the notorious impaler.

Legend has it that in 1462, when the Turks besieged Poienari Citadel, the Arefians helped Vlad Ţepeş to escape into the mountains. His wife, convinced they would not escape, flung herself from the turret. As an expression of gratitude, Ţepeş gave the Arefians their pasture lands. A document signed by Mircea Ciobanul (r 1545–52) in 1540 attests to the people of Arefu being granted 16 mountains and 14 sheepfolds by Ţepeş.

Just 1km north of the fortress lies the artificial **Lake Vidraru**, which was dammed between 1961 and 1966 to feed the hydroelectric power plant. From here the towering **Transfăgărăşan road**, a mountain pass that peaks at 2034m, crosses the Carpathians into Transylvania. The tunnel cutting between the Negoiu and Moldoveanu peaks is 845m long. The pass, allegedly built by the army as a training exercise, is only open for about three months of the year during summer. A sign at the side of the road south of Poienari Citadel shows whether the pass is open or shut.

Surrounding villages are teeming with *pensiunes* (B&Bs) and homes displaying *cazare* (accommodation) signs. Villagers in Arefu open their homes to travellers. Ask at the *biblioteca* (library) for *agroturism* members, or knock on the following doors.

In Căpăţânenii village, 1km south of Poienari, is **Pensiunea Dracula** (☎ 0740-757 400; r with/without bathroom €23/17) . Breakfast is not included.

The **Tomescu family** (☎ 730 102, 0743-678 365; per person €25) at house 229 has three clean rooms and, without a word of spoken English, manages to host Romanian feasts and *ţuică*-fuelled sing-alongs around the campfire. Rooms are also available at houses 53a, 330, 348 and 384. It is a 10-minute hike up the hill from the library – take the first right, then start asking people.

Cabana Cumpăna (☎ 0745-910 023; d/tr €31/34) is situated on the western side of Lake Vidraru. Bookings can also be made through Hotel Posada (opposite) in Curtea de Argeş.

The chalet-style hotel **Valea Cu Peşti** (☎ 0742-020 129; d €40) lies on the eastern side of Lake Vidraru.

Public transport to Arefu is limited to twice daily state buses and whimsical maxitaxis from Curtea de Argeş. To reach Poienari, alight in Căpăţânenii village – the citadel is a 1km hike north.

NĂMĂIEŞTI

Some 11km north of Câmpulung Muscel (itself 50km north of Piteşti) is one of Romania's most unusual sights: a monastery built into a mountain cave, above the Târg River Valley. Legend has it that **Nămăieşti Monastery** (Nămăieşti Mănăstire), dating from 1547, was founded by a shepherd who dreamt of a great church inside the rock face. It is claimed that a 16th-century icon here shows the only 'real' face of the Virgin Mary and it apparently works miracles. Nămăieşti is open to visitors but only accessible by private transport.

WEST TO TÂRGU JIU

☎ 250

The main road leads west from Curtea de Argeş to the industrialised town of **Râmnicu Vâlcea**. At the northern edge of town, on the road to Sibiu, is the **Valcea Village Museum** (Muzeul Satului Valcean; ☎ 746 869; admission/photo/video €0.90/1/2.20; ⏱ 10am-6pm Tue-Sun), a sprawling open-air museum with 80 examples of classic country structures and settings typical of the Valcea region, featuring sheds, houses, stores, churches, an old well, cemetery and Orthodox shrines.

For accommodation, **Antrec** (☎ 749 706) has an office here and **Hotel Alutus** (☎ 736 601; Str General Praporgescu 10; s/d €43/47) is in the town centre.

From Râmnicu Vâlcea head north up the Olt Valley to **Călimăneşti-Căciulata**, a twin spa resort with 1200m-deep hot and cold mineral springs. It was awarded a gold medal for its mineral waters at Vienna in 1873 and was a favourite haunt of Napoleon III who had waters brought from here to treat his kidney stones. The old Roman town comes to life during the first week of August, when it hosts a large **folk music and crafts festival**. Accommodation can be arranged through **Călimăneşti-Căciulata SR** (☎ 750 270; Calea lui Traian 413).

Just 2km north is **Cozia Monastery**, built by Mircea cel Bătran in the late 14th century, which today shelters the Wallachian prince's tomb. The original fountain dates from 1517, to which another was added by Constantin Brâncoveanu in 1711. The church frescoes are in excellent shape. There is also a small **museum**.

Two kilometres north of Cozia is the turnoff for **Turnul Monastery**, which was quietly established around 1467, when two priests from Cozia hand-burrowed caves into solid stone. The first church wasn't erected until 1676, and it later burned down. The diminutive 18th-century church has few frescoes, but the adjacent two-level *biserică* (1900), built by Polish architect Anton Lapinski, has crisp frescoes completed in 1998.

There are two hiking trails leading from the monastery, one marked by red and white stripes (3½ hours) and the other by triangles (5½ hours) leading to cabanas and Stănisoara Monastery. These hikes are difficult in winter. Ask around the monastery for current conditions.

Turnul offers sex-segregated rooms free-of-charge for one or two nights, though church attendance is required.

Bistriţa & Arnota Monasteries

Bistriţa Monastery (Mănăstirea Bistriţa) is 8km north of Costeşti. The current Brâncoveanu-style building (1856) was built on the site of a former 15th-century monastery. The first book printed in Wallachia (1508) is preserved here. Until 1982 the monastery sheltered one of the country's largest schools for children with special needs, now housed in a separate building at the entrance to the estate. Some 800m from the main monastery building is the **Peştera Sfântul Gheorghe**, a hillside chapel hidden in the 'St George' cave in the hill face and previously used to keep the monastery's treasures safe.

From Bistriţa, a forest road leads 4km north to the smaller **Arnota Monastery** (Mănăstirea Arnota). Ancient crosses are carved in the sheer rock face lining the southern end of this road. Wallachian prince Matei Basarab, who started building the monastery in 1636 (it was completed in 1706), is buried here.

Horezu Monastery

Seven kilometres further west along the road to Târgu Jiu is splendid **Horezu** (1694) in its idyllic mountain setting. It is one of Romania's veritable treasures and a Unesco World Heritage site. A long, increasingly picturesque road leads up to the fortress. Built in a swift four years during the reign of Constantin Brâncoveanu, it is considered one of Romania's finest examples of the unique synthesis of Western and Oriental architectural styles for which he became famed. The church has an unusually large *pronaos* (temple entrances) and open porch supported by ornate stone-carved columns. The church's interior frescoes are underscored by the massive altar, carved in tea tree wood. The old rectory contains frescoes from 1705 and is only open for holy occasions (and impromptu tours if the sisters are feeling generous). Request a visit to the Princely Chapel – it's a treasure trove of religious artefacts.

During the 17th and 18th centuries Horezu housed the country's most prestigious fresco-painting school.

Nearby **Horezu village** is a centre for brown pottery. Tiny shops line the roadside.

The **Horezu Monastery** (☎ 860 071; r €23) complex boasts 20 modern, clean rooms (summer only) in possibly Romania's loveliest setting. However there's no food available. Calling ahead is requested. The monastery is signposted 3km east of Horezu village.

Antrec arranges rooms in private homes for €10 to €15 a night; in Horezu village contact the **Drăgiţu family** (☎ 860 183) or the **Figura family** (☎ 860 113).

Polovragi & the Women's Cave

From Horezu a dirt road heads 30km west to the 18th-century **Polovragi Monastery** (Mănăstirea Polovragi), founded by Radu the Handsome (r 1474–75) in 1470. Every year in June the monastery hosts a **folk craft fair**.

The **Women's Cave** (Peştera Muierilor; adult/child €1/ 0.50; ⏰ 9am-7pm May-Sep), at the gateway to the Galbenul Gorges, 3km from Baia de Fier, contains the bones of women who used to retreat into the cave for safety during invasions in the Middle Ages. Guided tours (in Romanian) of the four-million-year-old cave are given every hour. Wear a jumper, as it's 10°C year-round.

TÂRGU JIU

☎ 253 / pop 100,360

Târgu Jiu is home to the internationally famed modernist sculptures of Constantin Brâncuşi (1876–1957).

Frequent strikes in the Jiu Valley mining region from the 1980s onwards paralysed industrial activity, forcing the communists to give in to the miners' militant demands. The miners' mass descent upon Bucharest in 1990 ended in bloodshed and their 1991 rampage led to the fall of Petre Roman's first post-Revolution government.

In early 1999, 10,000 striking miners smashed their way through police barricades as they marched towards Bucharest, protesting layoffs and low wages. After a 17-day strike, a deal was struck for pay rises and the pits were reopened. The government then reneged on the deal, sparking more violent protests and riots.

Protest leader Miron Cozma was sentenced to 18 years in prison over the 1991 protests. This harsh sentence was intended to show the International Monetary Fund (IMF) that the government was determined to forge ahead with plans to close hundreds of coal mines and loss-making factories, and pay off Romania's staggering US$3 billion foreign debt.

During WWII Târgu Jiu prison was home to communist party leader Gheorghe Gheorghiu-Dej, Nicolae Ceauşescu (the then secretary-general of the Union of the Communist Youth) and Ion Iliescu, who replaced Ceauşescu as president in 1990.

Should you unfathomably find yourself in the area on the third Sunday in February, bundle up for the **Enchanted Water Springs Music Festival** (weather permitting), featuring Gorj county's folk ensembles and miners' brass bands. Contact Gorj Tourism for more information.

Orientation

Târgu Jiu centre, east of the Jiu River, is a 15-minute walk from the bus and train stations. As you leave the station, turn right along Str Nicolae Titulescu, which becomes B-dul Republicii, until you reach Str Unirii, the main thoroughfare. Head 500m west along Str Unirii then turn right onto Calea Victoriei. The main hotels, shops and restaurants are dotted along the pedestrianised area.

Information

There's a currency exchange service inside the Gorj Tourism office.

Central post office (Str Vasile Alecsandri; ⏰ 7am-7pm Mon-Fri) Near Str Traian.

Central telephone office (Str Traian 1; ⏰ 7.30am-9pm Mon-Fri) Near the central post office.

Gorj Tourism (☎ 224 320; ⏰ 8am-6pm Mon-Fri, to 1pm Sat) Opposite the train station; sells regional maps (€3).

Raiffeisen Bank (⏰ 8am-5.30pm Mon-Fri) In the centre on Calea Victoriei.

Sights

Târgu Jiu's Brâncuşi tour starts in **Central Park** (Brâncuşi Park; ⏰ 6am-10pm May-Dec, 7am-8pm Jan-Apr), at the western end of Calea Eroilor, with three of the four sculptures (1937–38) that Brâncuşi created in memory of those who died during WWI. The entrance to the park is marked by his **Gate of the Kiss** (Poarta Sărutului), an archway reminiscent of Bucharest's Triumphal Arch constructed the year before. It is also in commemoration of the reunification of Romania. The stone archway bears folk art motifs from Brâncuşi's native Oltenia. Flip a coin on top of the archway for good luck!

Continue along the park's central mall to the **Alley of Chairs** (Aleea Scaunelor). The dwarf-sized stone stools are grouped in trios either side of the avenue.

The alley leads to the third sculpture, the riverside **Table of Silence** (Masa Tăcerii). Each of the 12 stools around the large, round, stone table represents a month of the year.

The small **Art Museum** (Muzeul de Artă; ☎ 214 156; Str Stadion; admission €0.60; ☼ 10am-5pm Tue-Sun) has a photographic exhibition on the life and works of Brâncuşi.

Brâncuşi's most famed sculpture, the **Endless Column** (Coloana Fără Sfârşit), endowed to the town in 1937, sits at the eastern end of Calea Eroilor. The 29.35m-tall structure, threaded with 15 steel beads, is considered as much a triumph of engineering as of modern art. According to the New York–based World Monuments Fund it ranks as one of the planet's top 100 works. Standing right underneath it is where his synthesis of heaven and physicality meet, with the column seemingly rising ad infinitum. The column was restored in 2000 at a cost of €4 million.

In front of the Elvira Godeanu Drama Theatre stands a **statue of Brâncuşi**, armed with his sculpting chisel.

The **Gorj County Museum** (Muzeul Judeţean Gorj; ☎ 212 044; Str Geneva 8; admission €0.60; ☼ 10am-5pm Tue-Sun) gained its name in 1996 after the city of Geneva presented Târgu Jiu with the **trio of clocks** that stand in front of the **statue of Tudor Vladimirescu**.

Sleeping

Gorj Tourism books rooms (about €10) in private homes.

Hotel Sport (☎ 214 402; s/d €16/21) Your back will not thank you for a night here. It's difficult to find, behind the stadium. Still, it's the cheapest place for 100km in any direction.

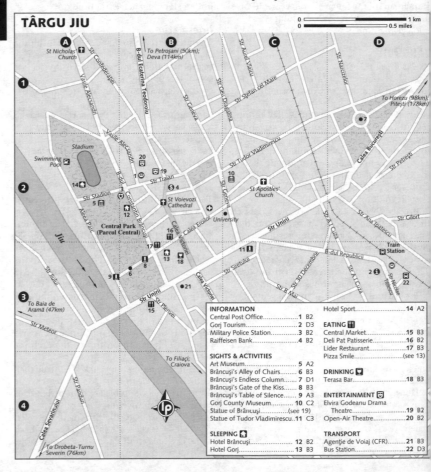

TÂRGU JIU

0 ———— 1 km
0 ———— 0.5 miles

INFORMATION	
Central Post Office	1 B2
Gorj Tourism	2 D3
Military Police Station	3 B2
Raiffeisen Bank	4 B2

SIGHTS & ACTIVITIES	
Art Museum	5 A2
Brâncuşi's Alley of Chairs	6 B3
Brâncuşi's Endless Column	7 D1
Brâncuşi's Gate of the Kiss	8 B3
Brâncuşi's Table of Silence	9 A3
Gorj County Museum	10 C2
Statue of Brâncuşi	(see 19)
Statue of Tudor Vladimirescu	11 C3

SLEEPING 🏨	
Hotel Brâncuşi	12 B2
Hotel Gorj	13 B3
Hotel Sport	14 A2

EATING 🍴	
Central Market	15 B3
Deli Pat Patisserie	16 B2
Lider Restaurant	17 B3
Pizza Smile	(see 13)

DRINKING 🍷	
Terasa Bar	18 B3

ENTERTAINMENT 🎭	
Elvira Godeanu Drama Theatre	19 B2
Open-Air Theatre	20 B2

TRANSPORT	
Agenţie de Voiaj (CFR)	21 B3
Bus Station	22 D3

Call ahead as it is often booked by groups. Breakfast not included.

Hotel Gorj (☎ 214 814; turism_ojt_gorj@yahoo.com; Calea Eroilor 6; s/d €30/37; 🖳) Skip the unrenovated rooms and the conditions here are acceptable. Internet (and wi-fi) available in some rooms.

Hotel Brâncuși (☎ 215 981; B-dul Constantin Brâncuși 10; s/d €37/40; 🖳) After a renovation this place now sparkles with Romanian grandeur. In-room internet is extra.

Eating & Drinking

Choice is limited in Târgu Jiu and often hotels are the best bet for a hearty meal. Hotel Brâncuși has the cleanest and nicest dining.

Pizza Smile (mains €2; 🕑 8am-midnight) This tiny place adjoining Hotel Gorj serves 18 kinds of fast-food-calibre pizza, best enjoyed on the terrace.

Lider Restaurant (☎ 219 002; Calea Eroilor 11; mains €4; 🕑 11am-midnight) This place serves hit-or-miss Romanian food. The Enigma bar downstairs is packed at weekends.

Deli Pat Patisserie (Calea Eroilor) Next door to Lider, this place is handy for a quick cup of coffee and a creamy cake.

Terasa Bar (Calea Victoriei) Behind Hotel Gorj, this bar offers an exquisitely placed terrace overlooking Calea Victoriei.

Stock up on fresh fruit and vegetables at the **central market** (Str Unirii), at the southern end of Central Park.

Entertainment

Open air concerts and theatrical performances are held in summer at the **open-air theatre** (Str Vasile Alecsandri 53). Close by is the **Elvira Godeanu Drama Theatre** (Teatrul Dramatic Elvira Godeanu; ☎ 216 494; cnr Str Stadion & Str Confederației).

Getting There & Away

BUS

The **bus station** (☎ 243 339; Str Nicolae Titilescu 5) is 100m south of the train station. A major service runs from here to Bucharest (257km, one daily), via Pitești (174km) and to Petroșani (57km).

Maxitaxi services run from the bus station to Timișoara (€10, four daily), Cluj-Napoca (€7, one daily), Alba Iulia (€5, one daily), Baia Mare (two daily), Drobeta-Turnu Severin (two daily) and Orșova (two daily).

TRAIN

The **Agenție de Voiaj CFR** (☎ 211 924; Str Unirii 2; 🕑 7am-7pm Mon-Fri) sells advance tickets.

From Târgu Jiu there are fast trains to Craiova (€3, three hours, four daily), Bucharest (€8, five hours, four daily) and Timișoara (€8, four daily). Northbound to Petroșani (1¼ to 1¾ hours), there are three local trains and one *accelerat* daily.

DROBETA-TURNU SEVERIN

☎ 252 / pop 106,599

Drobeta-Turnu Severin is on the bank of the Danube (Dunărea) River bordering Serbia. Though of ancient origin, the present town was laid out in the 19th century when its port was built. It's best known for the Iron Gates Museum's incredible scale model of the old Roman bridge that spanned the Danube to Serbia.

Orientation

From the train station, walk up to B-dul Republicii (B-dul Carol I). Follow this road to the east for 600m or so to Hotel Continental Parc, at the intersection of Str Bibiescu. The town centre lies one block north of here. The bus station is at the eastern end of Str Brâncoveanu.

Information

Banca Comercială Română (cnr Str Coștescu & Str Aurelian; 🕑 8.30am-5.30pm Mon-Fri, to 12.30pm Sat) Does everything but iron your jeans.

Post office (Str Decebal 41; 🕑 7am-8pm Mon-Fri, 8am-1pm Sat)

Telephone office (🕑 8am-8pm Mon-Fri, to 2pm Sat) Adjacent to the post office.

Sights

The **Iron Gates Museum** (Muzeul Porților de Fier; ☎ 325 922; B-dul Republicii; adult/student €1.70/0.90; 🕑 9am-4pm Tue-Sun) is housed in the former Trajan school for girls, dating from 1922. The museum was opened the day before the 1972 unveiling of the mammoth Porțile de Fier hydroelectric power station, 10km to the west. It contains a fine exhibition on the natural history of the Danube.

Other sections of the museum cover history, ethnography, astrology, popular art, the evolution of humans, and archaeology. Particularly impressive is the scale model of the Roman bridge constructed across the Danube in AD 103 by the Syrian architect Apollodor of Damascus, on the orders of the Roman emperor Trajan. The **Trajan Bridge** stood just below the site of the present museum, and

WALLACHIA

the ruins (ruinele podului lui Traian) of two of its pillars can still be seen towering beside the Danube. Northeast of the bridge ruins lie the remnants of **Castrul Drobeta**, a 2nd- to 6th-century Roman fort built to protect the bridge.

West of the castle ruins, also in the museum grounds, are the ruins of the 16th-century medieval **Severin Church** (Biserica Mitropoliei Severinului), including the remains of the crypt, which lie protected beneath glass.

In the basement of the Iron Gates Museum is a dingy **aquarium** displaying various fish species prevalent in the Danube, including the giant Somnul fish.

At the southern end of the town's main square, check out the huge metal **fountain**. It has 'arms' that spray water as they rotate, drawing crowds each night. The **old water castle**, standing a few blocks north of the square, looks deceptively medieval, but only dates from the early 20th century.

Eleven kilometres north of Drobeta is **Topolniţa Cave** (Peştera Topolniţa), which ranks among the largest caves in the world.

Sleeping & Eating

There are a number of faceless, overpriced three-star hotels in town.

Hotel Hip (☎ 312516; s/d €7.50/15) There's surprisingly clean bedding here, but the infinitesimal, smoke-infused rooms will challenge all but the hardiest of travellers. It's on the west side of the main square, above Café Ada-Kaleh.

Tropical Hotel (☎ 333 023; tropical_hotel@yahoo.com; I L Caragiale 39; s/d €27/29; 🖳) This hotel's poor location (2km northwest of the city centre) is compensated by comfortable rooms, a respectable on-site international restaurant and free wi-fi. Follow the signs from B-dul Vladiminescu (E70), heading towards Timişoara.

Hotel Continental Parc (☎ 306 730; drobeta@continentalhotels.ro; B-dul Carol I 2; s/d 2-stars €30/39, 3-stars €41/56; 🖳) The two-star rooms here are in commendable condition, particularly the bathrooms, while the three-star rooms are exceptional. Request a room facing the river. The restaurant offers a cheap menu with a shady terrace overlooking the park and river. There's an outside bar and café, which is packed in summer. In-room internet extra.

Aurora (Str Bibiescu) This is a café-bar with a covered pavement terrace; there's a small delicatessen adjacent. The opening times vary according to how the owners feel on the day!

Hala Radu-Negru indoor market (Str Coştescu) For fresh fruit and vegetables, head to this market near Str Unirii.

Getting There & Away

BUS

From Drobeta-Turnu Severin there is a service to Porţile de Fier (25 minutes, daily at 1.30pm).

Maxitaxis depart from the bus station. Services to and from Craiova and Băile Herculane stop at Drobeta-Turnu Severin (daily at 3.45pm except Sunday).

A private bus (€12, pay the driver) departs daily from outside the Drobeta-Turnu Severin train station to Negotin and Pojarevai in Serbia. Theoretically the bus is scheduled to leave at midnight. In reality it leaves when full. Return buses from Negotin and Pojarevai also depart for Drobeta-Turnu Severin when they are full.

TRAIN

Book tickets at the **Agenţie de Voiaj CFR** (☎ 313 117; Str Decebal 43; 🕑 7am-7.30pm Mon-Fri).

Most fast trains between Bucharest and Timişoara stop here. Services include those to Bucharest (€13, five hours, 10 daily), Craiova (€5, 1½ to 2½ hours, 10 daily), Timişoara (€9, 3½ hours, nine daily), Băile Herculane (€3, one hour, nine daily) and Orşova (25 minutes, four daily). In summer there are trains to Constanţa (€20, six hours, two daily).

PORŢILE DE FIER

The infamous **Porţile de Fier** (Iron Gates) at Gura Văii tower above the Danube 10km west of Drobeta-Turnu Severin. This monstrous concrete hydroelectric power station was a Romanian–Yugoslavian joint venture, conceived in 1960 and completed 12 years later. On top of the dam wall runs the road linking Romania to Serbia.

An area of 115,000 hectares around the power station has been conserved as the **Iron Gates National Park** to protect the flora and fauna of the region. A similar venture, the **Djerdap National Park**, sits across the river in Serbia.

The Porţile de Fier at Gura Văii stand on the site of **Old Orşova** (Orşova Veche), one of 13 settlements to be swallowed up by the artificial lake, created to curb this treacherous stretch of the Danube.

Sleeping

Motel Continental (☎ 252-342 144; drobeta@continental hotels.ro; s/d/ste €41/56/83; 🖳 🚷 🥢) About 12km east of Drobeta-Turnu Severin on the E70 to Băile Herculane, Motel Continental is unexpectedly flashy and a convenient stopping point for motorists heading to/from Serbia. Amenities include outdoor swimming pool, tennis and wi-fi (extra charge).

Getting There & Away
BUS

There is a bus service to Porţile de Fier from Drobeta Turnu Severin (25 minutes, daily at 1.30pm). The daily maxitaxi to/from Băile Herculane and Drobeta-Turnu Severin stops in Orşova.

TRAIN

Fast trains to/from Drobeta-Turnu Severin stop at Orşova (four daily).

CRAIOVA

☎ 251 / pop 311,586

The university town of Craiova, founded on the site of the Dacian stronghold of Pelendava, prides itself on its strong academic tradition and the wealth of prominent characters who have passed through on their journey to stardom: Wallachian prince Mihai Viteazul was born here, the world-famous sculptor Constantin Brâncuşi carved his first sculptures from scrap wooden crates in the town, and the first cartridge fountain pen was invented by Craiovan-born Petrache Poenaru (1799–1875). Today, Craiova is better known as the source of Craiova beer!

Prior to the war in Yugoslavia, IAR93 subsonic jet fighter-bombers were manufactured in Craiova for the Romanian and Yugoslav airforces. Production ground to a halt in 1992, however, after the UN imposed trade sanctions against Yugoslavia. Workers at the plant blocked the Craiova–Piteşti highway with a military plane in mid-1997 in a desperate bid to get their jobs guaranteed.

Following the outbreak of the conflict in Kosovo in 1999, UN sanctions against Yugoslavia were widened. With the conflict's end and the change of Yugoslav government, trade sanctions were finally lifted in late 2000.

Orientation

The northern bus station (Autogară Nord), the arrival and departure point for buses to and from most other towns, is next to the train station, 1km northeast of the centre on B-dul Carol I (B-dul Republicii). Bus 1 runs from the train station to the centre and the northern bus station. There are no buses to the southern bus station (Autogară Sud); a taxi from the centre should cost no more than €3.

Information

Banca Comercială Română (cnr Calea Unirii & Str Alexandru Ioan Cuza; ☯ 8.30am-5.30pm Mon-Fri)
Central Post Office (cnr B-dul Stirbei Vodă & Calea Unirii; ☯ 7.30am-7pm Mon-Fri, 8am-1pm Sat)
Mapamond Agenţie de Turism (☎ 415 071/73; travel@mapamond.ro; Str Olteţ 2-4; ☯ 8am-8pm Mon-Fri, 9am-2pm Sat, to 7pm Oct-May) Friendly, English-speaking staff hand out maps. Also an agent for Antrec.
Telephone Office (Calea Unirii 69; ☯ 7.30am-7pm)
TTC currency exchange (Str Olteţ 1; ☯ 9am-8pm Mon-Sat)

Sights
ART MUSEUM

The town's treasure is the **Art Museum** (Muzeul de Artă; ☎ 412 342; Calea Unirii; admission €0.90; ☯ 9am-7pm Tue-Sun), with an incredible collection of Brâncuşi's finest works, including *The Kiss*, *The Thigh* and *Miss Pogany*. It is housed in the Dinu Mihail Palace, built between 1900 and 1907 by the wealthy Romanian nobleman Constantin Dinu Mihail, and home to former Polish president Ignacy Moscicki in 1939 and later to Ceauşescu. The room of mirrors is worth the trip to Craiova alone.

HISTORIC CENTRE

Overlooking Calea Unirii, in the central square, is a **statue of Mihai Viteazul** who was born in Craiova. To its eastern side is the **prefecture**, bearing a memorial plaque to Craiova's victims of the 1989 revolution.

The **Natural History Museum** (☎ 419 435; Str Popa Şapcă 4; admission €0.80; ☯ 10am-5pm Tue-Sun), closed for renovations at the time of writing, has a tiny display of natural oddities. In the park opposite is the red-brick **Holy Trinity Church** (Biserica Sfânta Treime). Behind the church is the city's **Opera & Operetta Theatre** (p112), a former school that was a revolutionary hideout during June 1848.

Craiova's old town lies west of Calea Unirii around Piaţa Veche (Old Square). An excellent **Ethnographic Museum** (Muzeul Olteniei Secţia de Etnografie; admission €0.90; ☯ 9am-5pm Tue-Sun), in a former governor's house dating from 1699,

CRAIOVA

SIGHTS & ACTIVITIES
Art Museum	6 B2
Ethnographic Museum	7 A3
History & Archaeology Museum	8 A2
Holy Trinity Church	9 A2
Natural History Museum	10 B2
Opera & Operetta Theatre	11 A2
Prefecture	12 B2
St Hramul's Church	13 A2
Statue of Mihai Viteazul	14 B2

SLEEPING
Hotel Jiul	15 B1
Hotel Parc	16 A1

EATING
Amandina Pizzeria	17 A2
El Greco	18 B2

DRINKING
New York Café	19 B3
Niva	20 B3
Terasa Universitii	21 C2

ENTERTAINMENT
Agenţia Teatrală	(see 22)
National Theatre	22 B1
Oltenia Philharmonic	23 B2
Opera & Operetta Theatre	24 A2

TRANSPORT
Agenţie de Voiaj CFR	25 B1
Tarom Airlines Office	26 B1

INFORMATION
Banca Comercială Română	1 B2
Central Post Office	2 B3
Mapamond Agenţie de Turism	3 B2
Telephone Office	4 B3
TTC Currency Exchange	5 B2

stands on Str Hala at the end of Str Dimitru. Displayed inside **St Hramul's Church** (1928) is the Madona Dudu icon said to perform miracles for those who pray in front of it. Opposite the church is the **History & Archaeology Museum** (Muzeul Olteniei Secţia de Istorie şi Archaeologie; Str Madona Dudu 14; adult/student €0.90/0.50), which was closed for renovations at the time of writing.

Sleeping

Mapamond arranges rooms for €10 to €15 a night in private homes in surrounding villages.

Hotel Jiul (☎ 414 166; www.jiul.ro; Calea Bucureşti 1-2; s/d 2-star €27/36, 3-star €45/60; ☒) This is larger than Hotel Parc and popular with business travellers.

Hotel Parc (☎ 417 257; Str Bibescu 16; s/d €41/54) Here you'll find pleasant rooms set in lavish, abundant gardens.

Eating

Craiova's culinary options are limited to what you might like to wash down with a beer – and not the first beer. Try these or retreat to your hotel restaurant for sustenance.

El Greco (☎ 411 123; Str Alexandru Ioan Cuza 9; mains €3-5; ☒ 9am-1am) Proper pizza, spaghetti dishes, salads and Greek specialities are served with creamy milkshakes.

Amandina Pizzeria (Str Popa Şapcă; mains €3; ☒ 7.30am-11pm) This is a straight pizza joint with pastries and a full bar.

Drinking

Terasa Universitatii (Str Alexandru Ioan Cuza) Opposite the university, this bar is packed night and day with students and is a noisy and fun hang-out.

New York Café (☎ 419 198; Calea Unirii) Sink back in one of the many comfortable black lounges here and enjoy your favourite drink.

Niva (Calea Unirii; ☒ 9am-2am) This is a chilled cellar bar with pool, a short menu and several corners for idle coffee-slurping and smoking.

Entertainment

Highly recommended are performances at the impressive **National Theatre** (Teatrul Naţional; Calea Bucureşti) and the **Opera & Operetta Theatre** (Teatrul de Operă şi Operată; Str Ion Marinescu 12). Tickets for both are sold at the **Agenţia Teatrală** (☎ 413 755;

10am-12.30pm & 4-6.30pm), adjoining the main National Theatre building.

Classical concerts are performed by the **Oltenia Philharmonic** (Filarmonica Oltenia; Calea Unirii). The **ticket office** (☎ 411 284; 10am-1pm & 4-7pm) is inside the main Philharmonic building.

Getting There & Away

AIR
Craiova Airport (☎ 411 112; E70, Craiova-Bucureşti)
Tarom Airlines office (☎ 411 049; Complex Unirea, Piaţa Unirii,)

BUS
The **northern bus station** (Autogară Nord; ☎ 411 187; Str Argeş 13), next to the train station, is where the main daily services depart. Maxitaxis leave from here to Bucharest (€7, every 30 minutes), Piteşti (€3, two daily) and Calafat (€3, two daily). State buses run scant services to Râmnicu Vâlcea and Târgu Jiu.

Oz Murat travel agency (☎ 414 434), outside the northern bus station, runs a bus to Istanbul via Bucharest, departing at 10.30am daily except Saturday (€90 return).

The **southern bus station** (Autogară Sud; ☎ 428 065; Str N Romanescu), 5km south of town, runs rural routes around Craiova.

TRAIN
Book tickets at the **Agenţie de Voiaj CFR** (☎ 411 634; Complex Unirea; 7am-7.30pm Mon-Fri).

All fast trains between Bucharest and Timişoara stop at Craiova's **train station** (B-dul Carol I/B-dul Republicii). Services include trains to Bucharest (€12, three hours, 12 daily), Timişoara (€13, five hours, seven daily), Calafat (2½ hours, five daily), Budapest (€35, two daily) and Belgrade (€30, one daily).

CALAFAT
☎ 251
The small town of Calafat, on the Danube opposite Vidin in Bulgaria, makes a convenient entry/exit point to/from Bulgaria. Car ferries cross the river and there are frequent local trains between here and Craiova, from where you can catch a fast train on to Bucharest or Timişoara.

For cashing cheques and money withdrawals, there's a **Banca Commercială Română** (Str 1 Decembrie 3).

If you have some spare time, visit the unlabelled, but hard to miss, **Art Museum** (Muzeul de Artă; Str 22 Decembrie) and the **monument** to the

1877–78 War of Independence against the Turks.

The ferry landing is situated in the centre of Calafat, about four blocks from the train station.

There are local trains to/from Craiova (2½ hours, five daily). If you're continuing on to Bucharest or elsewhere, buy a ticket for your final destination and, as soon as you reach Craiova, go into the train station and purchase a compulsory seat reservation for your onward express train.

The car ferry to Bulgaria crosses the Danube here (€20 plus an additional €3 per person, cash only, 30 minutes) at least six times daily, and up to once per hour depending on traffic. Cars can spend several hours waiting to cross but pedestrians can avoid the queues and walk on in both directions.

In March 2000, after almost a decade of negotiations, the Romanian and Bulgarian governments agreed on the construction of a new bridge here over the Danube River (although Romania wanted the bridge to be built further east). The €155 million bridge, funded by the Bulgarian government and the European Union, will connect Calafat with the Bulgarian city of Vidin and was reported to be at least two years from completion at the time of writing.

GIURGIU
☎ 246
A typical dusty border town, Giurgiu is the main route from Bucharest to Bulgaria. Ferry services across the river have ceased in favour of the quick and easy bridge.

Giurgiu's train and bus stations are five minutes' walk from the centre. When you leave the station walk up Str Gării to the main street. Giurgiu's northern train station (Giurgiu Nord) is 5km out of town; local trains run between the two. Most trains heading for Bulgaria depart from the northern station.

The post office and central market are on Str Constantin Brâncoveanu. Turn right at the bridge crossing, then right onto Str Constantin Brâncoveanu. To get to the centre from here, turn left onto the main street.

Getting There & Away
If self-driving, take the main E70 highway from Bucharest to Giurgiu. This leads directly to the bridge crossing, signposted 'Punctul de frontieră Giurgiu'. To bypass the lengthy

queue of waiting lorries (semis), drive up the left side of the median to the administrative building in the centre of the road as you approach the customs control zone where toll tickets are sold. It's €6 per car and €2 per motorbike or bicycle. A compulsory €10 ecological tax is levied by the Bulgarian authorities. You are not permitted to cross at Giurgiu without transport.

Most Giurgiu–Ruse trains (4km, every 15 minutes) depart from the northern train station. The daily *Bosfor* train to Istanbul from Bucharest passes through the northern train station at 3.32pm, and leaves in the other direction on its way to Bucharest at 3.30pm. The daily *Bulgaria Expres* from Bucharest stops at Giurgiu at 9.33pm, and leaves on its way to Bucharest at 4.50am. The daily *Transbalkan* train from Bucharest stops at the northern train station at 1.35pm, and leaves for Bucharest at 5.56pm.

CĂLĂRAŞI, OSTROV & AROUND

Industrial Călăraşi offers yet another exit point. A ferry goes across the Danube to Ostrov (still in Romania) from where you can cross the border to Silistra in Bulgaria.

Travellers are allowed to cross here on foot. The border is 8km south of Călăraşi, and is served by a maxitaxi (€0.50).

The ferry takes cars (€6), motorbikes (€1.50) and foot passengers (€0.30); tickets are sold at the small green hut. The journey takes 30 minutes and the ferry generally operates between 6am and 7pm daily, but sometimes goes 24 hours, departing when full. In summer services can be disrupted if the level of the Danube is low. Restaurant Monica and a sorry looking camp site (open in summer only) are just west of the port. There is a maxitaxi service from the port to the centre of town. Negotiate with the driver for onward transport to the train/bus station.

Once in Ostrov you can continue east to the Black Sea coast, or cross the border into Silistra. As you come off the ferry a one-way street leads you directly to the customs control point. Continuing past the border control, the eastbound road to Dobrogea follows the Romanian–Bulgarian border for a further 200m.

Ostrov village proper is 5km east of the ferry terminal and border crossing. From here, the eastbound road follows the twists and turns of the magnificent Danube River, making it one of the most scenic drives in Romania. This majestic riverside stretch peaks at the **Derveni Monastery** (Mănăstirea Derveni), which overlooks Lake Bugeaculi, south of the Danube. The road continues east into northern Dobrogea.

Transylvania

Locals sometimes shake their heads over the 'Dracula connection', but there's no denying a sense of spookiness about this broad, mountainous, culturally rich region, which fills the bulk of Romania's centre. But really the Dracula thing (p23) is such a small part of a visit here, and you're likely to forget about it along the way. Saxon towns such as Sighişoara, Sibiu, Cluj-Napoca and Braşov evoke medieval life; all make fine hubs, with hikes, ski runs, horse markets and cute villages within an hour or two. Much of the fun comes from hikes through the interlocking Carpathians (sometimes called the Transylvanian Alps), which create a U-shape on all of Transylvania's sides but the north. Skiing is best in the Bucegi Mountains' Prahova Valley, but outdoors enthusiasts debate what's best for summer fun – hiking to underground rivers of the Apuseni, rock climbing at Piatra Craiului National Park, biking atop the flat Bucegi plateau, exploring the largely unknown Retezat or hiking the knee-torturing Făgăraş.

Transylvania, part of Romania only since 1918, benefits from its diverse ancestors. Saxons occupied southern Transylvanian towns, and most villages you pass are dotted with fortified churches that date back half a millennium. Going an hour north into Székely Land, where ethnic Hungarian communities are the majority, feels like going into a different country. Throughout you're likely to spot many Roma villagers – identifiable by black cowboy hats on the men and extravagant red dresses on the women – who sometimes usher passers-by in for meals.

So much is in Transylvania – it's no surprise that it's often the only part of Romania experienced by tourists.

TRANSYLVANIA

HIGHLIGHTS

- Saxon it up in the 'big three' towns of medieval glory: **Braşov** (p127), the real Dracula's birthplace at **Sighişoara** (p143) and **Sibiu** (p153)
- Enter the **Bucegi Mountains** (p122), where novices can bike or hike the flat plateau
- Wander Saxon Land's backroads by car or bike, stopping at **Saxon fortified churches** (p148) such as Viscri, where you can stay overnight in a traditional 'Saxon bed'
- Venture north into **Székely Land** (p163), where signs are in Hungarian and towns such as **Târgu Mureş** (p171) boast Habsburg's finest architecture
- Hang out with sheperds in *ag   i m* guesthouses such as **Sibiel** (p163) or the Hungarian **Huedin Microregion** (p196)

TRANSYLVANIA

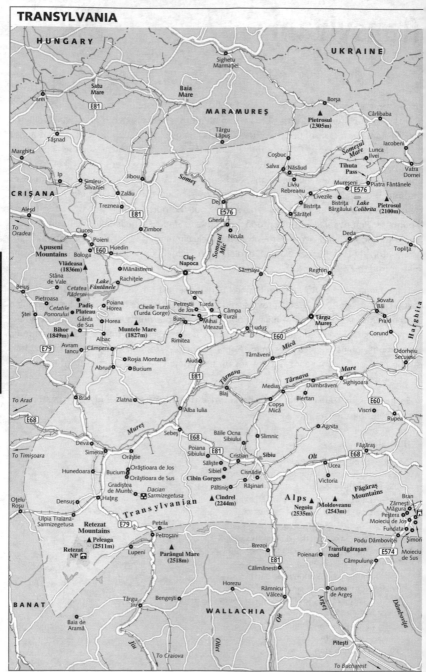

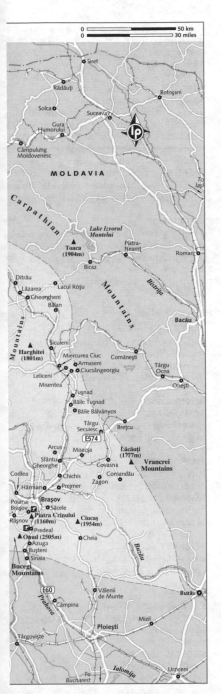

'We are in Transylvania; and Transylvania is not England. Our ways are not your ways, and there shall be to you many strange things.'

Dracula

HISTORY

For a thousand years, up till WWI, Transylvania was associated with Hungary. In the 10th century a Magyar (Hungarian) tribe, the Székelys, settled in what it called Erdély ('beyond the forest' – the literal meaning of Transylvania). In the 12th century Saxon merchants arrived to help defend the eastern frontiers of Hungary. The seven towns that they founded – Bistriţa (Bistritz), Braşov (Kronstadt), Cluj-Napoca (Klausenburg), Mediaş (Mediasch), Sebeş (Mühlbach), Sibiu (Hermannstadt) and Sighişoara (Schässburg) – gave Transylvania its German name, Siebenbürgen (both the origin and meaning of the term are disputed, but it roughly means 'seven boroughs').

Medieval Transylvania was an autonomous unit ruled by a prince responsible to the Hungarian crown. The indigenous Romanians were serfs. After the 1526 Turkish defeat of Hungary the region became semi-independent, recognising Turkish suzerainty.

In 1683 Turkish power was broken and Transylvania came under Habsburg rule four years later. The Catholic Habsburg governors sought to control the territory by favouring first the Protestant Hungarians and Saxons and then the Orthodox Romanians. In 1848, when the Hungarians launched a revolution against the Habsburgs, Romania sided with the Austrians. After 1867 Transylvania was fully absorbed into Hungary. In 1918 Romanians gathered at Alba Iulia to demand Transylvania's union with Romania.

This unification has never been fully accepted by Hungary and from 1940 to 1944 it set about re-annexing much of the region. After the war, Romanian communists moved to quash Hungarian nationalist sentiments. Currently, however, feelings of resentment have subsided somewhat and Romania's relations with its western neighbour continue to strengthen. Still, one feels an extant mistrust between the communities, and the Hungarians publish maps of the region with only Hungarian place names (even street names), as if they were not located in Romania, making things confusing for non-Hungarian tourists.

GOOD/BAD DRIVES

Dense Transylvania is plied by myriad maxi-taxi and train routes listed in this chapter. But if you're driving yourself, know that some routes are nicer than others. The main highway routes (eg Braşov–Sibiu, Braşov–Târgu Mureş, Sibiu–Cluj-Napoca, Cluj-Napoca–Bistriţa) are, unsurprisingly, rarely as nice as the, often rougher, roads off it – with the Cluj-Napoca–Bistriţa route edging out Cluj-Napoca–Sibiu for our vote for Transylvania's grimmest drive.

Some good ones, useful for pan-regional itineraries, include:

- Gheorgheni–Bicaz
- Gheorgheni–Târgu Mureş
- Sfântu Gheorghe–Miercurea Ciuc
- Sighişoara–Sibiu via Agnita
- Deva–Turda via Brad

PRAHOVA VALLEY

Wallachia turns into Transylvania in this narrow valley at the foot of the fir-clad Bucegi Mountains, as dramatic a scene as any in Romania. Everyone going from Bucharest to Braşov cuts through here; many stop. Sinaia, a king's summer retreat a century ago, is the finest town, but the real draw is up, way up, with hiking and biking trails along the flat plateau atop the mountains, and ski trails that carve down the mountain sides.

If you're looking for just a taste, it's possible to day-trip from Braşov (p127) to take a cable-car ride up and make a short hike. But it's easier if you stay a night or two.

SINAIA

☎ 244 / pop 14,640

Backed by the Bucegi, Prahova's shining star is Sinaia (see-*ni*-ya). Named for Mt Sinai and once home to Romania's first king, Sinaia boasts many century-old villas and hotels, built to impress the king's gaze. None outweighs the marvel of King Carol I's Peleş Castle, one of the region's highlights, along with the hiking, biking and skiing in the mountains above.

The setting's superb. Much of the town centre is a bit quiet (not exactly the 'Pearl of the Carpathians' it claims to be), but even

those without a car can hop in the cable car and head up to 2000m to access brilliant trails and ski runs of the impressive Bucegi Mountains (p122).

The resort earned its biblical moniker when a Romanian nobleman holidayed in Israel in 1695 and founded the Sinaia Monastery here. Sinaia eventually boomed as a major resort when King Carol I made his summer residence here in 1875. Until 1920, the Hungarian–Romanian border ran along Predeal Pass, just north.

For readers' convenience, this area has been included in Transylvania, even though Sinaia is administratively part of Wallachia.

Orientation

The train station is directly below and a couple of blocks north from the centre of town. From the station climb up the stairway across the street to busy B-dul Carol I, which leads left past hotels, banks, travel agencies and the cable car.

MAPS

For hiking maps see p122. The best map is SunCart's *Sinaia* (€2.50), which also includes Buşteni. You'll find posted city maps (with hiking routes) around town, including outside the tourist information centre.

Information
BOOKSHOPS
Flower Power (B-dul Carol I; ☼ 8am-6pm Mon-Fri) Carries area maps, man.

EMERGENCY
If you run into problems in the mountains or need to check weather conditions, contact **Salvamont** (☎ 313 131; Primărie, B-dul Carol I) which has an another branch at cota 2000 at the top of the chairlift.

INTERNET ACCESS
Internet Café (Str Aosta 3; per hr €0.90; ☼ 9am-11pm) Sign points to side of building.

LAUNDRY
Eco Laundry (☎ 0788-660 788; B-dul Carol I 31; per load €2.30; ☼ 7am-11pm) Drop-off laundry behind the big grey building.

MEDICAL SERVICES
SensiBlu Pharmacy (Hotel Sinaia, B-dul Carol I 8; ☼ 8am-10pm Mon-Fri, 9am-9pm Sat, 9am-2pm Sun)

MONEY

Banca Transilvania (B-dul Carol I 14; ⊙ 9am-5pm Mon-Fri, 9.30am-12.30pm Sat) Has ATM; foreign exchange service next door.

POST

Central post office (☎ 311 591; B-dul Carol I 33; ⊙ 7am-8pm Mon-Fri, 8am-noon Sat)

TOURIST INFORMATION

Tourism information centre (☎ 315 656; CIPT _sinaia@yahoo.com; B-dul Carol I 47; ⊙ 9am-4.30pm Mon-Fri, Sat 'optional') Snappy attendants soften with your persistence. Lots and lots of information and brochures and maps, but can't book rooms or arrange tours.

TRAVEL AGENCIES

Dracula's Land (☎ 311 441; B-dul Carol I 14; ⊙ 9am-5 or 6pm) It hides its tacky name from the street (the sign says 'Tourist Office'), but some chummy blokes inside can help find a villa or hotel room for you, arrange hiking guides or change money. Schedule depends on 'how we feel…very elastic'; Mondays, they're sometimes off fishin'. Several other agencies are around too.

Sights
PELEŞ CASTLE

Full of pomp and brimming with confidence of a new Romanian monarchy, the magnificent century-old **Peleş Castle** (☎ 310 205; compulsory tour adult/child €3.50/1.50; ⊙ 11am-5pm Wed, 9am-5pm Thu-Sun), a 20-minute walk up from the centre, is really a palace (see p138). Fairytale turrets rise above acres of green meadows and grand reception halls fashioned in Moorish, Florentine and French styles, while heavy wood-carved ceilings and gilded pieces overwhelm our wee mortal minds. Even if you're bent on chasing 'Dracula', it's hard not to get a thrill visiting this castle.

The first European castle to have central heating, electricity and vacuuming(!), Peleş was intended to be the summer residence of Romania's longest-serving monarch, King Carol I (the hand-to-hip statue of him outside looks a little sassy). Construction on the 3500 sq metre edifice, built in a predominantly German-Renaissance style, began in 1875. Some 39 years, more than 400 weary craftsmen and thousands of labourers later, it was completed, just months before the king died in 1914. King Carol I's wife Elisabeta was largely responsible for the interior decoration.

During Ceauşescu's era, the castle's 160 rooms were used as a private retreat for leading communists and statesmen from around the globe. US presidents Richard Nixon and Gerald Ford, Libyan leader Moamar Gaddafi and PLO leader Yasser Arafat were all entertained by the Romanian dictator here.

The 40-minute tour, which begins regularly, takes in about 10 rooms on the ground floor – bedrooms upstairs are off-limits. In the first Armoury Hall (there's two) look for one of the 11 medieval knight suits with the long pointed boots. Rembrandt reproductions line the walls of the king's office, while real Gustav Klimt works are in the last stop, a theatre/cinema behind the entry.

Guides will point out a secret door in the small library; all rooms have such a door apparently. Queen Elisabeta painted and wrote some 43 books in her life under a pseudonym; the paintings in the poetry room depict 'fairy-tale' scenes she wrote about in one book. In the Council Room, panels made from 14 kinds of wood bore witness to the signing of Romania's neutrality for the last two years of WWI.

Peleş Castle was off-limits to the public from 1947 to 1975, when it was reborn briefly as a museum. Extensive renovation was completed in 1990.

Tickets are sold either at the ticket counter at the nearby Pelişor Palace or under the arches in the centre of the building where a door is signposted 'foreign languages'. Guides speak English, French, Russian and German.

PELIŞOR PALACE

About 100m uphill from the castle, the German-medieval **Pelişor Palace** (☎ 310 918; compulsory tours adult/child €0.60/0.20; ⊙ 11am-5pm Wed, 9am-5pm Thu-Sun) has a hard time competing with its neighbour. King Carol I planned this house for his nephew (and future king) Ferdinand (1865–1927) and wife Marie (who didn't get on well with King C and loathed Peleş). Marie picked the design – pretty pastel decorations in simple Art Nouveau style. Most of the furniture was imported from Vienna. Marie used four apartments while Ferdinand had just one. Marie died in the arched golden room, the walls of which are entirely covered in gilded leaves.

At the western end of the Peleş estate is the Swiss-chalet-style **Foişorul Hunting Lodge**, built as a temporary residence by King Carol

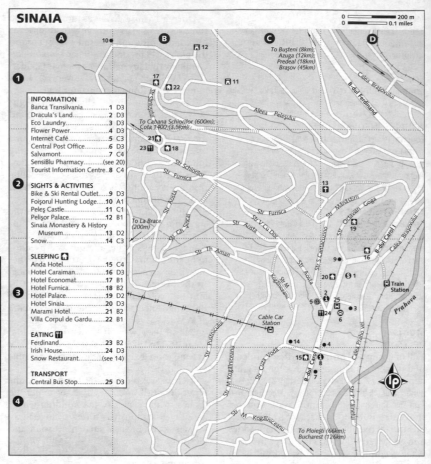

SINAIA

To Bușteni (8km),
Azuga (12km),
Predeal (18km),
Brașov (45km)

INFORMATION
Banca Transilvania..............**1** D3
Dracula's Land..................**2** D3
Eco Laundry....................**3** D3
Flower Power...................**4** D3
Internet Café...................**5** C3
Central Post Office.............**6** D3
Salvamont......................**7** C4
SensiBlu Pharmacy..........(see 20)
Tourist Information Centre....**8** C4

SIGHTS & ACTIVITIES
Bike & Ski Rental Outlet.....**9** D3
Foișorul Hunting Lodge.....**10** A1
Peleș Castle....................**11** C1
Pelișor Palace..................**12** B1
Sinaia Monastery & History
    Museum.....................**13** D2
Snow............................**14** C3

SLEEPING ⌂
Anda Hotel......................**15** C4
Hotel Caraiman.................**16** D3
Hotel Economat................**17** B1
Hotel Furnica...................**18** B2
Hotel Palace....................**19** D2
Hotel Sinaia....................**20** D3
Marami Hotel..................**21** B2
Villa Corpul de Gardu.........**22** B1

EATING 🍴
Ferdinand.......................**23** B2
Irish House......................**24** D3
Snow Restaurant............(see 14)

TRANSPORT
Central Bus Stop..............**25** D3

To Cabana Schiorilor (600m);
Cota 7400 (3.5km)

To La Brace
(200m)

Cable Car
Station

Train
Station

Prahova

To Ploiești (66km);
București (126km)

I before Peleş Castle was completed. Marie and Ferdinand's son, the future King Carol II, briefly lived here with his mistress Elena Lupescu. During the communist era, Ceauşescu used it as his private hunting lodge. The building is closed to visitors.

SINAIA MONASTERY

Half way between Peleş and the centre, the **Sinaia Monastery** (Str Mănăstirii; admission by donation; ☾ 8am-8 or 9pm), home to 20-some monks, is well worth a look. Inside the gate, the large Orthodox church ('biserica mare') before you dates from 1846; two icons inside were presented by Russia's Tsar Nicholas II in 1903.

Beside the church is a small **History Museum** (Muzeul de Istorie; admission €1.20; ☾ 8am-5pm summer)

in which some of the monastery's treasures are displayed, including the first translation of the Bible into Romanian (in the Cyrillic alphabet), dating from 1668.

Back towards the mountains, a passageway leads to a smaller church ('biserica veche') from 1695. Monks retreated into the Bucegi Mountains from the 14th century but it was not until the late 17th century that they built a monastery.

The **tomb of Tache Ionescu**, the head of a transitional government for a few months in 1921–22, is in the building next to the small church. Stricken with cholera as a child, Ionescu came here. Quotations from his speeches are carved in stone on the mausoleum's interior walls.

Activities

Skiing, hiking and biking are big deals in the Bucegi.

Skiers either drive, bus or cable-car to Cota 1400, a festive scene with sleds to hire, open-air grills to snack on, a ski-hire shop (about €9 per day for skis) and a chairlift (one/five rides €2.80/10). From here you can also take the second cable car to Cota 2000 to access some 40km of wild skiing around Mt Furnica (at Cota 2000); the 2.5km Carp trail, descending from Mt Furnica to Cota 1400 is the toughest. There are also several other trails of intermediate and beginners' levels. Located on top of the Bucegi plateau above the Sinaia resort is an 8km cross-country route, as well as a 13-bend bobsled track.

In summer these trails welcome hikers, and many can be biked.

A good source of equipment and information in town, **Snow** (☎ 311 198; www.snow-sinaia.ro; Str Cuza Voda 2a; ☯ 9am-6pm), near the cable-car station, hires skis (€10 per day) and bikes in summer. It offers ski instruction services. Check out the 1930s skis on the walls of the shop.

Another **rental outlet** (☎ 314 906; Str Octavia Goga 1; ☯ 8am-7pm) rents bikes for €2.30 per hour, €11.50 per day; skis are about €9 per day, snowboards €11.50.

Sleeping

Hotels tend to be overpriced. Travel agencies around town can find you a room in one of the countless villas (generally family vacation homes with a few available guesthouse-style rooms). Rates start at around €20 to €25 and it's really the only option for budget travellers in town.

If you want the sense of the outdoors, opt for up the hill, such as the area around La Brace restaurant (p122) or towards Peleş. The only real advantages of being near the centre are sugary treats, the cable car and the internet.

Cazare (private rooms) are cheaper, but apparently police are cracking down on independent entrepreneurs at the train station.

See p124 for some information regarding cabanas in the mountains.

CENTRE

Hotel Caraiman (☎ 313 551; palace@rdslink.ro; B-dul Carol I 4; s/d/apt €33/44/61) Of the faded-glory century-old hotels – and Sinaia teems with them – we like the 1881 red-and-white Caraiman most, for being less royal ball and more rustic and laid-back. Rooms are simple – beige carpets, tiled bathrooms with standing showers, half looking west towards the mountains over a small park.

Hotel Sinaia (☎ 302 900; www.hotelsinaia.ro; s/d from €41/50; ☐ ☡) With gum-chewing attendants and 1970s aura running rampant, the Sinaia nevertheless booms with energy – lobby internet and ping-pong, basement disco – but its staff and rooms' green carpets and wall-bolted TVs may be in need of a pep talk. Pool use is extra.

Hotel Palace (☎ 312 051; palace@rdslink.ro; Str Octavian Goga 4; 3-star s/d €42/62, 4-star s/d €58/79; ☒ ☐) There's a little bit of *The Shining* in this glorious 1911 building, with halls that stretch and stretch before you and a wide low-lit lobby lounge that is often empty. Go four-star if you stay, for more space and newer furnishings. All have new bathrooms.

Anda Hotel (☎ 306 020; www.hotelanda.ro; B-dul Carol I 30; s €63-74, d €80-91; ☒ ☐) Set up for business, and rather modern for the mountains, the Anda Hotel's higher-priced rooms are worth the extra cost for more light and balconies.

UP THE HILL

Hotel Furnica (☎ 311 151; Str Furnica 50; s €19, d €26-37) Built by the Peleş architects, the century-old, faux-Jacobean 26-room Furnica gives you a sense of royalty for cheap. Rooms are clean but dated (bedspreads are thoroughly floral), with varied layouts, some overlooking the interior courtyard with restaurant.

Hotel Economat (☎ 311 151; fax 311 150; Aleea Peleşului 2; s €23-33, d €46) Right outside the Peleş gate, this place has just slightly nicer rooms in a better setting. First-time visitors approaching Peleş sometimes mistake this for the castle! The gate below actually served as the royal stables. You can stay in a few 'Villa Turistica' choices there. The best is the two-star Villa Corpul de Gardu (☎ 311 151; s/d €26/37).

Marami Hotel (☎ 315 560; www.marami.ro; Str Furnica 52; s/d/ste €50/55/60; ☒ ☐) The chalet-style frame looks a little cheap, but inside the Marami's 17 rooms are probably Sinaia's best midrange options. The vibe is slightly Art Deco, with pink-sand bedspreads and rust-coloured carpets. The 'suite' isn't much larger; stick with the regular rooms and ask for the 4th floor facing the mountains. Peleş is a 300m leafy walk away.

TRANSYLVANIA

Eating

There are a few fast-food stands and pizza places along B-dul Carol I. The best restaurants are further up, such as Ferdinand and La Brace.

Irish House (☎ 310 060; www.irishhouse.ro; B-dul Carol I 80; mains €2-6; ☺ 10am-midnight) Guinness is on tap (€1.60), ceilings are green and the menu has a few token Irish dishes, but everything else in this two-room rustic spot is pretty much Romanian or Italian. Everyone looks little, as the tables are too high for the chairs. Irish House also has a guestroom upstairs.

Ferdinand (☎ 0722-526 110; Str Furnica 63; mains €2.50-4; ☺ 11am-midnight) On the way to/from Peleş, Ferdinand's rustic dining room is an ante-upped option; chicken in raspberry wine sauce is the house speciality.

Snow (☎ 311 198; Str Cuza Voda; mains €2.90-5.80; ☺ 8am-midnight) Near the cable car, Snow gets busiest with ski and bike rentals, but its outdoor/indoor Romanian restaurant is about as good as the centre gets. There are ham-and-cheese pancakes and a vegetarian platter (€4), plus several breakfasts (but skip the disappointing coffee).

La Brace (☎ 310 348; Str Coştilei 27; mains €3.20-9; ☺ 10am-midnight Sun-Fri, to 1am Sat) Amidst trees, and near where the cable car passes, this fun multifloor place gets busy for pizza mostly – and the oven-baked pies are well done. It's a 15-minute walk from the centre; follow the many signs.

Getting There & Away

Sinaia is on the Bucharest–Braşov rail line – 126km from the former and 45km from the latter – so jumping on a train to Bucharest (1½ hours) or Braşov (€3.60, one hour) is a cinch.

Buses and maxitaxis run every 45 minutes between roughly 7am and 10pm from the central bus stop on B-dul Carol I to Azuga and Buşteni (€0.50, 10 minutes), some all the way to Bucharest (€3.80, 1½ hours) or Braşov (€1.40, one hour). Rates are less than the train; pay the driver when you board. There's little room for luggage usually.

BUCEGI MOUNTAINS

The Bucegi Mountains may not be part of the world traveller's everyday lingo, but they're no secret to Romanians. And for trekking they're as good as it gets, with a well-marked network of trails (some that can be biked) and many cabanas open year-round to shelter hikers and cross-country skiers. An added bonus is the flat-top plateau, above the horseshoe-shaped range that stands between Bran and Snaia.

Two problems of note: for one, the weather. As one guide told us 'You're the only thing moving up there'. When winds come you know it; winter is severe, avalanches close wild skiing options during the thaw and summer thunderstorms are common. Wind can often cause lift closures.

The other problem is crowds. In summer cable-car rides up from Buşteni (p124) and Sinaia (below) can bottleneck, particularly from Buşteni, which sometimes sees two-hour lines to go up (there are extra cars in the afternoon to bring people back).

The best hiking map by far is the Hungarian Dimap's fold-out *Five Mountains from the Carpathian's Bend* (covering the Piatra Craiului, Bucegi, Postăvarul, Piatra Mare and Ciucaş ranges, plus a Braşov city map; €2.50), with English text.

Hiking & Biking

The two most common starting points are from the cable-car stations at Cota 2000 (from Sinaia) or from Cabana Babele (from Buşteni). If it's just a day trip, consider Buşteni (where the bulk of hikes are); if you want to spend a couple of days up there, many people start from Sinaia.

GETTING INTO BUCEGI

The easiest way into the Bucegi from Sinaia is up two cable-car rides: one from the centre to the Cota 1400 station, then another up to Cota 2000 station. In the centre, the 30-person **cable-car** (☎ 311 764, 311 872; to Cota 1400 adult/child one way €2.90/1.75, return €5.20/2.90, to Cota 2000 one way €5.45/2.90, return €10.20/5.10; ☺ 8.30am-4 or 5pm Tue-Sun) leaves half-hourly with two station points marked by elevation. Lines are more likely to be open in winter than summer.

Buses outside Snow, just below the station, also go up to Cota 1400 (€1.50) when full; a taxi there is about €5.75.

See above for information.

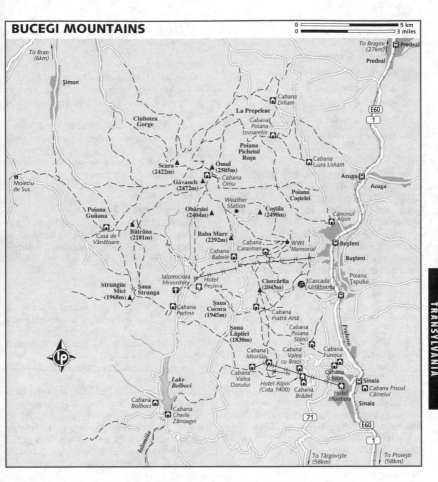

BUCEGI MOUNTAINS

From Bușteni take the cable car up to **Cabana Babele** (2206m). From Babele a trail leads to the giant WWI memorial cross at 2284m (one hour, marked with red crosses). From here a path (red crosses) leads to the top of Caraiman Peak (2384m). On the peak the path becomes wider, turning into a trail that continues towards Omu Peak across Bucegi Plateau. It gets close to the Coștila Peak (2490m) on top of which is a rocket-like TV transmitter (out of bounds to the public); nearby is a weather station that has accommodation.

Alternatively a trail (three to four hours, blue crosses) leads from **Cabana Caraiman** (2025m), where you can pick up the trail to the WWI cross (30 to 45 minutes, red circles).

Cabana Babele is the best starting point for **biking** around the Bucegi – you can take your bike on the cable car, but have to buy an extra ticket for the space.

From Cabana Babele you can hike south following a yellow-stripe trail to **Cabana Piatra Arsă** (1950m). From here you can pick up a blue trail that descends to Sinaia via **Poiana Stânii** (three hours). An even more interesting destination is the **Ialomiciora Monastery**, accessible by trail (1½ hours, blue crosses) or via a second cable car from Babele, where you'll find a small hermitage built partially inside the Ialomița cave. Visitors are welcome to spend the night there; there is also the Hotel Peștera nearby.

A more ambitious expedition involves taking the cable car from Bușteni to either of the

> **HIKING TIMES**
>
> ■ **Babele to Bran** nine hours
> ■ **Babele to Cota 2000** seven hours
> ■ **Babele to Omu** two or three hours
> ■ **Cota 2000 to Omu** four or five hours
> ■ **Cota 2000 to Bran** 14 to 16 hours
> ■ **Omu to Bran** eight hours

two cable-car stations and hiking northwest across the mountains to **Bran Castle** (p139). You can do this in one strenuous day if you get an early start from Babele, but it's preferable to take two days and free camp or spend a night at **Cabana Omu**. From the TV transmitter, there is a trail (two hours, yellow-marked) leading to Cabana Omu on the summit (Bucegi's highest point, at 2505m). North of Babele the scenery becomes dramatic, with dizzying drops into valleys on either side.

From Omu to Bran Castle is tough but spectacular – a 2000m drop through the tree line into thick forest, then onto a logging road leading to the castle (five hours, yellow triangles). Don't even think of climbing up from Bran to Omu.

A particularly nice route from Sinaia (seven to 10 hours, yellow and blue stripes) starts at either Cota 1400 or Cota 2000 at **Cabana Miorița**, to the **Cabana Piatra Arsă**, down to the Ialomiciora Monastery and then up to the Omul peak (where there's also a cabana).

Sleeping

No one hires out camping equipment, but last-second campers should be able to find cheap 'Chinese tents' (about €15) and sleeping bags (from €30) in Sinaia and Buşteni. Cabanas provide blankets. It's sometimes hard to reserve a spot in cabanas, but they'll always make space.

FROM BUŞTENI

Cabana Babele (☎ 315 304; dm/d €6/23; ☯ year-round) Perched high at 2206m, this simple hikers' refuge dates from 1937. Private doubles have private bathroom; there's a restaurant on the premises.

Cabana Omu (☎ 0744-567 290) This is a simple electricity-free refuge with beds. The nearby weather station has heat and electricity.

Another one open from May to September is Cabana Caraiman (2025m).

FROM SINAIA

Cabana Schiori (☎ 313 655; Str Drumul Cotei 7; r from €25) Walkable from Sinaia's centre, this is pretty fancy for a cabana, with a swank restaurant on site too.

Cabana Valea cu Brazi (☎ 313 605; bed €6) This is a so-so cabana at 1510m, a 10-minute walk up from Cota 1400.

Near the Cota 1400 cable-car station, Cabana Brădet was closed at research time but may reopen.

Getting There & Away

Aside from the cable cars from Buşteni and Sinaia, rough roads wind up from the south of the mountains all the way to Cabana Babele – these are for 4WD vehicles only.

BUŞTENI
☎ 244 / pop 11,790

Framed by absolutely towering peaks – the Caraiman (2384m) and Coştila (2490m) to the west are Europe's highest conglomerate cliffs – Buşteni is a bewildering mix of communist dreariness and Bucegi's greatest beauty. Still, it's a good starting point to reach Bucegi's wondrous scenes.

Most visitors keen on hitting the mountains by day, and bars or restaurants by night, will enjoy Sinaia (5km south) more, which also has a cable car accessing Bucegi's trails. Unlike Sinaia, where truck and commercial traffic is forced to go around the centre, Buşteni's central B-dul Libertăţii is rife with traffic and exhaust fumes.

Orientation

The train station backs onto the main street, B-dul Libertăţii. The cable car, Hotel Silva, post office and commercial complex are at the southern end of town (turn left from the train station, walk 200m past Hotel Caraiman, then right for 300m on Str Telecabinei).

There's a large-scale town map on B-dul Libertăţii in front of the post office. The best available map is Suncart's *Buşteni* (€2.50), which includes Sinaia and Bucegi Mountains.

Information

In case of emergency on the mountain, call **Salvamont** (☎ 320 048; Primărie, B-dul Libertăţii 91). Email emergencies are solved at **ILCOFON**

Internet (☎ 321 780; cnr B-dul Libertăţii & Str Fantanii; per hr €0.60; ☼ 9am-10.30pm), next to a small park, just across and south from the train station.

There are a few banks, 100m south of the train station on B-dul Libertăţii, including **BRD** (☼ 9am-5pm Mon-Fri, 9am-1pm Sat).

The **post office** (B-dul Libertăţii 93; ☼ 7am-9pm Mon-Fri, 8am-2pm Sat) is 50m south of the train station.

Travel information is hard to come by; check at Casa Achim (see Sleeping, below).

Sights

Between the wars, Buşteni was home to Romanian novelist Cezar Petrescu (1892–1961), whose realist works attempted to reflect a 'psychology of failure' in modern Romanian life. His house is now a **memorial museum** (Str Tudor Vladimirescu 2), which was closed at research time but likely to reopen. Turn right (north) out of the train station; Str Tudor Vladimirescu is the fourth street on the left (about 500m).

Activities

To get to Bucegi Mountains' hiking, ski and mountain-bike trails, take the 25-person **cable car** (☎ 320 306; adult/child return €5.40/2.60; ☼ 8am-3.45pm Jul–mid-Sep, Tue-Sun mid-Sep–Jun), a trip in which is a major experience in and of itself. In summer it can be busy, sometimes with three-hour waits or more. Arrive early (some even queue by 6am).

From Buşteni, it's also possible to **hike** 8km south to Sinaia or 10km north to Predeal.

Hotel Silva hires skis and bikes. In summer bike-hire stands are set up on B-dul Libertăţii as well.

Buşteni's small ski run **Calinderu** is over a kilometre west of the train station (go south 100m, turn left after the stream at Str Valea Alba for 1km). A nine-ride lift ticket is €12, while ski hire costs €6 Monday to Friday, €12 Saturday and Sunday.

Sleeping

Those wanting to get something out of their nights tend to prefer staying in Sinaia. See opposite for cabanas accessible from the cable-car above Buşteni. In town, you'll find dozens of rooms to rent up Str Caraiman and south along Str Unirii.

Casa Achim (☎ 321 693; Str Caraiman 7; r €17) This is a so-so guesthouse between B-dul Libertăţii and the cable-car lift (turn right the street before Str Telecabinei). When around, the English-speaking manager is a super source of travel information – even for drop-by visitors.

Pensiunea Cetatea Caraiman (☎ 323 222; r €17) Made up like a fricking castle, this basic guesthouse has small windows (only) to take in jagged peaks, mini-golf carpets and a little TV room. Walk south of the train station, then take the first left that winds north and over a stream; the castle is in a group of buildings to the right. It's about a 500m walk.

Hotel Silva (☎ 320 027, 321 412; www.hotelsilva .ro, in Romanian; Str Telecabinei 24; s/d from €36/51) This mammoth 1980 building lords over a hill right in front of the cable car. Rooms have gotten a fix up, with green or blue carpets and modern lounge chairs. All have balconies looking over the scene of hiker and skier swarms.

Eating

You can stock up on supplies in the commercial complex at the southern end of B-dul Libertăţii or at the cluster of shops at the foot of the cable-car station.

Bistro (☎ 0721-065 315; B-dul Libertăţii 146-148; pizzas €2.60-4.60; ☼ 8am-10pm) This is a rustic place 100m south of the train station with big windows, wood benches, €1.20 burgers and all-day omelettes.

Ristorante Falco Bianco (☎ 320 347; B-dul Libertăţii 109; ☼ 10am-midnight Fri-Sun, to 9 or 10pm Mon-Thu) Run by an Italian guy who likes the Stones, this two-floor tavern, south of the train station, churns out excellent, authentic pasta and pizza (word is that the British ambassador in Bucharest comes up for meals).

Getting There & Away

Buşteni has no Agenţie de Voiaj CFR. Buy tickets at the train station on B-dul Libertăţii. Buşteni is on the main Bucharest–Cluj-Napoca line, with all local trains between Braşov and Bucharest stopping.

From Buşteni, buses to Azuga and Sinaia depart every half-hour between about 6am and 8pm from the main bus stop on B-dul Libertăţii. All maxitaxis heading to and from Braşov (€1.40, 50 minutes) can be flagged down on the main street.

Open-bed trucks marked 'Gura Diham' depart for Cabana Gura Diham from Hotel Miorita (just south of the train station). They run daily in summer, at weekends in winter, leaving hourly or half-hourly between 7am and 10pm from outside the train station.

TRANSYLVANIA

PREDEAL

☎ 268 / pop 6740

The first skiing you hit heading south from Braşov, this ski resort is, at 1033m, higher than Poiana Braşov or Sinaia, but the runs aren't as long and it misses the most popular access points into the Bucegi Mountains. On occasion hordes of local kids on school camps (winter and summer) delight in Predeal, yet things seem quieter here than elsewhere and there are some good hikes. Just south of town is the official beginning of Transylvania.

Watch for Predeal's mascot, a red, yellow and blue bird named Toto.

Orientation & Information

The train station and bus/maxitaxi stop are right on the main street. B-dul Mihai Sălescu, which goes north to Braşov and south to Sinaia and Bucharest. The lifts are a 10-minute walk southeast. Some plush hotels are in the Trei Brazi district, a 20-minute walk northwest.

The friendly **Tourist Information Centre** (☎ 455 330; www.predeal.ro; ☿ 8am-8pm Mon-Fri, to 4pm Sat & Sun summer, 8am-4pm Mon-Fri, 9am-2pm Sat & Sun winter), in a modern building with huge glass windows in front of the train station, is a good first stop. It can offer prices of the dozens of hotels, villas and *pensiunes*, as well as a brochure with map and excellent info on hikes and bike rides.

Across B-dul Mihai Sălescu, the blue-and-white **Banca Comercială Română** (☿ 8.30am-5pm Mon-Fri, to 12.30pm Sat) has a 24-hour ATM. There is an **Internet Café** (Str Şoimului; per hr €0.60; ☿ 9am-midnight) behind the modern-looking white church, just north of the bank. Another 100m north is a post office; south of the bank is a de facto 'centre' with sports shops, cheap pizza and a travel agent.

In case of emergency, call **Salvamont** (☎ 0726-686 696).

Activities

Clăbucet Zona de Agrement (☎ 456 541) runs the eight-run mountain with two chairlifts and several drag lifts. A 10-point lift ticket costs €11/7 per adult/child; the chairlifts count for two points, but the drags as one. You can hire skis and snowboards near the base of the mountain.

A good hub for winter and summer activity is **Fulg de Nea** (Snow Flake; ☎ 456 089; Str Telefericului 1), close to the ski lift, which is Predeal's central ski school, but also offers ice skating, sleigh riding and hiking, plus biking and tennis in summer. It runs a villa.

There are several **hiking** trails in the area. The loop from near Fulg de Nea up the mountain to the southern end of Str Poliştoaca takes about two hours. Trails north of town are open for **cycling** too.

Sleeping

There are many options to stay in *cazares*. The tourist information centre can find you villas for as little as €12 or €15.

Fulg de Nea (☎ 456 089; Str Telefericului 1; r from €18) Just behind the ski centre, this 21-room villa is often filled with groups. Breakfast is not included.

Hotel Cabana Vânătorul (☎ 455 285; www.maroma .ro/cabanavanatorilor; Str Trei Brazi 3; r from €20) Some 3km northeast of the train station on the road to Trei Brazi, this is a lovely place with 24 rooms, and meat lovers will find their paradise in the restaurant.

Vila Fragilor (☎ 456 605; Str Nufarului 1; summer/winter r €23/29) This is a nicely renovated three-floor home with plain wooden floors and modern furnishings. Each of the six rooms has a TV, rug and writing desk (two share a bathroom). The top floor rooms have atmospheric wooden beams and diamond-shaped windows. There's no breakfast, internet or English, but the huge kitchen is for your use. It's across from the train station; zigzag your way up 60m behind the white church.

Hotel Carmen (☎ 456 656; Str Mihai Săulescu 121; s/d €25/37) If you're wheeling your luggage from the train station, head left 50m to get to this slightly faded, but cheerful enough, hotel with loud carpets, big wardrobes and small entries to each room. There's a travel agent here too.

Eating

Most hotels have a restaurant of sorts, and there are plenty of fast-food options along Str Mihai Săulescu. There are a few good restaurants at the southern end of B-dul Libertăţii (which reaches the main street 100m east of the train station), and the restaurant at Hotel Cabana Vânătorul serves tasty local fare.

Getting There & Away

The **Agenţie de Voiaj CFR** (☎ 410 233, ext 194601) is inside the train station building.

Predeal is on the main Cluj-Napoca–Braşov–Bucharest line and you'll never wait long for a train heading to Braşov (€1.70 to €2.60, 40 minutes) or Bucharest (two hours). Outside, buses or maxitaxis show up about every half-hour in the train station parking lot where you can get to Braşov (€1.20, 30 minutes), Sinaia (€1.20, 30 minutes) or Bucharest (€4.30, two hours).

BRAŞOV

☎ 268 / pop 321,460

The heart and hub of Transylvania, this popular, Saxon-rich town is an inviting base with a week's worth of day trips to castles, villages and mountains. Flaunting its medieval glory, Braşov's historic centre, still largely surrounded by medieval stone walls still not pierced by new-fangled paved roads, cobbles its way around tiny alleys and baroque façades and churches with (legend goes) sword marks on its walls. One new German resident said, 'It looks just like a German town, just that it hasn't been perfected yet. It's actually dangerous to walk under some buildings. I love it.'

There are hills all around – most popularly Mt Tâmpa shooting up outside the city's medieval walls, now sporting a 'Hollywood' Braşov sign that lights up as dusk hits – and plenty of kick-back bars, open-air cafés and fine eateries serving more than pizza. It's a bit touristy – too much for some visitors – but it's hard to miss.

See Around Braşov (p136) and Prahova Valley (p118) for scores of day-trip options including that eye-rolling, must-do 'Dracula castle' in Bran.

History

Established on an ancient Dacian site in the 13th century by Teutonic knights, Braşov became a German mercantile colony in the 13th century named Kronstadt (Brassó in Hungarian). The Saxons built ornate churches and townhouses, protected by a massive wall that still remains. The Romanians lived at Schei, just outside the walls, to the southwest.

One of the first public oppositions to the Ceauşescu government flared here in 1987. Thousands of disgruntled workers took to the streets demanding basic foodstuffs. Ceauşescu called in the troops and three people were killed in the scuffle.

Orientation

Str Republicii, Braşov's pedestrian-only promenade, is crowded with shops and cafés. At its north end is B-dul Eroilor, with museums and hotels; the boulevard also links two other main thoroughfares, Str Mureşenilor (the main entry thoroughfare to the centre) to its west and Str Nicolae Bălcescu to its east. The train station is 2km northeast of the town centre, past grey block-housing neighbourhoods.

MAPS & PUBLICATIONS

Amco's *Braşov City Plan* (€3.40) is the best available map; it surely beats the glossy ad-filled *Braşov City & County Map* (€2.80). The information centre hands out a useful, free *Sam's City Guide* with maps of Braşov and Poiana Braşov.

The free, biweekly Romanian magazines *Zile şi Nopţi* (*Days and Nights*; www.zilesinopti.ro) and *24-Fun*, found in bars and cafés, are worth picking up for the most up-to-date listings.

Pick up the bimonthly *Braşov Visitor* (www.brasov-visitor.ro) at the tourist information centre for English articles from visitors and expats about the Transylvanian experience.

Information

Check www.brasovtravelguide.ro or www.brasov.ro for basic information.

BOOKSHOPS

At the following you can find some Romania-themed books and maps, plus a smattering of English-language guidebooks.

Librărie George Coşbuc (☎ 444 395; Str Republicii 29; ⏰ 9am-7pm Mon-Fri, 10am-4pm Sat)

Librărie Ralu (Str Muresenilor 12; ⏰ 8am-8pm Mon-Fri, 10am-6pm Sat, 11am-4pm Sun)

FROM BRAŞOV WITH LOVE

Between 1950 and 1960, when Romania still considered itself Moscow's buddy, Braşov was named 'Oraşul Stalin', with the Russian dictator's name emblazoned into the side of Mount Tâmpa thanks to artistic deforestation. At the time, the name was sadly apt, as ruthless, forced industrialisation yanked thousands of rural workers from the countryside and plunked them down on the city in an attempt to crank the totalitarian motor of industry.

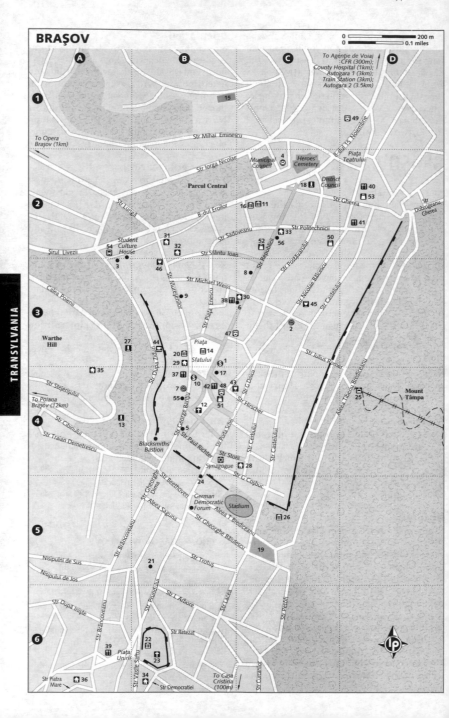

BRAȘOV

TRANSYLVANIA

0 _____ 200 m
0 _____ 0.1 miles

To Agenție de Voiaj
CFR (300m);
County Hospital (1km);
Autogara 1 (3km);
Train Station (3km);
Autogara 2 (3.5km)

To Opera
Brașov (1km)

Str Mihai Eminescu

Str Iorga Nicolae

B-dul 15 Noiembrie

Municipal
Council

Heroes'
Cemetery

Piața
Teatrului

Parcul Central

District
Council

Str Gherea

Str Dobrogeanu
Gherea

Str Lunga

B-dul Eroilor

Str Sadoveanu

Str Politechnicii

Student
Culture
House

Șirul Livezii

Str Sfântu Ioan

Str Republicii

Str Poștavarului

Str Nicolae Bălcescu

Str Michael Weiss

Str Mureșenilor

Str Piața Enescu

Str Castelului

Calea Poienii

Warthe
Hill

Str Julius Romer

Piața
Sfatului

Str Stejerișului

Str Dupa Ziduri

To Poiana
Brașov (12km)

Str Cibinului

Str Chiaci

Str Hirscher

Str Porta Scrii

Str Castelului

Str Traian Demetrescu

Mount
Tâmpa

Aleea Tiberiu Brediceanu

Blacksmiths'
Bastion

Str George Barițiu

Str Paul Richter

Str Cerbului

Str Beethoven

Str Gheorghe
Dima

Aleea Sigura

Synagogue

Str Storii

Str G Coșbuc

German
Democratic
Forum

Str Braicoveanu

Aleea T Brediceanu

Stadium

Str Gheorghe Bărnuțiu

Nisipului de Sus

Str Trotuș

Nisipului de Jos

Str Dupa Iniște

Str Prundului

Str L Arbore

Str Lacea

Str Fetzii

Str Bărncoveanu

Str Retezat

Piața
Unirii

Str Vasile Saftu

Str Curcanilor

Str Piatra
Mare

Str Democrației

To Casa
Cristina
(100m)

CULTURAL CENTRES

Alliance Française (☎ 412 179; www.afbv.home.ro; B-dul Eroilor 33; ⊗ 9am-5pm Mon, Wed & Fri, 1-8pm Tue & Thu) Hosts French classes and events.

British Council (☎ 419 338; B-dul Eroilor 33; ⊗ 9am-4pm Mon, Wed & Fri, 1-8pm Tue & Thu) Library and English club.

EMERGENCY

Salvamont (☎ 471 517, 0725-826 668; Str Varga 23) Emergency rescue service for the mountains.

INTERNET ACCESS

Blue Net Club (☎ 0740-839 449; Str Michael Weiss 26; per hr €0.40-0.60; ⊗ 24hr)

Internet (Str Gheorghe Bariţiu 8; per hr €0.60; ⊗ 24hr)

LEFT LUGGAGE

Train station (per day small/big bag €0.60/1.80; ⊗ 24hr) The left-luggage office is in the underpass that leads out to/from the tracks.

MEDICAL SERVICES

County Hospital (☎ 333 666; Calea Bucureşti 25-27; ⊗ 24hr) Northwest of the centre.

Europharm (☎ 411 248; Str Republicii 15; ⊗ 9am-6pm Mon-Fri, 8am-3pm Sat) Well-stocked pharmacy.

MONEY

You'll find numerous ATMs, banks and 24-hour exchange offices on Str Republicii and B-dul Eroilor. **Raiffeisen Bank** (Piaţa Sfatului; ⊗ 9am-6.30pm Mon-Fri, to 2pm Sat) charges 5% commission for changing travellers cheques; it's only 1.5% (US$5 minimum) at **Banca Comercială Română** (Piaţa Sfatului 14; ⊗ 8.30am-5pm Mon-Fri, to 12.30pm Sat).

POST & TELEPHONE

The **central post office** (☎ 411 609; Str Iorga Nicolae 1; ⊗ 7am-8pm Mon-Fri, 8am-1pm Sat) is opposite the Heroes' Cemetery.

TOURIST OFFICES

In the gold city council building, the English-language speaking staff at the **Tourist information centre** (☎ 419 078; www.brasovcity.ro; Piaţa Sfatului 30; ⊗ 9am-5pm) can point you to tour services, offer free brochures and track down hotel vacancies (there's no private accommodation though). The centre shares space with the history museum – hopefully museum attendants will lose that confused/shocked look they give to travellers seeking something called 'information'.

TRAVEL AGENCIES

Some travel agencies around town are geared for getting Romanians out of the country, but there are plenty focused on Braşov too.

   DiscoveRomania (☎ 472 718; www.discoveromania .ro; Str Paul Richter 1; ⊗ 10am-3pm Mon-Fri) This agency (aka Aventours), led by English-speaking

TRANSYLVANIA

TRANSYLVANIA

BRAŞOV HIGHLIGHTS

- Mt Tâmpa (opposite)
- White Tower (opposite)
- Piaţa Sfatului (below)
- Auld Scots Pub burger and beer (p134)
- Black Church (right)

guides, offers tailor-made tours and oodles of information on the area. It's a great place to start for little or big things – like finding someone hiring cross-country skis in Zărneşti or full-on week-long hikes with guides. Staff can help even if you're not planning to take a tour.

An Englishman runs **Roving România** (☎ 0744-212 065; www.roving-romania.co.uk), an out-of-home agency for personalised, usually small-scale tours – great for birding, 4x4 trips. Email for sample itineraries.

Sights

Braşov is an outdoor type of place, best seen by DIY rambles around its medieval core.

PIAŢA SFATULUI

This wide square is the heart of medieval Braşov. In the centre stands the 1420 **council house** (Casa Sfatului), topped by a **Trumpeter's Tower**, in which town councillors, known as centurions, would meet. Some locals swear the joint's haunted; we were warned one worker there quit after 'hearing sounds'. Apparently the tower staged countless tortures, and the square outside supposedly staged the last witch burning in Europe.

This old city hall today houses the two-floor, by-the-numbers **Braşov Historical Museum** (☎ 472 350; www.istoriebv.turistic.ro; adult/student €0.90/0.60; 10am-6pm Tue-Sun summer, 9am-5pm winter), in which the history of the Saxon guilds is recounted (in limited English); they could certainly sex up the small torture room.

Opposite is the Renaissance **Hirscher House** (built 1539–45), also known as the 'Merchants House'. It was thoughtfully built by Apollonia Hirscher, the widow of Braşov mayor Lucas Hirscher, so that merchants could do business without getting rained on. Today it shelters a gallery.

On the square's western side stands the charming **Mureşenilor House Memorial Museum** (Muzeul Memorial Casa Mureşenilor; ☎ 477 864; admis-

sion €0.60, free Sat & Sun; 9am-5pm Tue-Fri, 10am-5pm Sat & Sun), which honours the family of Jacob Mureşan, the first editor of the Romanian-language *Gazeta Transylvania*, a political newspaper published in the 19th century. No English is spoken.

BLACK CHURCH

Braşov's main landmark, just south of the square, is the **Black Church** (Biserica Neagră; adult/child €1/0.50; 10am-5pm Mon-Sat, mass 10am Sun), the largest Gothic church between Vienna and Istanbul and still used by German Lutherans today. Built between 1383 and 1480, its name comes from its appearance after a fire in 1689. The original statues on the exterior of the apse are now inside (look back after you enter) and some 120 fabulous Turkish rugs hang from the balconies (gifts from merchants who returned from shopping sprees in the southern Ottoman lands). Worshippers drop coins through the wooden grates in the floor and hope for the best.

The church's 4000-pipe organ, built by Buchholz of Berlin in 1839, is believed to be the only Buchholz preserved in its original form. Since 1891, organ recitals have been held in the church during July and August, at 6pm Tuesday, Thursday and Saturday (€1.20).

Note the scrape marks outside the church; some locals swear it's from soldiers' sharpened swords from centuries past; others say 'nah, it was just a butcher sharpening his cleaver'. Also the original construction was intended to have a far larger bell tower (funds ran out); see how small it is in comparison to the mammoth base.

BEARS!

About 5000 black and brown bears call Romania home, and many have started relocating to Braşov. In recent years, un-collected rubbish bins in Braşov's outskirts have become new feeding areas for bears, delighting some tour operations that champion 'bear-watching' tours to trash heaps. Many are against it, as it can be dangerous for bears to become accustomed to associating with the human presence and, well, it's not very 'natural'.

In 2004 a rabid brown bear killed two hikers near Braşov.

IT'S A MOBILE WORLD AFTER ALL

The only thing more complex and comical than Romania's bus service is the government-fuelled fervour at building a Disney-like Dracula Land amusement park for US$60 million with the aim of attracting up to a million tourists a year.

It began in 2001 with thoughts of plopping the rides next to Vlad Ţepeş' birthplace in Coienari, outside Curtea de Argeş, but environmental concerns and criticism from folks such as Prince Charles pushed the site to a place even less prepared to take it: medieval Sighişoara. By 2003 the government moved the site to Bucharest – 'construction will begin in three months!' it claimed – then Braşov got into the act, proposing a rival park to be called Empire Dracula in 2004.

Plans for both fell by the wayside, with everything postponed indefinitely – or at least until the next great location is found.

EAST OF THE CENTRE

Between Piaţa Sfatului and the Mt Tâmpa cable car is Str Storii (Rope Street), which is 1.32m by 83m – one of Europe's narrowest 'streets'. The cobbled pedestrian-only alley has been scrubbed up, with nice views of the 'Braşov' sign on the mountain, and connects Str Porta Schei and Str Cerbului.

NORTH OF THE CENTRE

Running north of the square, the pedestrianised Str Republicii provides respite from the traffic that detracts from the charm of the rest of the Old Town. At the promenade's northern end is the wooden-cross **Memorial to Victims of 1989 Revolution**. Across B-dul 15 de Noiembrie is the **Heroes' Cemetery**, a memorial slab listing 69 local victims.

A block west, the **Art Museum** (☎ 477 286; B-dul Eroilor 21; adult/child €0.90/0.60; ☼ 10am-6pm Tue-Sun) and the **Ethnographic Museum** (☎ 476 243; adult/child €0.60/0.30; ☼ 9am-5pm Tue-Sun) adjoin each other. The former has a mishmash of Romanian paintings and decorative arts. The latter has laminated handouts (in English, German and French) explaining exhibits; ask for a demo of the early 20th-century eight-ribbon loom.

In 1524 a new wooden **citadel** (Cetate; admission free; ☼ 11am-midnight) was built in Braşov, on top of Citadel Hill just north, though the stone wall ruins you now see are from the 16th and 17th centuries. Today it houses a couple of beer patios.

AROUND THE WALL

Old Braşov is surrounded by a 12m-high and 3km-long 15th-century wall, built to defend the city from Turkish attacks. Seven bastions were also raised around the city at the most exposed points, each one defended by a guild whose members, pending danger, tolled their bastion bell.

The most popular viewing area is along the western section, which runs along a stream and pedestrianised Str Dupa Ziduri north to B-dul Eroilor. A good access point is 200m south of the Black Church. Above on the hillside are two towers – the **Black Tower** (Turnul Neagru) and **White Tower** (Turnul Alba); both are rather white actually – offering nice views, particularly when the setting sun casts a golden hue on Braşov.

On the wall's southeast corner, past the **Schei Gate** (Poatra Schei; 1825), is the 16th-century **Weavers' Bastion** (Bastionul Ţesătorilor; Str Castelui). Visit the **Weavers' Bastion Museum** (Muzeul Bastionul Ţesătorilor; ☎ 472 368; adult/child €0.90/0.60; ☼ 9am-5pm Tue-Sun), housed in Braşov's only 15th-century building. The simple exhibits – in German and Romanian only – include a fudge-coloured model of Braşov in the 17th century, made in 1896 by a German teacher in town.

MT TÂMPA

Towering above town from the east is Mt Tâmpa, where Braşov's original defensive fortress was built. Vlad Ţepeş attacked it in 1458, finally dismantling it two years later and – out of habit – impaling some 40 merchants atop the peak.

These days it's an easy, and irresistible, trip up. Many visitors go via the **Tâmpa cable car** (Telecabina Tâmpa; ☎ 478 657; one way/return €0.90/1.80; ☼ 9am-5pm Tue-Sun) offering stunning views from the top of Mount Tâmpa in a communist-era dining room. There's access to **hiking trails** up here. Walk south to reach the 'Hollywood'-style **Braşov sign**, with a viewing platform.

You can also hike to the top in an hour following zigzag trails from the cable-car station

TRANSYLVANIA

(red triangles) or from the northeastern edge of the wall.

SCHEI DISTRICT

In Saxon Braşov, Romanians were not allowed to enter the walled city but were banished to the Schei quarter in the southwest. Entry to this quarter from the walled city was marked by the Schei Gate. Passing through it, the sober rows of Teutonic houses change to the small, simpler houses of the Romanian settlement.

A block east, towards Mt Tâmpa, is a **Military Cemetery**, with Iron Crosses on tombstones from fallen locals who fought for the Germans in WWI.

Further south along Str Prundului is the first **Romanian Lycée** where the first Romanian opera *Crai Nou* (New Moon), written by Ciprian Porumbescu (1853–83), was performed in 1882.

Continue south to Piaţa Unirii to the black-spired Orthodox Church of **St Nicholas' Cathedral** (St Nicolae din Scheii; ⊙ 6am-9pm), first built in wood in 1392 and replaced by a Gothic stone church in 1495 by the Wallachian prince Neagoe Basarab (r 1512–21), later embellished in Byzantine style. In 1739 the church was enlarged and its interior heavily redecorated. Inside are murals of Romania's last king and queen, covered by plaster to protect them from communist leaders and uncovered in 2004.

Beside the church is the two-room 1495 **First Romanian School Museum** (☎ 511 411; adult/child €0.90/0.60; ⊙ 9am-5pm Tue-Sun), which packs a staggering far-reaching selection of old books and pieces, including the first Russian Bible (1581), King Ferdinand's coronation flag from 1922 (found in 2006), and 15th-century schoolbooks that warned 'he who will steal this book will be CURSED...his blood shall melt on his body...his left eye shall dry

out!' Resist the temptation then. No English; guides are available.

Activities

Hikes are everywhere – from atop Mt Tâmpa in town (see p129), Poiana Braşov (p136), Zărneşti (p141) or into the Bucegi Mountains (p122). Pick up maps from Himalaya (p135) or talk with a travel agent specialising in hikes (p129).

You can also ski on day trips to Poiana Braşov (p136), Predeal (p126) and Sinaia (p118).

ECO-S Paragliding (☎ 0723-333 193; www.parapanta.ro) offers 10-day paragliding classes for €180.

Festivals & Events

The best time in Braşov is during the **Days of Braşov** festival, the first week after Easter (late April/early May), finishing with the fantastic **Juni Pageant** (see the boxed text, below).

Braşov proudly hosts other events including the **International Chamber Music Festival**, which is usually held the first week in September in various venues around town, with a final concert at Bran Castle. Since 1968, the **Golden Stag Festival** (Cerbul de Aur; www.cerbuldeaur.ro), held in late September, has put one-time subversive pop music on the stage – folks like James Brown, Joe Cocker and Ricky Martin have performed.

Etnovember is an imaginative festival, held in November since 1998, that highlights traditions of Romanians and many ethnic minorities.

Sleeping

BUDGET

Kismet Dao Villa (☎ 514 296; www.kismetdao.ro; Str Democratiei 2b; dm €10-11, d €24) Set up in a rather dorm-type building, the four-floor, six-room villa is a good budget choice, with video games

---

ROMANIAN BACHELOR PARTY

A centuries-old tradition, the Juni Pageant (Sărbătoarea junilor) still colourfully unfolds through the street of Schei in late April/early May. Groups of single young men don traditional Schei armour and, sword in hand, ride from Piaţa Unirii, through the Schei Gate, to Piaţa Sfatului, followed by the married men. The parade ends up on Mount Tâmpa for several hours of energetic folk dancing.

During Saxon domination, this was the one day of the year Romanians were allowed to enter the walled city. The costumes worn are seriously ornate, some over a century old and weighing several kilograms. The tradition was not meant to ensure that the single men found potential brides, but one can imagine how many trial runs were enacted as the party wound down.

on the TV, playful staff and good-value day trips to Bran and area attractions. Take bus 4 from the train station to the end of the line at Piaţa Unirii.

ourpick Beke Guesthouse (☎ 511 997; Str Cerbului 32; r incl likely jug of homemade wine €11-14) A lovely Hungarian-speaking couple runs this handful of simple rooms, each with its own feel and all with shared bath. Often they'll bring by a jug of homemade wine. The building has no sign – rooms are accessed from the vine-covered courtyard, shared with neighbours. No breakfast, no sign, no English. Two consecutive Lonely Planet researchers have hugged a Beke when leaving.

Hotel Aro Sport (☎ 478 800; Str Sfântu Ioan 3; s/d €11/16) Here's what Eastern European travel used to be about – old boxy rooms, a sink in the corner, a shower down the hall. It's quite clean and central though and the price is right. No breakfast.

Rolling Stone Hostel (☎ 513 965, 0744-876 970; www.rollingstone.ro; Str Piatra Mare 2a; dm/d €11/35; ⬛) Run by a long-time Braşov institution (Maria and Grig Bolea) – often found lingering at the train station – the Stone is a nice hostel with hidden doors opening to more dorm rooms (some in the arched attics) and a wading pool. You'll need energy to keep up with Maria and her two daughters' almost hyperactive attention. Check around before taking a tour (they're sometimes overpriced). They seem to save pennies on half-hearted breakfasts, rough toilet paper and no towels, but it's certainly homy. No internet access.

Hotel Postăvarul (☎ 477 448; fax 418 469; Str Republicii 62; s/d €19/27) Despite its 1910 German design, the gloriously faded grandeur of this 46-room hotel completes, by accident, a stereotypical vision of a 'Transylvanian hotel' – inside floors creak under green-and-white arched doors in a dated, mysterious hotel not for everyone. But rooms are vacuumed daily and have private toilets; shared showers are down the hall. Its adjoining Hotel Coroana is overpriced.

MIDRANGE

Casa Cristina (☎ 512 580, 0722-322 021; Str Curcanilor 62a; s/d €25/35) On a side street as the Schei district sneaks up into the hills, this six-room guesthouse is a homy spot, with views looking towards the centre. Three colour-themed rooms have private bathroom, plus there's a kitchen to use; breakfast is €3 extra. Staff can

point out the hike to Poiana Braşov nearby. It's south of the map extents, uphill slightly from Piaţa Unirii.

Montana (☎ 0723-614 534; Calea Polenii; s €42-44, d €52-54) Up above the White Tower, the Montana is a great convert of a Brady Bunch–style vacation home – a super frog-green six-room hillside guesthouse with slanted cedar roofs and seriously pastel room themes. Pay €2 more for rooms with refrigerator and balcony.

Bella Musica (☎ 477 956; www.bellamusica.ro; Piaţa Sfatului 19; s/d €63/77; ⬛ ⬛) Opened in 2005, the terrific 22-room Musica has very stylish rooms with soft lighting and textured orange walls and old-style wood desks to write poems on. Downstairs an 'invisible doorman' opens/closes the front door, which overlooks the main square. Its basement restaurant is excellent.

Casa Rozelor (☎ 475 212; www.casarozelor.ro; Str Michael Weiss 20; r €88; ⬛) Tucked away in a central alley, this German-run three-room guesthouse mixes up themes (one room has an upstairs loft with red-leather sofa next to a 15th-century brick wall). There are no TVs to clutter this edgy peek into the past and there are plans to expand.

TOP END

Hotel Aro Palace (☎ 478 800; www.aro-palace.ro; Str Mureşenilor 12; new hotel s/d €117/146, old hotel €70/90; ⬛ ⬛) This business-oriented hotel combines history (rather dated rooms in its 'old' wing, inside a lovely 1939 Art Deco front) and modern (its other wing follows the staid 'business hotel' template to a T). All rooms are overpriced, but a pool was in the works at last pass.

Eating

New eating spots open regularly. Just off Piaţa Sfatului, Str Hirscher is something of a 'restaurant row', with a few pizza places, a steak house and a lively pub. Fast-food options are more readily found on the pedestrian mall Str Republicii.

ROMANIAN

Casa Româneasca (☎ 513 877; Piaţa Unirii; mains €3-6; ⏱ noon-midnight) Deep in the Schei district, away from trolling tourists, this casa serves tasty *sarmalute cu mamaliguta* (boiled beef rolled with vegetables and cabbage) and a very meaty 'rustic tray' grab-bag. Live music adds to or subtracts from the experience, based on your taste.

Bella Musica (☎ 477 956; Str George Bariţu 2; dishes €3.40-10; ☻ 10am-midnight) Pretty much everyone's local favourite, this lovely cavernous basement restaurant of red brick and candlelight serves up a few Mexican dishes, but keeps the focus on very tasty Romanian fare; a popular starter is the meaty bean soup served in a bowl of bread (€2.10). Staff bring a 'music menu' for requests – the list includes 'best ballads' by Uriah Heap, Celine Dion, the Boss and Floyd.

INTERNATIONAL
Go to Auld Scots Pub (see Drinking, below) if you're looking for a burger.

Pizza Pasta Venezia (☎ 470 511; Str Hirscher 2; pastas & pizzas from €2.30; ☻ 11am-midnight or 1am) Wall-sized Venetian paintings and soft lighting – and cheaper prices – helps this cosy Italian restaurant fill before its similar-themed neighbours. The mozzarella-and-tomato salad seems particularly fresh.

Bistro de l'Arte (☎ 0722-219 980; Piaţa Enescu 11; mains €2.50-4.50; ☻ 9am-1am Mon-Sat, noon-midnight Sun) In the bottom of a cosy 15th-century building, the Bistro is the place for sit-back wine sessions, breakfasts with wi-fi for your laptop, or lively dinners with mingling Romanian couples (who sometimes come for plays). The menu drifts from French and includes daily fish dishes (€4.30), big salads (€3.60) and pasta (€3.70).

Hirscher Keller (☎ 472 278; Str Hirscher 2; mains €4.30-8.60; ☻ 9am-midnight) Gothic meets moderne in this stylish dining room that focuses on steaks – very tasty, very juicy steaks. There's a nice grilled vegetables plate with eggplant, cheese and tomato, and a wine cellar downstairs housing the luxe list of local wines. Breakfasts include €2.70 Eggs Benedict.

SELF-CATERING
Hard Discount (Str Nicolae Bălcescu; ☻ 24hr) This fully stocked supermarket is next to the indoor/outdoor fruit and vegetable market.

Drinking
CAFÉS
Cafeneaua Graft (☎ 0749-221 224; Str Dupa Ziduri; ☻ 11am-11pm) Part of the old wall lookout on the western wall, this smoky hipster spot revels in ice cream, coffee and drinks. There's an outdoor area above the wall too.

BARS
Auld Scots Pub (☎ 470 183; Str Hirscher 10; ☻ 11am-2am) Capturing local imagination, and plain one-upping the local Irish pub, the kilts and Connery on the walls of this inviting bar can be forgiven for its tasteful sitting areas, three-board dart room and far better-than-average pub fare. Good Romanian wine comes by the glass (€2) if you wish, while pints of Ursus beer are €1.50.

Festival 39 (☎ 478 664; Str Mureşenilor 23; ☻ 10am-1am) This cosy dark-lit room has brick walls, soft music, and dozens of candles and antiques. The bar area and tables are filled with 20- and thirtysomething locals, chatting and smoking.

Crama Vinoteca (Str Castelului 106; litre of wine €1.20-3; ☻ 10am-7pm Mon-Fri, to 3pm Saturday) Barrels and barrels of Romanian wine, and empty litre and half-litre bottles to fill and take to your own drinking spot.

Entertainment
CLUBS
Clubs are busier outside of summer, when students roll back into town and in need of some action. Grădina de Vară is an open-air disco sometimes held on summer weekends up on the hill in the citadel.

Aquarium (☎ 0740-915 843; Piaţa Teatrului 1) This is a popular disco, inside the Sică Alexandrescu Drama Theatre.

OPERA & BALLET
The **Gheorghe Dima State Philharmonic** (☎ 473 058; www.sfbv.home.ro; Str Hirscher 10) has a good reputation and performs mainly between September and May, as does the **Opera Braşov** (☎ 415 990; Bisericii Române 51), which stages mainly classics. Tickets for theatrical and classical music and ballet performances can be purchased at the **Agenţie de Teatrală** (☎ 471 889; Str Republicii 4; ☻ 10am-5pm Tue-Fri, to 2pm Sat), just off Piaţa Sfatului.

THEATRE
Sică Alexandrescu Drama Theatre (☎ 412 969; Piaţa Teatrului 1) Come here for plays, recitals and opera year-round.

Puppet Theatre (Teatrul de Păpuşi Arlechino; ☎ 475 243; Str Hirscher 10) This place stages creative shows for kids.

Shopping
The souvenir selection is surprisingly not in-your-face (yet). Try shops on Str Republicii or the shop at the Ethnographic Museum (p131).

Rom Filatelia (☎ 475 328; Str Republicii 41; ☒ 11am-5pm Mon-Fri, 9am-noon Sat) Find a souvenir backup at this swank (almost snooty) modern stamp shop, which sells artful stamps from the 1960s to the present.

Himalaya (☎ 477 855; www.himalaya.ro; Piaţa Sfatului 17; ☒ 10am-7pm Mon-Fri, to 2pm Sat) This great sports store has ski and hiking boots, sleeping bags, rock-climbing gear – pretty much whatever you forgot. Staff double as knowledgeable guides and they can sell you trail maps and point you to good DIY things too.

Doua Roti (☎ 0740-125 984; Str Nicolae Bălcescu 55; ☒ 8.30am-5pm Mon-Fri, 9am-1pm Sat) A great old-time shop selling used bikes and parts. The staff here can help you with repairs too.

Star (Str Nicolae Bălcescu; ☒ 9am-8.30pm Mon-Fri, to 8pm Sat) Four-floor department store.

Getting There & Away

Braşov is planning to have an airport built by the end of 2007.

BUS

Maxitaxis and microbuses are the best way to reach places near Braşov, including Bran, Râşnov, Sinaia, Hârman and Sfântu Gheorghe. Otherwise it's generally better to go by train as the bus situation is ever-changing.

The most accessible station is **Autogară 1** (☎ 427 267), next to the train station (reached by bus 4 from the centre), a ramshackle lot with a booming maxitaxi business (hourly jobs go to-and-fro on the Târgu Mureş–Sighişoara–Braşov–Buşteni–Bucharest route) and some long-distance buses.

From 6am to 7.30pm maxitaxis leave every half-hour for Bucharest (€5.25, 2½ hours), stopping in Buşteni and Sinaia. About four or five maxitaxis leave for Sibiu (€3.90, 2½ hours), stopping in Făgăraş town. Nine or 10 go daily to Sighişoara en route to Târgu Mureş (€5.70, four to five hours). A handful of buses go to Bistriţa (€8, seven to eight hours), and also Constanţa (€10) and Iaşi (€10).

Bus 4 reaches the centre from the train station (pre-buy your ticket). From the centre, hail a bus at the corner of Str Nicolae Bălcescu and Str Gherea.

Autogară 2 (aka 'Bartolomeu'; ☎ 426 332; Str Avram Iancu 114), a kilometre west of the train station, sends half-hourly buses to Râşnov (€0.45, 25 minutes) and Bran (€0.75, 40 minutes) from roughly 6.30am to 11.30pm; these are marked 'Moieciu–Bran'. A dozen daily buses go to

Zărneşti (€0.75, one hour), fewer on week-ends. Take bus 12 to/from the centre (it stops at the roundabout just north of the station).

A few daily buses leave from Autogară 2 to Sfântu Gheorghe (€1.20, 45 minutes), stopping just across B-dul Gării from the Autogară 1 (this may change). Separate, nearly hourly, buses go to Hărman (€0.40, 30 minutes) and Prejmer (€0.60, 30 minutes).

The main bus stop in town is the 'Livada Poştei' at the western end of B-dul Eroilor in front of the County Library (Biblioteca Judeţeană). From here bus 20 goes half-hourly to Poiana Braşov (€0.75, 20 minutes). Buy your ticket from the kiosk opposite the Student Culture House before boarding.

All European routes are handled by **Euro-lines** (☎ 475 219; www.eurolines.ro; Piaţa Sfatului 18; ☒ 9am-8pm Mon-Fri, to 4pm Sat), which sells tickets for buses to Germany, Italy, Hungary and other European destinations.

TRAIN

Advance tickets are sold at the **Agenţie de Voiaj CFR office** (☎ 477 015; Str 15 de Noiembre 43; ☒ 8am-7.30pm Mon-Fri).

Sample direct train services include the following (prices are for 2nd-class seats on rapid trains):

Destination	Price	Duration	Frequecy
Bucharest	€7.60	2½hr	22 daily
Cluj-Napoca	€11.70	6hr	5 daily
Iaşi	€10.60	8½hr	1 daily
Sf Gheorghe	€0.80-2	½hr	13-16 daily
Sibiu	€7.10	2¾hr	9 daily
Sighişoara	€6.70	2½hr	14 daily

International train services include three daily trains to Budapest (€40/71 seat/sleeper, 14 hours), two to Vienna (€75/100, 18 hours) and also one daily train to Prague (21 hours) and Istanbul (19 hours).

Getting Around

Bus 4 runs from the train station and Autogară 1 through the centre, stopping at Piaţa Unirii south of the centre. From Autogară 2, take bus 12 or 22 from the 'Stadion Tineretului' stop on nearby Str Stadionului (just north of the bus station).

Car-hire rates are higher in Braşov than Sibiu or Cluj-Napoca. **Kron Tour** (☎ 410 515; Str Gheorghe Bariţu 12; ☒ 9am-5pm Mon-Fri, 10am-1pm Sat)

TRANSYLVANIA

hires cars from €43 per day. **Budget** (☎ 474 564) has an office inside the Hotel Aro Palace that's sometimes staffed.

Transilvania Travel (☎ 477 623; www.transilvania travel.com; Str Republicii 62; ☷ 9am-5pm Mon-Fri, to 1pm Sat) also hires cars.

The taxi stand outside the train station has a good reputation. A couple of reputable companies include **Martax** (☎ 313 040) and **Tod** (☎ 321 111).

AROUND BRAŞOV

Though lumped together because of its proximity to Braşov, this region of castles and Saxon churches and ski lifts easily out-plays Braşov's own attractions – making it easy to stay in the area for a week or more. The most popular trip – usually done as a day trip from Braşov – is to see the 'Dracula castle' at Bran and the nearby castle in Râşnov, a simple DIY half-day trip with local buses. Many visitors prefer Râşnov, so try to fit it in.

On the third Sunday in April, in Apata village, 33km north of Braşov, you can witness the colourful Rooster Shooting (Impuscatul Cocosului), when dressed-up villagers read angry poems accusing a loud rooster of giving away their hiding place to Tartar invaders. Then they shoot it. The tradition dates from a 14th-century episode, and these days the rooster's made of wood.

POIANA BRAŞOV
☎ 268

An easy springboard for intermediate skiing or hiking on the back of the Bucegi Mountains, Poiana Braşov (1030m) is a resort, but often visited by day-trippers or the mountain-bound. Skiing is good, but has less advanced slopes than Sinaia. The cable car runs all year, leading to a panoramic view of Braşov and the surrounding Carpathians.

The newly built **St Ivan Butezatorul church** (Str Valea Dragă) in the centre is done in the Maramureş style (presumably for ski tourists who won't make it that far), and made entirely of wood and with a tall spire.

Orientation
The main road that runs through town from Braşov is called Str Poiana Soarelui, at the southern end of which is the cable-car station (Staţie Telecabină). At the very centre of town

is the unmistakable Capra Neagră restauran[t] and casino. Just north of here Str Poiana Ursului (the so-called 'old road' to Braşov) branche[s] off to the northeast, and the main car park where the central bus stop is located.

Information
There is no tourist information office in Poiana Braşov; check websites such as www.poiana-brasov.ro or www.poiana.info.ro. The local **Salvamont** (☎ 286 176; Cabana Cristianul Mare) will come to the rescue any time of the day in case of emergency.

Skiing
Best known as an intermediate mountain, Poiana Braşov's 12 runs – including two black slopes (each about 2km long) – are accessed by two cable-car lifts run by **ANA** (☎ 262 413) with a chairlift and five drag lifts higher up. The main cable car, a 15-minute walk up the road southwest from the bus stop (past the St Ivan Butezatorul church), operates all year. Another is next to Hotel Sport. To ride any of the mountain's six lifts it's €23 for 10 trips or €3.50 for one.

The ski season runs from December to March, sometimes later. Check out www.poiana-brasov.ro for ski conditions.

ANA all but runs a monopoly on the lifts and rental; you can rent from it for €12 per day, or €20 for two days. It also holds group and private lessons (it's about €20 per hour for two people) in English, French and German; check with its office situated at Hotel Sport. An alternative, **Club Rossignol** (☎ 0721 200 470; ☷ 9am-5.30pm), across from the main lift, also hires skis or snowboards for €12 per day.

Hiking
The Postăvaru Massif nestles between the Cheii Valley, Timişului Valley and Poiana Braşov, and has dozens of trails of varying levels of difficulty to choose from.

From Poiana Braşov you can hike to **Cristianul Mare** (1802m, three hours, marked with red crosses), the massif's highest peak (or just take the cable car up). From the top the trail (marked with yellow bar) leads to another (marked with red triangles), that leads east down to the road which links Timişu de Jos (on the Sinaia–Braşov rail line) with Timişu de Sus (2½ hours). Turn left for Jos, right for Sus.

You can also hike directly down to Timișu de Jos from Cabana Cristianul Mare in three to four hours. The trail is marked from the cabana with blue stripes, then blue crosses. Instead of following the blue-cross trail where the path diverges, you can continue following the blue-stripe trail, which eventually takes you over the top of Mt Tâmpa to **Brașov.** This trail (1½ hours) follows the old Brașov road.

From Poiana Brașov you can also easily hike to **Râșnov** (two to three hours, yellow crosses, then left on the road to the trail marked with blue stripes) or tackle the more strenuous hike to Predeal (five to seven hours, yellow stripes).

Sleeping

Most travel agencies in Brașov take bookings for hotels in Poiana Brașov. Except for a couple of weeks over Christmas and New Year, you can always find a room at the resort. Prices here are for during the peak season (between December and mid-March); prices at all but lower-end places fall by 25% or more at other times. Cheaper hotels don't raise their prices.

To get to the cheap end of the resort, follow Str Poiana Ursului away from the centre.

BUDGET

Cabana Postăvarul (☎ 0741-110 092, 101 036; r per person €9, r with private bathroom €34; 🖵) At 1585m (15 minutes downhill from the lift's exodus), this cabana has a prop-your-feet-up deck with full frontal views of Bucegi's glory. More than one skier missed half a day of skiing by lounging too long here. Rooms are simple, with two to four beds and wood-plank floors that creak. Some rooms have private bathroom. The restaurant buzzes as a skier lunch-break spot.

Cabana Critianul Mare, a chalet near the top of the slopes, was under renovation at research time.

MIDRANGE

Vila Diana (☎ 262 040; Str Poiana Ruia; s/d €52/80; ✖) If you've sworn off Swiss chalets, this eight-room guesthouse goes for a salmon-coloured nod to Miami Art Deco. The rooms are big – with cranberry carpets, peach bedspreads, work desks – plus there's a cosy basement bar, sauna and Jacuzzi. Breakfast is €5.75. It's just west of the Hotel Alpin (away from the lifts), about 150m from the bus stop.

Pensiunile Andreas (☎ 262 266; r/villa €52/155) Near the main lifts, this airy three-room villa can be rented by the room or as a whole. Two rooms share a bathroom. There's a laundry and nice TV sitting area.

Hotel Sport (☎ 407 333; www.anahotels.ro, in Romanian; s/d from €70/80; 🖵) The main one of three hotels run by ANA (by the second lift), is a little faded from all the tour groups checking in over the years, but has plenty of facilities (including tennis courts) and is popular with ski teams. It also runs the two nearby hotels, the Poiana and Bradul (hidden away by a thicket of trees).

Eating

There are a few OK places on the main road in town that serve pizza or grilled meat. It's hard to beat the outdoor seating facing the Bucegi Mountains up at Cabana Postăvarul (mains €2.30 to €4), with natural teas, soups and fries, in addition to meats and cooked breakfasts.

Getting There & Away

From Brașov, bus 20 (€0.75, 20 minutes, every 30 minutes) runs from the Livada Poștei bus stop, opposite the County Library at the western end of B-dul Eroilor, to Poiana Brașov.

RÂȘNOV

Râșnov, 18km south of Brașov, doubles the castle intake for those heading out to Bran Castle. The partially restored hilltop ruins of the 13th-century **Râșnov fortress** (Cetatea Râșnov; ☎ 230 255; adult/child €2.70/1.50; 🕙 9am-8pm summer, to 6pm winter), a 15-minute walk up the steps from central Piața Unirii, feel considerably less touristy than Bran's (despite the wooden Dracula set-up for photo opps). Visitors can wander the grounds, where there's a church, jail and nice views of the mountains. A small museum includes gruesome prints of torture, plus medieval cross bows and knightly knick-knacks. There's a 17th-century, 146m-deep well built by Turkish prisoners, who were promised freedom once completed (it took them 17 years!).

The fortress was built by the Teutonic Knights as protection against Tartar, and later Turkish, invasion. Indeed, almost immediately after its completion, the fortress suffered its first Tartar attack in 1335. The fortress was abandoned in 1850.

Sleeping & Eating

Casa Contelui (☎ 0723-005 378; www.casacontelui.ro; Str Bălcescu 16; r with shared/private bathroom €23/28) Green signs from Râşnov's centre point to this lovely fenced-off six-room farmhouse/guesthouse with an English-speaking owner who can arrange local activities.

Pensiunea Stefi (☎ 231 618; www.hotelstefi-ro.com; Piaţa Unirii 5; s/d €23/28) Spic-and-span, this five-room guesthouse on the main square has carpeted rooms and a wading pool out back. Breakfast is €3 extra.

Pub-Castel Restaurant (Piaţa Unirii 9; pizzas €2-3) This web of dark-wood rooms and arched brick-ways hops with locals eyeing pizzas and beer.

Getting There & Away

Buses bound for Bran come within 200m of the centre of Râşnov; a few 'Râşnov' buses go through it – finishing at the edge of town.

BRAN

☎ 268 / pop 5600

First things first: Bran Castle was by no means Dracula's or Vlad Ţepeş' castle, despite the image being encouraged by locals hawking bleeding-heart-bedecked 'I Love Transylvania' T-shirts and Vlad Ţepeş coffee mugs. The real Vlad may have passed through here in the 15th century, but this was not his home. (For real fake-Dracula country, see p211, for the 'real Vlad Ţepeş' castle, see p105, and for more on the Dracula myth, see p23). Still, the famed Bran Castle's sharp structure, with its fairy-tale turrets rising from an enveloping rocky bluff between two bodyguard-like hills, just looks too damn vampiric to not warrant a little 'ooh' at first viewing.

The area, as the plain settles into the merger of the Bucegi and Piatra Craiului ranges, is a nice spot, but most travellers find more rewarding bases in Braşov or natural ones in hill towns beyond (particularly Moieciu de Sus). By far the bulk of her visitors see Bran as a half-day trip, along with a stop at Râşnov Castle. Daring hiking trails down from the Bucegi wind up here too.

During the 15th and 16th centuries Bran was an important frontier town.

Orientation & Information

The centre of Bran lies on either side of the main north–south Braşov–Piteşti road (Str Principală), with villas, *pensiunes* and (surprisingly few) restaurants strung on and off the road. The entrance to Bran Castle, signposted 'Muzeul Bran', is on the left as you enter the town.

The bus stop is just south of the junction on Str Principală, next to the park, on the other side of which is Str Aurel Stoian. The central post is south of Bran centre, past the Vama Bran museum on the road to Moieciu. There's an **Internet club** (Str Principală 509; per hr €0.60; ☼ 9am-5pm Mon-Fri, to 1pm Sat) in the same building as the Antrec, 50m from the t-shirt stalls.

WHAT'S A CASTLE?

With medieval fortified walls and towers dotting its hilltops, Transylvania is full-blooded castle country. Or is it?

Many castle historians hilariously entangle themselves over the definition, prompted by 'sham castles' that 'use the c word' to help market their sites. Others insist it must be a residence, others don't care – as long as it's fortified…and, um, not too big.

Criticising the 'preposterous erections of the 20th century', historian Sir Charles Oman snapped in his 1926 book *Castles* that a castle 'is a military structure larger than a tower but smaller than a fortified town'. (Naturally!) Others argue the definition has fractured over the years, like the double-use of the French chateau for a big home or fort.

And what about Transylvania? Most of Romania's alleged castles date from the 15th and 16th centuries, slightly trailing the heyday of much of Europe. Bran's, built in the 16th century as a defence against Turks, is – by Oman's (and many others') strict definition – a castle. Râşnov's hilltop fort and Hunedoara's Corvin Castle (p181), built for military defence in the 14th century, surely are too. A fanciful, unfortified summer residence for a 20th-century king, Peleş Castle is not. The Hotel Castel Dracula in Bârgău Valley (p211), of course, is just an '80s tourist hotel with a fake coffin room and overpriced food. Good thing Sir Oman didn't live to see it.

By the way 'fortress' is a whole new debate. Don't ever get between enraged historians in that particular battle.

Sights

Facing the flatlands and backed by mountains, the 60m-tall **Bran Castle** (☎ 238 332; www.brancastle museum.ro; adult/student & child €2.90/1.45; ☑ 9am-6pm Tue-Sun, noon-6pm Mon May-Sep, 9am-4pm Tue-Sun Oct-Apr) is something to see. If you can manage to avoid bottlenecks from tour groups that seem to appear from nowhere, you may enjoy the largely renovated interiors and rather claustrophobic nooks and crannies.

All is signed in English, and for the most part manages to steer clear of the 'Dracula' swipe, though some guides often play up the eerie factor of the hidden steps to the 2nd floor (overheard: 'Dracula likes to feast on young beautiful virgin women... I see no one is missing').

Built by Saxons from Braşov in 1382 to defend the Bran pass against Turks, the castle may have housed Vlad for a few nights on his flight from the Turks in 1462, following their attack on the Poienari fortress in the Argeş Valley. From 1920 Queen Marie lived in the castle, and it served as a summer royal residence until the forced abdication of King Michael in 1947. It became a museum in 1957.

Many rooms have gone through a modern redecoration and look as if they are inhabited by rich eccentrics. Much of the original, fabulous furniture imported from Western Europe by Queen Marie is still inside the castle. A fountain in the courtyard conceals a labyrinth of secret underground passages.

Everyone seems to ignore the photo/video fees of €2.60/5.20.

Free guided tours are not regularly scheduled, but you're likely to stumble on one in English. Your ticket for the castle includes entrance to the open-air **village museum**, with a dozen traditional buildings at the foot of the castle.

The **Vama Bran Museum**, down the hill behind the castle (accessible by road too), was closed for renovation at research time. In the past, ticket entry included this small collection of archaeological pieces from the former customs house.

Opposite the former customs house are some remains of the old **defensive wall**, which divided Transylvania from Wallachia (best viewed from the soldiers' watchtower in the castle). On the southern side of the wall is an endearingly petite stone **chapel**, built in 1940 in memory of Queen Marie. The church,

> **KEYS TO THE CASTLE**
>
> After 60 years in communist/government hands, Bran Castle's keys were handed back to a relative of the original owners in 2006 – Dominic Habsburg, Queen Marie's grandson. Dominic, a New York–based architect (not a vampire), told the *Guardian* that the Dracula connection with the family castle was 'not OK'. Habsburgs never have any sense of fun.
>
> It's expected the castle will remain open as a museum.

now boarded up, is a copy of a church in the queen's palace grounds in Balchik, Bulgaria (formerly southern Dobrogea). A **memorial tomb** where the queen's heart lies has been carved in the mountain, on the north side of the wall.

Festivals & Events

The three-day **Sâmbra Oilor**, held in late September/early October, is a huge pastoral festival celebrated to welcome the sheep home from the hills.

Sleeping & Eating

Bran's pack of villas and *pensiunes* grows every year, and you'll see dozens of *cazare* signs in private homes if you need something cheaper. See www.ruraltourism.ro for detailed descriptions of several *pensiunes* in Bran. Surprisingly, there's not much choice for eating in Bran.

Antrec (☎ 236 340, 0788-411 450; www.antrec.ro; Str Principală 509; ☑ 9am-5pm Mon-Fri, to 1pm Sat) The home base of this nationwide organisation arranges accommodation in 4000 (and growing) private homes, starting at around €25 per room per night. It's a good idea to call or email in advance, as we've found the office hours are rarely adhered to.

Vila Bran (☎ 236 866; www.vilabran.ro; Str Principală 238; r €29-40) Bran's best spot, albeit a slightly cheesy one, brims with energy. This 58-room, hilltop five-building complex looks straight on to the castle. It caters to conferences and groups – with three restaurants, activities including a zip line over a creek(!), an indoor basketball court with 'slide' into nearby playhouse(!); and a petting zoo of two deer saved from dinner tables (one eats the shed roof!). Ask for room 5 for the best views, and avoid

TRANSYLVANIA

DRACULA VS VLAD!

We'll never know who'd win in a fight (well, it *is* easier to bite than impale in the confines of a ring…), but here's a comparison between the very-real Vlad Ţepeş (1431–76) and his later incarnation, Dracula.

Transylvanian?
Drac: Yes, Bram Stoker puts his home in the Bârgău Valley near Bistriţa, northeast of Cluj-Napoca.
Vlad: No, his real home is south of the Carpathians in Poienari, Wallachia.

Fearful feasts?
Drac: Yes, he ate people.
Vlad: Yes, he apparently ate steaks while captives wriggled on rectum-to-underarm stakes.

Bad breath?
Drac: In Jonathan Harker's words, 'his breath was rank' (congealed blood in the gums does that).
Vlad: Not sure, but he looked like a flosser.

Bi-curious?
Drac: Yes! The giveaway is when the fanged fluid-changer stops promiscuous female demons from devouring Jonathan Harker and cries out 'this man belongs to me!' – indeed.
Vlad: Probably (note his handle-bar moustache).

How did he die?
Drac: Wooden stake through the heart, followed by decapitation.
Vlad: No one's sure, but he may have died in battle or been assassinated by rival nobles; although eventually, Turks decapitated his body.

rooms 3 or 4 (which are past the 'bon voyage' sign). Rooms are rather basic, but are clean and have TV.

Popasul Reginei (☎ 236 834; www.popasulreginei.ro; Str Aurel Stoian 398; d €35; ☻) This 16-room villa-style hotel, across from the north end of the castle, is a plain, clean-tiled affair run by a peppy English-speaking manager (who is occasionally clad in a pink ski suit). The restaurant takes over the pool area at lunch, when hundreds of daytrippers come in and out to feast on some pretty good Romanian fare.

Cabana Bran Castle was closed for renovation at research time, but should now be open for business. The cabana is on a hillside about 600m from the castle (access via Str Aurel Stoian, a turn-off roughly where Str Principală begins to curve around the castle; a sign leads 50m past the yellow-painted hospital).

Getting There & Away

Bran's an easy DIY day trip from Braşov. Buses marked 'Bran–Moieciu' (€0.70, one hour) depart every half-hour from Braşov's Autogară 2. Return buses to Braşov leave Bran every half-hour from roughly 7am to 6pm in winter, and 7am to 10pm in summer. All buses to Braşov stop each way at Râşnov.

From Bran there are about a dozen buses daily to Zărneşti (€0.70, 40 minutes), and a few to Piteşti originating from Braşov.

AROUND BRAN

Perfect for leisurely drives past farms, shepherds and haystacks along ridges in the green hills, the villages south of Bran are enchanting in their rural attractiveness. Villas bring in business – check with Antrec in Bran or the great site www.ruraltourism.ro for options – but for the most part the wild landscape remains untouched. Be sure to stop for fresh cheese, as it and wool weaving remain vital parts of villagers' daily life here.

Some 3km southeast along a dirt track from Bran is the village of **Şimon**, with shoulder-to-shoulder villas and hiking trails leading into the Bucegi Mountains. **Mama Cozonacilor** (☎ 0745-151 424; www.branturism.ro; r €20) is a pleasant 25-room complex backed by a steep rising hill; staff arranges activities for all (including the frequent groups that check in).

Moieciu de Jos, 4km southwest of Bran on the road to Câmpulung, is known for its cheese with a pine aroma. It celebrates a **summer festival** at the end of June. From Moieciu de Jos, a dirt track leads northwest to **Peştera**, named after the village's 160m-long cave said to be full of bats. From Peştera, it's an easy 6km ride/hike north through **Măgura** to **Zărneşti**.

A few kilometres southeast of Moieciu de Jos is **Cheia**, home to one of the region's few intact 19th-century painted churches. Wool has been manufactured in this village since the Middle Ages. Continuing south along the upper course of the Moieciu River, you reach **Moieciu de Sus**, with another pretty village church. Hiking trails into the **Bucegi Mountains** are marked from here.

Staggering views of the mountains unfold along the road signposted to Câmpulung, proffering a breathtaking panorama of rolling green hills and farmhouses teetering on ridge tops at 1290m before reaching the minuscule **Fundata**, 25km south of Bran, where you can cross-country ski or bike. On the last Sunday of August this village holds the fascinating **Mountain Festival** (Nedeia Muntelui), bringing together local artisans.

Continuing south along the same road, you come to **Podu Dâmboviţei**, home to the **Peştera Dâmbovicioarei**. This 870m-deep cave is not particularly noteworthy but the drive to it is. Sheer rock faces line either side of the road, as do villagers, who frequently stand on the roadside selling homemade cheese (*caşcaval de casă*), sausages, smoked and dried meats, plus fresh milk.

ZĂRNEŞTI
☎ 268 / pop 26,500

This windswept and rather down-and-out town at the edge of the lovely, rugged Piatra Craiului National Park gives off a bit of a Twilight Zone vibe (maybe because one of Romania's largest arms manufacturers is based here). If only Nicole Kidman had hung around a little – or at all – when she was a couple of kilometres away filming *Cold Mountain*. (One *pensiune* owner lamented, 'She had a special bus to sleep in; we didn't see her.') Locals are particularly nice (10am beer-drinkers went out of their way to help us find things) and Zărneşti provides an excellent springboard to nearby hikes.

Orientation & Information

Buses stop at a roundabout, near the post office and about 100m past the city hall and centre along Str Metropolit Ion Meţianu. The train station is about 1km east (before) the city hall.

BCR (Str Metropolit Ion Meţianu 8; ☒ 8.30am-5pm Mon-Fri, to 12.30pm Sat) has a 24-hour ATM. You'll find an area map posted outside the nearby city hall. Nearby are small food shops and internet access.

The closed information centre (a pink building 50m east of the city hall) now houses **Salvamont** (☎ 0722-553 121; Str Metropolit Ion Meţianu 17; ☒ 8am-5pm), the scraggly local rescue team who can help point your way (in English).

The supremely helpful **Piatra Craiului National Park Office** (☎ 223 165; www.pcrai.ro; Str Raului 27; ☒ 8am-5 or 6pm Mon-Fri) is in a black-log cabin about 2km towards the mountains and west of the centre. It offers guide maps and can arrange bear-watching tours (from about €50) or guides (from €22 per day). Go up the stairs in the back building. Call ahead to arrange services at weekends.

Sleeping

There's also been a recent boom in guesthouses in the village of Mogura, 8km west.

Cabana Gura Raului (☎ 0722-592 375; s/d €8.60/17.20) A bit wobbly, but set at the outset of Zărneşti Canyon at the end of town (follow Str Raului 500m past the national park office), this fading cabana offers 17 boxy rooms – clean, pink walls, two beds, shared bathrooms. The bar downstairs serves some food. The grounds are a little trashy.

Pensiune Fabius (☎ 0722-523 199; Str Dr Senchea 7; r €19) Run by a lovely family (which includes *two* priests), the five-room Fab in town offers nice semi-rustic rooms with TV and private bath, and can arrange activities and meals (€7.20, breakfast €2.90). They speak English, French and German and have a small backyard, a ping-pong table, billiards and outdoor seats. The priests don't mind if you get blitzed. From the bus stop, go a block on Str Baiulescu, then right on Str Dr Senchea (about 50m total).

Getting There & Away

The bus stop is surprisingly active. There are 14 daily buses leaving on most hours weekdays to Autogară 2 in Braşov (€0.70, one hour), about half that at weekends. About five or six daily buses head to Bran (€0.70, 40 minutes).

Five daily trains link Braşov with Zărneşti (about €1, 50 minutes), stopping at Râşnov on the way.

PIATRA CRAIULUI NATIONAL PARK

Climbers, hikers and lovers of grandiose scenery rave about Piatra Craiului and its twin-peaked Piatra Mică ('Stone of the Prince' – no jokes), marked by a large stone cross, and La Om (2238m) – which offers climbers one of Romania's greatest challenges. The 25km-long range covers 14,800 hectares from Zărneşti down to Podu Dâmboviţei and rises from the ground in near-vertical limestone towers.

The national park office in Zărneşti offers information on the diverse levels of trails, guides and trail maps. Dimap's 1:70,000 *Piatra Craiului/Bucegi/Postăvarul/Piatra Mare Ciucaş i* (€4.25) has less detail.

In May/June and September, Piatra Craiului receives heavy rainfall. Summer storms are frequent and in winter much of the mountain cannot be accessed. Avalanches are common.

Hiking

Day-hike loops from Zărneşti are an option. For one that takes four to six hours, follow blue stripe markers south of town, past Cabana Gura Râului through the **gorge** where Jude Law got himself shot in *Cold Mountain*; the trail then veers northwest to **Cabana Curmătura** (☎ 0745-995 018; r per person €6), where you can follow yellow vertical stripe markers back to Zărneşti. An alternative return splinters east on the blue-dot trail up **Piatra Mică** (a 1816m peak).

Several trails meet up behind Cabana Curmătura, from where you can follow a blue-stripe trail in a looping direction west and north to **Colţul Chiliilor** peak (1125m, two hours). The blue-stripe trail back to the northwestern edge of Zărneşti from here is relatively flat (about two hours).

More experienced hikers eye the tougher stuff, back on the western side of the range. You should have a guide who knows the area (ask at the park office or in Braşov). From northwestern Zărneşti, a road marked with red-stripe signs goes 11km to 849m **Cabana Plaiu Foii** (r per person €11). It's best to hike as the road's pretty rough. From the cabana, a very difficult trail (red stripes, four hours) goes up limestone cliffs to **La Lanturi** (or 'to the chains', as you'll need cables to navigate some of the narrow canyon walls). Nearby is the vigorous climb up **La Om**.

Getting There & Away

By far the best access point to the park is from Zărneşti. If you're hiking from Bran, the quickest route is along the gravel road to Predulut, through the village of Tohaniţa.

NORTH OF BRAŞOV

After the dramatic approach to Braşov from Bucharest, things flatten out to the north, where you'll see little towns marked with a Saxon church. Good day-trip fodder lies out here – Hărman, Prejmer and up in Székely country Sfântu Gheorghe (p164) – all of which can be combined on a day trip, with a bit of effort, on public transport.

Hărman

Quiet Hărman (Honigburg in German – literally 'honey castle'), 12km north of Braşov and 7km from Prejmer, is a small Saxon village with a 16th-century peasant **citadel** at its centre. Inside the thick walls is a 52m weathered **clock tower** and a 15th-century **church** (admission by donation; ☉ 9am-noon & 1-5pm Tue-Sun summer, 10am-4pm winter). Hit the bell near the 'Bitte Läuten' sign on the door to the left of the main door if the gate's locked. The colourful houses facing the main square are typical of the Saxon era, with large rounded doors and few windows.

A block northwest of the church, the surprising two-room **Country Hotel** (☎ 367 051; www .thecountryhotel.info; Str Mihai Viteazu 441; r/apt €60/100 🖳 🖭) isn't in the country, but the converted 100-year attic is a great rustic-meets-modern base. Bedrooms, which can be hired separately, are hard-wood affairs with nice private bathrooms and exposed wood beams above the white-washed walls. The (private) common area has blue-velvet sofas and chairs facing the TV and traditional wood-fuelled oven. The fenced-off German Shepherds may bark at your Speedos if you dip in the small swimming pool.

Frequent microbuses and maxitaxis leave from Braşov's Autogară 2 and 3 here (€0.60, 20 minutes). If you're planning to visit Prejmer on the same trip, begin at the Autogară then take a Braşov-bound bus and exit at the Hârman stop (it's a 20-minute walk from the highway to the church on the lone entry road).

You can also come by train; walk 200m northeast, cross the highway, then walk 2km to the centre.

Prejmer

Several kilometres off the main highway north from Braşov, Prejmer (Tartlau) is an unspoiled Saxon town, first settled in 1240, with a picturesque 15th-century **citadel** (admission free; ☿ 9am-5pm Mon-Fri, to 3pm Sat summer, to 3pm Mon-Sat winter) surrounding the 13th-century **Gothic Evangelical church** in its centre (near where the microbuses stop). The fortress was the most powerful peasant fortress in Transylvania – and it has much more to investigate than the similar one in Hărman. Its 272 small cells on four levels lining the inner citadel wall were intended to house the local population during Turk sieges. You can walk up to the storage space, a dark high-ceiling 'attic' that runs around the complete complex. In parts were storage spaces for each peasant family, who were required to keep most of their goods here in case of attack. You'll also see open-hole toilets (no walls, as Saxons didn't blush), as the walls were built outward to allow refuse to drop freely to the ground (or on Turks' heads). The building's 4.5m thick outer defensive walls were the thickest of all the remaining Saxon churches. Underground tunnels were finally closed off in the 1970s. These fortified churches are listed collectively as Unesco World Heritage sites.

At research time, a tourist information centre was in the works, about 50m south of the citadel.

Frequent microbuses and maxitaxis leave from Braşov's Autogară 3 (€0.60, 30 minutes). Unfortunately there was no transport between Prejmer and Hărman. It's also possible to take the train from Braşov. The closest station is the Ilieni stop; walk south on Str Nouă for 500m, turn left on Str Alexandru Ioan Cuaz; turn left at the end to reach Str Şcolii on the right. The citadel is straight ahead. It's sure easier to bus there.

Vama Buzăului

☎ 268

If you're looking for a slice of traditional life, some hiking and very fresh cheese, this one-time customs point – now a rambling riverside village, 45km southeast of Prejmer by backroads – is that. *Agroturism* has moved in (there is a handful of *pensiunes*), but life remains quite old-school – a short-lived sculpture festival was aborted in 2006, after farmers complained that the creations scared their cows! It's possible to hike to the mountains just south, and the community is lobbying to make the area a national park.

A good guesthouse is **Pensiunea Floera** (☎ 288 547; d €14), a homy *pensiune* with rugs on the floor and keep-it-real vibe; says the owner, 'I never thought about changing anything.' Please don't!

It's possible to bus to Întorsura Buzăului, 6km north; otherwise you'll need your own wheels to get here.

SAXON LAND

No trip to Transylvania is complete without a ramble through the valleys and medieval villages and fortified churches in the area Saxons colonised from the 12th century. The area lies north of the Carpathians, between Transylvania's 'big three': Braşov (p127), Sighişoara and Sibiu (p153). In 2007, Sibiu's role of EU 'capital of culture' (along with Luxembourg) has prompted an expansive – and expensive – touch-up of the German-style city, while Sighişoara's evocative cobbled citadel remains a stand-out of Transylvania. The best way out of the region – if your timing's right – is a drive over the twists-and-turns of the Transfăgărăşan Road (p154), one of communism's brightest (only?) achievements.

SIGHIŞOARA

☎ 265 / pop 32,290

Dracula was born here. And for many visitors to this dreamy, medieval citadel town, seeing where Dracula, well Vlad Ţepeş actually, made his first steps is enough to justify a quick visit. But it's hardly the end of Sighişoara, with half-a-millennium-old townhouses of bright colours overlooking hilly cobbled streets and church bells that clang in the early hours. Cute museums uncover some colourful (and treacherous) local history. The low hills that flank the town lead to pastures and forests, which are home to traditional villages that conjure past eras, as well as Saxon villages (such as Biertan and Vişcri) you can bike, hike or drive to. Yes, bus tours come in and out in summer, and even some visitors feel that a day's enough – but some days are better than others.

Settled by the Romans, the town was first documented as Castrum Sex. Saxon colonists settled here from the 12th century and built it into a thriving crafts and trading town; today, there are fewer than 500 Germans here.

TRANSYLVANIA

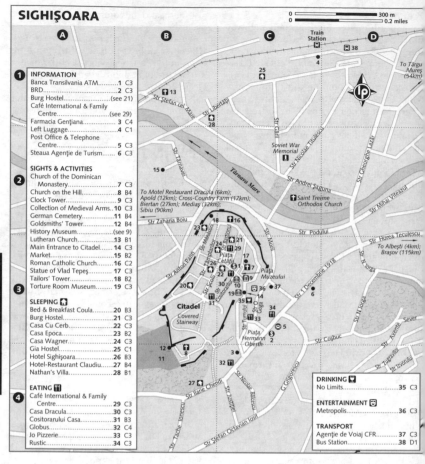

SIGHIŞOARA

0 — 300 m
0 — 0.2 miles

To Târgu Mureş (54km)

Soviet War Memorial

Saint Treime Orthodox Church

To Motel Restaurant Dracula (6km); Apold (12km); Cross-Country Farm (17km); Biertan (27km); Mediaş (32km); Sibiu (90km)

To Albeşti (4km); Braşov (115km)

Citadel

Covered Stairway

Piaţa Hermann Oberth

Sighişoara (Schässburg in German, Seges-vár in Hungarian) is in the midst of rejuvenation, prompted by a sudden influx of German investment, resulting in painted houses and new hotels and sidewalk cafés. Prince Charles, also, has played a part, rolling up his sleeves to assist with the Mihai Eminescu Trust (www .mihaieminescutrust.org), formed during the communist era to save the destruction of rural architecture.

In 2006, the municipality hired an 'announcer' – an artist/musician/teacher with traditional outfit and snareless drum to pat-pat-pat 'announcements' in various languages to passers-by (a practice borrowed from the citadel's olden days). A sample greeting: 'the gates of the citadel are open for you…welcome!'

The week-long Medieval Festival of the Arts in late July is more of a wild drinking party than anything cultural, but the colourful costumes are pretty to look at, especially through a beery daze.

For more on the Dracula myth, see p23.

Orientation

Follow Str Gării south from the train station to the unmistakably Soviet-era war memorial, where you turn left to the St Treime Orthodox church. Cross the Târnava Mare River on the footbridge here and take Str Morii to the left, then keep going all the way up to Piaţa Hermann Oberth and up into the citadel. Many of the facilities you'll want are found along a short stretch of Str 1 Decembrie 1918.

MAPS
Cartographia publishes the highly detailed, excellent *Sighişoara* fold-out map (€2.80), covering the city and environs.

Information

INTERNET ACCESS
Sighişoara is almost internet-free. If you can handle Christian pop, the basement of **Café International & Family Centre** (per hr €0.60; ☺ 8am-8pm Mon-Sat summer, 1-7pm Mon-Sat winter) is a good spot. There are also slow connections at **Burg Hostel** (per hr €0.60; ☺ 7am-midnight).

LEFT LUGGAGE
The **train station's information shed** (per day €0.90; ☺ 24hr) can hold your bags.

MEDICAL SERVICES
Farmacia Gențiana (Piața Hermann Oberth 45; ☺ 8am-8pm)

MONEY
There are numerous exchange offices lining the city's main street, Str 1 Decembrie 1918. **Banca Transilvania** (btwn Piața Cetății & Muzeului) Just an ATM and the only bank option in citadel.
BRD (Str 1 Decembrie 1918, 20; ☺ 9am-6pm Mon-Fri) 24-hour ATM.

POST & TELEPHONE
The **post office** and **telephone centre** (Str 1 Decembrie 1918, 17; ☺ 7am-8pm Mon-Fri) share the same funny yellow-panel building.

TRAVEL AGENCIES
Surprisingly, Sighişoara has no tourist information. Hotels and guesthouses can negotiate 'good' taxi drivers for a return trip to Biertan for around €17 to €20.
Café International & Family Centre (☎ 777 844; Piața Cetății 8; ☺ 8am-8pm Mon-Sat summer, 10am-6pm Mon-Sat winter) A multifunction non-profit agency (see also p147) founded by Nazarenes from Massachusetts. Doubles as a tourist office in summer (only); knows a lot

---

COMBO TICKET
It's not made clear, but you can visit the History Museum, the medieval arms collection, and the Torture Room Museum for a combined ticket price of €2.15 (about the same price as the student discounts for all three).

---

about the city, can arrange 1½-hour walking tours, hire bikes and can point you to an organic apple orchard in the hills outside town. Sales of local crafts go to help local homeless children and the elderly.
Steaua Agenție de Turism (☎ 772 499; Str 1 Decembrie 1918, 10; ☺ 9.30am-4pm Mon-Fri) Staff sells an ad-filled map of town, finds private accommodation (€10 per person per night) in the residential area northwest of the citadel, and sells fishing supplies.

Sights
Most of Sighişoara's sights are clustered in the compact old town – the delightful medieval **citadel** – perched on a hillock and fortified with a 14th-century wall, to which 14 towers and five artillery bastions were later added. Today the citadel, which is on the Unesco World Heritage list, retains just nine of its original towers (named for the guilds in charge of their upkeep) and two of its bastions. You'll have more than a couple of chances to get Dracula t-shirts and locally made brandy these days.

Entering the citadel, you pass under the massive **clock tower** (Turnul cu Ceas), which dates from 1280 and once housed the town council. Formerly the main entrance to the fortified city, the tower is 64m tall, with sturdy base walls measuring an impenetrable 2.35m. Inside, the 1648 clock is a pageant of slowly revolving 80cm-high figurines, carved from linden wood, each representing a character from the Greek-Roman pantheon: Peace bears an olive branch, Justice has a set of scales and Law wields a sword. The executioner is also present and the drum-player strikes the hour. Above stand seven figures, each representing a day of the week.

Inside the tower is the great little **History Museum** (☎ 771 108; Piața Muzeului 1; adult/child €1.50/1.10; ☺ 10am-6pm Mon, 9am-6.30pm Tue-Fri, 9am-4.30pm Sat & Sun mid-May–mid-Sep, 9am-3.30pm Tue-Fri, 10am-3.30pm Sat & Sun mid-Sep–mid-May), with small rooms that wind up to the 7th-floor look-out above the clock. On the 1st floor, don't miss the small exhibition on local hero Hermann Oberth; there are some English translations (as well as the sketch of Oberth's 'space suit'). A couple of floors up are 18th-century gingerbread wood blocks, a local tradition that dates from 1376. Above you can see the clock's famed figures, as well as the clanking innards behind.

Under the clock tower on the right (if heading out of the old town) is the small, dark

TRANSYLVANIA

LOCAL SPACE CASE

Cobblestones and Dracula we can understand, but what does Sighişoara have to do with space exploration? Heaps, it turns out. If it wasn't for one of Sighişoara's most beloved residents, space might still be 'out there'. Though he was born in Sibiu, Hermann Oberth (1894–1989), considered one of the fathers of modern astronautics and rocketry, is revered as a local boy (don't remind anyone that he only spent a few years here as a child).

Inspired by Jules Verne as a skygazing tyke, he started to design space rockets at the age of 14. Later, when studying medicine and physics in Munich, he wrote prolifically about the possibility and mechanics of space travel. Most of his dissertations were dismissed by the scientific community, but in 1929 he had what ended up being his big break: his designs were used to build model spaceships for the kitschy Fritz Lang film *Woman on the Moon*. That year, the German army launched a rocket research program. Hmm...

During WWII, he codeveloped the infamous V2 rocket for the Germans, then continued research in the US before retiring and publishing books on alternative energy sources and space exploration.

There is a Hermann Oberth Space Museum near Nuremberg, if you'd like to continue your Oberthian journey around Europe.

Torture Room Museum (admission €0.60; ☼ same as History Museum), which shows how fingers were smashed and prisoners burned with coals. The 'Spanish boot' was a happy little foot-crushing device. If it's closed, ask at the medieval arms collection for entry.

Towards Piaţa Cetăţii on the left, the small **collection of medieval arms** (adult/student €0.90/0.60; ☼ same as History Museum) has four rooms devoted to medieval helmets, shields, cross-bows, maces (aka 'whips for fight') and cannonballs. Somehow an illustration of Napoleon made the cut too.

Facing the museum is the 15th-century **Church of the Dominican Monastery** (Biserica Mănăstirii), which was closed for renovation at research time. The Gothic church became the Saxons' main Lutheran church in 1556. Classical, folk and baroque concerts have been held here in the past. Hidden away behind it is a **statue of Vlad Ţepeş**, showing the legend with a bewildered look and his trademark circa-1981 porno moustache.

Speaking of which, continuing west towards Piaţa Cetăţii, you come to the site where Vlad Ţepeş was born in 1431 and reputedly lived until the age of four. The pretty, all-renovated **Casa Dracula** is now a restaurant (see Eating, p148). Bubble-buster: the building is indeed centuries old, but has been completely rebuilt since Vlad's days.

The quiet, miniscule **Piaţa Cetăţii** is the heart of old Sighişoara. It was here that markets, craft fairs, public executions, impalings and witch trials were held.

From the square, turn left up Str Şcolii to the 172 steps of the **covered stairway** (scara acoperită), which has tunnelled its way up the hill since 1642, to the 1345 Gothic **Church on the Hill** (Biserica din Deal; ☼ mid-Apr–Oct), a 429m Lutheran church and the town's highest point. Facing its entry – behind the church when approaching from the steps – is an atmospheric, overgrown **German cemetery**.

Also behind the church are the remains of the **Goldsmiths' Tower**. The goldsmiths, tailors, carpenters and tinsmiths (the only craftsmen to have their guilds and workshops inside the citadel) existed until 1875.

From the church, head back down the hill, cross Piaţa Cetăţii, then head down Str Bastionul. At its northern end, are the **Roman Catholic church** (1896) and the **Tailors' Tower** (Turnul Cizmarilor).

Apart from their two churches in the citadel, Sighişoara's Saxon community had a third **Lutheran church**, deliberately sited well outside the city walls. The tin-spired church, sitting inauspiciously at a rail crossing just west of the train station off Str Libertăţii ('if that sermon don't knock the devil outa'em, the rattle of the trains will!'), was used in the 17th century as an isolation compound for victims of the plague and later of leprosy.

It's worth visiting the **market** on Wednesday and Saturday when Roma and villagers from outlying regions come into town on their horse-drawn wagons to sell their wares.

The drive to **Apold**, 12km south, is quite lovely.

Activities

The **Café International & Family Centre** (p145) rents bikes in summer, as do **Gia Hostel** and **Bed & Breakfast Coula**.

Cross-Country Farm (☎ 0744-500 457; www.cross -country.ro), 17km west of town, offers six-hour horse rides past traditional villages for €35 per person, or €45 for a lone rider. There are wagons for beginners and guides speak English.

Sleeping

IN THE CITADEL

Burg Hostel (☎ 778 489; www.ibz.ro; Str Bastionului 4-6; dm/s/d €7.25/11.50/17.25) Perhaps more focused on its basement lounge (rock music, internet) and restaurant, this very clean, slightly sterile hostel has nice rooms of various bed counts – all with their own private bathroom. Breakfast is €2.80.

ourpick Bed & Breakfast Coula (☎ 777 907; Str Tâmplarilor 40; r €15) Those looking for a homey budget base in the citadel will enjoy this place, an unsigned 400-year-old home run by an English-speaking family who can help arrange Saxon Land church trips, rent out bikes and sit with you at the family table in the big kitchen. There are six rooms (only one's in use in winter), and a vine-filled backyard with views to the hills northwest.

Casa Cu Cerb (Stag House; ☎ 777 349; Str Şcolii 1; s €35/d €40-50; ☒) First thing you see walking in this all-restored 1693 building is Prince Charles' mug – he stayed here a few days in 2002. It's a good choice, on the main plaza, with spacious rooms with white-washed walls, cast-iron bed frames and rattan rugs by the TV sitting area. No breakfast.

Casa Wagner (☎ 506 014; www.casa-wagner.com; Piaţa Cetăţii 7; s €40/d €45-50/ste €70) This 22-room beauty on the main square has a mix of rooms; singles are a bit cramped, but some of the others sprawl, with extras like wrought-iron candle holders, armoires, chests and antique benches. There's a back terrace and wine cellar that opens after 7pm or so. The ground-floor restaurant is quite good, often with live music in the evenings.

Casa Epoca (☎ 773 232; www.casaepoca.ro; Str Tâmplarilor 4; s/d/ste €40/50/75; ☒) On a quite central side street, the modern take on this building's 1678 roots evokes a pleasing, rustic vibe. The owner made many of the nine rooms' charmingly unfinished antique-style pieces, such as a kid's bed in a nook in the suite. Shoe-makers' stools look over a subterranean courtyard.

Hotel Sighişoara (☎ 771 000; www.sighisoarahotels .ro; Str Şcolii 4-6; s/d/apt €45/55/75; ☒ ☒) Tour groups seem to gravitate to this fine 29-room hotel with arched ceilings over cranberry carpets in faintly historic, mostly modern rooms. The basement wine cellar is a cavernous hangout spot, as is the back courtyard terrace and beauty salon.

OUTSIDE THE CITADEL

Nathan's Villa (☎ 772 546; www.nathansvilla.com; Str I libertăţii 8; dm/d €8/20) This traditionally popular choice (with free laundry and a bar) stays open from April to November only. It's 200m west of the train station.

Gia Hostel (☎ 772 486; giahouse@myx.net; Str Libertăţii 41; dm/r from €8.60/23; ☐) It backs onto the train tracks in a slightly dodgy area (about a 15-minute walk to the citadel), but this nine-room hostel has lots of good services (bike hire, car hire for €35 per day and internet access) and is good for an in-and-out, one-night stop. The rooms are a bit of a rush-job, with slapped down carpets, but two 'red rooms' go for the valentine effect. A new kitchen was in the works at last pass.

Hotel-Restaurant Claudiu (☎ 779 882; www.hotel -claudiu.com; Str Iarie Chendi 28; s/d incl breakfast €32/37; ☒) In a pinch, this 12-room modern spot, 100m west of buzzing Piaţa Hermann Oberth isn't bad. Rooms are boxy and rather uninspiring, but they're clean and come with private bathroom and breakfast.

Motel Restaurant Dracula (☎ 772 211; www.dracula .ro; r €35 & 43; ☒) On the bend of a creek, this 37-room three-complex resort on the edge of Daneş village, 7km west of town, has modern, comfy rooms with private bathroom and TV. The best are the top-floor, wooden-floored jobs in the old building – the new one (at €8.60 extra) ain't worth the extra shine in the bathroom tile. There's a pool, horses to ride, outside seating to eat brekky, and a five-room complex by a pool 5km away. It's slightly goofy (there's a painting of a hairy vampire attacking a woman), but pretty relaxing. A taxi ride here is about €4.

Eating

Cositorarului Casa (Str Cositorarilor 9; sandwiches €0.75; ☾ 9am-10pm) Near the citadel wall, this indoor/outdoor café focuses on sweets, coffee and brandy – but has a few sandwiches.

Jo Pizzerie (Piaţa Hermann Oberth; mains €1.75-5.75; ☾ 10am-midnight) Jo's huge terrace overlooks the busy square, with old tower views. The setting's great but the pizza's just OK. Focus on beer and ice cream (€1.75).

Café International & Family Centre (☎ 777 844; Piaţa Cetăţii 8; snacks €2-3.50; ☯ 8am-8pm Mon-Sat summer, 10am-6pm Mon-Sat winter) This two-room café, with chairs spilling onto the square in summer, is the perfect lunch spot, with daily made, mostly vegetarian fare, including quiche (€2), lasagne (€3) and lemon meringue pie (€0.85). No alcohol is served but you can bring beer to the outside tables.

Rustic (Str Decembrie 1, 7; mains €2.90-7.20; ☯ 8am-midnight) Wide-open windows hardly make a dent of light in this dark wood-and-brick 'man's man' bar-restaurant down from the citadel. Eggs are served all day, plus the usual grilled meats.

Casa Dracula (☎ 771 596; Str Cositorarilor 5; mains €4.30-8; ☯ 10am-midnight) The food can't compete with the restaurants in Casa Wagner or Hotel Sighişoara, but this three-room candlelit, totally remade restaurant is too tempting to pass by – breaded brains or juicy grills of pork or beef in Dracula's first home? Or maybe just a red wine in the bar.

The daily **market** (Str Târnavei) has a good selection of fruits, vegetables and cheese. **Globus** (Str Ilarie Chendi 4; ☯ 24 hr) is a small, but well-stocked grocery store.

Entertainment

Occasional classical concerts are held in the city's churches; check for posted adverts.

No Limits (☎ 518 961; Str Turnului 1; ☯ 8pm-4am) This slightly upmarket disco is to the right of the arched entry to the citadel, just below the Clock Tower. It borders on tackiness but gets steamy on weekends.

Metropolis (☎ 0740-025 907; Str Turnului; ☯ 10pm-late) Down the zigzag footpath left of the clock tower (from inside the citadel), this cavernous pink-walled joint has a large stage for jam sessions and themed dance nights. Stop by if you hear rehearsal and see if the manager's practising band has decided on a name yet.

Getting There & Away

About a dozen trains connect Sighişoara with Braşov (€3 to €8, two hours), nine of which (none of the slow ones) go on to Bucharest (€8 to €12, 4½ hours). Five daily trains go to Cluj-Napoca (€7.40 to €10, 3½ hours), while three passenger trains go to Odorheiu Secuiesc (€1, 1¾ hours).

You'll need to change trains in Mediaş to reach Sibiu (€1.85, 2½ hours), but the four daily trains are timed for easy transfers. Three daily trains go to Budapest (€38, nine hours), and the night train has a sleeper (from €50).

Buy tickets at the **train station** (☎ 771 886), which is a shambles, or at the central **Agenţie de Voiaj CFR** (☎ 771 820; Str Goga 6a; ☯ 8am-3pm Mon-Fri).

Next to the train station on Str Libertăţii, the **bus station** (☎ 771 260) sends buses of various size and colour to Bistriţa (€4.30, three hours, three daily), Budapest (€20, eight hours, two weekly), Făgăraş (€3.40, three hours, one daily), Odorheiu Secuiesc (€1.75, 2½ hours, one daily) and Sibiu (€3.50, 2½ hours, five daily). Maxitaxis pass by every couple of hours for Târgu Mureş (1½ hours) and Braşov (2½ hours). There are regular services to Daneş and Mediaş.

Getting Around

Taxis greet incoming trains; it should be about €1.50 to reach the citadel. Cars have to pay €2.90 to get in the citadel – taxis do not.

Gia Hostel (p147) hires cars for €35 per day. **Mokai Rent a Car** (☎ 777 113, 0744-605 816; www.rent acarsighisoara.com) charges about €40 per day, but often seems to need several days to track one down.

FORTIFIED SAXON CHURCHES

One of Romania's highlights is here in the belly of Saxon Land (aka the Târnave plateau) – stretching more or less 120km between Hwy 1 (between Braşov and Sibiu) to the south, and Hwy 13 (Braşov to Sighişoara) and Hwy 14 (Sighişoara to Sibiu) to the north. The rolling hills here are filled with fortified Saxon churches in towns that can easily feel lost in centuries past. Bus service is practically nonexistent; visitors come by hire car, taxi, bike or tour bus. If you get stares as you pull in, don't take it personally – they're just wondering who are the folks with a car!

A couple of highlights get nearly all the visits, notably Biertan and Viscri. It's best to just explore, particularly on weekends, when churches are usually open. On other days you may have to track down the caretaker to get entry (which is often possible).

Bring your own food or eat in Biertan or Mediaş – you won't find sushi bars (or any restaurant) in places like Aţel. Public transport here is limited – part of the charm is driving on your own.

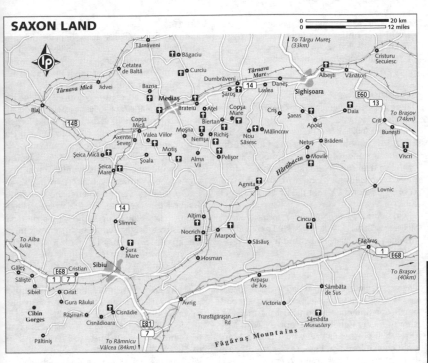

Much of the restoration in the area has been carried out by the Mihai Eminescu Trust.

History

In 1123 Hungarian King Geza II invited Saxons — mainly from the Franken region in western Germany – to settle here. In the 15th and 16th centuries, following the increased threat of Turkish attacks on their towns, the settlements were strengthened with bulky city walls and fortified churches. Defensive towers in the churches served as observation posts. Town entrances were guarded with a portcullis that could be quickly lowered.

Many Saxons left Romania during the communism period; some towns' villas became homes for the Roma population.

Biertan

☎ 269 / pop 1500

The undisputed king of the FSCVs (unofficially, Fortified Saxon Church Villages), and still far from developed, lovely Biertan (Birthälm is the Saxon name), 27km southwest of Sighişoara, is home to the region's grandest Saxon doublewalled church, which offers

some tasty views over terraced hill tops lined with vineyards. Plus you can have lunch.

Biertan hosts a Saxon Festival in mid-September.

SIGHTS

Biertan's fantastic 15th-century **church** (admission €1.30; ⏲ 10am-7pm Apr-Oct, closed Nov-Mar) was the site of the Lutheran bishop from 1572 to 1867 and has been listed as a Unesco World Heritage site since 1993. Its Viennese-style altar (1483–1550) has 28 panels and its three rings of walls stand up to 12m tall. This is the only fortified church in the region that holds regular services (once a month).

Near the altar in the church is the sacristy that once held treasure behind its formidable door with an even more formidable lock: it has 19 locks in one, and is such a marvel of engineering, it won first prize at the Paris World Expo in 1900. Inside the grounds are many buildings of interest, including a small bastion, which is famous in local lore: couples wanting a divorce were supposedly locked in here for two weeks as a last attempt to resolve differences. There was only one bed and one set of cutlery. The method has been so successful that only one couple decided to go through with divorce in 400 years!

You can't climb the towers, but there are plenty of views over the walls.

SLEEPING

There are a dozen guesthouses around town – not all are signed.

Pensiune Omi (☎ 868 119; Str Vlaicu 1; r incl breakfast €10) Above an old-time pharmacy in a 16th-century home on the main road 50m south of the central square, this simple three-room *pensiune* has homy rooms with shared bathroom – and one TV that the first arrivals get dibs on.

Casa Dornröschen (☎ 244 165; www.biertan.net; Str Gheorghe Cosbul 25; s/d/tr €19/29/39) These rather modern rooms are just behind the back citadel wall.

EATING

Unglerus Medieval Restaurant (Str 1 Decembrie, 1; mains from €4; ☺ 10am-10pm supposedly daily) Heart-shaped eggs over polenta surrounded by a moat of stewed meats – that's the average fare at this three-hall Gothic eatery, which is also your only choice in town. Eggs are served all day. Find it next to the church fort entry.

GETTING THERE & AWAY

Four daily buses connect Biertan with Mediaş (€1.20, 40 minutes). You should be able to hire a taxi from Sighişoara for about €20 for the day.

Around Biertan

Five kilometres south of Biertan is the small village of **Richiş**, likewise dominated by a fantastic stone church with a brook running by. From Biertan you can also head east for 3km along a dirt track to **Copşa Mare** (Grosskopisch), a quaint town in a tight valley. The church there dates from the early 14th century and was fortified to fend off Turkish and Tartar invasions in the 16th century, but failed to fend off Székely troops, who attacked the village in 1605 and pillaged the church.

A rough dirt road leads northwest from Biertan to **Aţel** (Heteldorf), but it's far easier to reach by looping back via the main highway. The church here, dating from the 14th century, was heavily fortified in 1471. In 1959 the northern tower was levelled to uncover a secret tunnel leading to a neighbouring farmstead.

Mediaş

Industry lives! Mediaş' dusty, hopeless-looking factories and power plants are a visual turn-off for new arrivals, but its centre scrappily evokes the town's medieval past and it's not a terrible base for Saxon Land day trips.

The fortified cream-coloured **Evangelical Church of St Margaret** (☺ 10am-3pm Mon-Fri) dominates the old town, just east of Piaţa Regele Ferdinand I. A church was built here in the 13th century, but this one was built in 1447. Note the altar, dating from 1485, which is considered one of Transylvania's most precious pieces of medieval Saxon art.

On Mediaş' central square, the new **Hotel Traube** (☎ 844 898; hotel.traube@dafora.ro; Piaţa Regele Ferdinand I 16; s/d/apt €46/57/130; ⊠ ⌂) has modern rooms in a bright yellow historic building – the apartment is massive, with a piano and towering wood-beamed ceilings.

It has little food, but the **Art Café** (Str Duca 44; ☺ 8am-midnight Mon-Fri, 10am-midnight Sat & Sun), a few blocks west (on the highway), occupies a medieval citadel tower. You can also find pizza on Piaţa Regele Ferdinand I.

Mediaş' bus station (300m west of the centre) sends four daily buses to Biertan and six to Sibiu. The train station, 100m west, has left-luggage facilities and trains to Sibiu, Cluj-Napoca and Sighişoara.

Around Mediaş

Bazna (Baassen in German), a small village first settled in 1302, is northwest of Mediaş (head north towards Târnăveni for 10km then west for another 5km). Its late-Gothic St Nicholas' Church was built at the start of the 16th century on the ruins of a 14th-century original. Its highlight is the three pre-Reformation bells (1404) in the church tower. From 1842 onwards the village developed as a small spa resort, following the discovery of natural springs, which released sulphurous gases.

Back on the Târnăveni road, go another 5km north, then take the road to 'Delenii' for 6km to reach **Băgaciu** (Bogeschdorf in German). The pre-Reformation, late-Gothic altar in its church, restored in Vienna in 1896, is considered to be the best-preserved Saxon church altar. Heading 4km south along the dirt track from here, **Curciu** (Kirtsch in German) has a decorative stone frieze above its 14th-century church's west door lined with apes and other animals.

TRANSYLVANIA

ROMANIA'S UGLIEST TOWN

If you've had enough of Transylvania's gorgeous self, stop in at **Copşa Micǎ** (pop 5200), 13km west of Mediaş. Blackened, rotting factory shells litter this haggard, one-time filthy industrial town, which serves as the junction between Sibiu and Sighişoara.

Throughout the communist period, carbon black factories spewed out soot all year until 1993; lead levels in factories often broke 1000 times the acceptable level. Evidence was everywhere: sheep wool and hanging laundry was blackened, the town recorded Europe's highest infant mortality rates, and two-thirds of children who survived showed signs of mental illness.

Euro-standard filters are now used on the metal works plant, and white snow was seen for the first time in decades. Cleaner now, it's still a sad place (no offence to the locals).

About 10km south from Mediaş on the way to Agnita, is **Moşna** (Meschen in German), with a 15th-century church built in late-Gothic style and an eight-storey bell tower.

About 5km south of Copşa Micǎ along a dirt track is **Valea Viilor** (Wurmloch in German). The village, dating from 1263, has a quaint fortified church, which was raised at the end of the 15th century and is surrounded by 1.5m-thick walls. The building is on Unesco's list of World Heritage sites.

Şeica Micǎ (Kleinschelken in German), first settled in 1316, is 3km west of a turn-off 11km south of Copşa Micǎ on the road to/from Sibiu. The village was engulfed by fire several times during the 16th century, but remarkably its local church, built in 1414, survived. Its beautiful baptismal font is late-Gothic (1447) in style and cast from iron.

Viscri

pop 450

Happy to play second fiddle to Biertan, locals in this quiet, fantastically Saxon town (about 30km southeast of Sighişoara) hope the 7km bumpy dirt road (it feels much longer than 7km) that keeps most tour buses away never gets paved. Up from town is a fortified church that Saxon colonists wrested from its Székely builders in 1185.

Attached to the one-room **fortified church** is a dark tower, with a rather frightening, open, creaking stairway leading to the top; if that's too scary, you can climb the bastions for lovely views of the Viscri valley too. It's recognised as a Unesco World Heritage site. About 25 Saxons still live in town.

None of the 10 (and counting) Viscri *pensiunes* have signs yet. Arrange a room in a traditional Saxon home by calling **Carolina Fernolend** (☎ 0740-145 397; Str Principǎla 13), who speaks English and can arrange accommoda-

tion for about €20 per person including meals and homemade wine. Plan ahead in July and August and ask for a traditional room, with a 200-year-old 'Saxon bed', which is an oversized cabinet with a pull-out mattress! Carolina can help arrange hikes and trips to visit shepherds or unlock the church. Most places have pit toilets – this is real-deal Saxon living. Shortly before our visit, allegedly, the Duke of Luxembourg got pissy about the conditions for his royal bowel movement.

You will need your own transport to get here.

FǍGǍRAŞ MOUNTAINS

☎ 268 / pop 40,100

Looking over bucolic Saxon Land and the zooming-by traffic of Hwy 1 between Braşov and Sibiu, the Fǎgǎraş Mountains look like an evil, impenetrable wall of doom, something like a *Lord of the Rings* outtake. The Transfǎgǎrǎşan Road – a real Transylvania highlight for those hiring wheels – sometimes opens only in early June, after the last of the snows melt from the road, closing by early October. Hikers with gusto (and strong knees) prefer mountain hikes here to the rest of Transylvania.

Access points from the north – namesake town and Victoria – are situated outside the mountains and lack any sort of mountain-air quaint punch.

Fǎgǎraş

☎ 268 / pop 35,400

Not pretty, but lively in its own way, Fǎgǎraş (fuh-guh-*rash*) town is 25km east of the start of the Transfǎgǎrǎşan Road, but has more services than any access point north of the mountain range. Maxitaxis stop on the main road, B-dul Unirii (a '70s-modern functional strip of white buildings), a block southeast of

TRANSYLVANIA

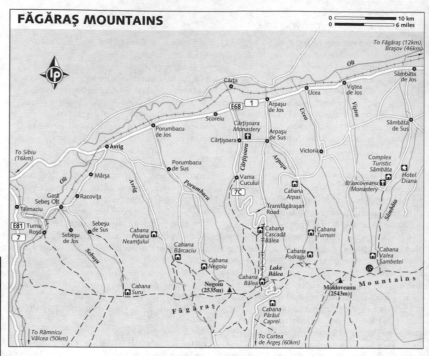

FĂGĂRAŞ MOUNTAINS

TRANSYLVANIA

the historic centre (Piaţa Republicii), where you'll find a bank and internet access, and 1km north of the train station and a very quiet bus station.

SIGHTS

The only attraction is a real-live, moat-surrounded castle, a block north of the roundabout, which houses the **Valeriu Literat Fâgâraş Museum** (☎ 211 862; adult/student €1.20/0.30; ☺ 8am-6pm summer, to 4pm Tue-Sun winter). The collection spans the town's history, highlighted by the 20th-century sculpture of local artist Virgil Fulicea. The castle was originally built in the 13th century, but what you see dates from the mid-17th century.

SLEEPING & EATING

A hotel was under construction at the northwestern edge of the roundabout at last pass. The best of the few present options is **Pensiunea Diana** (☎ 216 887; www.pensiuneadiana.ro; Piaţa Republicii; d €23-34/tr €40), a 15-room guesthouse with standard rooms facing the main square.

The best restaurant in town is **The Corner** (☎ 210 361; B-dul Unirii 1; mains €3.40-5.80; ☺ 10am-

midnight Mon-Sat, 2-11pm Sun), a modern pea-green place with castle views on the southwestern corner of the roundabout.

GETTING THERE & AWAY

From the roundabout (near the Universal Negoiu store, aka 'Big Store'), microtaxis go to Braşov (€2.10, one hour) and Sibiu (€2.10, one hour). Just east of the castle entrance, one daily bus leaves for Sâmbata de Sus (€1.10, 40 minutes) and Victoria (€1.40, one hour). Fâgâraş' train station sends half a dozen daily trains to Braşov and Sibiu, stopping at Ucea on the way. Taxis linger at the roundabout.

Victoria

☎ 268 / pop 10,900

Built to house a new breed of chemical factory workers in communist times, Victoria will disappoint travellers looking for an alpine flavour to their mountain base. Its rows of matching housing blocks jolt those who've been travelling untouched Saxon towns to the north. But it's friendly, and the best close base to the Transfâgâraşan Road.

HIKING FROM VICTORIA

If coming by train, one of the best stations to get off at is Ucea (59km from Sibiu), from where you can catch one of seven daily buses to **Victoria** or walk the 6km. From Victoria you can hike to **Cabana Turnuri** (1520m) in about six hours. The scenery is stunning once you start the ascent. The next morning head for **Cabana Podragu** (2136m), three or four hours south.

Cabana Podragu is a good base if you want to climb **Mt Moldoveanu** (2543m), Romania's highest peak. It's a tough uphill climb, but the views from the summit are unbeatable. Otherwise, hike eight hours east, passing by Mt Moldoveanu, to **Cabana Valea Sambetei** (1407m). From Cabana Valea Sambetei you can descend to the railway in Ucea, via Victoria, in a day.

On the central square, **Hotel Central** (☎ 241 609; www.hotelrestaurantcentral.ro; Str Libertăţii 20; r/apt €29/46) is a 24-room makeover of a '70s beast. Staff (if you can speak with them) can arrange pick-up from Ucea or tours into the mountains. It's standard but fine. There are *cazare* options available for less. The Central has a restaurant. Its DJ area is decorated with bear pelts and taxidermy flourishes.

Victoria is a walkable 6km south of the Ucea train station, which sees four or five trains between Sibiu and Braşov. A lone bus connects Victoria with Făgăraş. Buses supposedly meet all trains at Ucea. The bus station is at the southwestern edge of town, 200m along the looping road from the hotel.

Sâmbăta

At the foot of the mountains (20km by paved roads from Victoria, or 10km by dirt road), the Sâmbăta complex is home to one of Romania's wealthiest monasteries and a key access point for Făgăraş hikes. Ceauşescu liked it enough to build a villa here on the monastery grounds.

Popular with Romanians, the lavish 1696 **Sâmbăta Monastery** (aka Brâncoveanu Monastery; ☎ 241 237; admission free; ☼ 8am-6pm) is named for its original founder, Wallachian prince Constantin Brâncoveanu (r 1688–1714), who built the Orthodox monastery at the 16th-century site. Seen by the Habsburgs as the last bastion of Orthodoxy in the Făgăraş region, the

monastery was practically destroyed. Now 40 monks live here.

In 1926 restoration work started on Sâmbăta's ruins, finishing in 1936. Its fame today is derived from its workshops of glass icons, run by the monastery's monks, residents since the early 1990s. There is a **glass icon museum** (☼ 8am-5pm Mon-Sat, 2-4pm Sun May-Oct), with lovely examples of 18th-century glass icons and other relics.

SLEEPING

There are several signed *pensiunes* with rooms for around €25.

Complex Turistic Sâmbăta (☎ 241 927; per person €10; ☼ May-Sep) Just south of the monastery entrance, this plain collection of a dozen cabanas – with open-air bar-restaurant – is a popular start/stop point for Făgăraş hikers.

Academia Sâmbăta (☎ 241 494; r from €20) The monastery's slick rooms are in an adjoining complex with marble entry.

Hotel Diana (☎ 241 900; www.hoteldiana.ro; s/d €37/43) This is a pale-yellow hotel with 40 business-oriented rooms. It has a fitness centre, sauna and deck restaurant.

GETTING THERE & AWAY

The complex isn't convenient to train or bus stations. Sâmbăta is 9km south of Sâmbăta de Sus village, where roads go west to Victoria, or north to Sâmbăta de Jos village on Hwy 1 and on to Făgăraş (26km northeast of Sâmbăta de Sus).

SIBIU

☎ 269 / pop 170,000

Trailing Sighişoara, Braşov and Cluj-Napoca in travellers' appeal, Sibiu was once the king of the Transylvanian Saxon towns, serving as capital and dominating cultural activity. It still revels in the latter. Now, Sibiu is an EU-designated 'Capital of Culture' (along with Luxembourg), with year-long events putting lovely Sibiu on the map for even more visitors. The town is certainly enchanting enough on its own, with a just-scrubbed centre, newly cobblestoned squares and pedestrian malls, and the unique 'eyelid' rooftop windows looking over pastel-painted buildings.

Founded on the site of the former Roman village of Cibinium, Sibiu (Hermannstadt to the Saxons, Nagyszében to Hungarians) has always been one of the leading cities of Transylvania. During the peak of Saxon influence,

THE LONG & WINDING ROAD

Built out of Ceauşescu's fanatic zeal to conquer nature, the Transfăgărăşan Road (the 7C), Romania's highest asphalted road, provides an unforgettable experience behind the wheel. Boldly charging up and down one of Romania's highest mountains, this two-lane road sometimes has the narrowest of shoulders separating it from the edge of a cliff. Driving its length is an adventure in itself, with breathtaking scenery around every one of the dozens of twists and turns.

Why A Road?

The road – probably Ceauşescu's most (only?) celebrated project – was built in the 1970s over the course of 4½ short years (main stretches of it could only be worked on in the summer months). While the scheme fits well within Ceauşescu's overall megalomania, he also had more practical reasons for building it. Though other routes east and west of here cut an easier north–south route, he thought it wise to secure the Carpathian crossing at the traditional border between Wallachia and Transylvania, just in case the Soviets invaded (as they had Czechoslovakia in 1968).

And so the decree was ordered, and monumental work began: on the northern side alone, six million kilograms of dynamite were used to blast out 3.8 million cu metres of rock. Unofficially, 38 overworked soldiers died in accidents during its hasty construction. It was opened with great fanfare on 20 September 1974.

The Drive

Running from Piteşti via Curtea de Arges in the south to Hwy 1 in the north (118km in all), the Transfăgărăşan Road is most commonly accessed from the northern end, where a 35km drive will take you up to the haunting glacial Lake Bâlea (2034m), where even in midsummer there is snow.

Sibiu had some 19 guilds, each representing a different craft, within the sturdy city walls protected by 39 towers and four bastions. Under the Habsburgs from 1703 to 1791 and again from 1849 to 1867, Sibiu served as the seat of the Austrian governors of Transylvania. Much remains from this colourful history. In 2000 Johannis Klaus of the German Democratic Forum was elected mayor and has remained hugely popular ever since, placing the city once again under German leadership.

Orientation

The heart of Sibiu is three interlocking squares, Piaţas Mare, Huet and Mică. The pedestrianised Str Nicolae Bălcescu is the main artery running northeast into Piaţa Mare. The lower Old Town lies to the north of the main square.

MAPS

There are several fold-out city maps available including *Amco's Sibiu City & County Plan* (€3.40) and Stiefel's *Sibiu* (€2.50).

Information

The free biweekly *Şapte Seri* (www.sapteseri.ro) is a helpful Romanian listings booklet.

BOOKSHOPS

Librăria Humanitas (☎ 211 434; Str Nicolae Bălcescu 16; ☷ 10am-7pm Mon-Fri, 11am-5pm Sat) Best bookshop in town, with lots of maps.

Librăria Schiller (Piaţa Mare 7; ☷ 8am-3pm Mon-Fri) Good source for maps and many German-language titles on area history.

CULTURAL CENTRES

American Centre & Library (☎ 216 061; B-dul Victoriei 5-7)

British Council Centre & Library (☎ 211 056; bcu .britanica@ulbsibiu.ro; B-dul Victoriei 5-7; ☷ 8am-4pm Mon, Wed & Fri, 11am-8pm Tue & Thu) Organises events and has a reading room.

German Cultural Centre & Library (☎ 216 062, ext 124; B-dul Victoriei 5-7; ☷ 8am-7pm Mon-Thu, to 4pm Fri)

EMERGENCY

Salvamont (☎ 216 477, 0745-140 144; Str Nicolae Bălcescu 9; ☷ 8am-4pm Mon-Fri) Provides 24-hour emergency rescue service for hikers and skiers in trouble.

INTERNET ACCESS

Click (Str Ocnei 11; per hr €0.45; ☷ 9-2am Mon-Fri, 10-2am Sat, 2pm-2am Sun)

Schuponet (Str Lupas 21; per hr €0.45; ☷ 24hr)

Starting from Hwy 1 in the north, the drive gets interesting at Km12, when the road starts to sharply incline and begins a series of jagged turns through the lush forest. Deer are now more of a worry than cows or horse-drawn carts.

As you keep climbing, the trees start to shrink and thin out, their lifting veil replaced by unfolding views of sheer rock face. By Km20, your ears are popping. At Km22, you arrive at the *cascada* (waterfalls). The 360-degree panoramic views here are stunning; walls of mountains surround the area, and the distant waterfalls' slash of white appears like a lightning bolt in a grey sky. There are souvenir stands, a restaurant and the **Cabana Bâlea Cascada** (☎ 524 255), as well as a **cable car** (one way €2.90; ☿ 8am-5pm), which whisks you up to Lake Bâlea. Alternatively, follow the scenic blue-cross trail (2½ hours).

The remaining 13km up to Lake Bâlea is a maze of razor-sharp zigzags hanging over precipices framing breathtaking views.

The climax is Lake Bâlea, hovering like a mirror among the rocks, sometimes shrouded by clouds that come billowing over the peak above it. **Cabana Bâlea** (☎ 524 277) is here, one of the pricier cabanas in Romania, but one of the nicest as well. There's a decent restaurant and a few souvenir stands. The temperature here is easily near zero, even if it's steaming hot at the foot of the mountain, and the vegetation is minimal and miniature.

No public transport follows this route, which is closed from October to May (roughly). Some bikers and hikers walk up the road, but it's a maniacal venture, not to mention hazardous for the cars that must already be driven at a snail's pace.

After an 887m-long tunnel through rock under the Palţinu ridge, the road descends the (less impressive) south side along the Arges Valley. After re-entering forest, just when you think the fun is over, the road suddenly hugs the shores of the picturesque Lake Vidraru and crosses a 165m-high arched dam (1968). Beyond the lake, just off the road, is the Poienari Citadel, the real Dracula's castle (where Vlad Ţepeş ruled; see p105).

TRANSYLVANIA

LEFT LUGGAGE
Train Station (per day €0.85; ☿ 24hr) In 'ticket shed' across from station.

MEDICAL SERVICES
Farmasib (Str Nicolae Bălcescu 53; ☿ 7am-9pm Mon-Fri, 8am-9pm Sat & Sun)
Nippur-Pharm (Str Nicolae Bălcescu 5; ☿ 9am-7pm Mon-Fri, 9.30am-2pm Sat)

MONEY
ATMs are located all over the centre as well as in most hotels. The **Banca Comercială Română** (Str Nicolae Bălcescu 11; ☿ 8.30am-5.30pm Mon-Fri, to 12.30pm Sat) changes travellers cheques and gives cash advances.

POST
Post office (Str Mitropoliei 14; ☿ 7am-8pm Mon-Fri, 8am-1pm Sat)

TOURIST INFORMATION
For information on Sibiu's role as a 'cultural capital of Europe' in 2007, check www.sibiu 2007.ro.

A pioneer in self-organisation, the can-do **Tourist Information Centre** (☎ 208 913; www.sibiu .ro; Piaţa Mare 2; ☿ 9am-5pm Mon-Sat, 10am-1pm Sun) is slated to take over a primo spot in the ground floor of the new city hall for 2007 – that's true commitment to helping travellers. Staff provides events calendars and bus schedules, and can also book accommodation. It plans to have free exhibitions and project 24-hour videos of attractions in and around Sibiu.

TRAVEL AGENCIES
Carpathian Active Travel (☎ 0727-851 466, 101 167; www.reky-travel.de; Piaţa Mare 12; ☿ 9am-6pm Mon-Fri, 10am-3pm Sat May-Oct) Well-organised travel agent geared mostly to German visitors. Offers day trips to hang with shepherds or to Biertan (around €40 per person, including guide, transport and lunch).
Casa Luxemburg (☎ 216 854; www.kultours.ro; Piaţa Mică 16; ☿ 9am-9pm) Travel agent offering loads of city tours (€6 to €15) and day trips (€25 to €50); has a useful free map of the centre too.

Sights
Visitors with only a day should be able to fit in a look-see around the Old Town and a trip out to the Museum of Traditional Folk Civilisation (p158), 5km south.

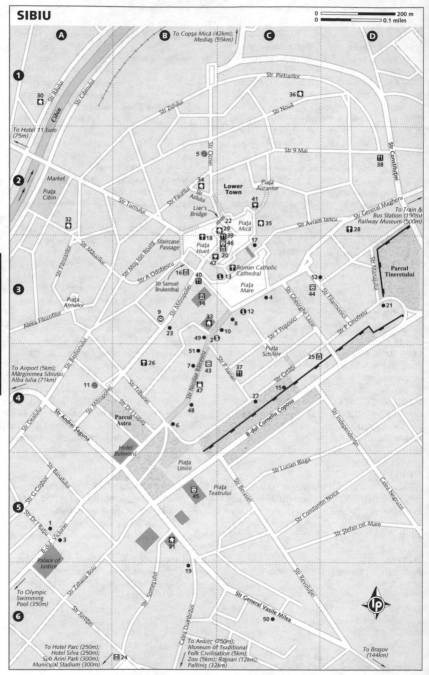

SIBIU

AROUND PIAŢA MARE

The centre of the old walled city, the expansive Piaţa Mare is a good start for exploring Sibiu. Climb to the top of the former **Council Tower** (Turnul Sfatului; admission €0.30; 10am-6pm), which links Piaţa Mare with its smaller sister square, Piaţa Mică. Clock clanks inside the white tower (1588) add to the views. It was originally built in 1370, but collapsed during a 1586 earthquake (killing a mural painter).

The **Brukenthal Museum** (217 691; Piaţa Mare 4-5; adult/child €1.80/0.90; 10am-5pm Tue-Sun) is the oldest (and likely) finest art gallery in Romania. Founded in 1817, the museum is in the baroque palace (1785) of Baron Samuel Brukenthal (1721–1803), former Austrian governor. There are excellent collections of 16th- and 17th-century Flemish, Italian, Dutch and Austrian paintings, including a giant painting of Sibiu from 1808. The floor filled with folk art, Romanian art and silverware was under renovation at research time.

Perhaps the square's most impressive building, however, is the new **city hall** (Banca Agricola; Piaţa Mare 2). Just west of here is the lovely **Primăria Municipiului** (1470), now the **City History Museum** (Str Mitropoliei 2), which was closed at research time but planned to re-open by mid-2007.

Nearby, on Piaţa Huet, is the Gothic **Evangelical Church** (9am-3pm Mon-Fri, 10am-4pm Sat, 11am-4pm Sun), built between 1300 and 1520,

its great five-pointed tower visible from afar. Don't miss the four magnificent baroque funerary monuments on the upper nave on the north wall, and the 1772 organ with 6002 pipes (it's Romania's largest). The tomb of Mihnea Vodă cel Rău (Prince Mihnea the Bad), son of a certain Vlad Ţepeş, is in the closed-off section behind the organ (ask for entry; it's the first of 67 tombstones). This prince, who ruled Wallachia from 1507 to 1510, was murdered on the square in front of the church after attending a service in March 1510. You can climb the **church tower** (admission €0.90) – ask for entry at Casa Luxemburg.

Housed in the nearby Piaţa Mică pharmacy (opened in 1600), the **Pharmaceutical Museum** (218 191; adult/child €1.20/0.60; 10am-6pm Tue-Sun) is a three-room collection packed with pills and powders, old microscopes and scary medical instruments (such as a 17th-century bone saw). Some exhibits highlight Samuel Hahnemann, a founder of homeopathy in the 1770s (Romania was one of Europe's first countries to legitimise the use of giving small doses of a disease's symptoms in order to fight the disease itself).

Named for a 19th-century collector from Sibiu, the great **Franz Binder Museum of World Ethnology** (218 195; Piaţa Mică 11; adult/child €1/0.45; 9am-5pm Tue-Sun) has an unexpectedly rich collection of North and Central African pieces (including a 2000-year-old mummy), picked

TRANSYLVANIA

TRANSYLVANIA

up by Franz during his 10-year stay in Egypt and Sudan. Temporary exhibitions include displays of Inuit art from Nunavut, Canada.

Heading northeast from Piaţa Mică, you come to the **St Ursuline Church**. Founded by Dominican monks in the 15th century, it was later transformed into a school, then turned over to the Ursuline order in 1728.

LOWER TOWN

To reach the lower town from Piaţa Mică, you can walk along the road that goes under the **Iron Bridge** (1859). The bridge's nickname is Liar's Bridge, after the tricky merchants who met here to trade and the young lovers who declared their 'undying' love on it.

While the lower town has less sights per se, it makes for a great strolling area. Here you can see many houses sporting eyeball-style windows popping out of red-tiled rooftops, a style particular to Sibiu. Enchanting courtyards and decorated garage doors and gates are also plentiful, particularly around little **Piaţa Aurarilor** (Goldsmith's Square).

STR MITROPOLIEI & OLD CITY WALLS

Str Mitropoliei extends southwest from Piaţa Huet. The standout feature is the 1906 **Orthodox Cathedral**, a miniature copy of Istanbul's Hagia Sofia. The street is lined with memorial plaques to Romanian notables who stayed there, however briefly. The **Memorandumists plaque** (Str Mitropoliei 19) honours the Transylvanian leaders of the Romanian National Party who addressed a memorandum to the emperor Franz Joseph in Vienna in 1892, calling for an end to discrimination against Romanians. In an apt response, 29 of their members were convicted of agitating against the state and imprisoned.

The influential Transylvanian Association for Romanian Literature & Culture, known as Astra, was founded in 1861 at Str Mitropoliei 20, in protest at the intense Magyarisation of Transylvania in the mid-19th century. Astra's nationalist calls for Romanians to stand up for their liberty and identity were voiced in *Tribuna*, Transylvania's first Romanian newspaper, written and printed in Sibiu from 1884. The group is memorialised by **Parcul Astra**, the quiet park near the end of the street.

CITY WALLS

South of Piaţa Mare, Str Cetăţii lines a section of the old city walls, constructed during the 16th century. As in Braşov, different guilds protected each of the 39 towers. Walk north up Str Cetăţii past a couple – the **Potters Tower** (Turnul Olarilor) and **Carpenters Tower** (Turnul Dulgherilor) – to reach the **Natural History Museum** (☎ 213 156; Str Cetăţii 1; adult/child €1.45/0.60; ❧ 9am-5pm Tue-Sat), an average collection of stuffed animals that dates from 1849.

Further north, the street curls around the **Haller Bastion**, which was named after the 16th-century city mayor Petrus Haller. When Sibiu was hit by the plague, holes were drilled through the walls to enable corpses to be evacuated more quickly from the city. The bastion was consequently dubbed the 'gate of corpses'.

OUTSIDE THE CENTRE

The so-called **Railway Museum** (Muzeul Locomotivei cu Abur; Str Dorobanţilor 22; admission negotiable; ❧ approx 7am-3pm Mon-Fri) is an open-air collection of a couple of dozen old trains right off the tracks. Don't pay any more than the posted €0.45 ticket price. Alternatively, the friendly depot worker in the hut next door happily explains (in limited English) how trains are managed and maintained; sit with him and chat a while. Get there by walking south from the train station; it's across the tracks, 300m south.

A 15-minute walk southwest of the centre, the **Museum of Hunting Arms & Trophies** (Muzeul de Arme şi Trofee de Vânătoare; ☎ 217 873; Str Şcoala de Înot 4) was under renovation at research time, but should have its collection of stuffed heads ready to devour by now. At the southern end of this street is the 21-hectare **Sub Arini Park** filled with tree-lined avenues, beautifully laid-out flower beds, a tennis court and swimming pool (open from May to September). There is also a **Municipal Stadium**, where Sibiu's football team plays.

Sibiu's top highlight is some 5km from the centre. The large **Museum of Traditional Folk Civilisation** (Muzeul Civilizaţiei Populare Tradiţionale Astra; ☎ 242 599; Calea Răşinarilor 14; adult/child €3.50/1.75; ❧ 10am-6pm Tue-Sun, to 8pm in good weather) is a sprawling open-air museum with 120 traditional dwellings, mills and churches brought from around the country. Many are signed in English, with maps showing where they came from; they're situated in a lovely forest around a lake. There's also a nice **gift shop** (❧ 9am-5pm Tue-Sun) and **restaurant** with creek-side bench seats. Trolleybus 1 from the train station goes there (get off at the last stop and keep walking for under 1km, or take the hourly Răşinari tram for a couple of stops), though it's an easy and pleasant bike ride there too.

Activities

Explorer Sport (☎ 216 641; Calea Dumbrăvii 14; ⌚ 9am-8pm Mon-Fri, 10am-2pm Sat) is a sport shop that rents bikes (about €5 a day), skis in winter, sells packs and boots, and repairs bikes.

Festivals & Events

Sibiu's cultural richness dates from its days as the Saxon capital. Some highlights include:

Mayfest (1 May) Sibiu's remaining 5500 German-speaking Saxons flock to Dumbrava forest for pagan frolicking and beer bingeing.

Sibiu Jazz Festival (May) In 2005 Sibiu resurrected its week-long jazz festival (www.sibiujazzfestival.com), which died, along with its first founder, in the early 1990s.

International Theatre Festival (May/Jun) See www.sibfest.ro.

International Country & Folk Music Festival (Jul)

National Festival of Folk Traditions (early Aug) Displays of craft traditions at Astra (aka Museum of Traditional Folk Civilisation), which holds many summer events.

International Opera Music Festival (late Sep) www.filarmonicasibiu.ro.

International Astra Film Festival (mid-Oct) Bi-annual event held on even-numbered years. See www.astrafilm.ro.

Sleeping

Sibiu's Old Town is sadly underrepresented by accommodation options, and the for-2007 hotel boom has eyed far less appealing areas outside the centre. At research time **Hotel Bulevard** (Piaţa Unirii 10) was undergoing a massive, long-overdue renovation. Check www.sibiu2007.ro for updates on accommodation.

Also, ask the tourist information office about the University of Lucian Blaga dorms around town, which it is planning to open for about €10 per person.

If you hang out at the bus or train station long enough, you're likely to get an offer of a private room. You can also call **Tourism & Hospitality** (☎ 0722-551 073; r €28), which books central rooms.

Antrec (☎ 233 503; turism@turism.sobis.ro; Str Cala Dumbrăvii 101; ⌚ 9am-5pm Mon-Fri) arranges rooms in *pensiune*-style accommodation in the countryside for €12 to €17 per person per night (including breakfast); call ahead.

BUDGET

Old Town Hostel (☎ 216 445; www.hostelsibiu.ro; Piaţa Mică 26; dm/d €11.50/26) In a 450-year-old build-ing with spacious dorm rooms looking over a main square, this simple hostel has the most atmospheric location in Sibiu. Dorms are better than the private room (which has four beds and no window). Breakfast is not included, but you can use the kitchen (plus there's table football!). Lots of transport and day-trip information is available, as is laundry service (€2).

Hotel 11 Euro (☎ 222 041; www.11euro.ro; Str Tudor Vladimirescu 2; s/d €22/33) The name's a lie – unless you count divisibles. This 27 room hotel (a former clothing factory) is slightly stranded, about 500m northwest of the centre, but has perfectly passable, if cheap rooms. Second-floor ones have the best views. Breakfast is €2.

Hotel Halamadero (☎ 212 509; Str Măsarilor 10; d/tr with shared bathroom €23/31.50) This friendly, family-run four-room deal is in a slightly unglam-orous patch of the Lower Town. Rooms are old-school, with TV and three or four beds. The family runs a beery patio café that's nice but no breakfast is served.

Hotel Podul Minciunilor (☎ 217 259; www.hotel-ela.as.ro; Str Azilului 1; d/tr €27/36) Located half a block from Liar's Bridge in Lower Town, this six-room guesthouse (run by the people behind Pensiunea Ela) is a bit cuter from the outside than the inside, but has basic clean rooms with TVs and a communal refrigerator. No breakfast is served.

ourpick Pensiunea Ela (☎ 215 197; www.hotel-ela.as.ro; Str Nová 43; s/d €29/37) One of Sibiu's best deals, this Lower Town guesthouse has just nine rooms, all clean and comfy, if a little small. Owners care for every detail (you're asked to remove your shoes in the room), and Lassie the German Shepherd is a sweet, quiet guy. A central courtyard isn't a bad sitting spot, though the breakfast is probably not worth €5. Laundry is available for €7.50.

MIDRANGE

Casa Luxemburg (☎ 216 854; www.kultours.ro; Piaţa Mică 16; s/d/tr €33/57/77) It's a little dormy, but this six-room job overlooks the Evangelical Church and Piaţa Mică.

Gasthof Clara (☎ 222 914; Str Răului 24; s/d €45/56) It's on an unappealing, dusty street, but all that evaporates once you're inside this cheerful six-room guesthouse with a terrace restaurant. The owner sometimes tells communist jokes.

Hotel Silva (☎ 243 985; www.hotelsilvasibiu.com; Aleea Eminescu 1; s/d €53/69) The Silva is a chalet-style hotel overlooking green Sub Airini Park.

Rooms are modern, but a recent renovation didn't cull the must. Half the rooms have balconies.

Hotel Continental (☎ 218 100; www.continental hotels.ro; Calea Dumbrăvii 2-4; s/d €56/77; ⊠ 🕃) Grey, grey, grey on the outside, this 13-floor, 182-room hotel is plain but quite well maintained inside, and rooms have nice views. It's on a busy street, five minutes from the Old Town. Word is that Ibis may take it over by 2008.

Hotel Împăratul Romanilor (☎ 216 500; Str Nicolae Bălcescu 2-4; s/d €56/78) Inside the green-tea exteriors, this hotel (founded in 1555 as a restaurant, rebuilt in 1985) looks fussy Louis XIV-style at first glance, but nicks on window ledges and scuffed carpets reveal that it's disappointingly maintained. A new heyday is sure to come: it's the only hotel in the centre.

Hotel Parc (☎ 424 455; www.hotelparcsibiu.ro; Str Şcoala de Înot 1-3; s/d €58/73; 🕃 🖵) This former grey blob 1.5km southeast of the centre went and did itself up, with a fresh gold exterior and 59 fully modern (if slightly unexciting) interiors. West-facing rooms get free views of the football games in the neighbouring stadium.

Eating

Sandwich & More (Str Brukenthal; sandwiches €0.90; 🕃 8am-8pm Mon-Sat) This window spot serves fresh veggie sandwiches and Asian-style pastas. It's by far Sibiu's best fast-food option.

Grand Plaza (Str 9 Mai 60; mains €2.30-3; 🕃 10am-11pm Mon-Sat) Not far from the train station, this simple and busy Romanian restaurant passes on the gimmicks and focuses on tasty Romanian food, which the locals file in for. Grilled meats are about €2.80, soups €1 to €1.80 and a Bulgarian salad costs €1.80.

Crama Sibiul Vechi (Str Ilarian; mains €2.30-6; 🕃 noon-midnight) This popular, evocative brick-cellar spot off the main crawl reels in locals for its tasty Transylvanian armoury of mutton, sausages, beef and fish. There's live music most nights.

La Piazzetta (☎ 230 879; Piaţa Mică 15; pizzas & pastas €3.15-5.70) Facing the square, this pizzeria is livelier than most, with smokers and passive smokers eating sizeable pizzas at red-chequered tables in the peach-walled interior or outside when the weather's nice.

Drinking

Piaţa Mică is the drinking HQ for Sibiu.

Go In (Piaţa Mică 10; 🕃 9am-3am) The Go In is a traditional-style bar with lots of 20-something

couples sharing tables over cocktails and beer.

Kulturkafe (Piaţa Mică 16; 🕃 10am-3am Mon-Fri, 1pm-3am Sat, 3pm-3am Sun) This place has the best table spots on the square.

Chill Out (Piaţa Mică 23; 🕃 10am-2am) Local students hightail it to this fun, loud, enigmatic cellar club with a well-lit room and a dark one, where themed nights and DJs rule the roost (one time it was pitch dark, with smooching couples dancing and a guy flashing a torch on the scene – now that's entertainment).

Art Café (☎ 0722-265 992; Str Filarmonicii 2; 🕃 8am-2am Mon-Sat, 10am-2am Sun) Saxon intellects and goofing teens discuss the world at side-by-side tables in this small café (coffee, beer, mixed drinks), which sometimes stages jazz and dance events. It has a very open vibe.

Entertainment

CINEMAS

Studionul Astra (Piaţa Mică 11) This place screens alternative art films; it also hosts the annual International Astra Film Festival in October.

THEATRE & CLASSICAL MUSIC

Agenţie de Teatrală (☎ 217 575; Str Nicolae Bălcescu 17; 🕃 10am-5pm Mon-Fri, 11am-3pm Sat) Tickets for major events are sold here.

Philharmonic (☎ 210 264; www.filarmonicasibiu.ro; Str Filharmonicii 2) Founded in 1949, this has played a key role in maintaining Sibiu's prestige as a main cultural centre of Transylvania.

Radu Stancu State Theatre (☎ 210 092; B-dul Spitelor 2-4) Plays here are usually in Romanian, with occasional productions in German on Wednesday. It hosts the International Theatre Festival in May/June.

Shopping

Franz Binder Museum Gift Shop (☎ 218 195; Piaţa Mică 11; 🕃 9am-5pm Tue-Sun) This shop stocks lots of traditional pieces, which make good souvenirs.

Antik (☎ 211 604; Str Nicolae Bălcescu 23; 🕃 10am-6pm Mon-Fri, to 2pm Sat) This is the best place to pick through old German knick-knacks.

Getting There & Away

AIR

Tarom (☎ 211 157; Str Nicolae Bălcescu 10; 🕃 9am-12.30pm & 1.30-5pm Mon-Fri) offers daily service to/from Munich (€280 return), plus five weekly flights to Vienna (€300) and three to Bucharest (€60/100 one way/return).

Carpatair (☎ 229 161; www.carpatair.ro), which has an office at the airport, offers service to Germany and Italy via Timișoara.

Austrian Airlines (www.aua.com) also flies between Vienna and Sibiu.

BUS

The **bus station** (☎ 217 757; Piața 1 Dec 1918) is opposite the train station. Daily bus and maxitaxi services include the following:

Destination	Price	Duration	Frequency
Alba Iulia	€3.40	2hr	10 daily
Brașov	€4.30	2½hr	13 daily
Bucharest	€8.50	5½hr	4-5 daily
Cluj-Napoca	€6	3½hr	9 daily
Deva	€4.50	2½hr	3-4 daily
Sighișoara	€3.50	2hr	4 daily
Timișoara	€9	6hr	2 daily
Târgu Mureș	€3.70	2½hr	13 daily

Three or four daily microbuses to Rășinari and Păltiniș (€1.15, 1¼ hours) leave from the roundabout in front of the train station, and buses to Cisnădie leave every half-hour from platform 9. Another microbus heads west a few times daily, stopping in Săliște (€0.30), 4km from Sibiel, and ending in Jina (€1.80).

Eurolines (☎ 213 536; sibiu@eurolines.ro; B-dul Vasile Milea 13; 9am-8pm Mon-Fri, to 4pm Sat) sells tickets to many European destinations.

Several international buses leave from the lot next to Hotel Parc, 2km southwest of the centre.

TRAIN

Sibiu lies at an awkward rail junction; often you'll need to change trains. But there are three daily direct trains to Brașov (€6.75, 2½ hours); three to Bucharest (€14, five hours) and Timișoara (€14, five hours); and one early morning one to Arad (€10.80, five hours). To get to/from Sighișoara or Cluj-Napoca, you'll have to change at Copșa Mică or Mediaș (about nine or 10 trains daily). For Alba Iulia, you have to change at Vințu de Jos.

Buy tickets at the **Agenție de Voiaj CFR office** (☎ 216 441; Str Nicolae Bălcescu 6; 7.30am-7.30pm Mon-Fri).

Getting Around

Trolleybus 1 connects the train station with the centre, but it's only a 450m walk along Str General Magheru.

TO/FROM THE AIRPORT

Sibiu airport (SBZ; ☎ 229 161; Hwy Alba Iulia 73) is 5km west of the centre. Trolleybus 8 runs between the airport and the train station.

TAXI

There's a taxi stand at the west end of Str Nicolae Bălcescu. To call a taxi dial ☎ 953.

CAR RENTAL

Toro (☎ 232 237; www.tororent.ro; Str Filarmonica 5; 8am-4pm Mon-Fri, to 1pm Sat) rents Dacias from €30 to €38 per day.

Advantage (☎ 216 949; www.patricia-rent.ro; Apt 5, Str Nicolae Bălcescu 37; 9am-8pm Mon-Fri, 11am-6pm Sat) has Dacias from €49 per day, or €10 less daily if you're renting for a week or more.

AROUND SIBIU
☎ 269

Many visitors fail to capitalise on Sibiu's great nearby attractions – quiet villages and hiking trails past glacial lakes. It's possible to hike across the Cindrel Mountains on a day trip, or rent a bike and go on trails from Păltiniș.

About 16km north of Sibiu, towards Saxon Land, in the town **Slimnic** is a great hilltop 15th-century fortified church that's fun to ramble around.

South of Sibiu

See Sibiu's transport section for bus service information.

CISNĂDIE

Forking west of the road to Păltiniș, about 12km south of Sibiu, is the Saxon fortified church of Cisnădie (Heltau in German, Nagydisznód in Hungarian). Work started on defensive walls around the church in 1430 but they were destroyed by a Turkish attack on the town in 1493. Ask in the village for the key to the bell tower, which looks over the town's red roofs.

RĂȘINARI

On the way to the Cindrel Mountains, the charming, rather well-to-do shepherd village of Rășinari, 12km south of Sibiu, is famed for its local carpentry, sheep farming and a lively Saturday market. This is also the birthplace of Romanian poet and politician Octavian Goga (1881–1939). The market lines one of the two small rivers running through town, around the centre; where the road forks (near the gold town

TRANSYLVANIA

hall and post office, just east of a small bridge), there's an information board with a town map of 11 local sites and day-hike information.

West of the centre (follow the signs), the small **Ethnographical Museum** (Str Grădiniţa De Copii 2) was under renovation at research time. 'It may move', a neighbour told us with an unsure shrug.

Across the stream, about 300m southeast of the city hall (veer left after the Orthodox Church up the hill), is the four-room, unsigned **Cioran Pensiune** (☎ 557 170; Str Emil Cioran 1503; r €20), at the home of an English-speaking family; breakfast is €3.

CINDREL MOUNTAINS

Not high on most travellers' lists, these lovely mountains – topped with Mt Cindrel (2244m) and Mt Frumoasa (2170m) – shelter two large glacial lakes, with excellent well-marked trails cutting across. Visitors could start from Păltiniş and make their way overland to Mărginimea Sibiului as a day hike.

From **Păltiniş**, some trails are perfect for mountain biking too. You can rent bikes from the Păltiniş reception centre and pick up trail maps.

There's a 4km trail to **Şanta**, where there's a refuge for campers to spend the night. The most popular route (3.5km, red circles) descends to the **Cibin Gorges** (Cheile Cibinului). From here the trail goes northeast, past **Cibin River** to **Cabana Fântânele**. The next day, continue in the same direction to **Sibiel** village (three to 3½ hours, blue crosses). Alternatively, follow another blue-cross trail to the neighbouring village of **Fântânele**. From Sibiel you can also take a 2½-hour walk to **Cetatea Sibielului** – it starts from the stream at the western end of the village.

Heading back south from Cabana Fântânele, a trail (red crosses and blue circles) cuts down a valley to **Şaua Şerbănei**, where you pick a separate trail leading to the **Cânaia refuge** (7½ to eight hours for the whole trip, blue circles).

More adventurous alpinists should follow the trail from **Cabana Păltiniş** south, past the Cânaia refuge (5½ to 6½ hours, red stripes) to the summit of **Mt Cindrel**. Heading northwards, red stripes also indicate the way to **Răşinari** village (six to seven hours), with its Cabana Mai.

Of all fun things, hourly (at most) tram 1 connects Răşinari with the southern part of Sibiu (take bus 1 from the train station to reach the tram). Yay, trams!

PĂLTINIŞ

Southwest of Răşinari, the road climbs up steeply, reaching after 20km the humble ski/summer resort Păltiniş. The collection of villas isn't all that much to see, but they are surrounded by hiking trails into the beautiful, forested Cindrel Mountains (also known as the Cibin Mountains).

Păltiniş hosts several interesting events: the **Snow Festival** (Sarbatori Zapezii), held in mid-April, includes soapbox derbies and build-your-own-sleigh competitions. In August, there's the **Mountain Days jazz festival** on the first weekend followed by the national off-road car rally.

Păltiniş' **Reception Centre** (☎ 574 035; www .scpaltinis.com; ☯ 8am-10pm) sells Cindrel trail maps, has an internet connection (per hour €1.70) and rents bikes (per hour €1.45) and skis. It also can book rooms in one of the handful of villas here, including the 57-room **Casa Turiştilor** (s/d €24.50/34.50), with a fitness centre and a Jacuzzi (€1.40). Breakfast costs extra.

By the ski lifts is the scrappy **Cabana Păltiniş** (☎ 0724-313 909; r per person with shared/private bathroom €10/14.50).

Halfway back towards Răşinari, **Curmătura Ştezii** (☎ 557 310; curmatura@hotmail.com; Km17; r/cabin €23/12) is a happy little lodge with heaps of pelts and an appealing streamside location. There are trails nearby and a good restaurant. Breakfast is extra.

Mărginimea Sibiului

The villages in the so-called Mărginimea Sibiului ('borders of Sibiu') represent the heart and soul of traditional rural (ie Romanian) Transylvania. Scattered throughout the region west of Sibiu, they have preserved an old way of life: here you see not only the ubiquitous horse and plough, but also artisans engaged in woodwork, carving and weaving. Painting icons on glass and colouring eggs are pastimes here as much as surfing the internet is in Bucharest, and the local cuisine includes a tasty shepherd's polenta (with loads of fresh cream and milk).

It's great to ramble around by bike – get a map to take quiet backroads from Sibiu, as the Sibiu–Alba Iulia highway is flooded with traffic.

Look up www.ruraltourism.ro for details (and photos) of many guesthouses in the area.

CRISTIAN

Lying 10km west of Sibiu is Cristian (Grossau in German, Kereszténysziget in Hungarian). This dusty village was settled by Saxons in the 14th century and is therefore not part of Mărginimea Sibiului, technically. Red-roofed houses and vibrant washed walls are overshadowed by a grandiose fortified church in the centre of the village. Sometimes visitors can climb the tower of the church for an aerial view. Local history is covered in the petite village **museum** (Muzeul Sătesc; ☺ noon-5pm Tue-Sun), next to the local prefecture in the centre of the village.

Also, watch out for storks – the town is known for its big stork population.

GURA RÂULUI

Just 9km south (via Orlat) is Gura Râului, a sleepy town with a massive dam several kilometres south. **Pensiune Țepeș** (☎ 572 324; Str Principăla 958; r per person €8) is one of a couple of dozen *pensiunes* in town; this one has a lovely backyard with chickens and gardens looking towards a mountain. Breakfast is €3, three big meals cost €13. After you enter the town, veer right at the fork in the road (with the crucifix altar) for about 1km.

SIBIEL

It's easy to settle in to wee Sibiel, just a few kilometres south of Saliște on the highway, but tucked out of sight and feeling worlds away. At the eastern edge of town, past the tree-lined stream and many century-old villas, is the **Zosim Oancea Icons Museum** (☎ 553 818; admission €0.85; ☺ 8am-8pm), one of Romania's largest icon museums, with some 700 icons collected by a priest who spent 17 years in prison during the communist reign for his religious deeds. Hiking trails loom in the hills to the east – follow the river upstream.

Firmly gripped by all things bucolic and peaceful, the highly recommended **Mioritica** (☎ 552 640, 0740-175 287; coldeasv@yahoo.com; r from €15; ☐) is 'paradise' to Sorian, the English- and German-speaking owner of this remarkable streamside four-room guesthouse. Three bridges go over the roaring stream, and a garden includes exhibitions of found objects that Sorian, a local history teacher, rescues from the ages (including a 'nostalgic' creekside exhibition of communist relics; 'it's important to remember your past', Sorian explains). Meals are provided, and he can point you to hiking trails, nearby villages and the icon museum in town. Sometimes local musicians drop by to play for drinks. It's located towards the hills, upstream from the village centre, and you'll find it hard to leave.

AROUND SIBIEL

From Sibiel, head 6km north to Săliște, another quaint village rich in local folklore. In Galeș, 2km west of Săliște, is a small ethno graphic and art museum. It is at the southern end of the village, across the bridge opposite a salami factory. A dirt track leads from Galeș to Poiana Sibiului, famed for its fantastic coloured eggs, which are decorated with bright, geometric motifs.

GETTING THERE & AWAY

See p161 for bus details for the region. Local trains from Sibiu to Sebeș stop at Cristian (15 minutes), Sibiel (25 minutes), Săliște (35 minutes) and Miercurea Sibiului (1¼ hours).

SZÉKELY LAND

Technically it's wrong to call this central patch of Transylvania on the eastern realms of the Carpathians 'Hungarian Transylvania', but going around much of Székely Land (Țara Secuilor in Romanian, Székelyföld in Hungarian) it can feel that way. So near to Saxon towns Brașov or Sighișoara, the pulse and nomenclature and spirit of many towns – such as Odorheiu Secuiesc (Székelyudvarhely in Hungarian) and Miercurea Ciuc (Csíkszereda in Hungarian), where ethnic Hungarians comprise the majority, or the even-split of Târgu Mureș (Marosvásárhely in Hungarian) – feel almost foreign. Some of it comes from the enthusiasm given to guests, as many Transylvania itineraries head between Cluj-Napoca and Sibiu, missing this lovely area altogether. Plus, we find the food in the area to be particularly tasty.

That should change: in 2006 budget airline Wizz Air started service from Budapest to Târgu Mureș, the region's largest city; while friendly Odorheiu Secuiesc and Sfântu Gheorghe make great day trips from Sighișoara and Brașov, respectively.

TRANSYLVANIA

The area is home to many Székelys, ethnic Hungarians who live and communicate almost exclusively in their Hungarian dialect. Highly organised as a group, they publish their own local booklets and maps (often with place names written in Hungarian only) and have nourished a flourishing cultural life. Yet this is mainly since 1990, as during the communist regime their population tended to be either roundly ignored or actively suppressed.

A good deal of tension still exists between Romanians and Hungarians, who battled each other during WWI and WWII. Some claim it's just politicians making the swipes, but mention of Székely Land or ethnic Hungarians not learning Romanian language in some parts of Romania brings out verbal editorials, as does any notion of Romania's treatment of the Hungarians in the 20th century for many locals here. One local defended a grandfather who shot at Romanians in WWII ('It was war'), then wondered why Romania never apologised for culling the spoils of victory, ie Transylvania. In Târgu Mureş' main Orthodox church you can see a peasant Jesus dressed in Romanian costume being tortured by nobility in Hungarian costumes. Statues of Romulus and Remus stress Romania's Latin roots, purposefully placed during communist times to undermine the Hungarians' claim. Things haven't settled. Tread lightly on the subject and you'll have no problems.

You could consider travelling with a Hungarian phrasebook here, but you'll find that most people know Romanian or some English.

History

The origins of the Székely (see-kay) people are disputed. Debates rage as to whether they are descendants of the Huns, who arrived in Transylvania in the 5th century and adopted the Hungarian language; or whether they are Magyars who accompanied Attila the Hun on his campaigns in the Carpathian basin and later settled there. Three 'nations' were recognised in medieval Transylvania: the Székelys, the Saxons and the Romanian nobles.

During the 18th century the Székelys suffered at the hands of the Habsburgs, who attempted to convert this devout Protestant ethnic group to Catholicism. Thousands of young Székely men were conscripted into the Austrian army. Local resistance throughout Székely Land led to the massacre of Madéfalva

in 1764, after which thousands of Székelys fled across the border into Romanian Moldavia.

Following the union of Transylvania with Romania in 1918, some 200,000 Hungarians – a quarter of whom were Székelys – fled to Hungary. It was during this period that the Székelys composed their own national anthem ('As long as we live/Peoples of Hungary/our spirit shall not be broken…Let us inherit our nation, the land of the Székely…'), in which they beg God for help in the survival of Transylvania. Today, many Hungarian tourists flock to the area, especially to the 'capitals' of Odorheiu Secuiesc and Miercurea Ciuc, to experience pastoral customs considered 'authentic' and already lost in their motherland.

Maps

Cartographia's *Ţara Secuilor, Székelyföld, Székely Land* map includes a detailed map of the region, complete with lengthy historical explanations in Hungarian.

SFÂNTU GHEORGHE

☎ 267 / pop 66,380

Only 32km north of Braşov, Sfântu Gheorghe (Sepsiszentgyörgy in Hungarian), on the gently sloping banks of the Olt River, is more 'housing blocks built in communist fervour' than a traditional Transylvanian-Hungarian stronghold. That said, this chummy town with a Hungarian majority (reading its own Hungarian daily newspaper, *Háromszék,* and attending one of Romania's two Hungarian State Theatres) makes for a fascinating day trip from Braşov.

First documented in 1332, Sfântu Gheorghe developed as a cultural centre for the Székelys from the 15th century onwards, when it became a free town. It was left devastated by Turkish attacks between 1658 and 1671, and a plague in 1717. Today its museum is the region's best place to investigate Székely culture.

A fun time to be around is during the three-day St George Days Fair, ending on the last Sunday in April.

Orientation

The bus and train stations are a 25-minute walk east of the centre along Str 1 Decembrie 1918, which begins at the stations and veers right (past Str Jozef Bem, at the St George Statue) one block before it hits the north end of Central Park at Piaţa Libertăţii. From there,

TRANSYLVANIA

Str Libertăţii begins southward, turning into Str Kós Károly after 300m.

Information

Banca Comercială Română (Str Jozef Bem; 8.30am-6pm Mon-Fri, to 12.30pm Sat) Opposite IT&T, a couple of blocks east of Central Park.

International Tourism & Trade (IT&T; ☎ 316 375; Str Jozef Bem 2; it&t@honoris.ro; 9am-5pm Mon-Fri) Travel agent offers day trips, rents cars and can fix you up for the night in Ceauşescu's former hunting lodge, Arcus Castle, 3km south of town (about €90).

Tourist Information Bureau (☎ 316 474; www.sep siszentgyorgy.ro; Str 1 Decembrie 1918, 2; 7.30am-3.30pm Mon-Wed, to 5pm Thu, to 2pm Fri) Offers useful free city map and guesthouse listings. Can point you to bike rentals.

Sights

About 200m south of Central Park, the **Székely National Museum** (Székely Nemzeti Múzeum; ☎ 312 442; Str Kós Károly; adult/child €0.40/0.20; 9am-5pm Tue-Sun) is housed in a building which is itself a masterpiece, designed by leading Hungarian architect Kós Károly between 1911 and 1912 (he designed many of the buildings around Central Park too). The three floors of exhibits are unfortunately not signed in English and sit under buzzing fluorescent lights. There's a war-torn Hungarian flag from the 1848 revolution, plus 17th-century knight suits, a cheerful stuffed boar in the animal room (the lynx looks like a dick though) and lots of Székely crafts and costumes. Outside are a few traditional gates and wooden houses.

A couple of blocks south (just behind a tennis club) is an interesting **outdoor market**. We have a soft spot for the **St George Statue** (Str 1 Decembrie 1918), a modern addition that one local likened in disgust to 'a mosquito being attacked by a dinosaur'.

North of the centre, following Str Kossuth Lajos and crossing a bridge over the Debren River, you'll come to the **Fortificată Reformată church**, in whose cemetery you can also see some lovely examples of traditional Székely wooden crosses and graveposts.

Sleeping

The tourist information centre can point out guesthouses to you.

Sugas Hotel (☎ 312 171; www.sugaskert.ro; St 1 Decembrie 1918, 12; s/d/apt €38/44/63;) Hidden behind some historic central buildings, the 28-room Sugas has bold graphic designs in its comfy rooms, with headboards and wardrobes in Székely traditional style. Its restaurant is a big hit with townies too.

Eating

Tribel (cnr Str 1 Decembrie 1918 & Piaţa Libertăţii; mains from €1.20; 7am-10pm Mon-Fri, 9am-10pm Sat & Sun) Quite homy for a fast-food spot, this place is half pizza-bar, half pick-and-point cafeteria (good for fish, chicken, potatoes and salads).

Szentgyörgy Pince (St George Cellar; ☎ 352 666; St Gábor Áron 14; mains €2.80-5; 9am-midnight) Through a tunnel of the gold building facing the heroic statue of Mihai Viteazul (at the northern end of Central Park), this basement spot offers the Székely slant to Transylvania cooking – a few spicy goulashes and lots of grilled meats.

Getting There & Away

The bus station is 50m north of the train station. Microbuses and maxitaxis go along Str 1 Decembrie 1918 (stops are marked); some finish at a stand north of the market. Frequent services go to Braşov (€1.20, 40 minutes) and Covasna (€1.20, 40 minutes). There's also service to Miercurea Ciuc, Piatra Neamţ and Târgu Neamţ.

Buy train tickets at the **Agenţie de Voiaj CFR** (☎ 311 680; Str Mikó Imre 13; 8am-3pm Mon-Fri). From Sfântu Gheorghe three trains daily go to Covasna (€0.70, one hour) and 16 to Braşov (€0.80, 30 to 45 minutes), with eight stopping in Hărman (€0.70, 30 minutes).

SPA TOWNS
COVASNA

The curative powers of mineral waters in the area around Sfântu Gheorghe – such as the 'Fairy Queen Valley' (Valea Zânelor) in Covasna (Kovászna in Hungarian), 28km east – draw an older steady crew of visitors seeking cures for what ails them. Up towards the hills in Covasna, **Hotel Montana** (☎ 067-340 290; Str Toth 23; r from €16) evocatively feels like stepping into a colour-faded *National Geographic* article from 1979, with lots of old-timers in robes awaiting treatments.

Check www.turismcovasno.ro for more information.

See above for information on transport here.

BĂILE TUŞNAD

About 40km north of Sfântu Gheorghe (en route to Miercurea Ciuc), more peaceful

Băile Tuşnad, in the volcano-made Harghita Mountains, features pools and springs in a lush valley. An InfoTur stand has listings of 15 *pensiunes* in town (about €12 to €18 per person); the nearby **Centrul de Informare Eco-Turistica** (🕙 9am-2pm Mon, Wed & Fri), 100m north of the bus station, offers accommodation information too.

Across the street is a **pool** (🕙 daily Jun-Sep). It's possible to hike 40 minutes up the path behind the train tracks to cliff-top **Stânca Soimilor** for a valley view.

About 24km southeast, St Anne's Lake is a pretty spot with boats and picnic grounds (no accommodation). An annual pilgrimage is held there on 26 July.

One hotel is **Astoria** (🕾 266 335 04; www.lacul ciucas.ro; Str Oltului 102; r €20), run by the folks who opened the great lakeside Lacul Ciucaş restaurant down from the main road.

Buses between Miercurea Ciuc and Sfântu Gheorghe stop here.

MIERCUREA CIUC

🕾 266 / pop 42,000

Known as being Romania's coldest city, or for its nationally loved Ciuc (pronounced chook) beer or the town's hockey fascination, Miercurea Ciuc (Csíkszereda in Hungarian) is a friendly, if rather dishevelled, historic city, where the population is over 80% ethnic Hungarian. If you're heading to Bicaz Gorges or Lacu Roşu in Moldavia, it's a useful stopoff, although few make this area a destination of its own.

Founded during the reign of Hungarian King Ladislaus I (r 1077–95) around a castle that the king built for himself, Miercurea Ciuc quickly developed into a prosperous commercial centre and the hub of Székely Land cultural activities. Ceauşescu left an imprint in the 1970s and '80s, knocking down century-old Habsburg buildings for a grey civic centre that takes up a chunk of the town's heart.

Traditional Székely villages such as **Leliceni** (4km southeast), **Misentea** and **Ciucsângeorgiu** (another 2km and 4km south), and **Armaseni** (2km north of the latter along a dirt track) lie within easy reach of Miercurea Ciuc.

Information

INTERNET ACCESS

Internet (cnr Str Petöti & Tudor Vladimirescu; per hr €0.30; 🕙 10am-midnight)

LEFT LUGGAGE

Train station (per 24hr €0.80; 🕙 24hr)

MONEY

Banca Comercială Română (Kereskedelmi Bank; 🕾 271 766; cnr Str Kossuth Lajos & Str George Coşbuc; 🕙 8.30am-6pm Mon-Fri, to 12.30pm Sat)

POST

Post office (Str Kossuth Lajos 3; 🕙 7am-8pm Mon-Fri, 8.30am-1pm Sat)

TOURIST INFORMATION

Tourist information centre (🕾 317 007; www.szereda .ro; Room 20, Piaţa Cetăţii 1; 🕙 8am-3pm Mon-Fri) Hiddenaway information office on 1st floor of city hall. Hands out free town map and may help with area info. 'Not many people visit', one employee lamented at last pass.

Sights

CITY CENTRE

Miercurea Ciuc's centrepiece, and proud source of the Ciuc beer logo, is its **Mikó Castle**, which today houses the impressive **Székely Museum of Csík** (Csíki Székely Múzeum; 🕾 311727; adult/student €1.40/0.70; 🕙 9am-5pm Tue-Sun). Built from 1623 to 1630, the castle was burnt down by Tartars in 1661 and rebuilt in 1716. It later played a role as defence for the Habsburg empire, housing the first Székely infantry in 1849. The museum, with labels in English, shows old weaponry (eg a three-bladed spring-action knife) and regional costumes and artefacts. In the back lot are a couple of relocated traditional buildings.

The **Palace of Justice**, built in 1904, and the baroque **city hall** (1884–98), both built in an eclectic style, and a **Soviet Army Monument** are on the opposite side of Piaţa Cetăţii.

Several blocks north, via B-dul Timişoara, is the city's **Civic Centre**, with a 'Pyongyang Square' feel; original houses were knocked down in 1976–77. One still standing is the canary-yellow, regal building from 1903, where the **National Bank of Romania** managed to survive – just. In 1984 the entire building was uprooted from its foundations and moved 128m east on rollers to make way for the **district library**, which has since been demolished.

Miercurea Ciuc is something of a hockey town. Its team frequently clashes against Steaua of Bucharest – many build it up as a Hungarian versus Romanian grudge-match. There's a heroic **hockey statue** in front of the town's rink, next to Hotel Fényo.

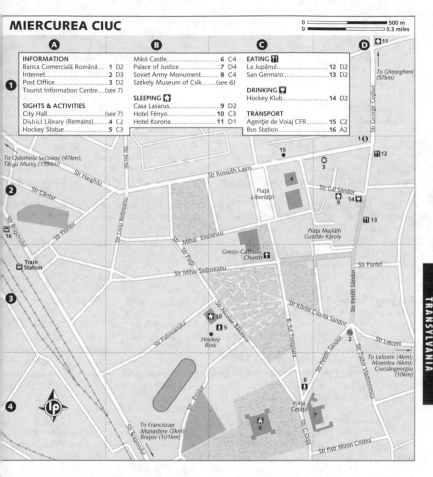

MIERCUREA CIUC

INFORMATION
Banca Comercială Română.... 1 D2
Internet.............................2 D3
Post Office........................3 D2
Tourist Information Centre....(see 7)

SIGHTS & ACTIVITIES
City Hall............................(see 7)
District Library (Remains)........4 C2
Hockey Statue.....................5 C3

Mikó Castle............................6 C4
Palace of Justice......................7 D4
Soviet Army Monument............8 C4
Székely Museum of Csík........(see 6)

SLEEPING
Casa Lasarus..........................9 D2
Hotel Fényo..........................10 C3
Hotel Korona........................11 D1

EATING
La Jupânul..........................12 D2
San Gennaro........................13 D2

DRINKING
Hockey Klub........................14 D2

TRANSPORT
Agenţie de Voiaj CFR...........15 C2
Bus Station..........................16 A2

FRANCISCAN MONASTERY

Two kilometres south of the centre in the Şumuleu district (Csíksomlyó in Hungarian) is a fine **Franciscan monastery**, built in 1442 by Iancu de Hunedoara (János Hunyadi), governor of Hungary from 1446 to 1452, to commemorate his great victory against the Turks at Marosszentimre.

The monastery today is the site of the city's main tourist draw, the **Pentecostal Pilgrimage**. About 300,000 Székelys flock here on Whitsunday (late May/early June) to celebrate their brotherhood.

Sleeping

Casa Lasarus (☎ 325 446; www.lasarushostel.ro; Str Gál Sándor 9; dm €8.60; 🖳) This hostel has eight spotless rooms, each with four beds, TV and private bathroom, and is the cheapest place in town. It's located on the 2nd floor of this religious organisation's offices. A kitchen is available.

Hotel Korona (☎ 310 993; Str Cosbuc 38; s/d/apt €26/43/52) This Habsburg-era building has been revamped with eight comfortable mustard-coloured rooms and lots of space. Free breakfast is served in a good restaurant downstairs.

Hotel Fényo (☎ 311 493; www.hunguest-fenyo.ro; Str Nicolae Bălcescu 11; s/d €57/67; ⛌ 🖳) Sitting near the citadel, this is a lovely place with 92 comfortable, business-friendly rooms and pluses like internet connection. Some rooms are equipped for wheelchair-bound guests.

TRANSYLVANIA

Eating & Drinking

The eating/drinking strip for Miercurea Ciuc is the pedestrian mall Str Petőfi Sándor.

San Gennaro (☎ 206 501; Str Petőfi Sándor 15; pastas & pizzas €2-4; ☻ 9am-midnight) This three-part Italian restaurant is the most popular of the pedestrian mall sidewalk eateries. The food's fine and the setting's great.

La Jupânul (☎ 0744-386 346; Str Coşbul 18; mains from €2; ☻ 9am-11pm) Cosy and popular with lively 20-something snackers and drinkers, this traditional restaurant has bench seats, hanging knick-knacks, painted wooden floors and good food (pork schnitzels, chicken breast etc).

Hockey Klub (Str Petőfi Sándor; beer €0.75; ☻ 9am-midnight) This well-lit bar-restaurant sells more beer than food, and has enough displayed hockey jerseys and pennants from around the globe (including US minor league team Oklahoma City Blazers) to keep the chit-chat puck-oriented.

Getting There & Away

The **Agenţie de Voiaj CFR** (☎ 311 924; 1st fl, Str Kossuth Lajos 12; ☻ 7.30am-2.30pm Mon-Fri) sells advance tickets. From Miercurea Ciuc there are 10 trains to Braşov (€2 to €4, two to 2½ hours) via Sfântu Gheorghe (€1.30, 1½ hours); three continue to Bucharest. There are also 11 daily trains to Gheorgheni (from €1.30, one hour), and one daily train to Budapest and Iaşi.

The **bus station** (☎ 324 334; Str Braşovului 1) is 50m north of the train station. A couple of daily buses go to Braşov (€2.80, two hours), three to Gheorgheni (€1.40, 1¼ hours), plus a handful to Sfântu Gheorghe, five weekly to Odorheiu Secuiesc, and five weekly to Budapest (for Budapest info call ☎ 372 311).

GHEORGHENI

☎ 266 / pop 20,000

The small town of Gheorgheni (gore-gen; Gyergyószentmiklós in Hungarian), 45km north of Miercurea Ciuc, has few sites of interest, but it makes an interesting quick break (particularly to see Lăzarea's castle) on the way to or from Lacu Roşu and the Bicaz Gorge, 26km east (p269).

Banks and hotels line the central Piaţa Libertăţii. **Tourlnform** (☎ 364 568; Str Balcescu 11; ☻ 9am-5pm Mon-Fri), about 250m northwest of Piaţa Libertăţii, sell maps (€0.40) and helps with transport times.

Sights

The **Tarisznyás Márton County Museum** (Város Tarisznyás Márton Muzeum; ☎ 365 229; Str Rácóczi 1; adult, student €0.90/0.45; ☻ 9am-5pm Tue- Sun), 400m east of Piaţa Libertăţii, is in an 18th-century Armenian trade house and well worth a visit to see the intricately carved wooden fence posts, craft-workers' tools, and other artefacts of Magyar and Székely culture.

It backs onto an **Armenian Church**, which dates from the 17th century, when many Armenians lived in town.

Just 6km north of Gheorgheni on the road to Topliţa is the tiny village of **Lăzarea** (Gyergyószárhegy in Hungarian). Dating from 1235 the predominantly Hungarian village is dominated by its 16th-century **castle** (admission €1.15; ☻ 9am-5pm Tue-Sat), on the rim of green forested hills. It was to Lăzarea Castle that Gábor Bethlen, later to become prince of Transylvania (r 1613–29), came seeking solace following the death of his son in 1590. There's a small museum and views of the area and the neighbouring monastery from the bastions.

Sleeping & Eating

Lázár Panzió (☎ 364 446; www.lazarpancio.ro; Str Fürdö 3; s/d €20/28) New and central, this seven-room guesthouse is in a three-storey building with white-picket fence surrounding a courtyard bar-restaurant. It's about 30m west of Piaţa Libertăţii.

Rubin Hotel (☎ 365 554; www.rubinhotel.ro; Str Gábor Áron 1; s/d/ste €25/30/45; ▢) A little plain but certainly comfortable, the 18-room Rubin is another central choice – and the only place in town that crafts 'white swan' towels or rose-coloured bedspreads.

In Lăzarea village, there are about 20 *pensiunes*, some with signs. One good one is **Emma Pap** (☎ 352 700; emitur@gmail.com; Str Szini; r per person incl meals €17); follow the 'information' signs.

Pizza Bank (Str Două Poduri 2; pizzas from €2; ☻ 10am-late) This place has pretty good pizzas and cold beer in a weird century-old building, 200m southeast of Piaţa Libertăţii.

Getting There & Away

The **bus station** (☎ 364 722) and **train station** (☎ 364 587) are 1.5km west of the centre via Str Gării. Three daily buses go to Braşov (€2.30, 2½ hours); one to Târgu Mureş (€4.60, four hours), continuing to Cluj-Napoca; three to Lacu Roşu (€1, one hour); and one to Odorheiu Secuiesc (€3.20, 2¼ hours). Trains or the rail line between Braşov and Satu Mare stop here. There is no public transport to the stations, so many people lug their bags out there by foot.

ODORHEIU SECUIESC

☎ 266 / pop 37,500

Of all Székely Land, nowhere is more 'Hungarian' than little Odorheiu Secuiesc (or as locals prefer, Székelyudvarhely). About 97% of the locals are ethnic Hungarians, and this lovely, prosperous town ('a car for every three residents', one local boasted) feels like a different country from Sighişoara, 1¼ hours' drive south. Surrounded by small hills, and inhabited by spirited, very welcoming locals, stepping into Odorheiu Secuiesc feels like the Eastern Europe of 1990, in the sense that locals may stop you to chat, absolutely charmed by your presence. Perhaps you'll bump into the teenager who introduced locals to dreadlocks, as we did.

Politics is often a part of conversation, and you're more likely to hear about the tensions between Romanian and ethnic Hungarian politicians here than elsewhere in Székely Land.

Settled on an ancient Roman military camp, Odorheiu Secuiesc developed as a small craft town between the 11th and 13th centuries. The Craftmen's Market, held in the citadel in mid-July, carries on the town's tradition of craft guilds set up by King Matthias Corvinus in 1485.

Orientation

The train and bus stations, reached via Str Bethlen Gábor, are a 10-minute walk north of the centre; the bus station is 100m southwest of the train station (west of the tracks). Street names – all names actually – get two names here – Hungarian and Romanian. We've included varying Hungarian names on the map in parentheses.

MAPS

Odorheiu Secuiesc (€1.75) published by Geocart can be bought at Herr Travel.

Information

There are ATMs and banks along Str Kossuth Lajos.

BOOKSHOPS

Corvina bookshop (☎ 217 637; Str Cetăţii (Var Ut) 2; 🕑 8am-8pm Mon-Fri, 9am-2pm Sat) Stocks maps and Hungarian-language books.

INTERNET ACCESS

Korona Panzió (see p170; per hr €0.60; 🕑 10am-11pm)

POST OFFICE

Post office (Str Kossuth Lajos 35; 🕑 7am-8pm Mon-Fri, 8am-1pm Sat)

TOURIST INFORMATION CENTRE

Tourinfo (☎ 217 427; www.tourinfo.ro; Piaţa Márton Áron 6) The office was closed during research time, but planning to open at this location.

TRAVEL AGENCIES

Herr Travel (☎ 102 342; www.guide2romania.ro; Piaţa Márton Áron 2; 🕑 8am-6pm Mon-Fri, 9am-1pm Sat) Ambitious agency arranges car service, biking, caving and culture tours around region, or walking tours in town (a one-hour looksee at otherwise-closed public buildings is €4 per person and well worth it); rents Dacia Solenzas (from €20 per day).

Sights

Odorheiu Secuiesc is more about being here, mingling with locals at a place like G Café than sightseeing. But there's enough to look at to occupy a good afternoon, or you can take up Herr Travel on one of their interesting walking tours.

At the western end of the main square, Piaţa Primeriei, stands the **Franciscan Monastery & Church** (Szent Ferencrendi Templom és Kolostor; ☎ 213 016; Piaţa Primeriei 15; 🕑 10am-6pm Tue-Sun), built from 1712 to 1779. Walk east past the impressive **city hall** (1895–96) to the 18th-century baroque **Hungarian Reformed Church** (Református Templom).

Behind the Hungarian Reformed Church is Piaţa Márton Áron. Just below the steps leading to the town's first **Roman Catholic church** (Római Katolikus Plébániatemplom; built 1787–91) is a statue of the square's namesake bishop, who received a life sentence for promoting Hungarian rights during the communist era. At the head of the park is a **WWI & WWII Monument.**

Odorheiu Secuiesc's medieval **citadel** (*vár*), built between 1492 and 1516, is almost fully intact today, and houses an agricultural college. Visitors can freely stroll the grounds around its inner walls.

South of the main square is the **Haáz Rezsó Museum** (Str Kossuth Lajos 42), which was in the process of moving to this new location at research time. The museum explains the town's colourful history.

TRANSYLVANIA

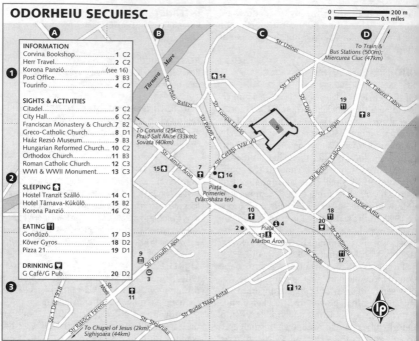

ODORHEIU SECUIESC

INFORMATION
Corvina Bookshop...............1 C2
Herr Travel.........................2 C2
Korona Panzió..................(see 16)
Post Office..........................3 B3
Tourinfo............................4 C2

SIGHTS & ACTIVITIES
Citadel...............................5 C2
City Hall.............................6 C2
Franciscan Monastery & Church.7 B2
Greco-Catholic Church.........8 D1
Haáz Rezső Museum............9 B3
Hungarian Reformed Church..10 C2
Orthodox Church................11 B3
Roman Catholic Church........12 C3
WWI & WWII Monument....13 C3

SLEEPING
Hostel Tranzit Szálló............14 C1
Hotel Târnava-Kükülő..........15 B2
Korona Panzió....................16 C2

EATING
Gondüzó.............................17 D3
Köver Gyros........................18 D2
Pizza 21.............................19 D1

DRINKING
G Café/G Pub......................20 D2

To Corund (25km);
Praid Salt Mine (33km);
Sováta (40km)

To Train &
Bus Stations (500m);
Miercurea Ciuc (47km)

Piaţa Primeriei (Városháza ter)

Piaţa Márton Áron

To Chapel of Jesus (2km);
Sighişoara (44km)

The town's best church lies 2km south of the centre on Str Bethlen Gábor. The small fortified **Chapel of Jesus** (Jézus kápolna; Str Bethlen Gábor) is one of the oldest architectural monuments in Transylvania, built during the 13th century. The chapel gained its name from Székely warriors who, during a Tartar invasion, cried to Jesus for help. It's usually locked, but you can ask for entry at house No 143 on the main road next door.

Sleeping

Herr Travel can arrange a room in university housing (pricey at €16 per person including meals).

Hostel Tranzit Szálló (☎ 213 755, 217 798; www.topnet.ro/tranzit; Str Tompa László 36; s/d with shared bathroom €8.60/14.30, with private bathroom €11.50/20) This hostel has a kitchen and seven simple clean rooms.

Korona Panzió (☎ 218 061; www.koronapanzio.ro; Piaţa Primeriei 12/2; s/d €21/32; 🖳) No doubt this is the best deal in town. The simple rustic style fits the country villa theme. The in-house restaurant serves up good dishes, and the bar is a popular hang-out for locals. There's free internet access in the morning (only for guests).

Hotel Târnava-Kükülő (☎ 213 963; www.kukullo.ro; Piaţa Primeriei 16; r €52-57; ✗) This standard business hotel's restaurant and bar (with free wi-fi access) teems with local life. Rooms are nothing special – carpeted floors, all the usual fittings (satellite TV, mini bar, phone, work desk). There's a small fitness centre.

Eating & Drinking

There are some fast-food joints along Str Bethlen Gábor north of Piaţa Márton Áron.

Köver Gyros (Str Sântimbru; gyros €1.60-3; 🕑 9am-11pm) This walk-away stand serves Odorheiu's juiciest, tastiest fast food.

Pizza 21 (Str Crişan; pizzas from €2.50 🕑 10am-midnight) This cute pizzeria, a couple of blocks north of the centre, is Odorheiu's favourite.

Gondüzó (Str Sântimbru; mains €3.50-6; 🕑 10am-midnight) For traditional Hungarian fare, this plainly formal spot offers a widely varied menu that delivers the goods, such as a roasted chicken breast with stewed fruit and rice. Selfless research methods attest to the delicious ice-cream-covered sponge cake, which should be shared. Vegetarians may have to stick with salads.

TRANSYLVANIA

ourpick **G Café/G Pub** (Str Sântimbru; 7.30am-1pm Mon-Fri, 9am-midnight Sat & Sun) This two-part bar-club gets our bet for Transylvania's best bar. Up top the crowd is 30-something, with jazz or live music soundtracking beer and cocktail drinkers in a parlour-style room with old newsprint and photos on the walls. Downstairs it's a bit edgier – graffitied walls – and younger people (sometimes staying till 2am). It's OK to bring in a gyro from Köver across the street.

Getting There & Away

Transport into Odorheiu is a little limited. From the **bus station** (217 979; Str Târgului 10), 100m southwest of the train station, there is only one daily bus to Sighişoara (€2, 1½ hours), five to Sovata (€2.25, one hour), seven to Miercurea Ciuc (€2 to €3, one hour), four to Târgu Mureş (€3, two hours) and a few to Budapest (€35, 12 hours). A few Hungarian-bound bus companies include **Csavargó** (249 253) and **Scorpion Trans** (218 495).

The **Agenţie de Voiaj CFR** (213 653; Str Bethlen Gábor 63; 5.30-6.30am & 7.30am-2.30pm Mon-Fri) is at the train station. Only three daily trains clank out towards Sighişoara (1½ hours) – at research time they left at 6am, 2.30pm and 10.20pm.

Check with Herr Travel about renting a car.

ODORHEIU SECUIESC TO TÂRGU MUREŞ

CORUND

Known for its green, brown and cobalt-blue pottery, the small village of Corund (Korund), 25km north of Odorheiu Secuiesc, is sometimes called the 'souvenir village'. Lines of open-air stands sell cowboy hats, sombreros, tablecloths and, of course, pottery.

Buses to Sovata go through here from Odorheiu Secuiesc.

PRAID

Some 8km further north on the road to Sovata, Praid is home to a **salt mine** (240 200; www.salinapraid.ro; Str Állomás 44; adult/child €2.90/1.90; 7am-6pm summer, 9am-2.30pm winter), a bizarre underground world with sculpture, swing sets, slides, a café selling soda and beer, and internet access(!). Locals come for extended underground treatments for bronchitis and other respiratory illnesses at the base, 120m below the surface. A bus leads down dark tunnels – it's almost apocalyptic.

There's a saltwater outdoor **pool** a couple of hundred metres west of the entrance.

SOVATA

This leafy, slightly faded, but fun lake resort town, 40km north of Odorheiu Secuiesc and 60km east of Târgu Mureş, has attracted vacationers to its reputedly curative waters since the early 19th century. Its most popular lake is saltwater **Lacu Ursu** (Bear Lake; mid-Jun–Sep), so-named for its shape – and the actual bears berry-picking in the hills to the north. It's also about 45°C, and apparently Europe's biggest heliothermic lake. Many of the villas are 100 years old; some can be rented out by the week or longer.

Sovata Tourist Information Centre (265 577 421; www.sovatatravel.ro; 9am-9pm Jun-Aug, to 5pm Tue-Sat Sep-May), 3km northeast of the crossroads and 750m from Lacu Ursu, helps find homes, hotels and *pensiunes*. It rents bikes for €6 per day. Profits support a local orphanage.

Past the lake as the road winds, **Teleki** (0265 577 625; www.tok.ro; Str Trandifilor 147; dm/d €5/32;) is a simple green villa hotel with nice rooms and great staff; ask for 'royal' on the top floor for a balcony. Breakfast is €3 extra.

Hotel Eden (0265 570 505; www.holliday-sovata .ro; Str Cireşului 2; chalets from €16), off the road near Lacu Ursu, is a group of chalets and a lodge surrounded by forest.

Five minibuses connect Sovata with Odorheiu Secuiesc (€2.25, one hour), and four with Sighişoara (about €3, 2½ hours).

TÂRGU MUREŞ

265 / pop 150,000

Lively if not jaw-dropping in beauty, Târgu Mureş – with its nearly even Hungarian and Romanian populations, as well as a sizeable Roma population – offers a different slice of Transylvania, past and present. Buildings in its centre sport a more colourful, even flamboyant, Habsburg spirit, with tiled rooftops of government buildings jutting over heroic statues and floral paint-jobs in well-maintained interior spaces. In July 2006 budget airline Wizz Air (www.wizzair.com) began service from Budapest, so more travellers are likely to treat this friendly central Transylvanian town as a hub. It's well worth poking about for a day.

Named literally for a 'market' on the Mureş River, Târgu Mureş (Marosvásárhely

TRANSYLVANIA

TÂRGU MUREŞ

0	300 m
0	0.2 miles

SLEEPING
Atlantic..........................20 A2
Hotel Concordia.............21 B2
Hotel Continental...........22 B1
Pensiune Ana Maria........23 D1

EATING
Emma Vendégco..............24 B1
Hotel Concordia Restaurant &
Bar.............................(see 21)
Kebab............................25 B2
Leo................................26 B2
Varan Varan....................27 C1

SIGHTS & ACTIVITIES
Citadel Information Office........7 C1
City Museum.........................8 C1
County Council Building............9 A2
Culture Palace.....................10 B2
Ethnographic Museum............11 B1
Greco-Catholic Cathedral........12 B2
Memorial to Victims of 1989
Revolution........................13 B2
Orthodox Cathedral................14 C1
Reform Church......................15 C1
Roman Catholic Church...........16 C1
Synagogue..........................17 B1
Teleki House.........................18 C1
Teleki Library/Bolyai Museum..19 C2

DRINKING
Teresa Scara........................28 B2

ENTERTAINMENT
Agenţie de Bilete..............(see 10)
Cinema Arta.........................29 B2
National Opera & Theatre.30 B1
Red Light District..............(see 27)
State Philharmonic............(see 10)

TRANSPORT
Agenţie de Voiaj CFR.......31 B1
Eurolines............................32 B1
Tarom................................33 C1

INFORMATION
Banca Carpaţi..........................1 C1
Complex Charis........................2 B1
Corbet Transair........................3 B2
Electro Orizont.........................4 B1
Librărie Hyperion.....................5 C1
Post Office..............................6 C1
Tourist Information Centre..(see 10)

in Hungarian, Neumarkt in German) was first documented as 'Novum Forum Siculorum' in 1322. It developed as a leading garrison town and later as an important cultural and academic centre. In 1658 it was attacked by Turks, who captured 3000 inhabitants and transported them back to Istanbul as slave labour.

During the Ceauşescu regime, Târgu Mureş was a 'closed city', with all ethnic groups other than Romanians forbidden to settle here, in an effort to dilute the Hungarian community.

In 1990 Târgu Mureş was the scene of bloody clashes between Hungarian students, demonstrating for a Hungarian language faculty in their university, and Romanians who raided the local Hungarian political party offices. The Romanian mob attempted to gouge out the eyes of playwright András Sütő, who remains blind in one eye. The violence was apparently stirred up by the nationalist political group Vatra, which paid Romanian peasants from outlying villages to travel to Târgu Mureş, and armed them with pitchforks and axes. Officials later scapegoated local Roma in their investigation of the conflict.

Today Hungarian seems to be undergoing a renaissance in Târgu Mureş, with many local songs being in Hungarian only or in both languages. Carnival comes on the last weekend in June, when the city hosts its Târgu Mureş Days. Felsziget Festival (www.felsziget.ro) is a big five-day rock/DJ festival at the end of July.

Orientation

To make the 15-minute walk into town from the train station, exit the station and head straight to Str Gheorghe Doja, turn right and walk 1km straight up to Piaţas Victoriei, Unirii and Trandafirilor, the main thoroughfare where most hotels and travel agencies are. The citadel is just northeast of Piaţa Trandafirilor.

From the bus station, turn right along Str Gheorghe Doja and follow the street north 1.75km to Piaţa Trandafirilor.

MAPS

SunCart's 1:15,000 *Târgu Mureş* (€2.30) is a nice map of the city and region, but the freebie offered at the Tourist Information Centre is just as good for getting around town.

TRANSYLVANIA

Information

BOOKSHOPS

Librărie Hyperion (Piaţa Teatrul; 🕑 8am-8pm Mon-Fri, 9am-3pm Sat) Down steps on north side of square; carries Lonely Planet guides.

INTERNET ACCESS

Complex Charis (cnr Str Arany Ianoş & Str Aurel Filmon; per hr €0.60; 🕑 9am-9pm Mon-Fri, 3-9pm Sat, 6-9pm Sun) A Christian organisation with a slick reading room with computers to check email.

Electro Orizont (☎ 268 806; Piaţa Teatrului 12; per hr €0.45; 🕑 8am-10pm Mon-Fri, 9am-10pm Sat & Sun) Barebone internet spot off small alley south of square.

LEFT LUGGAGE

There's left luggage at the bus station and train station (per day €1 or €2, depending on size).

POST

Post Office (☎ 213 386; Str Revoluţei 1; 🕑 7am-8pm Mon-Fri, 8am-1pm Sat)

MONEY

ATMs are easy to find in the centre, including at **Banca Carpaţi** (cnr Piaţa Trandafirilor & Str Mihai Viteazul; 🕑 8.30am-6pm Mon-Fri, 9am-12:30pm Sat).

TOURIST INFORMATION

Tourism Information Centre (☎ 365 404 934; www .cjmures.ro/turism; cnr Piaţa Trandafirilor & Str Enescu; 🕑 8am-8pm Tue-Thu, to 4pm Mon & Sat) Occupying the enviable corner spot of the Culture Palace, this superbly run centre offers free maps and information on the region. Its website lists lots of accommodation and getting-around info too.

TRAVEL AGENCIES

Corbet Transair (☎ 268 975; www.corbet-transair.ro; 2nd fl, Piaţa Trandafirilor 3¾; 🕑 9am-5pm Mon-Fri) This busy travel agency can arrange trips to Roma villages to hear live music, (expensive) car rental and a wealth of adventure trips around the area – though it sometimes is quick to suggest Sighişoara or Sibiu. The office is upstairs through first door to right in central courtyard.

Sights

PIAŢA TRANDAFIRILOR & AROUND

The lively, long central **Piaţa Trandafirilor** is filled with heroic statues, open-air cafés and restaurants, and plenty of stuff to see.

By far Târgu Mureş' top attraction dominates the square's southwestern corner, the **Culture Palace** (Palatul Culturii; ☎ 267 629; cnr Piaţa Trandafirilor & Str Enescu; adult/student €1.40/0.70; 🕑 9am-6pm Tue-Sun),

the city's beloved landmark. Built in 1911–13, the secessionist-style building is unlike anything you'll find around Transylvania. Inside its glittering, tiled, steepled roofs are ornate hallways, colourful walls, giant mirrors imported from Venice, and an often-used concert hall (with a dramatic 4463-pipe organ), not to mention several worthwhile museums (all included in the entry price). The best is the **Hall of Mirrors** (Sala Oglinzi), with 12 stained-glass windows lining a 45m hallway – a tape in various languages explains the Székely fairy tales each portrays. The **Art Museum** (2nd floor) houses many large late-19th- and early 20th-century paintings; the **Archaeological Museum** (1st floor) explains Dacian pieces found in the region (English subtitles).

Next door is the **County Council Building**, with a tiled roof and bright green spires. Its 60m watchtower *may* open for visitors, but presently the only glimpse of the building you can get is the grand, colourful entry with hand-painted ceilings and stained glass facing the grand staircase upstairs.

Close by on Piaţa Unirii, just past the Romanian Orthodox Greco-Catholic Cathedral, is a **Memorial to Victims of the 1989 Revolution**, made of five connected wood crosses in tribute to the eight locals killed here.

Heading halfway down Piaţa Trandafirilor, the side-street Str Bolyai leads east to the interesting **Teleki Library/Bolyai Museum** (☎ 261 857; Str Bolyai 17; admission by donation; 🕑 10am-6pm Tue-Fri, to 1pm Sat & Sun), a two-part museum that takes on two different angles to the city's past. More famous is Teleki Library, which includes 230,000 (and counting) rare books that stem from Samule Teleki's (Austrian chancellor to the city) donation to the city in 1802. Modest chickenwire encases simple displays. The adjoining Bolyai Museum is dedicated to Târgu Mureş sons Farks and János, 19th-century mathematicians and excellers in non-Euclidian geometry; if that's boring to you, father/son scalps and skull parts are displayed side by side.

At the northeastern end of Piaţa Trandafirilor are two very different churches. Dominating **Orthodox Cathedral** (1925–34) was designed to impress, with gold icons (as well as a politically charged mural of a 'Romanian peasant' Jesus being whipped by nobles in Hungarian costumes inside; look to the left and right after entering). Across the street is the airier, baroque-style **Roman Catholic church** (Biserica Sfântul Jonos), which dates from 1728.

On the square's western side, just past adjoining Piaţa Teatrul, is the simple **Ethnographic Museum** (☎ 250 169; Piaţa Trandafirilor 11; admission €0.30; ☺ 9am-4pm Tue-Fri, to 2pm Sat, to 1pm Sun), housed in the baroque Toldalagi Palace (1762). The collection of traditional fabrics, pots, looms and tools is dryly explained in English.

A block west is an ornate and well-preserved **synagogue** (Str Aurel Filmon 21) from 1900. Before WWII, 5500 Jews lived in Târgu Mureş; now only about 100 live here.

THE CITADEL & AROUND

A block northeast of Piaţa Trandafirilor, the huge citadel dates from 1492, but was rebuilt in 1602. The approach of huge stone walls and its seven towers is super, but it's less impressive inside. On its southern end, and accessed separately from the rest, is the Reform Church (1491), with the nicest grounds. Gates lead into the main area from either side, but it's easiest from the northeastern side. There are a couple of theatres as well as an army recruitment centre inside. The most appealing attraction, in the 1492 gate tower on the western wall, is a small **City Museum** (admission €0.30; ☺ 9am-4pm Tue-Fri, 10am-2pm Sat, 10am-1pm Sun), with pottery fragments and old decrees. There's a small **information office** (☎ 250 337; ☺ 8am-3 or 4pm Mon-Fri) near the northern gate; English-speaking staff can tell you if a concert or special exhibition is going on in the citadel.

Towards Piaţa Trandafirilor, on Piaţa Bernády György, is the yellow-painted, baroque **Teleki House** (built 1797–1803). Joseph Teleki served as governor of Transylvania between 1842 and 1848.

WEEKEND PARK

Târgu Mureş sure loves this **complex** (☎ 212 099, 214 080; cnr Str Luntraşilor & Aleea Carpaţi; admission per hr/day €0.25/1.50; ☺ 8am-midnight), 2.5km north of the centre. A bit scrappy, the complex is along a river-fed canal, with a couple of giant pools, a few kids' pools, beach volleyball area, and plenty of places for beer and meat. It's certainly where the action is on hot summer weekends. Take Str Revoluţiei north, then go left on Str Luntraşilor.

Sleeping

Târgu Mureş can surprise a late arrival with full hotels and guesthouses, particularly midweek if conferences are on in town. If desperate, pick up a *Zile şi Nopţi* weekly, which includes accommodation listings. Contact **Antrec** (☎ 269 343; mures@antrec.ro) for help finding *pensiunes* in the region.

BUDGET

Hotel Sport (☎ 231 913; Str Liviu Rebreanu 29a; r with shared/private bathroom €10/22) Crusty and a bit musty, this OK 44-room cheapie (five minutes north of the train station by foot) is for shoestringers only. No breakfast.

Weekend Park (☎ 212 099, 214 080; cnr Str Luntraşilor & Aleea Carpaţi; bungalows €12) You can rent bungalows here, or pitch a tent.

ourpick Pensiune Ana Maria (☎ 264 401; Str Al Papui Ilarian 17; s/d/apt €26/29/37) With aqua-blue 'chalet' roofs over white bedframes, lacy green curtains on either side of raised platforms filled with tall plants, and framed prints of weird-looking women or unlikely mountains, the 8-room Pensiune Ana Maria is something like a home for Elvis Habsburg. The playful eight-room guesthouse mixes a bit of green Vegas garishness and Austrian tradition. 'Special breakfasts' are huge and superb; specially prepared dinners include homemade ţuică liquor made at the owner's horse ranch outside town. The great staff can arrange laundry or help you pay parking tickets. Go past the citadel and turn right on Str AL Papui Ilarian.

MIDRANGE

Atlantic (☎ 268 381; www.atlantichotel.ro; Str Libertăţii 15; r €22 & €40; 🖳) Gutsy tile choices clash a little with this 10-room *pensiune*'s clean comfort and big space (in the €40 rooms), but there is a lovely garden gazebo and a very good restaurant.

Voiajor (☎ 250 250; www.voiajor.ro; Str Gheorghe Doja 143; s/d €29/34; 🖳 🖳) It's connected to the bus station, 1.5km outside the centre, but this clean, aqua-and-gold 33-room hotel isn't a bad place for a night. Carpeted rooms come with cable TV, and staff are nice.

Casa Adria (☎ 250 544; www.casa-adria.ro; Str Verii 49; s/d €35/40; 🖳 🖳 🖳) Up the hill 2km northeast of the centre, Casa Adria's 12 rooms provide a quieter base, with deck seats by a small pool and free wi-fi for the laptop crowd.

Hotel Continental (☎ 250 416; www.continental.ro; Piaţa Teatrului 6; s/d €56/74; 🖳 🖳) This 111-room minichain hotel smacks of '80s socialism (eg the old wood panelling in clean rooms), but it's better spruced up than some of the old hotels in town.

TRANSYLVANIA

TOP END

Hotel Concordia (☎ 260 602; Piaţa Trandafirilor 45; s/d €96/112; 🔀 🖵 🗪) London chic meets Transylvania. This 34-room hotel, one of Romania's most surprising boutique hotels, offers stark, giant, stylish rooms with zebra-print chairs and framed fashion prints. Jet-setting Mureşianos hang in the ground-floor restaurant and bar (which projects key football games onto a blank wall). There's a fitness centre with Jacuzzi.

Eating

Kebab (☎ 268 510; Str Bolyai 10; dishes €0.75-1.50; 🕑 6.30am-10pm Mon-Sat) The name's simple, and the food's great and cheap, plus there's seating. Go in, pick out kebabs (€1.50, with freshly squeezed juice) or cafeteria-style salads or hot dishes (including a veggie option or two), then sit inside or under the orange canopy on the footpath.

Emma Vendégco (☎ 263 021; Str Horea 6; mains €1-3; 🕑 11am-11pm) This low-key Hungarian restaurant-bar brings in the locals for its €1.50 borschts and €2.75 four-course dinners. Best of all is the chicken with cucumber sauce and polenta.

Leo (☎ 214 999; Piaţa Trandafirilor 36-38; dishes €2-7; 🕑 24hr) Covered streetside seats fill first in this buzzing all-hours restaurant, popular for tasty grilled meats (a speciality is the lovely grilled pork with corn grits, fried eggs and garlic sauce), pizzas, big salads, beer or ice cream.

Hotel Concordia (☎ 260 602; Piaţa Trandafirilor 45) Those wanting to be seen stick with the street side seats of the bar and restaurant here, where there are sandwiches (from €2) and business lunch specials (€4.25).

Varan Varan (Piaţa Trandafirilor; 🕑 7am-10pm Mon-Sat, 8am-6pm Sun) This is a central supermarket.

Drinking

Hotel Tinereului Café-Bar (☎ 217 441; Str Nicolae Grigorescu 17-19; 🕑 10am-10pm) Those collecting experiences should get a coffee or beer – and a free 1980s flashback – at this little, commie-era hotel café in the student quarter, 1km north of the citadel. (Rooms are stuffy and overpriced.)

Cuba Libre (Str Nicolae Grigorescu 17-19; 🕑 10pm-4am Thu-Sat) Next door to Hotel Tinereului, this basement club reels in the nearby students.

Teresa Scara (Piaţa Trandafirilor; 🕑 10am-10pm) Pretty much everyone who drinks beer (flirting uni students, middle-aged coworkers) drops in at this open-air place for €0.80 beers.

Entertainment

The lovely **Culture Palace** (☎ 267 629; cnr Piaţa Trandafirilor & Str Enescu) houses a **children's library** (🕑 9am-8pm Mon-Fri) filled with fanciful decorations and displays. Here too is the **Agenţie de Bilete** (☎ 212 522; 🕑 10am-1pm & 5-7pm Mon-Fri, 10am-1pm Sat & Sun), which sells tickets for a wide variety of shows, including opera, high-school talent shows and the **State Philharmonic** (☎ 262 548, 261 420; tickets €1-3.50) concerts, which are held Thursday nights.

National Opera & Theatre (☎ 264 848; Piaţa Teatrului 1; www.orizont.net/teatru) Events at this very-1978 venue are in Hungarian and Romanian.

Cinema Arta (☎ 263 180; Piaţa Trandafirilor; tickets €1.25-2) Next to McDonald's, this cinema plays Hollywood films in the original language.

Red Light District (☎ 0740-038 555; Piaţa Trandafirilor 53; 🕑 10am-4pm Tue-Sun) Hosts rock and punk shows in its graceful two-room cellar.

Getting There & Away

Wizz Air (www.wizzair.com) started three weekly flights to/from Budapest in July 2006; flights cost around €17 one way. The airport is 14km west of town (on the road to Cluj-Napoca). **Tarom** (☎ 250 170; Piaţa Trandafirilor 6-8; 🕑 9am-5pm Mon-Fri, to noon Sat) sells tickets to Bucharest (flights three times weekly).

The **bus station** (☎ 221 451; Str Gheorghe Doja) sends daily bus and maxitaxi services, including hourly maxitaxis to Sighişoara (€2, 1½ hours), continuing on to Braşov (€5.25, four hours) and Bucharest (€10, seven hours). There are also five daily buses to Bistriţa (€2.40, 2½ hours), three to Budapest (€57), five to Cluj-Napoca (€3.50 to €4, 2½ hours), two to Sibiu (€3.50, three hours), and frequent services to Sovata (€2, 1¼ hours).

The **Agenţie de Voiaj CFR** (☎ 266 203; Piaţa Teatrului 1; 🕑 7.30am-7.30pm Mon-Fri) sells advance tickets. From Târgu Mureş there are two daily trains to Bucharest (€15.70, 8½ hours) and Sibiu (€4, 5½ hours), and one each to Budapest (€37, 7½ hours), Cluj-Napoca (€6.75, 2¼ hours), Iaşi (€12.30, 6½ hours) and Timişoara (€9.15, 6½ hours).

Getting Around

Central Târgu Mureş is small enough to cover by foot. Bus 18 (€0.45) goes from the stop at Piaţa Teatrul and Piaţa Trandafirilor to the

TRANSYLVANIA

bus station; bus 5 goes to the train station. At research time no buses went to the airport; a taxi is about €6 or €7.

Eurolines (☎ 306 126; Str Călăraşilor 38; ☒ 9am-8pm Mon-Fri, to 4pm Sat) rents Dacia Logans from €43 per day.

SOUTHWEST TRANSYLVANIA

The patch of Transylvania between the Retezat Mountains and Apuseni Mountains, west of the Cluj-Napoca–Sibiu highway, is one of the region's least chartered and ventured-to areas, where Dacian ruins, mountain-top citadels, and one of Eastern Europe's greatest 'Dracula-style' castles (in Hunedoara) await those willing to deal with scarce sources of information and an often dodgy hotel scene.

The history is undeniable. The pre-Roman Dacia kingdom lived in full force in the area until Romans conquered the capital Sarmizegetusa in AD 106. The union of Transylvania with Romania occurred in Alba Iulia. Twice. Once in 1599 and again after WWI.

Those willing to drive on back roads – such as the lovely hilly drive from Deva to Abrud – will get a break from often-industrial, highly trafficked roads, such as the sometimes unpleasant ride between Sibiu and Arad, or around Hunedoara's steel mills.

ALBA IULIA

☎ 258 / pop 66,400

Hugely important to Romanians – the nation announced the union of Transylvania with Romania here in 1599 and 1918 – and less so to foreigners, dusty Alba Iulia is a good stop-off if you're heading between Cluj-Napoca and Sibiu. Its Unification Museum, located in the citadel, is one of Romania's most interesting history museums. Otherwise, the town's rather modern, concrete-dominated sprawl and disappointing lodging options make it easy to pass.

Alba Iulia was known by the Dacians as Apulum, serving both as the capital of Upper Dacia and later, during Roman times, as the largest centre in the Dacian province of the Roman empire. From 1542 to 1690 Alba Iulia was the capital of the principality of Transylvania. Romania's national day (1 December) is a time of major celebrations in Alba Iulia.

Orientation

The sprawling citadel – filled with churches and administrative buildings – lies between the new town to the west, and lower town to the east, which resembles a building site. Most of the town's older buildings were bulldozed under Ceauşescu to make way for a civic centre that never happened.

Many locals stubbornly refer to streets by their old names. Some you may need to know about: Str Dr Ioan Ratiu used to be Str Avantului; Str Rubin Patiţa used to be Str Primăverii; Str Frederic Mistral used to be Str Parcului.

The adjacent bus and train stations are some 2km south of the citadel.

Information
INTERNET RESOURCES
Internet Domino (☎ 834 981; Str Dr Ioan Ratiu 2; per hr €0.60; ☒ 24hr)

LEFT LUGGAGE
Train station (per day €1.70; ☒ 24 hr)

MONEY
Banca Comercială Română (B-dul Regele Carol I, 35; ☒ 8.30am-6pm Mon-Fri, to 12.30pm Sat) Cashes travellers cheques and gives cash advances.

POST
Post office (B-dul Brătianu 1; ☒ 7am-8pm Mon-Fri)

TRAVEL AGENCIES
Albena Tours (☎ 812 140; office@albenatours.ro; Str Fredric Mistral 2; ☒ 9am-5pm Mon-Fri, to 1pm Sat) Central travel agent, more keen to get you out of Romania, but can help with regional tours.

Sights
The imposing **Alba Carolina Citadel**, richly carved with sculptures and reliefs in a baroque style, is the dominant sight of the city of Alba Iulia – and worth stopping to see for a couple of hours. It was originally constructed in the 13th century, although the fortress you see today was built between 1714 and 1738 to a design of Italian architect Giovanni Morandi Visconti. There are English and French information panels placed throughout the citadel, making it quite easy to delve into its history without a guide.

Str Mihai Viteazul runs up from the lower town to the **first gate** of the fortress, adorned with sculptures inspired by Greek mythology. From here, a stone road leads to the **third gate**

TRANSYLVANIA

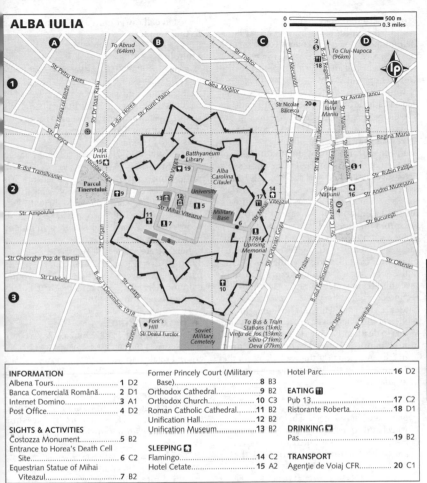

ALBA IULIA

TRANSYLVANIA

of the fortress, dominated by an equestrian statue of Carol VI of Austria. Above the gate is **Horea's death cell** (Celula lui Horea), where the leader of the great 1784 peasant uprising awaited his unpleasant end.

Just before you enter the third gate, a foot-path leads 500m south to an out-of-sight **Orthodox church** (Biserica Memorială Sfânta Treime). The wooden church, brought to Alba Iulia in 1990 from Maramureş, stands on the site of a former Metropolitan cathedral built by Mihai Viteazul in 1597 and destroyed by the Habsburgs in 1713.

Inside the gates, about 200m west in a park, is the Soviet-style 22.5m **Costozza monument**,

which commemorates the soldiers and officers of the 50th infantry regiment of Alba Iulia who were killed while fighting in the Habsburg army against Italy in the battle of Costozza in 1866.

Just west is the **Unification Hall** (Sala Unirii; 1900), built as a military casino. In this hall the act of unification between Romania and Transylvania was signed during the Great Assembly of 1 December 1918.

Facing the hall from the south is a large **equestrian statue of Mihai Viteazul** (Michael the Brave), ruler of Romania from 1593 to 1601. On 1 November 1599 he visited Alba Iulia to celebrate the unification of Wallachia,

Moldavia and Transylvania – a union that crumbled after his assassination a year later. Behind the statue is the **Princes Court**, former residence of the princes of Transylvania, which was built in several stages from the 16th century onwards.

Immediately west is the 18th-century **Roman Catholic Cathedral**, built on the site of a Romanesque church destroyed during the Tartar invasion of 1241. Many famous Transylvanian princes are buried here.

Inside the former Babylon building (1851) just west of Unification Hall is the impressive **Unification Museum** (Muzeul Unirii; ☎ 813 300; adult/child €1.20/0.60; ◷ 10am-7pm Tue-Sun summer, to 5pm Tue-Sun winter). The commie years are all that gets missed in this look at Romanian history (it goes from pre-Roman history to 1944). Many Roman sculptures, votives and pillars found in the area are subtitled in English (one of the Jupiter statues lost his penis over the years). One hallway celebrates various heroes you may recognise from street names. Don't miss the section devoted to the peasant revolutionaries Cloşca, Crişan and Horea. The highlight is a replica of the wheel used to crush Cloşca and Horea to death in 1785 (Crişan sensibly killed himself in prison before he could be tortured to death). A plaque on the wall recounts the orders issued by the judge who determined their ghastly death:

...they are to be taken to the torture place and there killed by being tied to a wheel and squashed – first Cloşca, then Horea. After being killed their bodies are to be cut into four parts and the head and body impaled on the edge of different roads for everyone to see them. The internal organs – their hearts and intestines – will be buried in the place of torture...

Near the western entrance of the citadel, the highly impressive **Orthodox Cathedral** (originally known as the 'Church of the Coronation') was built on the old site of the citadel guardhouse in 1921–22 for the coronation of King Ferdinand I and Queen Marie in 1922. Their frescoed portraits remain intact on either side of the doors as you enter. Designed in the shape of a Greek circumscribed cross, the cathedral is surrounded by a wall of decorative colonnades that form a rectangular enclosure with peaceful gardens within. A 58m-tall bell tower marks the main entrance to the complex.

Sleeping

Flamingo (☎ 816 354; Str Mihai Viteazul 6; r with private toilet €29, s/d with shared toilet €8.60/17.40) This old villa has six rooms and a loud bar-restaurant, right next to the eastern entrance to the citadel. It's simple; upstairs rooms have shared bathroom, but are further from the ground-floor bar noise. No breakfast.

Hotel Parc (☎ 811 723; www.hotelparc.ro; Str Primăverii 4; s/d in '2 star' wing €49/60, r in '4 star' wing €77; ▣) Still rather flippantly run, the scrubbed-up '70s hotel in the centre is definitely Alba Iulia's smartest. 'Four star' rooms are bright, with lots of space, while 'two star' are fine. All rooms have balconies, plus there's an indoor pool and fitness centre.

Hotel Cetate (☎ 811 780; Piaţa Unirii 3; s/d €50/70) Thrown-down carpets and raised prices hardly make-over this 10-storey, 113-room, commie relic. It's up the hill, at the citadel's west entrance. Lots of groups.

Eating & Drinking

Ristorante Roberta (☎ 819 980; B-dul Regele Carol I; pizzas & pastas €1.50-5.50; ◷ 9am-midnight) On a busy commercial strip, Roberta churns out Alba's favourite meals, which break the usual Italian mould (eg tagliatelle with rabbit and cream sauce). There are two sitting areas – plant-filled brick-floors up front, a bit dowdy and formal out the back. Sometimes it takes time for fresh meals to be made. (Our pasta took 1½ hours!)

Pub 13 (3rd Gate, Citadel; mains €2.30-5.15; ◷ 10am-2am) Built into the citadel's eastern wall near the 'third gate', this cavernous restaurant-bar has world flags flying over a cool brick-walled space that's big on grilled meats and pizza.

Pas (Str Varga 4; ◷ 8am-midnight or so) Pas is a very artful little bar in the citadel (papier-mâché torsos come out of the walls) attracting an indie-rocker crowd. Good for coffee or beer.

There is a small market selling fresh fruit and vegetables, as well as dried and tinned products behind the Banc Post building, next to the Agenţie de Voiaj CFR office.

Getting There & Away

Direct bus and maxitaxi services from Alba Iulia's **bus station** (☎ 812 967) include six to Bucharest (€10), 14 daily to Cluj-Napoca (€4, two hours), five to Deva (€1.70, 1½ hours),

13 to Sibiu (€1.70, 1½ hours), three to Târgu Jiu (€4.30), three to Târgu Mureş (€3.90, 2¼ hours) and three to Timişoara (€3.60). Local buses 3 and 4 run from the stations to the citadel and centre.

The **Agenţie de Voiaj CFR** (☎ 816 678; Calea Moţilor 1; ☯ 8am-4pm Mon-Fri) sells advance tickets. There are three daily trains to Bucharest (€9, 6½ to nine hours), Cluj-Napoca (€5, 2½ hours), Deva (€5, two hours), three to Timişoara (€10, five hours) and Sibiu (€5, 2½ hours). There are also a couple of daily trains to Prague (16 hours) and Vienna (12 hours).

DEVA
☎ 254 / pop 77,300

The area's key transport hub, Deva is a somewhat haggard mining town with a little spunk, much of it from the crumbling citadel looming above town. The historic citadel – nearly blown to bits in an 1849 explosion –is a popular haunt. Maybe it's the tug from the Hollywood-style Deva sign (which those copycats in Braşov seemed to like).

Romania's top gymnastics club, Cetate Liceul de Educaţie Fizica şi Sport Deva, trains young athletes for the elite Romanian Olympic team here.

Orientation & Information
The train and bus stations are five minutes' walk north of the centre at Piaţa Garii. It's easy enough to pop into town for a quick citadel look-around and a pizza, then get back on the road. The 'information' desk on the train station tracks keeps bags if you ask, with no set price.

Internet Club (B-dul Iuliu Maniu; per hr €0.50; ☯ 24hr) Follow the sign behind the building.

Post Office (B dul Decebal; ☯ 8am-8pm Mon-Fri, to 2pm Sat)

Raiffeisen Bank (B-dul Iuliu Maniu; ☯ 9am-6pm Mon-Fri) At train station.

Sights
Rising some 270m from town on a rocky hilltop, the 13th-century **Citadel** (admission free) crowns the mining town. A new **funicular** (☎ 220 288; return €1.45; ☯ 9am-9pm) saves visitors from the steep climb (which leads up behind Parcul Cetăţii at the west end of B-dul 1 Decembrie). At the top there are plenty of

TRANSYLVANIA

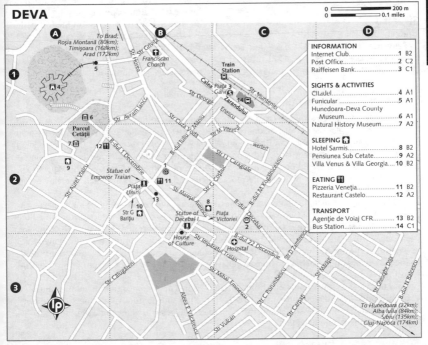

DEVA

0   200 m
0   0.1 miles

INFORMATION
Internet Club...................1 B2
Post Office.......................2 C2
Raiffeisen Bank................3 C1

SIGHTS & ACTIVITIES
Citadel............................4 A1
Funicular.........................5 A1
Hunedoara-Deva County
Museum.........................6 A1
Natural History Museum.......7 A2

SLEEPING
Hotel Sarmis....................8 B2
Pensiunea Sub Cetate........9 A2
Villa Venus & Villa Georgia....10 B2

EATING
Pizzeria Veneţia................11 B2
Restaurant Castelo............12 A2

TRANSPORT
Agenţie de Voiaj CFR...........13 B2
Bus Station.......................14 C1

To Brad;
Roşia Montană (80km);
Timişoara (168km);
Arad (172km)

Franciscan Church

Train Station

Calea Piaţa
Garii

Str Gheorghe

Str Crivita

Str Horea

Str Avram Iancu

Str Cuza Voda

Str Muntenei

Zarandului

Str George Enescu

Str M Viteaz

Parcul Cetăţii

Str G Cosbuc

Str IL Caragiale

B-dul M Kogălniceanu

B-dul 1 Decembrie

Str Aurel Vlaicu

Statue of Emperor Traian

Piaţa Unirii

Str Mareşal Averescu

Str G Baritiu

Statue of Decebal

Piaţa Victoriei

B-dul Decebal

House of Culture

Str Împăratul Traian

Hospital

B-dul 22 Decembrie

Str D Zamfirescu

Str Mihai Eminescu

Str Călugăreni

Aleea E Văcărescu

Str Vulcan

Str C Porumbescu

Str Carpaţi

Str Mărăşti

Str Gheorghe Doja

B-dul N Bălcescu

To Hunedoara (22km);
Alba Iulia (84km);
Sibiu (135km);
Cluj-Napoca (174km)

stone walls to ponder, arched gateways to walk through, and windows to look out over 360-degree views of the surrounding hills.

Work started on the stone fortress in 1250. Legend says the wife of the mason was buried alive in the walls to ensure its safekeeping. In 1453 Iancu de Hunedoara expanded the fort, just in time to imprison Unitarian activist Dávid Ferenc (1510–79), who died here.

In 1784, during the peasant uprising led by Horea, Crişan and Cloşca, the fortress served as a refuge for terrified nobles fearful of being killed by militant peasants. In 1849 Hungarian nationalists attacked Austrian generals held up in the fort. The four-week siege ended with the mighty explosion of the castle's gunpowder deposits, which left the castle in ruins.

Down by the park are two museums. Closed for renovation at the time of research, the **Hunedoara-Deva County Museum** (Muzeul Judeţean Hunedoara-Deva) is housed in the 17th-century Magna Curia Palace. Hopefully they're expanding their already great exhibition on Deva and the surrounding area's citadels.

Nearby is the OK **Natural History Museum** (Muzeul Ştiinţe ale Naturii; admission €0.35; ☻ 9am-5pm Tue-Sun).

Sleeping

Budget options are limited.

Pensiunea Sub Cetate (☎ 212 535; www.subcetate .ro; B-dul 1 Decembrie, 37b; s/d € 27/38; ☒) Family run, this excellent 10-room *pensiune* has a group

of rooms around a lovely patio and a garden that looks up to the Hollywood-style Deva sign. Best are the two front carpeted rooms with balconies. A couple come with a small kitchen. No English is spoken.

Hotel Sarmis (☎ 214 731; Str Mareşal Averescu 7; s/d €49.50/64.60) Vaguely shaped like a 1974 commie idea of an Aztec palace, this eight-floor, 113-room hotel is being renovated (at last). The best of the three stodgy hotels in the centre.

Villa Venus & Villa Georgia (☎ 212 243; www .villavenus.ro; Str Mihai Eminescu 16; r €55-75; ☒) Two neighbouring historic villas join to make Deva's nicest sleep. The six rooms mingle styles – chunky Art Deco beds or armoires in sprawling rooms with '70s-style carpets (new). One 'single' has a separate changing room and sitting area, each as big as Hotel Sarmis' double. A huge outside garden is filled with slides and play areas for kids. Next door's 'Villa Georgia' rooms are more modern – the apartment (€75) has a kitchen.

Eating

Restaurant Castelo (cnr B-dul 1 Decembrie & Str Avram Iancu; mains €2.25-4; ☻ 9am-midnight) Occupying a nice spot on the foot of the hill, locals cram in here for the €2.60 lunch specials, seating themselves on shaded bench seats out on the footpath.

Pizzeria Veneţia (B-dul Iuliu Maniu; pizzas €2.60-3.25; ☻ 9am-11pm) The Veneţia is a vaguely modern pizza spot in the centre, with orange walls and brick walls, plus outdoor seats.

DISAPPEARING MOUNTAIN

About 80km from Alba Iulia or Deva, the **Roşia Montană** (or 'Red Mountain') has long drawn the less charitable instinct of foreigners, from Romans to Canadian suits. Known for its gold and silver, mines here date from Dacian times 2000 years ago. In recent years Canadian mining company Gabriel Resources launched a plan to create the continent's largest opencast mine, a 16-year-project that would begin extracting 2000 tons of gold and silver by 2009. Many locals, riddled with unemployment, have sold plots of land to the company and plan to create a new village 15km away.

Tension peaked in June 2006, when Vanessa Redgrave was awarded a lifetime achievement award at the Transylvania Film Festival and lashed out at the company, which cosponsored the festival. Hungary backed her up, by asking for mining not to continue, citing a 2000 mining disaster in Baia Mare that spilled cyanide into waters feeding Hungarian rivers. Many critics worry that the ecosystem will be crushed, a mountain lost and that culturally important sites – such as a 400m-long stretch of **old Roman galleries** (which were indeed locked up during our visit) – lost forever.

In the village, 10km north of Abrud, there's a rather neglected **open-air mining museum** (admission free) with old stamps used to crush ore in the 18th century, plus some Roman tablets. It's just before the police station, off the main road; ask locals to point the way

Have a look before it's gone.

Getting There & Away

BUS

The **bus station** spills across the parking lot in front of the train station. Frequent buses and microbuses go to Oraştie (€1.15, 30 minutes) and Hunedoara (€0.75, 25 minutes). Other services include five to Cluj-Napoca, eight to Petroşiani, four to Sibiu, two to Târgu Mureş and four to Timişoara.

Minibus 6 also does a circuit of Deva, running when full and costing €0.30 per journey.

TRAIN

Deva has many train links. Daily service includes a few direct trains to Bucharest (€10.70, 6½ to 7½ hours), three to Cluj-Napoca (€7.75, 3¼ hours), three with changes to Sibiu (€6.75, 3½ to 4½ hours) and a couple to Timişoara (€7.75, 3¼ hours), plus three daily trains to Budapest (6½ hours). Buy advance tickets at **Agenţie de Voiaj CFR** (☎ 218 887; Block A, B-dul 1 Decembrie; ⏲ 8am-8pm Mon-Fri).

HUNEDOARA

☎ 254 / pop 79,200

One of Romania's most communist-looking cities, with skeletons of steel mills surrounding a surprisingly welcoming Soviet-style city of housing blocks, is also home to one of Eastern Europe's loveliest medieval castles. Other than that, Hunedoara is all about bowling apparently – it hosted the 2002 Bowling World Cup.

The adjacent bus and train stations are a few hundred metres from Hotel Rusca; take Str Avram Iancu for 200m a couple of long blocks east, then head right (south) on L-shaped B-dul Dacia to where it bends back towards the west.

The castle shop sells a Hunedoara map for €0.60.

Sights

With a tweak in promotion, the 14th-century **Gothic Corvin Castle** (Castelul Corvinestilor; ☎ 711 423; adult/student €1.20/0.60; ⏲ 9am-3pm Mon, to 6pm Tue-Sun May-Aug, to 3pm Mon, to 5pm Tue-Sun Sep-Apr) could trump Bran for Transylvania's premier (fake) 'Dracula castle' status. A drawbridge leads to three towering stone turrets over a rushing river. Inside you'll find iron gates, nooks into Gothic rooms, suspended walkways, and weapon displays of the glory days in the 14th and 15th centuries – it all seriously tugs an imaginative chord in all but the most jaded castle-hating visitors.

The fantastical monument stands as a symbol of Hungarian rule (both János Hunyadi and his son Matthias Corvinus, two famous Hungarian kings, made notable improvements), which made it pretty unpopular with Ceauşescu.

The fairy-tale castle walls, believed to be built on old Roman fortifications, were hewn out of 30m of solid rock by Turkish prisoners. The fortress was extensively restored by Iancu de Hunedoara (János Hunyadi in Hungarian) from 1452 onwards. Eventually Jules Verne included the castle in his *Around the World in 80 Days* itinerary in 1873 (no steel factories then).

From the bus or train station, the castle is about 1.5km southwest. Take B-dul Republicii south, then turn right on B-dul Libertăţii towards the steel works; it's across the river from Piaţa Libertăţii via Str Bursan.

Don't miss the striking **communist murals** inside the train station.

Sleeping & Eating

Hotel Rusca (☎ 717 575; www.hotelrusca.ro; B-dul Dacia 10; s/d €40/55) Three decades on, the Rusca's spruce-up has scrubbed away the scars, making it more fresh than many commie-era make-overs. Rooms are nice and it's in the heart of B-dul Dacia action.

Scorpion (☎ 714 511; B-dul Dacia 4-5; mains €2.30-4; ⏲ 10am-1am Tue-Sat, noon-1am Sun & Mon) About 200m north of Hotel Rusca, amidst housing blocks and tree-lined footpaths, the Scorpion is Hunedoara's best restaurant – with deliciously un-Romanian 'oriental chicken' with vegetables and rice, plus good pizzas.

Getting There & Away

The **bus station** (B-dul Republicii 3) sends maxitaxis every 15 minutes to Deva (€0.70, 30 to 40 minutes). There's a night bus to Bucharest (€17) and Timişoara.

The adjoining **train station** (☎ 719 238; B-dul Republicii 3) sees little action. About eight daily trains connect Hunedoara with Simeria (€0.50), where you can reach Braşov, Sibiu or Arad.

THE DACIAN & ROMAN CITADELS

Strewn across this area of Transylvania – from Orăştie to the foot of the Retezat Mountains – is an archaeologist's delight: Dacian and Roman ruins from fortresses recognised as Unesco

World Heritage sites, including the pre-Roman Dacian capital (Sarmizegetusa) and Roman-conquered Dacian capital (Ulpia Traiana).

The area is very undeveloped for travellers, with few accommodation options and very few tourist services, including guides or information centres.

South of Orăştie

About a dozen kilometres south of the historic town Orăştie (on the Sibiu–Deva highway) are two nearby Dacian sites that are tough to reach without 4WD or hiking boots and time to kill. It's not easy to make much of either without a guide.

Easiest to reach is **Costeşti fortress**, built to defend the larger town Sarmizegetusa from its spot on the banks of the Oraşului River. After the village Costeşti (10km south of Orăştie), when the paved road ends, veer right across the bridge; yellow-cross signs point to the fortress. It's a 40-minute walk, or you can drive on the rough dirt road.

Back where the paved road ends, a monster dirt road veers left into the wood, rambling 20km along the river to **Sarmizegetusa**, the Dacian capital from the 3rd century BC until the Romans conquered it in AD 106. The Dacian leader Burebista (r 70–44 BC) holed up here atop the 1200m hill from Romans after helping enemies of Caesar; both leaders were assassinated the same year (44 BC). Sarmizegetusa remained unconquered by the Romans until AD 106, when Roman forces led by Trajan forced the Dacians to retreat north. The Dacian city was divided into three parts – two civilian areas and the middle sacred zone, which contains the places of worship. Visitors are allowed to walk around the ruins. Our attempts to reach Sarmizegetusa through the muddy road by Dacia failed; the route is best tackled during the summer season, when it's clear of snow.

Orăştie itself is a pleasant little town, with a quiet central street a block south of the highway, with an **Orthodox Church**, an **Ethnographic & Art Museum** and heroic busts and murals of Dacian leaders Decebal and Burebista.

In Orăştie, **Mini Hotel Jorsa** (☎ 254 240 013; Str Bălcescu 30; s €14-21.50, d €26; ☐), halfway between the centre and the Deva–Sibiu highway, is a slightly run-down 13-room hotel that gets a little flair with potted plants, bright colours, a sauna and internet access. There are a couple of other options in town too.

Densuş & Around

About 13km west of the town Haţeg (43km southwest of Orăştie), and in full view of the Retezat Mountains, the **Densuş church** (admission free) is on Romania's top-10 list of fabulous historic treasures. A priest here will unlock the chapel.

The small stone church, built between the 11th and 12th centuries, stands on the ancient site of an edifice dating from the 4th century, which archaeologists believe to have been the mausoleum of Roman general Longinus (look for his name on the first pillar to the left inside). The church was constructed from stones taken from the Roman city of Ulpia Traiana-Sarmizegetusa.

Archaeologists conclude that the church, believed to have been built as a court chapel, was built by a Romanian noble family, only falling under Hungarian rule from the 14th century onwards. There are fragments of a 15th-century fresco inside the church, and Roman-era pieces outside.

To reach Densuş, head west of Haţeg, turning north at Toteşti. All roads are paved.

One of the better places to stay in the area is the **Art Motel** (☎ 254 772 344; B-dul Vladimirescu 15; s €23 d €29 & €37; ☒) in Haţeg. This stylish make-over of a ugly building next to the central square is an excellent bet, with eight small rooms decorated with 1920s B&W prints of town.

Contact the local **Antrec representative** (☎ 254 770 796; hunedoara@antrec.ro) for *pensiunes* in the area.

Ulpia Traiana (Sarmizegetusa)

Following the Romans' defeat of Decebal's forces in AD 106, they built up a spectacular array of towns, and set their capital of conquered Dacia in Ulpia Traiana, some 15km southwest of Densuş on the main Caransebeş road. To confuse things, the name of the former Dacian capital was added to the Roman city's name. It was now known as Ulpia Traiana-Sarmizegetusa or plain old Sarmizegetusa.

Only 2% of the city, which was home to 30,000 in its heyday, has been excavated. Just off the highway, you can see bits of walls and some pillars in the city that may have covered an area of 60 hectares.

During the early 14th century, the stones of the Sarmizegetusa ruins were used by local villagers to build churches and it was not until the 19th century that the dismantled ruins fell under the protection of the Deva

TRANSYLVANIA

Archaeological Society and later the National Museum of Transylvania. Remains of the Roman Forum, complete with 10m-tall marble columns, have already been uncovered; they're just south of the highway, past the main site.

Many tools, ceramics, ivory combs and other Roman treasures yielded from Sarmizegetusa are exhibited in the **museum** (☎ 254 776 418; adult/student €0.60/0.35; �9am-8pm summer, to 5pm winter), across the highway 150m west of the site.

Dani Delinescu chips in as an unofficial **tourist information service** (☎ 0747-038 145) for the town of 700. She can help find a room or a guide.

In summer archaeologists from Cluj-Napoca's **National History Museum of Transylvania** (p189) arrange digs around the area; contact them to see about volunteering opportunities.

Pensiunea Sarmis (☎ 254 776 572; www.pensiunea sarmis.webpro.ro; Ulpia Traiana 82; r €20-23) is a modern *pensiune* on a side road, southwest of the ruins. For something cheaper, the far more basic **Ulpa Traiana** (☎ 254 776 453; r per person €13) is nearby.

One lone bus goes between here and Deva in the early morning.

RETEZAT MOUNTAINS

Part of the Southern Carpathians, these glacially bent mountains gain their name ('Retezat' is Romanian for 'cut off') from the flat-topped pyramid shape of these peaks. Most of the stunning territory is covered by the **Retezat National Park** (www.retezat.ro), Romania's oldest (established in 1935). Covering 38,138 hectares (including some 80 glacial lakes), the area is considered a Unesco Biosphere Reserve. Carnivores large and small (especially the cute marmot) roam the region, as do black deer and chamois. The region is among Europe's last remaining largely untouched stretch of wilderness and provides unforgettable hiking experiences among its valleys, peaks, rivers and gorges.

East of the Retezat Mountains lies the Jiu Valley, Romania's largest mining region, centred on the towns of Petroşani, Petrila and Câmpii lui Neag in the northern end of the valley. Petroşani makes a potential base.

TRANSYLVANIA

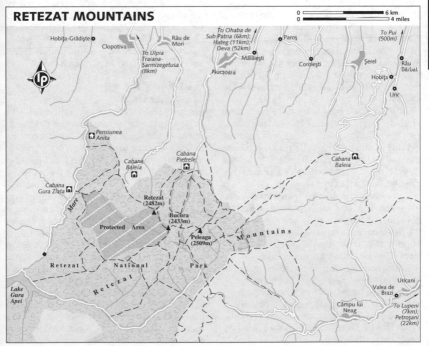

RETEZAT MOUNTAINS

From Petroşani you can head 57km south down the Jiu Valley to Târgu Jiu (p107). The southbound road running parallel to this road to the east is said to be the highest road in Romania, peaking at 2142m. It is only possible to cross the mountains along this road by 4WD vehicles.

From Târgu Jiu there are a few daily trains to Petroşani (1¼ to 1¾ hours). From Hunedoara and Deva, change at Simeria.

You can camp at designated tent sites for about €3 per person; cabanas cost about €6 to €10 per person.

Activities

Hiking is excellent here. The two main bases are Cabana Gura Zlata and Cabana Pietrele.

From Cabana Gura Zlata (the most popular cabin in the area), which is reached by paved road south of Cârneşti, there are oodles of well-marked hikes. Another 12km south of the cabin is **Lacu Gura Apei**, a glacial lake you can stick your feet in (it's cold). It's possible to hike here from Ulpia Traiana (Sarmizegetusa), northwest of the mountains, by taking the red-cross trail 20km (about seven hours).

Cabana Gura Zlata (☎ 0744-648 599; www.turismtur .ro; d €10) is a two-storey villa, with campsites 200m north (in a patch of woods across the river). Staff know some English, and cook up breakfast for €2 (plus other meals). A few kilometres on there is a home on the stream that can be rented out called **Pensiunea Anita** (☎ 0744-524 871).

Another good base is south of Nucşoara. Hikers can catch a local train from Simeria (36km), Petroşani (44km) or Târgu Jiu (94km) to Ohaba de Sub Patria, then follow the trail south, through Nucşoara, to **Cabana Pietrele** (six to seven hours, blue stripes). This can also be reached by car.

A trail between the two cabins takes eight to 10 hours. A popular hike is up **Mt Retezat** (2482m), which is roughly halfway between the two cabanas (a very full day trip). Another popular hike is the five-hour hike up **Mt Peleaga** (2509m) from Cabana Pietrele.

Other access points to the mountains are to the northeast and east of the mountains. From Ohaba de Sub Patria (9km), take a local train to Pui train station, from where you can hike 3km south along a paved road to Hobiţa. From Hobiţa a trail leads to **Cabana Baleia** (4½ hours, blue triangles).

A starting point from the east is Petroşani. Daily buses run to Câmpu lui Neag, 28km west of Petroşani. There is a cabana in Câmpu lui Neag. From here a 3½- to four-hour trail leads to Cabana Buta in the southeastern Retezat.

NORTHERN TRANSYLVANIA

Stretching north towards Maramureş, Transylvania's treats don't stop. Cluj-Napoca is a hopping student town many visitors rank as tops in Transylvania, and is a popular gateway to the caves and hikes of the Apuseni Mountains just southwest. Further north, the Bârgău Valley served as the perfect setting for Bram Stoker's *Dracula*.

During WWII, northern Transylvania fell under pro-Nazi Hungarian rule. Under the Diktat of Vienna of 30 August 1940, the Axis powers, Germany and Italy, forced Romania to cede 43,493 sq km and a population of 2.6 million to Hungary. During the four years of occupation, thousands of Romanians were imprisoned and tortured while entire villages were massacred. Northern Transylvania was not recovered until 25 October 1944 when, following the liberation of Satu Mare, the territory fell back into Romanian hands.

CLUJ-NAPOCA

☎ 264 / pop 318,030

Just one letter away from 'club,' Cluj isn't quite as pretty or mountainous as the Saxon towns to the south, but it earns much of its nationwide fame for the dozens of cavernous, unsnooty subterranean discos that blare and bounce with many of the city's thousands of university students. Outside the clubs, though, it's one of Romania's most welcoming and energised cities – a 'real' city where there's everything going on (football, opera, espresso, heated politics, trams), regardless of who visits or not. Its attractions don't hit you over the head like Dracula's 'birthplaces' do, but if you look closer Cluj's are some of Transylvania's most arresting.

It's also a great base for renting a car – it's cheaper than in Braşov – and has several good travel agencies, so it serves as a common shooting-off point for the Apuseni Mountains and the further-flung Maramureş.

History

Cut in two by the Someşul Mic River, Cluj-Napoca has long made it a crossroads, which explains its present role as an educational and industrial centre. Known as Klausenburg to the Germans and Kolozsvár to the Hungarians (ethnic Hungarians make up 20% of the population), Cluj has added the old Roman name of Napoca to its official title, in order to emphasise its Daco-Roman origin.

The history of Cluj-Napoca goes back to Dacian times. In AD 124, during the reign of Emperor Hadrian, Napoca attained municipal status and Emperor Marcus Aurelius elevated it to a colony between AD 161 and 180. German merchants arrived in the 12th century and, after the Tartar invasion of 1241, the medieval earthen walls of 'Castrenses de Clus' were rebuilt in stone. From 1791 to 1848 and after the union with Hungary in 1867, Cluj-Napoca served as the capital of Transylvania.

Orientation

Central Cluj can be seen by foot. The train station is 1km north of the town centre, where many of the sites and hotels are within walking distance of one another.

Bookstores around the centre carry a few Cluj maps. Good for the city is MicroMapper's 1:18,000 *Cluj-Napoca* (€1.60) or Cartographia's 1:12,000 *Cluj-Napoca* (€2.90), while SunCart's ad-filled 1:15,000 *Cluj-Napoca/Cluj County* (€2.90) and Amoco's *Cluj-Napoca/Cluj County* add to the area, including Turda and Huedin Microregion.

Information

Şapte Seri (www.sapteseri.ro), *Zile şi Nopţi* (www.zilesinopti.ro) and *24-Fun* are widely available, biweekly entertainment listings (in Romanian).

Check www.clujonline.com for some general information.

BOOKSHOPS

Gaudeamus (Map p188; ☎ 439 281; Str Iuliu Mariu 3; ☣ 10am-7pm Mon-Fri, 11am-2pm Sat) Has some maps, lots of art books and mainly Hungarian titles.

Librăria Humanitas (Map p188; Str Napoca 7; ☣ 10am-7pm Mon-Fri, to 6pm Sat)

Universităţii (Map p188; Str Universităţii & Piaţa Unirii; ☣ 8am-8pm Mon-Fri, 9am-4pm Sat) Maps and some Lonely Planet guidebooks.

ROMANIAN/HUNGARIAN TENSION

A lot of locals shrug it off – 'it's just politicians, there's no trouble between people' – but there's no denying there's been some tension between ethnic Hungarians and Romanians in Transylvania before and after communism fell. (And we're likely to get a few letters for just bringing it up.)

In 1992 Cluj elected ultranationalist Gheorghe Funar as mayor, and he made no secret of his feelings towards Hungarians. While reports that he stripped the 'Hungarian' before Matthias Corvinus' names in Piaţa Unirii aren't true (it apparently happened in 1944!), Funar did stage a mock funeral ceremony when Romania signed a friendship treaty with Hungary in 1996. In 2002 he refused to recognise a new law legalising the use of native languages in weddings of minorities – a law prompted by a Cluj wedding in which a registrar walked out when ethnic Hungarians confirmed their vows in Hungarian (then Romanian).

Cluj voted Funar out of office in 2004, but there are various 'works' that arose during his time in office visible around town. Here are some examples:

■ Blue, red and gold (ie the colours of the Romanian flag) rubbish bins, fire hydrants and poles facing Matthias Corvinus' statues.

■ Piaţa Libertăţii has been renamed Piaţa Unirii (Union Square) to stress the Transylvanian union with Romania after WWI.

■ Nearby at Corvinus' birthplace, a Hungarian-language plaque marks the site, while a rival one in Romanian and English calls the king 'Romanian' and dismisses the Hungarian claim as 'according to historical tradition'.

■ Three blocks from Piaţa Unirii, an expensive statue of Avram Iancu (a Romanian who fought Hungary) is dramatically lit, while the nearby Corvinus statue remains mostly in the dark.

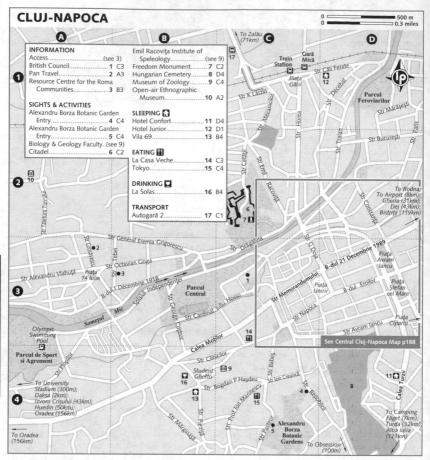

CLUJ-NAPOCA

INFORMATION
Access......................................(see 3)	
British Council...................**1** C3	
Pan Travel..........................**2** A3	
Resource Centre for the Roma Communities.................**3** B3	

SIGHTS & ACTIVITIES
Alexandru Borza Botanic Garden Entry...............................**4** C4	
Alexandru Borza Botanic Garden Entry...............................**5** C4	
Biology & Geology Faculty...(see 9)	
Citadel.................................**6** C2	

Emil Racoviţa Institute of Speleology...................(see 9)	
Freedom Monument.............**7** C2	
Hungarian Cemetery............**8** D4	
Museum of Zoology..............**9** C4	
Open-air Ethnographic Museum............................**10** A2	

SLEEPING
Hotel Confort...................**11** D4	
Hotel Junior......................**12** D1	
Vila 69.............................**13** B4	

EATING
La Casa Veche....................**14** C3	
Tokyo...............................**15** C4	

DRINKING
La Solas............................**16** B4	

TRANSPORT
Autogară 2.......................**17** C1	

CULTURAL CENTRES & LIBRARIES

American Studies Library (Map p188; Str Ion Brătianu 22; 1-7pm Mon, 8.30am-3pm Tue-Fri) University library open for the public.

British Council (Map p186; ☎ 594 408; www.british council.ro; Str Arany Janos 11; centre 9am-5pm Mon-Fri, library 1-7pm Mon, Wed & Thu, 10am-4pm Tue & Fri) First-floor library has good stock of books, magazines and CDs, plus internet access. A year's membership is €18/12 per adult/student, a day pass is €1.80.

French Cultural Centre (Centre Culturel Français; Map p188; ☎ 597 595; www.ccfc.ro; Str Ion Brătianu 22; library 2-7pm Mon, 10am-7pm Tue-Fri, to 1pm Sat Sep-Jul) Well-stocked library; hosts art, music and film events.

German Cultural Centre (Deutsches Kulturzentrum; Map p188; ☎ 594 492; www.kulturzentrum.ubbcluj

.ro; 1st fl, Str Universităţii 7-9; library 10am-2pm Mon, Wed & Fri, 2-6pm Tue & Thu) Library with German periodicals; hosts cultural events and films.

Resource Centre for the Roma Communities (Map p186; ☎ 420 474; Str Tebei 21; office 9am-5pm Mon-Fri, library 3-8pm Mon & Wed, 10am-8pm Tue & Thu) Outgrowth of the Soros Open Foundation, with information and resources on minorities in Romania, especially the Roma.

United States Embassy Information Office (Map p188; ☎ 594 315; 1st fl, Str Universităţii 7-9; 9am-noon & 2-5pm Mon-Fri) Notary services and tax forms, plus a poster of Iraq's Most Wanted.

INTERNET ACCESS

Blade Net (Map p188; Str Iuliu Maniu 17; per hr €0.60; 7am-midnight)

Marghila Café (Map p188; Str Iuliu Maniu 1; per hr €0.40; ☺ 10am-midnight Mon-Sat, noon-midnight Sun) Adjoining Egyptian-style café with fast food.

Net Zone (Map p188; Piaţa Muzeului 5; per hr €0.30-0.45; ☺ 24hr 'approximately')

LANGUAGE COURSES

Access (☎ 420 476; www.access.ro; 3rd fl, Str Tebei 21; ☺ 10am-6pm Mon & Thu, 2-8pm Tue & Wed, 2-6pm Fri) Offers Romanian-language courses.

LAUNDRY

Perado Laundry (Map p188; Str Calera Turzeii 13; per load €4.20; ☺ 10am-7pm Mon-Sat) The ever-valuable, ever-rare wash-dry-and-fold service.

LEFT LUGGAGE

Plan ahead: the train station had no official left luggage service at research time.

MEDICAL SERVICES

For a well-stocked and central pharmacy, try **Clematis** (Map p188; Piaţa Unirii 11; ☺ 8am-10pm).

MONEY

Steer well clear of the leather-clad money-changing toughies on the streets. The city is full of ATMs and legitimate exchange offices. The **Banca Comercială Română** (Map p188; Str Gheorghe Bariţiu 10-12; ☺ 8.30am-6pm Mon-Fri, to 12.30pm Sat) gives cash advances and changes travellers cheques.

POST & TELEPHONE

Central post office (Map p188; Str Regele Ferdinand 33; ☺ 7am-8pm Mon-Fri, 8am-1pm Sat) The main **telephone centre** (☺ 9am-6pm Mon-Fri, to 1pm Sat) is in the building attached to the back, facing Caragiale Park.

TRAVEL AGENCIES

The municipality has long delayed its promises to open a tourist information centre; Cluj surely could benefit from one. Retro Hotel (p191) organises enjoyable, good-value trips. Also see p190 for other associations that can help plan trips.

Pan Travel (Map p186; ☎ 420 516; www.pantravel.ro; Str Grozavescu 13; ☺ 9am-5pm Mon-Fri), a top-notch outfit led by the engaging Andrei, can book accommodation, provide English- or French-speaking guides (€15 to €30 per day) and car rentals (from €30 per day), and arrange trips to the Apuseni or around Maramureş. It's best to contact them ahead, via website or telephone. The trips themselves are authoritative and unstaged – a more 'knock on door'

approach than a pre-planned artificial event. Bus 30 goes from near Piaţa Unirii.

Transylvania Ecological Club (Clubul Ecologic Transilvania; ☎ 431 626; www.greenagenda.org, www.cdtcluj .ro), one of Romania's most active grass-roots environmental groups, operating since the mid '90s, focuses on promoting ecotravel in the Huedin region and Apuseni mountains as an alternative to the booming timber industry. It can provide trail maps and find guides. It often works in collaboration with Green Mountain Holidays (p190). At research time, it was looking for a new location.

Sights
PIAŢA UNIRII

The vast 14th-century **St Michael's Church** (Map p188) dominates Piaţa Unirii. The neo-Gothic tower (1859) topping the Gothic hall church creates a great landmark and the church (built in four stages) is considered to be one of the finest examples of Gothic architecture in Romania. The three naves and vestry were the last to be completed at the end of the 16th century. The choir vaults, built in the 14th century, were rebuilt in the 18th century, following a fire. Daily services are in Hungarian and Romanian, and evening organ concerts are often held.

Flanking the church to the south is the bulky 1902 equestrian **statue of Matthias Corvinus** (Map p188) – the famous Hungarian king and son of Iancu de Hunedoara (János Hunyadi). It served as a focal point of nationalist mayor Funar's efforts to undermine Cluj's links with Hungary. See p185.

On the eastern side of the square is the **National Art Museum** (Map p188; ☎ 496 952; Piaţa Unirii 30; adult/child €1.30/0.65; ☺ noon-7pm Wed-Sun Jun-Oct, 11am-6pm Wed-Sun Nov-May), housed inside the baroque Banffy Palace (1791). The couple of dozen rooms are filled with paintings and artefacts, including a 16th-century church altar and many 20th-century paintings. The inner courtyard (free entry) sometimes stages outdoor shows, as do the ground floor halls.

Here's why we travel – for superb, fully rewarding, ever-surprising quirks such as this, the small three-room **Pharmaceutical Museum** (Map p188; ☎ 597 567; Str Regele Ferdinand 1; adult/child €0.60/0.30; ☺ 10am-4pm Mon-Sat). It's housed in Cluj's first – and Romania's fourth – apothecary (1573), as a bronze-plate map painstakingly attests. Tours are led by a hilarious pharmacist in a white lab coat, who points like a game-show model towards (seemingly

TRANSYLVANIA

CENTRAL CLUJ-NAPOCA

TRANSYLVANIA

ho-hum) glass cases of ground mummy dust, medieval alchemist symbols and painted 18th-century aphrodisiac bottles. He speaks some English. If you utter a 'wow' you may get a deadpan 'For you... interesting... for me... *it is normal*'!

By the time you reach the medieval labs in the basement, you're hooked. Hopefully Mr Radu-Mihai will still be there when you drop by. Perhaps you'll even get a fist-pump and shouted farewell of your home (eg 'Okla-homa!'), as we did.

An **Ethnographic Museum** (Muzeul Etnografic al Transilvaniei; Map p188; ☎ 592 344; Str Memorandumului 21; adult/child €1.20/0.60; ☺ 9am-5pm Tue-Sun) was under renovation at last pass, but its collection of folk costumes and decorations should be re-

opened before your visit. The museum's more popular **open-air section** (secţia în aer liber; Map p186; adult/child €1.20/0.60; ☺ 10am-6pm May-Sep, 8am-4pm Oct-Mar) is northwest of the centre in the Hoia forest (take bus 27 from the train station). The display includes traditional sawmills, wells, wine and oil presses, roadside crosses, fruit dryers and potters' workshops.

NORTH OF CENTRE
Around Piaţa Muzeului, a couple of blocks north of Piaţa Unirii, this charming neighbourhood is pleasant to explore on foot, letting you dip into courtyards for a peek at local life and seeing remnants of archaeological digs that have been going on here since 1991 in the southern and northeastern sections of

the square. On the eastern side of the square is a beautifully decorated 15th-century **Franciscan church** (Biserica Franciscanilor), one of the city's oldest structures. Services are held in Hungarian.

The **National History Museum of Transylvania** (Map p188; ☎ 495 677; Str Constantin Daicoviciu 1; adult/child €0.70/0.35; ☺ 10am-4pm Tue-Sun), which dates from 1859, is only half open. The history stops when things start to get interesting (and controversial) – when Hungarians and Romanians started living in the same neck of the woods (that wing should be re-opened in 2007). In these quiet halls you can see a mummy from Egypt, lots of Roman pieces, ghoulish remains of three humans from the area's first tombs (they were probably Indo-Europeans, as Dacians cremated corpses), and a map that tries to make sense of migration in the area.

A block south is the politically charged **birthplace of Matthias Corvinus** (Map p188; Str Matei Corviri 6), a 15th-century Hungarian king. Note the side-by-side plaques. Romanian authorities allowed the Hungarian community to put up the first, then placed the rather flip second one in Romanian and English, which claims that the '*Romanian* Matthias Corvinus' was born here 'according to historical tradition'.

At research time, the **Emil Racoviţa Institute of Speleology Museum** (Map p188; ☎ 591 273; Str Sextil Puşcariu; admission free; ☺ noon-4pm), a fascinating collection of works by internationally renowned Romanian biologist Racoviţa (1868–1947), was moving to a new location. After joining an 1897 expedition to Antarctica, Racoviţa explored some 1400 caves and created the world's first institute devoted to caves here in Cluj. It's hoping to have an entrance at Piaţa Unirii at some point. The museum was formerly in the Biology and Geology Faculty.

Northwest of the square, on the banks of the river you'll see the **Hungarian State Theatre & Opera**, one of only two in Romania today – and the only one to have held ballet classes taken by pre-'Touch My Bum' Cheeky Girls (see p193). By crossing the footbridge west of the theatre, or the bridge across Str Regele Ferdinand to the east, you can climb **Citadel Hill** (Map p186), for nice views; take any of the footpaths that wind up towards the eyesore that is Hotel Belvedere, towering pathetically on top of the citadel. There is a **freedom monument** (Map p186) in memory of those who died during WWI. Some ruins of the 15th-century citadel (enlarged in 1715) still remain, but you'd have to be an archaeologist or detective to find them.

TRANSYLVANIA

Head back down the hill then bear north along Str Horea to the **Synagogue of Deportees** (Map p188; Str Horea 23). This grand Moorish-style building is just one of three remaining synagogues in Cluj-Napoca. This was built in 1987 in memory of the 16,700 Jews who were deported to Auschwitz from Cluj-Napoca in 1944.

SOUTH OF PIAŢA UNIRII

The **Babeş-Bolyai University** (Map p188; ☎ 405 300; www.ubbcluj.ro; Str Mihai Kogălniceanu 1b), home to some 43,000 students, is the largest university in Romania (after Bucharest). Founded in 1872, Hungarian was the predominant language here until 1918. Internationally, it's famed for being the home of the world's only university institute of speleology (the study of caves). It's a lovely building, with its gold-brick centre courtyard, which you can peek into rather freely.

A couple of blocks east, on Str Mihail Kogălniceanu, is a **Hungarian Reformed Church** (Map p188) built by the king of Hungary, Matthias Corvinus, in 1486. The statue of St George slaying the dragon in front of the church is a replica of the 14th-century original, carved by the Hungarian Kolozs-vári brothers; the original is now displayed in Prague. Organ concerts are sometimes held in the church.

Further east is the sprawling Piaţa Ştefan cel Mare, lined with wall fragments of the original citadel. At the wall's south end is the smaller Piaţa Baba Novac on which there's a **statue of Baba Novac** (1975; Map p188) in front of the **Tailors' Bastion** (Map p188; Bastion Croitorilor). There's no entry, but you can peek inside. The bastion, dating from the 1550s, is the only one that remains from the medieval fortified city. The square on which it stands is named after one of Mihai Viteazul's generals, who was executed by Hungarian nobles here in the 17th century.

STUDENT GHETTO

The student ghetto, southwest of the centre, is inside the triangle formed by Calea Moţilor, Str Mărginaşă and Str Pasteur and is full of open-air bars, internet cafés, fast-food shops – and students. It has a completely different look (a lot of young people in lab coats) than elsewhere around the city, and is surrounded by the east and south, with some fine historic homes.

From the centre, walk west along Str Clinicilor, to where it branches left through a brick gate into the wooded **Biology and Geology Faculty**, where you'll find (100m up on the left, past the cocky statue of Emil Racoviţa) the surprisingly rewarding **Museum of Zoology** (Map p186; ☎ 595 739; Str Clinicilor 5-7; adult/student €0.45/0.23; ⏲ 9am-3pm Mon-Fri, 10am-2pm Sat & Sun), an L-shaped lab that looks like it hasn't changed since biologist Racoviţa donned his final lab coat here. Bird noise penetrates the huge windows, bringing some life to the silence (and death) of hundreds and hundreds of jarred and stuffed specimens, while invertebrates and fish sit vertically in filled tubes. We particularly like the display of a vulture feasting on dead rabbit. Oh, and someone needs to put an eye-patch on one of the boars.

West through the campus housing, head past fast-food joints up Str Bogdan P Haşdeu to Str Pasteur to reach the fragrant 1930 **Alexandru Borza Botanic Gardens** (Map p186; ☎ 592 152; Str Republicii 42; adult/student €1.20/0.60; ⏲ 9am-6pm), which covers 15 hectares, with shaded green lawns, a super Japanese garden and rose garden with some 600 different varieties, and an observation tower.

Just east of here, most easily reached from Str Avram Iancu down the hill, is an immense, highly memorable **Hungarian cemetery** (Map p186; Házsongárdi temető in Hungarian), where dozens of revered Hungarian notables are buried.

Activities

Cluj-Napoca is a popular centre for mountain biking and caving enthusiasts, with the Apuseni Mountains to the southwest offering a wealth of caves and trails. The northern access points are covered on p198, the southern on p226.

Clubul de Cicloturism Napoca (☎ 450 013; office@ccn.ro) is a group of outdoors-lovers who don't organise trips, but can help with all your two-wheeler questions. At research time, they were looking for a new office.

Green Mountain Holidays (☎ 418 691, 0744-637 227; www.greenmountainholidays.ro) is a terrific ecotourist organisation, recommended for an environmentally-friendly, activity-filled week or two. Check its website for caving, hiking and biking tours – such as the 13-day hike around the Apuseni Mountains, with guides, transport, meals and accommodation for €550, or an 11-day cycling trip for €600.

Daksa (☎ 0740-053 550; www.daksa.ro) is an experienced group offering horseriding excursions outside Cluj for €80 or €90 per person per day, including transport, accommodation, food and guides. Trips last three to seven days. Carriage rides are also available.

Festivals & Events

Cluj's biggest event is the **Transylvania International Film Festival** (www.tiff.ro), held in June. In 2006, the festival drew 40,000 visitors to see some 105 films from 25 countries. There is also a **Septemberfest**, a **Folk Crafts Fair** in May, a **music festival** in September/ October, and the nationwide **Festivinum Wine Festival** all May.

Sleeping

Cluj-Napoca's accommodation is generally more expensive than the rest of Romania, and you're likely to pay more for less, unless you're staying at a hostel. Pan Travel (p187) can help. The Cluj **Antrec representative** (☎ 406 363; cluj@antrec.ro) can help find a *pensiune* in the region.

BUDGET

Camping Făget (☎ 596 234; tent space/2-person hut €2.20/15) This hilltop collection of OK cabanas and tent spots in the trees is 7km south of the centre. Take bus 35 from Piaţa Mihai Viteazul south down Calea Turzii to the end of the line. From here it is a marked 2km hike.

Retro Hostel (Map p188; ☎ 450 452; www.retro .ro; Str Potaissa 13; dm/r per person €11/14; ☐) On a quiet lane amidst 16th-century citadel wall fragments, the happy, superbly run Retro is one of Romania's best hostels. Two colourful dorm rooms upstairs have gold walls, moonlight windows and sunshiny bedspreads. Things are a little tight (only a couple of bathrooms, and one private room is accessible through the other room). When things are full, it opens its second location nearby – there are 48 beds in all. At research time, the Retro was planning to open four more private rooms. Staff offers good-value day trips and sells area maps. Half an hour of internet access is free, while breakfast is €2.50.

Piccola Italia (Map p188; ☎ 536 110; www.piccolaitalia .ro; Str Racoviţă 20; s/d €22/25) On a rising slope of private villas, this two-building, nine-room complex isn't in the centre, but in many ways it's Cluj's best-deal guesthouse. Rooms are basic but comfortable; breakfast is served on the vine-covered deck.

Hotel Junior (Map p186; ☎ 432 028; www.pensiune -junior.ro; Str Câri Ferate 12; s/d €23/28) In a hot-pink building, with simple rooms, on a dusty, unappealing street just down from the trains, this place has no breakfast.

MIDRANGE

Vila 69 (Map p186; ☎ 591 592; vila69@email.ro; Str Haşden 69; s/d €29/38; ☐) Seventeen rather plain, modern rooms make up this happy little place – with restaurant and club. It's right off the main strip of the student ghetto.

Hotel Meteor (Map p188; ☎ 591 060; receptie @hotelmeteor.ro; B-dul Eroilor 29; s €35, d €40 & €44) This is a lightly faded modern hotel – some rooms are quite small, but the staff is nice and there's laundry service, plus the breakfast buffet at the next-door restaurant is a bonus. Some windows overlook the alley tables, and noise lingers on summer nights.

Hotel Confort (Map p186; ☎ 598 410; www.hotel confort.ro; Calea Turzii 48; s/d €39/52; ☒ ☐) This quite colourful place with shiny tile floors and rather basic modern furnishings is done up in pastel. Six of the 35 rooms have wall-of-glass windows and air-con. Back rooms catch bird calls, not engine burps, from the busy street. The website easily takes honours for Most Overly Dramatic Website in the Fairly Cheap Guesthouse category. It's a 10-minute walk from the centre.

Fullton (Map p188; ☎ 597 898; www.fullton.ro; Str Sextil Puşcariu 10; s €40-60, d €45-65; ☒ ☐) The closest to boutique style in Cluj, this back-street central inn has earth-toned walls, wrought-iron bedframes and a nice covered patio bar – in all, the most comfortable accommodation on offer. More expensive rooms have writing desks and extra space. Some rooms have air-con. Plug-in internet's free.

Villa Siesta (Map p188; ☎ 595 582; www.villa-siesta .ro; Str Gheorghe Şincai 6; s/d €47/57; ☒ ☐) Though here since the 1930s, it's hard to see the history of this 12-room villa beyond its 1980s décor. For the price, it's a bit frayed (old blue-chequered carpets, nicks on the floral wallpaper).

TOP END

Hotel Victoria (Map p188; ☎ 597 963; www.hotel-victoria .ro; B-dul 21 Decembrie 1989, 54-56; s/d €55/66) This 1986 hotel aims for modern fussiness, with fluffy, sparkling-gold fabrics. All's new; rooms have mini step-out balconies to watch the boulevard buzz by.

Hotel Agape (Map p188; ☎ 406 523; www.hotelagape.ro; Str Iuliu Maniu 6; s/d €59/70; ✗ ▢) Run by Hungarian locals, this 40-room hotel is quite a complex – *six* restaurants and a great self-service cafeteria with a skylight. Opt for a double, which sprawls with blonde wood floors and beige throw rugs, plus two leather chairs.

Eating
RESTAURANTS
Agape (Map p188; Str Iuliu Maniu 6; dishes €0.80-1.50; ☯ 11am-9pm Mon-Fri) This cafeteria-style restaurant, the best of the hotel's six, is more stylish than you'd expect and serves quick, tasty, Hungarian-style meals on the cheap.

Tokyo (Map p186; ☎ 598 662; Str Marinescu 5; sushi & rolls from €2.80; ☯ 11am-midnight) If you've been in Romania for a while, you'll want to come to this non-Romanian, non-Italian eatery. It's hard to miss, with its red Shinto gate façade west of the Botanical Gardens. Japanese pop on the stereo is a refreshing touch, as is the pretty good sushi, warm hand towels and imported green tea. Lunch specials start at €4.30.

La Casa Veche (Map p186; ☎ 450 583; Str Clinicilor 14; mains €4-8; ☯ 11am-11pm Mon-Sat, to 10pm Sun) This lovely three-room place serves Romanian fare and it feels like stepping back a stack of centuries. It has silver platters and rustic wooden floors inside, and outside seats on a brick courtyard face the nice backyard. It's best for steaks, but – this is Romania – there are a few pasta choices.

our pick **Roata** (Map p188; ☎ 592 022; Str Alexandru Ciura 6a; mains €4.25-8.50; ☯ noon-midnight Tue-Sat, 1pm-midnight Sun & Mon) Housed in a back-alley building, with tasty traditional Romanian dishes served in clay plates, this joint is best for sitting on the small terrace and vying for space amidst potted plants and moss-covered stones. Traditional music puts a little bounce into the air. People know it's good, and it's almost always busy.

Lugano (Map p188; ☎ 594 593; Str Clemenceau 2; mains €5.40-9; ☯ 11am-midnight) This ritzy little Italian restaurant is the best at the pasta game, with no pizza to clutter the menu or a long wine list. Trout is grilled with lemon and costs €8.50.

QUICK EATS
For fast-food outlets, follow students. There are heaps of good pizza, hamburger and kebab

options on Str Piezişă in the student ghetto and more centrally on Piaţa Lucian Blaga and along Str Napoca.

Caprice (Map p188; Str Memorandumului 10; pastries €0.60-0.90; ☯ 8am-9pm Mon-Fri, 9am-8pm Sat, 9am-7pm Sun) Baking since 1926, this three-room patisserie evokes ages past. Ice cream comes out in summer, but look for the 'frog' (choco biscuit covered in Kermit-green icing) year-round.

Speed/Alcatraz (Map p188; Str Napoca 4-6; pizzas €3.15, sandwiches €1.25-1.75; ☯ 24hr) Busy fast-food option with good seating options, including an outdoor deck and an enigmatic Alcatraz basement with seating in Al Capone-style cages.

SELF-CATERING
For fresh produce, stroll through the quite colourful **central market** (Map p188), behind the Complex Commercial Mihai Viteazul shopping centre on Piaţa Mihai Viteazul, which also houses **Mega Supermarket** (☯ 7am-9pm Mon-Fri, 8am-8pm Sat, 8am-7pm Sun). The **Sora supermarket & shopping mall** (Map p188; Str 21 Decembrie 1989, 5; ☯ 24hr) has cafés, a basement restaurant, €1.20 *shaorma* (kebab) and €0.80 fresh carrot juice.

Drinking
CAFÉS
Crema (Map p188; ☎ 0723-161 002; Piaţa Unirii 25; ☯ 9-1am) This place has masterpieces of Western Europe on the wall, and matching prices on the menu – espresso is €1.50, but then again, Crema *is* one of Cluj's hippest café-bars.

Flowers (Map p188; Piaţa Unirii 23; ☯ 8am-10pm Mon-Fri, 10am-10pm Sat & Sun) Stone-floored and twee, Crema's more chat-friendly neighbour offers loose teas and wi-fi access for its mostly 20-something, studious crowd. Tea is €0.75.

BARS & NIGHTCLUBS
Here you go. It's possible to just head to Piaţa Unirii and peek into surrounding streets and look for signs leading down to dozens of clubs that go a long way to perpetuating the 'vampire-only at night' stereotype Romania gets. Action runs along with darkness, and revellers come out around 11pm and stay till dawn in dozens of cavernous underground cellars and tomb-like bars, often with blood-red lights. Weekend nights sizzle, but things can be busy most of the week. Fun-seekers of all backgrounds, ages and sexualities jostle with minimal complexes. Don't limit yourself to the centre; in Cluj it pays to explore.

Diesel Bar (Map p1880; ☎ 493 043; Piaţa Unirii 17) It's obvious – right on the main square – but if you walk past the hipsters looking to be seen in the all-glass entry and go downstairs into a towering room, with red-spotlit tables and giant rooms, plus €4.30 gin-and-tonics, you can mix with the coolest of Cluj. 'It's chill-out on weekdays, DJs and live music on weekends', explained the nose-pierced bartenders.

Latino Club (Map p188; ☎ 0722-750 611; Str Memorandumului 23; ⏲ 6pm-4am) Blood-red lights and blood-red walls line this cavernous lounge with some salsa music and fancy cocktails.

Club Roland Garros (Map p188; ☎ 431 952; Str Horea 2; ⏲ 9am-late) Part pizza restaurant, part teenage weekend disco, Roland delivers for its riverside balcony seats, great for afternoon beer to watch fishermen.

Music Pub (Map p188; ☎ 432 517; Str Horea 5; ⏲ 9am-3am Mon-Fri, 11am-3am Sat, 5pm-3am Sun) A little Wild West up-front, this sprawling pub is a great casual place for buddy blokes to sit and drink, indie-poppers to flirt, and students to study on quiet nights. Lots of live shows on the small stage.

Obsession (off Map p188; ☎ 401 777; www.obsession club.ro; Str Republicii 109; entry about €10; ⏲ 10pm-late) One regular told us with boundless pride that the slick three-room Obsession, about 1km south of the centre, is 'definitely the hottest club in Transylvania'. It gets its cred with its blaring beats, wall-to-wall bodies, theme nights (including Magyar Night) and big-name DJ visitors.

The student ghetto, southwest of the centre (on/off Str Piezişă, reached by Str Clinicilor about 300m from Piaţa Lucian Blaga), teems with lively open-air bars, including **La Solas** (Map p186; Str Piezişă; ⏲ 10am-2 or 3am).

Entertainment

Şapte Seri (www.sapteseri.ro) and *24-Fun* are free biweekly booklets listing all the latest happenings (in Romanian). They're available in cafés, hotels and entertainment venues.

CINEMAS

Cinema Arta (Map p188; ☎ 596 616; Str Universităţii 3) This cinema plays Hollywood films in English.

THEATRE & CLASSICAL MUSIC

Hungarian State Theatre & Opera (Map p188; ☎ 593 468; Str Emil Isac 26-28) This company, close to the river, stages Hungarian-language plays and operas. Tickets are sold in advance at the box office inside the theatre.

> **CHEEKY IS DEAD, LONG LIVE CHEEKY**
>
> A UK poll in 2004 called their hit song 'Touch My Bum' the worst pop song of all time, and many Cluj locals roll their eyes and even apologise for them, but the Cheeky Girls remain the town's most famous export.
>
> Twin sisters Monica and Gabriela Irimia were born in Cluj in 1982, and studied gymnastics, karate and ballet (at the Hungarian Opera House – go visit these hallowed grounds, mortal).
>
> In 2002 they left with their mum for London, and somehow through a combination of reality-show failures and evil-star alignments they eked out a career based on 'dance hits' that plumbed the depths of shamelessness (eg a cover of Boney M's classic as 'Hooray Hooray! It's a Cheeky Holiday'). They never performed at Cluj's clubs – they've apparently never really performed 'their' songs 'live' – but certainly Cluj's clubs provided some background fodder for the CG's dance 'hits'.
>
> Anyone wanna bet they cover 2 Live Crew's 'Me So Horny' as 'We So Cheeky' next?

The **National Theatre Lucian Blaga** (Map p188; ☎ 590 272; Piaţa Ştefan cel Mare 2-4) was designed by the famous Viennese architects Fellner and Hellmer and performances here are well attended. The **Opera** (☎ 595 363) is in the same building. Tickets can be bought in advance from the **Agenţie de Teatrala** (Map p188; ☎ 595 363; Piaţa Ştefan cel Mare 14; ⏲ 11am-5pm Tue-Fri & before events). Tickets for classical concerts hosted by the **State Philharmonic** (Filarmonica de Stat; Map p188; ☎ 430 060) are also sold here.

Shopping

Romanian Folk Art (☎ 596 114; www.romanianfolkart .ro; Str Eroilor 1; ⏲ 10am-6pm Mon-Fri, to 2pm Sat) Cluj's best shop for traditional items from around Romania, this alley shop offers painted eggs, embroidered dresses and tablecloths, colourful masks and hats, and other pieces. Prices are a little lower than other shops and the quality's high.

The Ethnographic Museum (p188) also has a gift shop.

Atta (Map p188; ☎ 590 743; Str Calea Moţila 32; ⏲ 10am-7pm Mon-Fri, to 2pm Sat) Outdoors shop with maps, rock-climbing gear, tents and sleeping bags, hiking boots.

TRANSYLVANIA

Betix (Map p188; ☎ 598 933; Str Universității 8; ☉ 9am-5pm Mon-Fri, to 2pm Sat) Lots of neat hats are worn around these parts, some of them made here at this cute, 35-year-old shop. Lamb's wool shepherd hats are €60 to €70, felt jobbies are about €6.

Getting There & Away

AIR

Tarom has at least two daily direct flights to Bucharest (five-day advance ticket one-way/return €103/153). It also has several weekly flights to Milan, Bologna, Verona, Frankfurt, Munich and Vienna. Tickets can be bought at the airport or from the **Tarom city office** (Map p186; ☎ 432 669; Piaţa Mihai Viteazul 11; ☉ 8am-6pm Mon-Fri, 9am-1pm Sat).

BUS

Cluj's bus situation changes frequently. Have your guesthouse or hotel call ahead to check times/locations. At research time, daily bus services from **Autogară 2** (Autogară Beta; Map p186; ☎ 455 249) included the following: two daily buses to Braşov (€8), four to Bucharest (€12), five to Budapest (€18), one to Chişinău (€20), one to Iaşi (€12 to €15) and three to Sibiu (€5.70, three hours); they are useful as there's often tricky connections if going by train. There's also a handful of buses to Bistriţa (€2.90, 2½ hours). The station is 350m northwest of the train station (take the overpass). Note: there is no Autogară 1.

From a parking lot on Piaţa Mihai Viteazul, two companies run seven daily buses to Turda (€1.20) till about 8.30pm.

From Piaţa Unirii microbuses go via Oradea to Budapest's Ferihegy 2 Airport (€10, six or seven hours).

TRAIN

The **Agenţie de Voiaj CFR** (Map p188; ☎ 432 001; Piaţa Mihai Viteazul 20; ☉ 7am-7pm Mon-Fri) sells domestic and international train tickets in advance. Sample fares for *accelerat* trains include:

Destination	Price (€)	Duration	No of daily trains
Bistriţa	2.20	3½hr	3
Braşov	8.70	4hr	6
Bucharest	10.60	7½hr	6
Budapest	34.50	5hr	2
Huedin	2.25	45-75 min	13
Iaşi	10.60	9hr	4
Oradea	5.70	2¼-4hr	12
Sibiu	9.15	4hr	1
Sighişoara	7.30	3½hr	6
Suceava	8.70	7hr	4
Târgu Mureş	6.75 (rapid)	2¼hr	2
Timişoara	8.60	7hr	6
Zalău	5.70	4½hr	6 (not direct)

The smaller Gára Mică, 100m east of the central train station is for short-distance trains only.

Getting Around

TO/FROM THE AIRPORT

Cluj-Napoca airport (☎ 416 702) is 8km to the east of the town centre in the Someşeni district. Bus 8 runs from Piaţa Mihai Viteazul to the airport.

CAR

Cluj has some of the best car-rental rates in the country. **Pan Travel** (Map p186; ☎ 420 516; www.pantravel.ro; Str Grozavescu 13; ☉ 9am-5pm Mon-Fri) rents Dacias

---

STAY OUT OF THE WOODS!

Thank goodness the Transylvania Society of Dracula holds an annual symposium! In 2006, in Sighişoara, the fang-leaning congress met to explain all sorts of unexplained things, chiefly the 'Romania Bermuda Triangle', aka Hoia-Baciu Wood (HBW), outside Cluj.

And. It. Was. Explained. In. Frightening. Detail.

The pioneer in HBW research was Alexandru Sift, who in the 1960s and '70s took photographs of disc-shaped UFOs – and found many things revealed in photos not visible to the naked eye, including geometric flying objects and 'live' humanoid heads with faces resembling dead persons known to the beholder. The 'special active spot 3', which distorts photographic images, was identified…the same year Sift died (1993)!

It is not recommended to go into the woods, as, per the report, visitors there have complained of 'burns', 'thirst' and 'headaches'. Or maybe you can just take some water and aspirin.

Check www.benecke.com for updates.

for €30 per day. **Rodna** (☎ 416 773; www.rodna-trans.ro; Str Traian Vuia 62), towards the airport, rents newish Dacia Logans from €30 per day, and foreign cars for a bit more. **Pro Travel** (Map p188; ☎ 598 858; Str Napoca 2; ⏱ 9am-7pm Mon-Fri, to noon Sat) rents Daewoo cars from €25 (for four days or longer).

TAXI
Diesel Taxi (☎ 953, 946) is a well-regarded, meter-using local company. A ride from the train station to the centre is about €1.75.

TRAM, TROLLEYBUS & BUS
Trolleybus 9 runs from the train station into town. Bus 27 takes you within a 10-minute walk of the open-air ethnographic museum northwest of the centre in Horea forest. Single-ride tickets for either cost €0.35.

TURDA
☎ 264 / pop 60,400
A great and easy day trip from Cluj, the unfortunately named town of Turda (tur-*da*), 27km southeast, seems at first glance the last place to find deep, awe-inspiring drops made naturally by rivers (the massive Turda Gorge) or less naturally by human hands (the salt mine). Set in wide-open, rather flat farmlands, Turda was an important salt-mining town from the 13th century until 1932, when the main mine shut down. A quarter of the town's residents are Hungarian.

Michael the Brave hated Turda. He got himself decapitated here in 1601.

Orientation & Information
Turda's fun little central street, Str Republicii, is home to several banks, the post office, an internet café and a taxi stand at its north end (at Piaţa Republicii, near where the roads go around the 15th-century Catholic Church).

Stop by the **Tourist Information Centre** (☎ 314 611; Piaţa 1 Decembrie 1918; ⏱ 9am-6pm Mon-Sat), about 250m south of the church, where you can get a Turda map and advice on hikes.

The **Fundaţia Potaissa** (☎ 316 385; Piaţa 1 Decembrie 1918, 6a), a rock-climbing club, has info on rock climbing spots in Turda Gorge, or the smaller Turenia Gorge north of town.

Sights
SALT MINE
Salt mines, shmalt shmines, some say. But Turda's **salt mine** (☎ 311 690; Str Salinelor 54; adult/child €2.30/1.15; ⏱ 9am-3.30pm summer, to 1.30pm Mon-Fri,

to 3.30pm Sat & Sun winter) is different. A cool 10°C-12°C throughout, the handful of trapezoid and bell-shaped mines are reached by an eerie 500m tunnel with concentric circles created by the occasional light. The main mine to visit is the 13-storey Rudolf (40m deep – big but not the biggest), which you can encircle from above on creaking wood platforms teetering perilously over the edge (a little too Indiana Jones for a certain Lonely Planet researcher). Two sets of stairs lead to the dark bottom, passing dates on the way that mark when miners reached the depth; from the bottom you can look way down into the adjoining Terezia mine (dated from 1690, which goes down 70m to an 8m-deep lake).

The mine operated from 1271 till 1932, after which cheese was stored here briefly. Try to note the odour at the closed-off end of the tunnel; it's said it's not salt, but the lingering smell of decomposing horses who died decades ago from one salt-cart haul too many.

The mine is about 1km north from the centre, back towards Cluj; a sign points 200m off road. If driving from Cluj, veer left at the first fork in the village (a sign points to 'centru').

TURDA GORGE
Turda Gorge (Cheile Turzii) is a short but stunning break in the mountains 7 or 8km west (as the stork flies). You can hike the bottom of the gorge's length in an hour.

One way there is to walk. From the centre, walk west on a trail (marked with red crosses) about 90 minutes across rolling farmlands to the gorge. There's now a cement trail along one side of the gorge – which can get choked with day-trippers on summer weekends. You can follow the trail up and over the quite straight-up steep northern end (about one hour up).

Driving there isn't as easy as it looks on a map. Only locals (supposedly) are allowed to use the road to the south of the gorge from the road 2km west of Mihai Viteazul on the main Turda–Abrud road. Another way is via Săndulești, 5km northwest of Turda; take the road across from the highway out of town towards Cluj, and follow the (signed) dirt road about 10km to the gorge.

At research time the **Cabana Cheile Turzii** (450m), at the southern foot of the gorge, was closed. Ask at the tourist information centre if eating options have opened up; otherwise take what you need.

OTHER SIGHTS

In summer, locals go and float in the deep Durgâu salt lakes a few kilometres northeast of town. You can taxi or take bus 14 to the end of the line and follow the dirt road to the right.

Just off the trail towards the Turda Gorge are hill-top **Roman castle ruins** (Cetatea Romană) of the 5th Macedonian League, who stationed themselves here around AD 168; it's not easy to find, so ask at the tourist information centre.

A couple of kilometres east of the centre is the small, popular spa resort of **Băile Turda**, with an outdoor pool, allegedly built on the site of an old Roman salt mine. Bus 15 goes from Turda's centre here.

Sleeping & Eating

Hotel Potaissa (☎ 312 691; Str Republicii 6; s/d with shared bathroom €11.50/23, with private bathroom €27/36) The Potaissa is clean and central but a bit clunky, with loud carpets and a rendering of its 1947 opening in the lobby.

Hunter Prince Castle (aka 'Dracula Hotel'; ☎ 316 850; www.huntercastle.ro; Str Sulutiu 4-6; r €51 & €65; 🔀) A dramatic 'Transylvania castle' hotel, on an unlikely dusty central spot in a town with no Dracula links, this place can't quite decide to go for vampires or hunters, so splits the difference. It has creatively campy rooms, with rock walls separating spiked cast-iron beds, sitting areas and antlers on the wall. The restaurant (mains €4.30 to €11.50), with outdoor seating, has murals of head-cuttings and lots of furry pelts. It's good, but watch out for extra items on the bill.

Getting There & Away

Maxitaxis leave frequently from the centre to Cluj-Napoca's Piaţa Mihai Viteazul (€1.15, 40 minutes) until 8.30pm or so. A taxi back is about €15. Dacos buses leave from the 'Transit Stop' just north of the Catholic church, heading for Alba Iulia, Sibiu and Bucharest. Buses to the Arieş Valley – for stop-offs at Apuseni Mountain hubs to the south – are less frequent.

RIMITEA
☎ 264

West of Turda, Hwy 75 leads along the southern access points of the Apuseni Mountains (see p226). About 26km southwest is a pocket of paradise. This ethnic Hungarian village of distinctive white-washed homes faces Piatra Secuiului (1128m), a lone bluff that can be climbed (blue crosses). **Vajda Şara** (☎ 517 610; r per person incl meals €13) is a lushly traditional home you can stay in. Nearby, by a brook, is an old water mill.

Four kilometres south, from the village of **Colţeşti**, are ruins of a medieval castle on the hill to the west, which you can climb up to.

HUEDIN MICROREGION (KALOTASZEG)
☎ 264

Just off the Cluj–Oradea highway – like a more accessible Maramureş, – this bucolic paradise near the Apuseni Mountains includes 40 (chiefly) Hungarian villages bundled under the names 'Huedin Microregion' or Kalotaszeg. With a car, there's much to explore – as men in Austrian-style hats and women in headscarves on horse carts return your waves as you bounce and weave towards superb mountain hikes and waterfalls.

The Kalotaszeg is much beloved by Hungarian folklorists as a stronghold of pastoral Transylvanian Magyar culture. In Budapest's Ethnography Museum, there is a huge, seven-room exhibit devoted entirely to Kalotaszeg. Centuries-old traditions persist here – staying at a home can open up makeshift tours of horseshoe makers' workshops, shepherd huts and wooden churches – plus (from May to October), you can see how sheep-milk cheese is made.

You can plan trips with Davincze Tours in Sâncraiu or Green Mountain Tours (see p190).

Restaurants are not to be found in much of the area; plan on eating at Huedin or your guesthouse.

Along the Highway

Seven kilometres east of Huedin, **Izvorul Crişului** is known as Körösfő to Hungarians, or just as 'souvenir village' to everyone else, as the roadside is lined with stalls selling traditional handicrafts.

The area's namesake, **Huedin** (Bánffyhunyad in Hungarian), 52km west of Cluj-Napoca, is an unengaging highway town that nevertheless can fill your cellphone with credits, tummy with food, wallet with lei. You're better off heading to Sâncraiu or Mănăstireni for accommodation, but the highway **Hotel Montana** (☎ 353 090; d €20.80), at the northern end of town, has fine rooms and a pretty good restaurant.

Twelve kilometres west of Huedin is the small village of **Poieni**, 2.8km from Bologa. The ruins of a 13th-century **medieval fortress** tower above it. Equally interesting is the old **watermill** *(moară de apă)*, still in use today. The entrance to the mill is 3km from the main road on the left in the centre of the village.

Ciucea village, 22km west of Huedin, is principally a place of pilgrimage for Romanians and Hungarians alike, having been home to Romanian poet and politician Octavian Goga (1881–1939) and to Hungary's most controversial 20th-century poet, Endre Ady (1877–1919). There's a small museum and 16th-century **wooden church**, moved here from near Cluj to preserve it.

In villages around Ciucea, on the first Sunday in May, are irresistible **Measurement of the Milk Festivals** (Masurisul Laptelui), when shepherds bring in their flocks and milk them for a comparative contest – along with a lot of eating, dancing and merriment. Buses go to villages such as Magura Priei, 10km north of Ciucea, from Huedin for the festival.

Near Huedin

These places are quickly accessed in a two-hour leg-break on long drives, or serve as stepping stones to the Apuseni. Six kilometres south of Huedin, **Sâncraiu** is set at the base of sweeping hills, with a few dozen homes turned into guesthouses. Many are signed, though not all. Stop by **Davincze Tours** (☎ 257 580; www.davincze.ro; No 291), a crafty travel agency (across from the Reformed Church), which handles accommodation and tours. Rooms are €8 per person, €18 including all meals. They speak English.

A good spot for DIY exploration, **Mănăstireni** (Magyargyerömonostor in Hungarian) is 16km southeast of Huedin via Căluta or 21km via Izvorul Crişului. It's a quaint village noted for its 13th-century **church**, built by the Gyeröffy family, with a Gothic apse added in the 15th century. Inside an adjoining room you can see the old steeple with bullet holes from Turk guns. You may have to ask the priest for the keys – he's usually at the large, modern wood home 50m southeast.

During the 1848 revolution, 200 Hungarians died at the battle of Mănăstireni. They were buried in a mass grave, which today rests beneath lake waters at **Lake Beliş** – at low water levels, you can see the church top coming up for air.

A superb guesthouse in Mănăstireni is **Bogdan Erzsebet** (☎ 375 221; No 279; r per person incl meals €15), run by a lovely English-speaking family who can arrange tours. Take the road to Râşia and follow the handmade signs to 'turist info' for 150m.

On the roads between Huedin and Mănăstireni, **Căluta** has a little **restaurant** at the south end of town.

Towards the Mountains

If you don't want to rough it in the Apuseni but want to hike, the best (and last) base with guesthouses is **Rachiţele**, a largely Romanian mountain village with farms on hillsides and a rushing creek passing through. Seven kilometres east, reached by a patchy dirt road, is Rachiţele Falls. Most area hikes to Padiş start about 20km down the road (see below for hiking information).

There's a small **tourist information centre** (☉ 10am-1pm Thu, noon-3pm Fri-Sun) by the bridges in the centre, and eight (and growing) *pensiunes* to stay in, including **Pensiunea Bogdan** (☎ 0729-016 278; No 167; r per person from €10), about 100m towards the falls. English is harder to come by out here.

A nice approach to the Apuseni is the 50km ride southwest from the main-highway town Gilău (16km west of Cluj) to Lake Beliş. It's possible to find accommodation in towns such as Ruseşti, Mărişel and Lake Beliş.

Getting There & Around

See Cluj (p194) for bus or train links to Huedin. Note that international trains don't stop here.

Huedin has taxis that can drop you off into villages; another option is hitchhiking. Bus trips around the area may be possible, but are unpredictable and few and far between.

APUSENI MOUNTAINS (NORTH)

Southwest of Cluj-Napoca, the popular Apuseni are dotted with caves and forested trails, with a world of subterranean rivers and a 3500-year-old underground glacier. It's a lovely area that draws fervent fans.

There are two distinct parts, and ways to get there. Most travellers head straight for the central Padiş Plateau – reached from the north or south – to camp or bunk at a cabana and make a week's worth of day trips from there. See p226 for information on the southern access points to the Apuseni Mountains and highlights such as the Bear Cave and Scărişoara Ice Cave.

TRANSYLVANIA

Information

We hear information centres are in the works, but considering the area straddles county lines, disorganisation may continue. Check www.padis.ro for details on the plateau. One regional map is Dimap's *Munţii Apuseni* (€5), which has limited trail details.

It's worth considering going with a guide. Based in Oradea, **Apuseni Experience** (www.apuseni experience.ro) leads full week-long hiking, cultural, caving and underground rafting trips from €55 per day. Other good guides work with Green Mountain Tours or Pan Travel in Cluj (p187).

Padiş Plateau

From Cabana Padiş the most popular circuit leads southwest along the polluted Ponorului River to the fantastic Cetăţile Ponorului (Cetatea Ponorului; 2½ hours one way, blue circles). The cave takes its name from a fortress because of its towering entrance. You'll need good boots and a torch to make much of the damp chamber underground. The river sinks its ways through the chamber's numerous holes – some as deep as 150m.

Another trail, marked first by red stripes then by red circles, leads from the cabana north for three or four hours to a meadow at **Poiana Vărăşoaia**. From here, red circles bear east two hours to the **Rădesei Citadel** (Cetăţile Rădesei), another underground chamber with impressive rock formations (and tent sites). The route then circles **Someşul Cald**, a river in a deep gorge, before heading back south to the cabana. If you continue to follow the red stripes north through the Stâna de Vale ski resort you'll arrive at **Cârligatele Peak** (1694m).

Sleeping

There are a couple of camping places in Padiş plateau. **Cabana Padiş**, where many trails start from, is rather run down; one Apuseni regular said 'a tent is better'. Newer, and in far better shape, is **Cabana Cetăţile Ponorului** (☎ 0722-760 190; www.padis.ro; per person €9), near its namesake attraction. This 40-bed place has bathrooms and a restaurant; reserve online.

Getting to the Plateau

The best access road to Padiş is south of Huedin from Rachiţele (p197). It's 21km from Rachiţele to Ponor and a further 10km to Padiş. Another option is slower going – from Pietroasa in the west (it's 16km to Boga then 6km to Padiş).

These can be difficult roads to ride, but many people make it in regular cars.

These roads can be hiked, as can trails from **Gârda de Sus** (five to six hours, blue stripes) or the lesser-used trail from **Stâna de Vale** in the northwest (six to seven hours, red stripes).

ZALĂU

☎ 260 / pop 62,700

Heavy on '70s housing blocks and light on cheap accommodation, Zalău, 86km northwest of Cluj-Napoca, is understandably missed by most travellers' itineraries. It's worth popping by on a loop between Apuseni and Maramureş, however, as the Roman-Dacian town nearby is the first town chronicled in Transylvania.

The town fills a broad valley coming down from the foothills of the Meşes Mountains. The steep decline into town from Cluj-Napoca along hairpin turns is about the most exciting part of the place.

Orientation & Information

The **bus station** (Str Mihai Viteazul 54) is 1km north of the centre. Bus 1 runs from the centre to the train station, which is 6km north of the centre in the village of Crişeni. Bus 23 goes from centre to the south end of town. The centre stretches between Piaţa Iuliu Maniu and, a block east, Piaţa 1 Decembrie 1918, where you can find banks and ATMs.

Sights

Zalău's main site is about 10km east of town, the hilltop ruins of **Porolissum**, which was a Roman town that stood on the ultimate northern boundary of Roman Dacia. Dating from AD 106, the settlement was rapidly fortified, following which it developed as a leading administrative, economic and civilian centre. By AD 193, it had been granted the status of a municipality. It's an excellent way to break up a drive between Maramureş and Cluj or Huedin.

The 'Municipium Septimium Porolissensis', which some historians believe could even have briefly served as the capital of Dacia, was built within the walls of a giant castle. The 20,000 inhabitants who lived behind the walls were defended by some 7000 soldiers.

These days, nice views (some claim you can see Cluj on clear days) add to the thrill of walking around the 300m by 200m site, past crumbled and recreated walls, former roads and an amphitheatre that probably hosted gladiator games for 5500 blood-thirsty spectators. Most sites are signed in English and Romanian. Sorin, a friendly chap who has worked at the site since 1977 and lives at the white house (No 229) just before the road reaches the ruins, will lead you around the site (donation appreciated).

From Moigrad, keep going up the road south up the hill, ignoring a couple of left turns – eventually it ends at the site gate. It's about a half-hour walk uphill from the village.

In Zalău centre, the **County Museum of History & Art** (☎ 612 223; Str Unirii; adult/student €0.35/0.20; ☒ 9am-5pm Tue-Sun), just east of Piaţa Iuliu Maniu, also covers Porolissum.

Sleeping & Eating

Hotel Meses (☎ 661 050; www.hotelmeses.ro; Str Unirii 11; s/d €53.50/65) Set back from central Piaţa 1 Decembrie 1918, this is a nice yellow hotel with 34 comfy but standard rooms.

Villa Vlad (☎ 619 183; Str Gheorghe Doja 159; s €51-57, d €60-66; ☒ ☒) Just past the south entrance to town, this is something of a 'boutique hotel' (with its own gas station out front!). Rooms have stylish leather seats and platform beds – room four has good balcony views. When the manager's away, you can get online in her office.

There's pizza in the centre. A nice spot near Villa Vlad is the **Hanul Drumeţilor** (Str Gheorghe Doja; mains €2.90-7.10; ☒ 24hr), with windows overlooking the valley, standard Romanian dishes and ice cream.

Getting There & Away

See p194 for train and microbus links between Cluj and Zalău. Train connections are a little inconvenient, with changes required at Jibou. Microbuses from Cluj stop at various points in town, finishing at the bus station; from there five or six daily buses go to Moigrad (€1.15),

near the Porolissum ruins. There are buses also to Huedin, Baia Mare and Oradea.

Call 633633 to arrange a taxi; a ride to Porolissum is about €12 to €15.

CLUJ-NAPOCA TO BISTRIŢA
☎ 264

Don't think this road, past many industrial towns, with trucks racing past you, is going to be a lovely leisurely experience. Still, there are a few places worth stopping off at if you're headed north towards Bistriţa, Maramureş or Southern Bucovina.

Bonţida

Thirty kilometres northeast of Cluj, this village is home to a Banffy Castle that will be under renovation for several years. You're free to wander by and inside the medieval 16th-century walls. During summer, a café is open Friday to Sunday. To find it, veer right past the river when you reach the central monument. The village is 3km east of the highway.

Gherla

About 45km northeast of Cluj, the highway passes through this small market town that, in the 17th century, was known as Armenopolis when it was predominantly Armenian. It has a pretty Renaissance-style castle and a baroque **Armenian Catholic Cathedral** (1784–1798) on the central square Piaţa Libertăţii. It is also the only town in Romania whose original city planning utilised a grid system. A small **history museum** (Str Mihai Viteazul 6) is a block north, on the street parallel to the highway.

The town is best known, however, for its prison. Still functioning, **Gherla prison** (Str Andrei Mureşan 2), about four blocks north of the square (on the west side of the highway), gained notoriety in the 1950s for its so-called 're-education program'. Using severe psychological pressure

GLASS ICONS

Painted-glass icons can be found all over Transylvania, but the small village of **Nicula**, 7km east of Gherla, is famous for them. Icons were painted here for centuries, but it took a miracle to get the honours.

Visitors to this hilltop 16th-century monastery can see examples of the age-old folk art that dates from the 11th century. Icons of saints were painted and put in peasants' houses to keep evil spirits at bay. Nicula earned its fame only in the 18th century after, per legend, an icon of the Virgin Mary miraculously shed tears for 26 days in 1699. Afterwards, Nicula-made icons became highly sought items.

Some 300,000 believers make a pilgrimage here every 15 August, St Mary's Day.

and physical torture, hundreds of dissident students were tormented until they ratted on friends and allies and were then made to torture them in turn. Conditions inside remained harsh even after re-education programs ceased in 1951. In 1970, during floods, 600 prisoners drowned in their cells after the prison director ordered the inmates to be locked in before fleeing the building himself. Just north is a **memorial** (a grey crucifix) to those who died.

SLEEPING & EATING

Cola Pensiunea (☎ 243 178; Str Mihai Eminescu 9; r €17) This small guesthouse is on the main street, with a popular restaurant. No breakfast is served.

Pensiunea Iona (☎ 213 451; www.pensiuneaiona .ro; Str Clujului 4; r €17 & €23) This modern 18-room complex on the main road, a couple of kilometres south of the centre, has no breakfast.

Sic

On the dirt backroads between Bonţida and Nicula, Sic (Szék in Hungarian) is an interesting, predominately ethnic-Hungarian village home to the recently opened, EU-funded **Sic Reedbed Nature Reserve** (☎ 410 720; www.arpmcluj.ro, in Romanian; admission free). Here you can wander on woodplank walkways across a marshy reef – the last thing you expect to see in Transylvania – where bird life can drown out the sounds of your footsteps. Large fish sometimes startle visitors, including Lonely Planet researchers, with sudden splashes just beneath the walkway. It's a 30-minute walk across.

The road winds along low-lying hills. At the north end is a nice, seven-room **pensiune** (☎ 228 392, 094 594 788; r about €12).

BISTRIŢA

☎ 263 / pop 81,470

Bistriţa would hardly catch a passing gaze from travellers if not for the work of an Irishman who never made it here. Bram Stoker overnighted his Jonathan Harker in a hotel here on the eve of St George's day before riding on east to Dracula's castle. Some local businesses understandably try to cash in on the accidental fame, but with the museum half-closed and tourist information centre shut down, Bistriţa (about 108km northeast of Cluj) is more of a village trapped in the form of a town. It feels a little sad at times – as if it knows its time in the sun has passed – but the people are nice and the medieval centre is worthy of a little stroll

after lunch, before heading towards greater glories at Tihuţa pass, Lake Colibiţa or the cheesy Dracula Castle (p211).

First chronicled in 1264, Bistriţa (Bistritz in German) was one of the seven towns founded by the Saxons, whose presence still lives on in the old town's quaint 15th- and 16th-century merchants' houses (only about 370 Saxons still call Bistriţa home). Witch trials were common events in Bistriţa during medieval times.

In August, the city hosts the International Folk, Dance and Traditions Festival *Nunata Zamfirei*. The central streets seem a lot busier than you'd expect for a town of 80,000; good luck trying to figure out the complex web of 'right-of-way' at various intersections.

MAPS & PUBLICATIONS

The ad-filled *Bistriţa-Năsăud County* map (€2.10) includes a city map. A local 200-page colour guide *Bistriţa Năsăd Travel Guide* has some useful information on county sights in English.

Information

BOOKSHOPS

Librăria Radu Petrescu (Str Petru Rareş 1; ☻ 8am-7pm Mon-Fri, 10am-2pm Sat) Sells books.

INTERNET

Club Internet (Str Ursului 14; per hr €0.45; ☻ 10am-midnight Sun-Thu, to 6am Fri & Sat)

MONEY

Banca Comercială Română (Piaţa Petru Rareş; ☻ 8.30am-6pm Mon-Fri, to 12.30pm Sat) Cashes travellers cheques and has an ATM.

Raiffeisen Bank (Piaţa Uniri 1; ☻ 9am-6.30pm Mon-Fri)

TRAVEL AGENCIES

A former tourist information centre has closed; a city hall rep told us another may open at some point in the future.

Coroana Tourist Company (☎ 212 056; www.dracula transylvania.ro; Piaţa Petru Rareş 7a; ☻ 8am-5pm Mon-Fri, 10am-1pm Sat) is very happy to sell you flights to Italy or to book Black Sea trips in Romania, but is far less useful providing information around the region.

Transylvanian Society of Dracula (☎ 231 803; 1st fl, Piaţa Petru Rareş 7; ☻ 8.30am-4.30pm Mon-Fri), part of Coroana, is a chapter of the nonprofit

(Continued on page 209)

Glass ceiling and dome above Pasajul Vilacrosse (p72), Bucharest

Jukebox nightclub (p85) in Bucharest

Palace of Parliament (p68) and fountains in Piața Unirii (p70), Bucharest

Last Judgement fresco from Suceviţa Monastery (p278), Moldavia

'Welcome to Mamaia' sign, Black Sea coast (p287), Northern Dobrogea

Next page:
History & Archaeological Museum (p289), Conştanta, Northern Dobrogea
RUSSELL YOUNG / JOHN ARNOLD IMAGES / ALAMY

DIANA MAYFIELD

NICHOLAS PITT / ALAMY

208

DAN HERRICK

Chişinău (p318), Moldova

JEFF

Orthodox wedding ceremony,
Chişinău (p318), Moldova

(Continued from page 200)

organisation for a world group of vampire fanatics. It stages some events, usually tagged along with package trips. One employee:'To be honest, I don't understand how this society works'.

Sights

The towering **evangelical church** (Biserica Evanghelică) dominates Piața Centrală, though is rarely open for visitors to see. Built by the Saxons in the 14th century, and today in a state of perpetual renovation, the 76.5m Gothic-style church still serves Bistrița's small Saxon community.

Facing the church on the north side of Piața Centrală is the fine **Șugălete** row of terraced buildings, which in medieval times was bustling with trading activities. Built between 1480 and 1550, the 13 houses were bound together with stone arches and in the 16th century, a portico was added. There is a bar, restaurant and a couple of shops worth peeking into, including the **Galeriile de Arta** (☎ 0745-454 032; Piața Centrală 24; ☼ 11am-

2pm Mon, 4-7pm Tue-Sat), with regularly changing exhibitions.

An **Orthodox church** (1270–80) is the centrepiece of Piața Unirii. The open courtyard of the half-closed **County Museum** (Muzeul Judetean; ☎ 230 046; B-dul General Grigore Bălan 19; adult/student €0.60/0.30; ☼ 10am-6pm Tue-Sun) has a wooden church and plenty of crosses to see. The museum proper's collection of minerals and stuffed animals is hardly worth a look; hopefully they'll reopen the history section some day.

What remains of the city's 13th-century walls lies south of the town along the north-west side of the **municipal park**. Bistrița suffered numerous attacks by the Turks and Tartars during the 16th and 17th centuries and the citadel and most of the bastions intersecting the city wall were destroyed. In 1530, Wallachian prince Petru Rareș (r 1541–46) besieged Bistrița, forcing its Saxon inhabitants to finally surrender. The **Coopers' Tower** remains at the east of the park.

Activities

To cool off or lounge about, there's the **Codrișor swimming pool**, an outdoor pool on the south side of the river.

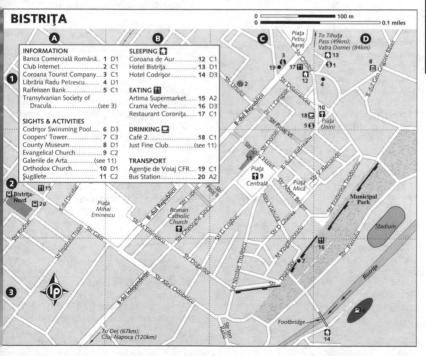

BISTRIȚA

INFORMATION	
Banca Comercială Română.. **1** D1	
Club Internet........................**2** C1	
Coroana Tourist Company.. **3** C1	
Librăria Radu Petrescu....... **4** D1	
Raifeissen Bank.................. **5** C1	
Transylvanian Society of Dracula.........................(see 3)	
SIGHTS & ACTIVITIES	
Codrișor Swimming Pool..... **6** D3	
Coopers' Tower.................. **7** C3	
County Museum.................. **8** D1	
Evangelical Church.............. **9** C2	
Galeriile de Arta...............(see 11)	
Orthodox Church.............. **10** D1	
Șugălete.......................... **11** C2	

SLEEPING	
Coroana de Aur...............**12** C1	
Hotel Bistrița.................. **13** D1	
Hotel Codrișor................ **14** D3	
EATING	
Artima Supermarket......**15** A2	
Crama Veche................. **16** D3	
Restaurant Coronița...... **17** C1	
DRINKING	
Café 2............................**18** C1	
Just Fine Club.............(see 11)	
TRANSPORT	
Agenție de Voiaj CFR.... **19** C1	
Bus Station.................... **20** A2	

TRANSYLVANIA

Sleeping

Hotel Bistriţa (☎ 231 056; www.hotel-bistrita.ro; s €23, d €33; 🕱) Tucked behind a bank and government building across from the Coroana de Aur, this modest yet stylish 44-room hotel is the town's best deal. Older rooms have wood floors, rugs and are fresh enough, despite the years; the new ones are swank (for Bistriţa), with gold walls, standing lamps and little balconies.

Hotel Codrişor (☎ 233 814; coroana@bistrita.ro; Str Codrişor 28; s/d €26/31.50) Right across a footbridge, and next to a large open-air swimming pool, this bright yellow hotel has 19 rather boxy, but colourful rooms, and is adding 10 more bigger ones. The terrace restaurant draws many locals in summer.

Coroana de Aur (☎ 232 667; www.hotel-coroana-de -aur.ro; Piaţa Petru Rareş 4; s/d €31.50/46) Prince might dig the purple façade, but Bram Stoker's character Jonathan Harker may have turned back if he had had to stop at this disappointing (and inevitable) cash-in attempt based on the fictional hotel Harker stopped at before heading to Dracula's castle. Oh, the 130 rooms are fine and comfy enough, but suffer from a very '70s decor (as in 1970s not 1870s).

Eating

Crama Veche (☎ 218 047; Str Albert Berger 10; mains €2.30-5.70; 🕑 noon-midnight) A better-than-average Romanian traditional restaurant, this evocatively traditional place – with oodles of wood carvings and unfinished wood tables and a live act – is a nice setting for Romanian, German and Hungarian fare off the grill. Hunter's goulash with venison is €5.70; start with the cauliflower, pepper and pickle salad served in an earthenware bowl (€1). Best is in summer, when the outdoor terrace fills with happy locals. It's set in the basement, at the back of the Casa de Cultura.

Restaurant Coroniţa (Piaţa Petru Rareş 4; mains from €2.90; 🕑 10am-11pm) The atmosphere's stuffy and tacky, but if you're craving breaded brains and Golden Mediaş wine try this place, adjoining the Coroana de Aur hotel.

Artima Supermarket (Str Garii; 🕑 8am-10pm Mon-Sat, 9am-7pm Sun) This big supermarket is across from the bus station.

Drinking

Just Fine Club (Piaţa Centrală 21; 🕑 10am-1am) This is the town's premier chill-out club, in a cave-like cellar with dim lighting, couches and lounge music.

Café 2 (Piaţa Unirii 2; 🕑 9am-10.30pm Mon-Sat, noon-10.30pm Sun) This cool-kid coffee and drink lounge has electronic beats and glass-panel floors exposing coffee beans.

Getting There & Away

BUS

The scrappy **bus station** (☎ 233 655) sends five daily buses to Braşov (€8, seven to eight hours), four to Cluj (€2.90, 2½ to three hours) and Oradea (€8.60), two to Satu Mare (€7.20), three to Sibiu (€8, six hours), one to Suceava (€6) and seven to Târgu Mureş (€3.45, 2½ hours). There are as many microbuses to Braşov, Oradea and Sibiu, and more to Cluj; call ☎ 213 938 for more information.

TRAIN

The **train station** (☎ 223 572) sends one overnight daily train to Bucharest (€10, 10 hours), four daily trains to Cluj (€2.20, three to four hours) and one to Vatra Dornei (€2.90, five hours). It's easier to reach Lunca Ilvei from Cluj. To reach Suceava (€10, eight hours) you must change trains in Beclan Someş. You can also buy tickets at the **Agenţie de Voiaj CFR** (☎ 213 938; Piaţa Petru Rareş; 🕑 9am-4pm Mon-Fri).

BÂRGĂU VALLEY
☎ 263

Retracing Jonathan Harker's trip up to the lovely Tihuţa Pass is irresistible for the fang-inclined, but anyone can appreciate some of the area's beauty, particularly west of the pass itself (and the 'Hotel Dracula'), Lake Colibiţa and little lost Lunca Ilvei. Eventually the pass leads to Vatra Dornei in Moldavia.

To fully access the region, you'll need your own wheels, or to be on a tour.

Lake Colibiţa

The first 20 or so kilometres from Bistriţa pass dusty, rather industrial towns before climbing and turning past fir trees and hill-clinging farms. A well worthwhile (bumpy) detour is 15km southeast from the village of Prundu Bârgăului to Lake Colibiţa (www.locolibita .ro), a dam-made blue lake with lovely summer homes, boats to borrow, islands to swim to, and a few places to stay.

On the water, near the lake's west end, the dreamy **Lumina Lacului** (Light of the Lake; ☎ 265 570; www.luminalacului.ro; r with shared/private bathroom per person €10/14.50) is a lovely spot with simple rooms, a restaurant and boats. Best are the rooms with shared bathroom, with balconies looking over the water. Meals are extra. Just up the hill is **Pensiunea Ariniş** (☎ 0740-407 954; d €17), with a handful of rooms, some with private bathroom, and terrace restaurant overlooking the west end of the lake.

'Dracula's Castle'

After Mureşeni (29km east of Bistriţa) the road starts to climb steeply on its approach to the Tihuţa Pass, which peaks at 1200m. A trail (red circles) leads from here to Piatra Fântânele at the top of the pass.

The main reason most people break their journey at Piatra Fântânele is not so much for the fine hiking that it offers but rather for the tacky, 53-room **Hotel Castel Dracula** (☎ 266 841; www.hotelcasteldracula.bn.ro; s/d € 52/65, apt €86-100). The castle/hotel, better known as Dracula's Castle, towers 1116m high on the spot where Stoker sited his fictitious Dracula's castle. Stoker got the setting right: the views of Tihuţa Pass are great. The architect who designed the jagged-edged building in the early 1980s clearly studied Dracula movies. Rooms sport a lot of cranberry-blood colour with dragon motifs – but are not overly camp. The 'highlight' of a visit is a peek into **'Dracula's room'** (admission €0.30), down dark creaky steps, where visitors are given a short, candlelit tour around his 'coffin'. A 'surprise' occurs near the end of the tour designed to give visitors a little jolt (it's not much of one, but a Canadian visitor had a heart attack on the spot in the mid-1990s).

There's tennis and a small ski lift next door. There are several **hikes** that pass by the area, though maps are hard to come by.

A couple of daily buses between Bistriţa and Vatra Dornei pass by here.

Lunca Ilvei

Reached by 4WD vehicles from Piatra Fântânele on a forestry road, or via a 30km very rough ride from the Năsăd–Sângeroz-Bău highway to the west (in all 71km from Bistriţa), the laid-back valley village of Lunca Ilvei is worth the effort for those seeking leisurely hikes past shepherd huts and haystacks up forested mountains, winter skiing and horse rides.

Run by a Brit here since 1999, the **Riding Centre** (☎ 378 470; www.riding-holidays.ro; Str Bolovanul 340) offers five-day riding trips to Dracula's castle and the mountains, staying in village guesthouses and moving luggage for you. A trip, including all meals and accommodation, costs €780; riding is €15 per hour. There are rooms for €25 per person (including all meals).

On the other end of town, **Casa Alexandra** (☎ 378 117, 0722-218 295; www.ecolunca.go.ro; Str Principală 44; r per person incl meals from €10) is a bucolic farm by the river with six rooms run by a sweet English-speaking family who provide meals.

Personal trains between Cluj and Suceava stop here. It's less convenient getting here from Bistriţa by train.

TRANSYLVANIA

Crişana & Banat

The areas of Crişana (north of the Mureş River) and Banat (to the south) have a lively, spiritual autonomy found nowhere else in Romania, driven by their sense of regional identity, ethnic diversity and tangible Habsburg influence. Oradea, Arad and Timişoara were once large military fortresses marking the southeastern extent of Austria-Hungary, while being culturally and politically married to Yugoslavia's Vojvodina and Hungary's Great Plain. Following WWI, Crişana and Banat were dealt out to Romania, despite their predominantly Hungarian populations, and even now they have more in common with Subotica (Serbia) and Szeged (Hungary) than with the rest of Romania.

It was in the stylish city of Timişoara that the seeds of the 1989 revolution were sown, a fact that has left these charming and proud people with a scarcely concealed grin. Hungarian and Yugoslav TV have given the region stronger links to the West, evidenced by cutting-edge restaurants, clubs and a forward-looking society.

While flaunting three of Romania's most 'European' cities, in both essence and crumbling Habsburg architecture, the regions are also sprinkled with tempting offerings such as the soaring Apuşeni Mountains, ski runs, deep caves, gorges, waterfalls and curative thermal waters. Zigzag from giddying excitement to recuperative leisure all within a few hours' drive.

HIGHLIGHTS

- Stew in the soothing thermal waters of Băile Herculane's **Roman baths** (p221)

- Look at (but don't touch!) the ancient stalactites and stalagmites in the magnificent **Bear Cave** (p227) and the surreal **Scărişoara Ice Cave** (p227)

- Eavesdrop on a candle-lit service in Timişoara's beautiful **Metropolitan Cathedral** (p218)

- Ski, hike, cycle or gaze stupidly at the western **Apuşeni Mountains** (p226)

- Indulge in a lazy day in Timişoara, starting at the **outdoor pools** (p218), then clean up for an evening at the **opera** (p219) and finally take a nightcap in a **Piaţa Victoriei** (p216) bar

Bear &
Ice Caves

Western
Apuseni
Mountains

Timişoara

Băile
Herculane

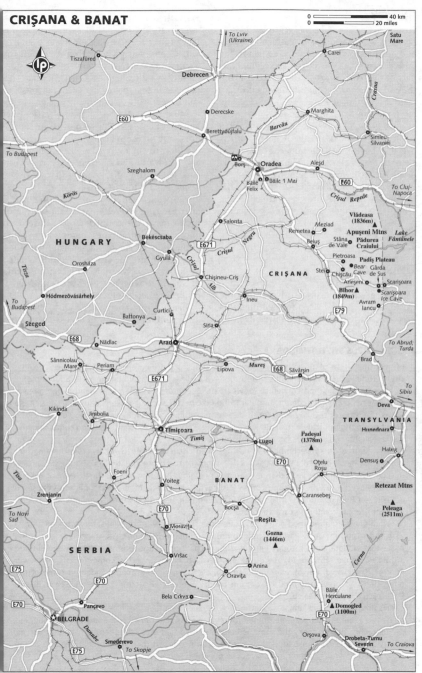

HISTORY

Historical Crişana and Banat are today divided between western Romania, eastern Hungary and northern Yugoslavia. First settled in the 6th century BC, by AD 106 the region was part of the Roman province of Dacia. From the end of the 9th century until the Ottoman conquest of Crişana and Banat in 1552 the region was under Hungarian rule.

In 1699 the Turks relinquished Hungary to Austria but held Crişana and Banat until their defeat by Habsburg prince Eugene of Savoy in 1716. In 1718 Crişana and Banat became part of the Austro-Hungarian empire.

The Treaty of Trianon in 1920 split the territory among Romania, Hungary and Yugoslavia, setting Crişana and Banat's current borders.

BANAT

TIMIŞOARA

☎ 256 / pop 321,930

Timişoara (tee-mee-*shwa*-ra) stunned the world and disrupted sleep for evil dictators everywhere when its incensed residents insti-gated the 1989 revolution. Romania's fourth largest city is known by locals as Primul Oraş Liber (First Free Town), for it was here that anti-Ceauşescu protests first exceeded the Securitate's capacity for violent suppression, eventually punching Ceauşescu's ticket to Hell (see boxed text, below). Less courageous, but still noteworthy achievements include being the first city in Europe to have electric street lamps (1884) and the second to introduce horse-drawn trams (1867). With its charming Mediterranean air, regal Habsburg buildings and a cultural and sporting scene that's un-equalled in Romania, it's a city that's loved by residents and tourists alike.

Timişoara, dubbed the 'city of flowers' after the ring of pretty parks that surrounds it, is one of the country's most developed and multicultural cities, comprising strong Hungarian, German and Serbian minorities. In recent years the city has been designated as 'Romania's economic showcase', spurring debate as to whether the 'Timişoara Model' can be applied to other cities.

In addition to being superior to Bucharest as a Romanian road/rail access point from

---

DON'T MESS WITH TIMIŞOARA

Even at the height of his power, Timişoara gave Ceauşescu the creeps. The dictator's visits to the city were few, brief and required surreptitious, dread-fuelled travel and sleeping arrangements to allay his assassination concerns. So, when the Securitate overplayed its hand in the already truculent city by trying to deport popular Hungarian pastor and outspoken Ceauşescu critic László Tőkés, the dictator should have sensed disaster looming. However, like most megalomaniacs, he didn't grasp the full scale of his folly until he was being shoved in front of a firing squad, looking genuinely stunned, 10 days later on Christmas Day 1989.

What started on 15 December 1989 as a human chain of Tőkés' parishioners protecting him from arrest mushroomed and lost all focus – many of the protesters that joined the initial rally mistakenly thought they were demonstrating for religious freedom, not for the defence of Tőkés – until it peaked as a full-scale, anti-communist revolt on 20 December. Overconfident Ceauşescu actually left Romania during this time for a visit to Iran, leaving his wife Elena and various sub-ordinates to cope with the escalating protests.

When Ceauşescu returned a few days later, the situation was critical. Factory workers, armed with clubs brought in by Party officials to crush the demonstrations, spontaneously joined the protesters in Piaţa Operei (today Piaţa Victoriei), chanting antigovernment slogans and singing an old Romanian anthem ('Wake up, Romanians!') banned since the communists took power in 1947. The crowd, now over 100,000 strong, overpowered then commandeered some of the tanks that had previously fired on demonstrators. Protests ensued in Bucharest (see p28) and Ceauşescu's fate was sealed.

Despite the events in Timişoara leading to the revolt being confused and directionless, there's no denying that the people were primed for rebellion. While other cities are said to have mounted similar revolts in the weeks and months before, only to be hastily subdued by Securitate forces, it was the tenacious Timişoarans that first successfully defied their government, leading to the undignified downfall of their least favourite guest.

the west, Timişoara is the hub of Carpatair (p220), Romania's thriving semi-budget airline. 'Flashpackers' and people with an aversion to spine-jangling overnight train trips will want to make Timişoara their Romanian base of operations.

Orientation

Confusingly, the northern train station (Timişoara-Nord) is west of the city centre. From here, walk east along B-dul Regele Ferdinand (which becomes B-dul Republicii) to the Opera House and Piaţa Victoriei. To the north is Piaţa Libertăţii; Piaţa Unirii, the old town square, is two blocks further north. Timişoara's bus station is beside the Idsefin Market, three blocks from the northern train station. Take B-dul General Drăgălina south from the train station to the canal, cross the bridge and head west to the next bridge.

MAPS

Hotfoot it around Timişoara with Amco Press' *City Plan* (1:10,000; €3), sold in most bookshops. There is a tourist map in the bilingual city guide *What? When? Where? Timişoara*, available free all over the city. Be aware that many street names have changed but many maps and locals still use the old names.

Information
BOOKSHOPS
Humanitas (Map p217; ☎ 433 180; Str F Mercy 1; ☯ 9am-7pm Mon-Fri) Sells some English-language books about Romania.
Librăria Mihai Eminescu (Map p217; ☎ 494 123; Piaţa Victoriei 2; ☯ 9am-7pm Mon-Fri, to 1pm Sat) Stocks a less exhaustive range than Humanitas.

CULTURAL CENTRES
British Council (Map p217; ☎ 497 678; Str Paris 1; ☯ 1-7pm Mon, Tue & Thu, 9am-3pm Wed & Fri)
French Cultural Centre (Centrul Cultural Francez; Map p217; ☎ 490 544, 201 453; B-dul CD Loga 46; ☯ 10am-6pm Mon, Wed & Fri, 2-7pm Tue & Thu, 10am-1pm Sat)

INTERNET ACCESS
Internet Café (Map p217; per hr €1; ☯ 9am-1am Mon-Fri, to 3pm Sat) It's located inside Cinema Timiş.
Internet Java (Map p217; ☎ 432 495; Str Pacha 6; per hr €1; ☯ 24hr) Inside the Java Coffee House.

MEDICAL SERVICES
Farmacie Remedia (Map p217; B-dul Revoluţiei 1989; ☯ 7am-8pm Mon-Fri, 8am-3pm Sat)

Sensi Blu Pharmacy (Map p217; ☎ 406 153; Piaţa Victoriei 7; ☯ 8am-8pm Mon-Fri, 9am-8pm Sat & Sun)

MONEY
Currency exchange (☯ 8am-6pm Mon-Fri, to 1pm Sat) Inside Hotel Continental.
HVB Bank (Map p217; ☎ 306 800; Piaţa Victoriei 2; ☯ 9am-4pm Mon-Fri)
Volksbank (Map p217; ☎ 406 101; Str Piatra Craiului 2)

POST & TELEPHONE
Central post office (Map p217; ☎ 491 999; B-dul Revoluţiei 2; ☯ 8am-7pm Mon-Fri, to noon Sat)
Post office (Map p217; Str Macieşilor; ☯ 8am-7pm Mon-Fri) This branch near B-dul Revoluţiei is useful when the central PO's too busy.
Telephone office (Map p217; Str N Lenau 4; ☯ 7am-9pm) Has fax facilities.

TOURIST INFORMATION
City Centre Travel Agency (Map p217; ☎ 292 960; www.aerotravel.ro; B-dul Republicii 4; ☯ 9am-6pm Mon-Fri) A can-do kind of agency with people exclusively dedicated to all varieties of domestic tourism, car hire and flight bookings.
Qual Tours (Map p217; ☎ 294 411; office@qualtours.ro; Str Nicolaus Lenau 10; ☯ 9am-6pm Mon-Fri, 9am-noon Sat) Staff speak excellent English and French, and can organise car hire, regional tours and guides.

Festivals
Like many cities in Romania, Timişoara hosts a raucous **beer festival** in October for the pure joy of public inebriation and live music.

Sights
PIAŢA UNIRII
In the heart of the old town, Piaţa Unirii (Map p217) is Timişoara's most picturesque square, featuring the imposing sight of the Catholic and Serbian churches facing each other. The eastern side of the square is dominated by the baroque **Roman Catholic Cathedral** (Catedrală Episcopală Romano-Catolică; ☎ 430 671; Piaţa Unirii 12), built in 1754. The main altar painting was completed by Michael Angelo Unterberger, director of the Fine Art Academy in Vienna. On the opposite side is the **Serbian Orthodox Church** (Biserica Ortodoxă Sârbă), built the same year as its Catholic counterpart; local Banat artist Constantin Daniel painted the interior.

The **Trinity Column**, in the square's centre, was erected by the people of Timişoara at the end of the 18th century in thanks to God for allowing them to survive the plague that hit

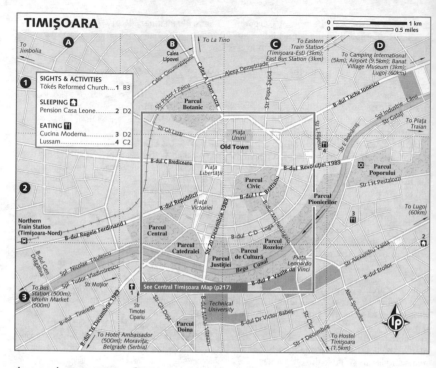

TIMIŞOARA

SIGHTS & ACTIVITIES
Tökés Reformed Church....**1** B3

SLEEPING
Pension Casa Leone..........**2** D2

EATING
Cucina Moderna..............**3** D2
Lussam.........................**4** C2

See Central Timişoara Map (p217)

the town between 1738 and 1739. Overlooking the square is the baroque **Old Prefecture Palace** (Palatul Vechii Prefecturi; 1754), suffering through major renovations at the time of writing. When open, it houses an **Art Museum** (Muzeul de Artă; admission €0.75; ☺ 10am-4pm Tue-Sun).

From Piaţa Unirii, walk east along Str Palanca to the **Banat Ethnographic Museum** (☎ 491 339; Str Popa Şapcă 4; admission €0.50; ☺ 10am-4.30pm Tue-Sun), housed in the oldest fortress in Timişoara, within the city's remaining 18th-century bastion. Allow an hour to drift through its 2000 exhibits, which include traditional costumes, 19th-century furniture, craft and 'spiritual culture' from the Banat region. Nearby is a landmark **fountain**, which has all the points of the compass round its circular design.

The **Great Synagogue** (Str Mărăşeşti 6) was built in 1865 and is an important keynote in Jewish history. Jews in the Austro-Hungarian empire were fully emancipated in 1864 (they could finally own land and have a profession), the year when permission was given to build the synagogue. It once hosted concerts by the Philharmonic Orchestra, which refused to play music by Nazi sympathiser Richard Wagner.

PIAŢA LIBERTĂŢII TO PIAŢA VICTORIEI

Walk south from Piaţa Unirii past the **town hall** (1734), built on the site of 17th-century Turkish baths, to **Piaţa Libertăţii** (Map p217). It was here that the leader of the 1514 peasant revolt, Gheorghe Doja, was tortured before being executed. Doja's peasant army, after an initial victory, was quickly quashed, captured and killed. Legend has it that, upon Doja's public execution, his followers were forced to eat parts of his body as an appetiser before their own executions. Look for the cannonball embedded in the wall of a building on Str Ungareanu, close to Piaţa Libertăţii.

The central **statue of Saint Nepomuk and the Virgin Mary** was made in 1756 in Vienna and brought to Romania in memory of plague victims. Mary holds a lily, the symbol of purity. Her gold star-studded halo was added during restoration in 2000.

Continue south along Str Lucian Blage to the 14th-century Huniades Palace. Built between 1307 and 1315 by the Hungarian king Carol Robert, Prince of Anjou, it was redesigned under the Habsburgs in the late 18th century. It houses the **Banat History Museum**

CENTRAL TIMIŞOARA

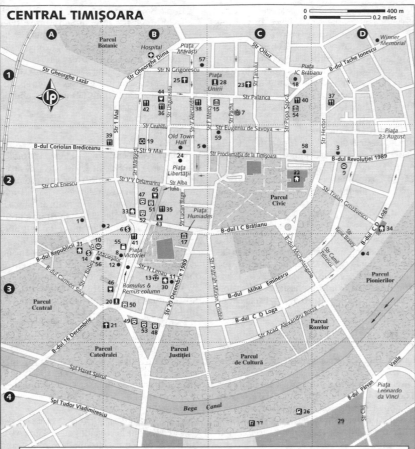

0 — 400 m
0 — 0.2 miles

(Muzeul Banatului; ☎ 491 339; Piaţa Huniades 1; admission €0.60; ⌚ 10am-4.30pm), which is worth visiting for its enormous displays on natural history, geology, armour, weapons, archaeology, ceramics, tools, an authentic wooden fishing boat and scale-model countryside shelters. In nearby Piaţa Victoriei note the column topped with the classic scene of **Romulus and Remus** feeding from the mother wolf, a gift from the city of Rome.

Head west to the marble 18th-century **National Theatre & Opera House** (opposite). It was here that thousands of demonstrators gathered on 16 December 1989, following the siege on László Tőkés' house (see boxed text, p214). A memorial plaque on the front of the Opera House reads: 'So you, who pass by this building, will dedicate a thought for free Romania.'

At the southern end of Piaţa Victoriei there are **memorials** to those who died during the revolution and the Orthodox **Metropolitan Cathedral**, built between 1936 and 1946. Unique to the church are its electrical bells cast from iron imported from Indonesia. A collection of 16th- to 19th-century icons is displayed in the basement.

SOUTH OF THE CENTRE

The 1989 revolution began at the **Tőkés Reformed Church** (Biserica Reformată Tőkés; Map p216; ☎ 492 992; Str Timotei Cipariu 1), where Father László Tőkés spoke out against the dictator. Today, Tőkés' small apartment is privately inhabited. On the southern bank of the Bega Canal is the **University of West Timişoara** (UWT; Map p217; ☎ 490 009; B-dul Vasile Pârvan 4), established in 1944.

NORTH OF THE CENTRE

The **Banat Village Museum** (Muzeul Satului Banaţean; ☎ 225 588; Str Al CFR 1; ⌚ 1-8pm Tue-Sun Jun-Sep, 10am-4pm Nov-Feb), 6km northeast of the centre, exhibits more than 30 traditional peasant houses dating from the 19th century. The open-air display was created in 1917. Take tram 1 (black number) from the northern train station.

Activities

For swimming, the **Terasa Eminescu Complex** (Map p217; ☎ 229 212; admission €3; ⌚ 10am-7pm) has loud pumping music and hordes of students, making this a social rather than sporty day-out. The **Strand Complex** (Map p217; ☎ 203 663; admission €3; ⌚ 24hr) is just as popular for a quick dip.

Book boat trips on Bega Canal (which flows through the city) and on Mureş River through adventure company **Pepetour** (☎ 354 924; office@pepetour.ro; half-day/full-day tours per person €10/20). Extreme-sports lovers can get their thrills thanks to the tour agency **Latura Extremă** (www.latura.ro), which organises water sports, ballooning, paintballing, tandem paragliding and adventure trips.

Sleeping

BUDGET

Camping International (☎ 208 925; campinginternational@yahoo.com; Aleea Pădurea Verde 6; tent sites €2.50, chalets s/d/q €34/46/63) This excellent camping ground – and mildly expensive restaurant – is nestled in the Green Wood forest. The main entrance is on Calea Dorobanţilor. From the train station catch trolleybus 11 to the end of the line, 50m from the camping ground.

Hostel Timişoara (☎ 293 960; Baron Bldg, Str Arieş 19; dm €9) Two kilometres from the city centre, take tram 8 from the northern train station to this four-room, bare-bones, dorm-style hostel situated on the top floor of a university building.

Pension Casa Leone (Map p216; ☎ 292 621; www.casaleone.ro; B-dul Eroilor 67; d/tr €30/45) This lovely seven-room *pensiune* offers exceptional service and individually decorated rooms. Take tram 8 from the train station or call ahead to arrange transport. Breakfast not included.

MIDRANGE

Hotel Cina Banatul (Map p217; ☎ 491 903; B-dul Republicii 3-5; s/d €29/40) The best-value pad in Timişoara, this hotel has clean, ultramodern rooms and a good restaurant.

Hotel Central (Map p217; ☎ 490 091; www.hotel-central.ro; Str N Lenau 6; s/d €40/46) Recent renovations have left this place glistening, modern and comfortable.

Villa International (Map p217; ☎ 499 339; B-dul CD Loga 48; s/d €50/60) Part villa, part curiosity. The Ceauşescus only slept here for two nights, but their apartments still contain 'personal effects', free for guest use. The villa has an unusual faded glory, underscored by an eerie ambience. Rooms are achingly outmoded and bare, but clean. A sneak peak at the dated lobby is highly recommended.

Hotel Timişoara (Map p217; ☎ 498 852; Str 1 Mai 2; s/d €50/62) Inside this soaring Soviet delight are simple, zealously priced three-star rooms, though the location is superb.

Hotel Continental (Map p217; ☎ 494 144; www .hotelcontinental.ro; B-dul Revoluţiei 3; s/d €74/80; ⏏) Hiding in this Soviet eyesore are clean, large four-star rooms. Synchronize watches with the functioning giant landscaped clock near the entrance.

TOP END
Hotel Ambassador (☎ 306 880/81/82; www.ambassador .ro; Str Mangalia 3; s/d €120/140; ⏏ ⏏) Book here when work is paying. This is a plush, opulently furnished business hotel, with a sauna, gym and outdoor terrace. While economy and standard rooms lack tangible luxury, business class and above boast large rooms, gold trim, paintings and bathtubs. A taxi to/from the centre should cost about €2.

Eating
RESTAURANTS
Corona (Map p217; Str Ungureanu 7; mains €2-3) This cosy dark-wood restaurant is a good choice for pizza and Romanian favourites.

La Tino (☎ 226 455; Calea Aradului 14; mains €4) Classy Italian food and a wide choice of delicious pizzas are offered here.

Cucina Moderna (Map p216; ☎ 202 405; Str Socrates 12b; mains €4) International-style dishes with a Spanish twist using Romanian ingredients.

Intermezzo (Map p217; ☎ 432 429; Piaţa Unirii & Str V Alecsandri; mains €6; ◷ noon-midnight) This place has great pizzas and even better pastas. Dine on the terrace on Piata Unirii or in the cellar restaurant.

Crama Bastion (Map p217; ☎ 221 199; Str Hector 1; mains €6) Romanian dishes vie with the wine list for attention at this traditional restaurant housed in an 18th-century fortification.

Restaurant Lloyd (Map p217; ☎ 294 949; Piaţa Victoriei 2; mains €8-12) Dine here on exquisite international/Romanian dishes of shark, smoked salmon and spit-roast.

CAFÉS & QUICK-EATS
There are plenty of lovely terrace cafés lining Piaţa Unirii and Piaţa Victoriei where you can kill time or plot the next revolution.

Chicago B (Map p217; Str Alba Iulia 1; ◷ 10am-11pm) This Austrian-style café serves coffees, including lattes and cappuccinos.

Lussam (Map p216; ☎ 496 872; B-dul Tache Ionescu 55; ◷ 24hr) This is an infamous after-bar pizzeria.

Java Coffee House (Map p217; ☎ 432 495; Str Pacha 6; ◷ 24hr) Gulp caffeine with one hand, check email with the other.

Pizzeria Horse (Map p217; ☎ 229 666; Str Popa Şapcă 4; mains €3) Come here for slabs of mouth-watering pizza starting at €1!

SELF-CATERING
Timişoara has a colourful central produce **market** (Map p217; Str Brediceanu Coriolan) near Str 1 Mai. There is also the well-stocked **Stil Supermarket** (Map p217; Str Mărăşeşti 10; ◷ 24hr).

Drinking
Meet sociable locals at the terrace café-bars on Piaţa Victoriei, downing bottles of the local Timişoreana Pils beer for around €1 a bottle. Violeta Bar, at the southern end of the square, is particularly popular.

Lemon (Map p217; Str Alba Iulia 2; ◷ from 10pm) This club in the cellar of a piano bar has hip-hop and house DJs.

Club 30 (Map p217; ☎ 201 115; ◷ 6pm-3am Fri & Sat) Cruise to the blues in this jazz joint inside Cinema Timiş.

Komodo (Map p217; Str Ungureanu 9) So trendy it hurts, this large, colourfully lit eclectic bar has techno/house DJs on weekends.

Discoland (Map p217; ☎ 490 008; Piaţa Iancu Huniade 1; ◷ 11pm-5am) Dance in, stagger out. This is where partying professionals test their stamina. It also has salsa nights. It's next to the sign that says 'Firestage'.

Entertainment
CINEMAS
Timişoarans are devoted film-lovers and there are plenty of screens in town. Films are shown in their original language at these cinemas (tickets cost €2 to €3): **Cinema Timiş** (Map p217; ☎ 491 290; Piaţa Victoriei 7); **Cinema Capitol** (Map p217; ☎ 493 396; B-dul CD Loga 2); and the brilliant outdoor **Cinema de Vară** (Map p217; B-dul CD Loga 2).

THEATRE & CLASSICAL MUSIC
The **National Theatre & Opera House** (Teatrul Naţional şi Opera Română; Map p217; ☎ 201 284; Str Mărăşeşti 2) is highly regarded. Buy tickets in the nearby **Agenţia Teatrală** (Map p217; ☎ 499 908; tickets from €1.50; ◷ 10am-1pm & 5-7pm Tue-Sun).

Close by is the **German State Theatre** (Teatrul German de Stat; Map p217; ☎ 201 291; Str Mărăşeşti 2). Get tickets at its **box office** (◷ 10am-7pm Tue-Sun), at the Str Alba Iulia entrance.

Classical concerts are held most evenings at the **State Philharmonic Theatre** (Filharmonia de Stat Banatul; Map p217; ☎ 492 521; B-dul CD Loga 2). Tickets (from €1.50) can be bought at the box office inside the Philharmonic Theatre or from the Agenţia Teatrală.

Event details are generally advertised in the local press and on posters around town.

Shopping

Galeria Helios and **Hermestim** (Piaţa Victoriei; ☾ noon-6pm Mon-Fri, 1-3pm Sat) are adjacent shops, selling artwork (from €15), jewellery (from €30), handcrafts and ceramics (from €12).

Banat Ethnographic Museum (p216) offers handmade crafts, costumes and carvings.

Getting There & Away

AIR

Tarom (Map p217; ☎ 200 003; B-dul Revoluţiei 3-5; ☾ 8am-8pm Mon-Fri, 7am-1pm Sat) has four daily flights to Bucharest (US$75 plus tax US$5; Tarom does not accept euros) from Timişoara, as well as international flights weekly to European cities, and a daily flight to Milan.

Carpatair (☎ 300 900; www.carpatair.com) strangely doesn't have an office in its hub city, only out at the airport. It serves nine Romanian cities and a growing list of international destinations.

Austrian Airlines (Map p217; ☎ 490 320; all-tsr-to@aua.com; Piaţa Unirii 6) has daily flights to Vienna for about €200.

Yugoslav Airlines (JAT; Map p217; ☎ 495 747; Str Eugeniu de Savoya 7) runs daily international flights to Europe, Turkey and Ukraine.

BUS

The small, shabby **bus station** (autogară; ☎ 493 471; B-dul Maniu Iuliu 54; ☾ 6am-8pm Mon-Fri) has six platforms from where slow state buses run daily to Campeni, Arad, Sibiu and Rimincu Valcea. Maxitaxis run daily to Oradea, Arad, Deva and Campeni.

International buses leave from the **east bus station** (autogară est), which is merely a few kiosks cluttered outside the eastern train station. **Atlasib** (☎ 226 486) goes to Italy, Spain and even Sweden. **Eurolines** (☎ 288 132; Timişoara .ag@eurolines.ro) goes to Budapest, Greece, Switzerland and Portugal, among other destinations. Call **Murat** (☎ 0744-144 326) – no English spoken – for bus tickets to Istanbul (€100).

TRAIN

All major train services depart from the **northern train station** (Gară Timişoara-Nord; Map p216; ☎ 491 696; Str Gării 2). You can purchase tickets in advance from the **Agenţie de Voiaj CFR** (Map p217; ☎ 491 889; cnr Str Măcieşilor & Str V Babeş; ☾ 8am-

8pm Mon-Fri, international tickets 9am-7pm Mon-Fri). The station's **left-luggage office** (☾ 24hr) is in the underground passageway to the tracks.

Daily fast trains include eight to Bucharest (€22.50), one to Cluj-Napoca (€11.50), five to Băile Herculane (€8.40), one to Baia Mare via Arad (€12.60) and three sadistically slow runs to Iaşi (16 hours), aka 'the Horror Train'. Additionally, three go to Budapest (€38) and one to Belgrade (€14), which leaves from Timişoara at 5.08am.

Getting Around

TO/FROM THE AIRPORT

Timişoara **airport** (☎ 491 637; Calea Lugojului) is 12.5km northeast of the centre. Bus 26, which stops outside Hotel Continental, also goes to the airport.

CAR

Avis (☎ 203 234) has an office at Timişoara airport. Cars can also be hired at Qual Tours and City Centre Travel Agency (p215).

TRAM, TROLLEYBUS & BUS

All public transport runs between 4.45am and 11.15pm. Tickets (€0.30) are sold at kiosks next to tram and bus stops. Tram 1 runs from the northern train station (Gară Timişoara-Nord) to Piaţa Libertăţii, Hotel Continental and the eastern train/bus station (Gară Timişoara-Est). Tram 4 runs from Hotel Continental to Piaţa Traian (Piaţa Romanilor). Trolleybus 11 and 14 travel from the northern train station east down B-dul Regele Ferdinand I, then turn north on Str 1 Mai.

BĂILE HERCULANE

☎ 255

Take your train-beaten body to this spa resort for some pampering and fresh mountain air. Legend has it that Hercules himself bathed in the natural springs that still flow today in Băile Herculane. The first baths were built by Roman legions following their invasion of Dacia. Inspired by the incredible healing powers of the springs, they named the resort Ad Aquas Herculi Sacras, meaning 'the Holy Water of Hercules'.

The waters here are said to cure eye disorders (conjunctivitis), stomach disorders (gastritis) and rheumatism, among other ailments. You should avoid these baths if you have glaucoma, ulcers or heart conditions. Hotels have physicians on staff for consultations.

During the early 19th century, Băile Herculane developed as a fashionable resort, attracting royal visitors such as Habsburg emperor Franz Josef. Sadly, most of the grand hotels and baths now stand empty and neglected. Renovation work is under way, but still several years from completion. Meanwhile, a collection of dilapidated Soviet-era monstrosities and new yet unpretentious budget hotels are filling the void.

Mt Domogled (1100m) towers over Băile Herculane to the west, dominating the Cerna Valley in which the resort lies. This forest reservation, which has been protected since 1932, includes rare trees, turtles and butterflies.

Orientation

Băile Herculane lies on either side of a road that follows the Cerna River. The train station is at the junction of the main Drobeta-Turnu Severin –Timişoara highway and the Băile Herculane turn-off.

The resort is split into three parts: the residential area is at the western end of the resort on Str Trandafirilor; the concrete blocks of the newer satellite resort are 2km east of the residential area; and the oval-shaped historic centre is at the resort's easternmost end (8km from the train station).

Information

There's no tourist office in Băile Herculane. Try the **Agenţia de Turism** (☎ 560 454) inside Hotel Hercules, where some of the staff speak English.

Banca Comercială Română (Str Castanilor 13c; ☼ 8.30am-5pm Mon-Fri) is across from Dacia Hotel. There's also a **currency exchange office** (☼ 10am-7pm Mon-Fri) on the 3rd floor of Hotel Roman (p222).

The central post office is next to the **CFR office** (Piaţa Hercules 1; ☼ 7am-8pm Mon-Fri) and has the same opening hours.

Sights

All sights lie in the historic centre. Many Roman baths were destroyed during the Turkish and Austrian-Hungarian occupations, but a few stand well preserved in the **Roman Bath Museum** (admission €0.30) inside Hotel Roman. Feel the heat from the natural 54°C water running under the hotel. One of the exhibits is a 2500-year-old carving of Hercules. People have broken off parts and chewed them (his genitals are notably damaged as men have chewed these chunks for sexual potency!). The 2000-year-old baths are still used – the water is cooled down to 37°C and masseurs line the small marble baths.

Next to the hotel flows the **Hercules II spring** (Izvorul Hercules), one of several springs from which drinking water flows – believed to be good for stomach problems – throughout the historic centre.

The resort's **central pavilion** (Str Cernei 14) was built during the 1800s by the Habsburgs as a casino and restaurant. Today it houses a few small shops and a small **History Museum** (Muzeul de Istorie; admission €0.30; ☼ 10am-4pm Tue-Sun). Beside the steps leading up to the museum entrance stands a 200-year-old **Wellingtonia Gigantea tree**, famed for its enormous size. On the opposite side of the river stand the derelict **Austrian baths**. Despite their decaying appearance, the grand hotels are certainly worth the energy it takes to stroll past them.

Activities

THERMAL POOLS

Wallowing in a thermal pool or being pummelled into oblivion by a masseur is all part and parcel of a stay in Băile Herculane.

Hotel Roman (p222) has a thermal **swimming pool** (admission €2), which is open to non-guests. Hotel Cerna (p222) also has a **thermal pool** (adult/child €0.60/0.30) and treatment centre.

The Seven Springs (Izvoare 7) thermal pool and camping ground is 4km to the north of Hotel Roman, from where you catch a maxitaxi (€0.25). Seven Springs is a summer-only attraction, and tends to be crowded and noisy.

DAY TRIPS

Day trips to **Hobiţa**, to see Brâncuşi's memorial house, **Tismana Monastery** and other sites leave from Hotel Cerna (p222) at 9am on Sunday (returning at 6pm). The trips cost €8 per person; ask at reception for information.

HIKING & CLIMBING

Directly behind Hotel Roman stands **Brigands' Cave** (Peştera Haiducilor), named after the thieves who would hide in the cave, waiting for their prey to roll by. A path leads up to the cave from the hotel. A second path (2.5km), marked with blue stripes, leads to the **Grota cu Aburi Cave**. A trail (3km) marked with red stripes, starting from the centre of Băile Herculane at the **Brasseria Central** (Str Izvorului 1), leads

CRIŞANA & BANAT

to the **Munk natural spring** (Izvorul Munk), east of the Grota cu Aburi Cave.

Southeast of the resort, the **White Cross** (Crucea Albă) is a popular hiking trail (marked with yellow stripes). It starts from Str 1 Mai next to Hotel Cerna.

The rock face behind Hotel Roman is a favourite for climbers in summer.

Sleeping

Most hotels in Băile Herculane have costly short-stay rates (one to three days) and cheaper long-stay rates (three to 21 days). All prices listed are short-stay rates. If you plan to stay longer, negotiate! Top hotels fill up in July and August, and the resort is very quiet from mid-September to mid-May.

BUDGET

Popas Flora camping ground (☎ 560 929; Str Castanilor 25; bungalows per person €4; ☾ May-Oct) Located between the old and new resorts, this place has two- and four-bed bungalows overlooking the Cerna River. Communal showers and toilets.

Hotel Cerna (☎ 560 436; Str 1 Mai 1; s/d without bathroom €9/12, d with bathroom €15) This yellow ornate building has old-fashioned but reasonable rooms.

MIDRANGE

Hotel Geta (☎ 560 043; Str Trandafirilor 40; s/d/ste €23/29/43) Opened in late 2005, this is the best value for this price range. The bright rooms have balconies with river and mountain views. Breakfast isn't included, but a reasonably priced restaurant is on-site.

Hotel Hercules (☎ 560 880; Str Izvorului 7; s/d €28/41) Average, clean rooms await you at this dated complex with a sauna.

Hotel Roman (☎ 560 390; argirom.tour@rdsnet.ro; Str Română 1; s/d €35/49) Built into the side of the mountain on the site of a natural spring, this concrete vision is long overdue for renovations. Amenities include massage and sauna, the ancient baths and a reasonable restaurant.

Hotel Ferdinand (☎ 561 131; office@hotel-ferdinand .ro; Piaţa Hercules; s/d/ste €44/60/103) This is the resort's newest and best hotel – classy luxury, good prices and the most charming mountain-side wooden terraces, which are candle-lit at night.

Eating

Băile Herculane has few restaurants beyond those inside its hotels. The in-house restaurants of Hotel Ferdinand (main course €7)

and Hotel Roman (mains €2 to €4) serve the best food.

Entertainment

Next to the minimarket is the popular Bar Cezar, but the hottest nightspot in town is **Club 69** (Str Izorului).

Youngsters also hang out at the *discotecă* in the basement of the old **Central Pavilion** (Str Cernei 14).

Getting There & Away

BUS

Maxitaxis run daily, except Sunday, between Craiova, Băile Herculane and Drobeta-Turnu Severin from outside the post office in Piaţa Hercules. The timetable is posted to a tree. The Drobeta-Turnu Severin service leaves daily at 2.30pm (€1).

TRAIN

The train station is 5km southwest of the satellite resort. The **Agenţie de Voiaj CFR** (☎ 560 538; Piaţa Hercules 1) is in the historic centre.

Băile Herculane is on the main Timişoara–Bucharest line and has many daily fast services, including seven to Bucharest and Timişoara, one to Budapest (3.33am), one to Constanţa and two local trains to Orşova.

Getting Around

Maxitaxis run all day to/from the train station, along the 8km length of Băile Herculane to the centre, stopping at the residential area and satellite resort (€0.30).

CRIŞANA

ORADEA

☎ 259 / pop 209,571

Elegant Oradea, the capital of Crişana, lies a few kilometres east of the Hungarian border, at the edge of the Carpathian Mountains. Inhabited since the Bronze Age, the area has been an important commercial, trade and communications point since the 11th century.

In the 18th century, Viennese engineer Franz Anton Hillebrandt planned the city in baroque style, leading to the construction of many contemporary landmarks such as the Roman Catholic Cathedral and the Bishop's Palace (now the Museum of the Land of the Criş Rivers). The river Crişul Repede runs

ORADEA

INFORMATION
24-Hour Pharmacy	**1** B2
Eurom Bank	**2** C3
Game Star Internet Café	**3** B1
HVB Bank	**4** A2
Panda Tours	**5** B2
Post Office	**6** B1
Telephone Office	**7** B2

SIGHTS & ACTIVITIES
Culture House	**8** C3
Endre Ady Museum	**9** B1
Orthodox Moon Church	**10** A2
Statue of Mihai Eminescu	**11** B2
Statue of Mihai Viteazul	**12** A2
Town Hall	**13** A2
Vulturul Negru Mall Entrance	**14** B2
WWI Memorial	**15** B3

SLEEPING 🏠
Hotel Atlantic	**16** B2
Hotel Continental	**17** C2
Hotel Parc	**18** B2
Hotel Vulturul Negru	**19** A2
Pension Gobe	**20** D3

EATING 🍴
Capitolium	**21** A3
Hotel Atlantic Restaurant	(see 16)
Restaurant Vegetarian Çris	**22** C1

DRINKING 🍸
Irish Kelly's Pub	**23** B2
Lion Café	**24** A2

ENTERTAINMENT 🎭
Puppet Theatre	**25** B2
State Philharmonic	**26** B1
State Theatre	**27** B1

TRANSPORT
Agenție de Voiaj CFR	**28** B2
Tarom	**29** A2

through the city centre, accentuating the architectural beauty of the area.

Of all the cities of the Austro-Hungarian empire, Oradea has best retained its 19th-century romantic style. It was ceded to Romania in 1920 and has since taken on an air of arresting but faded grandeur.

Orientation

The train station is a couple of kilometres north of the centre; tram 1 and 4 run south from Piața București (outside the train station) to Piața Unirii, Oradea's main square. Tram 4 also stops at the northern end of Calea Republicii – a five-minute walk south to the centre.

The main square north of the river is Piața Republicii (AKA Piața Regele Ferdinand I).

Information

The Romanian tourist information office deficiency continues here. Panda Tours has English-speaking staff. Some hotels have city maps.

24-Hour Pharmacy (☎ 418 242; Str Libertății) At the junction with Piața Ferdinand.

Eurom Bank (☎ 210 023; Piața Independenței 35; 🕙 9am-4pm Mon-Fri)

Game Star Internet Café (Str Mihai Eminescu 4; per hr €0.40; 🕙 24hr)

HVB Bank (☎ 406 700; Piața Unirii 24; 🕙 9am-4pm Mon-Fri)

Panda Tours (☎ 477 222; Str Iosif Vulcan 6; 🕙 9am-7pm Mon-Fri, to 1pm Sat)

Post Office (☎ 136 420; Str Roman Ciorogariu 12; 🕙 7am-7.30pm Mon-Fri)

Telephone Office (Calea Republicii 5; 🕙 8am-8pm)

Sights

Oradea's most imposing sights are on its two central squares, Piaţa Unirii and Piaţa Republicii. The **Orthodox Moon Church** (Biserica cu Lună; Piaţa Unirii), built in 1784, has an unusual lunar mechanism on its tower that changes position in accordance with the moon's movement.

In the centre of Piaţa Unirii stands an equestrian **statue of Mihai Viteazul**, the prince of Wallachia (r 1593–1601), who is said to have rested in Oradea in 1600. East of the statue, overlooking the Crişul Repede River, is the **Vulturul Negru** (Black Vulture; 1908) hotel and shopping centre. The mall, with its fantastic stained-glass ceiling, links Piaţa Unirii with Str Independenţei and Str Vasile Alecsandri. A **statue of Mihai Eminescu**, the 19th-century poet, sits on the river's southern bank.

In Central Park (Parcul Central) is the **Culture House** in front of which is a large **monument** to soldiers who fought for Romanian independence during WWI.

Across the bridge from Piaţa Unirii the neoclassical **State Theatre** (Teatrul de Stat), designed by Viennese architects Fellner and Hellmer in 1900, dominates Piaţa Republicii. Nearby, in the centre of Traian Park, stands a small **museum** dedicated to the Hungarian poet Endre Ady (1877–1919), who lived for four years in Oradea before dying of syphilis.

The **Roman Catholic cathedral** (Str Stadionului), 1.4km from north of the centre, was built between 1752 and 1780 and is the largest in Romania. Organ concerts are occasionally held here.

The adjacent **Bishop's Palace** (Episcopia Ortodoxă Română; 1770) boasts 100 fresco-adorned rooms and 365 windows, and houses the **Museum of the Land of the Criş Rivers** (Muzeul Ţării Crişurilor; ☎ 412 725; B-dul Dacia 1-3; admission €0.60; 10am-5pm Tue-Sun), with history and art exhibitions relevant to the region. Immediately outside the museum entrance, busts of Romania's leading statesmen and kings stand on parade. To the right are busts of Wallachia's princes.

Note **Canon's Corridor** nearby, a series of archways along Str Stadionului that dates back to the 18th century.

The **citadel**, south of the river, built in the 13th century, now serves as government offices.

Sleeping

BUDGET

Camping Venus (☎ 318 266; tents & 2-3 bed bungalows per person €10) This camping ground is only 500m from Strandul cu Voluti. Take a southbound tram 4 (black number) from the train station or an eastbound tram 4 (red number) from Piaţa Unirii to the end of the line, then catch bus 15 to the last stop.

Hotel Parc (☎ 411 699; Calea Republicii 5-7; s/d €14/23) Ignore the crumbling façade – the large rooms here are worn, but reasonably clean. It's the best (and now only) budget hotel in town. Singles have shared toilet.

Strandul cu Voluti (cabins/tent sites per person €14.50/3; May–mid-Sep) In Băile 1 Mai, this place is 9km southeast of Oradea.

Pension Gobe (☎ 414 845; Str Dobrogeanu Gherea 26; s/d €30/40) This family owned *pensiune* has several charming rooms, a small restaurant and a bar.

MIDRANGE

our pick **Hotel Atlantic** (☎ 426 911; www.hotelatlantic .ro; Str Iosif Vulcan 9; s/d/ste €45/50/60) Looking for a special place to stage a party or romantic weekend? Call off the search. These spacious, classy, contemporary rooms sport *huge* marble bathrooms, some with spas, and your own private bar! No, not 'minibar' (though they have those too); this is a full-on bar, complete with tools and stools! Not impressed? Did we mention that the Blue Suite has a bed the size of a trampoline? Standard rooms are also notably large and bar-equipped. Bring ample booze.

Hotel Vulturul Negru (Black Vulture; ☎ 450 000; www .vulturulnegru.ro; Str Independenţei 1; s/d/ste €63/85/140) This former backpackers' institution has been reborn into a fashionable four-star hotel. Every nook of the 1908 Art Nouveau building has been beautified with stained-glass windows, crystal chandeliers and Italian décor. Guest or not, the glass-ceilinged day bar should be visited for a cup of coffee and 30 minutes of sheer elegance.

TOP END

Hotel Continental (☎ 418 655; www.continentalhotels.ro; Aleea Ştrandului 1; s/d €76/90;) This is a nine-storey business hotel with masseur, thermal pool, nightclub and – dare we say it – horrendously outdated blue interiors à la motorway service station. In-room internet extra.

Eating & Drinking

Calea Republicii is a stroller's paradise, lined with cheerful eateries and cafés. Most of Oradea's terrace cafés and restaurants double as bars in the evening.

Restaurant Vegetarian Çris (☎ 441 593; George Enescu 30; mains €1.50; ☻ 9am-9pm Sun-Thu, to 4pm Fri, closed Sat) This is the one and only vegetarian restaurant in Romania. Choose from a tantalizingly affordable menu featuring hearty soups, stuffed peppers, minced pumpkin balls, lentils, macaroni and cabbage, celery schnitzel, mushroom haggis, and soy, soy, soy!

Hotel Atlantic Restaurant (☎ 414 953; Str Iosif Vulcan 9; meals €5) This elegant restaurant offers the best menu in town, with hearty goulash, Mexican chicken and speciality steak dishes.

Capitolium (☎ 420 551; Str Avram Iancu 8; mains €5; ☻ 8am-12am) Bask in doting service and huge portions at this Romanian restaurant.

Lion Café (Str Independenţei 1; ☻ 7am-1am) This place is trendy by day, packed by night.

Irish Kelly's Pub (☎ 413 419; Calea Republicii 2) This pub hosts a rowdy crowd on its outside terrace.

Entertainment

Tickets for performances at the recently renovated State Philharmonic (Filarmonica de Stat; ☎ 430 853; Str Moscovei 5; tickets €2) can be purchased from its ticket office (☻ 10am-6pm Mon-Fri) inside the State Theatre (Teatrul de Stat; ☎ 130 885; Piaţa Republicii 4-6; tickets €3-12; ☻ 10-11am & 5-7pm).

Kids big and little will enjoy the shows at Oradea's Puppet Theatre (Teatrul de Păpuşi; ☎ 433 398; Str Vasile Alecsandri 8).

Shopping

Lotus Mall, 2km southeast of the centre on Str Nufărului, has a modern cinema, bowling alley, supermarket and a number of boutiques.

Getting There & Away

AIR
Tarom (☎ 131 918; Piaţa Republicii 2; ☻ 8am-6pm Mon-Fri, 10am-1pm Sat) operates three flights a week to Baia Mare, two flights to Satu Mare and daily flights to Bucharest from Oradea airport (☎ 416 082; Calea Aradului). Fares are US$75/112 one-way/return, plus taxes (Tarom does not accept euros).

BUS
From Oradea bus station (autogară; ☎ 418 998; Str Războieni 81), there are daily services to Beiuş, Deva, Cluj-Napoca and Timişoara, via Arad. Maxitaxis run throughout the day to/from Băile Felix. Four daily go to Baia Mare, via Satu Mare (€4.50, four hours).

There are daily services to Budapest leaving from outside the train station: a state bus (€17, 10 hours) – pay the driver – and maxitaxis (€20).

CAR & MOTORCYCLE
The border crossing into Hungary for motorists at Borş, 16km west of Oradea, is open 24 hours.

TRAIN
The Agenţie de Voiaj CFR (☎ 130 578; Calea Republicii 2; ☻ 7am-7pm Mon-Fri) sells advance tickets for internal and international train trips.

Daily fast trains from Oradea include three to Budapest (€28), two to Bucharest (€22), five to Băile Felix, three to Cluj-Napoca (€11), one to Braşov and three to Timişoara (€7).

Getting Around

Oradea airport (☎ 416 082) is 6km west of the centre on the Oradea–Arad road. Transport between the airport and town is limited to taxis.

BĂILE FELIX
☎ 259

Băile Felix, 5km southeast of Oradea, is a famous year-round spa resort where city dwellers flock to splash in thermal pools. It has a rowdy package-holiday feel so forget napping in the sun. There's a large open-air thermal swimming pool and several smaller pools covered by the rare Nymphea lotus thermalis, a giant white water lily.

The waters here are said to ease rheumatism, head trauma, some paralysis and stomach illnesses. People with certain medical conditions should not partake in the treatments – each hotel has a doctor for consultations.

The most popular public pools are Strand Apollo and Strand Felix (admission €2; ☻ 8am-7pm, closed Nov-Apr), by the Staţia Băile Felix bus stop, which have the same opening hours.

Sleeping

The nearest official camping grounds are 3km away at Băile 1 Mai (see opposite), but many camp in the resort's main car park.

Hotel Muncel (☎ 318 460; r €20) This hotel has a pool and treatment centre, as well as a travel agency, Turism Felix (☎ 318 321).

Pensiunea Veronica (☎ 318 481; Str Băile Felix 9; s/d €23/43; 🖵) This recently renovated, pink chalet, off the main drag, has the best rooms in the resort. Breakfast not included.

Termal Hotel (☎ 318 214; s/d €55/73, 💻) This drab building hides a modern and comfortable spa resort. The rooms reek of cleanliness, with firm beds and balconies (request a forest view).

Eating

Club Art Pizzaria (mains €5; 🕑 noon-5am) At the town's only intersection, this place has a central dance floor with nightly DJs (summer only).

Restaurant Union (mains €4; 🕑 8am-midnight) Across the road from Club Art Pizzaria, feast on a full menu with Romanian and Italian food on the summer terrace here.

Getting There & Away

Maxitaxis run every 15 minutes or when full between Oradea and Băile Felix (€2). Local trains also run daily from Oradea, stopping first at Staţia Băile Felix, then at the major hotels.

BEIUŞ & MEZIAD CAVE

Sixty-three kilometres southeast of Oradea, approaching the western fringe of the Apuşeni Mountains, is the small market town of Beiuş, from where you can visit the **Meziad Cave** (Peştera Meziad; adult/child €0.85/0.30; 🕑 9-11am & 2-4pm), discovered in 1859. The cave features an enormous opening and entrance tunnel, which has equally enormous stalactites with a curved shape. Bring a torch as there's no electric light in the cave. If you arrive outside visiting hours, the massive entrance hall (25m high, 40m wide) is open and satisfactorily illuminated by natural light. The guide is required to enter the *real* cave, which is split into three levels, the main passage being the middle. Good shoes are recommended for the slippery climbs and descents.

From Beiuş's town centre, follow the signs for Peştera Meziad for 11km. When you get to the village of Remetea, bear right at the fork next to the Cămin Cultural building and continue for 9km until you reach Meziad. Turn left at the first fork, then cross the small white bridge to a gravel road. The main office for the cave is 4km along this road. The cave entrance is a further 1.5km and not accessible by car.

Sleeping

Wild camping is permitted around the cave. Alternatively, you could hike on from the cave for three hours (path not accessible by car) to Coada Lacului (Tale of the Lake) where camping is permitted by the lake.

One kilometre from Beiuş is **Motel Desira** (☎ 259-322 420; d €29), which has five clean rooms and offers currency exchange.

Getting There & Away

Beiuş' train and bus stations adjoin each other on the southern edge of town. Its scant train services include daily local trains to Ploieşti (€8), Arad (€3), Cluj-Napoca (€4), Bucharest (€8) and Oradea (€2, three daily).

From Oradea there are two daily buses to Stâna de Vale via Beiuş. Services are greatly reduced on weekends.

STÂNA DE VALE

Scenic Stâna de Vale is a small alpine resort (1300m) in the Pădurea Craiului Mountains 27km east of Beiuş in the Bihor Massif. A delightfully quiet summer hiking and health resort, it is transformed into a bustling ski centre between December and February. The 550m slope is rather tame, best suited for beginner to intermediate skiers. It's worth a night's stay to breathe in the pine-scented air and amble through wooded glades.

The **ski lift** is next to the camping ground, where it's possible to hire skis and have lessons. A couple of **hiking trails** lead into the Apuşeni Mountains (maps are available in the hotels). One of the trails (six hours), marked with red stripes, takes you to **Cabana Padiş** in the heavily karstic Padiş Plateau. The blue-cross trail leads to Devil's Mill Waterfall (Cascada Moara Dracului; six hours), which is cinematically blanketed in violet crocuses in the springtime. Another more challenging trail marked with blue triangles leads past the Saritoarea Bohodei Waterfall (Cascada Saritoarea Bohodeiului; eight hours return), the highest waterfall in Romania (100m). This trail loops back to Stâna de Vale on a different path, a route that is strongly recommended as the blue triangles are difficult to spot if you double back the way you came. Alternatively, this trail continues on and terminates at the **Meziad Cave** (left), six hours from Stâna de Vale. Don't attempt this hike in bad weather or in winter. Nearby is the source of Romania's Wonder Spring (Izvorul Minunilor), a popular brand of bottled water.

Sleeping & Eating

In summer it's best to bring your own tent and pitch it in the **camping ground** (cabins per person €12) at the western end of the resort.

Those seeking total immersion can submit to one of the nearby shepherds offering a meal of *plăcintă* (baked pie with cheese or jam) and a room in their **huts** (per person €1.50), which have pit toilets in the garden.

Both Cabana Padiş and **Cabana Cetatile Ponorului** (www.padis.ro; d €9) have clean accommodation in dorms with between two and 10 beds, and a restaurant.

The resort's main hotel is **Hotel Iadolina** (☎ 0744-599 334; d 2-star €35, 3-star €40, 4-star villa €85); breakfast is not included. Cerbul Vila & Restaurant, opposite Hotel Iadolina, is open in winter only. The **ICCR Beiuş Restaurant** (mains €2) has a simple menu but good, fresh food.

Getting There & Away

The dusty train and bus stations are huddled together at the southern end of the resort. There are two daily buses between Oradea and Stâna de Vale via Beiuş (€2). Otherwise, hitch or hike. Local trains link Băile Felix to Beiuş, from where you can get to Stâna de Vale and surrounding villages.

BEAR CAVE

Named after skeletons of the extinct cave bear *(Ursus spelaeus)* found by quarry workers in 1975, the **Bear Cave** (Peştera Urşilor; tour adult/child €1.50/1; around 10am-5pm) is one of Romania's finest. It's well worth a day trip from Oradea, 82km northwest.

The magnificent galleries of the cave (182m) extend over 1000m on two levels. Stupendous stalactites and stalagmites loom, creating uncanny shapes in the half-darkness. The stalactites, many of which are believed to be 22,000 to 55,000 years old, grow 1cm every 20 years.

Compulsory guided tours allow you to spend an hour or so exploring the cold (a constant 10°C) stalactite-filled chambers of the cave. Note that the formations are delicate and must not be touched.

The idyllic camping ground **La Fluturi** (☎ 259-329 085; cabins €11), in the town of Chişcău, sits near a bubbling stream and has six wooden cabins. Breakfast not included.

At the foot of the Bear Cave, **Pensiunea Daniadis** (☎ 0722-699 847; d €14) is a wooden chalet with seven rooms, each with shared bathroom, and a charming restaurant. Breakfast not included.

Without private transport the region around the cave is tricky to navigate. There's one daily bus running between Beiuş, Chişcău and Stei. From Oradea by car, head south through Beiuş, follow Hwy E79 for a further 8km along the Crişul Negru River, then turn left at the turn-off for Pietroasa and Chişcău. Continue 4km along this road; the cave is signposted on the right.

Hotel Muncel (p225) in Băile Felix runs day tours to the Bear Cave.

SCĂRIŞOARA ICE CAVE

Cave buffs should head straight to this fantastic **ice cave** (Peştera Ghetarul de la Scărişoara; adult/child €1.50/1; 10am-4pm Tue-Sun).

The cave was first documented in 1863 by Austrian geographer Arnold Schmidt. This enabled the Romanian scientist and speleologist Emil Racoviţa (1868–1947) to pursue further explorations between 1921 and 1923. Believed to be one of only 10 of this kind in Europe, the cave is filled with 7500 cu metres of ice. The ice, at an altitude of 1150m, dates back to the Ice Age when the Apuseni Mountains were covered in glaciers.

The maximum temperature inside the cave in summer is 1°C; in winter it drops to -7°C. Safety precautions inside the cave are not up to Western standards, and lighting is nonexistent. Bring your own torch or ask the keeper for an oil/carbon lamp (*lampă cu carbid*).

To get there from Beiuş, head south to Ştei. Two kilometres further south turn left, following the signs for Arieşeni and Gârda de Sus. From Gârda de Sus a rough gravel track leads to the ice cave. The track is impassable by car after 6km, so you must hike the remaining 13km in the Arieş Valley. It's impossible to access the cave from Scărişoara village.

GÂRDA DE SUS & AROUND

The village of Gârda de Sus lies in the Arieş River valley in the Apuseni Mountains. Until 1932 it was classified as part of Scărişoara village. Traditional folk costumes, resembling those worn by early Dacian tribes, are still worn in the village for festivals.

Arieşeni, about 8km away, is a village renowned for its traditional folk customs and wooden church. Two kilometres west of Arieşeni, on the border of the Bihor and Alba counties, is a 753m-long **ski slope** (9am-6pm Dec-May), signposted 'Teleschi Vârtop'.

About 20km south of Gârda de Sus is the village of **Avram Iancu**, formerly known as Vidra de Sus.

The nearby **Roşia Montană Eurogold mine** (☎ 254-233 680), the biggest gold reserve in Europe (a Canadian joint venture), has attracted fierce criticism from scientists, geologists and environmental campaigners for polluting the local water sources with chemicals and deposits. On the other hand, people in nearby Gârda de Sus rely on the mine for employment and are just as fiercely opposed to shutting down the site.

Sleeping

The Belgian charity Opération Villages Roumains has helped Gârda de Sus establish its own *agroturism* scheme whereby tourists can stay in villagers' homes. The local representative in Gârda de Sus is **Ioan Stefanuţ** (☎ 258-778 065, 0744-700 871; ☾ 9am-5pm) at house 31. In Arieşeni, ask for **Marta Maghiar** (☎ 0744-278 219) at house 13. If a house has a sign reading 'Retea Turistica' in the window it means it has rooms to rent.

Mama Uţa (☎ 258-778 008; cabins/tent sites €20/1) This popular summer spot, at the western end of Gârda de Sus, has 14 wooden cabins and a noisy bar and grill.

Hotel Apuşeni (☎ 258-779 023, 0744-187 256; www.hotelapuseni.net.tf; Bubeşti 87a; d/apt €23/40) This friendly hotel, about 3km east along the road to Arieşeni, has fantastic views, gorgeous rooms and a sun terrace with hill views.

Cabana Vârtop (☎ 0744-560 427, 0745-776 541; d €29) Amid rolling hills in Arieşeni, this chalet has amazing views and its own ski run.

Casa Noastrâ (☎ 258-779 122, 0744-322 215; r €35; 🏊) This luxury chalet has a trout farm and swimming pool.

Getting There & Away

From Gârda de Sus, hikers can head north to the Padiş Plateau. A trail marked by blue stripes (five to six hours) leads from the village to Cabana Padiş.

ARAD

☎ 257 / pop 172,269

The gateway to Hungary, Arad is situated in lush winemaking country on the banks of the Mureş River, which loops around the city. Arad developed as a major trading centre during Turkish occupation of the city between 1551 and 1687. Much of the centre boasts elegant late-19th-century architecture, the charming legacy of the Austro-Hungarian empire. Arad's tourist attractions will only fill half a day, but idle strolling and an evening show are strongly recommended.

Orientation

The train station is a few kilometres north of the centre, with the international bus station two blocks west of B-dul Revoluţiei on Str Corneliu Coposu. To reach town, take tram 1, 2 or 3 south down B-dul Revoluţiei (known simply as 'the boulevard').

Information

There is an ATM outside Supermarket Ziridava.

Banca Commercială Română (☎ 254 460; B-dul Revoluţiei 72; ☾ 9am-4pm Mon-Fri)

Banca Ţiriac (Piaţa Avram Iancu 11; ☾ 9am-3.30pm Mon-Fri, to 12.30pm Sat)

Club Pro Net (☎ 270 533; pronet@pro-net.ro; B-dul Revoluţiei 67; internet per hr €0.90)

Info Tour Arad (☎ 270 277; turism@primariaarad.ro; B-dul Revoluţiei 84-86; ☾ 9am-6pm Mon-Fri, to 2pm Sat) The wonderful staff here veritably bury you in free city maps, brochures and contacts with *agroturism* homestay organisation Antrec.

Internet Café (Str Tribunal Dobra 8; per hr €0.70; ☾ 9.30am-midnight Mon-Fri, 10am-midnight Sat & Sun)

Post office (☎ 232 222; B-dul Revoluţiei 46-48; ☾ 7am-7pm Mon-Fri)

Telephone office (B-dul Revoluţiei 44; ☾ 8am-8pm)

Sights

Arad's large, star-shaped **citadel** was built under the orders of the Habsburg empress Maria Theresa between 1763 and 1783. The Austrian architect and general Filip Ferdinand Harsch was commissioned to design the Vauban-style six-pointed star. It stands on the site of an old fortress built in 1551 by the Turks. Today the citadel houses a military base and is closed to the public.

After crushing the liberal revolution of 1848, the Habsburgs hanged 13 Hungarian generals outside the citadel. A **monument** to these men stands outside the southern walls of the citadel.

The U-shaped, neoclassical **town hall** (B-dul Revoluţiei) is Arad's most impressive building. The clock ticking on the tower atop the 1876 building was purchased in Switzerland in 1878. Framing the town hall is the steepled **Cenad Palace** (Palatul Cenad), constructed by the Arad Cenad Railway Company at the end of the 19th century, and the **Aurel Vlaicu University** building, decorated in Viennese rococo

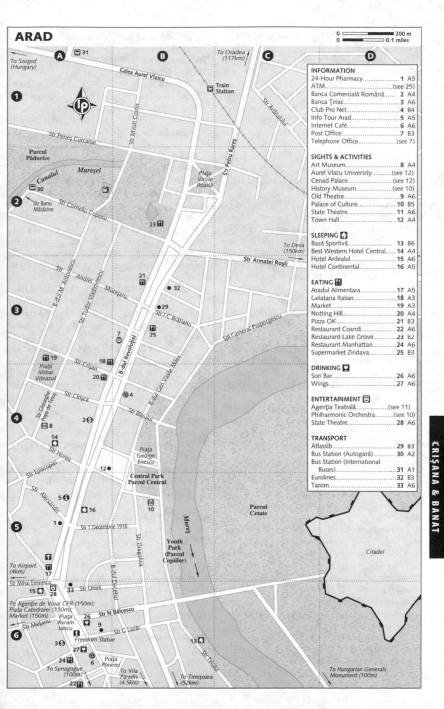

ARAD

0 — 200 m
0 — 0.1 miles

INFORMATION
24-Hour Pharmacy	**1** A5
ATM	(see 25)
Banca Comercială Română	**2** A4
Banca Ţiriac	**3** A6
Club Pro Net	**4** B4
Info Tour Arad	**5** A5
Internet Café	**6** A6
Post Office	**7** B3
Telephone Office	(see 7)

SIGHTS & ACTIVITIES
Art Museum	**8** A4
Aurel Vlacu University	(see 12)
Cenad Palace	(see 12)
History Museum	(see 10)
Old Theatre	**9** A6
Palace of Culture	**10** B5
State Theatre	**11** A6
Town Hall	**12** A4

SLEEPING
Bază Sportivă	**13** B6
Best Western Hotel Central	**14** A4
Hotel Ardealul	**15** A6
Hotel Continental	**16** A5

EATING
Aradul Alimentara	**17** A5
Gelataria Italian	**18** A3
Market	**19** A3
Notting Hill	**20** A4
Pizza OK	**21** B3
Restaurant Coandi	**22** A6
Restaurant Lake Grove	**23** B2
Restaurant Manhattan	**24** A6
Supermarket Ziridava	**25** B3

DRINKING
Sori Bar	**26** A6
Wings	**27** A6

ENTERTAINMENT
Agenţia Teatrală	(see 11)
Philharmonic Orchestra	(see 10)
State Theatre	**28** A6

TRANSPORT
Atlassib	**29** B3
Bus Station (Autogară)	**30** A2
Bus Station (International Buses)	**31** A1
Eurolines	**32** B3
Tarom	**33** A6

CRIŞANA & BANAT

motifs and built to house the local adminis-tration's treasury.

Near the town hall, in front of Central Park (Parcul Central), is the local **History Museum** (Muzeul de Istorie; ☎ 281 847; Piaţa George Enescu 1; admission €0.60; ⊙ 9am-5pm Tue-Sun), which has some inter-esting photos and artefacts from Arad county. It is based inside the **Palace of Culture** (built be-tween 1911 and 1913), also home to Arad's Philharmonic Orchestra (opposite). Busts out-side the building pay homage to leading liter-ary figures, including Romanian poet George Coşbuc (1866–1918) and post-romantic histo-rian Alexandru Xenopol (1847–1920).

To the east of the museum, along the Mureş River, lies **Youth Park** (Parcul Copiilor). At the southern end of B-dul Revoluţiei is the 1874 neoclassical **State Theatre** (opposite). Across Piaţa Avram Iancu is the ailing but still kicking **Old Theatre** (Teatrului Vechi; ☎ 211 918; www.culturaarad.ro; Str Gheorge Lazar 1-3, tickets €3-10), built in 1817, where poet Mihei Eminescu worked alongside famous actors of the time. Lengthy renovations have not slowed the show one bit. Productions are popular, particularly the annual Underground Festival in May, attended by independent thea-tre companies from the US, Hungary, Poland and France, among others. South of the theatre is the Jewish community's **synagogue** (Str Dobra 10). It was built between 1827 and 1834 in typically Moorish style. Enter via Str Cozia.

The **Art Museum** (Muzeul de Arte; ☎ 257 503; Str Gheorghe Popa de Teiuş 24; admission €0.60; ⊙ 9am-5pm Tue-Sun) has paintings and photos by Romanian and Hungarian artists.

Sleeping

Antrec arranges rooms in private homes in and around Arad for about €15 to €20, in-cluding breakfast. Book through Info Tour Arad (p228).

Bază Sportivă (☎ 251 059; Str Teiului 1; r €6) These rooms above the sports club are cheap-as-chips and basic but clean. If full, try the alternative Bază Sportivă further north along the river, by Restaurant Perla. No English spoken.

Hotel Ardealul (☎ 280 840; B-dul Revoluţiei 98; s/d unrenovated €21/27, renovated €30/39) This lovely con-verted concert hall, dating from 1841, has a music room where Brahms, Liszt and Strauss once performed.

Vila Paradis (☎ 287 377; Str Molidului 5; s/d €25) Five kilometres south of the centre, this is a good choice with simple, clean and comfy rooms. Breakfast not included.

Best Western Hotel Central (☎ 256 636; central@inext.ro; Str Horea 8; s/d €60/80) This five-storey hotel has all the mod-cons and a lovely terrace café overlooking its summer garden.

Hotel Continental (☎ 281 700; fax 281 832; www.continentalhotels.ro; B-dul Revoluţiei 79-81; s/d €72/89; 🖳 🖧) Arad's upmarket choice has inter-national standards of accommodation and service. In-room internet extra.

Eating
RESTAURANTS

Pizza OK (B-dul Revoluţiei 26-38; mains €3; ⊙ 10am-2am) This standard pizza joint serves up 28 varieties.

Restaurant Lake Grove (☎ 254 366; Pădurice Park; meal €4; ⊙ 10am-3am) Set in a nice spot on a lake in the park, with leafy, decked gardens, this restaurant is popular with tour groups; the menu has everything from pasta to pudding. Live music on Saturdays.

Restaurant Manhattan (Piaţa Avram Iancu 9; mains €4-10; ⊙ 10am-midnight) This splurge-worthy wood-lined restaurant was conceived by en-thusiastic foodies, sommeliers and tourism professionals.

Restaurant Coandi (☎ 214 999; Piaţa Avram Iancu 11; mains €7) This is a popular Romanian eatery with large tables, so expect to be seated with people of all nationalities for a noisy, fun feed. Portions are huge.

CAFÉS

B-dul Revoluţiei is lined with cafés and bars.

Notting Hill (cnr B-dul Revoluţiei & Str Crişan; ⊙ 11am-11pm) Offers standard Romanian meals.

Gelateria Italian (B-dul Revoluţiei) This spot has 20 different flavours of *bella* Italian ice cream, including bubblegum and cola.

SELF-CATERING

Arad has two open-air **markets**, one on Piaţa Mihai Viteazul and another on Piaţa Cate-dralei, at the western end of Str Meţanu. For groceries, go to the large Western-style **Supermarket Ziridava** (B-dul Revoluţiei; ⊙ 8am-8pm Mon-Sat) or the well-stocked **Aradul Alimen-tara** (⊙ 24hr), at the southern end of B-dul Revoluţiei.

Entertainment
BARS

Piaţa Avram Iancu is the place to head for ter-race café-bars. One of these is the bikers' joint, Wings, at the southern end of the square.

CRIŞANA & BANAT

Sori Bar (☎ 281 478; Str Nicolae Bălcescu 2) This is a popular drinking spot, with a small terrace and some café-style meals (€4).

THEATRE & CLASSICAL MUSIC

The Municipal House of Culture web site (www.culturaarad.ro) is wondrously complete, though some Romanian will be needed to decipher the schedules. Alternatively, ask for assistance at Info Tour Arad.

The **Philharmonic Orchestra** (tickets from €2), inside the Palace of Culture (opposite), holds concerts on weeknights at 7pm. Tickets are sold at the **box office** (☎ 280 519) two hours before performances begin. Arad's **Agenţia Teatrală** (11am-1pm Tue-Sun), which sells tickets to local theatre performances, is at the back of the **State Theatre** (Teatrul de Stat; ☎ 280 018; B-dul Revoluţiei 103).

Getting There & Away

AIR

At the time of writing, the only airline serving forlorn Arad Airport, 4km west of the centre, was budget airline **Blue Air** (www.blueair-web.com), with twice-weekly services to both Verona, Italy and Valencia, Spain.

Tarom (☎ 211 777; www.tarom.ro; Str Unirii 1; 8am-8pm Mon-Fri, 9am-2pm Sat) has three flights a week to Bucharest out of Timişoara airport (US$75/107 one-way/return, plus taxes; note that Tarom does not accept euros), about 64km away.

BUS

Arad has two bus stations, one for **international buses** (Str 6 Vânători 2) and the domestic **autogară** (☎ 273 323; Str Banu Mărăcine), two blocks west of the train station.

Daily internal buses from the *autogară* include two to Timişoara (€3), one to Bucharest (€12) and one to Craiova. State buses go to Szeged (€10) and Budapest (€15).

Private companies selling tickets for international buses to (for example) Hungary, France and Spain line B-dul Revoluţiei. These buses are considerably more comfortable than the state buses, with air-con, clean seats and free tea and coffee; prices are obviously higher. Try **Atlassib** (☎ 270 562; B-dul Revoluţiei 35), which has express coaches running twice-weekly to Germany and Austria, or **Eurolines** (☎ 250 397; arad@eurolines.ro; B-dul Revoluţiei 31), which has buses to nearly everywhere.

CAR & MOTORCYCLE

The border crossing into Hungary is 52km west of Arad, in Nădlac. This is the major road crossing from Romania into Hungary, so it can get congested. It's open 24 hours a day.

TRAIN

Tickets for trains to Hungary and Austria have to be bought in advance from the **Agenţie de Voiaj CFR** (☎ 280 713; Str Meţanu 16; 8am-8pm Mon-Fri).

Arad train station (☎ 230 633; Piaţa Gării 8-9) is a major railway junction. Daily fast services include five to Budapest (€26), five to Vienna (€57), five to Bucharest (€27), five to Timişoara (€11), one to Constanţa (€21) and one to Cluj-Napoca (€14).

To get to Hunedoara from Arad, you have to get a train to Deva and then take a bus from there to Hunedoara.

Getting Around

Currently, the only way to Arad airport is by taxi (about €3).

Maramureş

Dismount from the horse-drawn cart and tip your chauffeur in cigarettes. You've found one of the last places where rural European medieval life remains intact. Where peasants live off the land as countless generations did before them. Where tiny villages, steeped in local customs and history, sit among rolling hills and dreamy landscapes. Where the word 'cappuccino' elicits a bewildered stare. Even Romanians joke that nothing has changed here for 100 years – welcome to Maramureş.

The last peasant culture in Europe is thriving here, with hand-built ancient wooden churches, traditional music, colourful costumes and festivals. Villagers' homes are still fronted with traditional giant, ornately carved wooden gates, and ear-smoking, 100-proof ţuică (plum brandy) stills percolate in the garden, tended by a rosy-cheeked patriarch. Discovering this part of the world is a time-travel adventure, verily stunning Western visitors.

The region was effectively cut off from Transylvania by a fortress of mountains and has remained largely untouched by the 20th century (and the 19th century, and the 18th century…). It escaped the collectivisation of the 1940s, systemisation of the '80s and the Westernisation of the '90s and as such is living history.

Medieval Maramureş exists in the Mara and Izei Valleys. Eight of its churches – in the villages of Bârsana, Budeşti, Deseşti, Ieud, Plopis, Poienile Izei, Rogoz and Surdeşti – are on Unesco's list of World Heritage sites.

HIGHLIGHTS

- ■ Find God (or don't) while facing fiery visions of hell at **Poienile Izei church** (p246)

- ■ Knock on the wooden churches of **Budeşti** (p242), **Surdeşti** (p237) and **Ieud** (p246)

- ■ Enjoy the beauty and humour of death through the painted wooden crosses in **Săpânţa's Merry Cemetery** (p244)

- ■ Get your medieval on at homestays in the **Izei** (p244) and **Mara Valleys** (p243)

- ■ Ride up through the Vaser Valley on a narrow-gauge railway from **Vişeu de Sus** (p246)

Săpânţa ★
Mara Valley ★   Izei Valley ★   Vaser Valley ★
Budeşti ★ ★ ★ Ieud
Surdeşti ★
Poienile Izei

History

Maramureş, with Baia Mare as its capital, was first documented in 1199. Prior to this, Dacian tribes are thought to have settled here around 1000 BC; today's inhabitants believe they are descended from these tribes. When the Roman emperor Trajan conquered the rest of Romania in AD 106 , his forces never made it over the range of mountains protecting the Maramureş villages.

Hungary gradually exerted its rule over the region from the 13th century onwards. Tartar invasions of the Hungarian-dominated region continued into the 17th and 18th centuries, the last documented battle being on the Prislop Pass in 1717. Numerous churches sprang up in Maramureş around this time to mark the Tartars' final withdrawal from the region.

Maramureş was annexed by Transylvania in the mid-16th century, then ceded to the Austrian empire in 1699. It was not until 1918 that Maramureş was returned to Romania, albeit only part of it – the remainder went to what is now Ukraine.

Between 1940 and 1944 the Maramureş region – along with northern Transylvania and parts of Moldavia – fell under pro-Nazi Hungarian rule, during which time the entire Jewish population of its capital, Sighetu Marmaţiei, was shipped to Nazi Germany's concentration camps.

Ceauşescu's rule had little effect on the area. Indeed, he curiously encouraged the people here to maintain their traditional culture, contrary to his systemisation policies for the rest of Romania.

BAIA MARE

☎ 262 / pop 141,611

Baia Mare (Big Mine), at the foot of the Gutâi Mountains, is the seat of Maramureş County. The town was first documented in 1329 and developed as a gold-mining town in the 14th and 15th centuries. In 1446 the town became the property of the Iancu de Hunedoara family. In 1469, under the rule of Hungarian king Matthias Corvinus (Iancu de Hunedoara's son), the town was fortified.

Baia Mare gained notoriety during Ceauşescu's regime as home to the Romplumb and Phoenix metallurgic plants which released more than 5 billion cu metres of residual gases into the atmosphere each year, smothering the town with a sulphur-dioxide/metal powder smog. In the early 1990s, a new

> ### GETTING INTO & AROUND MARAMUREŞ
>
> Accessing Maramureş and then getting around can be a resolve-testing struggle. Train entry often requires visitor-challenging transfers in small, lazily marked stations and maxitaxis are, well, maxitaxis. The same goes for the sparse and limited options for getting around, though the upshot is you will rarely enjoy more genial hitchhiking conditions in Europe. For DIY touring, car hire is strongly recommended, preferably from Suceava or Cluj, meaning you'll have nary a transport dilemma throughout your visit – deficient countryside signage notwithstanding. A detailed map of the region is essential. Alternatively an organised tour (p244) will alleviate virtually all of the above.

smoke stack was built in an attempt to alleviate air pollution.

The town was again thrown into the environmental hot seat in early 2000, when a poisonous spill from the Aurul gold mine caused one of Europe's worst environmental disasters. On 30 January a tailings dam burst, causing cyanide-contaminated water to leak from the gold mine – part-owned by Australian company Esmeralda Enterprises – contaminating the Someş and Tisa Rivers before spilling into the Danube and finally the Black Sea.

With six neighbouring countries affected, the water supply of 2.5 million people contaminated and the rivers' ecosystems devastated, the full impact of the spill may not be known for another two decades. Drinking water remains unpotable and fish stocks polluted.

On a lighter note, at the time of writing Baia Mare was in full renovation mode. Piaţa Libertăţii in particular will likely be a whole new, nightlife-focused hub of good vibrations by the time you read this. The city's museums are unexpectedly arresting and the superior hotels are a good place to reintegrate with the 21st century after staying in the villages.

Despite its lacklustre name, the **Chestnut Festival** (last weekend in September) is a lively bash, with concerts, dancing, sports events, people carousing in costume and dodgy-looking carnival rides.

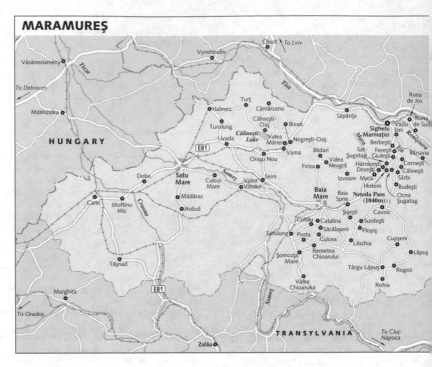

MARAMUREŞ

Orientation

The train and bus stations, west of the centre on Str Gării, are a 15-minute walk from Piaţa Libertăţii, Baia Mare's central square. The Şasar River flows across the north of the town.

Information

INTERNET ACCESS

At the time of writing, the city was suffering from a scarcity of internet cafés. Those with wi-fi enabled devices can plunder service from Hotel Rivulus while dining in Oaza Italiana (p236) – sit on the hotel side of the restaurant.

MONEY

Banca Commerciala Română (B-dul Unirii 15; 8.30am-1pm Mon-Fri)
Banca Post (☎ 220 350; B-dul Traian 1B; 8.30am-5pm Mon-Fri, 8.30am-noon Sat)
West Bank (☎ 224 586; B-dul Unirii 7; 8.30am-4.30pm Mon-Fri)

POST

Central post office (B-dul Traian 1B; 7am-8pm Mon-Fri) Has fax and cash transfer facilities.

TOURIST INFORMATION

Mara Holidays (☎ 226 656; office@hotelmara.ro; B-dul Unirii 11; 9am-5pm Mon-Fri) Helpful, English-speaking staff arrange car hire, walking, trekking and horse-riding tours, provide maps, and can book accommodation through Antrec.

Sights

Transylvanian prince Iancu de Hunedoara (János Hunyadi in Hungarian), royal governor of Hungary between 1446 and 1453, lived in the now-crumbling, 15th-century house **Casa Iancu de Hunedoara** (Piaţa Libertăţii 18). In 1456 he successfully thrashed the Turks on the banks of the Danube close to Belgrade. Hunedoara died of the plague in Belgrade that same year. Today, his house has temporary exhibitions arranged by the local history museum.

Hunedoara's life story – and that of Baia Mare – is told in the local **History & Archaeology Museum** (Muzeul de Istorie şi Arheologie; ☎ 211 927; Str Monetăriei 1; admission €1.50; 8am-4pm Tue-Fri, 10am-2pm Sat & Sun). This expansive complex houses excavation displays, including the mother of all clay pot collections, extensive weapons exhibitions, tools, weathered documents, bronze

fragments and rooms devoted to literature, sports, industrial equipment and clocks.

Looming above Piaţa Libertăţii is **Stephen's Tower** (Turnul Ştefan). The 14th-century Gothic-style tower was initially topped with a bell but this was replaced by a mechanical clock in 1628. Behind the tower is the **Cathedral of the Holy Trinity** (Catedrala Sfânta Treime; Str 1 Mai), close to the local **Art Museum** (Muzeul de Artă; ☎ 213 964; Str 1 Mai 8; ☽ 10am-4pm Tue-Sun) with 250 exhibits tracking local artists from 1896 to the present.

The **central market** (cnr Strs 22 Decembrie & Vasile Alecsandri) is surrounded by the only remaining part of the 15th-century city walls and is beneath the **Butchers' Tower**, where famous brigand Grigore Pintea Viteazul was shot in 1703.

Heading north from the market across the footbridge over the Şasar River, the **Dealul Florilor Stadium** (Stadionul Dealul Florilor) is home to the Baia Mare football club. Open-air Masses are often held on Sunday next to the WWI **Romanian Soldiers Monument** (Monumentul Ostaşilor Români) in the park to the west of the football stadium.

Northwest of the football stadium is the **Ethnographic Museum** (Muzeul Etnografic; ☎ 212 845), in which all the traditional trades of the Maramureş region are represented.

Nearby, the **Village Museum** (Muzeul Satului; €1; ☽ 10am-5pm Tue-Sun, closed 16 Oct-14 May) displays traditional wooden houses and churches, for which the region is famed.

Baia Mare has a small **zoo** (admission €1; ☽ 10am-5pm Tue-Sun) adjoining an **amusement park** (Str Petőfi Sándor 28).

The **Mineral Museum** (Muzeul de Mineralogie; B-dul Iraian 8) houses a monument to the Jews deported from Baia Mare to Auschwitz during WWII. Until 1848, Jews were not allowed to live in the city because of a 17th-century law forbidding them from settling in Hungarian mining towns.

Sleeping

Baia Mare has no budget accommodation options except for homestays which must be booked in advance.

Mara Holidays (☎ 226 656; office@hotelmara.ro; B-dul Unirii 11; ☽ 9am-5pm Mon-Fri) This is an agent for Antrec and arranges rooms in private homes in the region for €15 to €20 per night, including a home-cooked breakfast.

Hotel Maramureş (☎ 216 555; Str Gheorghe Şincai 37; s/d €32/49) Grand three-star hotel with faded charm but comfortable rooms. Some rooms have balconies.

Euro Hotel (☎ 222 405; www.eurohotel-bm.ro; B-dul Bucureşti 23; s/d 2-stars €35/49, 3-stars s/d €47/58; 🖳 🐾) Wi-fi, pool, sauna, fitness centre, bar, restaurant, bowling – a few nights here will expunge all memories of village outhouses. Best value in town.

Hotel Rivulus (☎ 216 302; Str Culturii 4; s/d 2-stars €34/43, s/d 3-stars €43/52; 🖳 ♿) Overlooking Piaţa Revoluţiei, this landmark monstrosity has newly renovated rooms, all with balconies. Two-star rooms are virtually identical to the three-star rooms, minus the refrigerator. Wi-fi is (officially) only available in three-star rooms.

Hotel Mara (☎ 226 660; www.hotelmara.ro; B-dul Unirii 11; s/d €50/60; 🖳 🐾) Weary travellers can treat themselves to power showers, comfortable beds, swimming pool and massage here. Discounted rates are available on their web site.

Eating

Restaurant Dunarea (cnr Piaţa Libertăţii & Str 1 Mai; mains €2-3) A former favourite, this place was engulfed

BAIA MARE

INFORMATION		DRINKING
Banca Comercială Română........... 1 C4	SLEEPING	Butoiasul Cu Bere...............................29 C3
Banca Post...................................... 2 B4	Euro Hotel.............................21 B4	Café Dali...30 C3
Central Post Office........................3 B4	Hotel Mara............................22 C4	XXL Cafe Bar....................................31 C3
Fortuna Currency Exchange...... 4 C4	Hotel Maramureş....................23 C3	
Mara Holidays...........................(see 22)	Hotel Rivulus.........................24 C3	ENTERTAINMENT
Post Office....................................5 B3		Cinema Dacia....................................32 C3
Post Office....................................6 B4	EATING	Teatrul Dramatic...............................33 C3
West Bank.....................................7 B4	Casa Rustic............................25 B4	
	Maracarn...............................26 C3	TRANSPORT
SIGHTS & ACTIVITIES	Millenium Restaurant Pizzeria........(see 28)	Agenţie de Voiaj CFR..........................34 B3
Art Museum.................................. 8 D3	Oaza Italiana.........................27 C3	Bus Station.......................................35 A4
Butchers' Tower............................9 D3	Restaurant Dunarea...............28 C3	Maxitaxis to Budapest........................36 B3
Casa Iancu de Hunedoara............10 C3		Tarom..37 B3
Cathedral of the Holy Trinity...........11 D3		
Central Market.............................12 C3		
Dealul Florilor Stadium.................13 C2		
Ethnographic Museum...................14 C2		
History & Archaeology Museum.....15 C3		
Mineral Museum...........................16 B4		
Romanian Soldiers Monument 17 C2		
Stephen's Tower..........................18 C3		
Village Museum............................19 C2		
Zoo..20 C2		

in the Piaţa Libertăţii facelift project at the time of writing.

Maracarn (Str Victoriei 5; 8am-midnight; mains €2-4) A local favourite for Romanian cuisine.

Oaza Italiana (214 913; Str Culturii 4; mains €2-6) Large pizzas, pumping music and drinks make this modern eatery on Piaţa Revoluţiei a noisy winner.

Millenium Restaurent Pizzeria (Piaţa Libertăţii; 10am-midnight; mains €2-6) A modern, classy place mixing Romanian food with pasta and pizza.

Casa Rustic (Calea Unirii 14a; mains €5) Fabulous, cheap restaurant, with fish, soups and salads and whole roasted piglet or chicken.

Restaurant Salamandra (237 600; B-dul Traian; meals €5-10) Traditional Maramureş dishes are served here.

Drinking

Café Dali (Piaţa Revoluţiei) Get yourself a Dirty Bitch (Baileys and vodka; €1) at this cocktail heaven.

XXL Café Bar (Str Gheorge Şincai 23; 7.30am-10pm Mon-Fri, 7am-midnight Sat & Sun) A basement bar with records glued to the ceiling, frequented by English-speaking twentysomethings.

Butoiasul Cu Bere (Str Gheorghe Şincai 13) Beer cellar–style bar in this revamped, cobbled part of the old town.

Entertainment

Plays are performed in Romanian at the **Teatrul Dramatic** (211 124; Str Crişan 4). Tickets can be bought in advance at the **Agenţia Teatrală** (10am-noon & 4-6pm Tue-Sun) in the lobby.

See English-language films with Romanian subtitles at **Cinema Dacia** (☎ 214 265; Piaţa Revoluţiei 7; tickets €2).

Getting There & Away

AIR

Tarom (☎ 221 624; B-dul Bucureşti 5; ☺ 9am-6pm Mon-Fri, 9am-noon Sat) operates three flights weekly between Baia Mare and Bucharest (one-way US$75, return US$124, plus tax). Tarom doesn't accept euros.

BUS

Infrequent services run from the **bus station** (☎ 431 921; Str Gării 2) to outlying villages. There are two daily buses to Satu Mare (€2), two to Cluj-Napoca (€4), and four to Sighetu Marmaţiei via Baia Sprie (€2). Bus 8, which stops just outside Hotel Mara, goes to Baia Sprie.

Maxitaxis run twice daily (except Sunday) to Satu Mare (€1.50) and once daily to Bistriţa (€5). There's a daily maxitaxi to Budapest, leaving from outside McDonald's, on Str Dragoş Vodă, at 10pm (€16, six hours).

TRAIN

Advance tickets are sold at **Agenţie de Voiaj CFR** (☎ 219 113; Str Victoriei 5-7).

From Baia Mare **train station** (☎ 220 950; Str Gării 4) there is one daily train to Budapest (€20, eight hours) at noon; 10 daily to Satu Mare; one to Bucharest via Cluj-Napoca and Braşov; and one to Timişoara (€9).

Getting Around

The **airport** (☎ 223 394) is 9km west of the centre at Tăuţi Măgherăuş. A taxi should cost about €7.

AROUND BAIA MARE

Baia Sprie

Baia Sprie, 10km east of Baia Mare, is a small mining town first chronicled in 1329. The mine still operates today, mining approximately 145,000 tonnes of copper, lead and zinc ore annually.

A **roadside cross**, in memory of political prisoners who died in the mine during the communist purges of 1950–56, stands at the foot of the track that leads to the mine. During this period an estimated 180,000 people were interned in hard-labour camps such as those by the Danube–Black Sea canal, or in high-security prisons such as Piteşti, Gherla

and Sighetu Marmaţiei. Between 1947 and 1964, some 200 to 300 political prisoners were committed to forced labour at the Baia Sprie mine, including Corneliu Coposu, secretary to National Peasant Party leader Iuliu Maniu, who was himself imprisoned at Sighet (see p241).

The **village church**, bearing a traditional Maramureş tiled roof dating from 1793, is next to a new church in the centre. The village stages its very own pint-sized **Chestnut Festival** in September/October, if the one in Baia Mare gets too debauched for you.

Surdeşti & Around

Approaching Surdeşti from Baia Sprie, you pass through **Şişeşti** village, home to the Vasile Lucaciu Memorial Museum. Vasile Lucaciu (1835–1919), appointed parish priest in 1885, built a church for the village supposedly modelled on St Peter's in Rome. The church was ceremoniously named, and dedicated to, the Union of all Romanians (Unirii Tuturor Românilor).

The towering church at **Surdeşti**, southwest of Baia Sprie, is one of the most magnificent in the Maramureş region and well worth the hike. Though some damage was caused by a botched renovation job, the all-original wall and ceiling paintings remain impressive. The tiny church's disproportionately giant church steeple (72m) was considered the tallest wooden structure in Europe until the recent construction of the church in Săpânţa (p243) – though purists say the new church's stone base disqualifies it from contention. The church, signposted 'Monument' from the centre of the village, was built in 1724 as a centre of worship for the Greco-Catholic faithful and it remains a Uniate church today. The priest and his wife, who live in the house below the church, will gladly open it for you.

Two kilometres south in **Plopiş** is another fine church with a towering steeple. Ask for the key at the lone house nearby. A further 14km south is the town of **Lăschia**. Its church dates from 1861 and has a bulbous steeple. Note the motifs carved on the outer walls, which are like those traditionally used in carpets.

The last wave of nomadic Tartar tribes from the Eurasian steppe settled in the mining town of **Cavnic**, 8km northeast of Surdeşti, as late as 1717. A monument known as the Tartar stone stands in the centre of the small town, first documented in 1445. In 1952 and 1955, political prisoners were sent to the gold and silver mines here.

Heading north from Cavnic along the mountainous **Neteda Pass** (1040m) towards Sighetu Marmaţiei, you'll pass a small memorial plaque to those who died in the mines under the communist purges.

Baia Mare to Izvoare

North of Baia Mare a dirt road twists and turns through the remote villages of **Firiza**, **Blidari** and **Valea Neagră**, culminating 25km north of Baia Mare at **Izvoare**, where there are natural springs.

Viewing churches is not on the agenda here; wallowing in the mountainous rural countryside dotted with delightful wooden cottages and ramshackle farms is. Izvoare is dominated by pine forests and the rather ugly **Statiunea Izvoare complex**. The complex is closed between mid-June and mid-September, when it is transformed into a summer holiday camp for students. The rest of the year it is open to travellers. In winter, a ski lift offers aerial views of the **sculpture park** spread throughout the grounds of the complex.

This route is not served by public transport and hitching is difficult as few vehicles pass by. A **hiking trail** (five to six hours, marked with red triangles) leads from Baia Mare to Izvoare; it starts about 3km north of Baia Mare along the Baia Mare–Izvoare road.

Sleeping & Eating

Complex Turistic Şuior (☎ 262-262 080; s/d €26/49) This complex of three new hotels is 1km further along the same road from Mogoşa Chalet. It boasts a ski lift and a swanky bar-restaurant in a lovingly created, peaceful setting.

Mogoşa Chalet (☎ 262-260 800; www.mogosa.ro; d/ste €34/69) The chalet overlooks Lake Bodi, 731m above sea level. Campers can pitch their tents by the lake. In summer you can hire boats or swim in the lake, and in winter you can skate on the lake or rent skis; there is a nearby chairlift and two ski lifts (open 10am to 4pm, Tuesday to Sunday). The chalet is located 6km northeast of Baia Sprie. Follow the road to Sighetu Marmaţiei and turn right at the signpost for Mogoşa.

ŢARA CHIOARULUI

The Ţara Chioarului region in the south-western part of Maramureş takes in the area immediately south of Baia Mare. The numerous villages, most of which boast traditional wooden churches, form a convenient loop – ideal for a two-hour driving tour by private transport.

Sights & Activities

Follow the main road south from Baia Mare to Cluj-Napoca for 14km to Satulung. Three kilometres south of Satulung, take the unmarked turn-off on the left opposite Cabana Stejarul to Finteuşu Mare and continue for 5km until you reach the village of **Posta**. At the top of the hill towers a small wooden church dating from 1675.

Şomcuţa Mare, 24km south of Baia Mare, is home to the annual **Stejarul (Oak Tree) Festival** (July), which attracts bands and choirs from all over the region. The small **Vălenii Şomcuţei Cave** (Peştera de la Vălenii Şomcuţei), 4km away, is signposted from the centre of the village.

Nine kilometres south of Şomcuţa Mare lies **Valea Chioarului**, the southernmost village in Ţara Chioarului. Its delightful, tall church stands next to the bus stop in the centre of the village. Beside the church is a bust of Mihail Viteazul (1994).

From Şomcuţa Mare, a minor road winds its way to **Remetea Chioarului**, 12km northeast. Its tiny church, dating from 1800, is the highlight of Ţara Chioarului. It stands majestically beside the village's extraordinarily ugly, seven-spired, modern church (1996).

Culcea, about 5km northwest of here, has an unremarkable plastered church built in 1720 and renovated in 1939. **Săcălaşeni**, 2km further north, has a small church built in 1442, but sadly a modern church dominates the village.

From **Catalina**, just north again, head west 2km to the predominantly Hungarian village of **Coltău** (Koltó in Hungarian). Hungary's most celebrated poet, Sándor Petőfi (1823–49), lived in the village in 1847, prior to leading the revolution against Habsburg domination of Hungary (1848–49). There's a small memorial house in the centre of Coltău where the poet spent a few months. In the garden stands the giant, 300-year-old cypress tree under which Petőfi sought inspiration.

SIGHETU MARMAŢIEI

☎ 262 / pop 41,425

Sighetu Marmaţiei is the northernmost town in Romania. Almost touching the Ukrainian border, it lies on the confluence of the Tisa,

FESTIVITIES & CULTURE

Outside of carefree, ţuică-swilling wintertime, the most noteworthy celebration in Maramureş is the **Hora de la Prislop** folk music festival, held annually on the second Sunday in August. The festival's *hora* dancers stamp their feet, swing their upper body, and clap vigorously to the rhythm of a *ţăpurituri*, a chanted rhyme drummed out by three musicians on a traditional *zongora* (a type of viola), a *cetera* (shrill violin) and a *doba* (bongo made from fir or maple wood, covered with goat or sheep hide).

Additionally there is **Tânjaua de pe Mara**, a celebration of peasant work and diligence held in late April or early May in the villages of Hărniceşti, Hoteni and Sat-Şugatag. Revellers, young and old, are 'watered' in the river for purification, before retiring to a feast and party. Tourists are welcome. Other notable festivals include **Sanzienele** (St John's Day/Midsummer Day) in the third week of June, which revolves around rejoicing in the regenerative power of nature, the **Maramusical Festival** in July and the **Saint Maria's Pilgrimage** in Moisei on 15 August.

The **Winter Festival** (27 December) is the undisputed high point of the year, featuring food, music, masks, a parade of colourful peasant costumes and oxen carrying baked cakes between their horns!

Family life is the source of many customs and rites of passage. Birth is seen as the passing of the soul from the unknown world to the known, or 'white', world. A *botejunea* (party) is held to celebrate each birth. Marriage ceremonies mix ancient and Christian rituals. The ceremonies begin at the homes of both parties and they make their way to the church separately. It is not until the couple are bound that the revelling begins – and the party doesn't end until dawn.

Death is bound in as many rituals. When someone dies their body is washed, dressed in traditional clothing, then laid out in their home for three days. The burial service takes place on the fourth day and is accompanied by a poetic verse recounting the person's personality and deeds. If an unmarried boy or girl dies they are given a symbolic wedding at the burial to assure they lived a full life.

While colourful folk outfits are the rule for ceremonies and festivals – and most Sundays, come to that – the daily garb in this region is often a less decorative version of the same outfits. Women wear linen ankle-length 'shirts' and sometimes vests on top with one or two wool red and black striped aprons (*zadii*) covering the waist down, with colourful scarves covering their hair. Men also wear linen shirts, wide trousers (*gaci*), peasant sandals (*opinca*), traditionally with pigskin soles, and a mirthful straw hat (*clop*) that resembles an inverted funnel. In winter this is accessorised with a short coat (*guba*), made of wool, and trimmed with a black velvet border at the collar and the pockets.

There are several regional myths, including those about Marţolea, a mythical woman who punishes other women if they work on Tuesday evenings, and Vârcolac, a man who turns into a werewolf at full moon and attacks people.

Iza and Ronişoara Rivers. Its name is derived from the Thracian and Dacian word *seget*, meaning 'fortress'.

Sighet (as it is known locally) is famed for its vibrant Winter Festival. Its dusty streets bustle with markets, tucked beneath the domes of churches of all denominations.

Sighetu Marmaţiei's former maximum-security prison is now a museum, a sobering and informative highlight of any visit to northern Romania.

Information

ATM (Piaţa Libertăţii) Outside Hotel Tisa.
Banca Comercială Română (Str Iuliu Maniu; ⊙ 8.30am-2.30pm Mon-Fri)

BRD (Str Ioan Mihaly de Apşa 24; ⊙ 9am-5pm Mon-Fri) Has an ATM, cash transfer and exchange facilities.
Millennium (Str Corneliu Coposu; per hr €1.40; ⊙ 9am-10pm Mon-Sat, noon-10pm Sun) For internet access.
Post & telephone office (Str Ioan Mihaly de Apşa 39) Opposite the Maramureş Museum.

TOURIST INFORMATION & TRAVEL AGENCIES

There is no official tourist office. The region's best source for beds, books and information is **Fundaţia OVR Agro-Tur-Art** (☎ 330 171; www.vaduizei.ovr.ro), in Vadu Izei (6km south). In Sighet, there's **MM Pangeae Proiect Turism** (☎ 312 228; Piaţa Libertăţii 15; ⊙ 9am-4pm Mon-Fri), which offers simple maps and group tours.

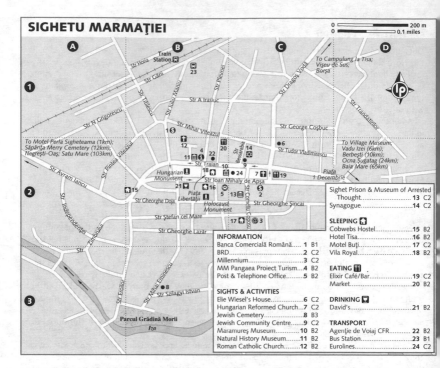

In nearby Campulung la Tisa, 12km northwest of Sighet, there is the all-purpose **Tourist Info Office** (☎ 0747-255 001; House 246; free domtimiro@hotmail.com; ☼ 24hr) run by Timea Homei, offering internet service, meals, a peaceful garden and help with any tourism needs in the region. Look for the banner in the village centre.

Sights

Sighetu Marmaţiei, first documented in 1328, was a strong cultural and political centre, being the birthplace of the Association for the Romanian Peoples' Culture, founded in 1863. On Piaţa Libertăţii stands the **Hungarian Reformed church**, built during the 15th century. Close by is the 16th-century **Roman Catholic church**.

Off the square is Sighet's only remaining **synagogue** (Str Bessarabia 10). Before WWII there were eight synagogues serving a large Jewish community which made up 40% of the town's population. Jews first settled in Sighet in the 17th century.

Next door is the **Jewish Community Centre** (☎ 311 652; Str Bessarabia 8; ☼ 10am-4pm Tue-Sun),

where you can purchase tickets to visit the **Jewish Cemetery** (Str Szilagyi Istvan), a couple of blocks south of the centre (follow Str Mihai Eminescu south, then turn left into Str Szilagyi Istvan). The cemetery isn't hard to find – just look for the 6m-high stone wall.

Elie Wiesel, the Jewish writer and 1986 Nobel Peace Prize–winner who coined the term 'Holocaust', was born in (and later deported from) Sighet. **Elie Wiesel's house** is on the corner of Strs Dragoş Vodă and Tudor Vladimirescu. His autobiography, *La Nuit* (The Night), was the first account ever published of the horrors of the Nazi concentration camps in WWII. On Str Gheorghe Doja is a **monument** to the victims of the Holocaust.

Maramureş Museum (Piaţa Libertăţii 15; admission €0.50; ☼ 10am-6pm Tue-Sun) displays colourful folk costumes, rugs, ceramics, regional paintings and carnival masks.

The decrepit but interesting **Natural History Museum** (Muzeul de Istorie şi ştiintele Naturii; Str Traian; admission €0.90; ☼ 9am-3pm Mon-Fri) is stuffed with dead animal exhibits. Knock on the door to enter.

Visit traditional peasant houses from the Maramureş region at the open-air **Village Museum** (Muzeul Satului; ☎ 314 229; Str Dobăieş 40; adult/child/photo/video €0.90/0.50/0.90/2.90; ☺ 9am-4pm), southeast of Sighet's centre. Allow at least half a day to wander through the incredible constructions. Children love the wooden dwellings, cobbled pathways and 'mini' villages. You can even stay overnight in tiny wooden cabins for €5.50.

Sleeping

Budget and midrange accommodation options are sprouting at a startling rate in Sighet. Keep an eye out for newer options. For homestays in the area check out www.ruraltourism.ro and www.pensiuni.info.ro.

Cobwobs Hostel (☎ 0745-615 173; www.cobwobs.com; Str 22 Dec 1989 42; dm/d €10/18) Run by an English/Romanian husband and wife team, like it was their home - because it is. They cook a mean meal out of the garden and arrange tours of the area.

Motel Buţi (☎ 311 035; Str Ştefan cel Mare 6; s/d/tr €21/28/41) This charming villa has spotlessly clean but small rooms, as well as a bar and pool table downstairs.

Hotel Tisa (☎ 312 645; Piaţa Libertăţii 8; d/tr €24/29) Smack-bang in the centre of Sighet, the ailing rooms here were enjoying renovation at the time of writing.

Motel Perla Sigheteana (☎ 310 613; www.perlasigheteana.ro; Str Avram Iancu 65; d €25) This place is out of town on the road to Săpânţa.

Vila Royal (☎ 311 004; www.vilaroyal.ro; Str Ioan Mihali de Apşa; s/d €32/37) Also dead centre, this eight-room villa is one of the city's newer options, housed in a classic building circa 1885. The rooms have been plasticised, but are comfortable.

Eating & Drinking

David's (Str Ioan Mihaly de Apşa; ☺ 7am-10pm; mains €3) The lively bar-of-the-moment, with a menu long on drinks and short on food.

Elixir Café/Bar (Str Traian) Get cosy with the locals at this busy, smoky joint that serves snacks and beer.

Hotel Tisa has a large, reasonably priced restaurant, which does good breakfasts. The town's **market** (Piaţa Agroalimentara) sells fresh fruit and veg.

Getting There & Away

BUS

The **bus station** (Str Gării) is opposite the train station. Several local buses leave daily to Baia Mare (€2, 65km), Satu Mare (€2.50, 122km), Borşa (€1), Budeşti (€1), Călineşti (€1) and Vişeu de Sus (€1.50), and one bus daily to Bârsana, Botiza, Ieud and Mara. A bus leaves

---

SIGHET PRISON: A SUFFERING NATION

In May 1947 the communist regime embarked on a reign of terror; slaughtering, imprisoning and torturing thousands of Romanians. While many leading prewar figures were sent to hard-labour camps, the regime's most feared intellectual opponents were interned in Sighet's maximum-security prison. Between 1948 and 1952, about 180 members of Romania's academic and government elite were imprisoned here.

Today, four white marble plaques covering the barred windows of the prison list the 51 prisoners who died in the Sighet cells, notably the academic and head of the National Liberal Party (PNL), Constantin Brătianu; historian and leading member of the PNL, Gheorghe Brătianu; governor of the National Bank, Constantin Tătăranu; and Iuliu Maniu, president of the National Peasants' Party (PNŢ). Many simply died of starvation; the prisoners were given 700 calories a day to survive on - the average person needs between 2000 and 2500 - an impossible task in Romania's feared winters.

The prison, housed in the old courthouse, was closed in 1974. In 1989 it reopened as the **Museum of Arrested Thought** (Muzeu al Gândirii Arestate; ☎ 314 224; Str Corneliu Coposu 4; admission free; ☺ 9.30am-6.30pm Mon-Fri 15 May-15 Oct, 9.30am-4.30pm 15 Oct-15 May). Photographs are displayed in the torture chambers and cells. The memorial plaque outside reads 'In memory of the young, intelligent people at the forefront of Romanian intellectual life who were imprisoned because they did not believe in communism and died, through torture, in this odious prison'.

Possibly the most heart-rending sight is the bronze sculptures in the courtyard, dedicated to those who died. Figures shielding themselves, imploring, covering their mouths in horror, all naked and missing limbs look to the heavens in a frozen symbol of their agony.

for Săpânţa every hour between 8am and 2pm, returning at 4pm and 5pm.

Eurolines (☎ 319 322; sighet@eurolines.ro; Str Traian; ☷ 9am-8pm Mon-Fri, 9am-4pm Sat) has a new office in the town centre.

TRAIN

Tickets are sold in advance at the **Agenţie de Voiaj CFR** (☎ 312 666; Piaţa Libertăţii 25; ☷ 7am-2pm Mon-Fri). There's one daily fast train to Timişoara (€20), Bucharest (€20, 12 hours), Cluj-Napoca (€12.50, six hours) and Arad (€18). Three trains a week (Monday, Wednesday and Friday) head into Ukraine – this journey is only open to those not needing visas, as there are no visa-issuing facilities at this border crossing.

MARA VALLEY

The Mara Valley (Valea Mara), with its beautiful rolling hills, is the heart of Maramureş. It takes its name from the Mara River which runs southwest through the valley from Sighetu Marmaţiei to Baia Mare. Villages here are famed for their spectacular churches and carved gateways.

Giuleşti & Around

Heading south from Sighetu Marmaţiei, you reach the tiny village of **Berbeşti**, famed for the 300-year-old *troiţă* (crucifix), a large, Renaissance-style cross carved with solar emblems, which stands by the roadside at the village's northern end. Traditionally, travellers prayed by the cross to ensure a safe journey.

Continuing south you'll find **Giuleşti**, the main village in the Mara Valley, notable for its crumbling wooden cottages with 'pot trees' in their front yards, on which a colourful array of pots and pans are hung to dry. It was here in 1918 that the revolutionary poet Ilie Lazăr summoned delegates from all over Maramureş prior to their signing Transylvania's Union agreement with Romania. Ilie Lazăr's house is preserved and open to tourists as a memorial museum. During the communist crackdown in the early 1950s, Ilie Lazăr was arrested and imprisoned at Sighet prison (see p241).

The village of **Deseşti** is a few kilometres southwest of Giuleşti on the road to Baia Mare. Its tiny Orthodox church, built in 1770, was struck by lightning in 1925, destroying much of the outer walls and the steeple. It has since been repaired and fitted with a lightning conductor. Its interior paintings, by Radu

Munteanu, date from 1780 and feature Sodom and Gomorrah.

Close to the church is an oak tree, hundreds of years old and measuring about 4.5m in diameter. It has been preserved as a monument to the extensive oak forest that once covered the area before people felled the trees to build their homes.

Mara, just a couple of kilometres south of Deseşti, is best known for its elaborate wooden fences. These porches are a unique architectural feature of the Maramureş region. In more recent times, the spiritual importance of these outside porches has been overridden by the social status attached to them; see p245.

Sat-Şugatag & Around

Seven kilometres south of Giuleşti is **Sat-Şugatag**, home to a church dating from 1642. The church is famed for its fine, ornately carved wooden gate. Sat-Şugatag was first documented in 1360 as the property of Dragoş of Giuleşti.

Mănăstirea is 1km east of Sat-Şugatag. The church here was built by monks in 1633. By 1787 just one monk and four servants remained, and during the reign of Austro-Hungarian King Joseph II the monastery was closed. The original monks' cells are on the northern side of the church. Several 18th-century icons painted on glass and wood have been preserved, as have some of the frescoes on the outside western wall of the church, normally seen on the monasteries of northern Moldavia.

Three kilometres south of Mănăstirea is the small spa resort-village of **Ocna Şugatag**, built on a hilltop in 1321. The village is named after its former salt mine, which was exploited until the 1950s (*ocnă* means 'salt mine').

Four kilometres south of Ocna Şugatag is **Hărniceşti**, home to a marvellous Orthodox church dating from 1770. A footpath, signposted 'Spre Monument', leads from the village's primary school to the hillside church.

Nine kilometres southeast of Ocna Şugatag is **Hoteni**, known for its **Tânjaua de pe Mara** folk festival held from 1 May to 14 May to celebrate the first ploughing (see p239).

Eastern Mara Valley & Cosău Valley

Heading south from Sighetu, bear left at **Fereşti** along the road leading to Maramureş' least accessible villages. From Baia Mare, you can approach this area through Cavnic, across the Neteda Pass.

Corneşti, the first village along this stretch, has a small 18th-century church with interior paintings by Hodor Toador. **Călineşti**, 7km further south, is where in 1862 archaeologists uncovered a cache of bracelets and ankle chains, believed to date from Roman times. Călineşti has two churches, known as Susani (*sus* meaning 'up') and Josani (*jos* meaning 'low'). The Susani church (1683) is on the left side of the road as you enter the village from the north. But the Josani church, built 20 years earlier, is more spectacular. To get to this church, turn right at the road for Bârsana and continue until you reach house No 385. A small path opposite this house twists and turns its way to the church; follow the upper path when you come to the fork.

From Călineşti a mud track leads to **Sârbi**, inhabited since 1402. Its two churches are built from oak. The Susani church dates from 1667, with interior paintings by Al Ponehachile. Sârbi's Josani church dates from 1665. A traditional 'natural launderette', ingeniously constructed by villagers to utilise the water power from the stream, is still used to wash clothes and blankets. Just follow the pumping sound. A wooden thresher and loom sit nearby, as well as a *ţuică* (plum brandy) 'factory' that welcomes visitors – look for the large white house or accost people with '*ţuică fabricat?*' until you home in on it.

Budeşti, 4km south of Sârbi, is one of the most beautiful villages in Maramureş. Its Josani church, built in 1643, features four small turrets surrounding the main steeple, signifying its role as local law courts. Inside the church is a small collection of icons on glass and wood, dating from 1766. Other exhibits include a glass box containing a real-life miracle – a hunk of wood sliced in half to reveal a perfect blackened cross image. The church's most prized piece, however, is the 18th-century painting of the Last Judgment, preserved in its entirety. The church also houses the undershirt of its most famous 17th-century inhabitant, Grigore Pintea Viteazul (a local Robin Hood), allegedly purchased from the local Romanian community in Budapest for 1000 forint. If the church is locked, inquire at the church up the hill for the key.

Blueberries and 'little angels', or red berries, grow in abundance on the fields surrounding the track.

Budeşti is impossible to reach without private transport or a long day of dedicated hitching. Pack a lunch as food here is scarce. There's a small *pensiune* down the hill from the church if you're too tired to hitch back to Sighet.

Sleeping & Eating

Fundaţia OVR Agro-Tur-Art (☎ 262-330 171; www .vaduizei.ovr.ro) In Vadu Izei, Fundaţia OVR Agro-Tur-Art arranges accommodation in private homes in the area for around €20 per night, including breakfast and dinner, or do it yourself at www.ruraltourism.ro and www .pensiuni.info.ro.

Camping Complex (tent sites/bungalows €2/10) Owned by Sind Romania (Union Romania), this complex has beautifully carved wooden bungalows sleeping up to six people.

Hotel Craiasca (☎ 262-374 059; www.craiasca.ro; s/d €15/20) This place has two restaurants, a bar and a disco, and offers spa treatments for €3 and three meals per day for an extra €10.

Hotel Salina (☎ 262-374 362/034; s/d incl spa treatments €29/34) This health resort, also owned by Sind Romania, has four salt pools and it's a bargain. It offers cheap holidays to Romanian workers and retirees.

SĂPÂNŢA

☎ 262

Săpânţa village has a unique place in the hearts of Romanians. It boasts the 'Merry Cemetery', the church graveyard famous for the colourfully painted wooden crosses that adorn its tombstones. Shown in art exhibitions across Europe, the crosses attract busloads of visitors who marvel at the gentle humour and human warmth that created them. Villagers seem utterly untouched by the fame that the crosses have created. Life carries on as normal: old women sit outside their cottages, colourful rugs are hung on clotheslines and beaten clean with wire swatters and the odd horse and cart trundles past. The village itself lies 12km northwest of Sighetu Marmaţiei, just 4km south of Ukraine.

Five hundred metres down a gravel road, a **new wooden church** claiming to be the tallest wooden structure in Europe (75m) is being built with a controversial stone base. This pips the stone-free church in Surdeşti (p237) by 3m and has subsequently sparked a peevish debate about the legitimacy of stone bases. Ask the resident nun to open the basement chapel.

MERRY CEMETERY

Săpânța's **Merry Cemetery** (Cimitirul Vesel; €0.50) was the creation of Ioan Stan Pătraș, a simple wood sculptor who, in 1935, started carving crosses to mark graves in the old church cemetery. He painted each cross in blue – the traditional colour of hope and freedom – and on top of each he inscribed a witty epitaph to the deceased.

Prior to his death in 1977, Pătraș carved and painted his own cross, complete with a portrait of himself and a lengthy epitaph in which he wrote of the 'cross' he bore all his life, working to support his family since his father's death when he was 14 years old. Pătraș' grave is directly opposite the main entrance to the old church.

Every cross tells a different story, and the painted pictures and inscriptions illustrate a wealth of traditional occupations: shepherds tend their sheep, mothers cook for their families, barbers cut hair, and weavers bend over looms.

Since Pătraș' death, Dumitru Pop, his apprentice, has carried on the tradition. He lives and works in Pătraș' former house and studio, using the same traditional methods. He makes about 10 crosses each year, depending on the mortality rate in the village.

The house where Pop lives and works is also a **museum** (donation €0.30). In one small room, various pictures carved in wood and painted by Pătraș are displayed. These include portraits of members of the Executive Committee of the Communist Party, and a portrait of Nicolae and Elena Ceaușescu carved in honour of Ceaușescu's visit to Săpânța in 1974. The interior of Săpânța's old church (1886), next to the cemetery, is adorned with painted frescoes.

Camping Poieni (☎ 372 228; tent sites/cabins per person €1.50/3; ☼ 1 Jun-31 Aug) is 3km to the south of Săpânța and has an excellent trout restaurant.

Villagers rent out their rooms in the Săpânța area. The owners at the green-tiled **Pensiunea Ileana** (☎ 372 137; per person €14) don't speak English.

Pensiunea Stan (☎ 372 337; d €20) is opposite the cemetery entrance and has five double rooms. Breakfast not included.

There's a new bar and terrace by the cemetery entrance.

Buses run every hour (8am to 2pm) from Sighet bus station and return at 4pm and 5pm. The wooden church is signposted off the main Sighet/Negrești-Oaș road, though it's easier to just look up and follow the steeple.

IZEI VALLEY
☎ 262/pop 3000

The lush Izei Valley (Valea Izei) follows the Iza River eastward from Sighetu Marmației to Moisei. The soul of ancient Romania lurks among the valley's tiny rural villages, inside its thatched roofs, tall wooden church steeples, 'pot trees' and wooden gates outside every home. Traditional crafts are still practised by wood carvers, blanket weavers and glass painters and there's ample opportunity for you to join in.

In mid-July Vadu Izei, together with the neighbouring villages of Botiza and Ieud,

hosts the **Maramuzical Festival**, a lively four-day international folk music festival.

Vadu Izei

Vadu Izei is at the confluence of the Iza and Mara Rivers, 6km south of Sighetu Marmației. Its **museum** is in the oldest house in the village (1750). If you visit a private home in this village – and the whole region – you'll quickly realise that little has changed since the 18th century – including the state of indoor plumbing: nonexistent.

Vadu Izei has been supported since the early 1990s by the Belgian charity Opération Villages Roumains, which originally started out as an international pressure group against Ceaușescu's systemisation programme. More recently, the village gained financial backing from the European Union's Phare programme to develop infrastructure.

The village tourism society, **Fundația OVR Agro-Tur-Art** (☎ 330 171; www.vaduizei.ovr.ro; house 161), at the northern end of the village, is an unrivalled source of local information. Additionally, **Nicolae Prisăcaru** (☎ 330 093, 0721-046 730; prisnic@conseco.ro) or the lovely **Ramona Ardelean** (☎ 0744-827 829; aramona@gmx.de) arrange excellent guided tours (in French or English, full day €25 plus €0.25 per kilometre), as well as picnics, wood-carving and icon-painting workshops.

Contact any of the individuals listed above to arrange accommodations (around €20 per person, breakfast and dinner included) or just show up and take your pick of the dozens of homes displaying *cazare* signs. Alternatively, www.ruraltourism.ro and www .pensiuni.info.ro list an array of homestays available in Maramureș.

Bârsana

From Vadu Izei continue for 12km through Oncești to the village of Bârsana (formerly Bîrsana), dating from 1326. In 1720 it built its first church, the interior paintings of which were created by local artists Hodor Toador and Ion Plohod.

The famous and enchanting Orthodox **Bârsana Monastery** (Mănăstirea Bârsana) is a popular pilgrimage spot in Maramureș. It was the last Orthodox monastery built in the region before Serafim Petrovai – head of the Orthodox Church in Maramureș – suddenly converted to Greco-Catholicism in 1711. The 11am service is a magical experience among the rolling hills and wildflowers.

Maria Pașca (☎ 331 165; house 377; bed without/with full board €20/30) has rooms to rent at her home.

Rozavlea

Continue south through Strâmtura to Rozavlea, first documented under the name of Gorzohaza in 1374. Its fine **church**, dedicated to the archangels Michael and Gabriel, was constructed between 1717 and 1720 in another village, then erected in Rozavlea on the site of an ancient church destroyed by the Tartars. The flower-strewn graveyard is a testament to the area's anarchic splendour.

Botiza

From Rozavlea continue south for 3km to Șieu, then take the turn-off right for idyllic Botiza. Botiza's **old church**, built in 1694, is overshadowed by the giant **new church**, constructed in 1974 to serve devout Orthodox families.

The 9am Sunday service is the major event of the week in Botiza. The entire village flocks to the church to partake in the religious activities which continue well into the afternoon.

Opération Villages Roumains runs a local *agroturism* scheme, which offers half/full board in local homes for €15/18 per night. Bookings can be made through the local representative, **George Iurca** (☎ 334 110, 0722-942 140; botizavr@sintec.ro; house 742; ☟ 8am-10pm), whose house is signposted. George is a licensed guide for all regions of Romania, running tours in German, French and English (€10 to €15 per day, depending on the number of participants). He also rents out mountain bikes (€5 per day), vehicles with a driver/guide (€45 per day) and organises fishing trips (€20, plus licence, transport and accommodation).

WOODEN MARAMUREȘ

Even now, wood is everywhere in Maramureș. The region has a long history of using wood to build houses and churches using logs and/or thick beams with incredible joins and no nails. Traditionally the homes of the Mara, Cosău and Izei Valleys used oak, while in Bârsana pine was used, and this is still the case. Roofs are tall and steep, the oldest covered in thatch.

Immense carved wooden gates fronting average homes are common now, often used to illustrate the social status and wealth of the inhabitants, yet originally they were built only by royal landowners to guard against evil. The gates were the symbolic barrier between the safe interior and the unknown outside world, and people placed money, incense and holy water under them for further protection against dark forces. Gate carvings include the Tree of Life, the snake (guardian against evil), birds (symbols of the human soul) and a face (to protect from spirits). Sacalas Gheorghe (1860–1934) was one of the region's most gifted carvers.

Maramureș is particularly famed for its wooden churches, many of which are Unesco World Heritage sites. The Orthodox churches are divided into the ante-nave, nave and altar. Gothic-style towers rise up to 50m above the churches and it is a testament to the builders' technical expertise that they continue to survive the harsh winters of the region.

Wood is still the main raw material used for a variety of purposes such as gourds at weddings, carved religious seals and painted icons. Wooden crosses also dot the landscape; the wooden crucifix in the village of Berbești (p242) is of great historical importance as it is the oldest of its kind in the region.

Alternatively, ask for **Iaon Costinar** (☎ 334 044, 334 066; house 790; bed without/with full board €8/19), who can also organise accommodation.

Poienile Izei

From Botiza a track leads west to Poienile Izei, home of a church with the most dramatic frescoes of hell you are ever likely to encounter. The church, with its thatched roof, was built in 1604. Its interior frescoes, dating from 1783, have a depiction of hell symbolised by a ferocious bird waiting to swallow up sinners. Australian Aboriginal–style paintings depict the torments inflicted by the devil on sinners who fail to obey the rules represented in the frescoes. To visit, ask for the key at the priest's house – a large wooden house in the centre of the village with an ornately carved terrace.

There are rooms for rent at the homes of **Florentina Petreuş** (☎ 334 204; house 77; bed without/ with full board €18/25), and **Donita Ilies** (☎ 334 383; house 135), who speaks French and does excellent home-cooking.

Four kilometres further north along the same dirt track is the village of **Glod**, the birthplace of the popular Maramureş folk-singing duo, the Petreuş Brothers.

Ieud

The oldest wooden church in Maramureş is in Ieud, 6km off the road south from Şieu. Century-old customs are still firmly intact in this fervently Orthodox village. Between 1787 (when the first marriage was registered) and 1980 there were no divorces in the village.

Ieud was first documented in 1365 but evidence suggests the village was inhabited as early as the 11th century by Balc, Dragoş Vodă's grandson and later Prince of Moldavia. In 1364 Ieud's fabulous Orthodox '**Church on the Hill**' (Biserica de Lemn din Deal) was built on castle ruins. It is made from fir-wood and used to house the first document known to be written in Romanian (1391–92), in which the catechism and church laws pertaining to Ieud were coded. The church is generally locked but you can get the key from the porter's house in the centre of the village, distinguishable by its simple, wooden gate.

Ieud's other **church** (Biserica de Lemn din Şes), today Greco-Catholic in denomination, was built in 1717. The church, at the southern end of the village, is unique to the region as it has no porch. It houses one of the largest collections of icons on glass found in Maramureş.

You can make accommodation bookings through Opération Villages Roumains' representative in Botiza, **George Iurca** (p245), or go straight to **Vasile Chindris** (☎ 336 197; house 201; bed without/with full board €12/25), **Liviu Ilea** (☎ 336 039; house 333; bed without/with full board €12/18) or **Vasile Rişco** (☎ 336 019; house 705; without/with full board €12/18).

Bogdan Vodă

The former village of Cuhea was renamed Bogdan Vodă in 1968 in honour of the Moldavian prince (r 1359–65) from Maramureş, who marched southeast from Cuhea to found the state of Moldavia in 1359. Some of the interior paintings in the village church, built in 1718, draw upon the traditional method of painting on linen, while others are painted on wood. The church, dedicated to St Nicholas, is on the left as you enter the village from the north.

Dragomireşti

Four kilometres south of Bogdan Vodă lies the village of Dragomireşti, whose church (1722), in fine Maramureş fashion, was uprooted in 1936 and moved to Bucharest's National Village Museum (p76). The villagers have since built a new wooden church, on the same site, immediately to the left of the village entrance.

A further 4km east is **Sălişzea de Sus**, first documented under the name Keethzeleste in 1365. It has two old churches, dating from 1680 and 1722, along with two new multi-spired, concrete churches.

VIŞEU & VASER VALLEYS
☎ 262

The wooded mountains rise to dizzying heights around the picturesque Vişeu Valley (Valea Vişeu), which tracks the Vişeu River on its journey south. Breathing in the fresh Alpine air here is enough therapy for a lifetime. A railway line links this stretch, from Rona de Jos in the north to Borşa in the south, making it more accessible for travellers without private transport.

The twin villages of **Rona de Jos** and **Rona de Sus**, 19km southeast of Sighetu Marmaţiei, lie just a couple of kilometres apart. Continue south through the unremarkable Petrova and Leordina, and you eventually come to the spectacular logging village of Vişeu de Sus.

Vişeu de Sus

This gateway to the wonders of the Vaser Valley was first chronicled in 1363 and is growing

---

STEAMED UP!

Since its construction in 1925, the narrow-gauge railway has been used to carry wood down the mountains. Steam engines were originally used as logging trains on this route. These days, the job's done mostly by diesel engines but there are still four steam engines making the arduous climb.

More than 4000 cu metres of fir wood *(brad)* are felled each month by the lumberjacks, who are ferried by train each morning 42km up the valley to the logging camp at **Comanu**, close to the Ukrainian border. Once up in the hills they barter cigarettes and vodka for freshly made cheese from the hilltop shepherds.

Tourists can also make the daily journey up past forests filled with elusive wolves and lynx. It's possible to pitch a tent 32km away at the camping grounds of **Făina** or **Valea Babii** (6km further on), but the cabanas are now reserved for workers. From Făina there's a well-marked hiking trail but it should only be undertaken in summer as there are few highly detailed maps of this region. Be wary not to stray near the border as border police are armed.

At **Novaţ** there's an artists' camp where you'll find sculptors in action and hear much frenzied late-night debate under the stars.

A tourist-only train leaves daily at 8.30am and begins its homeward journey at about 5pm, except Sundays and holidays. Tickets cost €8 and are bought at the station before boarding the train.

To get to the wood factory *(fabrica de lemn)* and **train station** (☎ 262-353 535), turn left opposite Hotel Brad on the corner of Str 22 Decembrie and Str Iuliu Maniu, continue along Str Carpaţi for 2km and they're on the left. The tourist information office in Vişeu de Sus sells a good map of the Vaser Valley trails (€1).

---

yearly into a mecca for travellers and nature-lovers. Logging is the town's traditional industry – and it's this tradition which is the catalyst for its newest industry: tourism.

Vişeu de Sus's unique **narrow-gauge railway** winds up and into the Vaser Valley and is still used to bring wood down from the mountains. The original steam engines now have several diesel locomotive companions (see 'Steamed Up!', above).

Aside from the railway line, the town's main axis is Str 22 Decembrie. The Vaser Valley railway stop is northeast of the town centre.

The **tourist information centre** (☎ 352 285; Str Libertaţii 1; ☼ 9am-6pm Mon-Fri), situated in the library, opens and closes at whim, despite posted hours. When reachable, they sell maps of the region, arrange accommodation and book steam train tours. The supply of hiking maps is frustratingly low, but you'll find one good map of the valley's trails here (€1).

Hotel Gabriela (☎ 354 380; www.hotel-gabriela.ro; s/d €17/29; ☐) is two kilometres from Hotel Brad, on the road to Borşa. This three-star chalet-style option has internet facilities.

Hotel Brad (☎ 352 999; cnr Strs 22 Decembrie & Iuliu Maniu; s/d €19/32) has simple rooms that must be booked in advance as they fill up quickly during summer.

Moisei

Moisei lies 9km southeast of Vişeu de Sus, at the foot of the Rodna Massif. Known for its traditional crafts and customs, Moisei gained fame in 1944 when retreating Hungarian (Horthyst) troops gunned down 31 people before setting fire to the entire village.

Hungarian forces captured the 31 people and detained them in a small camp in Vişeu de Sus without food or water for three weeks. On 14 October 1944, the Hungarian troops brought the prisoners to a house in Moisei, locked them inside, then shot them through the windows. Of the 31, 29 were killed, leaving only two survivors. Before abandoning the village, the troops set it on fire, leaving all 125 remaining families homeless.

Only one house in Moisei survived the blaze; the one in which the prisoners were shot. Today, it houses a small **museum** (Expoziţia Documentar – Istorică Martirii de la Moisei 14 Octombrie 1944), in tribute to those who died in the massacre. Photographs of the 29 who died as well as the two who survived the bloodbath adorn its walls.

Just opposite the museum is a circular **monument** to the victims, its 12 upright columns symbolising the sun and light. Ten columns are decorated with a traditional carnival mask

MARAMUREŞ

and two are decorated with human faces based on the features of the two survivors.

The museum and monument are at the eastern end of the village. If the museum is locked, knock at the house next door and ask for the key.

Each year, on 15 August, the **Feast of the Assumption** shuts down the area. Villagers from around the county, walking in groups for up to two days or more, carry crosses and holy pictures to Moisei's monastery. The singing, jubilant groups flood the narrow roads, testing the wafer-thin patience of heathen Romanian drivers.

Borşa

Ore has been mined at Borşa, 12km east of Moisei, since the mid-14th century. The area was colonised in 1777 by German miners from Slovakia; eight years later, Bavarian-Austrian miners moved to **Baia Borşa**, 2km northeast of the town, to mine copper, lead and silver.

The **Complex Turistic Borşa**, a small ski resort and tourist complex 10km east of Borşa town proper, is a main entry point to the splendid **Rodna Mountains**, part of which forms the Pietrosul Rodnei Nature Reservation (5900 hectares).

Hiking information is scarce in this hikers' heaven, largely because too few people make the effort to get here, but there are clearly marked trails leading from the top of the ski lift. Trails include a two-hour hike (in good weather) to the Prislop Pass and a pleasant one-hour hike signposted 'Cascada Cailor', which leads to the 40m high 'Horse' waterfall. If you want to stretch your legs before starting on the trails, there's a path leading up underneath the **ski lift** (Str Brădet 10; ☉ 7am-6pm).

In winter the Complex Turistic Borşa boasts the largest natural ski run in Europe (2km, beginner to intermediate). The small, relatively unspoilt resort is fast becoming a haven for travellers and skiers who wish to avoid the crowds in the Carpathians. Unfortunately, ski hire is not available.

Staff at the hotels or chalets of the complex are generally helpful. **Hotel Mia** (☎ 342 347; Str Al Cuza 237a) has clean, nice rooms as does **Hotel Iezer** (☎ 343 430; Str Decebal 2), **Hotel Perla Maramuresului** (☎ 342 539; Str Victoriei 27) and nearby **Hotel Mihali** (☎ 0742-797 599; Str Victoriei 65). At the Complex Turistic ski resort, **Pensiunea Focus** (☎ 344 038), near the chairlift, is the most attractive of the bunch.

Buses run between Borşa proper and the Complex Turistic throughout the day.

PRISLOP PASS

From Complex Turistic Borşa, a tight, winding road climbs for 10km to the remote Prislop Pass. Hikers can trek north into the Maramureş Mountains or head south into the Rodna Mountains and onward to Moldavia. Red triangles, then blue stripes lead to the peak of the Gargalau Saddle (1925m, two hours). Then either continue east (red stripes) to the Rotunda Pass, then southeast to Vatra Dornei, or west to the highest part of the massif and on to La Cruce (4½ hours). From here the weather station on the summit of Mount Pietrosul (2305m, blue stripes) is only 90 minutes away, which among the mind-bending views, allows for a good long gaze into Ukraine without the hassle of border checks. At this point, it's a direct hustle back down to Borşa (2½ hours).

Cabanas are scarce in this area, come prepared to camp out. Do not attempt to stray too far from these trails without a good map and compass.

SATU MARE

☎ 261 / pop 116,180

Satu Mare (Big Village), frequently clumped into the Maramureş region for the sake of guidebook simplicity (ahem), actually resides in Satu Mare county. Having spent a large part of modern history within Hungarian borders, the area has a substantial ethnic Hungarian population; many people still refer to the town by its former Hungarian name, Szatmar. It's also a strong contender for 'Ugliest Town in Romania' – a grand, communist architectural experiment which went horribly wrong. Nonetheless it has a certain charm because of its dubious looks, and demoralised locals are sincerely surprised and thrilled when travellers pass through. Still, you won't be buying postcards.

Orientation

The train and bus stations are adjacent at the northern end of Str Griviţei, to the east of the centre. South of the centre, the Someş River crosses the town from east to west.

Information

CULTURAL CENTRES

Culture House (Centre Socio Cultural Franco Romanian; ☎ 0766-784 080) Has a film club and French library.

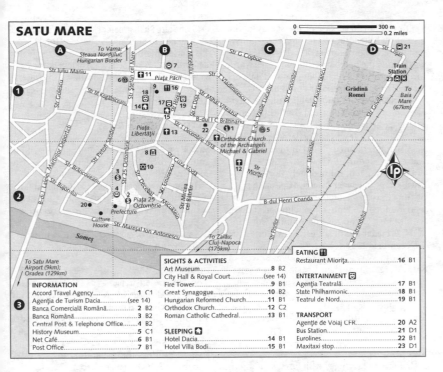

SATU MARE

SIGHTS & ACTIVITIES
Art Museum	**8** B2
City Hall & Royal Court	(see 14)
Fire Tower	**9** B1
Great Synagogue	**10** B2
Hungarian Reformed Church	**11** B1
Orthodox Church	**12** C2
Roman Catholic Cathedral	**13** B1

SLEEPING
Hotel Dacia	**14** B1
Hotel Villa Bodi	**15** B1

INFORMATION
Accord Travel Agency	**1** C1
Agenţia de Turism Dacia	(see 14)
Banca Comercială Română	**2** B2
Banca Română	**3** B2
Central Post & Telephone Office	**4** B2
History Museum	**5** C1
Net Café	**6** B1
Post Office	**7** B1

EATING
Restaurant Mioriţa	**16** B1

ENTERTAINMENT
Agenţia Teatrală	**17** B1
State l'hilharmonic	**18** B1
Teatrul de Nord	**19** B1

TRANSPORT
Agenţie de Voiaj CFR	**20** A2
Bus Station	**21** D1
Eurolines	**22** B1
Maxitaxi stop	**23** D1

INTERNET ACCESS

History Museum (B-dul Vasile Lucaciu 21; admission €0.75, per hr €0.30; 10am-5pm Tue-Sun)

Net Cafe (Ştefan cel Mare 4; per hr €0.50; 9am-1am) Situated just off Piaţa Libertăţii.

MONEY

Banca Română (Str 25 Octombrie; 8.30am-4.30pm Mon-Fri) Cashes travellers cheques, gives cash advances on Visa/Mastercard and has an ATM.

Banca Comercială Română (Str 25 Octombrie; 9am-5pm Mon-Fri) Has the same facilities as Banca Română.

POST & TELEPHONE

Central post and telephone office (Str 25 Octombrie; 7am-7pm Mon-Fri)

Post office (Piaţa Păcii; 7.30am-7.30pm)

TOURIST INFORMATION & TRAVEL AGENCIES

Accord Travel agency (737 915; www.accord-travel .ro; B-dul IC Brătinanu 7) These people speak the daylights out of English, sell maps of the region, arrange tours of Maramureş and rent cars. They can arrange private accommodation in rural homes for €15 to €20 per night.

Agenţia de Turism Dacia (710 060; Piaţa Libertăţii 8; 9am-4pm Mon, Wed & Fri, 9am-5pm Tue & Thu, 10.30am-1.30pm Sat) Situated in Hotel Dacia, this agency sells tickets for international buses to Bucharest.

Sights

Satu Mare's sights are centred on or around Piaţa Libertăţii.

The town's **art museum** (cnr Str Cuza Vodă & Piaţa Libertăţii; admission €0.90; 9am-5pm Tue-Sun) is large enough to make it worth spending some time checking out local works.

PUTTING THE 'UG' IN UGLY

Since you're surrounded by them anyway, why not turn the tables and admire Satu Mare's pitiable buildings for their glorious tastelessness? Seek out, rank and even pose in front of the city's top eyesores. Popular opinion is that the prefecture building reigns Ugly Supreme, but keep an eye out for the building on Piaţa Libertăţii that is so shameful that they've tried to completely cover it with commercial banners.

MARAMUREŞ

On the northern side of the square is the former **city hall and royal court**, which now houses Hotel Dacia. Continuing north down the alleyway next to the hotel, you come to a courtyard, in the centre of which stands a 45m-tall **fire tower** (Turnul Pompierilor), built in 1904.

A **Roman Catholic cathedral** lies on the eastern side of Piaţa Libertăţii. Building began on the cathedral in 1786; its two towers were added in 1837. It was badly damaged during WWII and remained closed until restoration was completed in 1961.

On Piaţa Păcii, immediately north, is the town's large **Hungarian Reformed Church**. In front of the church is a statue of Ferenc Kölcsey, who founded the Hungarian school next door. Satu Mare's Orthodox community worships at the **Orthodox church** at the eastern end of Str 1 Decembrie 1918.

Prior to WWII about 13,000 Jews lived in Satu Mare, which then boasted eight synagogues and a school. Most Jews were deported to death camps in 1944 and most of their synagogues destroyed, although the **Great Synagogue** (1920), located on Str Decebal, is still in use today.

Sleeping

Piaţa Libertăţii is ringed with three-star hotels. There are a few motels and camping north of the city.

Hotel Dacia (☎ 714 276/7; Piaţa Libertăţii 8; s/d 2-stars €25/32, s/d 3-stars €36/47; 🖳) *Grande dame* of the lush, leafy square, with stately rooms.

Hotel Villa Bodi (☎ 710 861; villabodi@villabodi.ro; Piaţa Libertăţii 5; s/d €51/69; 🖳) This plush 'villa' is dressed in an elegant 19th-century European style. It also has a sauna and Jacuzzi.

Eating & Drinking

Hotel Dacia (Piaţa Libertăţii 8; mains €4; ☘ 7am-midnight) This gorgeous, stately room looks primed for a royal reception – though the music suggests 'wedding reception'.

Restaurant Miorița (Str Mihai Viteazul 5; mains €4) Here, local cuisine is served in a sunny, green environment. Live bands play most nights.

Teatrul de Nord (☎ 715 876; Str Horea 5) This theatre has a popular outside bar during summer.

Entertainment

Posters advertising what is on where in the city – including underground dance parties – line walls and bollards.

The **State Philharmonic** (☎ 712 616; Piaţa Libertăţii 8) is tucked in an alleyway beside Hotel Dacia. Plays in Romanian are performed at the **Teatrul de Nord** (☎ 715 876; Str Horea 5). Tickets for both venues are sold at **Agenţia Teatrală** (☎ 712 106; Str Horea 6; ☘ 10am-4pm Mon-Fri), opposite the Teatrul de Nord.

Getting There & Away

AIR

Satu Mare airport (☎ 768 640) is situated 9km south of the city on the main Oradea–Satu Mare road.

Tarom (www.tarom.ro) flies to Bucharest (single/return US$75/124 plus about €4 tax each way) daily except Sunday. Tarom do not accept euros.

Carpatair (www.carpatair.ro) flies to Timişoara and beyond three times a week.

BUS

The **bus station** (autogară; ☎ 768 439) is a 10-minute walk east of the centre. Local daily services include 10 buses to Baia Mare (59km); and one each to Negreşti-Oaş (50km), Oradea (133km) and Turţ (35km).

Eurolines (☎ 710 995; satu.mare@eurolines.ro; Str IC Brătinanu 5) offers the usual dazzling network of connections to everywhere.

A daily maxitaxi leaves from the **maxitaxi stop** outside the train station (Gara) for Budapest (€13).

TRAIN

Agenţie de Voiaj CFR (☎ 721 202; Str Bujurului; ☘ 7am-7pm Mon-Fri) sells all train tickets.

There is one daily train to Budapest departing at 1.57am (€35). There are 10 daily trains to Baia Mare; one to Timişoara via Oradea (€9); three to Bucharest via Oradea or Baia Mare (€15); one to Cluj-Napoca (€8); and one daily to Constanţa (summer only).

A taxi from the station to Piaţa Libertăţii costs €1.

ŢARA OAŞULUI
☎ 261

Ţara Oaşului, literally 'Land of Oaş', refers to the geographical depression in the eastern part of Satu Mare district. The origin of the name is unclear although some say that Oaş is derived from the Hungarian word *vos* (iron), named after the supposed brutish, ironlike nature of the region's inhabitants. It certainly has a Wild West feel.

Several villages in the region cut loose in May/June during the **Festival of Sâmbra Oilor**, which curiously celebrates the sheep departing for mountain pastures.

Turţ

The northern village of Turţ, 27km northeast of Satu Mare, is a colourful small town with houses painted chocolate-box pastels. Its centrepiece is a magnificent, new **Orthodox church** built and paid for by the town's 2300 families. Seven domes grace it and the interiors are painted with stunning scenes from the Old and New Testaments. It took five years to build and was finished in 2001.

Turţ once boasted Romania's finest **pălincă factory**, producing the fiery plum brandy almost identical to traditional Romanian *ţuică* except that it was distilled more than three times. The now-deserted factory is opposite strawberry fields, at the southern end of the village.

The remainders of the town's mining history lie in the southeastern part of Turţ. From Satu Mare, follow the northbound Budapest road to Turulung village. Turţ is signposted on the right just after the village. There's no hotel or restaurant here.

Negreşti-Oaş & Around

Heading southeast from Turţ, through the lakeside **Călineşti-Oaş**, you come to **Negreşti-Oaş**. The main reason for stopping in this small village is to visit the **Open-air Museum** (Muzeul Satului Oşenesc; admission €0.30; 10am-5pm Tue-Sun). Its small collection includes a traditional farm and pig sty from Moişeni, a wine press from nearby Oraşu Nou, and a felting mill and washing whirlpool, methods still used by villagers to wash clothes and rugs. There's also a small **Oaş History Museum** (Muzeul Ţării Oaşului; Str Victoriei) in the village.

Four kilometres south of Negreşti-Oaş is **Vama**, historically a ceramics and pottery centre of which little evidence remains today. **Valea Măriei**, 2.5km west, is a small Alpine resort.

Four kilometres northwest of Negreşti-Oaş (off the Călineşti road) is **Bixad**, a 200-year-old hilltop monastery. It has great views and a beautiful church, which has just completed renovation work.

Sleeping & Eating

Popas Turistic Lacu Albastru (☎ 839 047; cabins €15) Located 1km southwest of Călineşti-Oaş, opposite Albastru Lake, Popas Turistic has nine four-bed cabins, communal showers and a small bar–grill. You can camp at Popas Turistic or on the field opposite for €3.

Cabana Pintar (☎ 857 155; s/d/ste €17/23/29) As well as providing accommodation, this cabana, in Valea Măriei, also has a restaurant.

To reach the more attractive **Cabana Valea Măriei** (☎ 857 155; d/apt €23/29) and **Cabana Teilor** (d/apt €23/29), turn right along the forest track, immediately opposite Cabana Pintar. Cabana Teilor, at the end of the left fork, has a tennis court and a restaurant. Breakfast not included.

Getting There & Away

There are buses daily except Sunday from Satu Mare to Negreşti-Oaş (1½ hours), from where they continue to Turţ. This area is difficult to reach without private transport, so you may have to flag down a lift or jump on a horse and cart.

Moldavia

With thickly forested hills and tranquil valleys undulating off into the horizon, Moldavia mixes the rich folklore, beauty and turbulent history of Transylvania and the quietly appealing, bucolic paradise of Maramureş into its own fusion of the best of Romania. Cavort through the countryside on horse-drawn carts, stopping to gawk at the world-famous medieval painted monasteries. Hike or ski over eye-popping mountain terrain. Then urbanise in Iaşi and Suceava, where the first generation to have no vivid memories of Ceauşescu is rapidly developing a taste for fine food, shopping and late-night indulgence.

In 1359, under Prince Bogdan of Cuhea, Moldavia became the second Romanian principality to divorce itself from the Hungarians. During the 18th century the region served as a refuge for thousands fleeing persecution in Hungarian-ruled Transylvania. Ştefan cel Mare (Stephen the Great) and his son Petru Rareş erected fortified monasteries and churches throughout Bucovina, many of which have survived centuries of war and enjoy Unesco World Heritage status. Mired under Turkish rule after Petru Rareş' defeat in 1538, Moldavia was finally united with Wallachia by Alexandru Ioan Cuza in 1859. Almost immediate cultural and economic growth followed and the modern Romanian state was born, with Iaşi as its capital.

Moldavia used to be much larger. Bessarabia, the area east of the Prut River, was annexed by Russia in 1812. Despite being recovered from 1918 to 1940 and again from 1941 to 1944, Bessarabia is now split between Ukraine and the Republic of Moldova. Northern Bucovina is now in southwestern Ukraine.

Romanians refer to Moldavia as 'Moldova' (the Slavic form of Moldavia), a Stalinist legacy and point of confusion for visitors. Neighbouring Moldova is referred to as the 'Republic of Moldova'.

HIGHLIGHTS

- Hike (or ski) the dizzying **Ceahlău** (p268) and **Rarău** (p280) mountains

- Endeavour to keep the car on the road while driving into the mind-bending **Bicaz Gorges** (p269) and its 'neck of hell'

- See if the dead tree stumps outnumber wild ducks in mysterious **Lacu Roşu** (p269)

- Ponder the beauty and longevity of the **painted monasteries** (p275) around Suceava

- Delve into small-town life and bond with endearing locals in **Rădăuţi & Marginea** (p278)

★ Rădăuţi & Marginea

★ Painted Monasteries

★ Rarău Massif

★ Ceahlău Massif

★★ Bicaz Gorges

Lacu Roşu

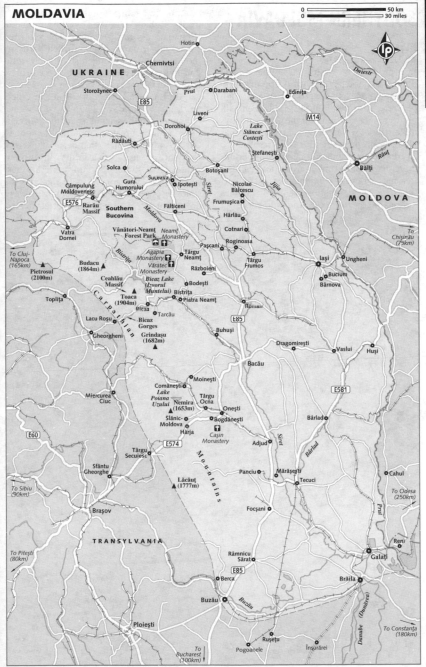

MOLDAVIA

| 0 | 50 km |
| 0 | 30 miles |

UKRAINE

Hotin
Chernivtsi
Storožynec
E85
Prut
Darabani
Ediniţa
M14
Liveni
Dorohoi
Rădăuţi
Lake Stânca-Costeşti
Ştefaneşti
Botoşani
Bălţi
Solca
Gura Humorului
Suceava
Ipoteşti
Nicolae Bălcescu
Câmpulung Moldovenesc
Rarău Massif
E576
Southern Bucovina
Frumuşica
Hârlău
MOLDOVA
Fălticeni
Cotnari
To Chişinău (75km)
Vatra Dornei
Vânători-Neamţ Forest Park
Neamţ Monastery
Paşcani
Roginoasa
Iaşi
Ungheni
To Cluj-Napoca (165km)
Pietrosul (2100m)
Budacu (1864m)
Agapia Monastery
Vărateç Monastery
Târgu Neamţ
Războieni
Târgu Frumos
Bucium
Bârnova
Ceahlău Massif
Bicaz Lake (Izvorul Muntelui)
Bodeşti
Bistriţa
Toplita
Toaca (1904m)
Piatra Neamţ
Roman
Bicaz
Tarcău
Lacu Roşu
Bicaz Gorges
Buhuşi
E85
Gheorgheni
Grindaşu (1682m)
Dragomireşti
Vaslui
Huşi
Bacău
Moineşti
Comăneşti
Lake Poiana Uzului
Târgu Ocna
E581
Miercurea Ciuc
Nemira (1653m)
Oneşti
Bârlad
Slănic-Moldova
Bogdăneşti
E60
Hârja
Caşin Monastery
Adjud
Târgu Secuiesc
E574
Mărăşeşti
Tecuci
Cahul
Sfântu Gheorghe
Lăcăuţ (1777m)
Panciu
Siret
Bârlad
To Odesa (250km)
To Sibiu (90km)
Focşani
Braşov
Mountains
TRANSYLVANIA
Reni
To Piteşti (80km)
Râmnicu Sărat
Galaţi
E85
Berca
Brăila
Buzău
Buzău
Danube (Dunărea)
To Constanţa (180km)
Ploieşti
To Bucharest (100km)
Ruşeţu
Pogoanele
Însurăţei

Carpathian Mountains
Bistriţa
Moldova
Siret
Jijia
Prut
Prut
Răut
Dniestr

MOLDAVIA

SOUTHERN MOLDAVIA

IAŞI

☎ 232 / pop 326,502

Iaşi (pronounced 'yash') has an energy and depth of character that would be instantly giddying if one had the power to see through concrete. Those without this endowment will need a few days to pinpoint the numerous joys of Romania's second-largest city. Iaşi's past as Moldavia's capital (since 1565) has resulted in a city dotted with fabulous buildings, important monasteries, parks and unpretentious cultural treasures. As one of Romania's largest university towns, its population seemingly doubles during the academic year, when students from

around the country flood the streets with a liveliness that defies their position in one of Romania's poorest provinces. The youthful, cosmopolitan atmosphere, fuelled partly by thousands of foreign students, is quickly extinguishing the lingering socialist ways and blasé attitude of the town's service industry. Moreover, it's the perfect staging area for travellers heading into Moldova, 20km away.

Founded in the second half of the 14th century, Iaşi has a great cultural tradition due to the stream of scholars that began clustering here in the early 17th century. Prominent names from the city's prolific literary past such as Vasile Pogor, Ion Creangă and the riotously popular poet Mihai Eminescu adorn dozens of streets, busts, memorial houses,

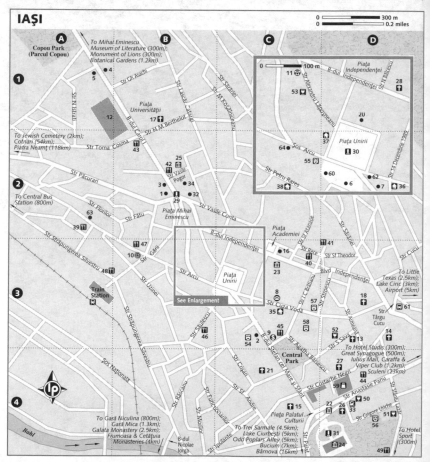

museums and an old linden tree. The first Romanian language newspaper was published here in 1829 and the country's first university was founded in 1860.

Iaşi's map-dot ballooned after being named the capital of modern-day Romania, when Moldavian ruler Alexandru Ioan Cuza united Wallachia with Moldavia in 1859 and christened the new university after himself. Bucharest usurped Iaşi in 1862, but it was relinquished briefly when the government, following the lead of King Ferdinand and Queen Marie, sought refuge here during WWI. During this period, Iaşi's notorious history of anti-Semitism took root with the birth of the League of National Christian Defence – the predecessor of the despicably fascist Iron Guard.

Modern Iaşi is among Romania's most vibrant cities, teeming with beautiful people, restaurants, bars and hot night spots. Each year the university honours its librarian-turned-celebrated-poet at the National Mihai Eminescu Symposium. For something less cerebral, try to catch Iaşi Days during the second week in October. Originally a week-long religious event devoted to Saint Parascheva, it has mushroomed into a street party, fuelled by a river of *must* (p53).

Orientation

To reach Piaţa Unirii from Iaşi's Gară Centrală train station, walk northeast along Str Gării two blocks, then turn right onto Str Arcu. From Piaţa Unirii, B-dul Ştefan cel Mare runs southwest past the Mitropolia Moldovei (Moldovian Metropolitan Cathedral) to the Palatul Culturii (Palace of Culture). The bus station (Autogara Vest) is one kilometre west down Str Străpungerea Silvestru from the train station.

MAPS & PUBLICATIONS

Amco Press' *Iaşi* city map (€3.35) is satisfactory but, for anal-retentive detail, indulge in Cartographia's *Iaşi* (€5.50). Free entertainment listings *24-Fun* and **Tot o Dată** (www.totodata .ro in Romanian) are found in shops, cafés and restaurants throughout the city.

Information

For general information and directory assistance, dial ☎ 951. Or better yet, get your host to dial. it's all in Romanian.

BOOKSHOPS

Eurolibris (☎ 210 858; B-dul Carol I, 3-4; ✆ 9am-5pm)
Junimea (☎ 412 712; Piaţa Unirii 4; ✆ 10am-6pm Mon-Fri, 9am-4pm Sat)

CULTURAL CENTRES

British Council (☎ 316 159; Str Păcurari 4; ☺ 1-7pm Mon, Tue & Thu, 10am-4pm Wed & Fri) In the same attractive building as the Mihai Eminescu Library.

French Cultural Centre (☎ 267 637; www.ccf.tuiasi .ro in French; B-dul Carol I, 26; ☺ 9am-noon & 1-6pm Mon-Thu, 9am-4pm Fri) Holds film screenings, theatre workshops and concerts and has a *mediathèque*.

Goethe German Cultural Centre (☎ 214 051; info-goethezentrum@catv.embit.ro; B-dul Carol I, 21; ☺ noon-6pm) Organises cultural events and has an extensive library.

EMERGENCY

For any emergency within in the city, dial ☎ 112.
Sfântu Spiridon University Hospital (☎ 240 822; B-dul Independenţei 1) The city's largest hospital.

INTERNET ACCESS

Bar-Cafe Internet (B-dul Ştefan cel Mare 8; per hr €1.50; ☺ 24hr) Inside the mall; smoky, dark and full of glassy-eyed gamers.
Take Net (Şoseaua Arcu 1; per hr €0.60; ☺ 24hr)

MONEY

ATMs are abundant in the centre.
Raiffeisen Bank (B-dul Ştefan cel Mare 2; ☺ 8.30am-6.30pm Mon-Fri, 9am-2pm Sat)

POST

Post office (☎ 212 222; Str Cuza Vodă 10; ☺ 8am-7pm Mon-Fri, 8am-1pm Sat) Iaşi's poste restante.
Telephone centre (Str Alexandru Lăpuşneanu; ☺ 8am-8pm Mon-Fri, 8am-3pm Sat) Has fax services.

TOURIST INFORMATION

Iaşi has no official tourist office.
Cliven Turism (☎ 258 326; www.reservation.ro; B-dul Ştefan cel Mare 8-12; ☺ 9am-6pm Mon-Fri, 9am-2pm Sat) The adept English-speakers here can arrange Antrec rural accommodation, wine tours, trips to the Bucovina monasteries and car hire.
Meridian Turism (☎ 211 060; meridian_turism@ yahoo.com; B-dul Ştefan cel Mare 1C; ☺ 9am-5pm Mon-Fri, 9am-noon Sat) Also agents for Antrec.

Sights

PIAŢA UNIRII TO PIAŢA PALATUL CULTURII

Standing in the ubiquitous Piaţa Unirii (Union Square), start your tour by sidling into the newly refurbished **Hotel Unirea** and taking the elevator to the lucky 13th-floor cafeteria where – weather permitting – you'll be able to identify many of the city's notable landmarks all the way to the hilltop monasteries on the

southern outskirts. In front of Hotel Unirea stands a bronze **statue of Prince Alexandru Ioan Cuza** (1820–73), unifier of Wallachia and Moldavia.

On the western side of the square is **Hotel Traian** (1882), a neoclassical building designed by Gustave Eiffel, who went on to build a somewhat popular tower in Paris a few years later. The **Natural History Museum** (B-dul Independenţei 16; ☎ 201 339; admission adult/child €1.10/0.90; ☺ 9am-3pm Tue, Thu & Sat, 9am-4pm Wed, Fri & Sun) has a modest collection of stuffed beasties, in addition to hosting travelling exhibitions. Alexandru Ioan Cuza was elected prince here in 1859. Opposite is the baroque **Costache Ghica House**, where Romania's first university was founded in 1860 – now serving as office space.

One block west at B-dul Independenţei 33 is **St Spiridon's Monastery** (1804). The body of Grigore Ghica III, killed in 1777 for opposing the Turks, lies inside the monastical complex, minus the head, which presumably came to rest in the sultan's sitting room.

The hectic, tree-lined B-dul Ştefan cel Mare leads directly southeast from Piaţa Unirii to the monumental Palace of Culture (opposite). Along this way is the prominent **Moldavian Metropolitan Cathedral** (built between 1833 and 1839). With a cavernous interior painted by Gheorghe Tattarescu, it's Romania's largest Orthodox cathedral and thus a busy place of worship. You can forget seeing its interior during Iaşi Days, when most of Moldavia's able-bodied pilgrims flock here to stand in line day and night for the chance to view the body of their beloved St Paraschiva, the patron saint of the cathedral and Moldavia. The saint's body is trundled out for this brief period each year. Additionally, the cathedral has a coffin said to contain the bones of St Friday.

Opposite is the **central park**, lined with bronze busts of eminent literary figures, where proud boyfriends pay artists to sketch portraits of their girlfriends and painters vend their work. Across the park is the **National Theatre** (1894–96). A majestic statue of its founder, poet Vasile Alecsandri (1821–90), monitors the front entrance for scalpers. The theatre was built according to the designs of Viennese architects Helmer and Fellner.

The boulevard's main attraction is the fabulous **Church of the Three Hierarchs** (Biserica Sfinţilor Trei Ierarhi; ☺ 9.30am-12pm & 1-5.30pm), which is currently suffering from acute scaffolding-itis both inside and out, due to years'-long painstaking

ŞTEFAN CEL MARE

It's a rare day when a Romanian doesn't speak the name 'Ştefan cel Mare' (Stephen the Great, 1457–1504), not only because he was the closest thing to a superhero that Moldavia has ever had, but his name adorns squares, boulevards, streets, statues and landmarks in virtually every city. During his reign as Prince of Moldavia, he repulsed forces from Poland and Hungary and his heroic resistance against the Ottoman Empire was admired throughout Europe. Pope Sixtus IV awarded Ştefan the Atheta Christi (*Champion of Christ*) award. Although it's said that he untiringly fathered over 20 illegitimate children, Ştefan was nevertheless considered holy enough for canonization by the Romanian Orthodox Church under the name 'The Right-believing Voivod Stephen the Great and the Saint'. When he wasn't building a battle record of 34 and two, he erected 44 churches and monasteries, several of which are now Unesco World Heritage sites. Strong, battle-savvy leadership ran in Ştefan's family; his cousin Vlad (Dracula) Ţepeş, though distinctly less pious in temperament, also fought – or, more accurately, frightened off – the Turks during his reign as Prince of Wallachia.

restoration. Fortunately, the unique exterior, embroidered in a wealth of intricate patterns in stone, can be appreciated – if not satisfactorily photographed – through the obscuration. In its original form, the exterior was covered in gold, silver and lapis. Built in 1637–39 by Prince Vasile Lupu, ostensibly to buy his way into heaven, it was damaged by Tartar attacks in 1650, but its dizzying mix of western Gothic, Renaissance and eastern motifs has been carefully restored.

Inside the church are the marble tombs of Prince Vasile Lupu and his family (to the left), Prince Alexandru Ioan Cuza (to the right), and Prince Dimitrie Cantemir. The adjacent Gothic hall is a **museum of 17th-century frescoes** (admission €0.60; ☉ 10am-4pm Tue-Sun). In 1994 the church reopened as a monastery. The three saints are celebrated here on 30 January with an all-monk choir performance.

At the southern end of B-dul Ştefan cel Mare stands the giant neo-Gothic **Palace of Culture** (Palatul Culturii; ☎ 218 383; admission adult/child per museum €0.70/0.50, all four museums €2.25/1.50; ☉ 10am-4.30pm Tue-Sun). Although many of the 365 rooms are closed to visitors, a combined ticket allows entry to its four museums.

The **Gheorghe Asachi Library**, and the four admirably stocked museums it houses, provide a superb diversion. The **Ethnographic Museum**, one of the best in the country, has exhibits ranging from agriculture, fishing and hunting to winemaking, as well as traditional costumes and rugs. The **Art Museum** is split into two galleries: the Galeria de Artă Românească, with over 20 works by Romanian artist Nicolae Grigorescu and others including Moldavian Petre Achiţemie; and the Galeria de Artă Universală,

exhibiting foreign works. Highlights of the **History Museum** include portraits of all of Romania's rulers since AD 81. Various mechanical creations and musical instruments are displayed in the less colourful **Science & Technical Museum**. Lastly, the furnishings and staircase in the entrance and main hall are something of an attraction in and of themselves, when they aren't being sullied by the kiosks and floor-to-ceiling display booths that sprout during frequent conventions and expositions.

The Palace of Culture was built between 1906 and 1925 and was formerly the administrative seat of the town. It was built on the ruins of the **old princely court**, founded by Prince Alexandru cel Bun (r 1400–32). Some remains of the court have been preserved beneath the concrete flooring of the neighbouring outdoor Summer Theatre.

In front of the palace on Piaţa Palatul Culturii is an equestrian **statue of Ştefan cel Mare**, unveiled in 1883. A **memorial** to Iaşi's heroes who died in 1989 stands by the entrance to the palace grounds. Opposite is the **Museum of Old Moldavian Literature** (☎ 0747-499 403; Str Anastasia Panum 54; admission €0.25; ☉ 10am-5pm Tue-Sun), housed inside the 17th-century Dosoftei House. Dosoftei was the metropolitan ruler of Moldavia between 1670 and 1686 and was responsible for printing the first church liturgy in the Romanian language (1679).

Behind Dosoftei House is **St Nicolas' Royal Church** (Biserica Sfântul Nicolae Domnesc), founded by Ştefan cel Mare in 1492. Little remains of the original church, which was restored and extended by Prince Antonie Roset in 1677, then rebuilt by French architect André Lecomte de Noúy in 1884.

JEWISH IAŞI

In the 19th century Iaşi was one of the great centres of Jewish learning in Europe. The world's first professional Jewish theatre opened here in 1876. A **statue** of its founder, Polish composer and playwright Avram Goldfaden (1840–1908), stands in the central park on B-dul Ştefan cel Mare. More than one third of the city's population at this time was Jewish, served by 127 synagogues. The most (in)famous Jewish scapegoat to come out of Iaşi was Magda Lupescu (1896–1977). During her time as the unlikely mistress-then-wife to King Carol II and head of the goon-squad arm of his National Renaissance Front, she was something of a scourge to the quickly growing anti-Semite group, the Iron Guard, enthusiastically using their own thuggish tactics against them, including murder. The press referred to her as 'the she-wolf'. Lupescu and Carol II fled Romania in 1940, just ahead of Hitler.

Today only two synagogues remain open in Iaşi. The **Great Synagogue** (1671) is barely visible amid the concrete apartment blocks surrounding it at Str Elena Doamna 15. There is a small museum inside the synagogue, but contact the **Iaşi Jewish community** (☎ 214 414) in advance to visit it. In front of the synagogue is a monument to the victims of the 1941 pogrom.

Many of the victims of the Iron Guard's pogroms were buried in four concrete bunkers in the **Jewish Cemetery** (Cimitirul Evreiesc; admission €2.85) on Mountain Hill (Dealul Munteni), west of the centre off Str Păcurari. There's another pogrom monument there, as well as the second, very small synagogue. It's a €2 taxi ride from the centre.

MONASTERIES & CHURCHES

Iaşi has a motherlode of religious architecture: there are 47 Orthodox churches, seven monasteries, three Catholic cathedrals, one Lippovan church and two synagogues, with several more churches standing half-built and forlorn, waiting for donations so that they can be completed. Entry to all churches and monasteries is free.

In addition to the churches and monastery mentioned in the previous section, the fortified **Golia Monastery** (Str Cuza Vodă), built in late-Renaissance style and surrounded by rose gardens, is definitely worth a visit. The monastery's walls and the 30m-high tower at the entrance shelter a weathered 17th-century church, noted for its vibrant Byzantine frescoes and intricately carved doorways. The bastions of the surrounding wall were added in 1667. The complex was damaged by fire several times and closed completely between 1900 and 1947. It regained monastery status in 1992 and is still undergoing major reconstruction.

Within the complex is a **memorial house** to writer Ion Creangă (1837–89), renowned for his short stories based on Moldavian folklore. He lived here between 1866 and 1871.

From Golia Monastery, head south along Str Armeană. On the right at No 22 you'll pass a small stone-and-brick **Armenian Church** (Biserica Armeană; 1395), considered the oldest church in Iaşi. Extensive renovations – which

have begun anew – have stripped off most of the original Armenian architecture. At the southern end of Str Armeană, turn right to **St Sava's Monastery** (Mănăstirea Sfântul Sava; Str Costache Negri 41), a small painted-brick church (1625). If instead you turn left along Str Costache Negri, you'll come to the 19th-century **Bărboi Monastery**. The church was built in 1841 on the site of a 17th-century church. Not only is the trompe l'oeil–painted interior worth a lingering gander, but the grounds are refreshingly free of construction activity!

UNIVERSITY & AROUND

B-dul Carol I is unsurprisingly a zoo of student activity, with people racing around campus, studying in parks and cafés and squashed into trams and maxitaxis, far beyond Geneva Convention directives. They hustle to and from student ghettos where up to six people share 16-sq-metre dorm rooms during the academic year (ponder *that* the next time you're complaining about a few nights in a full hostel!). An assortment of university buildings and literary museums hold worthwhile treasures, ranging from fascinating to kitschy.

Behind the **Student Cultural House** on Piaţa Mihai Eminescu is the Students' House park, the centrepiece of which is the **Voievodes Statuary**. These fantastic crumbling statues of Moldavia's princes were moved here from the university courtyard in the 1960s. In pairs stand Moldavia's first prince, Dragoş (r 1352–

53), and Alexandru cel Bun (r 1400–32); Moldavia's greatest prince, Ştefan cel Mare (r 1457–1504) with Mihai Viteazul (r 1600); Petru Rareş (r 1527–38) and Ion Vodă cel Viteaz (r 1572–74); and Vasile Lupu (r 1634–53) with Dimitrie Cantemir (r 1693). The boys, and everyone scurrying down Carol I, are supervised by a nearby massive **statue of Mihai Eminescu**, in a possible homage to the vigilant spirit of librarians everywhere.

One block north, along the serene Str Vasile Pogor, is the **Pogor House Literary Museum** (Casă Pogor; ☎ 410 340; Str Vasile Pogor 4; admission €0.30; 10am-5pm Tue-Sun), Vasile Pogor's 1850s mansion, where meetings of the literary society were held from 1871. On its lovely grounds stand **rows of busts** of some of the more eminent members of the society, including dramatist Ion Luca Caragiale (1852–1912) and poet Vasile Alecsandri (1821–90).

Another block further north is the heart of Iaşi's student life. On the east side of the boulevard is Piaţa Universităţii, backed by the **Forty Saints Church**, and on the west is the huge neoclassical **Alexandru Ioan Cuza University**, where the founder of the fascist Iron Guard, Corneliu Codreanu (1899–1938), once studied. The arcades of the main hall (aka The Hall of the Lost Footsteps) are decorated in frescoes by the painter Sabin Balasa.

Further north is **Copou Park** (Parcol Copou), laid out between 1834 and 1848 during the princely reign of Mihail Sturza. Poet Mihai Eminescu (1850–89) allegedly wrote some of his best works beneath his favourite linden tree in this park. The tree still stands, behind a 13m-high **monument of lions** opposite the main entrance to the park. A bronze bust of Eminescu sits in front of it.

Nearby is the **Mihai Eminescu Museum of Literature** (☎ 0747-499 405; admission €0.30; 10am-5pm Tue-Sun), housed in a distressingly modern white building. The museum recalls the life and loves of Eminescu, Romania's most cherished writer and poet. Though he was married, his great love was Veronica Micle, herself married to a vicar. They outlived their spouses but never married each other due to Eminescu's deteriorating health – he also considered himself too poor to offer Veronica what she deserved (sniff, sniff). A **bust** of Veronica faces another of her lover and his favourite linden tree at the end of Junimea Alley in the park.

Iaşi is home to Romania's first and largest **Botanical Gardens** (Grădină Botanică; admission €0.50;

10am-9pm), on the western side of Parcul Exposiţiei. Dating from 1856, they offer 21km of shady lanes, rose and orchid gardens, greenhouses, natural springs and a lake. Also on the grounds is Vasile Lupu's 'Church of the Living' (1638). While the landscaping isn't winning any awards, these are the city's premier strolling and picnicking grounds.

SOUTH OF THE CENTRE
Heading out of town along Şoseaua Bucium (DN 224), you pass the **Odd Poplars Alley**, lined with 25 poplar trees and marking another spot where poet Mihai Eminescu sought inspiration and brooded over late library books.

Southwest of the centre in the Nicolina district are three of Iaşi's most tranquil monasteries, which make for a pleasant hike (or take a short ride on Bus 9 downhill from the Palace of Culture). All of these monasteries are open for visitors (admission free), though there's a sporadically enforced photo fee at Cetăţuia Monastery. Perched on top of Miroslavei Hill is the 16th-century fortified **Galata Monastery**, founded in 1582 by Prince Petru Şchiopul, who is buried in the church. The ruins of the monks' living quarters and a Turkish bath are all that remain today. Though the new church, built in 1847, lacks extravagant frescoes and overdone ornamentation, it's still an impressive brick and stone edifice, with a devilishly sensitive echo that will reduce visitors to tiptoes and lip-reading conversations.

East of Galata at the northern end of Str Cetăţuia are the ruins of **Frumoasa Monastery** (1726–33). Built by Prince Grigore Ghica II, it served as a royal residence in the 18th century. From here, go south along Str Cetăţuia and follow the steep, narrow, resolve-testing road to the top of Dealul Cetăţuia to the impressive **Cetăţuia Monastery**. Founded in 1669, it's one of the few structures from this time to survive wholly intact. Numerous Moldavian paintings and frescoes done in the neo-Byzantine tradition remain within the church, though some were damaged by Ottoman Turkish reprisals. The 17th-century royal palace is now a museum of religious art, while the Gothic Room features its original hexagonal brick pavement. The complex also has wine cellars and a Turkish bath.

Activities
There's a serviceable **swimming pool** (piscină; Str Anastasie Panu 29-31; admission €4.20; 1-5pm & 6-10pm

Mon, Wed & Thu, 8.30am-noon & 1-5pm & 6-10pm Fri-Sun) around the corner from Hotel Moldova. **Lake Ciric**, at the city limits on the road to the airport, may look innocuous, but the water is generally too dirty for a proper swim. However, it's still a serene place for a stroll. A bus that passes the lake departs east of the centre, just off Str Sărăriei. **Lake Ciurbeşti**, 5km south of the city near the village of Ciurbeşti, is better for a dip and the surrounding area is a favourite weekend escape for city-weary locals.

Sleeping

Despite taking a few gratifying steps forward in recent years, Iaşi's accommodation options remain sub-par. Be prepared to fork out more money than you'd planned for reasonable comfort. Visit www.antrec.ro for rural accommodation at around €10 to €20 per person.

Hotel Sport (☎ 232 800; Str Sfântu Lazăr 76; d/tr €17/19.30) You'll need an athlete's fortitude to stomach this grotty, musty but cheap place directly behind the Palace of Culture. Call ahead as it is often booked with visiting athletes.

Casa Bucovineana Hostel (☎ 222 913; Str Cuza Voda 30; s/d/ste without bathroom €19.60/30/56) Recent renovations have made the rooms here more palatable. Some doubles have in-room showers. Breakfast not included.

Hotel Continental (☎ 211 846; Piaţa 14 Decembrie 1989; s/d with bathroom €30/40.50, without bathroom €25.50/30) Following the city-wide trend, the rooms here have been freshened up, but then so have the prices. Shared bathrooms are clean, private bathrooms are new and immaculate – worth the upgrade. Get a room away from the noisy street.

Hotel Studis (☎ 0332-107 152; www.hotelstudis.ro; Str Otilia Cazimir 10; d €31.50; 🖳 🕭) Brand new, with the aroma to prove it, this hard-to-find place lurks at the end of a tiny alley behind the giant Universitatea Petre Andrei building. All rooms have internet. Breakfast not included.

Majestic Pension & Restaurant (☎ 255 557; www.pensiuneamajestic.ro; Str Petru Rares 7; s/d €47/57; 🖳) Just completed, this modern, family-owned four-star *pensiune* is impeccably central. Moody, low-lit rooms have minibar, internet and large bathrooms. The on-site restaurant has a French-trained chef.

Little Texas (☎ 272 545; Str Moara de Vant 31; s/d €65/78; www.littletexas.org; 🖳 🔀) Located halfway between the city and the airport (10 minutes' drive from the centre) and run by Lone Star state expats, this four-star hotel embraces all things Texas, including a certain president. Plunder such amenities as internet, cable television, minibar, balcony with panoramic city views, room service, laundry service and an authentic Tex-Mex restaurant, serving the richest mud cake in Romania.

Hotel Traian (☎ 266 666; Piaţa Unirii 1; s/d/ste €63/79/97) The multilingual staff here will make you feel at home in this elegant hotel, designed by Gustave Eiffel. The high-ceiling rooms are awash in old-world comfort, with large, modern bathrooms.

Eating

The gruff, Soviet-style service that once prevailed in Iaşi eateries is fading fast. Restaurants are appearing at an eye-popping rate, staffed by fresh-faced university students who will invariably speak passable English.

CAFÉS & QUICK EATS

There are fast-food courts inside and across the street from the huge Western-style Iulius Mall, 3km southeast of the centre.

our pick Family Pizza (☎ 262 400; Str IC Brătianu 31; mains €1-2.50; 🕑 8am-11pm) With the rest of Europe gaily butchering pizza – Italy notwithstanding, obviously – you might not expect Romania to be home to some of the best pizza in the world. Family Pizza stands out, offering 25 types of pizza and an adjoining pastry shop. The terrace is the perfect summertime hangout, while waitresses in dangerously short skirts serve up pizza heaven to a backdrop of Romanian pop music. Delivery service available.

Casa Universitatilor (☎ 340 029; B-dul Carol I, 9; mains €1-3) Meals are geared for destitute students, but the lime-tree–festooned terrace is great for a lazy beer.

La Cao (☎ 240 485; Str Arcu 8; mains €2-3; 🕑 11am-11pm) An excellent Chinese restaurant with a lengthy English menu and speedy service.

Metro Pizza (☎ 276 040; Str Străpungerea Silvestru 8; mains €2-3; 🕑 9am-1am) Resist that just-off-the-train McDonald's urge and dine at this joint opposite the station.

RESTAURANTS

Trei Sarmale (☎ 237 255; Str Bucium 52; mains €1.20-5; 🕑 9am-2am) Revel in your touristness! This traditional Romanian restaurant embraces kitsch with its folkier-than-thou décor and live music, but the food is mouthwatering. Set inside a 17th-century inn about 5km south of the town centre, this could be a fun place for a small group if you get into the mood. The Bucium winery (p263) outlet shed is across the road. Call before you head out there as it is often booked by tour groups. Take a taxi (€3) or bus 30 or 46 from Piaţa Mihai Eminescu and ask the driver for Trei Sarmale.

Pub Baron (☎ 254 547; Str Sfântu Lazăr 52; mains €2-4; 24hr) It looks like a pub, with its cosy wooden interior impregnated with beer suds, but it's also a great eating option, particularly the summer terrace. The menu is heavy on fresh grills, cooked in brick ovens, but there are many salads and fish dishes too.

Casa Pogor (☎ 243 006; Str Vasile Pogov 4; mains €2-4; 11am-midnight) Where to sit? In the insanely cosy (if damp) basement that used to house the famed Junimea wine cellar; the elegant main dining hall furnished with antiques; or on the multi-tiered terrace overlooking a quiet square? Focus on the great atmosphere and ignore the dreadful service. While not extraordinary, the food is good and the menu (with some veggie meals) unexpectedly varied.

Ginger Ale (☎ 276 017; Str Săulescu 23; mains €2-5; 11am-1am) This place feels like an old-fashioned lunch café with antique furniture and a cosy dining room. Take advantage of 20% to 50% discounts daily from noon to 4pm. Dinner is classier, with reservations recommended on weekends.

Casa Bolta Rece (☎ 212 255, Str Rece 10; mains €2-6; 11am-11pm) Set in a 1786 house, Iaşi's formerly top dining experience has been overshadowed by spunky newcomers, but is still worth a novelty visit. The patchy service ranges from curt to slap-you-on-the-back friendly. Eat in the wine cellar or on the pleasant terrace and skip the starchy dining room. English, both written and spoken, is adventurously scant.

Caraffa (☎ 262 626; 2nd level, Iuliuis Mall, B-dul Tudor Vladimirescu; mains €3-7; 11am-11pm) The menu offers Italian and Mexican, but you should aim for the Romanian dishes and the salads, which are startlingly fresh. Try the *Tochitura Moldovenesca* – roughly 'Moldovan Heart Attack' – with pork, traditional cheese, polenta, eggs, bacon and sausage. Time of death…

Casa Lavric (☎ 229 960; Str Sf Atanasie 21; mains €4.60; 11am-11pm) Up the hill from Casa Bolta Rece is one of Iaşi's newest dining options, owned by singer-musician Laura Lavric and decorated in classic musical instruments. The menu – including a short vegetarian page – is devoid of English, but the staff's language skills more than make up for this. Reservations required on weekends.

SELF-CATERING

The central **market** (8am-4pm) is your fresh fruit and vegetables source. Below street level, it has entrances on Str Costache Negri and Str Anastasie Panu (look for the glass dome). There's a small supermarket above in Hala Centrala. **Billa** (Str Arcu 29; 8am-10pm Mon-Sat, 9am-6pm Sun) is a fully stocked supermarket with takeaway food and communist-era long lines. Smaller, 24-hour markets line B-dul Ştefan cel Mare.

Drinking

Quinta Café (☎ 268 447; Str Sfântu Sava 10; admission Sat & Sun €3.50; noon-midnight Sun-Thu, noon-5am Fri & Sat) High ceilings, cushy sofas, antique furniture and wood panelling give this lounge bar a familiar feel; in fact, this is a restored grand house. The weekday subdued music and lighting gives way to pounding bass and darkness on weekends.

City Café (Str Sfântu Lazăr 34; 24hr) A distinctly more adult crowd frequents this high-tech, blue-lit, ultracool bar to imbibe its many cocktails.

Terasa Corso (☎ 276 143; www.corsoterasa.ro; Str Alexandru Lăpuşneanu 11; 11am-midnight Mon, 9am-1am Tue-Sun) The concept of a bar is stretched in this huge, amphitheatre-shaped pub with a well-tended garden in the middle. Its spaciousness is great for large groups. Free wi-fi.

Blackout (☎ 0744-900 604; Str Grigore Ureche 1-3; 8am-2am) This basement bar-cum-discotheque has the ventilation of a bank vault, but it flouts cookie-cutter Euro-Pop for refreshingly varied music sets that bounce from Madonna and Katrina and the Waves to Ray Charles and Fat Boy Slim.

Entertainment

Vasile Alecsandri National Theatre (☎ 316 778; Str Agatha Bârsescu 18) and the **Opera Română** (☎ 211 144) are in the same impressive neo-baroque building. Alternative performances are held in the smaller studio hall (*sală studio*) upstairs, which has its entrance on Str Cuza Vodă. For advance bookings go to the **Agenţia de Opera** (☎ 255 999; B-dul Ştefan cel Mare 8; 10am-5pm Mon-Sat). Tickets cost from €1.50, with 50% student discounts.

Luceafărul Theatre (☎ 315 966; Str Grigore Ureche 5) Behind Hotel Moldova, this theatre puts on very interesting pieces geared to children and young people.

Philharmonic (Filarmonica; ☎ 212 509; www.filarmonicais.ro; Str Cuza Vodă 29; ☯ box office 10am-1pm & 5-7pm Mon-Fri) When the much-revered Iaşi State Philharmonic Orchestra is in town its concerts are massively popular; it performs 200 concerts per season, across Romania and abroad. Concerts of some kind are usually held on Friday nights. Tickets start at €2 with 50% student discounts.

Viper Club (Iulius Mall; ☯ 24hr, disco 11pm-4am) This rainy-day entertainment emporium features bowling alleys, billiards and video games. Come night-time it turns into a house-music haven.

Cinema Victoria (☎ 268 012; Piaţa Unirii 5; tickets €1.50) See your favourite Hollywood schlockbuster, with Romanian subtitles, in this massive, stark theatre with a megaphone-quality sound system.

Shopping

Str Alexandru Lapusneanu, leading from the northwest corner of Piaţa Unirii, has interesting used book and antique stores.

Hala Centrala (Str Anastasie Panu) Has kiosks selling jewellery. Look for dirt-cheap pieces made from Romanian amber (*chihlimblar*) set in Turkish silver – glass and knick-knacks.

Iulius Mall (B-dul Tudor Vladimirescu) Fully westernised, it will alleviate the strongest case of culture shock.

Moldova Mall (Str Anastasie Panu) This flashy new place was nearing completion at the time of writing.

Getting There & Away
AIR

Tarom (☎ 267 768; www.tarom.ro; Str Arcu 3-5; ☯ 9am-5pm Mon-Fri) has daily flights to Bucharest. **Carpatair** (☎ 215 295; www.carpatair.ro; Str Cuza Voda 2; ☯ 9am-6pm Mon-Fri) has flights to Timişoara and onwards from Monday to Saturday.

BUS

The **central bus station** (Autogara Iaşi Vest; ☎ 214 720), completely hidden behind the Auto Centre building, has become busier in recent years with all the private maxitaxi firms opening, so it has started to expand – in chaos. Buses, microbuses and maxitaxis leave from the main lot, but some companies have started using the Billa supermarket parking lot, a kilometre away. Innumerable daily buses or maxitaxis leave for Târgu Neamţ (€2.85), Suceava (€5.15), Bucha-

rest (€11.40), Bacău (€4.60) and Piatra Neamţ (€4.30). Occasional maxitaxis to Târgu Neamţ depart from Billa and a mishmash fleet of regional maxitaxis leaves at whim from a parking lot directly across from the train station – ask any of the touts on hand for details.

Maxitaxis to Chişinău leave from outside the Billa supermarket five times daily, while up to six daily buses (*much* slower) to Chişinău (€5.70) depart from the bus station. If you don't acquire a Moldovan visa (p355) in advance, have a completed visa application (www.travisa.com/Moldova/moldova_visa.pdf) ready at the border or risk being left behind by an impatient bus driver.

Tickets for the daily bus to Istanbul (€80, 24 hours), which departs from Billa, are sold at **Ortadoğu Tur** (☎ 257 000; Str Arcu) across the street.

TRAIN

Characters from a Kafka novel must have devised Iaşi's train station system. Nearly all trains arrive and depart from the Gară Centrală **train station** (Str Garii), which is also called Gară Mare and Gară du Nord. Trains to Chişinău, however, depart from the Gară Niculina (also called Gară International) on B-dul Nicolae Iorga, even though tickets for the trip must be bought from the so-called Gară Mică (the one with the sign saying 'Niculina' on it), 500m south on Aleea Nicolina. The **Agenţie de Voiaj CFR** (☎ 242 620; Piaţa Unirii 10; ☯ 7.30am-8.30pm Mon-Fri) sells advance tickets, while the train station only sells tickets one hour before departure.

There are six daily trains to Bucharest (€14.50, seven hours), one to Galaţi and Mangalia and three slow, crowded trains to Timişoara (16 hours), affectionately known as 'Horror Trains' by locals. Trains throughout the day go to Ungheni, a border town just 21km away. *Do not* take this train unless you already have a visa for Moldova, as there are no visa processing facilities at this crossing.

If you are planning to visit the monasteries in Southern Bucovina, take a train to Suceava (two hours) then change trains, or take a train bound for Oradea and get off at the Gura Humorului stop. To get to Târgu Neamţ from Iaşi you have to change at Paşcani.

Getting Around
TO/FROM THE AIRPORT

Sadly a taxi – or possibly an entrepreneurial airline-crew van-driver – is your only option for getting into the city. A taxi to Piaţa

Unirii should cost about €4.50. Don't let a van driver charge you more than five lei (€1.50) per person. You'll probably be dropped at Hotel Traian on Piaţa Unirii.

Bus 35 and any number of maxitaxis run between Piaţa Eminescu and Copou Park, stopping outside the university en route. Tram 3 runs between the bus and train stations and the centre.

AROUND IAŞI

Rolling hills, lush vineyards and pretty villages surround Moldavia's 'town of seven hills'. At the **Bucium winery**, 7km south of Iaşi, though no organised tours are available you can taste a variety of sweet wines as well as Bucium champagne out of the tiny roadside outlet shop across from Trei Sarmale (p260). Bring an empty water bottle, the bigger the better, which can be filled with the wine of your choice for a pittance. At weekends, Iaşi residents picnic in **Bârnova Forest**, 16km south of the city, accessible by train.

Cotnari

Cotnari is 54km northwest of Iaşi. Its **vineyards**, dating from 1448, are among the most famed in Romania, producing four to six million bottles of sweet white wine a year and exporting to the US, Canada, England, Italy, Spain and Japan, among others. Legend says Ştefan cel Mare described it as 'wine given by God'.

There was a Geto-Dacian stronghold on Cătălina Hill (280m) in Cotnari from the 4th century BC. In 1491 Ştefan cel Mare built a small church in the village and in 1562 a Latin college was founded. During this period French monks arrived bringing grape stocks, which they planted in the village, and by the end of the 19th century Cotnari wine had scooped up prizes at international exhibitions. King Michael I started building a small **royal palace** here in 1947, abandoning it half-complete the same year. It was restored in 1966 and today houses Cotnari Winery's administration.

The **Cotnari Winery** (☎ 232-730 393; www.cotnari.ro; ☼ 7am-3.30pm) hosts wine-tasting sessions and tours of its cellars and factory (by appointment only). Every year on 14 September, wine connoisseurs flock to Cotnari to get ripped in celebration of the harvest.

The winery's most popular wines include white table wines such as *frâncuşa* (dry), *cătălina* (semisweet), and the sweet, golden *grasă* and *tămâioasă* dessert wines.

From the Cotnari shop in the village, continue on the road towards Botoşani and Hârlău. The factory is 200m further on the left.

Visit **Cliven Turism** (☎ 258 326; www.reservation.ro; B-dul Ştefan cel Mare 8-12; ☼ 9am-6pm Mon-Fri, 9am-2pm Sat) or go to www.antrec.ro to arrange private rooms in Cotnari. There are *cazare* (room) signs in windows throughout the village.

Three local trains from Iaşi to Hârlău stop at Cotnari daily (1¾ hours). Maxitaxis leave hourly.

TÂRGU NEAMŢ
☎ 233 / pop 20,496

You know that notoriously dusty, god-awful town 40km from where you grew up that made everyone audibly gag at the mere utterance of its name? That's Târgu Neamţ (literally, German Market Town). The only reasons to come here are to visit the impressive ruins of a 14th-century citadel and stock up before heading to the Neamţ, Agapia and Văratec Monasteries.

Considered Moldavia's finest fortress, **Neamţ Citadel** (Cetatea Neamţului; ☎ 0744-702 415; admission adult/child €0.80/0.40; ☼ 10am-6pm Tue-Sun), perched just high enough above town to make you wish there was a chairlift, is admirably huge, sufficiently ancient and fun to poke around in. Built by Petru I Muşat in 1359, it was attacked by Hungarians in 1395 and by Turks in 1476, and then conquered by Polish forces in 1691, which explains its semi-ruined state. To get there, follow signs for 'Cetatea Neamţului' along B-dul Ştefan cel Mare. You must park your car at the foot of the citadel and take the calf-blasting but pleasant hike up the hill.

Casa Arcaşului (☎ 790 699; Str Cetaţii 40; s/d/tr €19.80/22.70/25.50) is a bright hotel-restaurant with a quiet, exotic location at the foot of the citadel. Rooms are simple but decent, equipped with cable TV, comfortable beds and small shower-toilet hybrids. The adjoining restaurant (mains €1.50 to €3.50) serves Romanian fare and has live music nightly.

Doina (☎ 790 270; www.hotel-doina.ro; Str Mihail Kogalniceanu 6-8; d €28.30), closer to the bus station, is an unremarkable place. Each of the tired but comfortable rooms has a balcony, minibar and cable TV. Breakfast is not included. The attached restaurant has a nice summer terrace.

After exiting Târgu Neamţ's **bus station** (☎ 790 474; Str Cuza Vodă 32), turn right for B-dul Mihai Eminescu and B-dul Ştefan cel Mare and turn left for the train station (1.2km away). There are eight daily buses and maxitaxis to Piatra Neamţ, six to Iaşi, two to both Braşov and Suceava, and five weekly to Bucharest. To reach the monasteries, there are five daily buses to Agapia, four to Văratec, three to Neamţ, and one each to Sihastrea and Gura Humorului. The train station is a lonely place, with only four daily trains to Paşcani, where changes to Iaşi and other destinations are possible.

MONASTERIES AROUND TÂRGU NEAMŢ

☎ 233

Târgu Neamţ is ringed by beautiful monasteries noted not for their outstanding artistic treasures but rather as Romania's most active religious centres. Agapia and Văratec are called monasteries even though they house nuns. Visitors to this area are still regarded as strange and even inauspicious by the locals. It's best to lock your car, as theft and vandalism are not uncommon. In the villages of Agapia and Văratec, dozens of attractive homes have *cazare* signs in their windows, and guesthouses abound. To access the Văratec, Agapia and Sihla monasteries comfortably on foot, aim for a guesthouse on the road to Agapia, which offers a shortcut back-road leading to Văratec.

Neamţ Monastery

Neamţ Monastery is the oldest and the largest male monastery in Romania. Founded in the 14th century by Petru I Muşat, it doubled as a protective citadel. Ştefan cel Mare built the large church we see today; it remains a classic example of the Moldavian style initiated in his time. The painting in the porch and narthex dates from Muşat's time, while in the altar, the nave and the room in which the tombs are located, the painting dates from 1497. In the fortified compound are a **medieval art museum** and a **memorial house** to novelist Mihail Sadoveanu (1880–1961). The library, with 18,000 rare books, is the largest of any Romanian monastery.

Three daily buses make the 15km journey from Târgu Neamţ, yet you'll probably find it easier to hitchhike along the road (15B) toward Ceahlău.

Agapia Monastery

The turn-off for **Agapia Monastery** (☎ 244 736; admission adult/child €0.80/0.50) is 4km south of Târgu Neamţ towards Piatra Neamţ. Within the confines of the monastery walls live 400-plus nuns who toil in the fields, tend vegetable gardens, weave carpets and make embroideries for tourists.

Agapia consists of two monasteries. The larger and flashier **Agapia din Vale** (Monastery in the Valley) is at the end of the village of Agapia itself. Built by Gavril Coci (Vasile Lupu's brother) between 1642 and 1644, its current neoclassical façade dates from reconstructions between 1882 and 1903. Between 1858 and 1861, the young Nicolae Grigorescu (1838–1907) painted every reasonable square centimetre of the church's interior with stunning murals, featuring heebie-jeebie eyes that stare at you whichever way you turn. A small **museum** (☽ 10am-7pm) off to the right contains icons from the 16th and 17th centuries. The main buildings are modern and of little architectural interest, but wandering around the grounds, past the well-tended gardens of the nuns' houses, is a treat. Slow, funds-starved construction is ongoing at Agapia din Vale, disrupting their usual capacity to house visitors.

Agapia din Deal (Agapia on the Hill; admission free), also called Agapia Veche (Old Agapia), is the second monastery, 2.2km from the main monastery complex (follow the road to the right, go through the charming old section of Agapia, full of wooden homes, to the signposted dirt road veering off to the right). It's absolutely worth the trip uphill to see this quiet, humble monastery – but only in a powerful car and not after rain, as some sections of the gravel road are extremely steep. Less ornate than Agapia din Vale, and with only modern frescoes, it nonetheless charms with its peaceful ambience and wooden buildings. It was built by Lady Elena, wife of Petru Rareş, from 1642 to 1647.

A dirt road in front of the lower monastery veers to the left towards the small and highly worthwhile **Sihla Monastery** (Schitu Sihlei; admission free). Some 30 monks live here, on a small plateau in the hills. The central church is small, wooden and sombre, almost touching in appearance. Mother Nature's assistance has made this one of the area's more visually pleasing religious sites, mainly due to the nearby cave of Pious Saint Teodora. Teodora supposedly lived in a small cave for 60 years; it's possible to visit her 'home', eerily lit by candles, among the rocks and boulders above the hermitage. Seeing the slab of rock she called a 'bed' certainly gives one pause. Her relics are now in Pecherska Monastery in Kyiv.

Sihla can house a limited number of visitors but, with no phone, reservations have to be made through divine channels.

Take care not to disturb, or be disturbed by, the clutch of *pustnici* (extreme hermit monks) in the area, who regularly drop to their knees in prayer when the urge strikes – side of the road, middle of the forest, the loo – and remain in that position for hours, day and night.

All buses between Târgu Neamţ and Piatra Neamţ stop in Săcăluşeşti village, from where it is a 6km hike along a narrow road to the lower monastery; the upper monastery is a further 30-minute walk uphill.

Three daily buses also go from Târgu Neamţ to the lower monastery, listed on bus timetables as 'Complex Turistic Agapia'. From Piatra Neamţ, there are two buses daily.

Văratec Monastery

Six hundred nuns live at **Văratec Monastery** (admission free), 7km south of the Agapia turn-off along 15C. Founded in 1785, the complex houses an **icon museum** and a small embroidery school. The **grave of poet Veronica Micle**, Mihai Eminescu's great love, lies within the monastery walls. She committed suicide on 4 August 1889, two months after Eminescu's death. Whitewashed in 1841, the main church incorporates neo-classical elements in its design. Compared to other nearby monasteries, Văratec looks like a modern villa crossed with a small botanic garden. The interior is lavishly decorated in paintings, frescoes, silver and bronze impressions and an opulent chandelier.

You can hike to Văratec from Agapia (two hours) and to **Secu, Sihăstria and Schitu Sihlei Monasteries** along clearly marked trails. There are four daily buses to Văratec from Târgu Neamţ.

Vânători-Neamţ Forest Park

The forest and woods surrounding these monasteries and stretching north to the village of Groşi are protected as the **Vânători-Neamţ Forest Park** (☎ 206 001; www.vanatoripark.ro). Its headquarters and information centre are in Văratec, on the main road to the monastery. A visit to the **information centre** (☺ 8am-4pm Mon-Fri) is highly recommended before any drive or hike through the region; it has detailed maps of hiking trails and can alert you as to whether any side roads have been closed or blocked. Within the park is the small Dragoş

Vodă Bison Reserve, where six bison live in semicaptivity in an enclave open to visitors. There are also small reserves protecting old patches of oak and birch forest.

PIATRA NEAMŢ
☎ 233 / pop 107,875

Piatra Neamţ (German Rock), 43km south of Târgu Neamţ, is a pleasant, picturesque town, sunk in a valley and embraced by velvety round hills. Perched above the town to the east is the rocky Pietricica Mountain. To the southwest stands Cernegura Mountain, flanked by an artificial lake, Lake Bâtca Doamnei, at its westernmost foot. Cozla Mountain, which towers over Piatra Neamţ to the north, is now a huge park. It has enough going for it to offer a happy day's wandering, and makes a nice base for exploring the surrounding landscape.

The area around Piatra Neamţ has been settled since Neolithic times. In the 15th century Ştefan cel Mare founded a princely court here.

Orientation & Information

B-dul Republicii leads north from Piaţa Mareşal Ion Antonescu towards Piaţa Ştefan cel Mare, where most facilities are located. The old town is located immediately northwest of this square, at the foot of Cozla Mountain.

ATMs can be found, among other places, in hotels and along Piaţa Ştefan cel Mare; change travellers cheques at **Raiffeisen** (Piaţa Ştefan cel Mare 3; ☺ 8.30am-6.30pm Mon-Fri, 9am-2pm Sat).

Even if you don't need to post any letters, it's worth popping into the **post office** (☎ 232 222; Str Alexandru cel Bun 21; ☺ 7am-8pm Mon-Fri, 10am-1pm Sat) for its old-fashioned wooden interiors. There are several internet cafés in town – try super-cool **Tavernet** (Piaţa Ştefan cel Mare 1; per hr €0.60; ☺ 9am-midnight).

There's a tourist office in the lobby of **Hotel Ceahlău** (☎ 219 990; Piaţa Ştefan cel Mare 3; ☺ 7am-8pm) that is staffed by ladies short on English but long on the desire to help. If you become lost in translation, summon the infallibly helpful Gaby from the hotel's front desk.

Sights

Piaţa Ştefan cel Mare is the city's heart and one of Romania's more picturesque central squares. A **statue** of the beloved Ştefan cel Mare stands proudly among landscaped flowerbeds. Just west of here is a small pedestrianised square where the remains of Piatra Neamţ's historic

MOLDAVIA

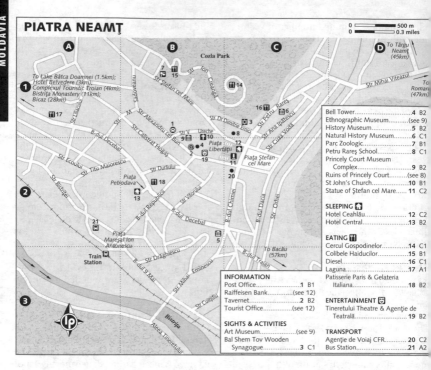

PIATRA NEAMŢ

0 — 500 m
0 — 0.3 miles

heart lie in a series of museums and historical buildings that are grouped into the **Princely Court Museum complex** (Curtea Domnească; ☎ 216 808; www.neamt.ro/cmj in Romanian; admission adult per museum €0.40; ☉ 10am-6pm Tue-Sun), founded in 1497 by Ştefan cel Mare.

Towering over the square is the lovely, sombre 1498 **St John's Church** (Biserica Sfântu Ioan) with its 10m-high bell tower. Just opposite are the small **Art Museum** and **Ethnographic Museum**. The art museum has mostly landscapes and still lifes, but the abstract art on the upper floor and modern, fanciful cityscapes in the 1st-floor section are interesting. Ask inside the museums for entrance to the archaeological digs across the street under the **Petru Rareş School** (Liceul Petru Rareş), where ruins of the princely court were found. Directly behind the school is **Bal Shem Tov Wooden Synagogue** (☎ 223 815; Str Dr Dimitrie Ernici; donations requested; ☉ 8am-noon Mon, Thu & Sat or by appointment). A visit here is very nearly a day trip, as arranging entrance can take half the day and the kindly old man who finally appears will jabber at you (in Romanian) for the other half. The original synagogue on this site was built in 1450 (only the foundation remains). The current

wooden structure dates from 1760. The tiny cluttered interior, decorated with Jewish artefacts and paintings, will be beautified with funding from the World Monuments Fund Jewish Heritage Grant Programme. If you have trouble rousing anyone at the synagogue, try sticking your head in the wooden gate 20 metres down the hill and knocking on the office door.

The local **History Museum** (☎ 218 108; Str Mihai Eminescu 10; admission €0.40; ☉ 10am-6pm Tue-Sun) runs through the area's history from the Stone Age onwards. There is also a small **Natural History Museum** (Muzeul de Ştiinţe Naturale; ☎ 224 211; Str Petru Rareş 26; admission €0.40; ☉ 9am-5pm Mon-Sat).

Cozla Park is a sprawling, forested park north of the centre, popular with strollers and city-type hikers. On the way along Str Ştefan cel Mare is the tiny **Parc Zoologic** (admission €0.30; ☉ 9am-7pm), a seasonal, outdoor, surprisingly pleasant mini-zoo, with wolves and baboons

Festivals & Events

Every year at the end of May, Piatra Neamţ hosts a week-long **International Theatre Festival**, attracting theatre companies from all over Europe.

Sleeping

Search **Antrec** (www.antrec.ro) for lovely *pensiunes* guesthouses) outside the city; in general, they are more pleasant than the accommodation you'll find in town.

Hotel Ceahlău (☎ 219 990; Piaţa Ştefan cel Mare 3; s/d/ste €23/45.50/71; ⊠ ☐ ♿) Marring the town's skyline is this 12-storey three-star hotel. The upshot is that the bluer-than-blue rooms have balconies with excellent views. The 12th-floor bar is a family-friendly scenic outlook by day and a bachelor-only lap-dance bar by night.

Hotel Belvedere (☎ 261 470; Str Petru Movilă 325; s/tr €25/30) Another three-star, overwhelmingly blue hotel option is the Belvedere, 3km north-west of the city, with an attached restaurant-bar (mains €1.50 to €3). The bright rooms have soft beds, refrigerator and cable TV.

Complexul Turistic Troian (☎ 241 444; eurotipo@ umbra.ro; Str Petru Movilă 270; d/tr/ste €30/38/48) Just 4km west of the city, this large 17-room complex has quiet, spacious, rustic-themed rooms and a fun two-floor dining hall with live music courtesy of a geezer with a Casio keyboard. All maxitaxis and buses from Piatra Neamţ to Bicaz will stop here upon request. Lake Bâtca Doamnei, a good swimming spot, is nearby. Breakfast is not included, but the restaurant does a fair-priced spread.

Hotel Central (☎ 216 230; www.hotelcentral.ro; Piaţa Petrodava 1-3; s/d/ste 38/54/70; ⊠ ☐) This huge concrete tower looks less dreary when lit up at night. Rooms are comfortably fur-nished, though due for renovation. Skip the exorbitantly priced post-communist dining room.

Eating & Drinking

There are several small cafés and pizzerias along Piaţa Ştefan cel Mare.

Patisserie Paris & Gelateria Italiana (☎ 234 330; B-dul Decebal 14; ⊠ 9am-9pm) Choose between su-perb *gelato* on one side and sumptuous pas-tries on the other.

Cercul Gospodinelor (☎ 223 845; Str Ion Creangă; mains €2-5; ⊠ noon-10pm) Located at the top of the road up to Cozla Park, this is a more modern Romanian option favoured for its panoramic views and tasty food.

Diesel (☎ 222 424; Str Petru Rareş 21; mains €3; ⊠ 9am-2am) A slick, pseudo high-tech place adorned in chrome and black leather, it has a wide and varied menu of inexpensive meals and slaps them out to the tune of thumping pop tunes;

the thumping turns to pounding late at night when it doubles as a bar/disco.

Laguna (☎ 232 121; B-dul Decebal 67; mains €4.50; ⊠ 10am-midnight) A recommended pizza joint, this modern place decorated in neon red and blues also has a few billiard tables. In the evening it doubles as a popular bar. It's on the second level, above the kids store.

Colibele Haiducilor (☎ 213 909; Str Ion Creangă 1; mains €4.50; ⊠ 8am-12am) An outdoor pub-restau-rant with oddly folk-costumed waitresses, set among an otherwise pleasant lush forest. The menu is limited to standard Romanian fare.

Entertainment

Performances at **Tineretului Theatre** (☎ 211 036; Piaţa Ştefan cel Mare 1) are usually held on week-end evenings; get your tickets at the Agenţie Teatrală adjoining the theatre.

Getting There & Away

The **Agenţie de Voiaj CFR** (☎ 211 034; Piaţa Ştefan cel Mare 10; ⊠ 7am-7.30pm Mon-Fri) sells tickets for the nine daily trains to Bacău, of which only the red-eye ends at Bucharest. There are also five daily trains to Bicaz. The **bus station** (☎ 211 210; Str Bistriţei 1) is near the train station. There are 11 daily maxitaxis to Bacău (€2.20) and Bu-charest (€9.40), and 11 buses and maxitaxis to Târgu Neamţ (€1.40). Two daily buses also go to Agapia and one to Gura Humorului. Other buses head to Suceava, Iaşi, Braşov, Miercurea Ciuc, Vatra Dornei and Gheorgheni.

BICAZ & THE CEAHLĂU MASSIF

☎ 233

This dizzyingly beautiful corner of western Moldavia is a relatively unexplored region offering great hiking opportunities and pic-turesque mountains and valleys. Together with the Bicaz Gorges and Lacu Roşu (p269), this area offers a varied tableau of Romanian landscapes.

Heading 24km west from Piaţa Neamţ, there's an unassuming turn-off to the rela-tively well-off village of **Tarcău**, which spreads out for 4km along a beautiful valley nestled between the Măgura Tarcău and Câmpilor mountain peaks. It feels cut off from time as it stretches lazily along the little Tarcău River. There's a pretty church and not much more here than peace, quiet and bucolic scenery.

Bicaz (population 9000), 4km further west on the confluence of the Bicaz and Bistriţa Rivers, is a sorry-looking town with little to

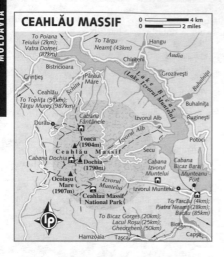

CEAHLĂU MASSIF

offer. Locals depend on the nearby giant and scary-looking concrete and (German-owned) asbestos factories west of town for survival, and it feels like a struggling industrial town. However, just north of here, along the road to Vatra Dornei is **Lake Bicaz** (Lacu Izvorul Muntelui; Mountain Spring Lake), which sprawls northward over 30 sq km. The hydroelectric dam (baraj) at the lake's southern end was built in 1950, with several villages being submerged in the process and the villagers relocated.

Near the dam, at the junction 4km north of Bicaz, is a turn-off for the twisting mountain road to Ceahlău (chek-lau). A right turn immediately after the bridge will bring you to **Munteanu Port** (☎ 671 350) on the western shores of the lake. There are paddle boats for hire here and nice picnic spots, too.

Next is the village of Izvoru Muntelui, which has no shops, so acquire any supplies you'll need, including water, in Bicaz. From here hiking trails begin to climb the stunning Ceahlău Massif, Moldavia's most spectacular mountain range. Go through the gate in the fence and after a five-minute climb you reach a little flat section with picnic tables, where two of the tracks begin, each going in opposite directions. A posted map illustrates how the trails meet at the peak of the Massif, without any cross-over, allowing for two unique hikes during ascent and decent. The menacing skull and crossbones on the map only applies to wintertime. With an early start and the requisite fitness level, the Ceahlău

Massif can be done in a single day. Be warned that going down can be just as punishing or weaker knees as going up. For those wanting to take it slower, **Cabana Dochia** (2-cot room, €4) sit welcomingly at the top with single and double rooms (though no showers) and a passable restaurant. You can also start/finish the hike in Durău and Ceahlău.

Durău (800m), on the northwestern side o the mountain, has a relatively strong touris infrastructure built around its spa and winte sports. A steep track (red stripes, one hour leads to **Cabana Fântânele** and from there oth ers lead towards Toaca Peak. There is also the small **Durău Monastery** (1830), a comple comprising two churches and quarters for the 35 nuns who inhabit it today. Visitors are welcome. The annual **Ceahlău Folk Festival** take place here on the second Sunday in August Shepherds come down from the mountains while locals don traditional dress.

In **Ceahlău** (550m), 6km north of Durău, are the remains of a palace built between 1639 and 1676, and an 18th-century wooden church.

Bypassing the mountain road from Bicaz and continuing north for another 24km, you come to **Grozăveşti**, a village with a wooden church typical of those in Maramureş. The church was built during the 20th century after the old church fell into the lake. Apparently, the day the church drowned the local village priest received a postcard from Maramureş. The postage stamp featured a wooden Maramureş church, thus inspiring him to build his new church in that style.

Sleeping

Campers can pitch their tents for free outside **Cabana Bicaz Baraj**, the first cabana you pass when entering Durău (430m) at the foot of the dam wall. The cabana has no rooms but serves snacks in its small café. **Cabana Izvorul Muntelui** (797m) has a few basic rooms. **Cabana Paulo** the first cabana you pass on the main road to Durău, has 16 places in one large room within a wooden chalet-style house. Cabanas in the area generally charge under €10 per person.

Durău itself has plenty of accommodation choices, from hotels to the numerous pensi-unes lining the main road.

Durău Monastery (☎ 256 583; www.ccpdurau.go.ro r per person €10) The nuns still take in the weary and blistered in the church-quiet villas or the nearby Pilgrim House. Rooms are basic but clean.

Pensiune Igor Ghinculov (☎ 256 503; s/d €10/20) Roughly 50m beyond Cabana Paulo, this friendly home has five double rooms with shared bathroom. Igor, who arranges accommodation in private homes elsewhere in the area, is talking retirement in the coming years, so be aware of a possible name change.

Hotel Bistriţa (☎ 256 578; s/d €16/20) On the first plateau of the mountain, this 40-room hotel-restaurant is up for complete renovation in time for the 2007 season. Be among the first to jump on the new beds!

Motel Gară (☎ 253 382; Str Republicii 8; s/d €18/18.50) Right beside the train station in Bicaz, it has a new modern wing of rooms. Breakfast is not included, but there's an on-site restaurant.

Getting There & Away

Five daily trains run between Bicaz and Bacău, all of which stop in Piatra Neamţ, and two of which continue to Bucharest. Buses and maxitaxis link Bicaz with Piatra Neamţ throughout the day; buses between Piatra Neamţ and Poiana (six daily), Gheorgheni (once daily) and Braşov (two daily) stop at Bicaz. All of these buses also stop at Tarcău and one daily bus trundles on to Izvoru Muntelui; otherwise it's a 4km hike to the village. From Durău, two buses go to Târgu Neamţ daily.

BICAZ GORGES & LACU ROŞU

Together with Transylvania's Transfăgărăşan road (see boxed text, p154), the road that slices through the **Bicaz Gorges** (Cheile Bicazului) 20km west of Bicaz is among Romania's most staggering and spectacular. The gorge twists and turns steeply uphill for 5km, cutting through sheer, 300m-high limestone rocks on its journey through the mountains. The narrow mountain road runs directly beneath the overhanging rocks in a section known as the 'neck of hell' (Gâtul Iadului). Dozens of artisans sell locally made crafts from stalls set up beneath the rocks and there are several places to park your car and sway around, head arched back in wonder. This entire stretch is protected as part of the Hăşmaş–Bicaz Gorges National Park (Parcul Naţional Hăşmaş–Cheile Bicazului).

A few kilometres west, you cross into Transylvania's Harghita County and immediately hit another splendid site of natural beauty, the resort of **Lacu Roşu** (Red Lake; Gyilkos tó in Hungarian). The lake is strangely filled with dead tree stumps that jut out of its murky waters at 45-degree angles and is considered one of Romania's weirdest natural wonders. Legend has it that the 'red lake' or 'killer lake' was formed from the flowing blood of a group of picnickers who had the misfortune to be sitting beneath the mountainside when it collapsed, crushing them to death. In fact a landslide did occur in 1838, eventually flooding the valley and damming the Bicaz River.

This thriving Alpine resort sprang up in the 1970s and is still a magnet for partiers and hikers from both Transylvania and Moldavia. There are dozens of hotels and villas here, as well as 24-hour stores, tourist markets and even a police station. It's a village without permanent residents. Though the resort is open all year round, in summer the area surrounding the lake can get noisy.

Lacu Roşu falls administratively under the Székely-dominated Harghita County, and the ever-resourceful Hungarians here have produced several useful multilingual guides and maps of the surrounding mountains, replete with trails and lots of useful information. These are available at the information kiosk by the side of the lake. The kiosk also has **boat hire** (2-person rowing boat per hr €2). There's even a trilingual sign posting the environmentally conscientious dos and don'ts of wild camping – rare in Romania.

A flat scenic track circles the lake, and other more demanding trails shoot up to the various peaks, all of which offer stunning views. Compared with the oft-travelled hiking trails of Transylvania, hikers and foreign tourists are relatively sparse here.

The main road continues another 26km to Gheorgheni (p168) via the Bucin mountain pass, another twisting snarl of beautiful mountain scenery.

Sleeping

Wild camping is permitted, every other house displays a *cazare* sign and there are plenty of hotels and villas to choose from.

Vila Bradu (☎ 0266-380 042; per person €9) Seconds from Lacu Roşu, near the church, this property has rooms and cabins available. Breakfast not included.

Jasicon Hotel (☎ 0266-380 080; s/d 23/29) This 40-bed hotel isn't a bad option, slightly away from the resort's busy centre along the uphill road near the police station. Rooms aren't anything to write home about, but there's a

MOLDAVIA

decent restaurant and bar, and hiking trails start directly outside the front door.

Getting There & Away

In addition to a daily bus from Gheorgheni, the daily Miercurea Ciuc–Piatra Neamţ and the twice daily Braşov–Piatra Neamţ buses all stop at Lacu Roşu.

SOUTHERN BUCOVINA

Southern Bucovina rivals Maramureş as a rural paradise, with the added perk of its plentiful Unesco-recognised painted churches, considered among the greatest artistic monuments of Europe. Wondrous religious art and fantastic churches notwithstanding, Southern Bucovina is bursting with folklore, picturesque villages and endless bucolic scenery.

Southern Bucovina embraces the northwestern region of present-day Moldavia; Northern Bucovina is in Ukraine. In 1775 the region was annexed by the Austro-Hungarian Empire and remained in Habsburg hands until 1918, when Bucovina was returned to Romania. Northern Bucovina was annexed by the Soviet Union in 1940 and incorporated into Ukraine, splitting families apart.

While coordinating transport between the remote villages can be challenging, there are plenty of alternatives to allow you to get the most out of your visit, including hitchhiking, biking, car hire or arranging a private tour.

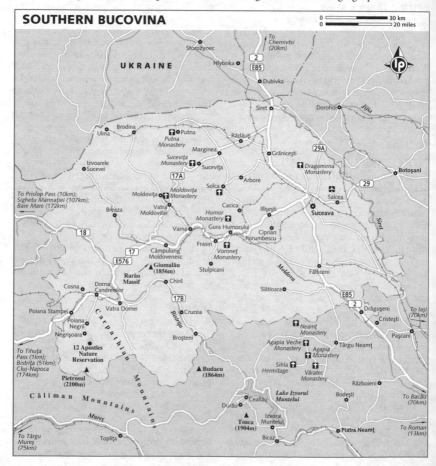

SUCEAVA

☎ 230 / pop 111,200

Barring the inevitable *ţuică* binge, Suceava won't exactly make your ears smoke with excitement. At first glance, it appears to be one concrete block connected to another by crumbling concrete promenades. Yet there's a palpable charm to the city that, combined with its worthwhile attractions, should leave visitors fulfilled. Furthermore, its stout and exceptional tourism infrastructure, unmatched outside of Transylvania, caters to every possible tourism desire in Bucovina and beyond.

The capital of Moldavia from 1388 to 1565, Suceava was a thriving commercial centre on the Lviv–Istanbul trading route. By the end of Ştefan cel Mare's reign in 1504, Suceava had approximately 40 churches. It fell into decline after the Turks bulldozed through in 1675.

During the Ceauşescu regime in the 1980s, Suceava became notorious for its toxic pulp and paper works (still in operation), which churned out 20 tonnes of cellulose and fibre waste a day, causing respiratory and nervous disorders known as Suceava Syndrome. Recognising that having the word 'syndrome' affixed to the city name was bad for PR and morale, civic leaders eventually installed new filters and pollution has greatly decreased. The local economy is still dependent on forestry, wood-processing, chemical production and mining for its survival.

The colourful Moldavian Furrier Fair is held here every year in mid-August. Alternatively there's Suceava Days (late June), yet another religious-holiday-turned-street-party, with biblical amounts of beer, street food and music.

Orientation

Piaţa 22 Decembrie is the centre of town. Suceava has two train stations, Suceava and Suceava Nord, both north of the centre and easily reached by trolleybus or maxitaxi.

From Suceava station, cross the street and buy a ticket at a kiosk for buess 2 and 4 or maxitaxis 6 and 9 to the centre of town. From Suceava Nord take bus 5 or maxitaxi 1 and 12 (pay the driver).

MAPS & PUBLICATIONS

Amco's *Suceava* includes a county map showing the location of the monasteries. There are several booklets and guides to the monasteries, some of which have rudimentary maps. A nicely illustrated and helpful booklet is *Bucovina…The Monastic Archipelago* (€3) published by Tipo and available at local bookshops.

Information

BOOKSHOPS

Alexandria (☎ 530 337; Str Mihai Viteazu 23; ✆ 8am-7.30pm Mon-Fri, 9am-5pm Sat)
Casa Cărţii (☎ 530 337; Str Nicolae Bălcescu 8; ✆ 9am-6pm Mon-Fri, 9am-2pm Sat)

INTERNET ACCESS

Assist (☎ 523 044; Piaţa 22 Decembrie; per hr €0.50; ✆ 9am-11pm) Also provides a range of printing and digital services.

MONEY

There are several ATMs on Piaţa 22 Decembrie and along Str Ştefan cel Mare.
Raiffeisen Bank (Str Nicolai Bălcescu 2; ✆ 8.30am-6.30pm Mon-Fri, 9am-3pm Sat) Provides the usual services.

POST & TELEPHONE

Post office (☎ 512 222; Str Dimitrie Onciu; ✆ 7am-7pm Mon-Fri, 8am-4pm Sat)
Telephone office (cnr Str Nicolae Bălcescu & Str Onciu; ✆ 7am-9pm Mon-Fri, 8am-4pm Sat)

TOURIST INFORMATION

Suceava is bursting with tourist resources. Start while you're still at home by visiting www.lasuceava.ro.
Ciprian Slemcho (☎ 0744-292 588; www.mtour.go.ro) Leading tours around Suceava and Maramureş for eight years, Ciprian is a specialist in both religion and history. He's a can-do kind of guy; if it's humanly possible he'll make it happen, including booking a room at no charge.
Infoturism (☎ 551 241; infoturism@suceava.rdsnet.ro; Str Mihai Eminescu 8; ✆ 8am-8pm) This is the official tourism office of Suceava county, headed by multilingual dynamo Mircea Tănase. It's *the* source on all things Romanian.
Unita Tour Suceava (☎ 523 024; unitatour.sv@unita-turism.ro; Str Nicolae Bălcescu 2; ✆ 8am-8pm Mon-Fri, 8am-5pm Sat) Inside Hotel Suceava, this small office can arrange day-long monastery tours with multilingual guides with just a few hours' notice for about €80 to €90 (€20 to €25 extra for guide) per group.

Sights

The bulky **House of Culture** (Casa de Cultură) is at the western end of the city's main square, Piaţa 22 Decembrie. North of the bus stop along B-dul Ana Ipătescu lie the foundations of the 15th-century **Princely Palace**. To the west

MOLDAVIA

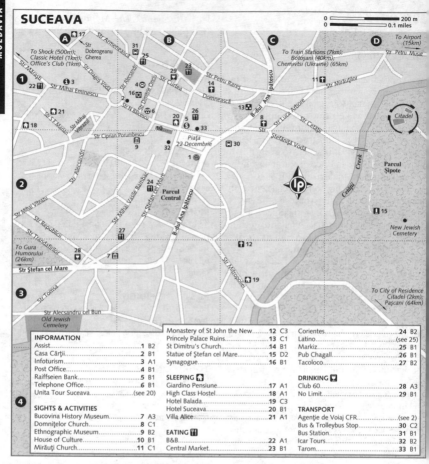

SUCEAVA

0 — 200 m
0 — 0.1 miles

is the impressive **St Dimitru's Church** (1535), built by Petru Rareș in an exciting, clubbed Byzantine style typical of 16th-century Moldavian churches. Traces of the original exterior frescoes can still be seen and the interior has been recently restored.

Approximately 250m northeast is the lovely **Mirăuți Church** (1375–91), the original Moldavian coronation church, which was rebuilt in the 19th century. This was the original seat of the Moldavian bishop, and it was here that Ștefan cel Mare became Moldavia's ruler. Of particular note is the *Prayer on the Mount of Olives* fresco in the nave. Another outstanding church is on the corner of B-dul Ana Ipătescu and Str Ștefaniță Vodă. Built by Vasile Lupu in 1643, **Domnițelor Church** (Princesses' Church)

is one of the city's loveliest monuments, despite its unfortunate location on a busy street. There is an old well in the small graveyard surrounding it.

West of Piața 22 Decembrie is Hanul Domnesc, a 16th-century guesthouse that now houses an **Ethnographic Museum** (☎ 216 439; Str Ciprian Porumbescu 5; admission adult/child €0.60/0.30; 9am-5pm Tue-Sun), with a good collection of folk costumes. Next to the post office on Str Dimitrie Onciul is the town's only surviving **synagogue** (1870). Prior to WWII, 18 synagogues served the local Jewish community.

Following Str Ștefan cel Mare south past **Parcul Central** (Central Park) is the worthwhile **Bucovina History Museum** (Muzeul Național al Bucovinei; ☎ 216 439; Str Ștefan cel Mare 33; admission adult/child

€0.90/0.30; 9am-5pm Tue-Sun). The exhibits trace life here from prehistoric times but come to an abrupt end at 1945. Old paintings hang in rooms that formerly glorified the communist era.

The **Monastery of St John the New** (Mănăstirea Sfântu Ioan cel Nou; 1522) off Str Mitropoliei, was the ultimate destination for pilgrims during Suceava Days. The paintings on the outside of the church are badly faded but give you an idea of the church frescoes for which Bucovina is famous.

CITY OF RESIDENCE CITADEL

At the end of the winding Str Mitropoliei, 3km from the centre, is the 1388 **City of Residence Citadel** (Cetatea de Scaun; admission adult/child €0.45/0.30; 9am-6pm), a citadel fortress that in 1476 held off Mehmed II, conqueror of Constantinople (now Istanbul). It's a vast complex and the highlight of many visitors' trips to Suceava. Massive stretches of the rectangular structure remain. A tacky disco and outdoor terrace have been set up nearby.

The original fortress, known as Muşat's Fortress, was built by Petru I Muşat when Suceava was Moldavia's capital. It had eight square towers and was surrounded by defensive trenches. Ştefan cel Mare developed it further, building 4m-thick, 33m-high walls around it so it was impossible to shoot an arrow over. In fact it was never taken, despite many attempts. In 1675 the fortress was finally blown up by the Turks. A century later it was partially dismantled and the stones used to build houses. Restoration work started on the fortress in 1944 and continues to this day, in tandem with archaeological exploration. Today the fortress, which looks as if it has been sliced in half, is slowly sinking into the soft ground below.

The citadel is accessible by car by following Str Mitropoliei to the end or by foot via Str Cetăţii, crossing the bridge and following the footpath that leads to the huge **equestrian statue** (1977) of Ştefan cel Mare. The lavish New Jewish Cemetery is behind the statue.

Sleeping

High Class Hostel (525 213, 0723-782 328; www.classhostel.ro; Str Mihai Eminescu 19 & Str Aurel Vlaicu 195; per person €14.50;) Moldavia's only real hostel. Monica, your interminably good-natured, problem-solving host, can arrange monastery tours. The rural Str Aurel Vlaicu

location will close in November 2007 in favor of a city centre location: a flowery villa on Str Mihai Eminescu, five minutes walk from the bus station.

Villa Alice (522 254; www.villaalice.ro; Str Simon Florea Marian 1; s/d €14.50/23;) The welcome is curt, but the small bright rooms have comfortable beds, refrigerators and very clean bathrooms. Some rooms have balconies.

Hotel Suceava (521 079; www.unita-turism.ro; Str Nicolae Bălcescu 2; s/d unrenovated €25/34, s/d/tr renovated €32/43/52) Smack in the city centre, it has old-fashioned but perfectly comfortable rooms, with new bathrooms. Refrigerators available upon request. Reservations strongly recommended in summer.

Giardino Pensiune (531 778; www.giardino.ro; Str Dobrogeanu Gherea 2; s/d €28/35;) Opened in 2005, when we visited this three-star *pensiune* still reeked of brand new everything: bathrooms, communal kitchen, mattresses, towels, terrace with grill, you name it. The breakfast (included) is overwhelming. Just 200m from the bus station. Psst! 'Prices are negotiable for backpackers'!

Classic Hotel (510 000; www.classic.ro; Str Universităţii 32; d 2-star €38, s/d 3-star €61/65;) Rooms here are simple, modern and very clean. Cheap student bars are nearby, while the centre is about a kilometre away, easily accessible by maxitaxi. Show this book and get 10% off your room.

Hotel Balada (520 408; www.balada.ro; Str Mitropoliei 3; s/d/ste €59/70/111.50;) One of the top hotels in the region, this three-storey hotel offers elegance and comfort over pure luxury; rooms have everything you need but are simply furnished.

Eating

There are several fast-food joints on the eastern side of Piaţa 22 Decembrie. The **central market** (cnr Str Petru Rareş & Str Ştefan cel Mare) is close to the bus station.

Corientes (Str Ştefan cel Mare 56) Pastries, snacks, tiramisu and much loved cookies. The selection is refreshed twice a day. On the ground floor of Bucovina Mall.

Markiz (520 219; Str Vasile Alecsandri 10; mains €2-4; 8am-11pm) Its once grand reputation diminished, the prices at this Middle Eastern joint remain budget-friendly and the terrace is a favoured place to have a few drinks.

Latino (523 627; Str Curtea Domnească 9; mains €2-8; 11am-midnight) Hailed by locals as the best pizza in town. The classy, subdued décor is accented by impeccable service and a dazzlingly varied menu that runs the gamut from 25 different kinds of pizza (€5; with real mozzarella!), first-rate pasta (€4) and steaming fresh fish dishes (€5 to €8). Yes, they deliver.

Pub Chagall (☎ 0723-961 127; Str Ştefan cel Mare; mains €3-7; ☺ 11am-1am) At complete odds with the cold, massive concrete blocks surrounding it is this cosy cellar pub and diner. Though it has a full menu of tasty meals, it's mostly used as a drinking hole. Behind Leonardo shoe store.

B+B (☎ 523 554; Str Mihai Eminescu 18B; mains €4; ☺ 10am-10pm) This cosy restaurant, using fresh ingredients, is a top choice for backpackers. A massive prix fixe lunch is just €4.50 or order from the à la carte menu.

Tacoloco (☎ 220 032; Str Ştefan cel Mare 47; mains €4; ☺ 9am-11pm). Mexican, Turkish and the ubiquitous pizza are served up in this popular eatery near Central Park. Warning: 'salsa' means ketchup.

Drinking

Office's Club (www.officesclub.ro; Str Viitorului 11; 6pm-3am) Hard to get to and even harder to find – the club is hidden from street view, sandwiched between two huge buildings – this mature, but funky environment is nurtured by weekend DJs and good drinks. There are tiny couch alcoves for initiating, or escaping from, saucy trysts and the metal chairs are works of art. Take maxitaxi 1, 2, 3 or 4 and tell the driver 'Office's Club'.

ourpick Club 60 (☎ 209 440; Str Ştefan cel Mare; ☺ 1pm-1am) Emanating some of the smoothest vibes around, this loft-style lounge-bar has wooden floors, antique furnishings, comfy sofas and billiard tables. Soul and hip-hop reign, with the occasional appearance by live jazz and blues bands. Enter from the back of the Universal Department Store and climb the stairs to the 2nd floor.

No Limit (Str Curtea Domnească 3; mains €4; ☺ 8am-11pm) More restaurant than bar, this new establishment serves decent German food, yet keeps an admirable bar crowd with its good music and pleasant staff.

Shock (Al Saturn; admission €0.75, ladies free; ☺ 8pm-4am) The undisputed best club in Suceava for the young crowd. The music and party atmosphere here is becoming legendary. Near Piaţa Mica.

Getting There & Away

AIR

Suceava's **Ştefan cel Mare Airport** (www.aeroport suceava.ro) is about 15km northeast of the centre.

Tarom (☎ 214 686; www.tarom.ro; Str Nicolae Bălcescu 2; ☺ 9am-7pm Mon-Fri, 9am-2pm Sat) has four weekly flights to Bucharest. **Carpatair** (☎ airport 529 559; www.carpatair.com) doesn't have an office in Suceava, but flies to Timişoara and points beyond three times a week.

BUS

The **bus station** (☎ 216 089) is in the town centre at Str Armenească. Bus and maxitaxi services include 13 daily to Gura Humorului (€1.40), eight to Botoşani (€1.40), six to Rădăuţi (€1.40), five to Iaşi (€4.50) and Vatra Dornei (€3), four to Bucharest (€9.20) and three to Târgu Neamţ (€2.30). Tickets for international destinations are sold at window 4. Several daily buses go to Chernivtsi in Ukraine (€5.70) and three a week to Chişinău in Moldova (€8.60).

TRAIN

The stop for buses to the train station is east of Piaţa 22 Decembrie, across B-dul Ana Ipătescu, next to McDonald's.

Suceava's two train stations Gară Burdujeni (aka Gară Sud or Gară Principala) and Gară Nord, are north of the city centre. The **Agenţie de Voiaj CFR** (☎ 214 335; Str Nicolae Bălcescu 8; ☺ 7am-8pm Mon-Fri) sells advance tickets. The majority of trains will originate or terminate at the newly spruced Gară Burdujeni.

Train service includes ten to Gură Humorului (€2.10, 70 minutes) – get off at the Gură Humorului Oraş stop, six to Vatra Dornei (€7, 3¼ hours), eight to Iaşi (€4.20, two hours), five to Timişoara (€18, 14 hours) and five daily to Bucharest (€15.50, seven hours). To get to Moldoviţa, change at Vama.

Getting Around

The central bus and trolleybus stop is at the eastern end of Piaţa 22 Decembrie; all buses and trolleybuses to and from the two train stations arrive at/depart from here. Buses 2 and 4, and maxitaxis 6 and 9 run between the centre and Gară Sud (Burdujeni). To reach Gară Nord, take bus 5 or maxitaxis 1 and 12. Beware, these maxitaxi routes are notorious for lurking pickpockets.

Icar Tours (☎ 524 894; www.icar.ro; Str Ştefan cel Mare 24; ☺ 9am-6pm Mon-Fri, 9am-1pm Sat) has the largest fleet of hire cars in town and the best prices.

BUCOVINA MONASTERIES

☎ 230

Pilgrims and the wicked unite in their appreciation of the arresting beauty of Southern Bucovina's monasteries, many of which have the unusual distinction of being painted on the outside as well as the inside. While some can be accessed by public transport, and all can be visited on a private tour (see p271), your thumb plus a wad of 1 leu notes, cigarette donations and a little patience will get you within walking distance of the monastery of your choice. Smoking and wearing shorts and hats (for men) are forbidden and women are required to cover their shoulders. All monasteries have an extra charge during high-season for cameras and video cameras (about €2).

In addition to the accommodation options listed here, just about any tour agent in Suceava can book rural *pensiunes*. Alternatively, point-and-click your way to your bed at www.ruraltourism.ro or www.antrec.ro.

Dragomirna Monastery

In the village of Mitocul Dragomirna, 12km north of Suceava, is this lovely, small **monastery** (admission/camera €1.20/1.70; ⏲ 8am-8pm) founded in 1608–09 by the scholar, calligrapher, artist and bishop Anastasie Crimca. The intricate rope lacing around the side of the main church (1627) represents the unity of the Holy Trinity and the short-lived unification of the principalities of Moldavia, Wallachia and Transylvania in 1600. The church tower is 42m high.

Dragomirna's treasure, displayed in the **Museum of Medieval Art** in the monastery grounds, includes a beautifully carved candle made by Bishop Crimca, ornamental carved cedar crosses mounted in silver-gilt filigree, and a large number of missals and religious scripts.

Dragomirna remained inhabited during the Habsburg and later the communist purges on the Orthodox church. Crimca's

---

THE PAINTED BEAUTIES

The painted churches of Southern Bucovina were erected at a time when northern Moldavia was threatened by Turkish invaders. Great popular armies would gather inside the monasteries' strong defensive walls, waiting to do battle. To educate, entertain and arouse the interest of the illiterate soldiers and peasants, who were unable to enter the church or understand the Slavic liturgy, well-known biblical stories were portrayed on the church walls in cartoon-style frescoes.

Most amazing in these vast compositions are the realistic portrayals of human figures against a backdrop not unlike the local landscape (the forested Carpathian foothills). Some frescoes have been damaged by centuries of rain and wind, but more often than not the intense colours have been duly preserved, from the greens of Suceviţa to the blues of Voroneţ and the reds of Humor. Natural dyes are used – sulphur for yellow, madder for red, and cobalt or lapis for blue.

All Orthodox monasteries face the east, in keeping with the traditional belief that the light of God shines in the image of the rising sun. An outside porch, likewise tattooed with frescoes, is typical of the Bucovina monasteries. Within, they are divided into three rooms: the first chamber (*pronaos*), the tomb room, and the altar room (*naos*). Women are not allowed to enter the altar, shielded from public view by an iconostasis – a beautifully sculpted, gilded partition in the *naos*. The church domes are a peculiar combination of Byzantine pendentives and Moorish crossed arches with larger-than-life paintings of Christ or the Virgin peering down.

Each monastery is dedicated to a saint, whose patron day is among the most important feast days for the monastery's inhabitants. The nuns or monks are required to fast – no meat, eggs or dairy products – for several days leading up to any religious feast. Wednesday, Friday, Lent, the six weeks after Easter and the days preceding Christmas are likewise fast days.

Novices are required to serve three to seven years in a monastery before being ordained. Numerous penances have to be observed during this training period; many novices have to stand motionless in the street for several consecutive days, bearing a plaque indicating that they are waiting for cash donations towards the 'spiritual furthering' of their monastery.

Following the Habsburg occupation of Bucovina in 1785, most monasteries were closed and their inhabitants forced to relinquish their spiritual lives for a civilian one. They were equally persecuted under communism, and it is only since 1990 that the inner activity of these holy sanctuaries has matched the dynamism of their outer façades.

dying wish was that a day should not pass without prayers being said in his monastery. Thus seven elderly nuns defied communist orders and remained alone at the monastery throughout the 1960s and 1970s. Today about 60 nuns live here.

It's possible for travellers to stay at the monastery. It's best to hitch or take a taxi from Suceava; there are no buses.

Voroneţ Monastery

The wondrous size, scope and detail of the *Last Judgment* fresco, which fills the entire exterior western wall of the **Voroneţ Monastery** (admission adult/child €1.20/0.60; ☙ 8am-8pm) has earned near-universal accolades as being the most marvellous Bucovine fresco. It's also something of a miracle. At the top, angels roll up the signs of the zodiac to indicate the end of time. The middle fresco shows humanity being brought to judgment. On the left, St Paul escorts the believers, while on the right Moses brings forward the nonbelievers. Below is the *Resurrection*.

On the northern wall is *Genesis*, from Adam and Eve to Cain and Abel. The southern wall features another tree of Jesse with the genealogy of biblical personalities. In the vertical fresco to the left is the story of the martyrdom of St John of Suceava (buried in the Monastery of St John the New in Suceava, p273). The vibrant, almost satiny blue pigment used throughout the frescoes is known worldwide as 'Voroneţ blue'. As with the aforementioned miracle, with the exception of the northern wall, which has absorbed the brunt of centuries of Romania's punishing elements, the exterior frescoes remain implausibly vibrant. As the pigment is only 2mm thick, their robustness has thus far defied logical explanation.

In the narthex lies the tomb of Daniel the Hermit, the first abbot of Voroneţ Monastery (see p279 for more on Daniel). It was upon the worldly advice of Daniel, who told Ştefan cel Mare not to give up his battle against the Turks, that the Moldavian prince went on to win further victories against the Turks and then to build Voroneţ Monastery out of gratitude to God.

In 1785 occupying Austrians forced Voroneţ's monks to abandon the monastery. Since 1991 it has been inhabited by a small community of nuns.

The monastery is a 4km walk from the turnoff or 6km from Gura Humorului.

SLEEPING & EATING

The town of Gura Humorului is a perfect base to visit Voroneţ. More and more enterprising locals are taking in tourists and each year rates soar higher. The usual rate per person per night in an unlicensed 'vila' is about €15 or €20. Roughly 500m south of the bus station (follow the only path), there's wild camping on the south bank of the River Moldova, as well as a few cafés and a small tourist complex.

Pensuinea Lions (☎ 235 226; www.motel-lions.ro in Romanian; Str Ştefan cel Mare 39; s/d €23/29) Opened in early 2006, this three-star *pensiune*-restaurant minicomplex is warm, homely and clean. Beds are decent and all rooms have a balcony. Discounts offered for multinight stays. Traffic noise and music from the restaurant (open until 11pm) is audible from the rooms.

Hotel Simeria (☎ 230 227; Mihail Kogalniceanu 2; s/d per person €27/30) This is a modern, impeccably clean and pleasant three-storey hotel. Some rooms have balconies, all have refrigerator and TV.

Casa Elena (☎ 230 651; www.casaelena.ro; s/d €44/59) A quick 3.5km trip from Gura Humorului on the northern edge of Voroneţ Monastery, this four-star option has 31 rooms in five different villas, all in a large, luxurious complex. The hotel also has a billiard room, sauna and 24-hour restaurant.

GETTING THERE & AWAY

There are buses on weekdays from Gura Humorului to Voroneţ, departing at 7am, 12.30pm and 2.45pm. A lovely option is to walk the 6km to Voroneţ, much of it along a narrow village road. The route is clearly marked and it is impossible to get lost.

Humor Monastery

Humor (admission adult/child €1.20/0.60; ☙ 8am-8pm) counters the memorable exterior frescoes at Voroneţ with its own fantastic interior frescoes. It was founded by Chancellor Theodor Bubuiog in 1530 under the guidance of Moldavian prince Petru Rareş. Unlike the other monasteries, Humor is surrounded by ramparts, partly made from wood, with a three-level brick and wood lookout tower; its traditional Moldavian open porch was the first of its kind to be built in Bucovina. Slip into the tower for the memorable climb to the viewing deck. Squeezing up the final lean flight of stairs will feel like a literal rebirth for some, but the photo opportunity is well worth the effort.

Its exterior frescoes, dating from 1535, are predominantly red. Paintings on the church's southern exterior wall are devoted to the Holy Virgin, the patron saint of the monastery. There's a badly faded depiction of the 1453 siege of Constantinople, with the parable of the return of the prodigal son to the right. St George is depicted on the northern wall. On the porch is a painting of the Last Judgment: the long bench on which the 12 apostles sit, the patterned towel on the chair of judgment, and the long, horn-like *bucium* (pipe) used to announce the coming of Christ are all typical Moldavian elements.

Humor shelters five chambers. The middle one (the tomb room) has a lower ceiling than the others. This hides a treasure room (*tainiţa*) where monastery riches were traditionally kept safe. On the right wall as you enter the tomb room is a votive painting depicting the founder, Toader Bubuiog, offering, with the help of the Virgin Mary, a miniature replica of the monastery to Christ. The tombs of Bubuiog, who died in 1539, and of his wife, lie on the left side of the room; a painting of his wife praying to the Virgin Mary is above her grave.

The paintings in the first chamber (*pronaos*) depict various scenes of martyrs. Above the decorative border, which runs around the base of the four walls, is a pictorial representation of the first three months of the Orthodox calendar (*synaxary*).

SLEEPING

Dozens of homes here have rooms for rent. See also p275 for nearby options.

Maison de Bucovine (☎ 0744-373 931; 172 Mănăstirea Humor; d €23) Only a rosary bead's swing away from the monastery (30m), this unassuming-looking home is a comfortable place to spend the night. The bathrooms are clean and modern and the hosts a delight. Breakfast not included.

GETTING THERE & AWAY

Aside from hitching a ride for the 6km from Gura Humorului, you can take one of the maxitaxis that depart from next to the towering Best Western Hotel, at the start of the road towards the monastery.

Moldoviţa Monastery

In the middle of a quaint village, **Moldoviţa Monastery** (admission adult/child €1.20/0.60; ☽ 10am-6pm)

consists of a fortified quadrangular enclosure with towers, brawny gates and a magnificent painted church at its centre. The monastery has undergone careful restoration in recent years. Its frescoes are predominantly yellow.

The fortifications and surrounding buildings are as impressive as the exterior frescoes. A haunting atmosphere of tranquillity reigns here, partly thanks to the lovely tended grounds and beautiful stone buildings. On the church's southern exterior wall is a depiction of the defence of Constantinople in AD 626 against Persians dressed as Turks, while on the porch is a representation of the Last Judgment. Inside the sanctuary, on a wall facing the original carved iconostasis, is a portrait of Prince Petru Rareş, the monastery's founder, offering the church to Christ. All of these works date from 1537.

In the monastery's small museum is Petru Rareş' original throne.

SLEEPING

See www.ruraltourism.ro for some great places to stay in Vama, a small village 14km south of Moldoviţa on the main Suceava–Vatra Dornei road. Many homes have rooms to rent.

Mărul de Aur Camping Ground (☎ 336 180; camping free, cabins €3.50) The pitiable rooms at Mărul de Aur, located in Moldoviţa between the train station and the monastery, are not recommended, but this place also operates the camping ground, 3km out of town on the road to Suceviţa.

ourpick **Letitia Orsvischi Pension** (☎ 0745-869 529; orsivschiletita@yahoo.fr; Str Gării 20, Vama; r per person €25; 🖳) Follow the signs with painted eggs to this large two-house property, 250m off the main road in Vama. Letitia only speaks Romanian and French, but her house does most of the talking. Among its attractions are a massive painted-egg display, with samples from around the world, and a private ethnographic museum. Rooms are rustic and simple, but clean, with shared bathroom. Breakfast, dinner *and* internet included! The grounds are filled with flowers and a new covered terrace with grill is available for cookouts.

Casa Alba (☎ 340 404; www.casa-alba.suceava.ro; s/d/ste €46/54.50/77) You certainly won't feel a monastic asceticism in this lush, ultramodern and very comfortable villa. Prices are about €10 cheaper from September to June. Follow the one road heading south, 5km west of Frasin, which is about 3km east of Vama.

MOLDAVIA

GETTING THERE & AWAY

Moldoviţa Monastery is right above Vatra Moldoviţei's train station (be sure to get off at Vatra Moldoviţei, not Moldoviţa). From Suceava nine daily trains go to Vama (1¼ hours), and from Vama three trains leave daily for Vatra Moldoviţei (35 minutes).

Suceviţa Monastery

The winding, remote mountain road from Moldoviţa to Suceviţa (27km) offers breathtaking views across the surrounding fields and is reason enough to make the trip. It climbs 1100m and passes small Alpine villages. Yet the prize at the end of it is golden too: **Suceviţa** (admission adult/child €1.20/0.60; ⏱ 8am-8pm) is perhaps the largest and perhaps all-round finest of the Bucovina monasteries.

The church inside the fortified monastic enclosure, built between 1582 and 1601, is almost completely covered with frescoes. Mysteriously, the western wall of the monastery remains bare. Legend has it that the artist fell off the scaffolding while attempting to paint the wall and was killed, leaving his contemporaries too scared to follow in his footsteps. The exterior frescoes – predominantly red and green – date from around 1590.

As you enter you first see the *Virtuous Ladder* fresco covering most of the northern exterior wall, depicting the 30 steps from Hell to Paradise. The frescoes inside the arches above the open porch depict the apocalypse and the vision of St John.

On the southern exterior wall is the Jesse tree symbolising the continuity of the Old and New Testaments. The tree grows from the reclining figure of Jesse, who is flanked by a row of ancient philosophers. To the left is the Virgin as a Byzantine princess, with angels holding a red veil over her head.

Inside the church, in the second chamber, the Orthodox calendar is depicted. The tombs of the founders, Moldavian nobles Simion and Ieremia Movilă, lie in the tomb room. The last of the painted monasteries to have been built, this is the only one that wasn't built by Ştefan cel Mare or his family. Ieremia Movilă, who died in 1606, appears with his seven children on the western wall inside the *naos*. Apart from the church, there's a small museum at Suceviţa Monastery in which various treasures and art pieces from the monastery are displayed.

Suceviţa Monastery was first inhabited by monks in 1582. During the communist era, only nuns aged over 50 were allowed to stay at Suceviţa. Today, it is a relatively flourishing place.

SLEEPING

It's worth spending a night here and doing a little hiking in the surrounding hills. Wild camping is possible in the field across the stream from the monastery, as well as along the road from Moldoviţa. Homes with *cazare* signs abound.

Pensiunea Emilia (☎ 0740-117 277; Str Bercheza 173; d €14.50) Of the handful of *pensiunes* in the immediate area, this one is the most appealing. It only has five rooms, but all feel like home. Walk 700m up the road opposite the monastery.

Pensiunea Silva (☎ 417 019; www.pensiuneasilva .ro; Suceviţa 391; r incl full board per person €24; 🖳) The hunting lodge motif here is punctuated by the gaggle of taxidermy critters that meet you at the door. Located on the western edge of nearby Suceviţa village, it's an easy 3km walk to the monastery.

GETTING THERE & AWAY

Suceviţa is the most difficult monastery to reach on public transport. There are only two daily buses from Rădăuţi. Hitching or biking are your best bets. There's a beautiful hiking trail to the Putna Monastery from here (opposite).

Rădăuţi & Marginea

Rădăuţi (rah-*dah*-oots) is a lovely market town with a smattering of quaint attractions, the star of which being **Bogdana Monastery**, aka Saint Nicolas Church, built by Bogdan I in the mid-14th century, making it the oldest church in Moldavia. The interior frescoes look as if they haven't been touched up since Bogdan flung open the doors, but therein lies some of its charm. The church holds the decorative tombs of Moldavian rulers Bogdan I, Latcu, Roman Musat and Ştefan I.

Piaţa Unirii is dominated by an ambitious multidomed cathedral. Opposite is the extensive **Museum of Bucovina Folk Techniques** (☎ 562 565; Str Piaţa Unirii 63; admission adult/student €1.50/0.30; 🕒 8am-7pm), Moldavia's oldest ethnographic museum, with over 1000 items in 11 exhibition halls, highlighting pottery, for which the region is famous. The adjoining workshop of **ceramic artist Florin Colibaba** will likely spasm your impulse-buy muscles.

The tiny village of **Marginea**, 9km west of Rădăuţi, is renowned for its black earthenware and pottery, a custom dating back to the Neolithic Age. **AF Magopat Gheorghe** (☎ 560 845; www.ceramicamarginea.ro; house 1265; 7am-6pm) is a darling shop, with an adjacent exhibition of locally produced pottery, black and otherwise. Visitors are invited to view the pottery workshop next door that shows how the stuff is made. This entire area is a pleasure to explore by bike, as each village has its own charm.

SLEEPING

Pensiune Turistica Fast (☎ 560 060; Str Ştefan cel Mare 80; s/d €17/28.50) This basic *pensiune* and restaurant has an inexpressible scrubbed-down charm. Follow the 'Fast' signs from Piaţa Unirii in Rădăuţi, about 1km west.

Luxor (☎ 406 022; www.luxor-marginea.ro; Marginea 1435; s/d/apt €26/34/46) Across the road from the ceramic workshop in Marginea is this lovely oasis of comfort, with startlingly nice rooms and an excellent on-site restaurant (mains €3 to €5).

GETTING THERE & AWAY

From Rădăuţi you can catch a train to Putna or a bus to Suceviţa monastery. The bus station is on B-dul Ştefan cel Mare, a block north of Rădăuţi's train station on Str Gării. From the bus station, head east along B-dul Ştefan cel Mare until you reach Piaţa Unirii.

Five daily trains go from Rădăuţi to Putna (1½ hours) – two of which require a change at Gura Putnei – and six to Dorneşti (11 minutes) from where there are three trains to Suceava (1¼ hours).

Buses from Rădăuţi include six a day to Suceava, and two to Suceviţa and Guru Humorului. Oddly, there are none to Putna. Double-check posted times with a ticket clerk. Maxitaxis heading to all points south leave continuously, usually when full.

Southbound maxitaxis from Rădăuţi pass Luxor every 30 minutes.

Putna

Legend has it that, to celebrate his conquest of the fortress of nearby Chilia against the Turks, Ştefan cel Mare climbed to the top of a hill overlooking Putna village, 28km northwest of Rădăuţi, and fired three arrows. Where the first arrow landed in the valley below became the site of Putna Monastery's holy well; the second arrow decided the site of the altar; and the third the site of the bell tower. As you approach **Putna Monastery**, you can see the spot where Ştefan cel Mare stood, marked by a large white cross. The monastery, built between 1466 and 1481, is still home to a very active religious community, with groups of monks chanting Mass just before sunset.

In the large building behind the monastery is **Putna Museum**, where a wealth of treasures from the monastery and surrounding regions are displayed, including medieval manuscripts and the Holy Book that Ştefan cel Mare carried when he went to battle. Outside the church are three bells inscribed in Slavic. The largest of the three, dating from 1484, was strictly reserved for heralding royal deaths.

Compared to other Bucovina monasteries Putna is aesthetically lacklustre, but it's dear to the heart of Romanians as Ştefan cel Mare himself is buried in the tomb room of the church. Below is the grave of his third wife, Maria Voichiţa. On the left is the grave of their two children, Bogdan and Petru. Above the children's grave is that of Ştefan cel Mare's second wife, Maria of Mangop from Greece.

Some 60 monks live at Putna today, practising icon-painting, shepherding, agriculture and wood-sculpting.

Daniel the Hermit's Cave (Chilia lui Daniil Sihastrul), 2km from the monastery, is also worth visiting. Inside is a humble wooden table and memorial plaque to the hermit and seer Daniel Dimitru, born in a village near Rădăuţi in the 15th century. He became a monk at the age of 16 and later moved to Chilia where he dug himself a cave in the rock. To get to Chilia from the monastery, turn right off the main road following the sign for Cabana Putna. Bear left at the fork and continue until the second fork in the road. Turn right here, cross the railway tracks, and continue over a small bridge, following the dirt road until you see the rock, marked by a stone cross, on your left.

SLEEPING

Some people camp in the field opposite Daniel the Hermit's Cave at Chilia near the train station.

Ionas Pensiune (☎ 414 123; 272 Putna; d with/without breakfast €29/23) About 700m from the train station (sign posted) are a few nice homes owned by the Ionas family. All rooms share bathrooms.

GETTING THERE & AWAY

Local trains go to Putna from Suceava five times daily (1¼ hours). The large monastic enclosure is at the end of the road, nearly 2km from the station. From Putna there is also one direct train a day to Iaşi (six hours).

You can do as Prince Charles did in May 2003 and hike the 20km from Putna to Suceviţa Monastery in about five hours (though he went the other way). Follow the trail marked with blue crosses in white squares that starts near the hermit's cave. About 4km down the road you turn off to the left.

CÂMPULUNG MOLDOVENESC
☎ 230 / pop 20,076
This small 14th-century logging and fair town is tucked in the Moldavia Valley at an altitude of 621m. Câmpulung Moldovenesc is a good access point for hiking in the Rarău Mountains, 15km to the south. In winter, Câmpulung attracts cross-country skiers. There is also a short 800m ski slope served by a chairlift at the foot of the resort. Between 1786 and 1809 many German miners settled in the region at the invitation of the Habsburg authorities.

A winter sports festival takes place in Câmpulung Moldovenesc every year on the last Sunday in January.

Orientation & Information
The main street, Calea Transilvaniei, which runs into Calea Bucovinei, cuts across the town from west to east. The train station is a five-minute walk west of the centre at Str Gării 8. To get to the centre from the main Câmpulung Moldovenesc train station (do not get off at Câmpulung Moldovenesc Est stop), turn left along Str Gării and then right along Str Dimitrie Cantimir until you reach the post office on the corner of Calea Bucovinei. The bus station is at Str Alexander Bogza. From here cut through the market to the left of the station. As you exit, you'll see the sign for Hotel Zimbru. Follow that to reach the centre.

George Turism travel agency (☎ 312 801; www.george turism.ro in German; Str.Caprioarei 27; ⏰ 9am-6pm Mon-Fri) can help you with any of your questions.

Hotel Zimbru (☎ 314 356; www.rarau-turism.ro; Calea Bucovinei 1-3; ⏰ 8am-4pm Mon-Fri off-season, 24hr in summer) has a tourism office that can assist with guided tours to monasteries.

HIKING THE RARĂU MOUNTAINS

The Rarău Mountains, part of the Eastern Carpathians, offer fantastic hiking opportunities. From May to October you can access these mountains and the region's main base for hikers, **Cabana Rarău** (1400m; ☎ 0744-320 496; d €15), from Câmpulung Moldovenesc by car. There's a small restaurant and provisions shop there too. As you enter Câmpulung Moldovenesc from the east, a road on the left is signposted 'Cabana Rarău 14km'. Do not attempt to drive in bad weather unless you have a 4WD, as the road is narrow and extremely pot-holed and rocky in places. Hiking takes three to four hours (follow the red circles).

A second mountain road – slightly less pot-holed – leads up to the cabana from the village of **Pojorâta**, 3km west of Câmpulung Moldovenesc. Hiking takes four to five hours (follow the yellow crosses). This road is not marked on maps. Turn left at the fork after the village post office, cross the railway tracks, then turn immediately left along the dirt road. Note the large stones of Adam and Eve as you enter the village.

Cabana Rarău can also be accessed from the south in the village of **Chiril**, 24km east of Vatra Dornei on the main Vatra Dornei–Durău road. This is the best of the three road options for those determined to drive. Hiking takes three to four hours (blue circles). **Cabana Zugreni** (☎ 373 581; d with/without private toilet €15/8), 4km from Chiril on the Vatra Dornei road, is a good option. The adjoining restaurant serves traditional Moldavian meals.

From Cabana Rarău a trail (30 minutes) leads to the foot of Rarău's most prized rocks, the Lady's Stones or Princess' Rocks (Pietrele Doamnei). A clutter of crosses crowns the highest (1678m) in memory of angels the climbers it has claimed. The view from the top is superb.

A trail marked by red stripes and red triangles (five hours) leads from the cabana to the **Slătioara Forest Reservation**. From here another trail (red triangles) leads to the **Todirescu Flower Reservation**.

Sights

The unlikely highlight of Câmpulung Moldovenesc is its mirthful, but bizarrely intriguing wooden spoon collection, which is displayed in a small house. Love spoons, jewellery constructed from spoons and other cutlery delights collected by Ioan Ţugui are exhibited in the **museum** (Str Gheorghe Popovici 3; admission €0.30; 9am-4pm Tue-Sun). Other fun wooden objects are displayed at the **Wood Carving Museum** (Calea Transilvaniei 10; admission €0.30; 9am-4pm Tue-Sun).

Sleeping

Pensiunea Genţiana (313 165; Str Valea Seacă 19B; www.pensiunea-gentiana.go.ro in Romanian; d summer/winter €20/23;) Basic rooms, with TV and shared bathroom. Rates for single rooms are negotiable. Heading east from the main square, take the first right and follow the signs for 700m.

Hotel Zimbru (314 356; rezervari@rarau-turism .ro; Calea Bucovinei 1-3; s/d €29/34;) This is your typical state-run 10-storey concrete block that has characterless rooms but friendly service. Internet extra charge.

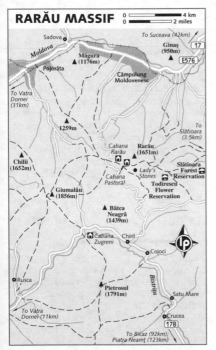

RARĂU MASSIF

Eden Hotel (314 733; www.hotel-eden.ro; Str Bucovinei 148; s/d/ste €34/46/80;) This lovely house has an oasis feel to it and its 17 simple but well-furnished rooms. Service is first-rate and the restaurant excellent. The hotel can also organise folk dance shows and car hire.

Getting There & Away

There are eight buses/maxitaxis daily to Vatre Domei and four to Suveaca. Four local (slow) trains go to Suveaca Nord and two to Vatra Domei. Four fast trains pause here while en route to both Timisoara and Iasi and one each to Cluj and Bucharest.

VATRA DORNEI

230 / pop 17,650

Nestled at the confluence of the Dorna and Bistriţa Rivers in the Dornelor depression, Vatra Dornei was a fashionable spa resort during Habsburg times. Today it looks and feels as if it's seen better days, but a mini construction and renovation boom signals that the town has not thrown in the mud wrap yet. Vatra Dornei is home to Romania's largest sparkling mineral water bottling plants.

Information

Internet (Str Luceafărilui 27; 9am-11pm; per hr €0.30)
Pharmacie (Str Mihai Eminescu 90; 8am-8pm Mon-Fri, 9am-7pm Sat, 9am-3pm Sun)
Post office (Str Mihai Eminescu 8; 8am-7pm Mon-Fri, 8am-noon Sat)
Raiffeisen Bank (Str Luceafărilui 23; 8.30am-6.30pm Mon-Fri, 9am-2pm Sat)
Tourist Centre & Salvamont (372 767; salvamont dorna@yahoo.com; Str Garii; 9am-6pm Mon-Fri) This is a good first stop; you can pick up free local maps, including one highlighting the 30-odd local hiking trails, and check weather conditions in the mountains. You can also book accommodation in hotels or private homes here.

Sights

Vatra Dornei's **park** (Parcul Staţiune) is beautifully laid out with sprawling avenues, well-groomed lawns and neatly arranged flower beds. Bronze busts of national poet Mihai Eminescu and composers George Enescu and Ciprian Porumbescu gaze out from beneath the trees.

You can taste Vatra Dornei's natural spring waters at the **drinking fountain** in the fairytale single-turreted castle in the park. The bicarbonated water is good for curing stomach ills but not recommended for those with high

MOLDAVIA

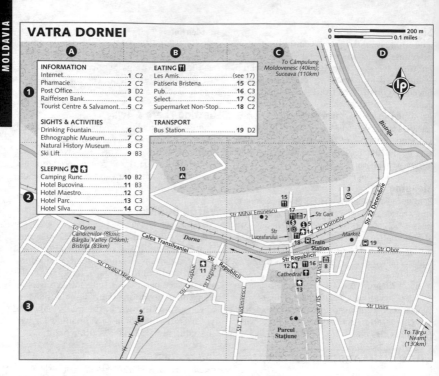

VATRA DORNEI

0 ——— 200 m
0 ——— 0.1 miles

INFORMATION	
Internet.........................1 C2	
Pharmacie.......................2 C2	
Post Office.......................3 D2	
Raiffeisen Bank..................4 C2	
Tourist Centre & Salvamont.....5 C2	

SIGHTS & ACTIVITIES	
Drinking Fountain................6 C3	
Ethnographic Museum............7 C2	
Natural History Museum........8 C3	
Ski Lift..........................9 B3	

SLEEPING	
Camping Runc....................10 B2	
Hotel Bucovina.................11 B3	
Hotel Maestro..................12 C3	
Hotel Parc......................13 C3	
Hotel Silva.....................14 C2	

EATING	
Les Amis........................(see 17)	
Patiseria Bristena...............15 C2	
Pub..............................16 C3	
Select...........................17 C2	
Supermarket Non-Stop........18 C2	

TRANSPORT	
Bus Station.....................19 D2	

To Câmpulung Moldovenesc (40km); Suceava (110km)

To Dorna Candrenilor (8km); Bârgău Valley (25km); Bistriţa (83km)

To Târgu Neamţ (130km)

---

blood pressure or an aversion to sulphurous water. Adjoining the park on Str Republicii is a grandiose baroque mansion, once home to a bustling casino in Habsburg times but now undergoing renovations.

The **Natural History Museum** (Muzeul de Ştiinţe Naturale şi Cinegetică; Str Unirii 3; admission adult/child €0.45/0.30; 10am-6pm Tue-Sun) displays flora and fauna from the surrounding Căliman and Rarău Mountains. North of the river is a small **Ethnographic Museum** (Str Mihai Eminescu; admission adult/child €0.45/0.30; 10am-6pm Tue-Sun).

The **ski lift** (telescaun; one way/return €2/3; 10am-5pm Tue-Sun) is open year round (but only runs with a minimum of 10 passengers) for those who want to enjoy a summer day's view or the valley's autumn colours.

Activities

It's not only people with aching whatsits who find reason to visit; the **hiking trails** directly north of town are lovely, and the downhill **skiing** scene on Dealul Negrii (1300m) is on the rise. The Black Hill and Parc slopes are accessed from the edge of town by the ski lift. Equipment hire shacks are nearby. Contact the Tourist

Centre & Salvamont for up-to-the-minute details on skiing and accommodation.

Sleeping

Camping Runc (371 892; campsite/cabin €4/7) This very nice campground is on a forest-covered hill overlooking the town. It has 43 wooden double cabins, with communal showers and toilets, and a restaurant-bar on site. Go west along Str Mihai Eminescu until you see a sign on the right.

Hotel Bucovina (375 005; Str Republicii 35; s/d €15/29) For the price, this is probably the best deal in town. Though the impressive Swiss-chalet exterior is not matched by the interior décor, it's a comfortable place with full services.

Hotel Parc (0744-964 307; Str Parcului; d €16;) Renovations will include a new hot tub at this bare-bones, light-blue lodge inside the main park. The café-cum-disco can get a little noisy with spontaneous all-night parties.

Hotel Silva (371 033; Str Dornelor 12; s/d €27/37) On the 2nd floor of a commercial complex, this modern hotel has a fitness centre and a nightclub.

Hotel Maestro (☎ 375 288; http://eis.go.ro; Str Republicii; s/d/tr €34.50/46/63) A great eight-room, modern place in the centre of town. It runs a popular terrace café out the front and hires out skis and snowmobiles. The same people run the lovely Cabana Schiorilor up in the mountains.

Eating & Drinking
There are many eating options along the pedestrianised Str Luceafărului.

Patiseria Bristena (☎ 372 338; Str Mihai Eminescu 28; mains €1-2; ☒ 8am-8pm) Does the word 'yum' mean anything to you? Great cakes, meat-filled pastries, pizza slices and cheap eats maintain an irresistible aroma and wide smiles in here.

Les Amis (☎ 375 280; Str Luceafărilui 19; mains €1-3; ☒ 9am-11pm) The lengthy menu and central location on the city's pedestrian mall makes up for the impertinent, cigarette-centric staff.

Pub (Str Republicii 1; mains €1-3; ☒ 10am-2am Mon-Fri, 10am-5am Sat) The no-frills name doesn't do justice to the best drinking hole in town. This relaxed hang-out, furnished top to bottom in wood, is the remedy to a day's skiing or hiking. There is live music on weekends and a basic sandwich and salad menu.

Select (Str Luceafărilui 19; ☒ 9am-1am) Upstairs from Les Amis, this trendy bar has an outdoor terrace, a couple of pool tables and limited cocktails.

For self-catering, **Supermarket Non-Stop** (Str Dornelor 10; ☒ 24hr) is a well-stocked store with some takeaway meals.

Getting There & Away
The **bus station** (☎ 371 252) is located at the eastern end of town on Str 22 Decembrie. There are eight buses or maxitaxis per day to Câmpulung Moldovenesc, seven to Gura Humorului, four to Suceava, three to Bistriţa, two to both Piatra Neamţ and Târgu Neamţ and one to both Cluj-Napoca and Rădăuti.

Tickets are sold in advance at the **Agenţie de Voiaj CFR** (☎ 371 039) inside the **train station** (☎ 371 197; Str Republicii 1). There are six daily trains to Suceava (3¼ hours) – four of which end up in Iaşi (5½ hours), three to Timişoara (10½ hours), and one to both Bistriţa (five hours) and Oradea (7½ hours.)

AROUND VATRA DORNEI
Vatra Dornei stands in the middle of Romania's most dramatic mountain passes, steeped in legend and famed for their wild beauty and savage landscapes. If you head southwest into Transylvania you cross the **Bârgău Valley** and the Tihuţa Pass (p210), or, if you've read Bram Stoker's *Dracula*, the Borgo Pass!

THE MUDDY VOLCANOES OF THE EASTERN CARPATHIAN MOUNTAINS

The tiny village of Berca, about 30km northwest of Buzau, is the staging area for the Muddy Volcanoes (Vulcanii Noroioşi) – or 'the gates of hell' as the locals call them – one of Romania's best known geological reserves. Mud replaces lava here through a less powerful geological reaction, but with similar effect. Volcano cones up to 6m high dribble mud with surprising colours – greys, browns, ochre or simply shining black – while the chocolate borders of the craters are adorned with the white crust of crystallised salt and belts of yellow sulphur mud. Mud bubbles release small amounts of methane into the air which one can independently (and judiciously) confirm by lighting a match and watching the blue flame dance. The mild stench of oil and the bloop-bloop noise of the gas bubbles coming up to the surface, creating eruptions ranging in size from marbles to sandpits, have stewed many local superstitions regarding the origin of the geological phenomenon.

As advertised, the Muddy Volcanoes are quite muddy. Wear sturdy shoes or sport sandals, tightly fastened, lest the mud snatch one off in mid-stride. There's a post-visit footwear scrubdown station at the entrance, with a visitor centre, restaurant and mini-motel.

Reaching the site without private transport is impossible. From Berca, follow the sparse but timely signs 14km to the Muddy Volcanoes.

While in the area, be sure to visit the Sculpture Camp in the village of Măgura. A large clearing is filled with 256 stone sculptures, a true in-nature museum, courtesy of the artists who used to meet here in the '70s and '80s. Yet further northwest are the Active Fires of Lopatari, blue flames that burn deep in the cracks of the soil at 700m above sea level.

In Dorna Candrenilor, 8km west of Vatra Dornei, you can access the **Căliman Mountains**. The highlight of these volcanic mountains is the anthropomorphic rocks, which form the **12 Apostles Nature Reservation** (Stâncile Doisprezece Apostoli). A trail (marked with blue triangles then red circles) leads from Vatra Dornei to its peak at 1760m. Only tackle this tough climb if you are experienced and have a map and the right gear.

A less challenging route if you have a car is to drive to Dorna Candrenilor, turn left along the road to Poiana Negrii and continue for 14km along road and dirt track until you reach Negrişoara. From here it is a three-hour walk (4km) along a path to the foot of the geological reservation.

Heading north you cross from Moldavia into the Maramureş region via the **Prislop Pass**, which peaks at 1416m (p248).

Northern Dobrogea

Northern Dobrogea is undeniably a kingdom unto itself within Romania. Despite their lack of prevailing Romanian icons (breath-taking mountains, ancient churches, the undead), the Danube River (Râul Dunărea) and the Black Sea coast (Marea Neagră) contain offerings ranging from all nature to *au natural*. The 193.5km coastline *(litoral)* attracts waves of wildlife and party animals alike. Equally, those seeking waterfront seclusion, archaeological stimulation and overwhelming numbers of exotic birds won't be disappointed.

Though widely considered to be the least 'Romanian' part of the country, ironically, this is where the strongest evidence of Romania's conspicuously proud connection to ancient Rome is found in the form of statues, busts, sarcophagi and other archaeological finds. The cultural distance from the rest of Romania can be partially explained by the unusually broad ethnic diversity in the area. Sizeable Turkish, Tatar, Bulgarian, Ukrainian and Lippovani/Old Believer settlements add to the mix, giving the area a refreshing burst of multiculturalism and the traveller a gratifying selection of cuisines.

History and culture notwithstanding, marine life still rules supreme here, despite tenacious attempts by humans to usurp the crown. On one hand we have the 65km stretch south of Mamaia where humans converge in beach resort towns to soothe their bodies with sunshine and curative mud. These restorative pursuits are then promptly annulled hours later by gluttonous feasts and some of the wildest clubbing in the country. Alternately, the calming and notably less opulent Danube Delta draws bird-lovers and seekers of solitude. A fantastic, tangled netowrk of ever-eroding canals, riverbeds and wetlands in Europe's second-largest delta boasts remote fishing villages and stretches of deserted beach, where the pelicans are abundant and the fish are nervous.

HIGHLIGHTS

- Test the limits of sun, carousing and your beach modesty around **Mamaia** (p294)
- Disregard prudence and wallow in stinky mud in **Eforie Nord** (p296)
- Relive ancient Rome in **Histria** (p300)
- Know the sound of thousands of pelicans in the canals and lakes of the **Danube Delta** (p302)
- Visit a tranquil fishing village such as **Sfântu Gheorghe** (p308)

NORTHERN DOBROGEA

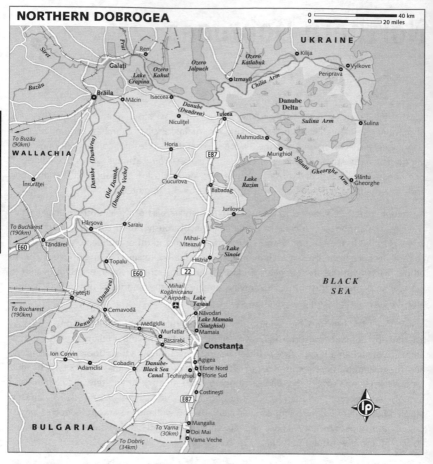

HISTORY

In 1878 Northern Dobrogea became part of Romania when a combined Russo-Romanian army defeated the Turks in Bulgaria. Southern Dobrogea was ceded to Bulgaria.

In antiquity the Dobrogea region was colonised first by the Greeks and then by the Romans, both of whom left behind much for visitors to admire. Histria, the oldest Greek settlement in Romania, was founded in 657 BC. From AD 46, Dobrogea was the Roman province of Moesia Inferior. At Adamclisi (Tropaeum Trajani) the Romans scored a decisive victory over the Geto-Dacian tribes, thus expanding into regions north of the Danube. Dobrogea later fell under Byzantine control and in 1418 was conquered by the Turks.

Once Romanian flags flew over Dobrogea, much was done to integrate it to the 'mainland' as soon as possible, and with the completion of the formidable bridge over the Danube at Cernavodă (1895), a vital rail link was established between Constanţa and the capital. At this time, the coast started to develop as a summer leisure destination; to this day, summer tourism is the backbone of the region's economy.

ECOLOGY
Litoral Beaches

There are no Blue Flag beaches here, though this is more a matter of bureaucracy and finances than cleanliness, as many beaches meet the 27 criteria (see www.blueflag.org

.uk). Beaches in northern Mamaia are judged to be quite clean and the ones closer to the Bulgarian border benefit from good water circulation. The beaches in southern Mamaia are among the least clean of the *litoral* – they are overcrowded and several big hotels discharge used pool water here. Beaches at Eforie Nord and Costineşti are gearing up to install waste-water management systems driven by EU funding. Meanwhile, a recycling collection program is in the works to help deal with the sizable quantity of beach trash.

Fifteen first-aid points were set up along the coast in 2003, staffed by volunteers, ensuring greater beach safety. Some 50 lifeguards are on duty in Mamaia alone.

Generally, swimming in the Black Sea is pleasant: there are no undercurrents to worry about, the sands are fine and golden, and water salinity is a decent 17%.

Mare Nostrum (☎ 0341-407 432; www.marenostrum .ro; Str George Enescu 32) is an NGO dedicated to promoting ecotourism and a greater awareness of environmental issues in the area, including actively working to keep the beaches and waters clean.

GESS (☎ 0213-124 051; mihai.baciu@gess.ro, gess@home .ro) is an ecological group headquartered in Mangalia whose mandate is to study ecology, marine biology and cave biology, as well as to promote awareness of ecological issues. It's an excellent source of information about these matters as well as info on diving options along the coast.

Danube Delta

The delta's ecosystems have been much maligned by humans, starting with the shortening of the Sulina canal at the end of the 19th century. In the decades following, dozens of small canals were dug throughout the region in an attempt to increase fish stocks and to facilitate transport. Frenzied reed cutting during the communist period disturbed the natural filtering process that reeds have for the river as well as unbalancing the habitat for birds, fish and insects. In addition to this, dams were built, which destroyed bird nesting grounds; sections of the delta were drained for agriculture; and exotic birds were enthusiastically hunted. Sadly, human meddling has irrevocably changed the delta. Whereas in the early 1900s there were 10 to 15 million birds in the region, there are now less than half a million.

Many strides have been made in the last decade. Pollution has been reduced and reed cutting has been vastly curbed. Ecotourism is continuing to develop as tourist options become more ecofriendly.

The headquarters of the **Danube Delta Biosphere Reserve** (DDBR; ☎ 240-518 945; arbdd@ddbra .ro; Str Portului 34A) is in Tulcea. The **Danube Delta Research Institute** (DDNI; ☎ 240-531 550; www.indd .tim.ro; Str Babadag 165), also in Tulcea, is a good source of information.

BLACK SEA COAST & LITTORAL

CONSTANŢA
☎ 241, 341 / pop 314,490

Constanţa is the gateway to Romania's seaside activities. Romanians and tourists alike arrive by the train- and bus-load all summer. Sharp annual price hikes have made a trip here fairly expensive, even by Western European standards, though staying in private homes, camping or cramming into hotel rooms can ease expenses. However, with minor planning, an affordable visit can be easily arranged that will effectively pacify one's need for sun, water sports and life-threatening amounts of clubbing.

While much of Romania's largest port and third-largest city is adorned with the familiar wide boulevards and piles of concrete, there are equal parts that evoke romantic notions of ancient seafarers, the Roman poet Ovid and even the classic legend of Jason and the Argonauts (they fled here from King Aietes). Constanţa's original name, Tomis, means 'cut to pieces'– a reference to Jason's beloved Medea, who cut up her brother Apsyrtus and threw the pieces into the sea near the present-day city.

Emperor Constantine fortified and developed the city and later renamed it after his sister. By the 8th century the city had been destroyed by invading Slavs and Avars. After Constanţa was taken by Romania in 1877, the town grew in importance, with a railway line being built to it from Bucharest. By the early 1900s it was a fashionable seaside resort frequented by European royalty.

The city beaches are more polluted than those in the resorts to the north and south, and areas away from the beach. Constanţa

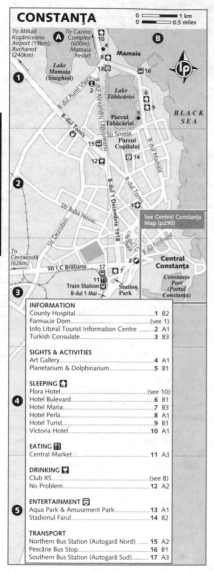

CONSTANŢA

0 ___ 1 km
0 ___ 0.5 miles

INFORMATION
County Hospital...1 B2
Farmacie Dom...(see 1)
Info Litoral Tourist Information Centre 2 A1
Turkish Consulate...3 B3

SIGHTS & ACTIVITIES
Art Gallery..4 A1
Planetarium & Dolphinarium.......................5 B1

SLEEPING
Flora Hotel...(see 10)
Hotel Bulevard...6 B1
Hotel Maria..7 B3
Hotel Perla...8 A1
Hotel Turist..9 B1
Victoria Hotel...10 A1

EATING
Central Market...11 A3

DRINKING
Club XS...(see 8)
No Problem..12 A2

ENTERTAINMENT
Aqua Park & Amusement Park...................13 A1
Stadionul Farul..14 B2

TRANSPORT
Northern Bus Station (Autogară Nord) 15 A2
Pescărie Bus Stop.....................................16 B1
Southern Bus Station (Autogară Sud)........17 A3

Constanţa hosts the annual **National Romanian Folk Festival** at the beginning of August. **Constanţa Days** are held around May 21; these days see concerts and general merry-making taking over the city.

Orientation

Constanţa's train station and main southern bus station (Autogară Sud) are 1.5km west of the old town. The northern bus station (Autogară Nord), serving destinations north towards the delta, is 3km north of the town centre, on Str Soveja.

Most facilities are on the main artery, B-dul Tomis, which runs from the new town in the north to the old town and towards the port in the south. The semi-pedestrianised Str Ştefan cel Mare is another main thoroughfare, the main focus of which is the large Tomis Department Store.

MAPS & PUBLICATIONS

There are few good maps of the city. The best of the lot, published by Amco Press, includes a city map, maps of all the resorts, and public transport routes. It is available in bookstores, major hotels and travel agencies.

The free English and German magazine *What Where When Constanţa* (www.bucuresti www.ro) contains helpful listings and news articles and can be found at most hotels, as can both *Best of Constanţa*, a free monthly listings booklet, and the weekly Romanian-language *Seara de Seara* (www.searadeseara .ro), which is the most comprehensive listings booklet for all the hot spots between Mamaia and Vama Veche.

Info Litoral Tourist Information Centre (Map p288; ☎ 555 000; www.infolitoral.ro; Constanţa Chamber of Commerce Bldg, B-dul Alexandru Lăpuşneanu 185; ☷ 9am-5pm Mon-Fri) publishes the excellent *Cultural Tourist Guide Dobrogea* (€2.65). This is a highly worthwhile guide in English and German that is chock-full of history, practical listings, suggested itineraries and resort maps.

Information
BOOKSHOPS
Librăria Sophia (Map p290; ☎ 616 365; Dragoş Vodă 13) The best bookshop for English- and French-language books.

CONSULATES
Russian Consulate (Map p290; ☎ 615 168; Str Mihai Viteazul 5)

itself can seem devoid of people even in mid-summer, as party-goers head to where the action is. However, the city offers a bit of everything: beaches, a picturesque Old Town, archaeological treasures and a peaceful Mediterranean air with the charm of dilapidated Venice back alleys. Its few excellent museums can be seen in an afternoon.

Turkish Consulate (Map p288; ☎ 611 135; B-dul Ferdinand 82)

Chinese Consulate (Map p290; ☎ 617 833; B-dul Carpați 7)

CULTURAL CENTRES & LIBRARIES

The **British Council** (Map p290; ☎ 618 365; Str Mircea cel Bătrân 104A; ⊗ 2-8pm Mon, Wed & Fri, 9am-3pm Tue & Thu) runs a small library located inside the Biblioteca Judeţeană Constanța (district library).

INTERNET ACCESS

Planet Games (Map p290; ☎ 552 377; cnr Str Ştefan cel Mare & Str Răscoala din 1907; per hr €0.65; ⊗ 24hr).

MEDICAL SERVICES

County Hospital (Map p288; Spitalul Judetean; ☎ 662 222; B-dul Tomis 145)

Farmacie Dom (Map p288; ☎ 519 800; B-dul Tomis 146; ⊗ 24hr)

Farmacie Ovidus (Map p290; ☎ 614 576; B-dul din Revoluției 22; ⊗ 8am-7.30pm Mon-Fri, 8am-1pm Sat) This is just off Str Remus Opreanu.

MONEY

Most hotels and travel agencies have exchange outlets, and there are numerous exchange offices, several of which are open around the clock, lining B-dul Tomis south of B-dul Ferdinand.

Banca Comercială Română (Map p290; ☎ 638 200; Str Traian 1; ⊗ 8.30am-5.30pm Mon-Fri & 8.30am-12.30pm Sat) changes travellers cheques (1% commission), gives unlimited cash advances on Visa and MasterCard and has an ATM. There's also a **Raiffeisen Bank** (Map p290; Str Traian 68).

POST & TELEPHONE

The **main post office** (Map p290; ☎ 552 222; B-dul Tomis 79-81; ⊗ 8.30am-8pm Mon-Fri, 8.30am-1pm Sat) and **telephone office** (⊗ 8.30am-10pm) share the same building.

TOURIST INFORMATION

Contur Travel (Map p290; ☎ 619 777; www.contur .ro;Piața Ovidiu 14 Block B; ⊗ 9am-5pm Mon-Fri) A truly helpful, multilingual bunch, Contur's speciality is developing tailor-made tourist circuits around the coast, the delta and elsewhere. It can also get you discounts in some hotels.

Danubius (Map p290; ☎ 615 836; excursion@danubius.ro; B-dul Ferdinand 36; ⊗ 9am-7pm Mon-Fri, 9am-2pm Sat) Though it mainly deals with groups, Danubius can also handle individual bookings. In a group, a day-trip to Histria will cost about €65; otherwise, a half-day trip to Histria for

up to three people will cost €100. Its second office (Map p290; ☎ 619 039; Piața Ovidiu 11) has the same opening hours but only sells airline tickets.

Latina Tourism (Map p290; ☎ 639 713; latina@latina .ro; B-dul Ferdinand 70; ⊗ 9am-5pm Mon-Fri) is a recommended travel agency with all the normal services.

Sights

Constanța's most renowned attraction is the **History & Archaeological Museum** (Map p290; ☎ 618 763; Piața Ovidiu 12; adult/child €3/1.50; ⊗ 9am-8pm Tue-Sun Jun-Sep, 10am-6pm Oct-May). There's something here for everyone. The kids will like the bones of a 2nd-century woman and the mammoth tusks; otherwise there are many 2nd-century Roman statues (discovered under the old train station in 1962) and 4th-century Roman coins. The centrepiece is a fantastic sculpture of the snake god Glykon, which is carved from a single block of marble.

Roman archaeological fragments spill over onto the surrounding square. Behind the museum is the 3rd-century **Roman mosaic** (Edificiul Roman cu Mozaic; Map p290; adult/child €0.60/0.30; ⊗ 9am-8pm Tue-Sun Jun-Sep, 10am-6pm Oct-May), discovered in 1959 and believed to have housed a commercial building. A staircase led from the museum's lower terrace to the public **Roman thermal baths** (Map p290), at the southern end of the cliff. Parts of its foundation remain today and are best viewed from Aleea Vasile Canarache.

The **statue of Ovid** (1887; Map p290; Piața Ovidiu) commemorates the outlaw-poet who was exiled to Constanța in the 8th century by Emperor Augustus. He looks lost in deep thought but he may simply be depressed; he reputedly disliked Tomis intensely and wrote some of his most self-pitying verses here.

South of the square is the imposing **Mahmudiye Mosque** (1910; Map p2900; Str Arhiepiscopiei), which has a 140-step minaret that you can climb when the gate is unlocked. This is Romania's main mosque, where the Mufti (the Muslim spiritual head) is located. The other mosque in the city is the **Geamia Hunchiar Mosque** (1868; Map p290; B-dul Tomis). Two blocks south of the mosque is the **Orthodox cathedral** (1885; Map p290; Decembrie 1989). A small **archaeological site** lies south of it, displaying walls of houses dating from the 4th to 6th centuries. Constanța's **Roman Catholic church** (Biserica Romano-Catolica Sfântul Anton; Map p290; Str Nicolae Titulescu 11) is one street west of the Orthodox cathedral.

Continue south to the small **Ion Jalea Museum** (Map p290; ☎ 618 602; Str Arhiepiscopiei 13; adult/

NORTHERN DOBROGEA

CENTRAL CONSTANŢA

0 ———— 200 m
0 ———— 0.1 miles

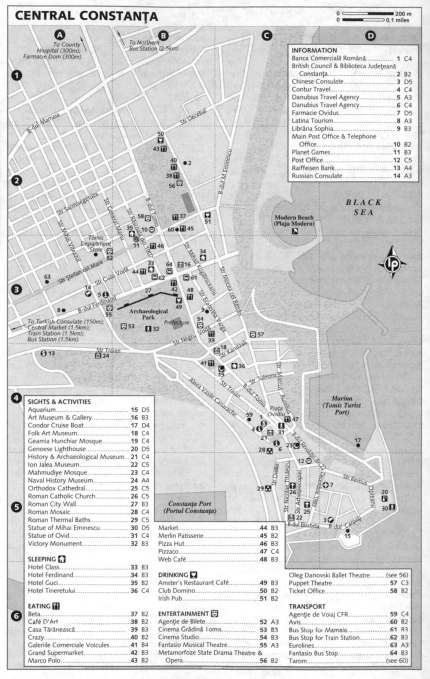

BLACK
SEA

Modern Beach
(Plaja Modern)

Marina
(Tomis Turist
Port)

Constanţa Port
(Portul Constanţa)

child €1/0.50; ☺ 10am-6pm Wed-Sun), which holds many of the local sculptor's works in a fabulous Moorish-style house.

A peaceful promenade meanders along the waterfront, offering sweeping views of the Black Sea. The humble **aquarium** (Map p290; ☎ 611 277; adult/child €2/1; ☺ 9am-8pm Tue-Sun Jun–mid-Sep, 10am-6pm mid-Sep–May) may be underwhelming for those over the age of five. Further along the promenade is the 8m-high **Genoese Lighthouse** (1860; Map p290) located off Str Remus Opreanu and a pier, which has a fine view of old Constanţa. Behind the lighthouse, a tragically poised **statue of Mihai Eminescu** (1934; Map p290) looks out to the sea.

Some museums in town worth checking out include the **Folk Art Museum** (Muzeul de Artă Populară; Map p290; ☎ 616 133; B-dul Tomis 32; adult/child €1.25/0.50; ☺ 9am-8pm Tue-Sun Jul-Aug, 10am-6pm Sep-Jun), which has handicrafts and costumes. Further north along the boulevard is the **Art Museum & Gallery** (Map p290; ☎ 617 012; B-dul Tomis 84; admission adult/child €1.75/1; ☺ 10am-6pm Tue-Sun), with mostly still-life and landscape paintings and sculptures. Contemporary exhibits are held in an adjoining art gallery. The **Naval History Museum** (Map p290; Muzeul Marinei Române; ☎ 619 035; Str Traian 53; adult/child €1.50/0.50; ☺ 10am-6pm Tue-Sun Jun-Sep, 9am-5pm Oct-May) is housed in the old Navy high school. The captions are presented in Romanian.

Near the city's main intersection, B-dul Ferdinand and B-dul Tomis, is the **Archaeological Park** (Map p290), which has remains of the 3rd-century **Roman city wall** and the 6th-century butchers' tower, loads of Roman sculptures and the modern **Victory Monument** (1968).

Heading north towards Mamaia, you pass Constanţa's **Planetarium & Dolphinarium** (Map p290; ☎ 831 553; B-dul Mamaia; adult/child €2/1; ☺ 8am-9pm Jun–mid-Sep & 8am-4pm mid–Sep-May), on the south-eastern shores of Lake Tăbăcăriei.

Activities

You can sail aboard the **Condor Cruise Boat** (☎ 0744-689 228; €5 per person per hr for a group of 14; ☺ around 9am May-Sep), moored at the marina known as the Tomis Turist Port (Portul Turistic Tomis), at the eastern end of Str Remus Opreanu, opposite the Yacht Club.

Delphi (☎ 0722-336 686) provides a flexible range of scuba-diving opportunities in the area to suit all budgets. Call for details.

Lake Tăbăcăriei has a pay-per-ride family **aqua and amusement park**. There is also a

beach, though the ocean beaches are much better. Food is limited to the fast and greasy kind, though there's plenty of beer to wash it down.

Sleeping

Constanţa is one of those cities where a small legion of people, usually pensioners with spare rooms, meet every arriving train to hawk cheap accommodation. Prices range from €5.75 to €11.50. The rooms are always plain but acceptable, though privacy is nonexistent. Agree on a price before getting in a cab and, as always, never hand over any money until you've seen the room.

The nearest camping ground is north of Mamaia (see p294).

Hotel Tineretului (Map p290; ☎ 613 590; fax 611 290; B-dul Tomis 24; s/d €24/26.50) This is the cheapest place in town for a reason. The rooms are worn, the bedding half-heartedly laundered, the bathrooms woeful and the reception indifferent.

Hotel Maria (Map p288; ☎ /fax 616 852; B-dul 1 Decembrie 1918; s/d €40/51.50; 🐾) This more modern option, situated across from the park that faces the train station, has lots of glass, chrome and deep blue to soothe your sun-withered nerves. There are only 12 rooms, so it's cosy and quiet.

Hotel Ferdinand (Map p290; ☎ 617 974; www.hotel ferdinand.ro; B-dul Ferdinand 12; s/d €56/64.50; 🐾 🖵) This clean and attractive three star hotel is within easy walking distance of virtually everything including the city beach. Rooms have internet ports, excellent beds and refrigerators.

Hotel Class (Map p290; ☎ 660 766; www.hotelclass .ro; Str Răscoala din 1907 1; s/d/ste €57.50/68.50/86; 🐾 🖵) Bang in the heart of the new town and open in January 2006, everything here is new or new-looking enough to make it worth the price.

Hotel Guci (Map p290; ☎ /fax 695 500; www.blacksea hotels.ro; Str Răscoala din 1907, 23; s/d/ste €62/70/90; 🐾 ✖) This modern, three-star business hotel offers full services, including Jacuzzi, sauna, laundry and massage.

Eating
RESTAURANTS

our pick Marco Polo (Map p290; ☎ 617 537; Str Mircea cel Bătrân 103; mains €2-5; ☺ 11am-midnight) This splendid Italian restaurant is cosily nestled in the back of the park near the Drama Theatre (see p293). On the terrace, each table is in its own foliage-encased nook. Tables are separated from each other by plants, making you feel like you're in a private garden, only one with doting waiters! The pizza, pasta, meat, fish and veggie dishes are delicious and the dessert menu irresistible. No credit cards.

Pizzaco (Map p290; ☎ 615 555; Piaţa Ovidiu 7; mains €3-5; ⏰ 24hr) While wood-fired pizza is their bread and butter, the menu also offers truffles, pasta, Buffalo wings, fish, salads and an inexpensive wine list, lovingly pieced together by the fixated sommelier-owner. The terrace allows for ample people watching on the *piaţa*.

our pick **Casa Tărănească** (Map p290; ☎ 665 606; Str Negru Voda 9; mains €3.50-7; ⏰ 24hr) This traditional restaurant stays open day and night, offering such Romanian comfort food as *sarmale*, *ciorbă*, *mămăligă*, knuckle of pork and, um, 'bear with wild sauce' (we dare you). Tourists and locals alike flock here for group outings or post-clubbing detox meals where the pictorial menu satisfactorily serves both non-Romanians and those too drunk to read.

Beta (Map p290; ☎ 673 663; www.la-beta.ro; Str Ştefan cel Mare 6A; mains €3-6; ⏰ 7am-1am) This modern food emporium and bar with a sprawling terrace is sure to satisfy all. Menu items include full breakfast, vegetarian dishes, pizza, salad and children's meals.

Amster's Restaurant Café (Map p290; B-dul Tomis 55; mains €4-6.50; ⏰ 8am-2am) Just opened at the time of writing, this cosy café has small wood tables and leather chairs from where you can plunder the free wi-fi service. The short, ambitiously priced menu deviates far from typical café fare.

Crazy (Map p290; ☎ 0726-779 292; Str Mircea cel Bătrân 97A; mains €4-11; ⏰ 9am-1am) This is an upscale eatery with a mature menu selection rarely found outside of Bucharest. The giant, overstuffed leather chairs, flat TVs and bar seating invite people to linger long past dessert.

CAFÉS & QUICK EATS
Café D'Art (Map p290; ☎ 612 133; B-dul Tomis 97; mains €1-3; ⏰ 9am-1am) This is an intimate place snuggled up to the Drama Theatre. Especially popular as an evening drinking hole (cocktails €2), it's also packed during the day by those seeking a good place to people-watch while enjoying a light meal.

Fast-food outlets serving kebabs, burgers and hot dogs are dotted all over town. There are some inside the modern **Galeriile Comerciale Voicules** (Map p290; off B-dul Tomis), and 24-hour joints can be found in the colourfully seedy

section of B-dul Tomis south of Str Traian.
Pizza Hut (Map p290; ☎ 518 430; Str Răscoala din 1907 10) delivers.

SELF-CATERING
Stock up on fruit, cheese and vegetables at the **central market** (Map p288; ⏰ 7am-4pm) between the train station and southern bus station. There is another **market** (Map p290; Str Răscoala din 1907) in the centre of town. The **Grand Supermarket** (Map p290; B-dul Tomis 57; ⏰ 24hr) has a good choice of cakes, biscuits and staple foods. Freshly baked breads and pastries are sold at the **Merlin Patisserie** (Map p290; Str Ştefan cel Mare), opposite Beta.

Drinking
Web Café (Map p290; B-dul Tomis 56; ⏰ 24hr; internet per hr €0.85) This is a simple bar-café with a couple of internet terminals. The pumping dance music makes for an invigorating afternoon coffee break or staging area for a big night out.

Irish Pub (Map p290; ☎ 550 400; www.irishpub.ro; Str Ştefan cel Mare 1; mains €4.50-8; ⏰ 9am-1am) The attractive, bright, orderly wood interior and exceptional menu miss the true mark of an Irish pub, but you can get your pint of Guinness here and that's what counts. The popular terrace almost overlooks the sea.

Club Domino (Map p290; ☎ 665 888; www.restaurant-domino.ro; Str Mircea cel Bătrân 105; club 10pm-4am Thu-Sun, café 10am-2am daily) They cover all the bases at Domino; a ground floor café, a first floor restaurant and, most importantly, one of only two nightclubs in Constanţa proper in the basement. The bright café is a trendy hangout for drinks and snacks. Theme parties are frequent in the club, with drink specials and guest DJs.

No Problem (Map p288; ☎ 513 377; B-dul Tomis 253; special events admission €3; ⏰ 10pm-5am Thu-Sat) These guys have finally dropped the pretence and switched to a full-on nightclub, competing with the daunting action at nearby Mamaia.

Entertainment
New foreign films are presented at **Cinema Studio** (Map p290; ☎ 611 358; cnr B-bul Tomis & Str Negru Voda). In summer, films are also screened at **Cinema Grădină Tomis** (Map p290; B-dul Ferdinand), an outside cinema in Archaeological Park.

Colourful cabarets, pantomimes and musicals are performed at **Fantasia** (aka Constanţa National Theatre; Map p290; ☎ 618 843; B-dul Ferdinand 11). The **Puppet Theatre** (Map p290; Teatrul de Copii şi Tineret Constanţa; ☎ 618 992; Str Karatzali 16) can be fun for the kids, even if performances are in Romanian.

The more literary should head to the **Metamorfoze State Drama Theatre & Opera** (Map p290; ☎ 615 268; Str Mircea cel Bătrân 97) in the central park. You can get tickets at the **ticket office** (Map p290; B-dul Tomis 97; ☼ 9am-6pm Mon-Fri, 9am-noon Sat, 5-6.50pm Sun). The theatre is also home to the Black Sea Philharmonic (Filarmonica Marea Neagră) and the **Oleg Danovski Ballet Theatre** (☎ 488 202). The **Agenţie de Bilete** (Map p290; ☎ 988 247; Str Ştefan cel Mare 34; ☼ 10am-5pm) also sells tickets for all performances.

FC Farul Constanţa, the city's cherished football team (they are six-time national champions), has its home ground at the 5000-seat **Stadionul Farul** (Map p288; ☎ 616 142; Str Primăverii 2) in Parcul Copilului (Children's Park).

Getting There & Away
AIR
During summer there are international flights from Athens and sometimes from Istanbul to Constanţa's **Mihail Kogălniceanu airport** (☎ 258 378), 25km from the centre.

As road and train connections with the capital are so good, **Tarom** (Map p290; ☎ 662 632; Str Ştefan cel Mare 15; ☼ 8am-6pm Mon-Fri, 8.30am-12.30pm Sat) has only a once-weekly flight to Bucharest (one-way adult/student €50/26). **Carpatair** (☎ 255 422; constanta@carpatair.com), located at Constanţa's airport, flies to Timişoara and beyond six days a week.

BUS
Constanţa has two bus stations. From the **southern bus station** (Autogară Sud; Map p288; ☎ 665 289; B-dul Ferdinand), buses to Istanbul (17½ hours, €40) depart daily. Tickets are sold in advance from **Özlem Tur** (☎ 514 053), just outside the bus station. There are three maxitaxis daily to Brăila (€5.60) and 10 daily to Galaţi (€6.70), each of which stop at Constanţa's **northern bus station** (Autogară Nord; Map p288; ☎ 641 379; Str Soveja 35) on the way. Maxitaxi 23 also departs to Mamaia from here.

From the northern bus station services also include at least one daily maxitaxi to Chişinău (€13, 9 hours) and Iaşi (€11.20, 7 hours), and four to Histria (€1.75, 1½ hours). Maxitaxis leave for Tulcea (€3.70, 2½ hours) every 30 minutes from 6am to 7.30pm.

If you're travelling south along the Black Sea coast, buses are infinitely more convenient than trains. Exit Constanţa's train station, turn right and walk 50m to the long queue of maxitaxis, buses and private cars destined for Mangalia, stopping at Eforie Nord, Eforie Sud, Neptun-Olimp, Venus and Saturn.

Eurolines (Map p290; ☎ 662 704; Str Ştefan cel Mare 71) sells bus tickets to European destinations and can arrange car rentals and sell last-minute plane tickets to Germany.

TRAIN
Constanţa's **train station** (Map p288; B-dul Ferdinand) is near the southern bus station, 1.5km from the town centre. The 24-hour left-luggage office is downstairs.

The **Agenţie de Voiaj CFR** (Map p290; ☎ 617 930; Aleea Vasile Canarache 4; ☼ 7.30am-8.30pm Mon-Fri & 8am-1pm Sat) sells long-distance tickets only; for the local train service (down the coast), buy your tickets at the train station. Student discount tickets are sold at the last window on the left.

There are 11 to 15 daily trains to Bucharest (€8.75, 2½ to 4½ hours), though some terminate at Bucureşti Obor. The fastest is the intercity 'Marea Neagră'. There are daily services to Suceava (via Iaşi), Cluj-Napoca, Satu Mare, Galaţi, Timişoara and other destinations. As many as 19 trains a day head from Constanţa to Mangalia (€1.30, 1¼ hours), stopping at Eforie Nord, Eforie Sud, Costineşti and Neptun.

There are one to two daily trains to Chişinău in Moldova (€20, 12 hours). The Ovidius train to Budapest also runs overnight (17 hours) via Bucharest and Arad.

In winter, services are reduced.

Getting Around
TO/FROM THE AIRPORT
Mihail Kogălniceanu airport (☎ 255 100) is 25km northwest of town on the road to Hârşova. Public buses headed into the city don't come right up to the airport – you have to go out to the road. All public buses to Hârşova (from the northern bus station) stop at the airport.

BUS & TROLLEYBUS
Public transport runs from 5am to 11.30pm. A ticket costs €0.80, good for two rides. Bus 100 links the train station and the southern bus station with the northern bus station. Buses 40, 41 and 43 go from the southern bus station to the centre of town. Bus 43 continues to the Stadionul Farul south of Lake Tăbăcăriei,

and the 41 goes to Mamaia. Bus 40 goes to the Pescărie bus stop at the southern edge of Mamaia. Nearly all of these routes are also covered by maxitaxis marked with the corresponding number from the bus route or simply the name of the destinations on a card in the front window.

Buses 42 (from the Fantasio bus stop on B-dul Ferdinand) and 43 go to the northern bus station.

CAR & MOTORCYCLE

Avis (Map p290; ☎ 616 733; Str Ştefan cel Mare 15; ◷ 8am-6pm Mon-Fri, 9am-1pm Sat) shares an office with Tarom. Travel agencies can also help in renting a car.

MAMAIA

☎ 241

Mamaia is where the real action is, if by 'action' you mean pretty beaches, pretty people and pretty dreadful hangovers. It's a mere 8km strip of beach between the freshwater Lake Mamaia (also known as Lake Siutghiol) and the Black Sea, but it's Romania's most popular resort, with golden sands, an aqua park, restaurants, nightclubs and a raucous atmosphere. There are over 60 hotels and tourist complexes squeezed together along the beach. If you're looking for a quiet, relaxing vacation, you've come to the wrong place!

According to legend, the resort gained its name from the desperate cries of a fair maiden, who, during the time of the Ottoman Empire, was kidnapped by a Turk and taken out to sea in a boat. As the wind howled, her frantic cries for her mother – 'Mamaia! Mamaia!' – could be heard for miles around. Today, cries of joy, or what have you, are heard from holidaymakers who come from around Romania to soak their bodies in sunlight and their livers in drink.

Mamaia hosts an annual **National Pop Music festival** (early Sep) which brings together bands from across Romania in catchy pop unity.

Information

Info Litoral Tourist Information Centre (Map p288; ☎ 555 000; www.infolitoral.ro; Constanţa Chamber of Commerce Bldg, B-dul Alexandru Lăpuşneanu 185; ◷ 9am-5pm Mon-Fri) is a highly recommended first stop – the friendly, well-informed staff can answer any questions. They also sell maps and booklets.

The **Gibraltar Travel Agency** (☎ 634 466; gibraltar travel@fx.ro; B-dul Mamaia 135-137; ◷ 9am-6pm), inside

the Millennium Business Centre, can help with car rental, accommodation and excursion bookings.

Danubius Travel Agency (☎ 480 350; Complex Pelican; ◷ 9am-7pm Mon-Fri, 9am-2pm Sat) is the headquarters of the Danubius offices for the Black Sea area.

Every hotel has a currency exchange, and ATMs are easy to find. To change travellers cheques you have to go to Constanţa.

The **telephone & post office** (◷ 8am-8pm Mon-Fri) are 200m south of the Cazino complex on the promenade.

Salvamar operates medical huts staffed with lifeguards on the beach between 15 June and 15 September.

Sights

Mamaia's number-one attraction is its wide, golden **beach**, which stretches the entire length of the resort. The further north you go, the less crowded it becomes, though the facilities become sparser, too.

In summer, **boats** (☎ 252 494; €3 return; every 30min 9am-midnight) ferry tourists across Lake Mamaia to **Ovidiu Island** (Insula Ovidiu, where the poet's tomb is located) from the Tic-Tac wharf opposite the Staţia Cazino bus stop. On the island, you can arrange boat tours and jet-ski rental (per hour €28).

A tall-spired **wooden church** from Maramureş has been brought to the area in an attempt to Romanianise the otherwise 'you-could-be-anywhere' surroundings and it now sits awkwardly on the eastern bank of Lake Mamaia.

Near Hotel Perla is an **art gallery** (Map p288; ☎ 547 389; B-dul Aurel Vlaicu). Head here to give your hedonistic, sun-drenched vacation a cultural edge.

Opposite Hotel Perla, **Aqua Magic** (◷ 8am-10pm mid-May–mid-Sep; adult/child under 12/child under 3 €10/6/free) keeps the crowds moistened. Adjacent is an **amusement park**.

Just north of Hotel Bucureşti, by the banks of Lake Mamaia, there is waterski and windsurf board rental (☎ 588 888; per 30 min €43-57).

Sleeping

Most unlicensed *pensiunes* will be a 15-20 minute maxitaxi ride from the beach; see p291 for info about alternative accommodation. Camping is no longer allowed on the beach in Mamaia proper.

Centrul de Cazare Cazino (☎ 831 200, 555 555; ◷ 10am-9pm mid-Jun–mid-Sep) Has lists of available accommodation. Booking hotel rooms through travel agencies can save you as much as 15% on the rack rate.

Popas Hanul Piraţilor (☎ 831 454; tent site/ 2-room huts €3/8) A camping ground 3km north of Mamaia's northern limit, this has shabby huts, but an on-site café and stretches of fine sand nearby. Bus 23 and maxitaxi 23E stop in front of it.

Hotel Turist (Map p288; ☎ 831 006; B-dul Mamaia 288; s/d € 32/41) This is good value, particularly for those wanting the beach scene without the beach nightlife blaring through the walls. It's off the main drag, about a 15-minute walk from the beach. Take bus 40 from the train station.

Hotel Perla (Map p288; B-dul Mamaia; ☎ 831 995; s/d/ste €43/48/75; 🔀 🖳 🕭) Lording over the resort's main entrance, this huge hotel is both a landmark and reliable service centre. It's a busy, efficiently run place, with top-to-bottom renovations completed in 2006. The small palm trees outside stay healthy throughout the year thanks to special hormone injections!

Hotel Bulevard (Map p288; ☎ 831 533; www.complex bulevard.ro; B-dul Mamaia 294; s/d from €49/58; 🔀 🖳 🕭) Next to Hotel Turist, this is a good choice among Mamaia's three- and four-star options. Modern, with a private beach and offering full services. Extra charge for in-room internet.

our pick **Flora Hotel** (☎ 831 059; d with/without breakfast €26/22.50) and neighbouring **Victoria Hotel** (☎ 831 028; www.hotelvictoria.ro; s/d €31.50/36) are just back from the beach, within staggering distance of Mamaia's legendary revelry. The hotels are virtually identical, except that Victoria has invested more in their lobby and restaurant. The rooms here are no-frills, but clean. Ever-frugal Romanian students take advantage of the large, chaotic properties by booking a double room and cramming in eight people for an extreme budget weekend at the beach. Hint, hint.

Eating

Almost every hotel has an adjoining restaurant and there are numerous fast-food stands and restaurants lining the boardwalk.

Orange Plazza (☎ 0722-500 577; mains €2-5; ⏱ 10am-6am) Located in the northern part of the resort, this is a good bet. It changes its menu every three months and has an eclectic international menu. There's also an on-site pub and disco.

Insula Ovidiu (☎ 252 494; mains €2-5; ⏱ 24hr) This famous restaurant on Ovidiu Island is worth

a visit. Seafood is the speciality of the house. They also have three-star accommodation.

Drinking

Some of the hottest discos on the strip are **Club XS** (Map p288; ☎ 831 212), next to Hotel Perla; Club XXI, 100m south of the casino; and the gigantic, slightly tacky **Cleopatra** (☎ 831 237). Entrance to these clubs is free or about €3 for special events.

Getting There & Away

Tickets for trains departing from Constanţa (see p293) can be purchased in advance at the **Agenţie de Voiaj CFR** (☎ 617 930), which adjoins the post and telephone office on the promenade.

The simplest and quickest way to travel between Constanţa and Mamaia is by maxitaxi. Maxitaxis 23, 23E and 301 depart regularly from Constanţa's train station and go north along Mamaia's 8km strip, stopping at major hotels. Maxitaxi 23 stops near Constanţa's northern bus station as well. Buses 41 and 47 also take you from Constanţa to the northern end of Mamaia.

In summer a shuttle runs up and down Mamaia's 5km boardwalk.

Bus 23 goes north to the neighbouring resort of Năvodari and the camp ground.

Currently, non-Constanţa-registered vehicles must pay a €0.50 road tax at the entrance to Mamaia, though this may be discontinued from 2007.

EFORIE NORD & LAKE TECHIRGHIOL
☎ 241

Eforie Nord, 14km south of Constanţa, is the first large resort south of the city. Beaches are below 10m to 20m cliffs and are as crowded as in Mamaia. Tiny **Lake Belona**, behind the southern end of the beach, is another bathing spot.

Within walking distance of the town centre is **Lake Techirghiol**, famous for its black sapropel mud, effective against rheumatism. Its waters are five times saltier than the sea (with 80g of mineral salt per litre; *tekir* is the Turkish word for 'salt'). The small town gets uncomfortably crowded throughout the summer, packed with restaurants, discos and thousands of revellers. However, the choice of accommodation is more varied than in Mamaia.

Eforie Sud, 4km south of Eforie Nord, is a more run-down (ie cheaper) version of its northern sister, but both have been privy to a €2.8 billion rejuvenation project, which will see building and beautifying works continuing through to 2011.

Orientation & Information

The train station is a few minutes' walk from the town centre. Exit the train station and turn right. Turn left at the roundabout then left onto B-dul Republicii, the main drag. Buses from Mangalia and Constanţa stop on B-dul Republicii near the post office.

Most hotels and restaurants are on Str Tudor Vladimirescu, which runs parallel to B-dul Republicii along the beach.

There is a currency exchange in practically every hotel. The **telephone office** (B-dul Republicii 11; 7am-9pm Mon-Fri, 11am-7pm Sat & Sun) is inside the **central post office** (8am-8pm Mon-Fri, 8am-6pm Sat).

Mud Baths

Wallow in black mud – and smell like… rotten eggs! From the train station, cross the tracks and head south for about 300m. To your right is the entrance to the **public mud baths** (admission €2; 8am-8pm) of Lake Techirghiol. Single-sex changing rooms lead to separate beaches where convalescence-seekers stand around nude, slather on the green-black glop with noses pinched and bask in the sun until it cracks. On-site massages cost €4.

Most of the major hotels offer mud baths at much higher prices.

Sleeping

Camping Meduza (742 385; tent site/d/2-bed hut €3/10/12) This cramped space is behind the Prahova Hotel at the northern end of town. Walk north along Str Tudor Vladimirescu and turn left after Club Maxim. The doubles are in a drab concrete building. The place is always noisy but it's close to the action and offers laundry service.

Bosfor Dan (743 042; Str Tudor Vladimirescu 1; d €20) Humbly sitting atop a fast-food joint, this four room option is one of the most economical in town. Though it's on a busy intersection, the comfortably equipped rooms aren't overly noisy. Bathrooms and showers are shared. Breakfast isn't included but the food stand downstairs has lots of goodies.

Pensiunea Colonial (741 561; B-dul Republicii 17; per person €35;) This three-star property has simple, clean rooms, a street-front terrace and a cosy common area. Breakfast not included.

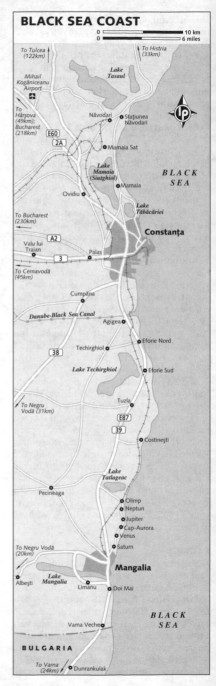

BLACK SEA COAST

Hotel-Restaurant Allegro (☎ 742 952; Str August 23, 15; d €50; ✿ ▯) A slightly swankier option, just 200m from the beach and Lake Techirghiol. Breakfast not included.

our pick Villa Horiana (☎ 741 388; Str Alexandru Cuza 13; s/d €40/60; ✿) This converted bungalow has only four rooms, but they're fully furnished and big enough for four persons. Some have their own balcony. The sumptuous home cooking by the super-friendly owners is almost reason enough to stay here.

Eating

The main market is 200m north of the bus stop, opposite the white orthodox church.

Cofetăria Pescăruş (B-dul Republicii; mains €1-3; ☽ 11am-1am) Opposite the post office, this caféteria-style joint is handy because you can point to the type of grease you want. It's good for a cheap fill-up and has live music from 9pm.

Nunta Zamfirei (☎ 741 651; Str Republicii; mains €2-6; ☽ 6pm-1am) This Romanian restaurant is famed for its folk song-and-dance shows. Walk north along B-dul Republicii and turn left onto the small track opposite the public thermal baths.

333 (☎ 742 333; ann_caramanian@yahoo.com; Str Andrei Mureşanu 1; meals €1-3; ☽ 8am-1am) This relaxed pub, café and bistro on the corner of Str Republicii doubles as a cool hangout. There is an attached three-star hotel.

Getting There & Away

The **Agenţie de Voiaj CFR** (B-dul Republicii 11; ☎ 617 930) is inside the post office building.

All trains between Constanţa and Mangalia stop at Eforie Nord, but you're better off taking a maxitaxi (€0.50; see p293).

FROM COSTINEŞTI TO SATURN

☎ 241

This stretch of the *litoral* extends the party mood from north to south at the resorts of Costineşti, Olimp, Neptun, Jupiter, Cap Aurora, Venus and Saturn. Costineşti, the only resort without a cliff backing, is synonymous with 'youth' due to the modern youth holiday compound and an international student camp; it's a rare sight to see anyone over 30 here.

Moving south, the double resort of Neptun-Olimp was until 1989 the exclusive resort of Romania's Communist Party. Ceauşescu had his own luxury villa here. Today, there's still a moneyed, elite air to these attractive resorts that cater to a slightly older clientele: chiefly affluent Romanians and some Western tourists. Two artificial lakes (Neptun I & II), ensconced in a lush forest, separate the resorts from the sea. If you arrive from (or depart for) Constanţa by maxitaxi, be warned that the main road is a 3km slog from the resort. Neptun-Olimp has plenty of restaurant, clubbing and shopping options.

Jupiter is yet another youth hang-out, with an artificial lake and a nice beach. Cap Aurora has some nice spots and benefits from being the coast's smallest resort. Venus is marginally more family oriented while Saturn has the least-expensive hotels on the coast, mainly in highrise concrete blocks. The latter has made a name for itself treating locomotor and gynaecological problems. Although Jupiter has seen some improvements recently, these four resorts are uniformly moribund compared to their northern neighbours.

Information

The Info Litoral Tourist Information Centre in Mamaia (see p294) can provide detailed information about these resorts, and it (or any travel agency) can help with hotel booking.

Changing money is not a problem at the resorts, with most hotels providing the service and numerous kiosks set up near the beaches. ATMs can be found as well.

Activities

Jet skis and boards for **wind surfing** (per 30 min €43-57) can be hired from the northern end of Neptun's beach or from the jetty in Costineşti. There is also a **yacht club** (☎ 752 395) on the beach in Neptun. Both resorts have **bowling alleys**.

The **Mangalia Stud Farm** (Herghelia Mangalia; ☎ 753 215) is at the southern end of Venus, 3km from Mangalia. It has a small racecourse and you can ride for an hour for about €6.

Festivals & Events

Costineşti hosts a **national film festival** in August. Contact the Info Litoral Tourist Information Centre for details.

Sleeping

In Costineşti, **Sim Val Car** (☎ 586 736) can help find you a room in someone's house for about €15 per person. In Neptun, try booking via **Rainbow Travel** (☎ 701 300; ☽ 24hr Jun-Sep), inside the Levent Market on the main street. In each resort, you'll also find many signs outside private homes advertising *cazare* (rooms).

There are numerous options along the strip, including finding a forest clearing and pitching a tent for free. In Costineşti, there's a camp ground at the resort's northern end. There are also camp grounds at the southern end of Lake Neptun II, at the northern end of Olimp and at the northern ends of both Jupiter and Saturn.

Hotel Amiral Nord (☎ 734 944; d without breakfast €28) Next to the train station in Costineşti, this two-star option differs from this resort's uniform mediocrity in that it's fairly new and untarnished.

Hotel Opal (☎ 731 374; www.hotelopal.ro; s/d without breakfast €25.60/32; 💻 🖭) This three-star place in Cap Aurora is good for seekers of kitsch and the exotic. It's a concrete giant built in the shape of a pyramid.

Sat Vacanta Liliacul (☎ 731 169; apt without breakfast €43-49) This is a fairly new, three-star bungalow complex in Jupiter's centre.

Hotel Cocor (☎ 701 042; www.hotelcocor.ro; s/d €64/86; 💻 🖭 👌) This is a swanky four-star option in the middle of the Neptun-Olimp resort. All rooms have internet, minibar and safe.

Most of the hotels in Olimp look out to sea. Try also the **Hotel Panoramic** (☎ 701 033; fax 701 133; s/d €45/69) and **Majestic Olimp Hotel** (☎ 701 030; www.pmg.ro; s/d €44/50).

Getting There & Away

By train, the Halta Neptun station is within walking distance of the Neptun-Olimp hotels, midway between the two resorts. The other resorts are best reached by the shuttle buses and maxitaxis that drive along the coast from Mangalia, through Saturn, Venus and Jupiter–Cap-Aurora, to Neptun-Olimp and Eforie Nord. The small maxitaxis stop in the centre of Saturn, Venus and Jupiter–Cap-Aurora.

MANGALIA

☎ 241 / pop 44,300

Ancient Greek Callatis is today a little town which, compared to the fanfare of its northern-resort cousins, has a pulse that's difficult to detect. It's better known for its several minor archaeological sites and health centres for elderly European tour groups who are bent on various cures. Mangalia is Romania's second-most important harbour, though mainly for military purposes and ship repairing.

Mangalia hosts an annual **Young Actors Festival** in the last days of August.

Orientation

Mangalia's train station is 1km north of the town centre. Turn right as you exit the station and follow Şoseaua Constanţei (the main road) south. At the roundabout, turn left for Hotel Mangalia and the beach, continue straight for the pedestrianised section of Şoseaua Constanţei, where most facilities are located, and then at the second roundabout make a right onto Ştefan cel Mare for the post office and central bus stop.

Information

There is a smallish tourist **information kiosk** (🕓 8.30am-4pm) outside the train station that gives out leaflets and can help with booking accommodation.

The multilingual reception of Hotel President can be helpful. The hotel's tourist office organises day trips to the Danube Delta and Murfatlar vineyards.

Most hotels have currency exchanges. One of the numerous **currency exchange offices** (Str Ştefan cel Mare 16; 🕓 7.30am-10pm) is opposite the post office. You can cash travellers cheques or get cash advances on Visa and MasterCard at the **Banca Comercială Română** (Şoseaua Constanţei 25; 🕓 8am-4pm Mon-Fri).

The **telephone office** (🕓 7am-10pm) and **post office** (🕓 7am-9pm Mon-Fri, 8am-4pm Sat, 11am-7pm Sun) is at Str Ştefan cel Mare 14-15.

La Maxim (per hr €0.65; 🕓 24hr) is an internet shack right on the beach, in front of Hotel Zenit. **Graphity** (☎ 758 284; Str Ştefan cel Mare 16; per hr €0.50; 🕓 24hr) is another option.

Sights

Mangalia's sights can be seen in two to three hours. The **Callatis Archaeological Museum** (☎ 753 580; Str Şoseaua Constanţei 26; 🕓 8am- 8pm) has a good collection of Roman sculptures. Just past the high-rise building next to the museum are remnants of a 4th-century **Roman-Byzantine necropolis**.

At the south side of Hotel Mangalia, along Str Izvor, are the ruins of a 6th-century **Palaeo-Christian basilica** and a **fountain** (Izvorul Hercules) dispensing sulphurous mineral water that, despite the smell, some people drink.

Cultural events take place in the **Casă de Cultură**, near Hotel President, which has a large socialist mural on the façade. One block east of the post office is the Turkish **Sultan Esmahan Mosque** (Moscheea Esmahan Sultan; Str Oituz; admission €0.65; 9am-8pm). Built in 1525, it's surrounded by a lovely garden and well-kept cemetery. It serves the 800 Muslim families living in Mangalia.

From here, head east down Str Oituz to the beachfront where, in the basement of Hotel President, remains of the walls of the Callatis citadel dating from the 1st to 7th centuries are open for all to see in the so-called **Callatiana Archaeological Reservation** (Muzeul Poarta Callatiana; 24hr). There's an adjoining **art gallery**.

Sleeping

The nearest camping grounds are in Saturn and Jupiter–Cap-Aurora. To get to Camping Saturn from Mangalia, follow Șoseaua Constanței 1km north from Mangalia's train station to the Art Deco Saturn sculpture, turn right, walk 50m then turn left.

Antrec (759 473; Str George Murnu 13, Block D, Apt 21; 24hr, calls only) It arranges rooms in private homes in Mangalia and other coastal resorts from €13 a night.

Hotel Paradiso (752 052; Str Rozelor 35; s/d €42.50/60;) A 1960s holdout, this is a popular choice. It's one of the few hotels on the coast with full wheelchair access; there are ramps onto the beach. There's a charge for 'extras' such as television and fridge (about €1.50).

Hotel President (755 861; www.hpresident.com; Str Treilor 6; s/d/ste from €53/91/147) This is the top place to stay south of Constanța – a four-star luxury hotel with a fully-fledged business centre. The lobby is breezy and dynamically decorated but the rooms are a tad drab.

Hotel Zenit (753 427; Str Teilor 7), **Hotel Astra** (751 673; Str Teilor 9) and **Hotel Orion** (751 156; Str Teilor 11) are surprisingly pleasant three-star options on the promenade. All have singles/doubles for €32/43, including private bath.

Eating

Cafe del Mar (0723-356 610; Str Treilor 4; mains €2-4; 24hr) You can't go wrong here. There's a great double-decker terrace, stylish interiors and one of the most varied, fanciful menus around – it's the only place on the coast you can get US-style Buffalo wings and potato skins!

Stock up on packed-lunch delights at the **food market** (Piața Agroalimentară; Str Vasile Alecsandri) behind Hotel Zenit.

For fast food, salads and soups try the self-service **Fast Food outlet** on the beach in front of Hotel President.

Getting There & Away

BUS

Maxitaxis from Constanța stop at Mangalia's train station and also in front of the post office, where all maxitaxis running up the coast to Olimp (every 20 minutes) and down the coast to Vama Veche stop. Maxitaxis to Constanța run regularly from 5am to 11pm, to Doi Mai every 15 minutes from 6am to 10pm, and to Vama Veche every hour from 6am to 7pm.

TRAIN

The **Agenție de Voiaj CFR** (752 818; Str Ștefan cel Mare 14-15; 7.30am-8.30pm Mon-Sat, 8.30am-1.30pm Sun) adjoins the central post office.

Mangalia is the end of the line from Constanța. From Constanța there are 19 trains daily in summer to Mangalia (one to 1¼ hours), five of which are direct to/from Bucharest's Gară Obor (€10, 4½ hours). In summer there are also express trains to/from Iași, Sibiu, Suceava, Cluj-Napoca and Timișoara.

DOI MAI & VAMA VECHE

241

This remote stretch of the coast near the Bulgarian border holds a special place in the Romanian consciousness, conjuring up images of a bohemian paradise with desolate stretches of windswept beaches, where nudists and nonconformists of all creeds come together. During the communist regime, Vama Veche (literally 'old customs point') was reserved for staff of the Cluj-Napoca university and developed its reputation as a haven for hippies, artists and intellectuals.

That was then. Vama Veche's parking lot is now crammed with expensive cars from Bucharest, free camping is a thing of the past, there are loud beachside bars for every musical taste, and nudists are the exception rather than the rule. A visible construction boom foretells big plans for the future.

Doi Mai has also been built up in the last few years but not as obviously as Vama Veche. Its beach is smaller and offers views onto a shipyard. It has retained a small-village charm and can make a pleasant base. Both towns are good alternatives to the more standard, noisier resorts to the north.

While the noise level is on the increase in Vama Veche, things rarely get wilder than on 10 August of every year, when the village hosts

House Parade, a festival of international DJs right on the beach. There is also a **jazz festival** in early September.

Activities

Patrician Activ (☎ 0722-846 876; office@patrician.ro) can hook you up with diving gear (starting at €150 for a 90-minute dip, discounts for larger groups) for dives both in the Black Sea and in a mountain lake. Also in Doi Mai, Casa Oana (see Sleeping below) rents bicycles for €1.50 an hour. **Jet Skis** can be rented on the northern end of the beach in Vama Veche for about €20 an hour.

Sleeping

There's free camping at the southern end of Vama Veche's beach, but not on the beach itself, only on the grasslands. The area is packed and uncomfortable. There are cold/hot showers (€0.40/0.65) near the centre of the beach.

Dispencerat Cazare (☎ 0722-889 087; www.vamaveche holidays.ro) Just around the corner from popular Bar Bibi in Vama Veche, this office can hook you up with a room in town for about €15.

Hotel-Restaurant Lyana (☎ 0744-671 213; d €20) This is right on the beach in Vama Veche. Its decent rooms promise a sea view – as well as the noise from all the beach discos. Its restaurant is the most elegant in the village.

our pick **Hellios Inn** (☎ 732 929; Str Gheorghe Bunoiu; www.hellios-inn.ro; s/d €25/32) One of the most pleasant options on the whole coast, this place is located in Doi Mai. Tastefully done up like a two-storey villa, with all 50 rooms facing an inner courtyard full of flowers, its rooms are small but cosy, with wood, stone or brick walls. The windows in some rooms are merely holes in stone. There's a huge bar and restaurant with open roof, a wine cellar and a large swimming pool. It's the last house on the street.

Casa Oana (☎ 743 900; Str Gheorghe Bunoiu 152; d €30) This is a bonafide B&B in Doi Mai – a lovely house with eight fully furnished, cosy rooms. Copious breakfasts are served in the garden.

Eating

Bar Bibi (☎ 0722-241 216; mains €2-4; ⏰ 10am-2am) This is one of the most popular hangouts and eateries in Vama Veche, on the main drag 50m from the beach. The meals are excellent and the first-floor pub is one of the saner places to be in the evening.

Dobrogean (cnr Str Kogalniceanu & Str Dobrogeanu; mains €2-4; ⏰ 8am-1am; ⏳) This is your best bet in

Doi Mai, though there are lots of cafés on Str Kogalniceanu, the main road. The décor is country-rustic, the menu is varied and there's internet access on site.

Getting There & Away

Maxitaxis serve Doi Mai and Vama Veche regularly from Mangalia (see p299).

TO BULGARIA

From the south end of Vama Veche you can walk or drive across the border into Bulgaria. The crossing is open 24 hours. If you cross on foot, be prepared for a 6km hike to Durankulak, the first settlement inside Bulgaria.

Motorists can also cross into Bulgaria at Negru Vodă, 15km west of Mangalia on the main Constanţa–Dobriø highway (E38). Kardam, the first village inside Bulgaria, is 5km from the border crossing.

THE DANUBE–BLACK SEA CANAL

The Danube Canal runs for 64km from Cernavodă (the site of Romania's nuclear reactor; a total of five reactors are planned for the area) in the west to Agigea on the eastern coast. The canal, which opened in 1984, shortens the sea trip from Constanţa to Cernavodă by 400km.

Murfatlar

As they approach Constanţa, the canal and railway pass through the Murfatlar area, where Romania's best-known dessert wines are produced. The profitable Murfatlar vineyards are northwest of the small town of Basarabi, some 14km west of Constanţa. Wine-tasting and guided tours of the factory are possible – but only for groups of 20 or more. Most travel agencies arrange group wine-tasting tours to Murfatlar.

HISTRIA

Histria, settled in 657 BC by Greek traders, is Romania's oldest town. It rapidly became a key commercial port, superseding Constanţa. But subsequent Goth attacks coupled with the gradual sandlocking of the harbour led to its equally rapid decline, and by the 7th century AD the town was abandoned. Its ruins were discovered in 1914.

Citadel

If you've seen the lost city of Pompeii, Histria Citadel (Cetatea Histria) may disappoint. If

THE DEATH CANAL

The Danube–Black Sea canal took 30,000 people around nine years to construct. Some 300 million cu m of land were manually excavated and 4.2 million cu m of reinforced concrete shifted by workers. This canal was only one part of a centuries-old dream to build an inland waterway linking the North and Black Seas, which was finally realised in 1992 when a 171km canal between the Main and Danube Rivers in Germany was opened.

Thousands of lives were lost during the communists' first attempt at building the canal – or 'death canal' *(canalul morţii)* as it was known – between 1949 and 1953. During the communist purges of this period some 180,000 political prisoners were placed in forced-labour camps in Romania; 40,000 of them were worked to death on the project.

The project was abandoned in 1953 and resumed again in 1975 when a more suitable route was followed.

Together with the Palace of the People in Bucharest, the canal has gone down in history as one of the communists' most costly follies – and not just financially.

you haven't, you will find the walls, baths and paved roads left at the **Histria Archaeological Complex** (☎ 618 763; admission €1.20; ☽ 9am-8pm) to be quite superb. Visitors are free to walk around the original streets of the ancient fortified city. Wild camping on the grounds is also permitted.

Archaeological relics uncovered at the site are displayed in the **Histria Museum** (☎ 618 763; free admission; ☽ 9am-8pm) at the entrance to the site. From the entrance, paths lead visitors through the ancient city's remains, and pass by the big tower into the western sector where most of the public buildings and thermal baths and the civil basilica stood. Close by is the Christian basilica, built with stones from the old theatre in the 6th century AD.

On the cliffs in the eastern sector is the 'sacred zone' *(zona sacră)* where archaeologists have uncovered remains of a Greek temple believed to be built at the end of the 6th century BC.

The complex is 4km south of Histria village. From Constanţa, turn east off the main road at the signpost for 'Cetatea Histria'. The complex is a further 7km along this road.

Getting There & Away

Getting to Histria is tough without private transport. Four buses depart from Constanţa's northern bus station, but the 4km hike from the stop puts many off. Taxis are hard to find here.

DANUBE DELTA

The Danube Delta (Delta Dunarii) is a marvellous world where water, fish and birds call the shots. While it remains a relatively small tourism centre, the area is developing rapidly in breathless anticipation of the tourism that EU membership is expected to attract. Most hotels, tourism agencies and even restaurants have private boats with tour packages, while three and four star boat hotels ('boatels') trundle through the major arteries, allowing for low impact, even plush delta tours. Yet hitching a ride with fishers or hiring a small boat to explore the minor waterways, floating arm's-length from the exotic wildlife, is indisputably one of the area's greatest pleasures.

At the end of its long journey across Europe the mighty Danube River spills into the Black Sea just south of the Ukrainian border. Here the Danube splits into three channels – the Chilia, Sulina and Sfântu Gheorghe arms, creating a 4187-sq-km wetland (3446 sq km of which are in Romania) that provides sanctuary for some 300 species of birds and 150 species of fish. Reed marshes cover 1563 sq km, constituting one of the largest expanses of reed beds in the world. Almost thirty different types of ecosystems have been counted.

This is Europe's youngest and least stable land. The river discharges an average of 6300 cu m of water per second, creating a constantly evolving landscape, made evident by the Sfântu Gheorghe lighthouse. Built by the sea in 1865, it now stands 3km from open waters.

The Danube Delta is protected under the DDBR (see Ecology on p286), set up in response to the ecological disaster that befell it during Ceauşescu's attempt to transform it, incredibly, into an agricultural region. There are 18 protected areas – 506 sq km (8.7% of the total area) including a 500-year-old forest and Europe's largest pelican colony. The delta is included in Unesco's World Heritage list.

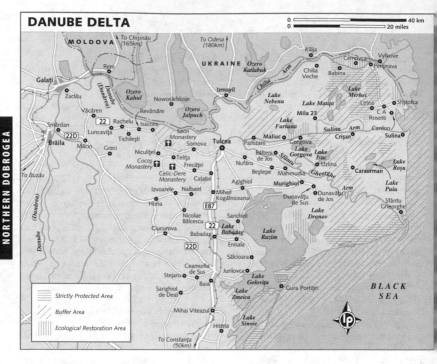

DANUBE DELTA

0 — 40 km
0 — 20 miles

Strictly Protected Area

Buffer Area

Ecological Restoration Area

Wherever you intend to go in the delta, stock up on supplies and mosquito repellent. Remember that the Danube is polluted water; although locals may use it to make tea and soup, do not drink it! (see p367 for what to do if you experience tummy trouble.) Still, sampling some Danubian cuisine is part of the experience of visiting the area. While fresh fish served in restaurants is generally fine to eat, some visitors report upset stomachs after eating fish in private homes that has not been cooked enough.

The delta's population incorporates large Ukrainian (24%) and Lipovan (13%) communities. Lipovanis form a majority in Mila 23, Jurilovca, Mahmudia, Periprava and a trio of remote villages north of Sulina: Sfiştofca, CA Rosetti and Letea. They are descendants of the Old Believers who left Russia around 1772 to avoid religious persecution. Lipovanis possess a traditional culture and are very skilled fishers. They continue to speak a Russian dialect as well as Romanian and in deference to their religion, they may be the only group of non-smokers in Romania!

Predominantly Ukrainian villages include Murighiol, Sfântu Gheorghe and Caraorman.

Climate

This is the most humid region in Romania, particularly during summer (July average 24°C). In spring up to 70% of the region is flooded. Winters are mild and it is extremely rare for the channels to ice over.

Bird-Watching

Halfway between the North Pole and the equator, the Danube Delta is a major migration hub for thousands of birds heading to/from Mongolia, Siberia, India, Africa and China. Prime times are mid-April to mid-May and late October, when half the world's population of red-breasted geese winter here. Long-tailed ducks, whooper swans, black-throated divers and clouds of white storks are equally abundant at this time.

Europe's largest white pelican and Dalmatian pelican colonies are also here, along with 60% of the world's pygmy cormorants.

Protected species typically found in the delta include the roller, white-tailed eagle, great white egret, mute swan, falcon and bee-eater.

Protected zones shield the largest bird colonies. Large green signs in most villages, most in Romanian, show visitors where these zones are and what birds can be found there. There are 65 observation towers dotted throughout the delta. Bird-watchers usually congregate around Lake Furtuna, Murighiol, the brackish areas around Lake Razim and Lake Babadag, and Histria.

Getting Around

In the delta proper it's easy to hire rowing boats from fishers. This is the only way to penetrate the delta's exotic backwaters.

NAVROM FERRIES

Navrom (☎ 511 553; www.navrom.x3m.ro, Romanian only) operates passenger ferries year-round to towns and villages in the delta. It also runs its own tours on weekends. On Saturday, tours head to Sulina, leaving at 8am and returning at 8pm (€4.80); on Sunday at the same hours tours sail to Sfântu Gheorghe (€4.80). You get to see the landscape but there is little time for true exploring.

There are now both fast and slow ferries to Sulina from Tulcea. Schedules change frequently, so check the website for current information. At the time of writing, the slow ferry departs Tulcea at 1.30pm (€5.20, Monday/Wednesday/Friday, four hours), returning at 7am (Tuesday/Thursday/Sunday) and the fast ferry leaves Tulcea at 1.30pm (€10, Tuesday/Thursday/Saturday, 1½ hours) returning at 7am (Monday/Wednesday/Friday). If you intend to return on the fast ferry, it's best to purchase a return ticket when boarding in Tulcea, as it's often sold out. Otherwise, if you're not in a rush, there's always some space on the slow ferry. The Tulcea–Sulina ferries stop at Partizani, Maliuc, Gorgova and Crişan (€2.65) on the way. To get to Mila 23 and Caraorman, disembark at Crişan and catch a local boat.

The slow ferry to Sfântu Gheorghe departs from Tulcea at 1.30pm (€5.75, Tuesday and Friday, 5½ hours), returning at 7am (Wednesday and Sunday). The fast ferry departs Tulcea at 1.30pm (€10.50, Monday and Wednesday, two hours), returning at 7am (Tuesday and Thursday). These boats stop at Bălteni de Jos, Mahmudia and Murighiol.

Ferries to Periprava from Tulcea depart at 1.30pm (€5, Monday, Wednesday to Friday, four hours), stopping at Chilia Veche. Return ferries leave Periprava at 6am (Tuesday, Thursday, Friday and Sunday).

> ### DELTA PERMITS
>
> In principle, visitors need travel permits to travel in the delta. If on a group excursion of any kind, these are automatically handled by the operator. If you hire a local fisher, ask to see their valid permit. The only time you'll need to buy one (€1) is if you go boating or foraging independently. The Information and Ecological Education Centre in Tulcea (see Tourist Information p304) can issue these for you. If inspectors (and there are many of them) find you without one, you can be liable for a fine of up to €200. You need separate permits to fish or hunt.

Ferry tickets are sold at Tulcea's Navrom terminal from 11.30am to 1.30pm. In summer the queues are long, so get in the correct line early (each window sells tickets to a different destination).

HYDROFOILS

Hydrofoils to Sulina (1½ hours, €5.25) depart from Tulcea's AFDJ Galaţia terminal, next to the floating ambulance, every day at 2pm. They stop in Maliuc (€1.80) and Crişan (€2.65) on the way. The return trip is at 7pm. Purchase tickets on board.

TULCEA

☎ 240 / pop 96,158

Tulcea (pronounced tool-*cha*) is usually passed through quickly en route to the delta, so most tourists miss its unassuming appeal. Despite reminders that Tulcea is mainly industrial (eg the billowing smoke from the brick factory outside town), it has a lively energy and an allure of its own, with hopping nightclubs and a sizeable Turkish population that lends a multiethnic flavour. For quiet strolling, there is a broad riverfront promenade where lovers hold hands and watch the sunset.

Tulcea was settled by Dacians and Romans from the 7th to 1st centuries BC, when it was called Aegyssus.

Orientation

The Tulcea arm (braţul Tulcea) of the Danube loops through Tulcea, cutting off the northern part of town (a sparsely populated area known as Tudor Vladimirescu, where the city's **beach** is located) from the main part of Tulcea where all the facilities are.

NORTHERN DOBROGEA

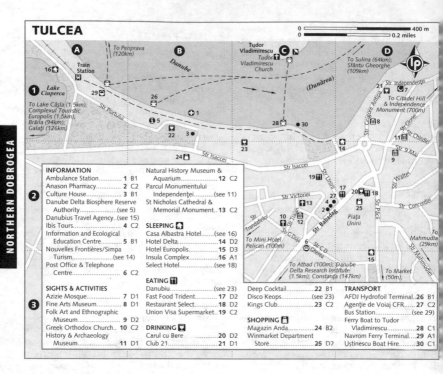

TULCEA

INFORMATION		
Ambulance Station............	1	B1
Anason Pharmacy............	2	C2
Culture House................	3	B1
Danube Delta Biosphere Reserve		
Authority................(see 5)		
Danubius Travel Agency..(see 15)		
Ibis Tours........................	4	C2
Information and Ecological		
Education Centre............	5	B1
Nouvelles Frontières/Simpa		
Turism..................(see 14)		
Post Office & Telephone		
Centre........................	6	C2

SIGHTS & ACTIVITIES		
Azizie Mosque................	7	D1
Fine Arts Museum............	8	D1
Folk Art and Ethnographic		
Museum........................	9	D2
Greek Orthodox Church..	10	C2
History & Archaeology		
Museum........................	11	D1

Natural History Museum &		
Aquarium..................	12	C2
Parcul Monumentului		
Independenţei...........(see 11)		
St Nicholas Cathedral &		
Memorial Monument..	13	C2

SLEEPING		
Casa Albastra Hotel.......(see 16)		
Hotel Delta....................	14	D2
Hotel Europolis............	15	D3
Insula Complex..............	16	A1
Select Hotel.................(see 18)		

EATING		
Danubiu.......................(see 23)		
Fast Food Trident............	17	D2
Restaurant Select..........	18	D2
Union Visa Supermarket..	19	C2

DRINKING		
Carul cu Bere	20	D2
Club 21........................	21	D1

Deep Cocktail................	22	B1
Disco Keops...............(see 23)		
Kings Club....................	23	C2

SHOPPING		
Magazin Anda..............	24	B2
Winmarket Department		
Store............................	25	D2

TRANSPORT		
AFDJ Hydrofoil Terminal..26		B1
Agenţie de Voiaj CFR......	27	C2
Bus Station.................(see 29)		
Ferry Boat to Tudor		
Vladimirescu................	28	C1
Navrom Ferry Terminal..29		A1
Uştinescu Boat Hire........30		C1

MAPS & PUBLICATIONS

The only city map you're likely to find is included in the *Tulcea Guide*, sold for €1 in museums. There are numerous detailed maps of the delta available at hotels and bookstores, including Amco's *The Danube Delta* (€1.90), which has many photos and detailed information about local marine life. The best delta map is Eco Touristic Map *Danube Delta Biosphere Reserve* (€2), published by Olimp.

Information

A floating **ambulance station** (staţia de ambulanţă; 24hr) is moored in front of Culture House on the riverfront. Some of its crew speak English.

Tulcea was suffering from an internet café deficiency at the time of writing.

At the **Anason Pharmacy** (513 352; Str Babadag 8), there's an all-night dispenser.

All the hotels have currency exchanges. The **post office** (512 869; Str Babadag 5; 7am-8pm Mon-Fri, 8am-noon Sat) and the **telephone centre** (7am-8pm) are situated within the same building.

TOURIST INFORMATION

Danube Delta Biosphere Reserve Authority (518 945; arbdd@ddbra.ro; 8am-4pm) Situated in the Information and Ecological Education Centre building (see below).

Danubius Travel Agency (/fax 517 836; Hotel Europolis; 8.30am-6.30pm Mon-Fri & 9am-1pm Sat) It arranges a variety of daytrips from Tulcea.

Ibis Tours (/fax 512 787; www.ibis-tours.ro; Str Babadag 6, Ap14) Arranges wildlife and bird-watching tours in Dobrogea and the delta, led by professional ornithologists, from €30 a day.

Information and Ecological Education Centre (519 214; www.deltaturism.ro; Str Portului 34A; 8am-6pm) This should be your first stop. Located inside the building opposite the AFDJ hydrofoil terminal, this office is a representative of Antrec and is run by the DDBR. It can book a range of accommodation and also provide helpful advice. It can also help you get fishing, hunting and travel permits. Booklets and maps are available here.

Nouvelles Frontières/Simpa Turism (/fax 515 753; office@simpaturism.ro; Hotel Delta) It organises numerous river tours (usually a few euro more expensive than at other travel agencies). Its boats hold around 80 to 100 people.

Sights

In front of the **St Nicholas Cathedral** (Str Progresului 37) there's a **memorial monument** to local victims of the 1989 revolution. Nearby is a fabulous **Greek Orthodox church** (Str G Doja). Northeast you'll discover the **Azizie Mosque** (1863; Str Independenţei), which the charismatic, elderly gatekeeper will open upon request. As you stroll along the river, note the **Independence Monument** (1904) perched regally on Citadel Hill, at the far eastern end of town. You can reach it by following Str Gloriei to its end.

All of Tulcea's museums are open Tuesday to Sunday from 9am to 6pm May to August and 8am to 4pm September to April. They charge €0.50 admission.

Some ruins of the old citadel can be seen in the archaeological site known as the **Parcul Monumentului Independenţei**, next to the **History & Archaeology Museum** (☎ 513 626; cnr Str Gloriei & Str Chindiei). The **Folk Art and Ethnographic Museum** (☎ 516 204; Str 9 Mai 4) has Turkish and Romanian traditional costumes, fishing nets, rugs and carpets among its exhibits.

The **Natural History Museum & Aquarium** (☎ 515 866; Str Progresului 32) highlights the delta's fauna with lots of stuffed birds and a basement aquarium. The **Fine Arts Museum** (☎ 513 249; Str Grigore Antipa 2) has over 700 wood and glass icons and a large collection of Romanian paintings and sculptures, including some surrealist and avant-garde works.

Festivals & Events

In August Tulcea hosts the annual **International Folk Festival of Danubian Countries**, where local songs, games and traditional activities are played out against a Danubian backdrop. Tulcea is also the site of December's **Winter Carnival**, where you can partake in Delta wintertime customs while nursing cups of hot mulled wine.

Sleeping

No camping is allowed within Tulcea's city limits. However, there are many areas where wild camping is permitted on the banks of the canal within a few kilometres of the city – ask at the Information and Ecological Education Centre for details.

The formerly stout boat hotel ('boatel') industry, with multiday Delta tours, was going through a lull at the time of writing. Keep an eye out for new companies opening to fill the void.

Hotel Europolis (☎ 512 443; www.europolis.ro; Str Păcii 20; s/d €24.50/34.50; ☒) These spacious rooms with huge bathrooms are popular year round so call ahead. For the same prices, you can stay at its Complexul Touristic Europolis from May to September, a resort-like hotel by Lake Câşla, 2km outside of Tulcea's city limits. Though favoured by groups, the site is lovely, in the thick of nature. Water-bikes and small boats can be rented and there are walking trails.

Mini Hotel Pelican (☎ 510 078; www.hotel-pelican.com; Str Trandafirilor 26; d/tr €26/37; ☐) Up the hill from central Tulcea on an unlikely residential street, this hotel has basic but comfortable rooms and a friendly, English-speaking staff. Request tiny rooftop room number seven for a sweeping view of the city out your door.

Select Hotel (☎ 506 180; www.calypsosrl.ro; Str Păcii 6; s/d €48/54; ☐) This is a mildly overpriced three-star business hotel, with big rooms, Swedish breakfast buffet, fitness centre, sauna and massage services.

our pick Hotel Delta (☎ 514 720; www.deltahotel.ro.com; Str Isaccei 2; s/d €48/60; ☐ ☒ ☒ ☒) While visiting the Danube Delta can be a peaceful, near-spiritual experience, upon return most people have a mind for soft beds, clean bathrooms and a good soak. Enter Hotel Delta. The building may be a city landmark of ugliness, but inside it boasts some of the most luxurious rooms in Dobrogea. There's a restaurant (mains €5) and a large, modern bar. Renovations have introduced a new heated swimming pool and a well-equipped fitness centre.

Other recommendations:

Insula Complex (☎ 530 908; Lake Ciuperca; s/d €26/35) Seconds from the train station, this two-star option has an onsite restaurant and pleasant rooms.

Casa Albastra Hotel (☎ 535 662; s/d without breakfast €16/20) Near the Insula Complex, this is a typical Romanian sport hotel.

Eating & Drinking

Carul cu Bere (Str Păcii 6; mains €1-3; ☺ 9am-midnight) This adjoins Restaurant Select and has a fun terrace that's great for enjoying a beer and people-watching. A lively crowd usually heads here to pull back a few. Meals are courtesy of Restaurant Select.

Fast Food Trident (Str Babadag; mains €2-4; ☺ 8am-11pm) This is an excellent spot for cheesy pizzas and pasta. It's opposite the Winmarket Department Store.

Restaurant Select (☎ 510 301; Str Păcii 6; mains €3-9; ☺ 9am-midnight) Treat yourself to a top-notch meal here; the cuisine is excellent and prices very reasonable. From its varied menu, choose from fish, frog legs, pizza and the local speciality, *tochitură Dobrogeana* (p53). The dining room is archly formal, but the best seating area is on the terrace.

There's a string of cafés and fast-food joints along Str Unirii.

Stock up on picnic supplies and fresh fruit at the **produce market** (Str Păcii) or the **Union Visa supermarket** (Str Unirii).

Club 21 (Str Grigore Antipa 10; 7pm-4am; terrace access 8am-11pm) A cosy bar with couches, art on the walls, low lighting and house music.

Deep Cocktail (waterfront; 8pm-2am) This is a two-level cocktail bar, with limited dance space available later in the evening. Theme parties and weekend drink specials are frequent.

King's Club/Disco Keops/Danubiu (514 732; www .danubiu.ro; Str Portului 2; noon-11pm restaurant, 10pm-4am clubs) This is your one stop eating, drinking and dancing emporium. Dine at Danubiu (mains €3-5), then hop next door to King's Club for drinking, DJs and appraisal of the opposite sex. Finally, cut loose for unbridled dancing in Keops. Reservations at King's Club are strongly recommended on Saturdays. The price of a reserved table (seating ten €29, seating five €14.50) is wholly applied to your bar tab, after which it's a cash bar.

Shopping

Magazin Anda (Str Isaccei 23; 9am-6pm) has camping gear and supplies.

Winmarket Department Store (Piaţa Unirii 1; 9am-7pm Mon-Fri, 9am-5pm Sat & Sun) has general supplies.

Getting There & Away

The **Agenţie de Voiaj CFR** (511 360; Str Unirii 4; 9am-4pm Mon-Fri) is on the corner of Str Babadag. From the **train station** (513 706; Str Portului) there are only two, slow trains to Constanţa daily (€5.10, five hours). There is one daily train to Bucharest (€9.80, six hours).

The **bus station** (513 304) adjoins the **Navrom ferry terminal** (Str Portului). As many as 15 buses and maxitaxis head to Bucharest (€9.80), at least nine to Galaţi (€3.15), five to Brăila (€3.15), nine to Murighiol (€1.20, via Mahmudia) and one a day to Iaşi (€12.60) and Piatra Neamţ (€13.70). There are two daily buses to Jurilovca (€1.80). Maxitaxis to Constanţa leave every half hour from 5.30am to 8pm.

One bus a day heads to Istanbul (€40).

Getting Around

Bus 4 departs from the bus and train stations, runs along Str Isaccei and heads down Str Păcii. A small motorboat continuously links the southern and northern sections of Tulcea (tickets €0.30).

Private motorboats lined up at the harbour cost upwards of €20 an hour for up to 10 people. **Ustinescu Boat Hire** (526 042) has a boat moored near the Tudor Vladimirescu ferry.

TULCEA TO PERIPRAVA

The 120km Chilia channel (braţul Chilia), the longest and largest channel, snakes along Romania's border with Ukraine before fanning out into some 40 tiny rivers forming a minidelta of its own. It's the least touristed of the delta's main arms.

Navrom ferries only call at **Chilia Veche** and **Periprava**, which is 30km from the sea. Immediately west of Periprava are the two islands of **Babina** and **Cernovca**, which were dyked by Ceauşescu in the late 1980s as part of his drive to turn the region into agricultural land.

South of Periprava lies the impressive **Letea forest** (Pădurea Letea), which covers 2.8 sq km. A national park since 1938, it is today protected by the DDBR. Tourists can visit Letea village nearby and spend a few days touring the surrounding waterways. Expect to pay local fishers at least €50 a day.

For information on **ferries** to/from Chilia Veche and Periprava, see above.

TULCEA TO SULINA

The Sulina arm, the shortest channel of the Danube, stretches 63.7km from Tulcea to Sulina. The Navrom ferry's first stop is at **Partizani**, from where you can find a fisherman to row you to the three lakes to the north: Tataru, Lung and Meşter. Next stop is **Maliuc**, where **Hotel Maliuc** (0748-200 372; hotelmaliuc2004@yahoo .com; bed & full board €40) sits directly across from

---

FLAPPING BY

Words you might (hopefully) hear on your Delta excursions: *barbiţă* (pelican); *vâtlan* (cormorant); *raţă mare* (great duck); *nagât* (lapwing); *lopătar* (spoonbill); *vultur codalb* (white-tail eagle); *ştiucă* (pike); *crap* (carp); *nisetru* (Black Sea sturgeon); *lotca* (wooden fishing boat) and *bors de peste* (traditional soup made with fish and vegetables).

the ferry stop, offering home cooking and rowboat tours and a camp ground with space for 80 people. North of Maliuc is **Lake Furtuna**, a snare for bird-watchers.

The ferry's next stop is the junction with Old Danube, 1km upstream from **Crişan**. There are several *pensiunes* in the village, all charging about €10 per person. Try **Pensiune Gheorghe Silviu** (☎ 511 279) or **Pensiune Pocora** (☎ 511 279). There is also the DDBR's **Crişan Centre for Ecological Information & Education** (☎ 519 214; office@deltaturism.ro; ✆ 8am-4pm Tue-Sun), which features wildlife displays, a library and a video room. At the main Crişan ferry dock, ask about side trips to **Mila 23** and **Caraorman**.

SULINA

☎ 240 / pop 5000

There's a faded romance to Sulina, and its position, dangling off the edge of Europe, gives it a poetic allure that's lived up to by its quiet **beach**, **lighthouse** (1870) and 19th-century British **cemetery**. First written about in AD 950, this is the delta's largest village, with some 50% of the population living here.

A canal dug between 1880 and 1902 shortened the length of the Tulcea–Sulina channel by 20km, ensuring Sulina's future as the delta's main commercial port. After WWI Sulina was declared a 'free port' and trade boomed. Greek merchants dominated business here until their expulsion in 1951. The village has been in a slow process of economic decay ever since.

There were plans to start a maxitaxi service from Sulina to Sfântu Gheorghe along a dyke, which would increase mobility options greatly, but the summer floods of 2005 have delayed this project indefinitely.

Orientation & Information

The ferry dock is located in the centre of town, with a few shops and bars to the west. There are no banks. The **DDBR office** (✆ 9am-noon & 4-7pm Tue-Sat, 9am-1pm Sun, May-Oct) is at house 1 near the dock.

Sleeping

There is a camping area on the road to the beach. As you get off the ferry, watch for people offering private rooms (around €10 per person).

Pensiunea Ana (☎ 543 252; s/d €12/14.50) has two clean rooms with a shared bath. A few hundred metres west along the riverfront from the Sulina Cinema is a small sign pointing to the friendly **Pensiune Astir** (☎ 543 379; s/d €10/20). The **Pensiune Delta Sulina** (☎ 0722 275 554; r with/without breakfast & dinner €40/30) is a comfortable, three-star option.

Getting There & Away

For information on ferries and hydrofoils see p303.

TULCEA TO SFÂNTU GHEORGHE

☎ 240

The Sfântu Gheorghe arm (braţul Sfântu Gheorghe) stretches 109km southeast from Tulcea to the fishing commune of Sfântu Gheorghe. A road runs along more than half of the Sfântu Gheorghe arm to Mahmudia, making it more accessible to travellers. From here a ferry is the only way to get to Sfântu Gheorghe.

From Tulcea, a potholed road – horrid even by Romanian standards – leads 13km southeast to **Nufăru**, a village boasting archaeological finds from the 12th and 13th centuries. The Navrom ferry's first stop is at **Bălteni de Jos**.

The ferry's second stop is at **Mahmudia**, 28km from Tulcea, developed on the site of the ancient Roman walled city of Salsovia (sun city). Emperor Constantine had his co-ruler and rival Licinus killed here.

Some ferries stop at **Murighiol** (Violet Lake), 45km from Tulcea, which was a Roman military camp in the 2nd century BC. It's a 3km walk to the river from the maxitaxi stop: keep walking in the same direction that the maxitaxi was travelling and turn left after the last house. The stacks of reeds you see piled up by the dock are exported, primarily to Germany; Germans big on folk-chic are the biggest importers of Delta reeds, used to make thatched roofs for their upscale country homes.

The most popular day trip from Murighiol is northeast to **Uzlina**, once reserved as an exclusive hunting ground for Ceauşescu. Just beyond is a trio of lakes – Uzlina, Isac and Isácel – that are popular for spotting pelicans, egrets and grey herons.

From Murighiol, the road continues 5km south to **Dunavăţu de Sus**.

Sleeping

In Mahmudia, there are numerous *cazares* and *pensiunes* to stay at, as well as one bonafide hotel, **Hotel Teo** (☎ 545 550; www.hotelteo.ro; s/d without breakfast €37/45), a large and modern full-service centre on the riverfront.

Murighiol has more options, the best of which is **Pensiune Riviera** (☎ 545 910; d with full board €15). Headquarted just 50m down the road from where the maxitaxi lets you off (further in the same direction), this B&B can easily arrange boat trips into the canals for about €15 an hour. Otherwise, **Camping & Hotel Pelican** (☎ 545 877; d with breakfast/hut/tent site per person €29/10/1.50), 3km from the maxitaxi stop, and 1.5km from the Navrom ferry port, has the advantage of being near the river but is otherwise a lonely, drab place. Some people camp wild by the riverbanks here.

Nouvelles Frontières/Simpa Turism (see Tourist Information on p304) will take bookings for rooms aboard the gleaming **Cormoran Hotel Complex** (☎ 0744-656 372, 515 753; www.cormoran .ro; s/d €40-60/50-75), a luxurious oasis smack in the middle of the delta at Uzlina. It has various types of accommodation in the area and prices vary accordingly. There is a restaurant, bar, disco and sunbathing terrace. Guests can waterski, windsurf, and hire small rowing boats or motorboats to explore the delta (at higher prices than elsewhere).

Getting There & Away

For ferry schedules to the area, see p303. There are nine daily maxitaxis from Tulcea to Murighiol (via Mahmudia; €1.20).

SFÂNTU GHEORGHE
☎ 240 / pop 1000

The ferry continues downstream from Murighiol, past Ivancea – one of the delta's largest geese-nesting areas – to the fishing village **Sfântu Gheorghe** (pronounced sfant-u gore-gay). First recorded in the mid-14th century by Visconti, a traveller from Genoa, this is one of the best places to sample traditional cooking; but the black caviar for which the village is famed (it is the only place in the delta where sturgeon are caught) is a delicacy reserved for religious feasts. Each August, the village hosts what is probably the world's most remote **film festival**. Check www.delta-resort.ro for info.

There are no tourist sights here and that is precisely the point. Highlights include spying on life in a traditional fishing village, listening to the frogs compete in the ponds, and making the 30-minute hike to the beach, where the Danube majestically enters the Black Sea. There are no beach services and few people – just deserted stretches of fine sand. From the dock, walk past the main square, then head

right, eastward. Alternately hop on the tractor or one of the private cars that shuttles people to the beach throughout the day.

Also of note is the architecture of the well-tended homes here, most of which have Byzantine-influenced porches under ornamental arches.

The only note of disharmony here is rung by the monstrous eyesore defacing the seascape to the north of Sfântu Gheorghe's beach. This was another Ceauşescu brainchild: believe it or not, it's a gigantic metal windmill. Meant to be among the planet's largest, it instead worked for two months before starting its main function: rusting.

Sleeping

Pensiune Mareea (☎ 0744-306 389; www.mareea.go.ro; s/d with full board €52/69) The best place around is a 250m walk straight from the dock. Aside from the comfortable lodgings and scrumptious home-cooked meals, the owners offer a full range of boat excursions, from €8 per person to €120 for a four-person, full-day trip into varied landscapes. From here, boats take in both sea and lake/canal ecosystems.

There are several *cazares* and *pensiunes* here: you can accept an offer from those who greet the boat, or ask around. Wild camping is possible on the beach, but it gets very windy and it's a long 2km hike in the dark.

Getting There & Away

At the time of writing, only ferries were making it out to Sfântu Gheorghe (see p303). The planned maxitaxi service over the dyke to Sulina has been delayed indefinitely due to the floods of 2005.

INTO MOLDAVIA

From the Danube Delta, the cities of Galaţi and Brăila, administratively part of Moldavia, are the gateways to further travel to Bucharest, Transylvania (via Braşov) or Suceava and Iaşi. Exiting the Danube Delta region involves a short ferry across the Danube River; this is included in bus and maxitaxi (p306) prices.

Galaţi & Brăila

Galaţi (pronounced ga-*lahts*) and Brăila are neighbouring cities near the confluence of the Danube, Siret and Prut Rivers. Perched in an unattractive backwater of Romania, at the jagged borders of Moldova and Ukraine, these two industrial cities 21km apart are merely used as transit points between Tulcea and Transylvania or Moldavia. The cities offer better connections eastwards than further north into Moldavia.

Galaţi (population 325,050), home to Romania's largest steel mill, has shabby shipyards scattered for kilometres along the riverside. Massive housing complexes fill the centre and cover entire hillsides. Brăila (population 230,687) is more pleasant, though still has a run-down, slightly aggressive air. Both were once important, flourishing ports. Romania's naval fleet is paraded in Galaţi in all its glory every year on Navy Day, the second weekend in August.

GETTING THERE & AWAY
In both cities, the bus and train stations are adjacent to each other. The most efficient mode of transport to and from here is via maxitaxis. There are no longer any ferries or hydrofoils to or from Tulcea.

From Brăila, there are 20 buses or maxitaxis to Galaţi, 10 to Bucharest, seven to Constanţa, five to Tulcea, three to Suceava and Braşov and two to Sibiu. Maxitaxis to Braşov, Constanţa and Galaţi leave from platform 1 across the street from the main bus station. Most of these buses and maxitaxis originate in Galaţi, from where there's also a thrice-daily bus service to Iaşi.

From both cities, there are five daily trains to Bucharest (four to six hours), two to Constanţa (six hours) and one to Braşov (five hours) and Oradea (17½ hours) via Suceava (seven hours), and Vatra Dornei (10 hours).

Moldova

Moldova

For a country that's only vaguely known in Europe and all but anonymous to the rest of the world, Moldova has a cultural, political and economic, erm, 'liveliness' equalled by few. Regrettably, news briefs that emerge from the region are punctuated by tales of civil war, breakaway republics, organised crime, human trafficking and a curious return to communism.

Landlocked and bounded by Romania and Ukraine, with the ethnic divisions to prove it, Moldova has come a long way in a short time and is arguably more advanced than EU-friendly Romania in many respects. The tourism focus is indisputably the country's wine industry, which produces staggeringly superb varietals and offers winery tours that will vanquish the stoutest of constitutions. Less celebrated are the attractions between the vineyards: sunflower fields, enormous watermelons, bucolic pastoral lands and the amazingly friendly people. Soberer diversions include remote monasteries cut into limestone cliffs and a rural backdrop inhabited by welcoming villagers.

What could have been a fascinating ethnic mix went horribly wrong in the early 1990s. The Turkic Gagauz and the Soviet-bent Transdniestr areas recognised the opportunity and declared their respective independences almost simultaneously, which culminated in a bloody civil war. Today, Gagauz maintains a calm truce with Moldova, while the alluringly bizarre Transdniestr region is on the brink of reopening old wounds (see boxed text, p336).

While still in contention for the title of Poorest Country in Europe, Moldova's prices (particularly for accommodation) are unexpectedly high. Coming from Romania, expect to pay about the same for almost everything.

MOLDOVA

HIGHLIGHTS

- Gorge on the many dining gems found in **Chişinău** (p325) before diving into its kick-ass nightlife

- Stagger through organised or improvised **wine tours** (p329) at the country's world-famous vineyards

- Contemplate the lifestyles of 13th-century monks in the fantastic cave monasteries at **Orheiul Vechi** (p331) and **Ţipova** (p332)

- Make a discreet visit to the living Soviet museum that is Transdniestr and its capital, **Tiraspol** (p337)

- Relax with likeminded Moldovans at the rural escapes of **Zimbet Camping** (p332) and **Satul Moldovenesc** (p331)

Ţipova ★

Orheiul Vechi ★ (Trebujeni)

Vadu lui Vodă ★

Wine ★ ★ ★ Chişinău Route

Tiraspol ★

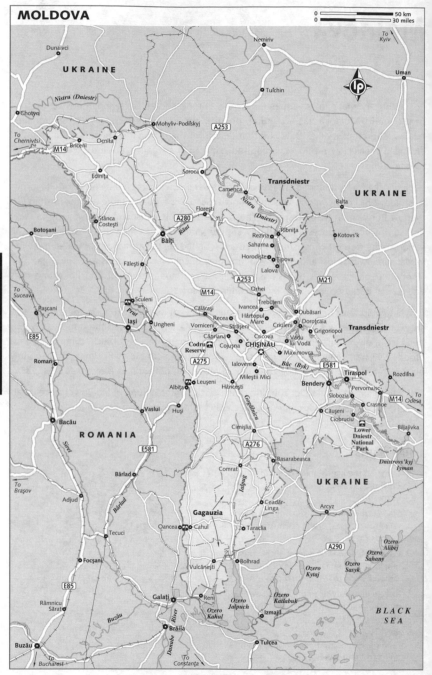

MOLDOVA

0 ▭▭▭▭ 50 km
0 ▭▭▭▭ 30 miles

History
BESSARABIA

As with so many Eastern European countries, Moldova has been sliced, diced and tossed from one owner to another in its long history of settlement. Today's Moldova straddles two different historic regions divided by the Dniestr (Nistru) River. Historic Romanian Bessarabia incorporated the region west of the Dniestr, while tsarist Russia governed the territory east of the river (Transdniestr) after defeating the Turks in 1792.

Bessarabia, part of the Romanian principality of Moldavia, was annexed in 1812 by the Russian empire. In 1918, after the October revolution, Bessarabia declared its independence. Two months later it decided to unite with Romania, angering Moscow.

In 1924 the Soviet Union created the Moldavian Autonomous Soviet Socialist Republic (Moldavian ASSR) on the eastern banks of the Dniestr and later moved the capital from Balta (in present-day Ukraine) to Tiraspol.

WWII & SOVIETISATION

In June 1940 Romanian Bessarabia was occupied by the Soviet army in accordance with the secret protocol attached to the Molotov-Ribbentrop Pact. The Soviet government immediately joined Bessarabia with the southern part of the Moldavian ASSR – namely, Transdniestr. This newly united territory was named the Moldavian Soviet Socialist Republic (Moldavian SSR). The remaining northern part of the Moldavian ASSR was given back to the Ukrainian SSR. Bessarabia experienced terrifying Sovietisation, marked by the deportation of 300,000 Romanians. In June 1941 alone, 5000 families from Bessarabia were deported to Siberia.

In 1941 allied Romanian and German troops attacked the Soviet Union. Bessarabia and Transdniestr fell into Romanian hands. Thousands of Bessarabian Jews were rounded up in labour camps in Transdniestr, from where they were deported to Auschwitz.

In August 1944 the Soviet army reoccupied Transdniestr and Bessarabia and continued where they had left off. In 1949, 25,000 ethnic Moldovans (Romanians) were deported to Siberia and Kazakhstan, followed by some 250,000 between 1950 and 1952. Street names were also changed and Russian-style patronymics were included in people's names. To this day, most Moldovans, though non-Slavic, have names like Andrei, Dimitri and Natasha – rarities in Romania.

Mikhail Gorbachev's policies of *glasnost* (openness) and *perestroika* (restructuring) from 1986 onwards paved the way for the creation of the nationalist Moldovan Popular Front in 1989. In short order, Moldovan written in the Latin alphabet was reintroduced as the official state language and the Moldovan national flag (the Romanian tricolour with the Moldavian coat of arms in its centre) was reinstated. Transdniestr stuck to the red banner.

In June 1990 the Moldovan Supreme Soviet passed a declaration of sovereignty. Following the failed coup attempt against Gorbachev in Moscow in August 1991, Moldova declared its full independence.

THE BLOODY 1990S

Counteracting these nationalist sentiments was an emerging desire for autonomy among ethnic minority groups. In Transdniestr the Yedinstivo-Unitatea (Unity) movement was formed in 1988 to represent the interests of the Slavic minorities. This was followed in November 1989 by the creation of the Gagauz Halki political party in the south of Moldova, where the Turkic-speaking Gagauz minority was centred. Both ethnic groups' major fear was that an independent Moldova would reunite with Romania.

The Gagauz went on to declare the Gagauz Soviet Socialist Republic in August 1990. A month later the Transdniestrans declared independence, establishing the Dniestr Moldovan Republic. In presidential elections, Igor Smirnov came out as head of Transdniestr, and Stepan Topal as head of Gagauzia.

Whereas Gagauzia didn't press for more than autonomy within Moldova, Transdniestr would settle for nothing less than outright independence. In March 1992 Moldovan president Mircea Snegur declared a state of emergency. Two months later, full-scale civil war broke out in Transdniestr when Moldovan

MOLDOVA

CURRENCY NOTE

All prices in this chapter are quoted in US dollars to keep in line with the practice of Moldovan businesses using dollars rather than euros in their price lists.

police clashed with Transdniestran militia in Bendery (then called Tighina), who were backed by troops from Russia. An estimated 500 to 700 people were killed and thousands wounded in events that shocked the former Soviet Union.

A cease-fire was signed by the Moldovan and Russian presidents, Snegur and Boris Yeltsin, in July 1992. Provisions were made for a Russian-led, tripartite peacekeeping force comprising Russian, Moldovan and Transdniestran troops to be stationed in the region. Troops remain here today, maintaining an uneasy peace.

Widely regarded as the poorest nation in Europe and one of the most corrupt countries in the world, Moldova is endeavouring to shake these stigmas. In late 2005 the country signed agreements committing itself to combat corruption and lock down people-trafficking. Average household income remains low and, with roughly one-third of the country's GDP comprising monies sent home from emigrants working abroad, an unproductive economic dependency is developing. Long-term domestic cultivation will be required to counteract this dependency.

In February 2001, Moldova became the first former Soviet state to elect a communist as its president.

National Parks & Protected Areas

Moldova has one nascent national park: the Lower Dniestr National Park (Parcul Naţional Nistrul Inferior), administered by the non-profit environmental organisation **Biotica** (☎ 22-498 837; www.biotica-moldova.org). Covering more than 50,000 hectares of land southeast of Chişinau, it hugs the Dniestr River southward to the border of Ukraine. Formal opening of the park has been delayed due to lack of government support. See p333 for more information.

In addition to this, there are five scientific reserves (totalling 19,378 hectares) and 30 protected natural sites (covering 22,278 hectares). The reserves protect areas of bird migration, old beech and oak forests and important waterways.

The Codru Reserve, Moldova's oldest and most frequently visited, boasts 924 plant species, 138 kinds of birds and 45 mammals. Biotica can provide information about trips to these sites.

Language

In short, the language is confusing. You might hear Moldovans referring to it as *limba de stat* (state language) or *limba nostra* (our language). Debate about whether or not there is such a language as Moldovan at all continues

---

NOT EXACTLY A NATIONAL SPORT

Did you know that Moldova is world famous for its underwater hockey teams? Well, OK, *infamous* then.

You wouldn't normally associate such a sport as underwater hockey with Moldova (come to think of it, there aren't any countries you'd associate it with, but that's another story...). However, in the 2000 Underwater Hockey Championships held in the world-renowned underwater-hockey metropolis of Hobart, in Tasmania, Australia, the Moldovan men's team puzzled referees and judges by not even knowing how to put their fins and flippers on properly. After being trounced by such stalwarts as Columbia 30-0 and Argentina 23-0, it came out that the entire team had filed for (and eventually received) refugee status with the Australian government.

It's a good thing for Moldovans that Canadians aren't known for their good memories or efficient bureaucracy. Two years later, after much hounding from a so-called Moldovan Underwater Hockey Federation based in Tiraspol (on probably the only occasion that Transdniestran officials called themselves Moldovan), the Canadian Embassy in Bucharest granted the women's team visas to participate in the world championships in Calgary.

There was much head-scratching as the Moldovan national anthem was played – and no team came out to play. But how could they? They were in Toronto, filing for refugee status. In this elaborate visa scam, each woman on the team (who no doubt wouldn't know what to do with an underwater puck even if it bit her) had paid organisers some $1200 – not bad for refugee status in Canada.

While this incident sadly spells out an uncertain future for the world of underwater hockey in Moldova, it does speak volumes about the creativity and persistence of Moldovans!

to rage among nationalist circles. The language spoken here is essentially Romanian, but nationalists wishing either to distance themselves from Romanians (who are not overly beloved here), or to snuggle up to Russia, doggedly insist there is such a language as Moldovan.

The debate was briefly rekindled after the publishing of the *Dicţionar Moldovenesc-Românesc* in 2003, a Moldovan-Romanian 'dictionary' by Vasile Stati, financed entirely by the Ministry of Culture in a politically (ic communist) motivated move to separate Moldova from Romania. More of a compendium of slang than an actual dictionary, its publication caused a passing scandal but was greeted overall with laughter and dismissal by the general population who know they speak Romanian, no matter what you call it.

The Soviet regime from 1924 onwards attempted to manufacture a 'new' language for its newly created Moldavian ASSR to pave the way for the incorporation of Bessarabia in 1940. Under Soviet 'tutelage', Romanian was written with the Cyrillic alphabet – until 1989! New words were also invented and lists of Romanian words 'polluting Moldovan' were drawn up. Some minor differences between Romanian and 'Moldovan' can be heard, and there are varied local expressions. Still, linguists agree that 'Moldovan' is at best a Romanian dialect; roughly equivalent to the difference between the English spoken in England and in America. The word *mântenesc* is sometimes used for 'thank you' instead of *mulţumesc*.

Recent changes to Romanian have been slow to take root in Moldova; thus you will still see the letter *î* rather than the contemporary *â*. Almost everyone in the republic speaks Russian fluently, and you'll find many flyers, posters and business cards written in Russian only, particularly in Chişinău. In Transdniestr and Gagauzia, Russian is what you'll see on most signs and hear on the street, though Romanian is generally understood.

Though it has been downplayed considerably since 2001 when the communists got back into power, 31 August remains National Language Day, a national holiday. Falling just after Independence Day and just before the first day of classes, it's mainly considered to be an extension of the former, serving as a convenient preparation day for students and, alas, devoid of flamboyant parades with monstrous inflatable dictionaries.

Dangers & Annoyances

While you might occasionally run into Soviet-style bureaucracy, it's much less an issue here than in Russia; people – even officials! – are generally open and accommodating. While street crime is low (there simply aren't enough foreigners to make this a viable occupation), flashing wealth around, as in any country, is not advisable, especially in places where you might stand out. Be wary of pickpockets on crowded buses and at train stations.

Travelling in the self-declared republic of Transdniestr can be wearying from a harassment-by-authorities perspective, but is still safe overall. Avoid sticking your nose into military objects and installations, no matter how pure your intentions.

Bucharest-style restaurant pricing scams are emerging in Chişinău, particularly in tourist-friendly basement joints with live music and wood-fire ovens (hint, hint). Never order anything, especially wine, without confirming the price *in writing* (eg on the menu) to avoid surprises on the bill, and be aware of the menu switcheroo. If you've been victimised, resist the urge to shred the receipts in a fury: save them for a police report.

Travellers are required to have their passports with them *at all times*. Cheeky police are prone to random checks.

Getting There & Away

Moldova is way off the beaten tourist track. Few trains and buses come here from further away than Romania, Ukraine and Hungary and, while flights from Western Europe are increasing, EasyJet won't be touching down here in the foreseeable future. While not a budget airline, **Carpatair** (www.carpatair.com) has begun service into Chişinău, via Timişoara, which is often cheaper than the competition, though occasionally Air Moldova under-cuts it. Most tourists find it easiest to enter via Romania, from where connections are frequent and easy. For an up-to-date list of all the open and traversable road borders into Moldova, see www.turism.md/eng/content/69.

People requiring visas for Moldova can usually pick one up upon arrival by air or road, but *not* when entering by train. If you try to enter by train and have not acquired a visa in advance, you will be turfed at the border and possibly arrested! The border crossing at Ungheni, Romania, does not have visa-issuing facilities. Cross at Sculeni.

BRIBE ME UP, BRIBE ME DOWN

The good news is that Moldovan police are getting a better income. The bad news is that a lucrative, tax-free second income is still hard to resist.

Whether you're a life-long resident or a fresh-faced visitor, submitting to police shakedowns for bribes is a fact of life in Moldova. Drivers are the most vulnerable, routinely being stopped for running 'red lights' or not yielding to cars tens of metres down the road. There's no attempt at subtlety; once the police have concluded with one slightly poorer driver, they stop the very next passing car and go to work on its driver, like an assembly line.

Travellers are occasionally stopped at random on the street for passport checks. It's important to know that *not having your passport on your person is a serious offence*, or so we're told. That settled, accusations may be levelled, with grimmer and grimmer consequences surfacing as the minutes wear on. As long as you haven't done something patently illegal you're not likely to get into much trouble, but particularly insistent officers have been known to throw defiant tourists in their cars and drive them around for hours for 'looking suspicious'. Note: staggering around drunk and alone after clubbing effectively invites this kind of harassment.

Expats living in Moldova report that the tap on the shoulder only happens once a month or so, but getting away without some kind of handout is virtually unheard of. Most problems can be solved with a $7 to $20 'fine', payable immediately. Just don't ask for a receipt.

Those requiring a letter of invitation to enter Moldova – which included people from Australia and New Zealand at the time of writing – will need to be carrying the original copy of the letter. Scanned, faxed or photocopied copies are not accepted.

If entering Moldova via some parts of Ukraine, you will pass through Transdniestr, where you might have to purchase a visitor's pass at the border. You will then be stopped when leaving Transdniestr to enter Moldova proper and made to pay a small fine. In this instance, make sure your passport gets a properly dated Moldovan entry stamp or there'll be trouble when you try to leave. For more information on visas, see p355.

CHIŞINĂU

☎ 22 / pop 664,325

In Chişinău (kish-i-now in Moldovan, kish-i-nyov in Russian) fleets of BMWs and Mercedes dominate traffic, while fashionably dressed youths strut down boutique-lined avenues and dine in fancy restaurants. How did this excessive wealth find its way to the capital of one of Europe's poorest countries? Answer: you don't wanna know and we ain't asking. The stunning contrast between rich and poor is only overshadowed by the conspicuously bold acts committed by individuals who are clearly above the law and shamelessly conduct themselves as such. While this dodginess may be inordinately distracting for visitors, citizens of this vibrant, good-natured city have long since dismissed these oddities in favour of what really counts: having a good time.

While photographs of Chişinău tend to show sprawling concrete esplanades smartly bookended by concrete apartment blocks, this is probably the cosiest of all the Soviet-style cities rebuilt after WWII (it was totally destroyed by bombardment and a 1940 earthquake). Just a block away from the main drag you don't feel the concrete at all through the lush foliage that holds the city in its embrace. First chronicled in 1420, Chişinău boasts wide avenues, pleasant parks, and is circled by yet more parks and lakes.

Visitors always marvel at how funky the city is; the communist government that's been in power since 2001 hasn't put a damper on the nightlife, which swings until the morning hours. One of the positive Soviet legacies the Moldovans inherited is a very Slavic attitude towards enjoying life – at all hours.

Jews used to comprise 35% of the city's population in 1913; today the figure is about 3%, though recent years have seen a reactivation of the community. In 1903 Chişinău was the scene of a pogrom that resulted in the murder of 49 Jews, with 500 injured and 1500 homes and shops vandalised; this was in response to rumours that Jews had ritualistically killed a Christian boy in Dubăsari to make unleavened Passover bread. See www.shtetlinks.jewishgen.org/kishinev/index for more information about Jewish Chişinău.

More than half of Chişinău's population today is Moldovan; Russians comprise 25% and Ukrainians 13%. As such, the Russian language is widely used in the city. The city celebrates – and how! – its City Day on 14 October, which bleeds into the Wine Festival, which takes place in the first weeks of October.

Chişinău's location in the centre of the country makes it an excellent base for day or several-day excursions to other parts of Moldova; it's usually possible to drive anywhere in the small republic and back in a day.

Orientation
Chişinău's street layout is a typically Soviet grid system of straight streets.

The train station is situated on Aleea Gării, a five-minute walk from the town centre. Exit the train station, turn right along Aleea Gării to Piaţa Negruzzi, then walk up the hill to Piaţa Libertăţii. From here the main street, B-dul Ştefan cel Mare, crosses the town from southeast to northwest. The city's main sights and parks radiate off this street.

MAPS & PUBLICATIONS
Some city and country maps are still around from the Soviet era, but they're as large as a city block. *Chişinău the Touristic Scheme* ($1.50), published by Strih SRL, is a good reference.

Strih SRL also puts out a user-friendly map of Chişinău and Moldova ($1.50), sold in most bookstores.

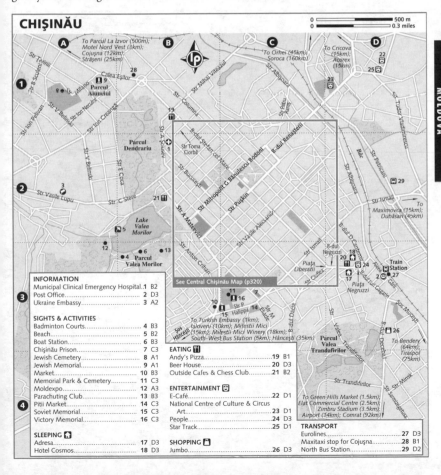

CHIŞINĂU

0 ——————— 500 m
0 ——————— 0.3 miles

INFORMATION
Municipal Clinical Emergency Hospital..1 B2
Post Office...2 D3
Ukraine Embassy.....................................3 A2

SIGHTS & ACTIVITIES
Badminton Courts....................................4 B3
Beach..5 B2
Boat Station...6 B3
Chişinău Prison...7 C3
Jewish Cemetery......................................8 A1
Jewish Memorial......................................9 A1
Market..10 B3
Memorial Park & Cemetery...................11 C3
Moldexpo..12 A3
Parachuting Club...................................13 B3
Piţii Market..14 C3
Soviet Memorial....................................15 C3
Victory Memorial..................................16 C3

SLEEPING
Adresa..17 D3
Hotel Cosmos...18 D3

EATING
Andy's Pizza..19 B1
Beer House...20 D3
Outside Cafes & Chess Club..................21 B2

ENTERTAINMENT
E-Café..22 D1
National Centre of Culture & Circus
Art...23 D1
People..24 D1
Star Track..25 D1

SHOPPING
Jumbo..26 D3

TRANSPORT
Eurolines...27 D3
Maxitaxi stop for Cojuşna.....................28 B1
North Bus Station.................................29 D2

To Parcul La Izvor (500m);
Motel Nord Vest (3km);
Cojuşna (12km);
Străşeni (25km)

To Orhei (45km);
Soroca (160km)

To Cricova (15km);
Acorex (15km)

To Turkish Embassy (1km);
Ialoveni (10km); Mileştii Mici
(15km); Mileştii Mici Winery (18km);
South-West Bus Station (5km); Hânceşti (35km)

To Maximovca (15km);
Dubăsari (45km)

To Bendery (64km);
Tiraspol (75km)

To Green Hills Market (1.5km);
Elat Commercial Centre (2.5km);
Zimbru Stadium (3.5km);
Airport (14km); Comrat (92km)

See Central Chişinău Map (p320)

MOLDOVA

MOLDOVA

Information

For directory assistance, dial ☎ 909 (in Romanian/Moldovan and Russian only).

BOOKSHOPS

Cartea Academica (Map p320; B-dul Ştefan cel Mare 148; ☻ 9am-6pm Mon-Sat)
Librărie Eminescu (Map p320; ☎ 295 922; B-dul Ştefan cel Mare 180; ☻ 9am-6pm Mon-Fri, 9am-5pm Sat)
Oxford University Press (Map p320; ☎ 228 987; Str Mihai Eminescu 64; ☻ 10am-6pm Mon-Fri, 10am-3pm Sat)

CULTURAL CENTRES

Alliance Française (Map p320; ☎ 234 510; Str Sfatul Ţării 18; ☻ 9am-6.30pm Mon-Sat) Has a well-equipped *mediathèque* and hosts regular cultural events.

EMERGENCY

For emergency assistance dial the following:
Ambulance ☎ 903
Fire ☎ 901
Police ☎ 902

INTERNET ACCESS

The central telephone office offers internet access for $0.60 per hour.
Internet (Map p320; Hotel National, B-dul Ştefan cel Mare 4; per hr $0.50)
Internet Club (Map p320; Str Teatrală 2/1; ☻ 8am-9pm; per hr $0.50; ☻ 24hr)

MEDICAL SERVICES

Contact the US embassy (p349) for a list of English-speaking doctors.

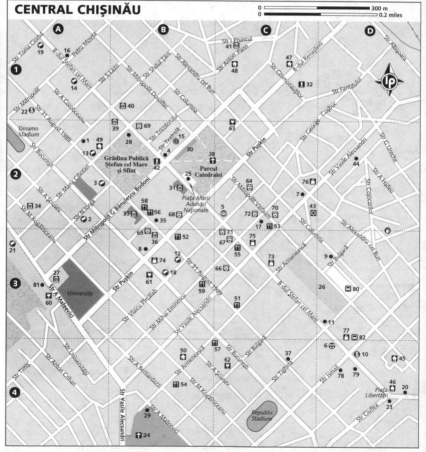

CENTRAL CHIŞINĂU

Felicia (Map p320; ☎ 223 725; B-dul Ştefan cel Mare 62;
🕒 24hr) Well-stocked pharmacy.
Hotel National (Map p320; ☎ 540 305; B-dul Ştefan
cel Mare 4) The emergency suite on the 4th floor provides
health care.
Municipal Clinical Emergency Hospital (Map p319;
☎ 248 435; www.ournet.md/~scmu; Str Toma Ciorba 1;
🕒 24hr) Provides a variety of emergency services and a
good likelihood of finding English-speaking staff.
Pharmacy inquiries (☎ 725 501; 🕒 24hr) Having
trouble finding your favourite brand? Call this free phone
service to find out which pharmacy stocks it.

MONEY

There are plenty of ATMs, in all the hotels
and shopping centres. Currency exchanges are
concentrated around the bus and train stations
and also along B-dul Ştefan cel Mare.
Eximbank (Map p320; ☎ 272 583; B-dul Ştefan cel
Mare 6; 🕒 9am-5pm Mon-Fri) Can give cash advances in
foreign currency.
Victoriabank (Map p320; ☎ 233 065; Str 31 August
1989 141; 🕒 9am-1pm & 2-4pm Mon-Fri) American
Express representative in Moldova.

POST & TELEPHONE

Central post office (Map p320; ☎ 227 737; B-dul
Ştefan cel Mare 134; 🕒 8am-7pm Mon-Sat, 8am-6pm
Sun) There is also a post office on Aleea Gării (Map p319;
open 8am to 8pm).
Central telephone office (Map p320; B-dul Ştefan cel
Mare 65; 🕒 24hr) Faxes and telegrams can be sent from
here. Receive faxes at ☎ 549 155.

TOURIST INFORMATION

There is no Western-style tourist information
centre in Moldova, but plenty of agencies can
give you information (see p322). Sometimes
travel agencies take a while to reply to emails
(if ever).

A better bet for pretrip contact would be
Marina 'Marisha' Vozian (☎ 488 258, 0691-557 53;
www.marisha.net), an independent guide based
in Chişinău. She's an all-around can-do dynamo and resource for business and pleasure
travellers. In addition to guiding, Marisha
juggles services like pretrip logistics, errand
running, research and arranging cheap and
comfortable homestays. Her website is a

MOLDOVA

MOLDOVA

treasure of pertinent Moldova information, where she offers prompt personal assistance (within reason) via email as a public service to her beloved country. While there are several excellent guides in Moldova, Marisha is the only one determinedly trying to reach out and help travellers prior to arrival.

Other good contacts:

Radu Sargu (☎ 0691-389 53; www.moldova-travel.com) Arranges apartment rentals and provides local information.

Valery Bradu (☎ 227 850, 0794-629 86; valbrdu@yahoo .com; guiding per hr incl car, gas & driver $19) A Chişinău-based guide since 2000.

TRAVEL AGENCIES

Most travel agencies will give general tourist information and offer discounted rates at some hotels.

Moldovar Tur (Map p320; ☎ 270 488; moldovatur@ travels.md; B-dul Ştefan cel Mare 4; ☺ 9am-5pm Mon-Fri) This official state tourist agency can arrange tours of the Cricova winery (see Wine Route, p329; slightly more expensive than dealing with Cricova directly, but with fewer headaches) and other vineyard tours. It can also find you chauffeured cars.

România Tourism Office (Map p320; ☎ 222 354; B-dul Ştefan cel Mare 4; ☺ 9am-5pm Mon-Fri) Get info about Romania and make advance bookings here.

Solei Tours (Map p320; ☎ 271 314; www.solei.md; B-dul Negruzzi 5; ☺ 8am-6pm Mon-Sat, 9am-5pm Sun) This very efficient organisation can book accommodation and transport tickets but is known for multiday excursions into remote Moldova, taking in monasteries and places of interest and incorporating rural homestays.

Voiaj International (Map p320; ☎ 547 769; www .voiaj.md; B-dul Negruzzi 7; ☺ 9am-6pm Mon-Fri, 10am-4pm Sat) This experienced, customer-friendly agency runs all sorts of tours throughout the country, books plane tickets and can get anything else you need done.

Sights & Activities

No one can accuse Chişinău of being overburdened with tourist sights. Lacking in 'must-sees', it's more a pleasant city to wander about in and discover as you go. Sadly, little remains of its historic heart due to heavy bombing during WWII. There are still some great museums and parks, however, and it is fun to see how communist iconography merges with symbols of Moldovan nationalism.

Begin smack in the centre, where Chişinău's best-known parks oppose each other diagonally, forming two diamonds at the city's core. The highlights here are the Holy Gates (1841),

more commonly known as Chişinău's own **Arc de Triomphe** (Map p320). To its east sprawls **Parcul Catedralei** (Cathedral Park; Map p320), dominated by the city's main **Orthodox Cathedral** (Map p320) with its lovely bell tower from 1836. On the northwestern side of the park is a colourful 24-hour **flower market** (Map p320).

Government House (Map p320; Piaţa Marii Adunări Naţionale), where cabinet meets, is the gargantuan building opposite the Holy Gates. Parliament convenes in **Parliament House** (Map p320; B-dul Ştefan cel Mare 123) further north. Opposite this is the **Presidential Palace** (Map p320).

Grădina Publică Ştefan Cel Mare şi Sfînt (Ştefan cel Mare Park; Map p320) is the city's main strolling, cruising area. The park entrance is guarded by a 1928 **statue** (Map p320) of Ştefan himself. The medieval prince of Moldavia is the greatest symbol of Moldova's strong, brave past. Every Moldovan will be happy to tell you that during Ştefan's 40-year reign, he lost a mere two battles (out of anywhere from 34 to 47, depending on your source's level of enthusiasm). In the northeast section of the park is the large **Cinema Patria** (Map p320; ☎ 232 905; B-dul Ştefan cel Mare 103), built by German prisoners of war in 1947, and still showing films to this day.

The **central market** (Map p320; Piaţa Centrală; ☺ 7am-5pm) spreads out across a huge area along Str Mitropolit Varlaam, around the bus station. The constant activity of the bustling crowds and tradespeople is reminiscent of Istanbul. Porters scurry around with trolleys to carry goods away, cars honk like crazy as they madly try to squeeze through the bustling crowds, women spit out sunflower seeds and old men huddle in groups haggling for the best bargain.

JEWISH CHIŞINĂU

North of the central bus station is a maze of run-down, dusty streets. Many of these formed the Chişinău Jewish ghetto. On the street leading east from B-dul Renaşterii to Str Fantalului is a **memorial** (Map p320) to the martyrs and victims of the Chişinău ghetto, inscribed in Hebrew, Moldovan and Russian. At Str Rabbi Ţirilson 4 are the remains of a **yeshiva** (Map p320), Chişinău's Jewish school, which functioned until WWII. Chişinău's only remaining working **synagogue** (Map p320) is close by at Str Habad Lubavia 8. Before WWII there were more than 70 synagogues in Chişinău, each serving a different trade. Glass blowers worshipped at this one.

The city's **Jewish cemetery** (Map p319; Str Milano) is northwest of the centre, next to Parcul Alunelul. Most graves are unkempt and overgrown. Ruins of an old synagogue lie next to the cemetery's surrounding stone wall. In Parcul Alunelul there is a **memorial** (Map p319) to the Jews killed in the 1903 pogrom. The remains of the victims were moved here after the cemetery in which they were buried was bulldozed by the communists in the 1960s. To get to the park and cemetery take bus 1 from B-dul Ştefan cel Mare and get off at the Parcul Alunelul stop. Cross the road and walk up the hill and along Str Milano.

MUSEUMS

The **National Archaeology & History Museum** (Map p320; ☎ 242 194; muzeum@mac.md; Str 31 August 1989, 121A; admission/photo $1.15/0.75; ☼ 10am-6pm Tue-Sat) is the granddaddy of Chişinău's museums, and well worth visiting. It has archaeological artefacts from Orheiul Vechi including Golden Horde coins, Soviet-era weaponry and a huge WWII diorama on the 1st floor, where you can speak to a man who spent 12 years as a political prisoner at a worker's camp in desolate Vorkuta in northern Siberia. A statue of Lupoaica Romei (the wolf of Rome) and the abandoned children Romulus and Remus stands in front of the museum. To Moldovans, this is a symbol of their Latin ancestry.

The **Muzeul de Arte Plastice** (National Museum of Fine Arts; Map p320; ☎ 241 312; Str 31 August 1989, 115; admission $1.15; ☼ 10am-6pm Tue-Sun) has an interesting collection of contemporary European (mostly Romanian and Moldovan) art, folk art, icons and medieval knick-knacks. Opposite is the **National Library** (Map p320; ☎ 221 475; Str 31 August 1989, 78a; ☼ 9am-5pm Sat-Thu).

National Ethnographic and Nature Museum (Map p320; ☎ 244 002; Str M Kogălniceanu 82; admission/tour in English $1.15/8; ☼ 10am-6pm Tue-Sun) has some pop art, lots of stuffed animals and exhibits covering the sciences of geology, botany and zoology. The highlight is a life-sized reconstruction of a mammal skeleton that was discovered in the Rezina region in 1966.

A few blocks south of here is the state university. Nearby is the **Chişinău History Museum** (Map p320; ☎ 241 584; Str A Mateevici 60A; admission $0.40; ☼ 10am-6pm Tue-Sun). It's a treat mainly for the old water tower (1892) it's housed in. The museum was inexplicably closed at the time of writing. This is the main meeting place for the Chişinău branch of the notorious **Hash House**

Harriers (www.ch3.md). Their bimonthly runs and drink-fests to oblivion start here.

Several blocks northeast of the central parks is the **Pushkin Museum** (Map p320; ☎ 292 685; Str Anton Pann 19; admission/tour in English $1.15/7; ☼ 10am-4pm Tue-Sun), housed in a cottage where Russian poet Alexandr Pushkin (1799–1837) spent an exiled period between 1820 and 1823. It was here that he wrote *The Prisoner of the Caucacus* and other classics – that is, when he wasn't involved in the amorous intrigues, hard drinking and occasional violence of his social circles in what was then a rough-around-the-edges distant outpost of the Russian empire.

SOUTH OF THE CENTRE

Bounded by Str A Mateevici and Str Ismail is a **memorial park** (Map p319), dominated by a **victory memorial** to the Soviet army in 1945. An eternal flame burns in the centre in memory of Chişinău's unknown soldiers who died in WWII. Soldiers' graves line the boundaries of the park and there is a small **military cemetery** at its northern end. In the centre of the park is a memorial to those who died during the fight for Moldovan independence in the early nineties. At the far northern end of the park is the **civil cemetery** (Cimitrul Central; Map p320), known locally as the Armenian cemetery, whose main entrance is on the corner of Str A Mateevici and Str Armenească. The blue-and-silver–domed **All Saints Church** (Map p320) in the centre of the cemetery dates from 1830.

The overcrowded **Chişinău Prison** (Map p319) is one block east, opposite the **Pitii Market** (Map p319; ☼ 7am-4pm).

South of the cemeteries, on the corner of Str P Halippa and Str Vasile Alecsandri, is another typically monstrous **Soviet memorial** (Map p319), with a small **market** (Map p319; ☼ 7am-4pm) opposite it.

A small **open-air military exhibition** (Map p320; cnr Str 31 August 1989 & Str Tighina; admission $0.10; ☼ 10am-6pm Tue-Sun) displays Soviet-made tanks, fighter planes and other military toys inherited by Moldova's armed forces. Kids like to swing from the plane wings and tank guns.

PARKS & LAKES

Chişinău locals' favoured haunt is **Lake Valea Morilor** (Map p319), just west of the centre. Steps lead to the lake and surrounding park from Str A Mateevici (opposite the university). Bus 29a from the city centre stops outside the university entrance to the park.

MOLDOVA

The **beach** (Map p319) on the lake's north-western shores gets packed with sunbathers and swimmers at weekends. You can hire canoes, rowing and paddle boats from the **boat station** (Map p319; per hr $2; 24hr Apr-Oct) on the lake's southern shores. There are **badminton courts** (Map p319) close to the university sports school on the southern shore. High-flyers should hike up to the **parachuting club** (Map p319; 223 563; per jump $2; 8am-11pm), just back from the southeastern side of the lake. Get strapped in and plummet 40m on the parachute jump machine – the views are great from the top, where your stomach is likely to remain.

Moldexpo (Map p319; 747 419; Str Ghiocelor 1), also inside Parcul Valea Morilor, is an enormous international exhibition centre hosting major expositions. Many tourists come here, however, to see the demoted communist triumvirate of Lenin, Marx and Engels guarding the entrance. Though they were ignominiously moved here from a prize spot in front of the Parliament building, the pedestals are often overflowing with flowers.

Northwest of the centre on the road to Cojuşna and Ungheni is Chişinău's largest park, **Parcul La Izvor**, on Calea Eşilor. It is dominated by three interconnecting lakes, which you can explore with hired **canoes and rowing boats** (per hr from $2). Opposite the park's southern entrance is a **cable-car station** (per trip $0.30; 7am-noon & 1-7pm Mon-Sat) that makes a three-minute journey across the valley. To get to the park, take trolleybus 1, 8 or 23 to the last stop. Maxitaxi (microbus) 11 runs from Str Studenţilor in the centre to Calea Eşilor.

Sleeping
BUDGET
Check out www.marisha.net for cheap home-stays in Chişinău.

Hotel Zarea (Map p320; 227 625; Str Anton Pann 4; s/d shared bathroom $10/20, 'deluxe' d $30) This drab high-rise has dour, smoky rooms that are priced appropriately. There's a bar and billiard club. Breakfast not included.

ourpick Adresa (Map p319; 544 392; www.adresa .md; B-dul Negruzzi 1; apt from $20; 24hr) For short or long-term stays, this reliable agency offers great alternatives to hotels, renting out one- to three-room apartments throughout the city. Though often in large concrete buildings, they are completely private, comfortable and have kitchens. It's also a great way to live

as the locals do, using rusty lifts or climbing staircases somewhat less than sparkling. Still, they're all safe and clean. Check out the photo album of options before you agree on one and see where the apartment is on the map. Most aren't right in the centre but are a short taxi ride away.

Hotel Turist (Map p320; 220 637; B-dul Renaşterii 13; s $26-50, d $25) For a cool blast of the Soviet past, try this friendly place: it overlooks a giant Soviet memorial to communist youth and sports a snazzy socialist mural on its façade. Rooms are comfortable, if slightly kitsch. The low-end singles are in tatty condition.

Motel Nord Vest (759 828; Calea Eşilor 30; s/d $38/51) This pleasant 100-bed motel is 3km to the northwest of the centre on the main Chişinău–Cojuşna highway. It has a tennis court, sauna and excellent restaurant and bar. Maxitaxi (minibus) 135 and 136 as well as all buses to Cojuşna stop right in front.

MIDRANGE
Hotel Naţional (Map p320; 540 305; www.moldovatur .travels.md; B-dul Ştefan cel Mare 4; s/d $47/60;) This 17-floor giant and its 319 ho-hum, mildly overpriced rooms is run by Moldova Tur. There are good services here like a small post office, a medical care room, shops, internet café, bar and restaurant.

Hotel Cosmo (Map p319; 542 757; cosmos@ moldova.net; Piaţa Negruzzi 2; s/d from $63/74;) There's no good reason to stay in this concrete tower with dull, plasticised, overpriced rooms save for access to the shopping centre downstairs, its full service desk and central location near the station.

TOP END
Mesogios (Map p320; 278 498; Str Armenească 23; apts $86-162;) Each of these beautiful, ultra-modern apartments is slightly different, some split level, some with restored furniture, and all of them fully equipped and with kitchenettes. The building, peeking through some trees on a quiet stretch of road, is a lovely example of Art Nouveau.

Flowers (Map p320; 260 202; hotelflowers@hotbox .ru; Str Anestiade 7; s/d $153/204;) If your credit limit's in good standing, this is the place. Enormous rooms with high ceilings are exquisitely decorated with tasteful restraint, incorporating paintings by local artists and, of course, a jungle's worth of plants and flowers. Public internet access included.

Jolly Alon (Map p320; ☎ 232 233; www.jollyalon.com; Str Maria Cibotari 37; s/d/ste $172/204/249; 🖥) The enticing sofas at reception are enough to make you want to check in immediately. Though the rooms aren't quite as luxurious, they are very spacious, some with balconies. Be sure to ask for one with a view over the park. In-room internet extra.

Eating

The assortment of great places to eat in Chişinau deserves a separate chapter; these are some of the best, but we encourage you to explore others that look interesting. See also Drinking (p326, as many pubs also have full menus.

CAFÉS & QUICK EATS

When the sun shines, outdoor cafés sprout like mushrooms. A popular terrace is outside the Opera & Ballet Theatre (p327). There are also some good outdoor cafés across the road from the main entrance to the university on Str A Mateevici and in the opposite courtyard leading to Parcul Valea Morilor. At the northern end of Str A Mateevici is another courtyard filled with outdoor cafés (Map p319) and chess fiends. The chess club is in the same courtyard.

For the cheapest of cheap eats, there are some kiosks and small 'cafés' around the bus station and central market, where a dish of mystery meat or meat-filled pastries is less than $1. Most go there for beer and vodka shots.

Café (Map p320; Str Puşkin 22; mains $1-2; ⏰ 11am-11pm) This no-name cafeteria serves surprisingly succulent food priced for the university crowd.

Andy's Pizza (Map p319; ☎ 210 210; B-dul Ştefan cel Mare 169; mains $2-4; ⏰ 7.30am-11pm) This popular chain has locations all around Chişinău, but this is its most stylish branch, with a high-tech look that makes it popular with a young, on-the-move clientele. The thick and gooey pizzas, spaghetti and chicken wings keep clients happily purring.

Green Hills Café (Map p320; ☎ 223 295; B-dul Ştefan cel Mare 77; mains $4-10; ⏰ 8.30am-10pm Mon-Sat, 10am-10pm Sun) Though the meals are delicious, most come here for a quick fix – great coffee, cocktails or beer, and of course to people-watch while sitting on the city's main drag.

our pick Cactus Café (Map p320; ☎ 504 094; www.cactus.md; Str Armenească 41; mains $4-8; ⏰ 9am-10pm) This is a true winner. The eclectic interior décor (Wild West meets urban bohemian, but with grace and humour) is matched by the city's most creative menu. There are incredible breakfasts (a rarity in these parts), lots of vegetarian meals (soy meat!), wild plates such as turkey with bananas and the country's most killer gazpacho.

RESTAURANTS

Class (Map p320; ☎ 227 774; Str Vasile Alecsandri 121; mains $4; ⏰ 11am-midnight) One of the country's rare Lebanese restaurants, Class doesn't disappoint with excellent starters, falafel and eggplant dishes. It offers waterpipes ($2.50), live music

MOLDOVA

MAKE NEW FRIENDS

As the locals are friendly and outgoing, you shouldn't have any trouble winning acquaintances in Moldova. However if you want to be instantly embraced, and possibly kissed, steer the conversation towards music, then casually drop these names: Zdob şi Zdub and Gândul Mâţei.

Zdob şi Zdub (zdob-shee-zdoob; www.zdob-si-zdub.com) have been together since 1995, working Moldovan audiences into a lather with their Romanian-folk-meets-the-Red-Hot-Chilli-Peppers sound fusion. In 2005, with little preparation and virtually no financial support from its own government, the group achieved a stunning sixth-place finish in the Eurovision Song Contest. They are now touring so ferociously that poor Moldova hardly hears from them. Your best chance is to catch a show in Romania.

Gândul Mâţei (gun-dool muts-ehee; www.gm.md) nimbly runs the gamut from lounge music to Coldplay-esque ballads to rocking *hard*. They're starting to break out of the Moldovan market, but still gig regularly in Chişinău.

Both bands have a very strong following in Moldova and locals aged between 15 and 35 are guaranteed to become unwound with breathless reverence at the mere mention of their names. Moreover, their shows are nothing short of fabulous and are a highly recommended experience.

every night and exotic dancing on Friday and Saturday evenings.

Green Hills Restaurant (Map p320; ☎ 220 451; Str 31 August 1989, 78; mains $4-10; ✦ 9am-midnight) This is run by the same bunch who operate the Green Hills café and supermarket, featuring the same menu. There's a large, extremely pleasant terrace that's perfect for a sit-down meal from the large selection of meat and vegetable dishes.

Oraşul Vechi (Old City; Map p320; ☎ 225 063; Str Armenească 24; mains $4-10; ✦ noon-midnight) One of your best bets is this stylish folk restaurant which doesn't overdo the folk theme. The grill house in the back has an open view into the glassed kitchen with wood-fire oven. Fish is the speciality with shark and octopus on the un-PC section of the menu.

Symposium (Map p320; ☎ 211 318; Str 31 August 1989, 78A; mains $5-10; ✦ 11am-midnight) Though not as expensive as some top-class restaurants in town, this can be called one of the city's top dining experiences in terms of elegance and refinement. In this cellar refitted with antiques, the French-style cuisine is succulent, with lamb dishes the speciality. There's a large selection of local wines.

Vila Vechi (Map p320; ☎ 225 526; Str Mihai Eminescu 44/1; mains $4-11; ✦ 11am-midnight) An elegant Moldovan restaurant, tastefully decorated in stone and modern art with a covered terrace done in a zebra-stripe motif.

El Paso (Map p320; ☎ 504 400; Str Armenească 10; mains $4-15; ✦ noon-11pm) To get your Mexican fix, head to this excellent, comfortable place. The menu runs the gamut from quesadillas to salmon in chilli sauce and pork with chocolate-almond sauce!

Mesogios (Map p320; ☎ 278 498; Str Armenească 23; mains $5-12; ✦ 12.30am-11pm) Seafood is the focus here, with fish imported from the Mediterranean. There are meat dishes and Moldovan specialities too in this elegant dining room which incorporates some Art Nouveau design elements to match the building's impressive exterior.

our pick **Beer House** (Map p319; ☎ 275 627; B-dul Negruzzi 6/2; mains $4-14; ✦ 11am-11pm) Of all Chişinău's hot dining places, you'll be returning to this brewery-cum-restaurant again and again – most likely for its delicious home-brewed beers, but also for its great menu, which ranges from chicken wings and soups to rabbit and chicken grilled in cognac. Its relaxed ambience and impeccable service add to the charm.

SELF-CATERING

The **central market** (Map p320; Piaţa Centrală; ✦ 7am-5pm) has since 1825 been the place where Moldovans haggle over prices for fresh produce. It's well worth a visit for its choice of fresh food and lively ambience. It sprawls out around the central bus station on Str Bendery and Str Armenească. There's always something going on here at all times of the day or night.

Slightly out of the centre is **Green Hills Market** (B-dul Decebal 139B; ✦ 9am-9pm) – one of the best-stocked supermarkets in town. Its B-dul Ştefan cel Mare 77 location (Map p320) has a good grocery section too, and is more convenient.

Drinking

Coliba Studenţilor (Map p320; ✦ 8am-11pm) This student hangout is opposite the university, just above the park. The terrace is a good place to bump into eager English speakers.

Dublin Irish Pub (Map p320; ☎ 245 855; Str Bulgară 27; pint of beer $5.50; ✦ noon-11pm) The atmosphere is always lively at this expensive but popular Celtic-cum-Moldovan Irish pub. While the bar is the highlight, the restaurant is a temptation as well with tantalising dishes such as Cock-a-leekie (leek with duck, chicken, prunes and veggies stewed in Guinness), 'slappy joe' and a classic Irish stew (mains $2.50 to $12).

Déjà Vu (Map p320; ☎ 227 693; Str Bucureşti 67; ✦ 11am-2am) This is a true cocktail bar, where the drinks menu is extensive and where the bartenders twirl glasses with aplomb. There is also a small dining hall serving meals, but most people come here to lounge about looking fabulous with multicoloured cocktails perched in their hands.

Robin Pub (Map p320; Str Alexandru cel Bun 83; ✦ 11am-midnight) A friendly local pub feel reigns supreme in this relaxed, tastefully decorated hang-out with an extravagant menu (mains $5 to $11). An ideal place to forget about the world for hours in a down-to-earth, unpretentious atmosphere.

Entertainment

Posters listing what's on where are pasted on the *teatrul concerte* noticeboard outside the Opera & Ballet Theatre on B-dul Ştefan cel Mare. The English-language magazine *Welcome* runs a fortnightly calendar of cultural events.

MOLDOVA

CLUBS

Chişinău rocks in all directions throughout the night, but be prepared to walk through metal detectors and deal with tough-guy posturing from goonish doormen at some of the larger clubs. Entry fees range from $3 to $12.

People (Map p319; ☎ 275 800; B-dul Negruzzi 2/4; ☾ 10pm-4am Thu-Sat) The best disco in town has lots of theme nights and special DJs. The doormen might try to lead male customers into the next-door strip club, but the real action is on the dance floor. The crowd is mainly early 20s, though 'middle-aged customers are also welcome'.

City Club (Map p320; Str 31 August 1989, 121; ☾ 10pm-2am) In the alley next to the Licurici Puppet Theatre, this 2nd-floor club is vying for the title of 'Hippest Place in Town'. You be the judge.

Star Track (Map p319; ☎ 496 207; Str Kiev 7; ☾ 10pm-4am Tue-Sun) The centrepiece of the Rîşcani district nightlife, its dark interior sports comfortable sofas and intimate booths where love-struck couples can smooch while scrutinizing the dance performances by lace-clad men and women. Under Star Track is the less titillating but equally popular Military Pub.

E-Café (Map p319; ☎ 0691-326 81; B-dul Moscovei 1/2; entrance $5) Also in Rîşcani, behind McDonald's, this club hosts jazz shows on Sunday nights (7pm).

CIRCUS

Itching to see the man on the flying trapeze? Head to the loftily titled **National Centre of Culture & Circus Art** (Map p319; ☎ 496 803; B-dul Renaşterii 33; ☾ box office 9am-6pm). Performances are held at 6.30pm Friday, and at noon, 3pm and 6.30pm on Saturday and Sunday. Bus 27 from B-dul Ştefan cel Mare goes there. Renovations were under way at the time of writing.

LIVE MUSIC

Classical concerts and organ recitals are held at the **Sala cu Orgă** (Organ Hall; Map p320; ☎ 225 404; B-dul Ştefan cel Mare 79) next to the Mihai Eminescu National Theatre. Performances start at 6pm; tickets are sold at the door.

Moldova's National Philharmonic is based at the **Philharmonic Concert Hall** (Map p320; ☎ 224 505; Str Mitropolit Varlaam 78).

SPECTATOR SPORTS

Moldovans are big football fans and Chişinau has three stadiums to prove it. The new **Zimbru**

Stadium is the city's first European regulation football stadium, located in Botanica. The **Republic Stadium** (Stadionul Republican; Map p320), south of the centre, has floodlighting. **Dinamo Stadium** (Stadionul Dinamo; Map p320) is north of the centre on Str Bucureşti. Moldovans like football so much, in fact, there's an American football team called the Chişinău Barbarians, who hold occasional matches, in full gear.

THEATRE, OPERA & BALLET

The **Opera & Ballet Theatre** (Map p320; ☎ 244 163; B-dul Ştefan cel Mare 152; ☾ box office 10am-2pm & 5-7pm) is home to the esteemed national opera and ballet company. It mainly stages classics but some modern pieces are occasionally performed. Tickets costs upwards of $3.

If your Romanian is up to snuff, you'll get a few belly laughs from the plays staged at the **Satirical Theatre** (Teatrul Satiricus; Map p320; ☎ 224 034; Str Mihai Eminescu 55). Contemporary Romanian productions can be seen at the **Mihai Eminescu National Theatre** (Map p320; ☎ 221 177; B-dul Ştefan cel Mare 79; ☾ box office 11am-1pm & 2-6.30pm) founded in 1933, while plays in Russian are performed at the **Chekhov Drama Theatre** (Teatrul Dramatic A Cehov; Map p320; ☎ 223 362; Str Pîrcălab 75), situated where Chişinău's choral synagogue was until WWII.

The **Luceafărul Theatre** (Poetic Star Youth Theatre; Map p320; ☎ 224 121; Str Veronica Micle 7) stages more alternative productions. Productions in Moldovan and Russian are held at the **Licurici Puppet Theatre** (Map p320; ☎ 245 273; Str 31 August 1989, 121; ☾ box office 9am-2pm Tue-Sun). Performances the kids will enjoy despite the language barrier usually start at 11am daily.

Various cabarets, musicals and local theatre group productions take place at the **National Palace** (Map p320; ☎ 213 544; Str Puşkin 21; ☾ box office 11am-5pm).

Shopping

Cricova (Map p320; ☎ 222 775; B-dul Ştefan cel Mare 126; ☾ 10am-7pm Mon-Fri, 10am-6pm Sat, 10am-4pm Sun) This commercial outlet of the Cricova wine factory is definitely worth a visit, especially if you won't be taking the winery tour (see p329). It stocks many types of affordable Cricova wines and champagnes (only $2 to $5 each), and the crystal glasses from which to drink them.

Mileştii Mici (Map p320; ☎ 211 229; www.milestii-mici .md; Str Vasile Alecsandri, 137; ☾ 9am-4pm Mon-Sat) This

MOLDOVA

major wine producer (also see p330) also has outlets on the 1st floor of the Elat Commercial Centre (4km southeast of the centre) and at the airport.

Ialoveni (Map p320; B-dul Ștefan cel Mare 128; 9am-6pm Mon-Fri, 10am-4pm Sat & Sun) The outlet for the Ialoveni sherry factory.

Unic Shopping Centre (Map p320; B-dul Ștefan cel Mare 8; 8am-7pm Mon-Sat) This main shopping centre is redolent of Soviet times but will have everything you need.

Galeria L (Map p320; ☎ 221 975; Str București 64; 10am-6pm Mon-Fri, 10am-5pm Sat) This place holds temporary art exhibitions but also sells small works of art and souvenirs crafted by local artists.

Jumbo (Map p319; B-dul Decebal) A midsized commercial centre with clothes, food and internet shops.

Getting There & Away
AIR
All international flights to Moldova use Chișinău (Kishinev) airport, Moldova's only airport, 14.5km southeast of the centre. Moldova has three national airlines.

Moldavian Airlines (Map p320; ☎ 549 339, airport 525 506; www.mdv.md; B-dul Ștefan cel Mare 3) located in the **Air Service** (www.airservice.md) travel centre offers 12 weekly flights to Timișoara and two daily flights to Budapest, from where it has connections to other European destinations. Also in the Air Service centre is **Carpatair** (www.carpatair.com), which flies to Timișoara and beyond six times a week.

Air Moldova (Map p320; ☎ 546 464, airport 525 506; www.airmoldova.md; B-dul Negruzzi 8) is the state carrier for Moldova, with direct flights to Amsterdam, Istanbul, Larnaca, Minsk, Moscow, Paris, Yekaterinburg, St Petersburg and Sofia.

Aerotour (Map p320; ☎ 542 454, airport 525 413; www.transaero.md; B-dul Ștefan cel Mare 4) has three weekly flights to Amsterdam and Rome, two to Paris and Prague, one or two daily flights to Bucharest, Moscow and Istanbul, two daily flights to Budapest, and a daily flight to Vienna.

Tarom (Map p320; ☎ 541 254, 272 618; tarom@mtc.md; B-dul Ștefan cel Mare 3; 9am-5pm) flies to Bucharest eight times a week.

BUS
Chișinău has three bus stations. The **north bus station** (Autogară Nord; Map p319; ☎ 439 489; Str Petricani) is where nearly all domestic and international

lines depart, except Transdniestr-bound lines, which depart from central. Services include 12 daily buses to Strășeni, and regular buses to Bălți, Recea, Edinița and Briceni. There are buses every half-hour between 9.15am and 10pm to Orhei.

There are daily buses to Bucharest ($14; 12 hours), Odesa ($4.15), Moscow ($31.50), St Petersburg, Kyiv and Minsk. You can buy advance tickets here or out of a tiny office at the train station. The information booth charges 1 leu ($0.07) per question.

Domestic and international maxitaxis operate out of the **central bus station** (Autogară Centrală; Map p320; ☎ 542 185), behind the central market on Str Mitropolit Varlaam. Maxitaxis go to Tiraspol and Bendery every 20 to 35 minutes from 6.30am to 6.30pm, with reduced services until 10pm.

Bus services to/from Comrat, Hâncești and other southern destinations use the less crowded **southwestern bus station** (Autogară Sud-vest; ☎ 723 983), 5km from the city centre on the corner of Șoseaua Hâncești and Str Spicului. Above each ticket window is a list of destinations covered by that ticket-seller. Daily local services include five buses to Comrat in Gagauzia and six to Hâncești. A fleet of private maxitaxis to Iași, Romania ($10, four hours) departs from here.

Eurolines (Map p319; ☎ 549 813, 271 476; www.eurolines.md; Aleea Gării) in the train station, offers regular routes to Italy, Spain and Germany (usually around $140 return).

TRAIN
The **train station** (Map p319; ☎ 252 737; Aleea Gării) is swelling with pride after major renovations have made it as modern as any in Western Europe. The **left luggage office** (24 hr) is 100m north of the main entrance alongside the platform. Ticket counters 13, 14 and 15 are for international destinations; 12 is for destinations within Moldova and the CIS.

International routes include three daily trains to Moscow ($46, 28 to 33 hours), one each to St Petersburg ($31.50, 37 hours), Bucharest ($29.50, 14 hours) and Lviv ($15.50, eight hours), and two a week to Minsk ($19.50, 25 hours). To get to Budapest, you must change in Bucharest.

Due to the train service interruption through Transdniestr, there were no trains to Bendery, Tiraspol or Odesa at the time of writing.

Five daily trains go to Comrat and four to Ungheni.

Getting Around
TO/FROM THE AIRPORT

Bus 65 departs every 30 minutes between 5am and 10pm from the central bus station to the airport. Maxitaxi 65 ($0.25) departs every 20 minutes from Str Ismail, near the corner of B-dul Ştefan cel Mare.

BUS & TROLLEYBUS

Bus 45 (and maxitaxi 45a) runs from the central bus station to the southwestern bus station. Bus 1 goes from the train station to B-dul Ştefan cel Mare.

Trolleybus 1, 4, 5, 8, 18 and 22 go to the train station from the city centre. Bus 2, 10 and 16 go to Autogară Sud-vest. Tickets, costing $0.15 for buses and $0.10 for trolleybuses, are sold at kiosks or direct from the driver.

Most bus routes in town and to many outlying villages are served by maxitaxis. These are faster but more expensive than regular buses ($0.25 per trip, pay the driver). Route numbers, displayed on the front and side windows, are followed by the letter *a* or *t*. Those with the letter *a* follow the same route as the bus of the same number. Those with a letter *t* follow the trolleybus routes. Maxitaxis run regularly between 6am and midnight.

CAR & MOTORCYCLE

Loran Car Rental (Map p320; ☎ 243 710; www.turism.md /loran; Str A Mateevici 79) has car-hire starting at €34 per day (Dacia Logan), including insurance. All payments must be made in cash (euros) and a deposit is required.

TAXI

Drivers at official taxi stands often try to rip you off. Calling a **taxi** (☎ 746 565/705/706/707) is cheaper. The official rate is $0.25 per kilometre.

WINE ROUTE

Though vineyards small and large are scattered throughout the country, the ones most often visited are in easy striking distance of Chişinău. Each of these places makes for a pleasant (and woozy) day trip, and some can be combined into an epic wine-tasting adventure that would do a sommelier proud.

Moldovan wines routinely grab highest honours at European tastings and beyond.

There is arguably no other place on Earth where you can sample the same quality of wine at such low prices.

Private transport is all but essential to get around in these parts. Buses of varying frequencies bring you to most of the villages, though not always near the wineries, which can be a sobering three to five kilometres distant. If you aren't on an organised tour with a travel agency (p322), you can always hire a car, preferably with a designated driver, and make the journey yourself. Hiring a private taxi in Chişinău is also an option, negotiating a fixed price with the driver. Most will be happy to do it for $40 to $60 for a six- to eight-hour day.

Cricova

The **Cricova winery** (☎ 22-277 378; www.cricova.md; Str Ungureanu 1; ⏰ 8am-4pm) is the grand duke of Moldovan wineries – and it knows it. This underground wine kingdom, 15km north of Chişinău in the village of Cricova, is one of Europe's biggest. It boasts 120km of labyrinthine roadways, 60 of which are used for wine storage, up to 100m underground. These 'cellars' are lined with wall-to-wall bottles and are kept at a temperature of 12°C to 14°C, with humidity at 96% to 98% to best protect the 1.25 million bottles of rare and collectible wine plus the 30 million litres of wine the factory produces annually (during Soviet times, the winery's output was two to three times this!). Tunnels have existed here since the 15th century, when limestone was dug out to help build Chişinău. They were converted into an underground wine emporium in the 1950s.

Cricova wines and champagnes enjoy a high national and international reputation. Legend has it that in 1966 astronaut Yuri Gagarin entered the cellars, re-emerging (with assistance) two days later. Russian president Vladimir Putin celebrated his 50th birthday here. Cricova's wines were among the top drops produced in the USSR. Its sparkling white was sold under the label 'Soviet Champagne'. Demand for its dry white sauvignon, muscadet and sweeter muscats remains high. Unique to the Cricova cellars is its sparkling red wine, made from cabernet sauvignon stocks and marketed as having a rich velvet texture and a blackcurrant and cherry taste. The *champenoise* method used to make sparkling wines here is unique to Moldova, France, Ukraine and Russia.

MOLDOVA

The most interesting part of your obligatorily guided tour is a visit to the wineglass-shaped cellar of collectibles, including 19 bottles of Gerhing's wines, a 1902 bottle of Becherovka, a 1902 bottle of Evreiesc de Paşti from Jerusalem and pre-WWII French red wines.

You must have private transport and advance reservations to get into Cricova. Regrettably, the winery is lax when it comes to answering emails, or the phone for that matter, hence booking through travel agencies in Chişinău and swallowing the booking fee is the path of least resistance. You can also try to make a booking at Cricova's Chişinău **headquarters** (Map p320; Str Vasile Alecsandri 111/7). The two-hour tour ($62 per person) includes trips down streets with names such as Str Cabernet and Str Pinot, wine tasting, a light meal and a few 'complimentary' bottles. Though the tour is admittedly worthwhile, Cricova's starch formality and astonishing aversion to customer contact puts off many visitors.

Acorex

Once you've finished at Cricova, head to **Acorex** (www.acorex.net; 9am-6pm), just down the hill. There's no tour, but its shop sells the winery's Legenda, Reserve, Select and other limited lines not available in most stores or outside Moldova. Acorex is one of the most internationally awarded wineries in Moldova, so don't miss a chance to pick up yet another mouth-watering bottle of fermented heaven!

Cojuşna

These spunky competitors to Cricova operate 12km northwest of Chişinău in the village of Cojuşna. This place is moribund in comparison with Cricova or even Ialoveni. However, the tours given here are first rate, down to earth and very friendly. What they lack in production they make up for with heart and charm. Sales have plummeted since Cojuşna's fabulous distribution network collapsed along with the USSR, and since most of its land was taken over and privatised (they reap the harvest of smaller wineries). Foreign investment will most likely be required to get the plant back up to its 12,000-bottle-per-hour capacity.

Cojuşna (22-744 820, 715 329; Str Lomtadze 4; 2-3hr tour per person Mon-Fri $17, Sat/Sun $20/40; 8am-6pm Mon-Fri, by appointment Sat & Sun), founded in 1908, is geared for tourists and is therefore very flexible – it will open its wine cellars and

wine-tasting rooms for you day and night. The cellars comprise six 'alleys', each 100m long. The wine tasting comes with a full meal, served in an impressive and seductively cosy hall decorated with wooden furniture carved by a local 17-year-old boy and his father.

Organising a tour of Cojuşna is a breeze: just show up! However, you'll need to give advance warning if you require a tour in English. You can buy wines ($2 to $12 per bottle) from the Cojuşna shop in the complex.

Bus 2 runs every 15 minutes from Str Vasile Alecsandri in Chişinău towards Cricova. Buses to Straseni stop at Cojuşna, or you can catch one of the frequent maxitaxis leaving from Calea Eşilor (Map p319); take trolleybus 1, 5 or 11 up Ştefan cel Mare, to the Ion Creangă university stop. Alight at the Cojuşna stop, ignore the turn on the left marked 'Cojuşna' and walk or hitch the remaining 2km along the main road to the winery entrance, marked by a tall, totem pole–style pillar.

South of Chişinău

Moldova's wine road sprawls south of Chişinău too. **Ialoveni**, 10km south of the capital, is home to **Vinuri Ialoveni** (737 838; www.wineialoveni.com; Str Alexandru cel Bun 4; 1-4hr tours $10-40; 8am-5pm Mon-Fri), known for its fine sherry called Heres. It's the only place in Moldova that makes this sweet drink. The premises aren't as impressive as Cricova's though here you get to see enormous 20,000L oak barrels up close.

At the **shop** (8am-1pm & 3-6pm Mon-Fri, 9am-2pm Sat) you can buy bottles of Heres and other wines for as little as $2. The Gloria line of sherry is particularly good, though it packs a wallop at 33% alcohol. Most prefer the dry matured Heres, which has a slight walnut taste. A range of tours is on offer, from a one-hour tour and tasting session to a four-hour excursion with a light meal and souvenir bottles.

While Cricova has the hype, **Mileştii Mici** (382 336, 382 333; www.milestii-mici.md; tours per person $11.50-39; 8am-5pm Mon-Fri), 8km east of Ialoveni, has the goods. Also housed in a limestone mine, these are *the* largest cellars in Europe, with a network of 'streets' more than 200km in length, some 55km of which are being used for storage. It was recognised by Guinness in 2005 for having the largest wine collection in the world – 1.5 million bottles – though at the time of writing the collection had surpassed the 2-million-bottle mark. Mileştii Mici specialises in producing and storing quality wine, sparkling wine and select collection wines, which have repeatedly won medals at national and international wine contests.

Tours, done by car, wind down through the cellars with stops at notable collections and artistically executed tourist points, terminating at the elegantly decorated restaurant, with a sea-bottom motif, 60m below ground. These tours, which include – naturally – wine tasting, are refreshingly informal and hilarious. Tours can be arranged directly with the winery. Officially, tour groups should have a minimum of four people; unofficially, this is negotiable. A Saturday or Sunday tour must have a minimum of 15 people.

To get here from Chişinău, take bus 35 from Autogară Sud-vest to Ialoveni. There are no buses between Ialoveni and Mileştii Mici but a local driver will take you there for around $2. There is one direct bus from Chişinău's Autogară Sud-vest to Mileştii Mici ($1.20).

ORHEIUL VECHI

Ten kilometres to the southeast of Orhei city lies Orheiul Vechi (Old Orhei; marked on maps as the village of Trebujeni), arguably Moldova's most fantastic sight. It's certainly among its most haunting places. The chimerical **Orheiul Vechi Monastery Complex** (Complexul Muzeistic Orheiul Vechi; 235-34 242; admission $1.15; 9am-5pm Tue-Sun), carved into a massive limestone cliff in this wild, rocky, remote spot, draws visitors from around the globe. The **Cave Monastery** (Mănăstire în Peşteră), inside a cliff overlooking the gently meandering Răut River, was dug by Orthodox monks in the 13th century. It remained inhabited until the 18th century, and in 1996 a handful of monks returned to this secluded place of worship and are slowly restoring it.

You can enter the cave via an entrance on the cliff's plateau. Shorts are forbidden and women must cover their heads inside the monastery. A small, highly atmospheric chapel inside acts as the church for three neighbouring villages, as it did in the 13th century. You can visit the area where up to 13 monks lived for decades at a time, sleeping on pure bedrock, each occupying a tiny stone bunk (keilies) that opens into a central corridor. This leads to a stone terrace, from where views of the entire cliff and surrounding plains are breathtaking. The cliff face is

dotted with what appear to be holes; most of these are other caves and places of worship dug over the millennia, as this region was a place of worship for Geto-Dacian tribes from before Christ's time. In all, the huge cliff contains six complexes of interlocking caves, most of which are accessible only by experienced rock climbers and many of which are out of bounds for tourists.

Ştefan cel Mare built a fortress here in the 14th century but it was later destroyed by Tartars. Archaeologists since WWII have uncovered several layers of history in this region; some of their finds are on display in Chişinău's National History Museum (p323). The area is rich in archaeological treasures.

In the 18th century the cave-church was taken over by villagers from neighbouring Butuceni. In 1905 they built a church above ground dedicated to the Ascension of St Mary. The church was shut down by the Soviets in 1944 and remained abandoned throughout the communist regime. Services resumed in 1996, though it still looks abandoned. Archaeologists have uncovered remnants of a defence wall surrounding the monastery complex from the 15th century.

On the main road to the complex you'll find the headquarters, where you purchase your entrance tickets. You can also visit a tiny **village museum** (235-34 242; 9am-5pm Tue-Sun) where several archaeological finds from the 15th and 16th centuries are presented. You can arrange guides (Russian and Romanian only) and get general information.

For an amusingly over-enthusiastic description of Orheiul Vechi, as well as excellent photographs and many details of the site, see http://orhei.dnt.md.

En route to Orheiul Vechi is **Ivancea**, which has an excellent **ethnographic museum** (Muzeul meşteşugirilor populare; 235-43 320; admission $1; 10am-5pm Tue-Sun) housed in a 19th-century stately mansion on beautiful grounds. Its eight halls are filled with traditional Moldovan costumes, musical instruments, pottery and folk art.

Sleeping

Orheiul Vechi Monastery Headquarters (235-56 912; d $23) Spending the night here is highly recommend. It has five pleasant rooms and a small restaurant. The rooms facing the monastery have spine-tingling views.

Satul Moldovenesc (248-36 136; http://moldovacc .md/satmoldovenesc; Hârtopul Mare; 1-room house $15-45,

2-room house $52) Only 30km northeast of Chiş-inau (head towards Dubăsari then north to Hârtopul Mare and follow the signs), this full-service complex in the middle of nature offers a very active programme of rest and relaxation! You can rent an island for $12, have a sauna, go horse riding (children can be 'accompanied on their ride of the don-key'), and swim or fish in one of the three lakes nearby.

Getting There & Away

A public transport–only trip to the monastery is an ordeal. Daily buses depart every half-hour from Chişinău going to Orhei ($1.50), but there's only a single daily bus from Orhei to Trebujeni at 6am (ask to be dropped off by the signposted entrance to the complex). Better yet, alight from the Orhei-bound bus at the Ivancea turn and taxi to Orheiul Vechi, striking a deal for there-and-back service, in-cluding a two-hour wait, for around $12, or one-way for about $6. There is a daily af-ternoon bus (3pm) to Orhei from Orheiul Vechi.

VADU LUI VODĂ

When Moldovans on a budget want to get away from it all, they head for Vadu lui Vodă and retire to **Zimbet Camping** (☎ 416 049, 0692-

005 70; 4-bed cabin/d without bathroom $11.50/31, r with bathroom $50). Fresh air, sports, walking, river recreation and enthusiastic beer drinking are the main pursuits here. Three square meals are available in the bar-restaurant for $11.50 per day or you can dine at several bars or restaurants by the beach. The cabins and dou-ble rooms are bare, but for the beds, and the shared bathhouse is reminiscent of summer camp, but you'll be in good company with droves of likeminded Moldovans. Bond with nature, kick around on the nearby football pitch, ride the river banana or just retreat to a shady tree with a book and a bottle of Moldovan wine.

Maxitaxis for Vadu lui Vodă leave regularly from Chişinău's Autogară Centrală through-out the day. Pay the driver.

BĂLŢI, REZINA & ŢIPOVA

Bălţi (*balts*, from the Romanian word for 'swamp'), 150km northwest of Chişinău, is Moldova's fourth-largest city, with a popu-lation of 143,630. A major industrial and mafia-influenced area, and predominantly Russian-speaking, it has little to offer be-yond being a convenient stopover en route to Ukraine. Although locals and expats alike report that they 'feel dirty just going into the city', it does have the advantage of the

---

THE LEGEND OF MAGNETIC HILL *Leif Pettersen*

At the insistence of my editor, I careened into the parking lot of the Safari Café just south of Orhei to test the legend of Magnetic Hill. Nazis were reputed to have buried Jews alive here, and strange happenings are alleged to occur in the area. Reportedly, if you park your car on the pavement right in front of the café, facing the main road, and slip it into neutral, the car will eerily advance, despite the slight uphill incline.

The legend is the high-point of the otherwise ho-hum town of Orhei, so locals are keen to encourage the hype. As I manoeuvred through the car park trying to identify the sweet spot, a waiter bounded out of the café to direct me. Finally positioned, I released the brake. And I moved. Indeed, as I advanced toward the hill the car accelerated, even as the incline increased. In the throes of a bug-eyed mind-screw, I repeated the experiment three times, once filming the experience from outside the car, nearly forgetting that I had to jump back into the car and stop it before it rolled into traffic.

That night, I couldn't sleep. I was deeply shaken.

Driving far off course, I returned to the Safari Café the following afternoon. I intended to test the phenomenon with a nonmetal object, a bottle of water. After one more indulgent test with the car, I climbed out and positioned the bottle at the end of the pavement.

I released the bottle and...

...to my utter consternation, it rolled 'uphill' too. I came to realise that the pavement, in fact, slopes *downhill* and Magnetic Hill is no more supernatural than the optical illusion that fuels it. I was hugely disappointed, but on the upside I slept like a baby that night.

best nightlife scene in Moldova outside of Chişinău.

Some 60km east of Bălţi on the western banks of the Dniestr River is the small town of Rezina. Seven kilometres south of the town is the Orthodox **Saharna Monastery**. Founded in 1495, the church used today dates from the 19th century and sits in a small valley. There are walking trails all around, some offering beautiful views of the entire monastery complex, and one leading to the Virgin Mary's footprint in rock (protected by a glass covering). There's also a lovely waterfall tumbling off an overhanging cliff. The **Day of the Holy Trinity** (8 September), a holiday throughout Moldova, is particularly lively here and includes evening concerts.

Some 12km further south is the marvellous **Ţipova Monastery**, Eastern Europe's largest cave monastery, another of Moldova's memorable highlights. It dates from the 10th to the 12th centuries, and is famous as the place where Ştefan cel Mare got married. Embedded in a large cliff, the caves are more accessible here than at Orheiul Vechi, as footpaths lead up the cliff. Services resumed here in 1994 after the monastery was closed and partially ruined during the Soviet period. Though busloads of tourists and visiting schoolchildren have left behind unsightly graffiti inside the caves, it's otherwise a lovely area, and the paths lead to a small, picturesque waterfall nearby.

Ţipova is in a remote corner of the country on the western banks of the Dniestr River. It's best accessed by car by following the turnoff to Lalova. The monastery is 4km past Horodişte at the far end of the village.

Hotel Basarabia (☎ 231-61 219; Str M Sadoveanu 1; d $25) is a 1960s holdout in central Bălţi. It's slightly run-down, as you might expect, but could be a convenient stopover while exploring northern Moldova.

Probably your best dining bet in Rezina is the restaurant-bar complex **Plai** (☎ 254-23 986; Str A Sciusev; mains $3; ⏰ 8am-3am).

Bălţi is well served by buses. Daily services include five to Tiraspol, eight to Soroca and seven to Ungheni. There are buses every half-hour to/from Chişinău ($3). One daily bus goes to Iaş i, Romania. It's possible to get to Ţipova by taking a bus from Chişinău to Rezina, and getting off 20km before Rezina at the turn-off to Lalova. It's a 12km hitchhike or just plain hike from there.

SOROCA

☎ 230 / pop 38,492

Soroca is the Roma 'capital' of Moldova. The large Roma population here, even in Soviet times, was renowned for living at a much higher standard than most Moldovans; hence part of the reason for the palpable prejudice that exists against them. Explanations as to how this unlikely distribution of wealth occurred range from shrewd entrepreneurial skills to drug trafficking. Stately mansions that the richer Roma have built for themselves line both sides of the road on the hilltop, some facing the river and Ukraine on the other side of it.

Yet people come here to see the outstanding **Soroca fortress** (☎ 230-24 873, 0693-23 734; http://soroca-fortress.nflame.net; admission free; ⏰ 9am-6pm Wed-Sun May-Oct, by appointment Nov-Apr). Visitors are thrown back to medieval times while wandering the grounds of this marvel, which gives a great impression of what life must have been like centuries ago between its nearly intact walls. Part of a medieval chain of military fortresses built by Moldavian princes between the 14th and 16th centuries to defend Moldavia's boundaries, it was founded by Ştefan cel Mare and rebuilt by his son Petru Rareş from 1543 to 1550. The limestone walls (18m high on the inside, 21m high on the outside) are more than 3m thick. Four towers plus a rectangular entrance tower still stand. Strategically placed at Moldavia's then most northeastern tip on the banks of the Dniestr River, Soroca (founded in 1499) was a key military stronghold.

The fortress is administered by the **Soroca Museum of History and Ethnography** (☎ 230-22 264; Str Independentei 68; admission $0.10; ⏰ 10am-1pm & 2-6pm Tue-Sun May-Oct, by appointment Nov-Apr). This well-designed museum is a real treat: its 25,000 exhibits cover archaeological finds, weapons and ethnographic displays.

The simple but clean and bright rooms at the **Nistru Hotel** (☎ 230-23 783; Str Mihiel Malmut 20; d $19.50) are your best bet in Soroca. The hotel is hidden down an improbable sidestreet one block east of the red-roofed Soroca city council building, which faces the park.

There are eight daily buses from Bălţi to Soroca and 12 daily buses from Chişinău's Autogară Nord.

LOWER DNIESTR NATIONAL PARK

The nonprofit organisation **Biotica** (☎ 22-498 837; www.biotica-moldova.org) has devised the Lower Dniestr National Park (Parcul Naţional

DIVINE COMMUNICATION

When Mircea Cerari, the king of Moldova's Roma community, died at the age of 59 in July 1998, it was not his death but his entrance into the afterlife that raised eyebrows. Determined to keep in contact with loved ones from beyond the grave, the king had made arrangements to be buried with his computer, fax and mobile phone.

The lavish funeral, held in Soroca in northern Moldova two weeks after his death, was attended by some 15,000 Roma who had gathered from the far reaches of Europe to pay their respects. Also in attendance was Mircea Cerari's son Arthur, who has since inherited Moldova's Roma crown.

The king's impressive white marble grave contained not only his communication equipment but also a bar stocked with – what else? – vodka!

Arthur – yes, that would be 'King Arthur' – is also now the main representative for the **Cultural Society of Roma of Moldova** (Map p320; ☎ 22-419032; Str Puşkin 33, Ap 69) in Chişinău.

Nistrul Inferior) in recent years, and is attempting to drive its gradual implementation. Unfortunately, at the time of writing, the project still had not come to fruition due to political and economic obstacles. Comprising more than 50,000 hectares of wetlands, forest and agricultural land, the proposed project encompasses some 40 sites of archaeological importance, observation points, many villages and some vineyards (at Purcari and Tudora for example). Though it is not yet fully set up with a tourist infrastructure, rural homestays already exist and excursions may be possible by the time you read this. Eventually, canoeing, hiking, wine tasting and camping will all be available in this lovely area, shimmering with possibility. Meanwhile, you can visit private vineyards and village artisans to see them at work making wicker baskets or furniture.

One guesthouse that caters to tourists is **Meşter Faur** (☎ 242-35 259; Str Ştefan cel Mare 100) in the village of Cioburciu. Run by Pavel Taranu, it can guarantee a splendid time in remote Moldovan countryside, with boat tours, visits to local village enterprises, wine tasting and relaxation galore. No English spoken.

TRANSDNIESTR

One of the most patently curious regions in Europe, the self-declared republic of Transdniestr (Pridnestrovskaya Moldavskaya Respublika, or PMR in Russian; population 555,500) is nevertheless a largely unknown enigma. The street credibility of being one of the world's last surviving communist bastions is wearing thin, however, as the illusion of a worker's paradise is being swiftly eclipsed by sweet, sweet capitalism! Monuments to Lenin and other Soviet heroes share high-profile street corners with expensive shops, while swanky hotels and stadiums pop up around Tiraspol, betraying a firm bling-centric platform on the part of business and political leaders. Meanwhile, simple folk struggle to get by in a land that the rest of the world knows nothing about.

Transdniestr defiantly occupies a narrow strip of land covering only 3567 sq km on the eastern bank of the Dniestr River, the scene of a bloody civil war in the early 1990s when the movement for independence from Moldova began. Independent in all but name, Transdniestr has its own currency, police force, army and borders, which are controlled by Transdniestran border guards. The predominantly Russian-speaking region boycotts the Moldovan Independence Day and celebrates its own independence day on 2 September.

On 6 July 2006, a bomb blast on a local bus in Tiraspol killed eight people. Transdniestran politicians were quick to blame 'Moldovan provocateurs'. Popular opinion in Moldova is that a would-be arms dealer probably lost control of his merchandise.

See http://geo.ya.com/travelimages/transdniestr.html for some excellent photos of the region.

Government & Politics

The generously eyebrowed Igor Smirnov was elected president of Transdniestr in 1991 following the region's declaration of independence four months earlier. In 1994 the Moldovan Parliament ratified a new constitution providing substantial autonomy to Transdniestr in regional affairs, as it did for Gagauzia. Transdniestrans, however, refused to recognise this autonomy as it didn't go nearly as far as they wanted. They insist it's an independent country and a sovereign state within Moldova. Most of the time, they push for the creation of a Moldovan federation, with proportionate representation between Moldova, Transdniestr and Gagauzia – on the condition, of course, that Smirnov would then become vice-president of Moldova.

Neither Smirnov's presidency nor the Transdniestran Parliament is recognised by the Moldovan – or any other – government, which has nonetheless been forced to engage in dialogue with the breakaway state, often brokered by Russian officials who still act as if the area is within their interests. The Russian 14th army, headquartered in Tiraspol since 1956, covertly supplied Transdniestran rebels with weapons during the 1992 civil war. The continued presence of the 5000-strong Russian 'operational group' in Transdniestr today is seen by local Russian-speakers as a guarantee of their security and is generally welcomed.

The Ministry of State Security (MGB), a modern day KGB, has sweeping powers and has sponsored the creation of a youth wing called the Young Guard for 16- to 23-year-olds who want to be indoctrinated into the happy world of xenophobia and military games in the hopes of building a dedicated nationalistic future generation. To observers, they are more akin to disenchanted skinheads than anything else.

Alongside a number of agreements between Moldova and Transdniestr since 1991, there have been countless moves by both sides designed to antagonise or punish the other. In 2003 alone, Smirnov, reacting to one of his demands having been refused by Moldova, slapped exorbitant tariffs on all Moldovan imports, instantly halting trade over the 'border' and making life more difficult for common people on both sides. In September 2003, Smirnov even got so huffy he severed phone connections, so that calls could not be made between the regions for a few weeks.

Though Smirnov and other officials have become contemptibly self-serving, a large subsection of locals still cannot be coaxed into criticizing their government, often deflecting probing questions with third-hand, conspicuously propagandistic stories about positive actions made by their government on behalf of the people. Direct questions on the current state of corruption are often met with indifference.

Political and economic attitudes aside, popular opinion still strongly supports independence from Moldova.

Economy

Transdniestr's economy has been disastrous, despite the fact that 40% of Moldova's total potential industrial output is concentrated in Tiraspol. After a brief period of improvement in metal production and light industry, political hostility in early 2006 appears destined to plunge the region into a new round of economic hardship (see the boxed text, p336).

Inflation is rampant and the local currency, the Transdniestran rouble, is worthless outside its borders. The average salary is approaching US$100 a month. State employers have been able to pay their workers more regularly than in the past, eliminating the need to earn a desperate living at the flea market, but a return to those difficult days seems inevitable.

It has been widely speculated that the mainstays of the economy – and why some people in Transdniestr are unfathomably rich – have included illegal arms sales (of old Soviet military machinery conveniently left on its territory), female slave trafficking, extortion of people trying to open businesses in the territory, money laundering and reaping profits from state-owned currency-exchange booths.

The region is dominated by a single company, Sheriff, owned on paper by Viktor Gushan, though it is rumoured that President Smirnov himself is actually behind the wheel. Nevertheless, the two are close; their sons careen through the streets of Tiraspol in matching black Hummers. Sheriff has a hand in almost everything, from the multimillion-dollar luxury hotel and football stadium on the edge of Tiraspol (until very recently, the only European regulation football stadium in Moldova) to bread factories, liquor stores and car showrooms. It is rumoured that, in order to start a business in Transdniestr, you have to talk to Sheriff.

Suffice to say that foreign investment in Transdniestr is a long way off.

Population

Two-thirds of Transdniestr's population is elderly and impoverished. Ethnic Russians comprise 29% of the population, ethnic Moldovans 34% and Ukrainians 29%. While the populace is tired of living in an area where

MOLDOVA

the average salary is less than that in neighbouring Moldova (itself often considered Europe's poorest country), organised anti-government protests are unheard of. People here tend to be more cautious and reserved than in the rest of Moldova, with the older generations particularly uneasy about openly speaking their mind against the government. The prevailing sentiment is that they must just accept their lot, no matter how dire, and try to stoically endure.

Language

The official state languages in Transdniestr are Russian, Moldovan and Ukrainian. Students in schools and universities are taught in Russian, and local government and most official institutions operate almost solely in Russian. All street signs are written in Russian, sometimes Moldovan and even Ukrainian.

Money

The only legal tender is the Transdniestran rouble (TR). There are 1, 5, 25, 50 and 100 rouble notes and 1, 5, 10 and 50 kopek coins. The notes are tiny, often dirty and disintegrating. All notes sport the much-revered and famous 18th-century Russian military general Alexander Suvorov on the front, while the back features different places of 'national' importance, such as the Kvint brandy factory on the 5-rouble note. Some taxi drivers, shopkeepers and market traders will accept payment in US dollars – or even Moldovan lei or Ukrainian hryvnia – but generally you'll need to get your hands on some roubles. All exchange offices are owned by the banks, so there's no shopping around for the lowest fee or best rate. Often you will find private citizens who will want to exchange dollars for roubles.

TREAD LIGHTLY IN TRANSDNIESTR *Leif Pettersen*

At the time of writing, rising political and economic turmoil was making a day trip into Transdniestr more hair-raising than it's been in years. The happy-go-lucky days of benign Kafkesque moments at the border and a time-travel stroll through Tiraspol have been replaced by social ostracism of foreigners and the creepy feeling of being watched at all times as renewed paranoia deepens. There have been accounts of people being reported and then detained by police for simply speaking English or giving blankets to the poor in Tiraspol. The taking of photographs, no matter how innocent – I was barred entrance to a café I intended to review for this book after the owner spied me taking a quick photo down the street. Frosty merchants rush through transactions without a word.

The source of the trouble is a very complex political predicament, the latest chapter in a four-way antagonising theatre of one-upmanship between Ukraine, Russia, Moldova and Transdniestr. Barring a sudden flash of diplomatic magic, the situation is expected to get far worse before it gets better.

The upshot is that the border can still be amusingly memorable, bobbing and weaving around invented infractions and creative interpretations of the law. Shaky political climate notwithstanding, border guards still have a vested financial interest (bribes) in letting you through – budget around $20 to $30 for this excitement, coming and going, depending on how dodgy you look or how big your camera bag is.

Entry permits are still (officially) $1 to $5 depending on your nationality, available at the border no matter what the guys on duty playfully tell you. If you stay under 24 hours, you needn't register with the authorities, and if you enter with a Moldovan national you can be listed on their entry permit (as several names can be inscribed on one) for a few pennies.

If you're staying for more than 24 hours, you'll need to register with the **OVIR** (Ulitsa Kotovskogo 2Ap338; ☎ 533-79 083; ☾ 9am-5pm Mon-Fri). Enter through the ominous, rusting prisonlike gate and inquire at the hidden white building with the red roof. At night or on weekends, register at **Tiraspol Militia office** (Map p338; ☎ 533-34 169; Roza Luxemburg 66; ☾ 24hr), though you'll probably be asked to follow up at the OVIR on the next business day. The registration fee is about $0.60. Some hotels won't even talk room availability with you until you've registered. Some high-end hotels will register you automatically.

As always, check the current political situation before heading into erratic territory.

Spend all your roubles before you leave, as no one honours or exchanges this currency outside Transdniestr, though you can probably find takers at the bus station in Chişinău if you somehow get stuck with a large amount.

EXCHANGE RATES

For the latest exchange rates, check out www .cbpmr.net. Exchange rates at the time of writing:

country	unit	rouble
euro zone	€1	TR10.59
Moldova	1 Lei	TR0.63
Russia	R1	TR0.31
UK	£1	TR15.48
Ukraine	1 hv	TR1.60
US	$1	TR8.30

Post & Telephone

Transdniestran stamps featuring Suvorov can only be used for letters sent within the Transdniestran republic and are not recognised anywhere else. For letters to Moldova, Romania and the West, you have to use Moldovan stamps (available here but less conveniently than in Moldova). If you bring your mobile phone to the territory, note that there is no roaming available here, save for Moldovan mobile phones.

Media

The predominantly Russian Transdniestran TV is broadcast in the republic between 6am and midnight. Transdniestran Radio is on air during the same hours. Bendery has a local TV channel that airs 24 hours a day.

The two local newspapers are in Russian. The *Transdniestra* is a purely nationalist affair advocating the virtues of an independent state; *N Pravda* is marginally more liberal.

TIRASPOL

☎ 533 / pop 183,678

Tiraspol (from the Greek, meaning 'town on the Nistru'), 70km east of Chişinău, is the second-largest city in Moldova – sorry, make that the largest city and capital of Transdniestr! Although it's as Soviet-licious as they come and still a candidate for World's Largest Open-Air Museum, nevertheless MTV and Red Bull are making their presence felt. Not surprisingly, the have/have-not divide is

glaring. Entering the outskirts from Bendery, you're confronted by the behemoth state-of-the-art football and sports stadiums and a five-star hotel (under construction at the time of writing). Built at a cost of untold hundreds of millions of dollars by Viktor Gushan, owner of the Tiraspol Sheriff football team, its intended customer base is still unclear. Locals who are lucky to earn $100 a month certainly won't be checking in soon, or even attending many games for that matter, and few visiting teams will be able to afford the rates.

The city was founded in 1792 following Russian domination of the region. Its population is predominantly Russian (41%), with ethnic Ukrainians comprising 32% and ethnic Moldovans 18% of the population.

Orientation & Information

The train and bus stations are next to each other at the end of ulitsa Lenina. From the stations, walk down ulitsa Lenina, past Kirov Park, to ulitsa 25 Oktober (the main street).

The **post office** (ulitsa Lenina 17; ⊙ 7.30am-7pm Mon-Fri) won't be of much use to you unless you want to send postcards to all your friends in Transdniestr (but if you do, be sure to bring your own postcards). At the **central telephone office** (cnr ulitsa 25 Oktober & ulitsa Kommunisticheskaya; ⊙ 7am-8.45pm) you can buy phonecards ($2.40 or $8) to use in the modern payphones (the old metal clunkers can only make local calls), send telegrams or make long-distance calls. Change money next door at the **Prisbank** (⊙ 8.30am-4.30pm Mon-Sat). **Bunker** (pereulok Naberezhnyi 1; per hr $0.40; ⊙ 9am-11pm) is a modern internet club.

Dom Knigi (ulitsa 25 Oktober 85; ⊙ 9am-7pm Mon-Fri, 9am-4pm Sat) is a big bookshop with a limited selection of Russian-only books (good luck finding any maps here).

Sights

At the western end of ulitsa 25 Oktober stands a Soviet armoured **tank** from which the Transdniestran flag flies. Behind is the **Heroes' Cemetery** with its Tomb of the Unknown Soldier, flanked by an eternal flame in memory of those who died on 3 March 1992 during the first outbreak of fighting. The Russian inscription reads 'You don't have a name but your deeds are eternal'. There's also an Afghan war memorial here. Other victims of the civil war are buried in the **city cemetery**, north of the centre, where a special alley has been allocated to the 1992 victims.

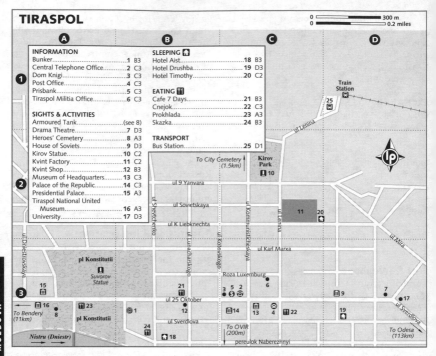

TIRASPOL

0 ——— 300 m
0 ——— 0.2 miles

INFORMATION
Bunker..............................1 B3
Central Telephone Office..........2 C3
Dom Knigi.........................3 C3
Post Office........................4 C3
Prisbank...........................5 C3
Tiraspol Militia Office............6 C3

SIGHTS & ACTIVITIES
Armoured Tank..................(see 8)
Drama Theatre.....................7 D3
Heroes' Cemetery..................8 A3
House of Soviets...................9 D3
Kirov Statue......................10 C2
Kvint Factory.....................11 C2
Kvint Shop........................12 B3
Museum of Headquarters...........13 C3
Palace of the Republic............14 C3
Presidential Palace...............15 A3
Tiraspol National United
    Museum........................16 A3
University........................17 D3

SLEEPING
Hotel Aist........................18 B3
Hotel Drushba.....................19 D3
Hotel Timothy.....................20 C2

EATING
Cafe 7 Days.......................21 B3
Cnejok............................22 C3
Prokhlada.........................23 A3
Skazka............................24 B3

TRANSPORT
Bus Station.......................25 D1

To City Cemetery (1.5km)
Kirov Park
Train Station
To Bendery (11km)
To OVIR (200m)
To Odesa (113km)
Nistru (Dniestr)
pl Konstitutii
Suvorov Statue

MOLDOVA

The **Tiraspol National United Museum** (ulitsa 25 Oktober 42; admission $0.30; ☎ 9am-5pm Sun-Fri) is the closest the city has to a local history museum, with an exhibit focusing on poet Nikolai Dimitriovich Zelinskogo, who founded the first Soviet school of chemistry. Opposite is the **Presidential Palace**, from where Igor Smirnov rules his mini-empire. The enormous ploshchad Konstitutii is bordered by ulitsa 25 Oktober and the park-lined concrete promenade along the Dniestr, a popular strolling area.

Ulitsa 25 Oktober, Tiraspol's backbone, is also its commercial strip, with most of the shops and restaurants. Fancy new stores blend with photo studios displaying hand-coloured portraits from the 1970s in their windows – a surreal mix. It's tree-lined, wide and impeccably clean, and people rush to and fro with their heads down. At night this street is virtually deserted, even on weekends.

The few Western foreigners who make it to Tiraspol love to capture images of the city's Soviet-style buildings and monuments – though be warned that conspicuous use of cameras, no matter the photographic subject,

is nearly guaranteed to invite suspicion from locals. That said, a must-snap is the **Palace of the Republic** (Dvorets Respubliki), slightly recessed south of the main street between ulitsa Kotovskogo and ulitsa Kommunisticheskaya. On it is a glorious relief of young communist men and women engaged in strange activities that surely have something to do with building a better world.

Change films before you get to the administration building, the neoclassical **House of Soviets** (Dom Sovetov), towering over the eastern end of ulitsa 25 Oktober. Lenin's angry-looking bust peers out from its prime location smack in front of the building. Inside the building is a memorial to those who died in the 1992 conflict. Close by is the military-themed **Museum of Headquarters** (ulitsa Kommunisticheskaya 34; admission $0.30; ☎ 9am-5pm Mon-Sat). The **Drama Theatre** is at ulitsa 25 Oktober, and close by is the **university**, founded in 1930.

The **Kvint factory** (☎ 37 333; http://kvint.biz; ulitsa Lenina 38) is one of Transdniestr's pride and joys. Since 1897 it's been making some of Moldova's finest brandies. There are no excursions, but a gander at the factory might be of interest. Buy some of its products either near the front entrance of the plant or at the **town centre store** (ulitsa 25 Oktober 84; 24hr).

Further north along ulitsa Lenina towards the bus and train stations is **Kirov Park**, with a **statue** of the Leningrad boss who was assassinated in 1934, conveniently sparking off mass repressions throughout the USSR.

Sleeping

If staying more than 24 hours you must register at the **OVIR** (ulitsa Kotovskogo 2A, Tiraspol; 533-79 083; 9am-5pm Mon-Fri) – see the boxed text, p336. Some hotels may staunchly refuse service until you've registered, no matter how long you're staying.

Hotel Drushba (34 266; ulitsa 25 Oktober 116; r/deluxe $20/40) Several dozen categories of rooms are on offer at this massive place that has hopefully seen better days. Some have hot water, TV, fridge, larger beds, private bathroom or shower. The atmosphere is rather dour but the rooms are fine and the staff the most pleasant in town.

Hotel Aist (37 174, 77 688; pereulok Naberezhnyi 3; d $25-40) Grass growing through cracks in the cement outside gives it a derelict feel, but the rooms are surprisingly nice. More expensive rooms have luxuries such as hot water, private toilet and TV.

Hotel Timothy (36 442; ulitsa K Liebknechta 395A; s/d $60/80;) The fanciest place in town is an ultramodern small hotel geared to business visitors (there's a business centre next door). The rooms are large, but plain and sparingly furnished. Some have spa baths. Yes, that framed portrait behind the check-in desk is of President Igor Smirnov, whose pals are probably the ones who use the hotel most frequently.

Eating

Cafe 7 Days (32 311; ulitsa 25 Oktober 77; mains $0.35-1.50; 9am-11pm) A great selection of tasty Russian fast food like blini (stuffed pancakes) and Western imports like pizza, as well as salads are on offer at this modern, pleasant café.

Cnejok (ulitsa Lenina 23; mains $1.50-3.30) A new and notably friendly bar-restaurant that looks primed for hosting receptions if you would like bragging rights to 'Wackiest Wedding Locale, Ever'.

Skazka (pereulok Naberezhnyi 1; mains $2-3.50; 10am-8pm) The offputting green and glass exterior hides a 'fairy-tale' place with half-hearted castle décor geared toward children, and a large Moldovan menu. The summer terrace faces the river.

our pick **Prokhlada** (34 642; ulitsa 25 Oktober 50; mains $2-4; 4pm-6am) This cavernous, sombre but friendly space is the best place in town for a meal or drink. Choose from six kinds of cognac as you view sports matches on a large TV screen. Dancing is encouraged, but often lonely. According to the sign outside you are not allowed to take in hand grenades, guns or gas bottles. But don't worry – that's just the old Transdniestran sense of humour in action!

Getting There & Away

BUS

You can only pay in the local currency for tickets to other destinations in Transdniestr, but you can pay in Moldovan lei or Ukrainian hryvnia for tickets to Moldova or Ukraine. Pay the driver.

From Tiraspol five daily buses go to Bălţi, 13 to Odesa and one to Kyiv. One bus a week goes to Berlin. Buses leave for Chişinău nearly every half-hour from 5.50am to 8.50pm, and maxitaxis run regularly from 6.30am to 6.10pm.

TRAIN

Tickets for same-day departures are sold in the main train station ticket hall. There is also an information booth – a question about national train services costs $0.05 and a question about services to CIS countries costs $0.10, though most tellers don't bother charging it. Buy advance tickets (24 hours or more before departure) in the ticket office on the 2nd floor.

Most eastbound trains from Chişinău to Ukraine and Russia stop in Tiraspol. There are seven daily trains to Chişinău ($0.90, 2½ hours), three to Odesa ($2, 2½ hours), two to Moscow ($31, 25 to 31 hours) and Minsk ($23, 23 hours) and one to St Petersburg ($28, 35 hours).

Getting Around

Bus 1 runs between the bus and train stations and the city centre. Tickets for trolley-buses ($0.10) are sold by the driver. Tickets for maxitaxis cost $0.20. Trolleybus 19 and maxitaxi 19 and 20 (quicker) cross the bridge over the Dniestr to Bendery.

MOLDOVA

MOLDOVA

BENDERY

☎ 552 / pop 123,038

Bendery (sometimes called Bender, and previously known as Tighina), on the western banks of the Dniestr River, has made something of a miraculous recovery in recent years. Physical and figurative scars from the bloodshed in the early '90s have noticeably healed. The centre in particular is a green, breezy and pleasant place, vastly more sociable and inviting than Tiraspol. Busy cafés, non-Soviet inspired sculptures and a palpably less guarded air make this place seem like it's sitting on the wrong side of the border.

During the 16th century, Moldavian prince Ştefan cel Mare built a large fortress here on the ruins of a fortified Roman camp. In 1538 the Ottoman sultan Suleiman the Magnificent conquered the fortress and transformed it into a Turkish *raia* (colony), renaming the city Bendery, meaning 'belonging to the Turks'. During the 18th century, Bendery was seized from the Turks by Russian troops who then massacred Turkish Muslims in the city. In 1812 Bendery fell permanently into Russian hands. Russian peacekeeping forces remain here to this day. The bloodiest fighting during the 1992 military conflict took place in Bendery and many walls of buildings in the centre remain bullet-pocked.

Information

Currency exchange (ulitsa Sovetskaya; ⏲ 7am-5pm) Next to Central Market.

Internet clubs (Central department store, cnr ulitsa Lenina & ulitsa Kalinina; per hr $0.50) There are two internet clubs on the top floor, opposite the main Hotel Dniestr.

Pharmacy (cnr ulitsa Suvorova & ulitsa S Liazo; ⏲ 8am-8pm Mon-Sat, 8am-4pm Sun)

Telephone Centre (cnr ulitsa S Liazo & ulitsa Suvorova; ⏲ 8am-6pm Mon-Fri, 8am-4pm Sat) Book international telephone calls here.

Sights

Bendery's main sight is paradoxically impossible to see. **Turkish fortress** was built by occupying Turks in the 1530s, replacing a 12th-century fortress built by the Genovese. It is now being used by Transdniestran military as a training ground and is strictly off limits. The best view of it is from the bridge going towards Tiraspol. At the entrance to the city,

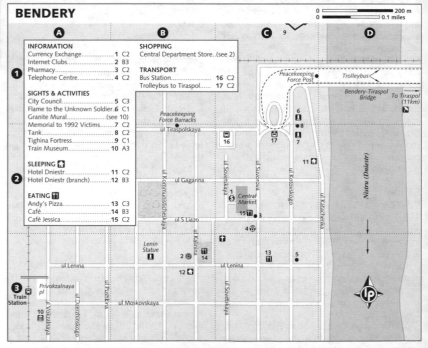

BENDERY

0 —— 200 m
0 —— 0.1 miles

INFORMATION	
Currency Exchange	1 C2
Internet Clubs	2 B3
Pharmacy	3 C2
Telephone Centre	4 C2

SIGHTS & ACTIVITIES	
City Council	5 C3
Flame to the Unknown Soldier	6 C1
Granite Mural	(see 10)
Memorial to 1992 Victims	7 C2
Tank	8 C2
Tighina Fortress	9 C1
Train Museum	10 A3

SLEEPING 🏠	
Hotel Dniestr	11 C2
Hotel Dniestr (branch)	12 B3

EATING 🍴	
Andy's Pizza	13 C3
Café	14 B3
Café Jessica	15 C2

SHOPPING	
Central Department Store	(see 2)

TRANSPORT	
Bus Station	16 C2
Trolleybus to Tiraspol	17 C2

close to the famous **Bendery–Tiraspol bridge**, is a **memorial park** dedicated to local 1992 war victims. An eternal **flame** to the unknown soldier burns in front of an armoured tank, from which flies the Transdniestran flag. Haunting memorials to those shot dead during the civil war are evident throughout many of the main streets in the centre. The **City Council** building is at ulitsa Lenina 17.

Fifty metres south of the train station is a **Train Museum** inside an old Russian CY 06-71 steam locomotive. The museum was closed at the time of writing. Alongside Bendery's only museum is a typically Soviet, oversized **granite mural** in memory of the train workers who died in the 1918 revolution.

Sleeping & Eating

A three-tier pricing system is intact here, with one level for the locals, another for the Moldovans, Ukrainians and Belorussians, and the highest for all other foreigners.

Hotel Dniestr (☎ 29 478; ulitsa Katachenka 10; r $20) The single rooms occasionally don't have hot water, but can be shared by two people as long as they are of the opposite sex (no funny stuff going on here!). The pricier doubles have hot water, TV and fridge – these are permitted to be shared by two people of any sex. There's an adjacent restaurant and terrace café. There's another branch of the hotel at ulitsa Kalinina 50 (closed for renovations at the time of writing), with similar prices, but you must register at the main ulitsa Katachenka hotel first.

Café (cnr ulitsa Kalinina & ulitsa Lenina; mains $1-2; ☺ 9am-11pm) In the park across from the department store, this small restaurant has a popular, pleasant terrace where grilled meat dishes are the favourite. It doubles as Bendery's favourite hang-out and bar.

Café Jessica (☎ 23 540; ulitsa S Liazo; mains $1-2.50; ☺ 10am-midnight) The year-round Christmas lights and the glow from the one-armed bandits in this dingy café provide a surreal atmosphere. Don't bother reading the menu, just ask what's on that day and stick with the tried and true *pelmeni* (similar to ravioli). There's 'surpriz' on the menu but we caution against risking finding out what it is. For dessert, indulge in lemon slices sprinkled with sugar.

Andy's Pizza (ulitsa Lenina 29; mains $2-4; ☺ 7.30am-11pm) Andy's has arrived in Transdniestr! Retreat here for a quick fix of familiar surroundings.

Getting There & Around

From the Privokzalnaya ploschad train station there are roughly 15 daily trains to Chişinău, including services from Moscow and Odesa.

The bus station is located on ul Tiraspolskaya. There are buses and maxitaxis every half-hour or so to Chişinău and two daily to Comrat, as well as two daily buses to Odesa and one to Kyiv.

Trolleybus 19 for Tiraspol ($0.10) departs from the bus stop next to the main roundabout at the entrance to Bendery. Maxitaxis regularly make the 20-minute journey ($0.20).

Local maxitaxis ($0.08) leave from outside the currency exchange office.

GAGAUZIA

Subordinate to Moldova constitutionally and for foreign relations and defence, Gagauzia (Gagauz Yeri) is an autonomous region covering 1832 sq km of noncontiguous land in southern Moldova. Unlike Transdniestr, the region eventually found its niche within Moldova through judicious mediation, but there's still simmering unrest between the two entities over language and economic issues. On a national level, Gagauzia is represented by the assembly's elected *başkan* (head, governor), a member of the Gagauz Halki political party who holds a safe seat in the Moldovan Parliament. Since 1995, this has been George Tabunshik.

Gagauzia comprises three towns and 27 villages dotted throughout three broken-up districts; Comrat, Ceadăr-Linga and Vulcăneşti. Wedged between these last two is the predominantly Bulgarian-populated district of Taraclia, which is not part of Gagauzia. Gagauz is further Swiss-cheesed by three Bulgarian villages in Ceadăr-Linga and a predominantly Moldovan village in Comrat district. Needless to say, there are no border controls at these atolls of territory.

The population of Gagauzia is 171,500, 78% of whom are Gagauz nationals; an additional 25,000 Gagauz live in other areas of Moldova, 20,000 more live in Greece and Bulgaria, and 32,000 in Ukraine. The Gagauz are a Turkic-speaking, Christian ethnic minority whose Muslim antecedents fled the Russo-Turkish wars in the 18th century. They were allowed to settle in the region in exchange for their conversion to Christianity. Their language

MOLDOVA

is a dialect of Turkish, with its vocabulary influenced by Russian Orthodoxy as opposed to the Islamic influences inherent in Turkish. Gagauz look to Turkey for cultural inspiration and heritage.

The republic has its own flag (blue, white and red stripes with three white stars in the upper left corner), its own police force, its own newspapers (Sabaa Ildyzy, Gagauz Vesti and Guneshhik), and its own university. The official languages here are Gagauzi, Moldovan and Russian, though Russian is used almost everywhere, including the university. Gagauzi is taught in 37 schools throughout Moldova.

Gagauz autonomy was officially recognised by the Moldovan government on 23 December 1994; that day is now celebrated annually as Independence Day. Unlike the more militant separatists in Transdniestr, the Gagauz forfeited independence for large-scale autonomy. Theirs is a predominantly agricultural region with little industry to sustain an independent economy. There are 12 vineyards on their territory producing fine wines, the profits for which Gagauzia accuses Chişinău of reaping.

COMRAT

☎ 298 / pop 25,197

Gagauzia's capital, 92km south of Chişinău, is no more than a dusty town with little of tourist interest apart from being an intriguing cultural and provincial oddity. In 1990 Comrat was the scene of clashes between Gagauz nationalists and Moldovan armed forces, pre-empted by calls from local leaders for the Moldovan government to hold a referendum on the issue of Gagauz sovereignty. Local protesters were joined by Transdniestran militia forces, who are always game for a bit of clashing.

Comrat is home to the world's only Gagauz university – so what if nearly all courses are taught in Russian? Most street signs are in Russian; some older ones are in Gagauzi but in the Cyrillic script. Since 1989 Gagauzi, alongside Moldovan, has used the Latin alphabet.

From the bus station, walk south along the main street, Str Pobedy, past the market to ploshchad Pobedy (Victory Square). St John's Church stands on the western side of the square, behind which lies the central park. Prospekt Lenina runs parallel to Str Pobedy, west of the park.

Change money at the **Moldovan Agrobank** (Str Pobedy 52; ☯ 8am-2pm Mon-Fri). A small currency exchange is inside the entrance to the market. You can make international calls at the **post office** (Str Pobedy 55; ☯ 8am-6pm Mon-Fri, 8am-5pm Sat). Surf the web at **IATP** (☎ 25 875; Str Lenina 160; per hr $0.40; ☯ 9am-6pm Mon-Fri).

The regional **başkani** (assembly) is on prospekt Lenina. The Gagauzi and Moldovan flags fly from the roof. Next to the assembly is the **Gagauz Culture House**, in front of which stands a statue of Lenin. West of prospekt Lenina at Str Galatsăna 17 is **Gagauz University** (Komrat Devlet Üniversitesi), founded in 1990. Four faculties (national culture, agronomy, economics and law) serve 1500 students. The main foreign languages taught are Romanian, English and Turkish. The university gets some funding from universities in Turkey.

On the eastern side of ploshchad Pobedy, **Hotel Aina** (☎ 22 841; Str Pobedy 127A; d 'deluxe' $23) is a fairly modern hotel. Its bar serves light meals, including delicious şaşlik (shish kebab) and salads. Nearby, **Yunosti** (☎ 24 447; Str Pobedy 52; mains $1-3; ☯ 9am-midnight) isn't a bad place to grab a meal or hang out for a few drinks.

Five daily return buses run from Chişinău to Comrat ($3.90). From Comrat there are two buses daily via Bendery to Tiraspol, and one only as far as Bendery.

Directory

CONTENTS

ACCOMMODATION

Though accommodation prices around Romania and Moldova have risen by 50% or more in the past few years, you're still likely to pay less than in Western Europe and some of Eastern Europe. Choice runs the gamut from seedy camping grounds and inviting family-run *pensiunes* (pensions) to communist relics with smelly lifts and business hotels offering wi-fi and boutique-style luxury.

USEFUL ACCOMMODATION WEBSITES

www.antrec.ro National listings.
www.pensiuni.info.ro For Maramureş.
www.rotravel.com Mostly Transylvania and Maramureş.
www.ruralturism.ro National.

PRACTICALITIES

- Videos you buy or watch will be based on the PAL system.
- Use a European two-pin plug to connect to the electricity supply (220V, 50Hz AC).
- The metric system is used for weights and measurements.
- Colour photographic film, flash cards and video cassettes are easily available in large centres; transparencies and black-and-white film are hard to find.

We list places to stay in budget order, broken down by type of accommodation or price category, and sometimes by their location in the town, depending on the situation. A 'single' means a single bed, usually a matrimonial bed, and a 'double' means two beds. The price usually stands regardless of whether it's one or two people in a single or double.

These days it's rare to find a double for under €30 in a hotel, but private accommodation is usually €15 to €20 including a meal or two.

Unless otherwise noted, breakfast is included in the prices quoted for both Romanian and Moldovan accommodation. For budget accommodation, we have noted when a room has a shared toilet down the hall, or a toilet but no shower. In midrange and top end choices, rooms have both toilet and shower. Even the grottiest hotels supply towels and soap.

There is no uniformity about discounted rates and periods. Many hotels in resort towns such as Poiana Braşov and Mamaia raise their prices during ski or summer seasons, respectively, but not all do. Some of the larger hotels in the midrange or top-end categories have weekend specials; others lower prices slightly on weekdays. Where possible this has been noted, but your best bet is to contact the hotel yourself.

Some hotels are open to bargaining, especially in low season or for extended stays. Occasionally tourist information centres keep information on accommodation – and can make reservations, and even arrange discounts.

BOOK ACCOMMODATION ONLINE

For more accommodation reviews and recommendations by Lonely Planet authors, check out the online booking service at www.lonelyplanet.com. You'll find the true, insider lowdown on the best places to stay. Reviews are thorough and independent. Best of all, you can book online.

Many hotels in Romania post their prices in euros, but you can pay in lei too. In Moldova, prices are listed in US dollars, but you must pay in lei.

You will be asked by officials to briefly present your passport upon registration in both countries.

Camping

While camping grounds *(popas turistic)* in Moldova are practically nonexistent, in Romania they tend to be grungy affairs; this book has recommended very few of them. Don't expect to find any Western-style camping grounds here. They usually comprise wooden huts *(căsuțe)*, which fit two to four people, and are packed side by side in a rather unatmospheric way. Bare mattresses are generally provided but you have to bring your own sleeping bag. Not very clean toilets and showers are shared, and hot water is a rarity.

Not only are these places often filled to the brim with local tourists who set up temporary homes for weeks or months on end, they tend to be dirty and cramped. Moreover, a few of them double as poorly disguised houses of prostitution.

The good news is that wild camping anywhere in Romania and Moldova is legal unless otherwise prohibited (in the Danube Delta there are allocated zones; along the Black Sea coast it is forbidden to camp on the beach; and obviously private property and areas in development are off limits). It's possible to spend the night in shepherd huts if you're in a pinch.

Mountain Huts

In most mountain areas there's a network of cabins or chalets (cabanas) with restaurants and dormitories. Prices are much lower than those of hotels (about €5 to €10) and no reservations are required, but arrive early if the cabana is in a popular location such as next

to a cable-car terminus. Expect to find good companionship rather than cleanliness or comfort. Many are open year-round. Cabanas invariably close for renovations at some time or other, so ask ahead.

You will also come across unattended, empty wooden huts *(refuges)* in the mountains. These are intended as shelter for hikers and anyone can use them. It is possible to camp free in the mountains and most cabanas allow camping in their grounds.

Homes & Farmstays

Nothing exposes the roots of rural Romanian home life more than a night, or more, in a private home. Often decorated earnestly in traditional rural style, these homes frequently have just a few rooms, and are found in cities, sizeable towns or (best) in the middle of nowhere. Meals (big ones) are arranged – usually dinner is extra – and welcoming host families often provide priceless, authentic extras like arranging visits to shepherds, arranging hikes or horse rides, or taking you to traditional workshops.

Many families rent rooms *(cazare)* as a way of supplementing income. This practice is almost nonexistent – so far – in Moldova, but you can arrange apartment rental in Chișinău (p324).

The trick is finding a good room. Travellers arriving at train stations and, to a lesser extent, bus stations, will be accosted by a gaggle of babushkas offering rooms (even teenagers are in on the act now, hoping to throw a modern spin on things). Make sure you understand exactly where the room is before you accept their offer, and don't part with cash until you've checked the room. Expect to pay €8 to €14 per person.

Most pleasing is *agroturism* (B&Bs in the countryside and villages), which has blossomed in recent years. A number of organisations are representing national or regional B&Bs, including the excellent source **Rural Tourism** (www.ruralturism.ro), which is put together by Pan Travel in Cluj-Napoca (p187). Its list of rural homes offers more detail than Antrec's (opposite). Contact Pan Travel if you have specific requests.

For comfortable places in the Apuseni Mountains, try www.greenmountains.ro or Opération Villages Roumains in Gârda de Sus (p228). Local travel agents can also usually help you find a private home.

The largest *agroturism* organisation in Romania is **Antrec** (National Association of Rural, Ecological & Cultural Tourism; www.antrec.ro), which started in 1994. It has 32 branches nationwide, but they vary wildly – often no one's around, sometimes staff are incredibly helpful, and sometimes travellers are disappointed.

A few travel agents in Chişinău (p321) arrange homestays around Moldova.

Hostels

Romania currently has 35 accredited Hostelling International (HI) hostels and more are opening all the time, as well as some independent ones. Some of the best and friendliest include the Retro Hostel in Cluj-Napoca (p191), Butterfly Villa in Bucharest (p82), and the High Class Hostel in Suceava (p273). Others range from great to shabby would-be hostels in run-down student dorms. The going rate is about €8 to €15 per person in rooms for four to eight people; most have private singles and doubles for higher prices.

There are no hostels in Moldova.

At Romanian hostels, you can count on internet access, good breakfasts, clean accommodation, laundry, lively surroundings and super-friendly, helpful and knowledgeable staff. Some offer reasonably priced local excursions.

Youth Hostels Romania (www.hihostels-romania.ro), based in Cluj-Napoca, lists contact information for Romania's HI-affiliated hostels; these provide discounts on certain rooms upon presentation of your HI card.

BUDGET BREAKDOWN

Unless otherwise noted in text, we use the following budget breakdown of accommodation in this guide:
Budget under €30 for a double
Midrange €30 to €75 for a double
Top End above €75 for a double

Hotels

Romanian hotels are rated by a government star system, which should be used as a rough guide at best. The top end of the scale (four and five stars) nearly guarantees semi-luxury with various levels of bells and whistles – though you're not going to find much to rival London boutique hotels here. The three-star category could be called 'anything goes'. Some three-star hotels are as comfortable as any four-star one, while others seem to be two-star variants that found an extra star on the ground and posted it. You can at least be assured of hot water, a phone, private bathroom and cable TV.

Not much separates one- and two-star hotels. Hot water *(apă caldă)* is common but not a given. In rural towns, it can be restricted to a few hours in the morning and evening. In rare cases, cold water *(apă rece)* will be restricted too. You can usually choose between a more expensive room with private bathroom or a cheaper one with shared bathroom. In Bucharest and Chişinău doubles cost €30 or more than elsewhere – those who want a little comfort may end up shelling out €80. Elsewhere such comfort comes for €40 or €50.

BUSINESS HOURS

There is considerable variety throughout the two countries, but banks can be expected to open from 9am to 5pm, with many closing for an hour around noon; some are open on Saturday mornings. Most shops are open from 9am or 10am to 6pm or 7pm, some closing on Sundays; museums are usually open from 11am to 5pm, most closing on Monday. Post offices are open from 8am to 7pm Monday to Friday, until 4pm on Saturday, and closed on Sunday. Most restaurants and cafés open from 8am or 9am and close at 11pm or later.

TOP FIVE DREAM SLEEPS

Five favourites from a big grab-bag that account for atmosphere first.

- Hotel Atlantic (p224) in Oradea: a party pad with giant beds, full-on bars and spas.
- Hotel Concordia (p175) in Târgu Mureş: of all things, London-chic in Székely Land.
- Mioritica (p163) in Sibiel: a B&B with its own private stream in a quaint Transylvanian village.
- Pensiunea Ruxi (p104) in Curtea de Argeş: sweet comfort in a homely B&B.
- Saxon pensions (p151) in Viscri: traditional 200-year-old beds with pull-out mattresses and outhouses out the back.

DIRECTORY

Theatrical performances and concerts usually begin at 7pm.

Some business change their hours for 'summer' (loosely June to September) and 'winter' (loosely October to May).

Where opening hours vary from standard, they are detailed in the regional chapters.

CHILDREN

If you can handle some bumps in the road and no highchairs in the restaurants, Romania is a superb destination for children. Sights are certain to bring on the dream factor, with 'Dracula castles', farm animals and shepherds to meet, weird underground worlds in salt mines or ice caves, horse-riding excursions through the mountains, plus fun on the beach or in aqua parks. Moldova offers fewer sights of interest to children, though visits to farms or orchards might help pass the time.

See p19 for kids-oriented destinations around Romania.

Challenges come with lack of children's menus, and toilets not equipped with nappy-change counters. Most malls don't have play centres for kids, and some hotels are more business- than child-oriented. But the X factor is the people, who are almost always willing to accommodate with smaller portions of food or a phone book to sit on. Family-run guesthouses may have toys around (or real-live kids!) for children to play with – and staff are often more than keen to join in too. Nappies and formula aren't tough to find, as most towns have Western-style, well-stocked supermarkets.

If you need to breastfeed, note that this is not something Romanians and Moldovans are used to seeing and doing in public; some discretion would be advised.

It would also be a good idea to have a talk with your children about the issue of orphans and child homelessness in Romania, as they are likely to see some street kids or child beggars and may be troubled by this. A visit to an orphanage might also be an eye-opening, life-changing experience for some children. In this case, bringing along a few extra toys or clothes to give away will make all involved feel good.

Contact the **Information and Cooperation Centre for Homeless Children** (☎ 21-212 6176; http://members .tripod.com/cicfa, Str Academiei 3-5) in Bucharest for information about this grave social issue and related charities. For information about the situation in Moldova and how you can help, see **Save the Children Moldova** (☎ 22 232 582; http:// scm.ngo.moldnet.md).

For more tips, see Lonely Planet's *Travel with Children*.

CLIMATE CHARTS

Temperatures can vary greatly in Romania and Moldova, depending not only on when but also where you go. Even in the summer,

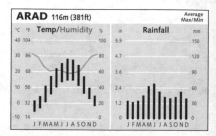

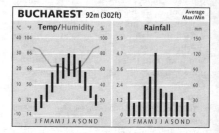

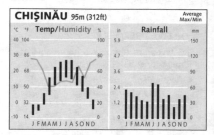

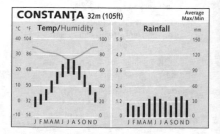

don't count on the 30° to 35°C heat that has befallen the region in recent years; if you plan to include trips into the mountains, be prepared for cold winds at high altitudes and cool nights everywhere else. Winters are fairly temperate, especially near the coast but, again, in the unpredictable mountains be prepared for virtually any conditions.

See p13 for more practical information on climate.

CUSTOMS
Romania

Officially, you're allowed to import hard currency up to a maximum of US$10,000. Valuable goods and foreign currency over US$1000 should be declared upon arrival. For foreigners, duty-free allowances are 4L of wine, 2L of spirits and 200 cigarettes. For more information, go to www.customs.ro.

Moldova

Moldova has more complicated customs procedures (Soviet legacies die slowly), but you shouldn't have any problems. Check 'How to Get There' at www.turism.md for the latest changes in customs regulations.

There is no limit to the amount of foreign currency you can bring into the country but, upon entering, the amount must be declared on a customs declaration sheet you'll be given, and then declared again upon exiting the country. You can leave Moldova with up to US$50,000 (greater amounts must leave via bank transfer). You might be asked to prove that you have at least $30 for each day of your stay.

You're allowed to cross the border either way with 1L of alcohol, 2L of beer and up to 200 cigarettes, though these rules are not strictly enforced (most tourists leave with several bottles of good, cheap wine!).

DANGERS & ANNOYANCES

Romania (and Moldova) can get a bad rap, but don't cancel your trip if you're worried about losing a wallet or getting a dog bite – it's not that extreme.

Prominent scams in the country are jacked-up prices for tourists in Bucharest and Chişinău restaurants, taxis that charge extortionate fares (call for a taxi with companies as recommended by your hotel), and a lifted wallet if you're not careful in public squares or jam-packed buses – like much

---

> **EMERGENCY NUMBER**
>
> Call ☎ 112 for an ambulance or other emergency services in Romania.

---

of the world. Outside the capital, and away from touristy zones like Braşov, you might end up being surprised you were ever concerned.

In Moldova, you should have US$5, US$10 and US$20 bills ready – it's hard to do much without some 'fees' (such as crossing the border: generally US$5). Don't expect police to offer any change. See the boxed text, p318, for more information on bribes in Moldova.

In the past guys in bogus uniforms have asked to see passports in Bucharest, and run off with them. Don't hand over your passport in public.

Also see Dangers & Annoyances sections throughout the book, which have been included where relevant.

To call the (Romanian-speaking only) police, dial ☎ 955. In Moldova, dial ☎ 902.

Stray Dogs

Stray dogs are all over Romania, but most evident in Bucharest, where packs of strays number anywhere from 100,000 to 200,000 – a legacy, apparently, of when Ceauşescu urbanised the city centre and owners no longer had yard (or indoor) space for the Fidos and Snoopys.

Most are harmless, but bites do happen. In 2005 a Japanese man died following a freak bite that severed an artery. During research we met a traveller who was bitten getting off the bus on his first day – some welcome to Romania! Mama dogs with pups can be snappy. Stay clear of packs, and bring earplugs if barking keeps you awake at night.

Should you get bitten, seek medical advice. See the Medical Services and Emergency sections in the regional chapters for places to call.

See also p367 for information on rabies.

Other Nuisances

Hay-fever sufferers will sneeze their way around the region in May and June when the pollen count is at its highest. Bloodsucking mosquitoes are rife in summer, particularly in the Danube Delta.

Probably Romania's biggest annoyance is getting change for your lei note – a communist legacy puts the burden on the buyer; we've walked away from sizeable purchases akin to €19 because the store didn't have €1 change.

DISABLED TRAVELLERS

Disabled travellers will find it difficult, if not downright impossible, to conquer Romania. Street surfaces are woefully uneven, ramps are rare (though more common in Sibiu, thanks to local government initiatives) and specially equipped toilets and hotel rooms are virtually unheard of. Consider joining a package tour that will cater to your specific needs. Some hotels on the Black Sea coast have wheelchair access, and spas in general may be more accustomed to disabled travellers.

Though there are laws providing for wheelchair access to public buildings, in reality little has been done. Only a quarter of the nation's 52,000 disabled children get any education, for example (and about one in five are abandoned). As the country is still economically and politically finding its footing, persons with disabilities and their problems have not been a priority. The **Romania Motivation Foundation** (☎ 21-493 2142; www.motivation.ro) in Bucharest has worked incredibly hard since its foundation in 1995 to provide access to wheelchairs for locals in need. They also started a wheelchair basketball organisation.

The situation for the disabled in Moldova is in even greater need of overhaul, and travellers will find obstacles all along their route. However, staff at hotels and restaurants will be obliging, and taking a wine tour at Cricova, for example, is entirely possible.

DISCOUNT CARDS

A Hostelling International (HI) card yields a token discount in some hostels. You can become a member by joining your own national Youth Hostel Association (YHA) or IYHF (International Youth Hostel Federation); see www.hihostels.com for details. Alternatively, you can buy an annual card for about €5 at one of Romania's HI-affiliated hostels.

Holders of the **International Student Identity Card** (ISIC; www.isic.org) are privy to many discounts in Romania and in Moldova (though only in Chişinău), and the **Euro<26 card** (www.euro26.ro in Romanian) entitles those under 26 years of age to some 600 discounts in Romania (none in

Moldova). Helpful hints for student travellers in Romania are found at www.studenttravel .ro including a list of all ISIC's discounts.

Elderly foreigners may obtain discounted entry to many museums and on some long-distance bus and train journeys, but not much more.

EMBASSIES & CONSULATES
Romanian Embassies & Consulates

Romanian embassies and consulates abroad:

Australia (☎ 026 286 2343; http://canberra.mae.ro; 4 Dalman Crescent, O'Malley, Canberra, ACT)

Bulgaria (☎ 02-973 3081; ambsofro@vip.bg; Mihai Eminescu 4, Sofia)

Canada Ottawa (☎ 613-789 5345; www.cyberus.ca /~romania; 655 Rideau St, Ottawa, Ontario); Montreal (☎ 514-876 1792; romcon@videotron.ca; 1111 St Urbain, Suite M01-04, Montreal); Toronto (☎ 416-585 5802; www .romaniacanada.com; 111 Peter St, Suite 530, Toronto)

France (☎ 01 47 05 10 46; www.amb-roumanie.fr, in French; 5 rue de l'Exposition, Paris)

Germany (☎ 030-212 39 202; www.rumainische -botschaft.de; Dorotheenstr 62-66, Berlin)

Hungary (☎ 01-384 0271; postmaster@roembbud .axelero.net; Thököly út 72, Budapest)

Ireland (☎ 031-668 1275; ambrom@eircom.net; 26 Waterloo Rd, Dublin)

Moldova (Map p320; ☎ 22-228 126; http://chisinau .mae.ro; Str Bucureşti 66/1, Chişinău)

Serbia (☎ 011-361 8327; embassy@romania.org.yu; Kneza Miloša 70, Belgrade)

UK (☎ 020-7937 9666; www.roemb.co.uk; 4 Palace Green, Kensington Gardens, London W8 4QD)

Ukraine (☎ 044-234 5261; romania@iptelecom.net.ua; ulitsa Mihaila Kotziubinskogo 8, Kyiv)

USA Washington (☎ 202-232 3694; www.roembus.org; 1607 23rd St NW, Washington DC); Los Angeles (☎ 310-444 0043; www.romanian.org/consulat/services.html; 11766 Wilshire Blvd, Suite 560, Los Angeles); New York (☎ 212-682 9122; www.romconsny.org; 200 East 38th St, New York)

Embassies & Consulates in Romania

Unless stated otherwise, the following foreign embassies are in Bucharest (city code ☎ 21).

Australia (Map pp62-3; ☎ 320 9802; don.cairns@ austrade.gov.au; B-dul Unirii 74)

Bulgaria (Map pp62-3; ☎ 230 2150; Str Rabat 5)

Canada (Map pp62-3; ☎ 307 5000; bucst-im@dfait-maeci .gc.ca; Str Nicolae Iorga 36)

France (Map pp62-3; ☎ 312 0217; www.ambafrance.ro; Str Biserica Amzei 13-15); Consulate: (Map pp62-3; ☎ 312 0991; Intrarea Cristian Tell 6)

Germany (Map pp62-3; ☎ 202 9853; www.deutsche botschaft-bukarest.org/ro/home; Str Rabat 21); Sibiu (Map p156; ☎ 269-211 133; Str Lucian Blaga 15-17, Sibiu); Timişoara (Map p216; ☎ 256-220 796; Hotel Continental, B-dul Revoluţiei 1989 3, Timişoara); *Consulates:* Sibiu (Map p156; ☎ 269-214 442; Str Hegel 3, Sibiu); Timişoara (Map p216; ☎ 256-190 495; B-dul Republicii 6, Timişoara)

Hungary (Map pp62-3; ☎ 312 0073; hunembro@ines.ro; Str Jean Louis Calderon 63-65); *Consulates:* (Map pp62-3; ☎ 312 0468; Str Henri Coandă 5); Cluj-Napoca (Map p186; ☎ 264-596 300; huconkol@codec.ro; Piaţa Unirii 23, Cluj-Napoca)

Ireland (Map pp62-3; ☎ 211 3967; Str Vasile Lascăr 42-4)

Moldova (Map pp62-3; ☎ 230 0474; moldova@customers .dirigo.net; Aleea Alexandru 40); *Consulate:*(☎ 410 9827; B-dul Eroilor 8)

Russia (Map pp62-3; ☎ 222 3170; Şoseaua Kiseleff 6); Constanţa (Map p288; ☎ 041-222 1389; Str Tuberozelor 4, Constanţa)

Turkey (☎ 210 0279; Calea Dorobanţilor 72); Constanţa (Map p288; ☎ 041-611 135; turkkons@fx.ro; B-dul Ferdinand 82, Constanţa)

UK (Map pp62-3; ☎ 201 7200; www.britain.ro; Str Jules Michelet 24)

Ukraine (Map pp62-3; ☎ 211 6986; Calea Dorobanţilor 16); *Consulate:* (Map pp62-3; ☎ 222 3162; Str Tuberozelor 5)

USA (Map pp62-3; ☎ 210 4042; www.usembassy.ro; Str Tudor Arghezi 7-9); *Consulate:* (Map pp62-3; ☎ 210 4042; Str Nicolae Filipescu 26); Cluj-Napoca Information Bureau (Map p186; ☎ 264-594 315; Str Universităţii 7-9, Cluj-Napoca)

Yugoslavia (Map pp62-3; ☎ 211 9871, consulate section 211 4980; Calea Dorobanţilor 34); Timişoara (Map p216; ☎ 256-590 334; gktyug@mail.dnttm.ro; Str Remus 4, Timişoara)

Moldovan Embassies & Consulates

Moldova has embassies and consulates in the following countries:

Bulgaria (☎ 02-981 7370; moldova@www1.infotel.bg; B-dul Patriarh Evtimii 17, Sofia)

France (☎ 01 40 67 11 20; ambassade.moldavie@free.fr; 1 rue Sfax, Paris) Also handles Spain and Portugal.

Germany (☎ 069-52 78 08; mongenmold@aol.com; Adelheidstrasse nr. 8, Frankfurt)

Hungary (☎ 1-209 1191; amrung@mail.elender.hu; Str Kazinthy 17, fsz 5-6, Budapest)

Romania (Map pp62-3; ☎ 230 0474; moldova@customers .dirigo.net; Aleea Alexandru 40, Bucharest) *Consulate:*(☎ 410 9827; B-dul Eroilor 8, Bucharest)

Russia (☎ 095-924 5353; moldemb@online.ru; 18 Kuznetskii most, Moscow)

Turkey (☎ 312-446 5527; ambmold@superonline.com; Kaptanpasa Sok 49, Ankara)

Ukraine (☎ 044-290 7721; moldovak@sovam.com; ulitsa Kutuzov 8, Kyiv) A consulate in Odessa was in the plans at research time.

UK (☎ 020 8995 6818; www.moldovanembassy.org.uk; 5 Dolphin Sq, Edensor Rd, Chiswick, London W4 2ST)

USA (☎ 202-667-1130; moldova@dgs.dgsys.com; 2101 S Street NW, Washington, DC)

Embassies & Consulates in Moldova

These countries have embassies or consulates in Chişinău (city code ☎ 22):

Bulgaria (Map p320; ☎ 237 983; www.bulgaria.bg/Europe /Chisinau; Str 31 August 1989 No 125)

France (Map p320; ☎ 200 400; www.ambafrance.md; Str Vlaicu Pîrcălab 6)

Germany (Map p320; ☎ 200 600; ambasada -germana@riscom.md; Str Maria Cibotari 35)

Hungary (Map p320; ☎ 227 786; huembkiv1@ meganet.md; B-dul Ştefan cel Mare 131)

Romania (Map p320; ☎ 22-228 126; http://chisinau .mae.ro; Str Bucureşti 66/1)

Russia (Map p320; ☎ 234 942; www.moldova.mid.ru; B-dul Ştefan cel Mare 153)

Turkey (Map p320; ☎ 242 608; tremb@moldova.md; Str Alexei Mateevici 57)

Ukraine (Map p319; ☎ 582 124; www.mfa.gov.ua; Str Vasilie Lupu 17)

UK (Map p320; ☎ 225 902; www.britishembassy.md; Str Nicolae Iorga 18)

USA (Map p320; ☎ 408 300; www.usembassy.md; Str A Mateevici 103A)

FESTIVALS & EVENTS

Romania has festivals going on all year round in all regions of the country, but Moldova is less festival-frenzied – perhaps because its citizens welcome any excuse to party throughout the year. Here is a calendar of many events. It's worth confirming dates before you show up, as they sometimes shift.

See p16 for a list of our favourites.

JANUARY
Winter Sports Festival Moldavia's Câmpulung Moldovenesc (last Sunday of January)

FEBRUARY
Enchanted Water Springs Music Festival Târgu Jui's folk music festival, held on the third Sunday in February

APRIL
Rooster Shooting Villagers denounce a (fake) rooster then shoot it; in Apata near Braşov (third Sunday in April)
St George Days Festival Three-day festival in Sfântu Gheorghe, Transylvania (last Sunday in April)

Tânjaua de pe Mara Maramureş peasant festival of fertility with river dunkings of young and old (late April/early May)

Days of Braşov & Juni Pageant Braşov's biggest festival begins in the first week after Easter (late April/early May)

MAY

Mayfest Sibiu's Saxon festival (1 May)

Constanţa Days Constanţa (around 21 May)

International Theatre Festival Week-long event in Piatra Neamţ (late May)

Festival of Sâmbra Oilor Celebrating the hill-bound exodus of sheep from Ţara Oaşului, Maramureş (May/June)

GayFest Romania's only gay festival, held in Bucharest (late May/early June)

Bucharest Carnival Week-long carnival with theatre, dance and music (late May/early June)

Sibiu Jazz Festival Weeklong jazz festival in Sibiu

JUNE

Fête de la Musique Bucharest's annual French music festival (21 June)

Suceava Days Street fair, with some religion thrown in, in Suceava (late June)

Dragaica Pagan pre-harvest celebration in Târgo Vişte (last week of June)

Târgu Mureş Days Carnival in Székely Land (last weekend in June)

Transylvania International Film Festival International player growing every year, in Cluj-Napoca (and also in Sibiu in 2007)

JULY

Maramuzical Festival Four-day folk music fest in Vadu Izei, Maramureş (mid July)

Felsziget Festival DJ/rock festival in Târgu Mureş (late July)

Medieval Festival of the Arts Sighişoara (late July)

AUGUST

National Romanian Folk Festival Constanţa (early August)

House Parade Vama Veche beach DJ festival (10 August)

Hora de la Prislop Folk Music festival held in Maramureş (second Sunday in August) and Bucharest (early August)

Ceahlău Folk Festival Shepherds don traditional outfits and head to Durău in Moldavia (second Sunday in August)

Craftsman's Fair Bucharest's Village Museum's heyday with guest craftsmen from around the country (15 August)

Moldavian Furrier Fair Suceava (mid August)

Mountain Festival Fundata (last Sunday in August)

National Film Festival Costineşti

International Folk Festival of Danubian Countries Tulcea

International Folk, Dance & Traditions Festival Bistriţa

Sfântu Gheorghe Film Festival In Danube Delta

SEPTEMBER

George Enescu Music Festival International event in Bucharest in 2008, runs the full four weeks of September

National Pop Music Festival National bands compete in Mamaia (early September)

Mioriţa Folk singer contest in Târgovişte (mid September)

Sâmbra Oilor Three-day welcoming home of the sheep, Bran (late September/early October)

OCTOBER

Wine Festival Chişinău's huge, messy, wine-splattered festival, scheduled around its City Day (14 October)

Iaşi Days Week-long religious event – and street party – in Iaşi (mid October)

Beer Festival Timişoara's sudsy sprawl with live bands

International Astra Film Festival In Sibiu in 2008

National Theatre Festival Bucharest's week-long event; sometimes runs in November

DECEMBER

De la Colind la Stea Four-day Bucharest music festival

Winter Carnival Mulled wine and winter customs, Tulcea

Gagauz Independence Day Moldovan Gagauz republic's independence day (23 December)

Winter Festival Sighetu Marmaţiei, Maramureş (27 December)

FOOD

Romanian restaurants are cheaper than Western European ones, but gone are the days when you could fill up for a euro or two. Some locals rarely eat out since communism failed and prices rose.

In this book we have listed prices for main courses (mains), which often start at €2 for a grilled sausage or two and rise up to €10 for something more substantial. Whether you add a garnish, soup, dessert, beer or alcohol, naturally, affects the meal price. Usually you can eat lightly for €5 or €6 per person, and rarely end up spending more than €10.

Chişinău has a surprisingly rich dining scene, with swank eateries that rival Bucharest's (in price too).

For more on food and drink, see p52.

GAY & LESBIAN TRAVELLERS
Romania

Romania's rather puritan attitude towards homosexuality has been reflected by its laws: only in 2001 it became one of Europe's last countries to decriminalise homosexual activity (in 1994 the Constitutional Court repealed Communist-era laws against homosexuality but in 1996 it was reinstated as a criminal offence). Until then, people were prosecuted and jailed even for acts in private between consenting adults.

Some homosexuals were tortured during the communist regime. Police harassment and brutality were commonplace – human-rights groups in Romania and abroad have reams of reports of violence, extortion and entrapment, even in the 1990s.

Not surprisingly, few gay and lesbian Romanians show affection in public. The Orthodox Church still considers homosexuality a sin. The situation is slowly getting more relaxed, especially in urban centres. Bucharest has, by far, Romania's most active gay and lesbian scene, represented by Bucharest-based **Accept** (☎ 21-252 5620; www.accept-romania.ro). In late May/early June Accept organises a six-day **GayFest**, with films, parties and conferences around Bucharest.

With its lively student population, Cluj-Napoca has gay nights in some nightclubs, and a far more open environment than most of Romania.

See also www.gaybucuresti.ro, which has a chat room.

Moldova

Before Moldova repealed its Soviet antigay law in 1995, it was one of only four European countries to still criminalise homosexuality. Now Moldova has one of the most progressively liberal laws on the continent: homosexual activity is legal for both sexes at 14, the same age as for heterosexual sex. A National Human Rights Plan, which would see the prohibition of discrimination against homosexuals, has been bounced around the government since 2003, but still has yet to pass.

There are annual **Gay Pride parades** in Chişinău in early May. However, homosexuality is still a hushed topic, and politicians still get away with antigay rhetoric. While most people take a laissez-faire attitude towards the notion of homosexuality, being visibly out is likely to attract unwanted attention.

There are no officially gay nightclubs in Moldova. Check out www.gay.md, run by GenderDoc-M (an information centre on gender studies), for the latest news.

HOLIDAYS

Public holidays in Romania are New Year (1 and 2 January), both Catholic and Orthodox Easter Mondays (in March/April), Labour Day (1 May), Romanian National Day (1 December) and Christmas (25 and 26 December).

Moldova's national holidays include New Year's Day (1 January), Orthodox Christmas (7 January), International Women's Day (8 March), Orthodox Easter (March or April), Memorial Day (27 April), Labour Day (1 May), Victory (1945) Day (9 May), Independence Day (27 August) and National Language Day (31 August).

If you travel during public holidays, it's wise to book ahead, as some hotels in popular destinations may be full.

INSURANCE

Though medical insurance is not compulsory in Romania and Moldova, a fully comprehensive travel-insurance policy to cover theft, loss and medical problems is strongly advisable, especially if you intend to do a lot of travelling. A policy that covers the costs of being flown out of the country for treatment is a definite bonus, given the still-limited local facilities.

See also car insurance (p359) and health insurance (p366).

INTERNET ACCESS

Internet cafés are all over Romania (even in smaller towns), often with sliding prices depending on the time of day. It usually costs €0.60 to €1.50 per hour. Speed is generally good, but the noise and cramp factor from ever-present computer-game enthusiasts can be distracting.

Many hotels say they have 'internet access' but actually only have a dial-up link for you to contact a local server if you know of one. Wi-fi access is on a slow-going rise, with a few hotels (including lobby bars) and cafés offering it, particularly around Bucharest.

Chişinău is also full of internet cafés that charge US$0.50 per hour; pickings are slim outside the capital.

For some internet resources, see p15.

LEGAL MATTERS

If you are arrested you can insist on seeing an embassy or consular officer straight away. It is not advisable to present your passport to people on the street unless you know for certain that they are authentic officials – cases of theft have been reported. Better still, carry a copy of your passport with you instead of the actual document while touring the city.

Romanians and Moldovans can legally drink, drive and vote (though not simultaneously!) at the age of 18. The age of consent in Romania is 15, in Moldova 16.

Romania and Moldova have high rates of incarceration, and drug possession is a criminal offence in both countries, so getting caught with drugs here is really not a good idea.

MAPS

If you are driving around the country, get a road map in a city bookshop – they are almost never available on the highway. Serious drivers should opt for Cartographia's 1:500,000 spiral-bound *Romania* (€9). Dimap's *Transilvania/ Erdély* (€6) has a little more detail of that region.

Regional maps and bookshops are recommended throughout the regional chapters.

MONEY

In both Romania and Moldova the only legal tender is the leu (plural: lei), though they are separate currencies in each country and have different exchange rates (see Quick Reference inside the front cover). In Romania you'll see many prices quoted in euros, while in Moldova people talk in US dollars. Consequently, this book quotes prices in euros for Romania, and in dollars for Moldova.

After tumultuous times of inflation and devaluation in the 1990s, both currencies are showing signs of stability. Joining the EU could mean a rise in prices in Romania, though many things have already risen to a level comparable to some EU members from Eastern Europe. For general costs, see p13.

ATMs

ATMs (cash points) are everywhere and give 24-hour withdrawals in lei on your Cirrus, Plus, Visa, MasterCard or Eurocard. Some banks, such as Banca Comercială Română, give cash advances on credit cards in your home currency.

It's easy to find ATMs in Chişinău, but not in other towns in Moldova.

Currency

Beginning in January 2007, the old Romanian lei (singular: leu) was taken out of circulation, and the new lei (abbreviated 'RON') – with four less zeroes – took over (ie 10,000 old lei equals one new leu). The new lei comes in denominations of 1, 5, 10, 50, 100, and 500. New ban coins come in 1, 5, 10 and 50 denominations; 100 ban equals one leu.

If someone offers the old notes, don't take them.

Exchanging Money

To change dollars, euros or pounds, you often need to show a passport. Be wary of changers with bodyguard goons out front. Some changers

---

BLOKE ON THE BILL

One strike against the EU is the standardised currency, which makes cross-Europe travel a little less exciting than it once was. For now, the portraits on Romania's money still tell a tale of its history.

1 leu: Nicolae Iorga (1871–1940) The cofounder of the Democratic National Party was renowned as a rare voice against fascism as WWII loomed. He was eventually tortured and executed and his body was left on the road. A copy of the paper that he wrote for had been stuffed down his throat.

5 lei: George Enescu (1881–1955) Famous for composing 'Romanian Rhapsodies' (1903), he left Romania after communism took over. Many of his works were lost because he rarely wrote them down!

10 lei: Nicolae Grigorescu (1838–1907) Romania's best-known painter progressed from Ruben copies to originals of traditional scenes around Romania.

50 lei: Aurel Vlaicu (1882–1913) The first Romanian to excel in flight (vampires included), he died in crash of his *Vlaicu II* in 1913.

100 lei: Ion Luca Caragiale (1852–1912) This playwright was happy to take the piss out of everyone with his rather ironic stabs at the modernising Romania at the end of the 19th century.

500 lei: Mihai Eminescu (1850–89) The mere mention of this national poet inspires Romanian pride. He suffered from manic-depressive psychosis, but probably died from syphilis (aged 38).

advertise juicy rates, but disguise a '9' as a '0' subtly etc. Count your money carefully.

Black market activity is not seen much. Don't change money on the street.

Travellers Cheques & Credit Cards

In theory it is possible to change travellers cheques at various Romanian banks, but in practice many banks are not able to do it. You may be better off relying on ATMs. The Banca Comercială Română, and the Eximbank in Moldavia, will give cash advances on major credit cards

Credit cards won't get you anywhere in rural areas, but they are widely accepted in larger department stores, hotels and many restaurants in Romanian cities and large towns. If you're planning to use a credit card, double-check ahead of time; some businesses have been known to put the 'Visa' sticker in the window because 'it looks nice.'

You'll need a credit card to hire a car, unless you're willing to pay a large deposit up front.

American Express is represented in Bucharest by Marshal Turism (p68). It has no representatives in Moldova.

POST

The reliable, but slow, **Romania Post Office** (www .postaromana.ro) sends a postcard or letter weighing less than 20g to Europe from Romania for €0.85; it takes seven to 10 days.

From Moldova, it costs US$0.35 to send a postcard or letter weighing less than 20g to Western Europe, Australia or the USA.

DHL (www.dhl.com) is the most popular international courier service in the region. It has offices in 22 Romanian cities; in Moldova there are offices in Chişinău, Balţi and Tiraspol.

SHOPPING

'Western-style' supermarkets and shopping malls are commonplace in much of Romania, so you should be able to find what you need. Local wines or Romanian ţuică (plum brandy) make good souvenirs – go for Kvint, a Transdniestrian brandy if you make it the region.

Other traditional purchases include embroidered blouses, ceramics, wooden sculptures, tablecloths and hand-woven carpets.

Some specific shopping suggestions are found in the appropriate sections in the regional chapters.

SOLO TRAVELLERS

There are no particular problems with travelling alone in Romania or Moldova, other than a head-shake of approving disbelief from the occasional local. Generally hotels charge cheaper rates for one person – sometimes a nifty 50% of a double – but your mouth may water at the (relatively) expensive bottles of wine enjoyed at neighbouring tables that you don't want to shell out for on your own.

TELEPHONE

For national and international phone codes and dialling codes, see Quick Reference inside the front cover.

Romania

Romania's international operator can be reached by dialling ☎ 971. Local numbers in Romania are five, six or seven digits; mobile phone numbers start with ☎ 07.

To make domestic calls in Romania, call ☎ 0 + area code; to call abroad dial ☎ 00 + country code + area code.

For an English-speaking operator abroad, call **British Telecom** (☎ 01-800 4444), **AT&T USA Direct** (☎ 01-800 4288), **MCI Worldwide** (☎ 01-800 1800) or **Sprint** (☎ 01-800 0877).

Romania's telephone centres and phone booths are a sad sight, almost completely ignored by mobile-phone revolutionaries. Many centres are closed or refashioned as mobile-phone stores. Phonecards costing €3 can be bought at newsstands and used at stranded, but still-kicking, phone booths for domestic or international calls.

European mobile phones with roaming work in Romania; otherwise you can get a Romania number from Orange or Vodafone, both of which have shops *everywhere*. The SIM card costs about US$5 including credit; calls are about US$0.10 to US$0.30 per minute.

Moldova

Any European mobile phone with roaming will work in Moldova, though reception inside Transdniestr is not a given. Mobile-phone service in Moldova is provided by Chişinău-based **Moldcell** (☎ 22-444 444; www.moldcell.md; Str Belgrad 3, Chişinău) and **Voxtel** (☎ 22-575 757; www .voxtel.md; Str Alba Iulia 75). SIM cards cost US$6 to US$8 for eight to 10 minutes of credit.

Moldtelecom, the state-run telephone company, sells pay cards which can be used to dial any number within Moldova only, for US$2.25 or US$3. These are sold at any telephone centre in the country. To make an international call using a prepaid card, you need to use a private company such as Treitelecom. Its cards cost from US$3.75 to US$35.

Prepaid telephone cards can be used to call locally, internationally or to mobile phones. Cards are sold in denominations of 50, 100 and 200 lei – available at telephone centres and street kiosks. Neotel also have good-value phone cards.

TIME

Both Romanian and Moldovan time is GMT/ UTC plus two hours, and both countries observe daylight savings time. Both also use the 24-hour clock. Dates are listed with the month first, followed by the day and year, ie 09/08/07 refers to 8 September 2007.

TOILETS

Let's just say that public toilets in these countries won't be among your highlights. We even heard a tale of the Duke of Luxembourg getting uppity over one in Transylvania. The toilets at train and bus stations are often smelly holes in vile pits that will make you rush out gasping for fresh air. While the vast majority are quite usable, the fact that many do not have a toilet seat (or have a cracked or soiled one) can be annoying for those not used to the squatting technique.

Though you might be handed a coarse piece of toilet paper by a WC clerk at the entrance for a nominal fee, this is where having some extra tissues comes in handy.

Many toilets have a plastic bin by their side. This is intended for used toilet paper. Women's toilets are marked with the letter F (*femei*) or with an s. Men's are marked B (*bărbaţi*) or t.

In Moldova most toilets bear Russian signs: Ж for women and M for men.

TOURIST INFORMATION
Local Tourist Offices

Amazingly, Romania still has no national tourist office network, making information tough to track down. A handful of highly efficient, independently run tourist centres – such as those in Sibiu, Târgu Mureş and Arad – have sprung up in the past couple of years (shockingly Bucharest is not represented.)

Many travel agencies cheerfully offer trips *out* of Romania, but occasionally help out with local information too. In each city section, we have recommended the places where you are most likely to get the best help.

Tourist Offices Abroad

Contrary to the disheartening lack of information locally, Romania runs 16 efficient tourist offices abroad, coordinated by Romania's **National Authority for Tourism** (www.turism.ro); but www.romaniatourism.com is the best site for government-provided information.

Some offices abroad:

France (☎ 01 40 20 99 33; roumanie@office-tourisme -roumanie.com; 12 rue des Gaillon, Paris)

Germany Berlin (☎ 030-241 9041; www.rumaenien -tourismus.de; Budapester Str 20A, Berlin); Munich (☎ 089-5156 7687; Dachauer Str 32-34, Munich)

Moldova (☎ 32-273 555; romtur@ch.moldpac.md; B-dul Ştefan cel Mare 151-153, Chişinău)

UK (☎ 020-7224 3692; www.romaniatourism.com; 22 New Cavendish St, London W1M 7ZH)

USA (☎ 212-545 8484; www.romaniatourism.com; 14 East 38th St, 12th fl, New York, NY 10016)

VISAS
Romania

In order to obtain a visa, you will need a passport that's valid for at least six months beyond the date you enter the country.

Citizens of all EU countries, USA, Canada, Japan and many other countries may travel visa-free for 90 days in Romania. Australians and New Zealanders no longer need to arrange a visa in advance. As visa requirements change frequently, check at the **Ministry of Foreign Affairs** (www.mae.ro) before departure.

Romania issues two types of visas to tourists: transit and single-entry. Transit visas (for those from countries other than the ones mentioned above) are for stays of no longer than three days, and cannot be bought at the border.

To apply for a visa you need a passport, one recent passport photograph and the completed visa application form accompanied by the appropriate fee. Citizens of some countries (mainly African) need a formal invitation from a person or company in order to apply for a visa; see www.mae.ro for details.

Regular single-entry visas (US$25) are valid for 90 days from the day you arrive. Single-entry visas are usually issued within a week (depending on the consulate), but for an extra US$6 can be issued within 48 hours.

Transit visas can be either single-entry (US$15) – valid for three days and allowing you to enter Romania once – or double-entry (US$25), allowing you to enter the country twice and stay for three days each time.

In Romania, you can extend your tourist visa for another 60 days at any county police office, but it can be trickier than just leaving the country and coming back in. Technically it takes a couple of days and shouldn't cost more than US$50. You may have to show you have US$100 per day for your stay. You must apply before your current visa expires. It's easier if you get a travel agent to help.

Check your visa requirements for Serbia, Hungary, Bulgaria and Ukraine if you plan to cross those borders. If you are taking the Bucharest–St Petersburg train you will need Ukrainian and Belarusian transit visas on top of the Russian visa.

Moldova

As this book went to press, Moldova was changing its sometimes vexing visa situation. It's a good idea to check www.turism .md (under 'How to Get To') for the latest changes on the visa rules.

Beginning in 2007, citizens of the EU, USA, Canada, Japan and Switzerland can enter Moldova without a visa. Visitors from Israel can present their passport (valid for six months after the visa's expiry date) and one photo to the nearest Moldovan consulate to obtain a visa. It's likely that citizens of Israel and Norway also will be able to visit without a visa by the time this book is published.

All other nationalities, including Australians and New Zealanders, require either a tourist voucher from an accredited travel agency or an invitation from a company, organisation or individual (difficult to get). Tourist vouchers ensure that you have a hotel prebooked and prepaid. Payments to the consulates are usually in the form of a bank deposit at a specified bank.

The main three border crossings from Romania are at Sculeni (north of Iaşi), Leuseni (main Bucharest–Chişinău border) and Cahul if arriving by bus or car from Romania – others have a history of being trickier to cross, though this may change with the easing of visa restrictions.

Visitors to Moldova no longer have to register with the police after their arrival.

Previously, an HIV-AIDS test was required for foreigners intending to stay in Moldova longer than three months. Certificates proving HIV negative status have to be in Russian and English.

COSTS & REGISTRATION

The price of a single/double-entry tourist visa valid for one month is US$60/75. Single/double-entry transit visas valid for 72 hours cost US$30/60. Special rates are available for tourist groups of more than 10 people, and for children, disabled travellers and senior travellers.

Visas can be processed within a day at the **Moldovan consulate** (☎ 4021-410 9827; B-dul Eroilor 8, Bucharest) in Romania.

VOLUNTEERING

England-based **Project New Life** (www.projectnewlife .org) is a religious nonprofit organisation that keeps religion out of its tireless efforts to help children in Romania and Moldova. Contact them about volunteering on their ongoing projects.

Clipa Siderala (www.clipa.md) is a Moldovan-based organisation run by volunteers that helps orphans.

Global Volunteers (www.globalvolunteers.org) offers one-week and two-week volunteering projects helping orphans and teaching English. Volunteers pay for the experience (a two-week slot is €1756 including lodging, food and insurance).

Sites like www.volunteerabroad.com list many other options.

Transport

CONTENTS

GETTING THERE & AWAY

ENTERING ROMANIA & MOLDOVA

Travellers entering Romania should not experience any trouble at customs and immigration, particularly if they come from a country which does not require them to possess a Romanian visa (see p354).

Moldova's a bit different. As a result of the Soviet legacy, travellers may experience some questioning on entering Moldova but, thanks to the same legacy, any potential complication is easy to resolve on the spot – most often by offering a few dollars (often about US$5 at the border).

AIR

Many airlines fly into Bucharest, but Carpatair's hub is in delightful Timişoara. Budget airline Wizz Air connects Budapest with Transylvania's Târgu Mureş.

Airports & Airlines

Flying is a popular way to enter Romania, though there are no direct flights from North America, Asia or Australia. Most international flights land at Bucharest's **Henri Coanda Airport** (formerly Otopeni; airport code OTP; www.otp-airport.ro; ☎ 201 4788; Şos Bucureşti-Ploieşti). An exception is discount airline Wizz Air, which uses the capi-

---

THINGS CHANGE

The information in this chapter is particularly vulnerable to change: prices for international travel are volatile, routes are introduced and cancelled, schedules frequently change and special deals come and go. Airlines and governments seem to take a perverse pleasure in making price structures and regulations as complicated as possible.

The details given in this chapter should be used as pointers and are not a substitute for your own careful, up-to-date research.

tal's older **Băneasa Airport** (airport code BBU; www.baneasa.aero; ☎ 232 0020; Şos Bucureşti-Ploieşti 40) for all flights. Wizz connects Bucharest with London (Luton) three times weekly. It also offers flights to Budapest, Rome, Barcelona and Dortmund. Wizz also connects Budapest with Târgu Mureş three times a week.

Carpatair sends planes from its hub in Timişoara to several cities in Germany and Italy, plus Paris and Chişinău. Tarom is Romania's struggling state airline.

Moldova's only airport is **Chişinău International** (airport code KIV; www.airport.md; ☎ 22-526 060). **Voiaj Travel** (www.voiaj.md) in Chişinău publishes the latest airport schedules. The national airline is Air Moldova, which serves Bucharest's Henri Coanda Airport too.

AIRLINES FLYING TO & FROM ROMANIA
Air France (airline code AF; ☎ 21-319 2705; www.airfrance.com)
Air Moldova (airline code 9U; ☎ 21-312 1258; www.airmoldova.md)
Austrian Airlines (airline code OS; ☎ 21-204 2208; www.austrianair.com)
British Airways (airline code BA; ☎ 21-303 2222; www.british-airways.com)
Carpatair (airline code V3; ☎ 256-300 900; www.carpatair.com)
ČSA (Czech Airlines; airline code OK; ☎ 21-315 3205; www.csa.cz)
KLM (airline code KL; ☎ 21-312 0149; www.klm.com)
LOT Polish Airlines (airline code LO; ☎ 21-314 1096; www.lot.com)

Lufthansa (airline code LH; ☎ 21-204 8410; www.luft hansa.com)

Swiss Airlines (airline code LX; ☎ 21-312 0238; www .swiss.com)

Tarom (airline code RO; ☎ 22-541 254, 0992 541 254; www.tarom.ro)

Turkish Airlines (airline code TK; ☎ 21-311 2410; www .turkishairlines.com)

Wizz Air (airline code W6; ☎ 403 6440 2000; www.wizz air.com)

AIRLINES FLYING TO & FROM MOLDOVA

AeroSvit Airlines (airline code VV; ☎ 422 237 682; www.aerosvit.ua) From Kyiv, Ukraine.

Air Moldova (airline code 9U; ☎ 21-312 1258; www .airmoldova.md)

Austrian Airlines (airline code OS; ☎ 22-244 083; www.austrianair.com)

Carpatair (airline code V3; ☎ 22-549 339; www.carpat air.com)

Moldavian Airlines (airline code 2M; ☎ 22-529 356; www.mdv.md)

Tarom (airline code RO; ☎ 22-541 254, 0992 541 254; www.tarom.ro)

Transaero (airline code UN; ☎ 22-542 454; www.trans aero.md)

Turkish Airlines (airline code TK; ☎ 22-527 078; www .turkishairlines.com)

Tickets

At better-known travel agencies you may pay slightly more than a rock-bottom fare in return for security and peace of mind.

www.cheapflights.co.uk Posts bargain flights out of the UK only.

www.dialaflight.com Offers worldwide flights out of Europe and the UK.

www.expedia.com Good site for checking worldwide flight prices.

www.lastminute.com Mostly deals in European flights, but has some worldwide flights including a link to an Australian version.

www.statravel.co.uk STA Travel's UK website. There are also websites in Australia (www.statravel.com.au) and the USA (www.statravel.com).

www.travel.com.au A good site for Australians to find cheap flights. From New Zealand try www.travel.co.nz.

For last-minute tickets online try **Skyauction** (www.skyauction.com). **Priceline** (www.priceline.com) tries to match the ticket price to your budget.

Australia & New Zealand

From Australia, expect to pay around A$1700 return during low season and upwards of A$2200 during high season. Austrian Airlines, British Airways and Qantas all have some good fare deals. Sometimes prices for

TRANSPORT

CLIMATE CHANGE & TRAVEL

Climate change is a serious threat to the ecosystems that humans rely upon, and air travel is the fastest-growing contributor to the problem. Lonely Planet regards travel, overall, as a global benefit, but believes we all have a responsibility to limit our personal impact on global warming.

Flying & Climate Change

Pretty much every form of motor transport generates CO_2 (the main cause of human-induced climate change) but planes are far and away the worst offenders, not just because of the sheer distances they allow us to travel, but because they release greenhouse gases high into the atmosphere. The statistics are frightening: two people taking a return flight between Europe and the USA will contribute as much to climate change as an average household's gas and electricity consumption over a whole year.

Carbon Offset Schemes

Climatecare.org and other websites use 'carbon calculators' that allow travellers to offset the greenhouse gases they are responsible for with contributions to energy-saving projects and other climate-friendly initiatives in the developing world – including projects in India, Honduras, Kazakhstan and Uganda.

Lonely Planet, together with Rough Guides and other concerned partners in the travel industry, supports the carbon offset scheme run by climatecare.org. Lonely Planet offsets all of its staff and author travel.

For more information check out our website: www.lonelyplanet.com.

TRANSPORT

flights from New Zealand can be disturbingly high – try NZ$15,000 return. If so, it may be cheaper to book a separate ticket to Sydney.

Eastern Europe

Bucharest is connected with regular flights to and from Prague, Budapest, Warsaw, Sofia and Moscow. Chişinău is connected with regular flights to and from Sofia, Minsk, Moscow, Budapest and Prague. In 2006 Wizz Air began a Budapest–Târgu Mureş service.

Romania & Moldova

Air Moldova and Tarom together operate daily flights between Chişinău and Bucharest (about €225 return), and Moldova's Transaero also has flights on that route. Air Moldova also has daily flights to Timişoara.

Turkey

Tarom and Turkish Airlines operate regular flights between Bucharest and Istanbul for about €200 return. Air Moldova connects Chişinău with Istanbul daily.

USA & Canada

Tarom has a flight at least once a week direct to/from New York. Peak season prices hover around US$1000, with off-season rates falling to US$600.

Western Europe

Bucharest is linked with all of the major European capitals, while Chişinău has direct flights from Amsterdam, Rome and Paris. Carpatair's Timişoara hub connects Romania with many places in Germany, Italy and Paris. Tarom also runs flights from Timişoara to Milan, from Sibiu to Munich and Stuttgart, and from Cluj-Napoca to Vienna, Frankfurt and Munich.

The big news for 2007 was Wizz Air's start-up of discount fares from London Stanstead to Bucharest; other airlines' London–Bucharest fares start around £170 return. For other Western European cities, expect to pay between €250 and €500 return.

Air Moldova travels daily to Vienna, four times a week to Rome, three times a week to Athens and five times a week to Frankfurt.

LAND
Border Crossings

When crossing the border by car expect long queues at Romanian checkpoints, particularly on weekends and public holidays. Carry food and water for the wait. Don't try bribing a Romanian official and beware of unauthorised people charging dubious 'ecology', 'disinfectant' or other dodgy taxes at the border. Though this is unlikely to happen, request a receipt if you are unsure. It is best to stick to the major border crossings, as staff at smaller ones may not always know how to process foreign visitors.

To avoid hassles entering Moldova, check the changing visa situation beforehand. Also see p355.

Bus
TO/FROM ROMANIA

Eurolines (www.eurolines.com) covers most bus routes across Europe, and has many links with central and western Europe. It has offices all over Romania. A one-way ticket to Vienna costs €65, Paris €125. Many routes offer a 10% to 15% discount for those aged under 26 or over 60. Children under 12 and under four years old receive additional discounts. Some passes, good for extended periods, are available.

There are many daily buses, on various bus lines, to Budapest from cities throughout Romania, including Bucharest, Arad, Braşov, Cluj-Napoca, Târgu Mureş and Satu Mare. There are no bus services from Moldova to Hungary.

Maxitaxis (see p360 go between Bucharest and Ruse, Bulgaria, but otherwise there are no buses to Bulgaria. Buses galore, however, trundle across Bulgaria on the 804km route between Bucharest and Istanbul in 19 hours. There are also some leaving from Constanţa.

BETWEEN ROMANIA & MOLDOVA

Maxitaxis connect Iaşi, Moldavia, with Chişinău across the border in Moldova five times a day. Daily buses connect Bucharest with Chişinău, a 12-hour trip.

TO/FROM MOLDOVA

Eurolines (www.eurolines.md) connects Moldova with Italy, Spain and Germany; offices are found all over Moldova.

Daily buses between Chişinău and Kyiv, Odesa or Moscow run through Transdniestr and Tiraspol; even if you have a Moldovan visa, local authorities are likely to make you pay for an additional transit permit. There are occasional buses to Istanbul.

Car & Motorcycle

The best advice here, and it's worth repeating, is to make sure all your documents (personal ID, insurance, registration and visas, if required) are in order before crossing into Romania and Moldova. A fairly easy access way is from Hungary at Oradea; crossing to/from Bulgaria isn't always easy due to border restrictions – the most popular route is into Ruse, south of Bucharest.

Driving into Moldova is possible but can bring on an extra dose of police 'fees' at the border (we've heard US$250!). Generally it's recommended to hire a car in Chișinău.

The Green Card (a routine extension of domestic motor insurance to cover most European countries) is valid in both Romania and Moldova. Extra insurance can be bought at the borders.

See p360 for more information on driving in Romania.

Train

International train tickets are rarely sold at train stations, but rather at CFR (Romanian State Railways) offices in town (look for the Agenție de Voiaj CFR signs) or at Wasteels offices. Tickets must be bought at least two hours prior to departure.

Those travelling on an Inter Rail or Eurail pass still need to make seat reservations (€3 to €4; €15 for a sleeper) on express trains within Romania. Whether you have a rail pass or not, practically all international trains require a reservation (automatically included in tickets purchased in Romania). If you already have a ticket, you may be able to make reservations at the station an hour before departure, though it's preferable to do so at a CFR office at least one day in advance.

BETWEEN ROMANIA & MOLDOVA

There's an overnight train service between Bucharest and Chișinău; at 12 or 13 hours, the journey is longer than taking a bus or maxitaxi (the train heads north to Iași, then south again), but is more comfortable. It also lets you experience a unique bogie change at the border. The train lurches, vibrates and clanks while the undercarriages are changed; to slow down a potential invasion, the USSR changed all its train tracks to a wider gauge and, to this day, trains entering and exiting the ex-Soviet Union must undergo this bizarre operation.

FROM BULGARIA & TURKEY

The train service between Romania and Bulgaria is slow and crowded but cheap. Between Sofia and Bucharest (11 hours) there are two daily trains, both of which stop in Ruse. Sleepers are available only on the overnight train; buy your ticket well in advance to guarantee yourself a bunk for the night.

The *Bosfor* overnight train travels from Bucharest to Istanbul (803km, 17 to 19 hours).

FROM HUNGARY

The Budapest Bucharest journey (873km) takes around 13 to 15 hours. To or from Arad it is a mere 28km to the Hungarian border town of Lököshaza, from where it is a further 225km (4½ hours) to Budapest. It's also possible to pick up the Budapest-bound train from other Romanian cities, including Constanța, Brașov and Cluj-Napoca. From Chișinău, you must go to Bucharest, then catch a Budapest-bound train.

FROM UKRAINE & BEYOND

Between Romania and Ukraine there is a daily Bucharest–Moscow train that goes via Kyiv. A second train, the Sofia–Moscow *Bulgaria Expres,* takes an alternative route through western Ukraine to Chernivtsi (Cernăuți in Romanian), and stops at Bucharest. Some wagons of this train continue to St Petersburg through Ukraine and Belarus (you will need transit visas for these countries).

From Chișinău, one daily train goes to Lviv and St Petersburg, two to Minsk and three to Moscow. Westbound, there are nightly trains to Romania and beyond.

FROM WESTERN EUROPE

There's only a direct train service to Bucharest from Vienna.

RIVER

There are ferry crossings into Vidin, Bulgaria, from Calafat (p113). Ferry crossings between Giurgiu and Ruse, Bulgaria, are no longer in operation.

TOURS

It's generally cheaper to use a Romanian-based operator if you want a prebooked tour (see p67). Here are a few recommended international tour agencies offering Romania tours:

Quest Tours (☎ 800-621 8687; www.romtour.com) US-based operator offers 'best ofs' and a week-long Dracula tour (€993, not including flight).

Transylvania Express (☎ 44-7798-932933; www.transylvaniaexpress.com) Beginning in 2007, this luxury 14-day train journey starts and ends in Budapest, but takes in much of Transylvania, plus Maramureş and Sucovina.

Transylvania Uncovered (☎ 44-1-539-531-258; www.beyondtheforest.com) UK-based operator books a variety of inclusive trips including a week chasing Dracula (from €1300) or a week's stay in a restored Saxon home (from €650).

GETTING AROUND

AIR
Airlines in Romania & Moldova
State-owned **Tarom** (www.tarom.ro) is Romania's main carrier. Based in Timişoara, **Carpatair** (www.carpatair.ro) also runs domestic flights. Sometimes return fares are only slightly more than one-way fares, which are usually €50 to €60.

BICYCLE
Romania
Cyclists are becoming a more frequent sight in Romania, particularly in Transylvania, Maramureş and Moldavia. And biking certainly offers an excellent way of seeing the country and meeting locals. Intercity roads are generally in decent condition but are often more trafficked than the hellish roads inside villages and towns. As so many places of interest require climbing steep roads, being in top shape is definitely a plus! Also, be aware that motorists are not as used to sharing roads with cyclists as in some western countries, and may drive accordingly.

It's possible to hire or buy bicycles in most major towns, for €5 to €12 per day. Many towns have bike-repair shops, but it's not a bad idea to bring spare parts.

Bicycles can be taken on trains. Most trains have a baggage car *(vagon de bagaje)*, marked by a suitcase symbol on train timetables. Bicycles stored here have to be labelled with your name, destination and the bicycle's weight. But it is easier and safer simply to take your bicycle on the train with you. On local and express trains there is plenty of room at either end of the carriage next to the toilet. Don't block passageways. You might be charged a minimal 'bulky luggage' fee.

Read more, if you speak German, at www.bikeromania.de.

See p46 for more information on biking in Romania.

Moldova
Being flat as a board, Moldova makes cycling an excellent way of getting around. That is, if it weren't for the bad condition of most of its roads, and for a lack of infrastructure – outside of Chişinău, you'll have to rely on your own resources or sense of adventure (and trying to enlist help from friendly locals) if you run into mechanical trouble.

BOAT
Boat is the only way of getting around much of the Danube Delta, where you can pick up ferries or hop in fishers' boats from Tulcea (p303).

BUS
A mix of buses, microbuses and maxitaxis combine to form the seriously disorganised Romanian and Moldovan bus systems spread across a changing array of bus companies. Finding updated information can be difficult without local help. Sometimes the bus stations *(autogară)* themselves move around, particularly the migratory lots from which maxitaxis depart. Posted timetables are often out of date; it's better to ask someone.

SUV-sized maxitaxis have emerged this decade. These guys usually fit 10 to 20 people and tend to rush along the same routes as buses, but often lack any real storage space – you may have to plop your bag on your lap. Some routes – such as Braşov–Sinaia or Sibiu–Cluj-Napoca – are more useful than others. Generally – not always – it's easier to plan on the train.

Fares are cheap and calculated per kilometre – it's about 1 lei (€0.29) per 10km; the 116km trip from Braşov to Sighişoara is about €3.50.

This chapter reflects the situation at research time; the routes should remain roughly the same, but don't get mad if you discover new fares and departure/arrival points.

CAR & MOTORCYCLE
Some day a video game will be made of a Sunday drive across Romania, considering all its hazards – strolling cows and sheep, slow-going horse carts filled with hay, bear-sized potholes, speed traps, unmarked curves, aggressive drivers. It can be draining. The

TRANSPORT

200km you're accustomed to driving back home can really drain hardenened drivers here. Many roads are best suited to 4WD; some mountain roads require it. But driving allows access to some pockets of rural villages and mountains that are hard to reach otherwise.

Only drive if your car is in good shape and has been serviced recently. Repair shops are increasingly used to the BMWs and Mercedes that the rich folks of Bucharest or Chişinău like to drive, but certainly know the abundant Dacias (and their identical Renault models).

Romania has only a few short stretches of motorway (*autostrada*). Some major roads (*drum naţional*) have been resurfaced, but many remain in a shockingly poor, potholed condition. Secondary roads (*drum judeţean*) can become dirt tracks, and mountain and forestry roads (*drum forestier*) can be impassable after heavy rain. While roads are being repaved all the time, roughly half of the country's roads are unpaved – and paved ones are sometimes rougher than dirt roads.

Western-style petrol stations are easy to come by (but fill 'er up before heading on long trips through the mountains or remote village areas). A litre of unleaded 95E costs about €1. Most stations accept credit cards.

If you're bringing your own car, most borders are open 24 hours. The most popular crossing is at Oradea, between Budapest and Cluj-Napoca.

Hire

Avis, Budget, Hertz and Europcar have offices in most cities and at Henri Coanda airport in Bucharest. Local companies are usually

TRANSPORT

SHOULD YOU DRIVE?

Lonely Planet remains divided on this, so much so that the co-authors have opposite viewpoints. Here's their thoughs on whether it's worth taking your wheels onto the highways.

No! Are you nuts?

Driving in Romania is more treacherous than I've seen in 40 countries. Indeed, I strongly discourage it for visitors. I was involved in several minor car accidents, mostly due to ice (ice/snow removal is still in its infancy here), and innumerable near-misses while researching this book. Despite the country's on-book driving regulations, in reality the situation is lawless. The prevailing belief is that racing along at the very edge of disaster is the pinnacle of skilled driving. Romanians routinely risk death just to gain three seconds on their journeys, even if they're just going to church. Moreover, anyone not conducting themselves in this unhinged manner is considered a menace, inviting abuse in the form of sustained horn blaring and curse words. And it doesn't end there. Hapless livestock, free-range pets, moonshine aficionados, sizable debris and even the crumbling, collapsing roads are against you. Even in good weather, this is white-knuckle driving of the first order. Passengers, particularly in maxitaxis, should consider tequila shots and blindfolds before long trips.

Leif Pettersen

With care & time, sure!

I always recommend to friends comfortable behind the wheel to get a car in Romania. I've driven cars and motorcycles in Vietnam, Bulgaria, Mexico, Guatemala and New York City, and Romania wasn't necessarily any tougher for me – particularly on back roads where some of my favourite Romanian experiences have come, on random routes. Just know that, while you can risk a few looks at the Pacific while driving California's Hwy 1, you can't here. But it's so worth it. Those on tours or who can bike like demons can get to back roads, but those dependent on bus won't see so much. With a car you dictate your pace and stops. You can stop to knock on doors to find the 'keymaster' for closed Saxon churches, or drive through the lovely Bicaz Gorge or on the summer-only Transfăgărasan road. I had some close calls, sure. One time, a very large tractor awaited around a blind curve I took too fast. I braked in time. Then the crew helped me steer between the rusting beast and a rocky cliff – a centimetre on either side of the car. I slowed down after that. You have to.

Robert Reid

ROAD DISTANCES (KM)

	Alba Iulia	Arad	Baia Mare	Bistrița	Brașov	Bucharest	Cluj-Napoca	Constanța	Deva	Iași	Miercurea Ciuc	Oradea	Piatra Neamț	Pitești	Ploiești	Satu Mare	Sibiu	Suceava	Târgu Mureș	Timișoara	Tulcea
Alba Iulia	---																				
Arad	236	---																			
Baia Mare	236	319	---																		
Bistrița	217	393	151	---																	
Brașov	229	429	392	267	---																
Bucharest	340	538	574	439	175	---															
Cluj-Napoca	94	270	142	123	281	432	---														
Constanța	581	809	781	648	383	243	662	---													
Deva	84	150	290	301	279	388	178	631	---												
Iași	458	686	508	355	307	389	428	432	586	---											
Miercurea Ciuc	288	522	349	209	99	272	261	486	378	258	---										
Oradea	247	117	202	276	434	528	153	815	190	581	411	---									
Piatra Neamț	358	620	383	244	236	342	310	425	422	118	140	463	---								
Pitești	231	431	467	375	147	107	325	349	281	454	246	478	383	---							
Ploiești	344	544	507	382	115	58	396	291	349	347	214	549	300	119	---						
Satu Mare	264	251	67	226	458	607	175	822	319	581	433	129	456	497	573	---					
Sibiu	73	274	322	271	156	265	167	538	126	413	255	320	295	188	271	343	---				
Suceava	408	588	318	191	328	434	300	562	492	140	247	467	107	475	392	403	406	---			
Târgu Mureș	137	378	227	93	174	347	106	554	221	321	151	260	201	282	289	282	124	284	---		
Timișoara	240	52	370	457	435	545	334	829	156	742	534	168	578	440	550	297	279	648	377	---	
Tulcea	600	813	777	591	384	304	665	147	666	335	406	817	345	401	262	846	540	437	558	825	---

cheaper. Car hire is well-priced in Bucharest (p87) and Cluj-Napoca (p194).

Because driving across the border to Moldova can be difficult and costly, consider hiring a car in Chișinău (p329).

Road Rules

Your country's driving licence or the International Driver's Permit are accepted here. Romania has a 0% blood-alcohol tolerance limit. Seat belts are compulsory for all seats; children under 12 are forbidden to sit in the front.

Speed limits are 90km/h on major roads and 70km/h inside highway villages and towns unless otherwise noted. A couple of motorways allow faster driving (such as the wonderfully smooth highway between Bucharest and Pitești). Speed traps – like the video ones between Brașov and Bucharest – are common; drivers warn each other with a flash of the headlights. Headlights need not be turned on in the daytime.

Romania's main automobile association is the **Automobil Clubul Român** (ACR; ☎ 21-222 2222; www.acr.ro in Romanian only), but it's mainly for Romanians to renew licences.

Moldova's intercity speed limit is 90km/h and in built-up areas 60km/h; the legal blood alcohol limit is 0.03%. For road rescue, dial ☎ 901. The **Automobile Club Moldova** (ACM; ☎ 22-292 703; www.acm.md) informs members of regulations and offers emergency assistance.

HITCHING

Hitching is never entirely safe in any country in the world. People who do choose to hitch will be safer if they travel in pairs and let someone know where they are planning to go. That said, hitching is very popular in both countries, where people usually stand along the main roads out of a city or town. It's common practice in Romania and Moldova to pay the equivalent of the bus fare to the driver.

LOCAL TRANSPORT
Bus, Tram & Trolleybus

Buses, trams and trolleybuses (buses run by electricity with wires overhead) provide transport within most towns and cities in Romania, although many are crowded. They usually run from about 5am to midnight, although services can get thin after 7pm in

DRIVING TIPS

Consider the following if you get behind the wheel in Romania or Moldova:

- Plan on it taking time. Kilometres here go slower than the kilometres you may be used to back home.

- A map is mandatory. A good one is Cartographia's 1:800,000 *Romania*; it's available in many bookshops, but highway petrol shops never carry maps.

- Stay alert. With all those potholes, sheep flocks and horse carts, don't expect to enjoy the scenery from behind the wheel.

- Let a...holes pass you. Some eager drivers like to crowd your bumper and pass cars on blind turns. If one's up on you, pull over and let them go.

- Hitchhiking is a part of life and you'll see old women, even children, hailing rides. Generally there are no problems; we 'enjoyed' the company of an extremely drunk man looking to go 500m.

- In most places, footpaths are fair game for parking your car. But look out for the '*P cu plata*' sign in some places, meaning payment is required. Usually a bloke patrols the area and charges €0.30 or €0.50 to park for a few hours.

more remote areas. Purchase tickets at street kiosks marked *bilete* or *casă de bilete* before boarding, and validate them once aboard. Some tickets are good for one trip; others are for two trips, each end of the ticket being valid for one ride. Tickets cost from €0.20 to €0.35.

If you travel without a validated ticket or with no ticket at all you risk a €10 on-the-spot fine.

In Moldova buses cost about US$0.15, trolleybuses US$0.10 and city maxitaxis US$0.25.

Horse Carts

In many rural parts the only vehicles that pass will be horse- or donkey-powered. Horse and cart is the most popular form of transport in Romania and you will see numerous carts, even in cities (although some downtown areas are off-limits to them).

Many carts will stop and give you a ride, the driver expecting no more than a cigarette in payment.

Metro

Bucharest is the only city to sport a metro; see p89 for details.

Taxi

Some Romanian taxi drivers, as in many places across the globe, are notorious rip-off merchants who have no scruples in charging you over the odds or driving you around in circles. It's always best (and cheaper) to call a reliable company either recommended by your hotel or by us in the regional chapters.

In Bucharest, cabs with reliable meters and reasonably honest drivers – identifiable by the yellow pyramid attached to their roofs and visible phone numbers – do exist. Their fixed meter rate is about €0.30 or €0.35 per kilometre, compared to €0.20 per kilometre in other cities and towns. If a taxi has no meter then bargain with the driver before roaring off to your destination.

In Moldova, avoid taking cabs from taxi stands, as some may try to overcharge you. The going rate is about US$0.25 per kilometre. Another way of getting a lift is waving down a private car and negotiating a ride.

TOURS

Considering how remote much of Romania remains, it's not always a bad idea to consider arranging a tour with local agencies – be it by bike, boot or car. Foreign agencies tend to plug Dracula more than locals. Often hostels and *pensiunes* arrange excellent day trips. We list agencies throughout the book; here are some of the stand-outs, who can help plan a trip before or after you arrive.

Aves Tours (☎ 266 215 555; www.avestours.com; Odorheiu Secuiesc) Experienced guides lead wildlife trips to Hungary and Romania, such as an inclusive nine-day birding tour (€900).

Contur Travel (p289; ☎ 619 777; www.contur.ro; Constanţa) Good for Black Sea and Danube Delta trips.

DiscoveRomania (p129; ☎ 268-472 718; www.discoveromania.ro; Braşov) Many active and cultural tours around Transylvania.

Green Mountain Holidays (p190; ☎ 418 691; www.greenmountainholidays.ro; Cluj-Napoca) Excellent hiking, biking and caving trips, chiefly around the Apuseni Mountains.

TRANSPORT

YAY, THE DACIA!

Found on dirt roads and new highways throughout Romania are noisy, communist-era Dacia models – like the 1300 – puttering alongside their more polished forebears, Dacia Solenzas or Dacia Logans. Why care? Very few communist-era car models survived *kapitalism* – the East German Trabant died off in 1991, the Czech Tatra stopped production in 1996 and the Soviet Volga is being phased out in 2007. Yet the Dacia remains a Romanian favourite.

It's always been as much French as Romanian. The French Renault company ran much of the production (Dacias are also produced in Turkey, and the new Logan is sometimes billed the Renault Logan). The first Dacia – the simple 1100 – rolled onto bumpy streets in 1968, but the enduring 1300 lasted longer. Because superior parts were used for export models in the 1980s – Dacia tried to tap into the UK market – some Romanians bought their Dacias in Hungary and drove them back.

These days you can find a mid-1980s 1300 for about US$1000 or more. Hiring a Dacia – particularly Solenzas and Logans – is a good idea. They're safe and dependable, and cheaper. If one should break down, flag down the next passing Dacia. Most Romanians are adept at dismantling the engine and fixing the burps and will be carrying the necessary tools with them!

Herr Travel (p169; ☎ 266-102 342; www.guide2 romania.ro; Odorheiu Secuiesc) Tours around Székely Land and Transylvania.

Marina 'Marisha' Vozian (p321; www.marisha.net; Chişinău) Best source of information and tours for Moldova.

Pan Travel (p187; ☎ 264-420 516; www.pantravel.ro; Cluj-Napoca) Engaging guides lead personalised, customised trips around Transylvania, Maramureş and Moldavia.

RoCultours/CTI (p68; ☎ 21-650 8145; www .rotravel.com/cti; Bucharest) Excellent cultural tours around Romania.

Roving România (p130; ☎ 0744 212 065; www.roving -romania.co.uk; Braşov) Personalised tours around Transylvania, including birding trips.

Transylvania Motorcycle Tours (www.tmtours.com) This Cluj-Napoca–based group offers a whirlwind of two-wheeled tours around Romania, including a nine-day

trip along the Black Sea coast, a six-day job across the Carpathians, and a month-long Romania trip.

TRAIN

Rail has long been the most popular way of travelling around Romania. **Căile Ferate Române** (CFR; Romanian State Railways; www.cfr.ro) runs trains over 11,000km of track, providing services to most cities, towns and larger villages in the country. Its website lists timetables. The national train timetable *(mersul trenurilor)* is published each May and is sold for €2 at CFR offices. Another excellent timetable source is www.bahn.de, a German website.

Sosire means arrivals and *plecare* is departures. On posted timetables, the number of the platform from which each train departs is listed under *linia*.

Classes & Types of Trains

In Romania there are five different types of train, all of which travel at different speeds, offer varying levels of comfort and charge different fares for the same destination.

The cheapest trains are the local *personal* trains. These trains are painfully slow. *Accelerat* trains are faster, hence a tad more expensive and less crowded. Seat reservations are obligatory and automatic when you buy your ticket. There's little difference between *rapid* and *expres* trains. Both travel at a fair speed and often have dining cars. Pricier InterCity trains are the most comfortable but aren't faster than *expres* trains.

Vagon de dormit (sleepers) are available between Bucharest and Cluj-Napoca, Oradea, Timişoara, Tulcea and other points. First-class sleeping compartments generally have two berths, 2nd-class sleepers generally have four berths and 2nd-class couchettes have six berths. Book these in advance.

Fares listed in this chapter generally indicate one-way 2nd-class seats on *rapid* or *accelerat* trains.

Buying Tickets

Tickets are sold in advance for all trains except local *personal* ones. Advance tickets are sold at an Agenţie de Voiaj CFR, a train-ticket office found in every city centre. When the ticket office is closed you have to buy your ticket immediately before departure at the station.

Theoretically you can buy tickets at CFR offices up to two hours before departure. Some-

COMPARING TRAIN COSTS

This chart is here to help gauge how train fares ebb based on speed and condition. In our experience, the 1st-class price wasn't worth the money; *personal* trains went nearly as quickly on some routes, but were scrappier and more crowded.

Trip	Personal	Accelerat	Rapid	InterCity
100km (1st Class)	€3.50	€6.40	€8.10	€9
100km (2nd Class)	€2.20	€4.40	€5.80	€6.65
Bucharest–Braşov (1st)	€5.70	€10	€11.20	€12.10
Bucharest–Braşov (2nd)	€3.50	€6.50	€7.90	€8.70

times they don't sell tickets for same-day trips, so try to plan a day ahead.

You can only buy tickets at train stations two hours – and in some cases just one hour – before departure. Queues can be horrendous. At major stations there are separate ticket lines for 1st and 2nd classes; you may opt for 1st class when you see how much shorter that line is. Your reservation ticket lists the code number of your train along with your assigned *vagon* (carriage) and *locul* (seat).

If you have an international ticket right through Romania, you're allowed to make stops along the route but you must purchase a reservation ticket each time you reboard an *accelerat* or *rapid* train. If the international ticket was issued in Romania, you must also pay the *expres* train supplement each time.

In a pinch you can board a train and pay the ticket-taker for the ride; ask how much. As one local told us, 'This is Romania – you can do anything if you pay for it.'

TRANSPORT

Health

CONTENTS

Travel health depends on your predeparture preparations, your daily health care while travelling and how you handle any medical problem that does develop. Romania and Moldova will not provide any major challenges to visitors' health.

BEFORE YOU GO

Prevention is the key to staying healthy while abroad. A little planning before departure, particularly for pre-existing illnesses, will save trouble later. Carry a spare pair of contact lenses and glasses, and take your optical prescription with you. Bring extra medications in their original, clearly labelled, containers. A signed and dated letter from your doctor describing your medical conditions and medications, including generic names, is also a good idea. If carrying syringes or needles, be sure to have a doctor's letter documenting their medical necessity.

INSURANCE

If you're an EU citizen, a European Health Insurance Card (EHIC) form, available from health centres or via www.dh.gov.uk in the UK, covers you for most medical care. Valid for three to five years, the EHIC will not cover you for nonemergencies or emergency repatriation. Citizens from other countries should find out if there is a reciprocal arrangement for free medical care between their country and the country visited. If you need health insurance, consider a policy that covers you for the worst possible scenario, such as an accident requiring an emergency flight home.

HEALTH ADVISORIES

It's usually a good idea to consult your government's travel health website before departure, if one is available:
Australia: www.dfat.gov.au/travel/
Canada: www.travelhealth.gc.ca
UK: www.dh.gov.uk/
USA: www.cdc.gov/travel/

INTERNET RESOURCES

The WHO's publication *International Travel and Health* is revised annually and is available online at www.who.int/ith/. Other useful websites include www.mdtravelhealth.com (travel health recommendations for every country; updated daily), www.fitfortravel .scot.nhs.uk (general travel advice for the layperson), www.ageconcern.org.uk (advice on travel for the elderly) and www.mariestopes .org.uk (information on women's health and contraception).

IN ROMANIA & MOLDOVA

AVAILABILITY & COST OF HEALTH CARE

Medical care is not always readily available outside of major cities, but embassies, consulates and five-star hotels can usually recommend doctors or clinics. They can also recommend where to seek treatment in smaller towns or rural areas. Note that there is an increased risk of Hepatitis B and HIV transmission via poorly sterilised equipment.

INFECTIOUS DISEASES
Bird Flu

In 2005 and 2006, several case of avian influenza were reported near Tulcea and other parts of the country, with poultry cases reported in May 2006. The Romanian government quarantined a number of towns, including Făgăraş in Transylvania, as a safety measure. No human cases were reported.

Tickborne Encephalitis

This is spread by tick bites. It is a serious infection of the brain and vaccination is advised for those in risk areas. Two doses of vaccine will give a year's protection, three doses up to three years' protection.

Typhoid & Hepatitis A

These diseases are spread through contaminated food (particularly shellfish) and water. Typhoid can cause septicaemia; Hepatitis A causes liver inflammation and jaundice. Neither is usually fatal but recovery can be prolonged. Hepatitis A and typhoid vaccines can be given as a single dose vaccine, Hepatyrix or Viatim.

Rabies

This is a potential concern considering the number of stray dogs running around Romania. If bitten by a homeless dog, seek medical attention within 72 hours (most main hospitals will have a rabies clinic), but don't panic – while rabies is transmitted via the animal's saliva, the rabies virus is present in saliva only during the final stages of the disease in the animal. It is therefore a relatively rarely transmitted disease. Still, do not take any chances and seek medical attention. Any bite, scratch or even lick from an unknown animal should be cleaned immediately and thoroughly. Scrub with soap and running water, and then apply alcohol or iodine solution.

TRAVELLER'S DIARRHOEA

If you develop diarrhoea, be sure to drink plenty of fluids, preferably an oral rehydration solution (eg Dioralyte). A few loose stools don't require treatment, but if you start having more than four or five stools a day, you should start taking an antibiotic (usually a quinolone drug) and an antidiarrhoeal agent (such as loperamide). If diarrhoea is bloody, persists for more than 72 hours or is accompanied by fever, shaking, chills or severe abdominal pain you should seek medical attention.

ENVIRONMENTAL HAZARDS
Hypothermia & Frostbite

Proper preparation will reduce the risks of getting hypothermia. Even on a hot day in the mountains, the weather can change rapidly, so carry waterproof garments and warm layers, and inform others of your route.

Hypothermia starts with shivering, loss of judgment and clumsiness. Unless rewarming occurs, the sufferer deteriorates into apathy, confusion and coma. Prevent further heat loss with warm dry clothing, hot sweet drinks and shared bodily warmth, and by seeking shelter.

Frostbite is caused by freezing and subsequent damage to bodily extremities. It is dependent on wind-chill, temperature and length of exposure. Frostbite starts as frostnip (white, numb areas of skin) from which complete recovery is expected with rewarming. As frostbite develops, the skin blisters and blackens. Adequate clothing, staying dry, keeping well hydrated and ensuring adequate calorie intake is the best prevention for frostbite.

Water

Tap water is generally considered safe to drink in Romania and Moldova. Beware drinking water from the polluted Danube River; some travellers have reported upset stomachs after drinking tea or eating soup or fish prepared with the Danube's waters. In this case, get yourself some Ercefuryl (200mg), an antibiotic available at any pharmacy; it will stop you from doubling over.

Any water found in the mountains should be treated with suspicion – never drink it without purifying (with filters, iodine or chlorine) or boiling it first, unless assured that it's safe to drink by a guide or local authority. At high altitude water boils at a lower temperature, so germs are less likely to be killed. Boil it for longer in these environments.

WOMEN'S HEALTH

Emotional stress, exhaustion and travelling through different time zones can all contribute to an upset in the menstrual pattern. If using oral contraceptives, remember some antibiotics, diarrhoea and vomiting can stop the pill from working and lead to the risk of pregnancy – remember to take condoms with you just in case. Time zones, gastrointestinal upsets and antibiotics do not affect injectable contraception. Travelling during pregnancy is usually possible, but always consult your doctor before planning your trip. The most risky times for travel are during the first 12 weeks of pregnancy and after 30 weeks.

Language

CONTENTS

Romanian (limba română), 'a Latin island in a Slav sea', is the official language of Romania and Moldova (where it's known as Moldovan, limba moldoveanească). It holds the intriguing status of being the only member of the Romance language family in Eastern Europe. As a descendant of Latin, it shares a common heritage with French, Italian, Spanish and Portuguese, but retains many aspects of Latin that no longer exist in the other Romance languages (such as noun cases).

Romanian's origins date back to the 2nd century AD when Emperor Trajan founded the Roman province of Dacia in the southwest of present-day Transylvania. The linguistic influence of the Romans ceased with their withdrawal by AD 275, and the void was filled with the arrival of the Slavs in the Balkans in the 6th century. The interaction with Bulgarian and Serbian (reflected in many loan words) was intensified from the 13th century through the shared Byzantine culture and the influence of Old Church Slavonic.

For language to help when ordering food and deciphering menus, see p56. For a more comprehensive language guide, get a copy of Lonely Planet's Eastern Europe Phrasebook. If you're keen to engage in further study, James Augerot's comprehensive Romanian/Limba Română – A Course in

ROMANIANLY SPEAKING
Romanian Pronunciation Guide

a	a	as the 'u' in 'cut'
e	e	as in 'tell'
i	ee	as in 'meet'
i	'	almost always silent at the end of a word (pronounce as a very short i)
ă	ə	a neutral vowel, like the 'a' in 'ago'
â/î	ew	like an 'ee' sound made with rounded lips
c	k/ch	as the 'k' in 'kit' before a, o, u, ă and â/î; as the 'ch' in 'chin' before e and i
ch	k	as 'k' before e and i
g	g/j	as in 'go' before a, o, u, ă and â/î; as the 'j' in 'jetty' before e and i
gh	g	as in 'go'
j	zh	as the 's' in 'treasure'
ş	sh	as in 'ship'
ţ	ts	as in 'cats'

Modern Romanian (2000) is a good resource. It is published by the Center for Romanian Studies in Iaşi and is available either in Romania or via the internet.

WRITING SYSTEM

The oldest record of written Romanian is a letter rendered in the Cyrillic alphabet to the mayor of Braşov dating back to 1521. There is also evidence of texts written in the Roman alphabet dating back to around 1700, but Cyrillic was used until 1859, when the Roman alphabet was officially adopted. During the period of Soviet rule, a Russian version of the Cyrillic alphabet was used in Moldova, but the Roman alphabet was reinstated in 1989.

Between 1953 and 1994 the letter â was replaced by the Slavic î. In 1994, the Romanian Academy decided to revert to the original â of the Latin orthography. The î is still used, mainly at the beginning of some words.

In place names, old spellings such as Tîrgu Mureş (instead of Târgu Mureş) still lurk on the odd map – this book uses the updated **â** spellings for all place names.

PRONUNCIATION

Written Romanian is more or less phonetically consistent, so once you learn a few simple rules you should have no trouble with pronunciation. In any case, you can always fall back on the pronunciation guides included with the words and phrases in this chapter (see the boxed text opposite, which covers the more difficult sounds).

At the beginning of a word, **e** and **i** are pronounced as if there were a faint 'y' preceding them, while at the end of a word a single **i** is almost silent, and **ii** is pronounced 'ee'. Word stress is marked in the pronunciation guides as italic.; it generally falls on the penultimate syllable.

ACCOMMODATION

Where's a ...?
Unde se află ...?   oon·de se *a*·flə ...
  camping ground
  un teren de camping   oon te·*ren* de *kem*·peeng
  guesthouse
  o pensiune   o pen·see·*oo*·ne
  hotel
  un hotel   oon ho·*tel*
  youth hostel
  un hostel   oon *hos*·tel

I'd like to book a room, please.
  Aş dori să rezerv o   ash do·*ree* sə re·*zerv* o
  cameră, vă rog.   *ka*·me·rə və rog

Do you have a ... room?
Aveţi o cameră ...?   a·*vets'* o *ka*·me·rə ...
  single
  de o persoană   de o per·so·*a*·nə
  double
  dublă   *doo*·blə
  twin (two-bed)
  cu două paturi separate   koo *do*·wə *pa*·toor' se·pa·*ra*·te

How much is it per ...?
Cât costă ...?   kewt *kos*·tə ...
  room
  pe cameră   pe *ka*·me·rə
  person
  de persoană   de per·so·*a*·nə

May I see it?
  Pot să văd?   pot sə vəd

CONVERSATION & ESSENTIALS

Hello./Hi.
  Bună ziua/Bună.   *boo*·nə *zee*·wa/*boo*·nə
Good night.
  Noapte bună.   no·*ap*·te *boo*·nə
Goodbye./Bye.
  La revedere./Pa.   la re·ve·*de*·re/pa
Yes.
  Da.   da
No.
  Nu.   noo
Please.
  Vă rog.   və rog
Thank you.
  Mulţumesc/Merci.   mool·tsoo·*mesk*/mer·*see*
You're welcome.
  Cu plăcere.   koo plə·*che*·re
Excuse me.
  Scuzaţi·mă.   skoo·*za*·tsee·mə
Sorry.
  Îmi pare rău.   ewm' *pa*·re rə·oo
How are you?
  Ce mai faceţi?   che mai fa·chets'
Fine. And you?
  Bine.   *bee*·ne
  Dumneavoastră?   doom·ne·a·vo·*as*·trə
What's your name?
  Cum vă numiţi?   koom və noo·*meets'*
My name is ...
  Numele meu este ...   *noo*·me·le *me*·oo *yes*·te ...
I'm pleased to meet you.
  Îmi pare bine.   ewm' *pa*·re *bee*·ne
Where are you from?
  De unde sunteţi?   de *oon*·de *soon*·tets'
I'm from ...
  Sunt din ...   soont deen ...
Can I take a photo?
  Pot să fac o fotografie?   pot sə fak o fo·to·gra·*fee*·e

DIRECTIONS

Where's the ...?
Unde este ...?   *oon*·de *yes*·te ...
Is this the road to (Arad)?
  Acesta e drumul spre   a·*ches*·ta ye *droo*·mool spre
  (Arad)?   (a·*rad*)
Can you show me (on the map)?
  Puteţi să·mi arătaţi   poo·*tets'* səm' a·rə·*tats'*
  (pe hartă)?   (pe *har*·tə)
What's the address?
  Care este adresa?   *ka*·re *yes*·te a·*dre*·sa
How far is it?
  Cât e de departe?   kewt ye de de·*par*·te
How do I get there?
  Cum ajung acolo?   koom a·*zhoong* a·*ko*·lo

SIGNS

Intrare	Entrance
Ieşire	Exit
Deschis	Open
Închis	Closed
Camere Libere	Rooms Available
Informaţii	Information
Secţie de Poliţie	Police Station
Interzis	Prohibited
Toalete	Toilets
Bărbaţi	Men
Femei	Women

Turn ...
Viraţi ...   vee·*rats'* ...
  at the corner
  la colţ   la kolts
  at the traffic lights
  la semafor   la se·ma·*for*
  left/right
  la stânga/dreapta   la stewn·*ga*/dre·*ap*·ta

It's ...
Este ...   *yes*·te ...
  far away
  departe   de·*par*·te
  left
  la stânga   la stewn·*ga*
  near (to ...)
  aproape (de ...)   a·pro·*a*·pe (de ...)
  right
  la dreapta   la dre·*ap*·ta
  straight ahead
  tot înainte   tot ew·na·*een*·te

by bus	*cu autobuzul*	koo a·oo·to·*boo*·zool
by train	*cu trenul*	koo *tre*·nool
on foot	*pe jos*	pe zhos
north	*nord*	nord
south	*sud*	sood
east	*est*	est
west	*vest*	vest

castle	*castel*	kas·*tel*
cathedral	*catedrală*	ka·te·*dra*·lə
church	*biserică*	bee·*se*·ree·kə
main square	*piaţa centrală*	pya·tsa chen·*tra*·lə
monastery	*mănăstire*	mə·nəs·*tee*·re
monument	*monument*	mo·noo·*ment*
museum	*muzeu*	moo·*ze*·oo
old city	*oraşul vechi*	o·ra·*shool ve*·ki
palace	*palat*	pa·*lat*
ruins	*ruine*	roo·*ee*·ne
statue	*statuie*	sta·*too*·ye

EMERGENCIES

Help!
  Ajutor!   a·zhoo·*tor*
It's an emergency!
  E un caz de urgenţă!   ye oon kaz de oor·*jen*·tsə
Could you help me, please?
  Ajutaţi-mă, vă rog!   a·zhoo·*ta*·tsee·mə və rog
Where's the police station?
  Unde e secţia de   oon·de ye *sek*·tsee·a de
  poliţie?   po·*lee*·tsee·e
Where are the toilets?
  Unde este o toaletă?   oon·de *yes*·te o to·a·*le*·tə
Go away!
  Pleacă!/Cară-te!   ple·*a*·kə/*ka*·rə·te
I'm lost.
  M-am rătăcit.   mam rə·tə·*cheet*

Call ...!
Chemaţi ...!   ke·*mats'* ...
  a doctor
  un doctor   oon *dok*·tor
  an ambulance
  o ambulanţă   o am·boo·*lan*·tsə
  the police
  poliţia   po·*lee*·tsee·a

HEALTH

Where's the nearest ...?
Unde se află cel mai   oon·de se *a*·flə chel mai
apropiat ...?   a·pro·*pee*·at ...
  dentist
  dentist   den·*teest*
  doctor
  doctor   *dok*·tor
  hospital
  spital   spee·*tal*

Where's the nearest (night) pharmacist?
  Unde se află cea mai   oon·de se *a*·flə che·a mai
  apropiată farmacie   a·pro·*pee*·a·tə far·ma·*chee*·e
  (cu program non-stop)?   (koo pro·*gram* non·stop)
I'm sick.
  Mă simt rău.   mə seemt *rə*·oo
I need a doctor (who speaks English).
  Am nevoie de un doctor   am ne·*vo*·ye de oon *dok*·tor
  (care să vorbească   (*ka*·re sə vor·be·*as*·kə
  engleza).   en·*gle*·za)
It hurts here.
  Mă doare aici.   mə do·*a*·re a·*eech*

I'm allergic to ...	*Am alergie la ...*	am a·ler·*jee*·ye la ...
antibiotics	*antibiotice*	an·tee·byo·*tee*·che
penicillin	*penicilină*	pe·nee·chee·*lee*·nə
peanuts	*arahide*	ara·*hee*·de

I have (a) ...	*Am ...*	am ...
asthma	*astm*	astm
cough	*tuse*	too·se
diarrhoea	*diaree*	dee·a·re·e
fever	*febră*	fe·brə
headache	*durere de cap*	doo·re·re de kap
nausea	*greţuri*	gre·tsoor'
pain	*dureri*	doo·rer'
sore throat	*durere în gât*	doo·re·re ewn gewt
toothache	*durere de dinţi*	doo·rer' de deents'

antiseptic	*antiseptic*	an·tee·sep·teek
condom	*prezervativ*	pre·zer·va·teev
contraceptives	*contraceptive*	kon·tra·chep·tee·ve
painkillers	*analgezice*	a·nal·je·zee·che

LANGUAGE DIFFICULTIES

Do you speak English?
Vorbiţi engleza?　vor·beets' en·gle·za
Do you understand?
Înţelegeţi?　ewn·tse·le·jets'
I (don't) understand.
Eu (nu) înţeleg.　ye·oo (noo) ewn·tse·leg
What does (azi) mean?
Ce înseamnă (azi)?　che ewn·se·am·nə (az')

Could you please ...?
Aţi putea ...?　ats' poo·te·a ...
　repeat that
　repeta　re·pe·ta
　speak more slowly
　vorbi mai rar　vor·bee mai rar
　write it down
　scrie　skree·ye

NUMBERS

0	*zero*	ze·ro
1	*unu*	oo·noo
2	*doi*	doy
3	*trei*	trey
4	*patru*	pa·troo
5	*cinci*	cheench'
6	*şase*	sha·se
7	*şapte*	shap·te
8	*opt*	opt
9	*nouă*	no·wə
10	*zece*	ze·che
11	*unsprezece*	oon·spre·ze·che
12	*doisprezece*	doy·spre·ze·che
13	*treisprezece*	trey·spre·ze·che
14	*paisprezece*	pai·spre·ze·che
15	*cincisprezece*	cheench'·spre·ze·che
16	*şaisprezece*	shai·spre·ze·che
17	*şaptesprezece*	shap·te·spre·ze·che
18	*optsprezece*	opt·spre·ze·che
19	*nouăsprezece*	no·wə·spre·ze·che
20	*douăzeci*	do·wə·ze·chi
21	*douăzeci şi unu*	do·wə·ze·chi shee oo·noo
22	*douăzeci şi doi*	do·wə·ze·chi shee doy
30	*treizeci*	trey·ze·chi
40	*patruzeci*	pa·troo·ze·chi
50	*cincizeci*	cheench·ze·chi
60	*şaizeci*	shai·ze·chi
70	*şaptezeci*	shap·te·ze·chi
80	*optzeci*	opt·ze·chi
90	*nouăzeci*	no·wə·ze·chi
100	*o sută*	o soo·tə
1000	*o mie*	o mee·e

SHOPPING & SERVICES

Where's the ...?
Unde este ...?　oon·de yes·te ...
　bank
　banca　ban·ka
　city centre
　centrul oraşului　chen·trool o·ra·shoo·looy
　market
　piaţa　pya·tsa
　police station
　secţia de poliţie　sek·tsee·a de po·lee·tsee·e
　post office
　poşta　posh·ta
　public toilet
　toaleta publică　to·a·le·ta poo·blee·kə
　tourist office
　biroul de informaţii turistice　bee·ro·ool de een·for·ma·tsee too·rees·tee·che

What time does it open/close?
La ce oră se deschide/închide?　la che o·rə se des·kee·de/ ewn·kee·de
Where can I buy ...?
Unde pot cumpăra ...?　oon·de pot koom·pə·ra ...
I'm looking for ...
Caut ...　kowt ...
Can I look at it?
Pot să mă uit?　pot sə mə ooyt
How much is it?
Cât costă?　kewt kos·tə
Can you write down the price?
Puteţi scrie preţul?　poo·tets' skree·e pre·tsool
That's too expensive.
E prea scump.　ye pre·a skoomp
What's your lowest price?
Care e preţul cel mai mic?　ka·re ye pre·tsool chel mai meek

Do you accept ...?
Acceptaţi ...?　ak·chep·tats' ...
　credit cards
　cărţi de credit　kərts' de kre·deet

debit cards
cărţi de debit   kərts' de de·beet
travellers cheques
cecuri de călătorie   che·koor' de kə·lə·to·ree·e

Where's ...?
Unde se află un ...?   oon·de se a·flə oon ...
　an ATM
　bancomat   ban·ko·mat
　a foreign exchange office
　birou de schimb valutar   bee·roh de skeemb va·loo·tar

Where's the nearest public phone?
Unde se află cel mai apropiat telefon public?
oon·de se a·flə chel mai a·pro·pee·at te·le·fon poo·bleek
I'd like to buy a phonecard.
Aş dori să cumpăr o cartelă de telefon.
ash do·ree sə koom·pər o kar·te·lə de te·le·fon
I'd like a SIM card for your network.
Aş dori un SIM card pentru reţeaua locală.
ash do·ree oon seem kard pen·troo re·tse·a·wa lo·ka·lə
Where's the local Internet café?
Unde se află cel mai apropiat internet café?
oon·de se a·flə chel mai a·pro·pee·at een·ter·net ka·fe

I'd like to ...
Aş dori ...   ash do·ree ...
　check my email
　să-mi verific e-mail-ul   səm' ve·ree·feek ee·meyl·ool
　get Internet access
　să accesez internetul   sə ak·che·sez een·ter·ne·tool

TIME & DATES
What time is it?
Cât e ceasul?   kewt ye che·a·sool
It's one o'clock.
E ora unu.   ye o·ra oo·noo
It's (two) o'clock.
E ora (două).   ye o·ra (do·wə)
Quarter past (one).
(Unu) şi un sfert.   (oo·noo) shee oon sfert
Half past (one).
(Unu) şi jumătate.   (oo·noo) sheezhoo·mə·ta·te
At what time ...?
La ce oră ...?   la che o·rə ...
At ...
La ora ...   la o·ra ...

am   *dimineaţa*   dee·mee·ne·a·tsa
pm (afternoon) *după masa*   doo·pə ma·sa
pm (evening) *seara*   se·a·ra
morning   *dimineaţă*   dee·mee·ne·a·tsə
afternoon   *după amiază* doo·pə a·mya·zə
evening   *seară*   se·a·rə

'STREET' ROMANIAN
Here are a few useful terms for getting around.

Aleea	a·le·ya	Avenue
Bulevardul	boo·le·var·dool	Boulevard
Calea	ka·le·ya	Road
Piaţa	pya·tsa	Square
Şoseaua	sho·sya·wa	Highway
Strada	stra·da	Street

Monday	*luni*	loon'
Tuesday	*marţi*	marts'
Wednesday	*miercuri*	myer·koor'
Thursday	*joi*	zhoy
Friday	*vineri*	vee·ner'
Saturday	*sâmbătă*	sewm·bə·tə
Sunday	*duminică*	doo·mee·nee·kə
January	*ianuarie*	ya·nwa·ree·e
February	*februarie*	fe·brwa·ree·e
March	*martie*	mar·tee·e
April	*aprilie*	a·pree·lee·e
May	*mai*	mai
June	*iunie*	yoo·nee·e
July	*iulie*	yoo·lee·e
August	*august*	ow·goost
September	*septembrie*	sep·tem·bree·e
October	*octombrie*	ok·tom·bree·e
November	*noiembrie*	no·yem·bree·e
December	*decembrie*	de·chem·bree·e

TRANSPORT
Public Transport
Is this the ... to (Cluj)?
Acesta e ... de (Cluj)?   a·ches·ta ye ... de (kloozh)
　boat
　vaporul   va·po·rool
　bus
　autobuzul   a·oo·to·boo·zool
　plane
　avionul   a·vee·o·nool
　train
　trenul   tre·nool

What time's the ... bus?
Când este ... autobuz?   kewnd yes·te ... a·oo·to·booz
　first
　primul   pree·mool
　last
　ultimul   ool·tee·mool
　next
　următorul   oor·mə·to·rool

Does it stop at (Galaţi)?
Opreşte la (Galaţi)?   o·presh·te la (ga·lats')

What time does it arrive/leave?
La ce oră soseşte/   la che *o·*ra so·*sesh·*te/
  pleacă?   ple·*a·*kə
Please tell me when we get to (Iaşi).
Vă rog, când ajungem   və rog kewnd a·*zhoon·*jem
  la (Iaşi)?   la (*yash'*)

One ... ticket (to Cluj), please.
Un bilet ... (până la Cluj),   oon bee·*let* ... (*pew·*nə la kloozh)
vă rog.   və rog
  one-way
  dus   doos
  return
  dus-întors   doos ewn·*tors*

How much is it?
Cât costă?   kewt *kos·*tə
How long does the trip take?
Cât durează călătoria? kewt doo·re·*a·*zə kə·lə·to·*ree·*a
I'd like a luggage locker.
Aş dori un dulap de   ash do·*ree* oon doo·*lap* de
  încuiat bagajul.   ewn·koo·*yat* ba·*ga·*zhool
Is this taxi available?
E liber taxiul?   ye *lee·*ber tak·*see·*ool
How much is it to ...?
Cât costă drumul   kewt kos·tə *droo·*mool
  până la ...?   *pew·*nə la ...
Please put the meter on.
Vă rog, daţi drumul la və rog dats' *droo·*mool la
  aparat.   a·pa·*rat*
Please take me to (this address).
Vă rog, duceţi-mă la   və rog doo·*chets'·*mə la
  (această adresă).   (a·che·*as·*tə a·*dre·*sə)

Private Transport
I'd like to hire a ...
Aş dori să închiriez o ...   ash do·*ree* sə ewn·kee·*ree·*ez o ...
  bicycle
  bicicletă   bee·chee·*kle·*tə
  car
  maşină   ma·*shee·*nə
  motorbike
  motocicletă   mo·to·chee·*kle·*tə

petrol/gasoline
  benzină   ben·*zee·*nə
I need a mechanic.
Am nevoie de un   am ne·*vo·*ye de oon
  mecanic.   me·ka·*neek*

I've run out of petrol.
Am rămas fără benzină. am rə·*mas* fə·rə ben·*zee·*nə
I have a flat tyre.
Am o pană.   am o pa·nə

TRAVEL WITH CHILDREN
Is there a/an ...?
Este/Există vreo/vreun ...
*yes·*te/ek·*sees·*tə vre·*o*/vre·*oon* ...
I need a ...
Am nevoie de ...
am ne·*vo·*ye de ...
  baby change room
  loc pentru a schimba un scutec pentru copil
  lok *pen·*troo a *skim·*ba oon *sku·*tek *pen·*troo ko·*peel*
  car baby seat
  scaun special în maşină pentru copil mic
  skown *spe·*chee·al ewn ma·*shee·*na *pen·*troo ko·*peel* meek
  child-minding service
  o persoană care să aibă grijă de copil
  o per·so·*a·*nə *ka·*re sə a·*ee·*bə *gree·*zhə de ko·*peel*
  children's menu
  meniu pentru copii
  me·*nyoo pen·*troo ko·*pee·*ee
  disposable nappies/diapers
  pampers/scutece de unică folosinţă
  *pem·*pers/*skoo·*te·che de *oo·*nee·kə fo·lo·*seen·*tsə
  infant milk formula
  lapte praf pentru copii
  *lap·*te praf *pen·*troo ko·*pee·*ee
  (English-speaking) babysitter
  un babysitter care vorbeşte engleza
  oon *bey·*bee·see·ter *ka·*re vor·*besh·*te en·*gle·*za
  highchair
  scaun special la masă pentru copil
  skown *spe·*chee·al la *ma·*sə *pen·*troo ko·*peel*
  potty
  oliţă
  o·*lee·*tsə
  stroller
  carucior de copii
  kə·roo·chyor de ko·*pee·*ee

Do you mind if I breastfeed here?
Vă deranjează dacă   və de·ran·zhe·*a·*zə da·*kə*
  alăptez aici?   a·*ləp·*tez a·*eech'*
Are children allowed?
Copii sunt acceptaţi?   ko·*pee·*ee soont ak·chep·*tats'*

LANGUAGE

Glossary

These handy Romanian words can also be used in Moldova. Hungarian (Hun) is included for key words.

ACR – Automobil Clubul Român
Agenţia Teatrală – theatre ticket office (Hun: színház jegyiroda)
Agenţie de Voiaj CFR – train ticket office (Hun: vasúti jegyiroda)
alimentară – food shop
Antrec – National Association of Rural, Ecological & Cultural Tourism
apă caldă – hot water (Hun: meleg víz)
apă rece – cold water (Hun: hideg víz)
astăzi – today
autogară – bus station (Hun: távolsági autóbusz pályaudvar)
autostrada – highway

bagaje de mână – left-luggage office (Hun: csomagmegőrző)
bandă roşie – red stripe (hiking)
barcă cu motor – motorboat
barcă cu rame – rowing boat
berărie – beer house
biserică – church (Hun: templom)
biserică de lemn – wooden church

cabana – mountain cabin or chalet
cale ferată – railway
cameră cu apă curentă – room with running water
cameră matrimonală – double room with a double bed
casă de bilete – ticket office (Hun: jegyiroda)
cascadă – waterfall
căsuţe – wooden hut
cazare – accommodation
CFR – Romanian State Railways
cheile – gorge
Crăciun – Christmas
crap – carp
cruce albastră – blue cross (hiking)

de jos – at the bottom
deschis – open (Hun: nyitva)
de sus – at the top
dispecerat cazare – accommodation office
drum – road, trip

en detail – retail (shopping)
en gros – wholesale (shopping)

floare de colţ – edelweiss

gară – train station (Hun: vasútállomás)
grădină de vară – summer garden
grind – sand dune

ieşire – exit (Hun: kijárat)
închis – closed (Hun: zárva)
intrare – entrance (Hun: bejárat)
intrarea interzisă – no entry (Hun: tilos belépni)

jos – low, down

mâine – tomorrow
mănăstire – monastery (Hun: kolostor)
meniu – menu
metropolitan – the head of a province of the church
muzeu – museum (Hun: múzeum)

noapte – night
notă (de plată) – bill (Hun: számla)

orar – timetable (Hun: menetrend)

păduri – forest
pâine – bread
parter – ground floor
pensiune – usually denotes a modern building or refurbished home, privately owned, that's been turned into accommodation for tourists
peron – platform
piaţa – square or market (Hun: főtér or piac)
piatră – stone, rock
plecare – departure (Hun: indulás)
popas – camping ground (Hun: kemping)
primărie – town hall
punct galben – yellow circle (hiking)

sală de concert – concert hall (Hun: hangversenyterem)
scaun de WC – toilet (Hun: toalett)
schimb valutar – currency exchange
scrumbie de Dunăre – Danube herring
Sistematizire – systemisation (Ceauşescu's scheme for bulldozing entire rural villages and shifting inhabitants into purpose-built agro-industrial complexes on city outskirts or into concrete block buildings)
şosea – road
sosire – arrival (Hun: érkezés)

spălătorie – laundrette (Hun: patyolat)
spălătorie auto – car wash
stradă – street
stufăriş – reed bed
sus – up

ţară – land, country
telecabină – cable car
teleferic – cable car
telescaun – chairlift
teleski – drag lift
terasă – terrace

toaleta – bathroom
traseu – hiking trail
triunghi roşu – red triangle (hiking)

vamă – customs (Hun: vámkezelés)
vilă – denotes a 19th- or 20th-century two- or three-storey house; many have been refurbished and turned into dwellings for tourists
vin alba – white wine (Hun: bor fehér)
vin roşu – red wine (Hun: bor vörös)

zi – day

Behind the Scenes

THIS BOOK

This 4th edition was written by Robert Reid and Leif Pettersen. The 1st edition of this guide was written by Nicola Williams, who, with the help of Kim Wildman, also researched and wrote up the 2nd edition. The 3rd edition was written by Steve Kokker and Cathryn Kemp.

This guidebook was commissioned in Lonely Planet's London office and produced by the following:

Commissioning Editors Fiona Buchan, Laetitia Clapton, Will Gourlay

Coordinating Editor Chris Girdler

Coordinating Cartographer Tony Fankhauser

Coordinating Layout Designer Tamsin Wilson

Managing Editor Imogen Bannister

Managing Cartographers Mark Griffiths, Adrian Persoglia

Assisting Editors Michelle Bennett, Janice Bird, Nigel Chin, Laura Gibb, Charlotte Harrison, Sally O'Brien

Cover Designer Rebecca Dandens

Project Manager Chris Love

Language Content Coordinator Quentin Frayne

Thanks to Sally Darmody, Craig Kilburn, Yvonne Kirk, LPI, Catalina Papuc, Trent Paton, Celia Wood, Monica Zavoianu

THANKS
ROBERT REID

Many thanks to the can-do travel agencies, hostels, hiking guides, national park guides, apple-givers, high-fivers, direction-pointers and pizza-makers around Romania. And to all the LP readers who sent in such great suggestions from the last edition.

Some big names to thank in Romania include Alis in Bucharest, Cipriani in Braşov, Alina at DiscoveRomania (Braşov), the USAID folks around Braşov, Mr Laurentiu of Făgăraş, Sorian of Sibiel, Andre and Mihaela at Pan Travel in Cluj, Robert and buddies of Odorheiu Secuiesc, Johan at Green Mountain Holidays, the party people from Oradea who warmly allowed me crash their weekend vacation plans and Saskia Bellem for photographing prehistoric bugs. LP-wise, thanks to Fiona Buchan for the gig, Will Gourlay for answering probs, Chris Girdler for editing, Tony Fankhauser for making the maps and Arsenal fan Stephen Palmer for dodging duty in London's LP office to accompany me a few days in Székely Land. Another big thanks to Leif for being a great coauthor and constant source of information, enthusiasm and humour. And thanks to Mai for letting me travel and making me get a cellphone.

LEIF PETTERSEN

Foremost thanks go to Catalina Papuc for her tireless efforts and assistance when I came a whisker away from being vanquished by Romanian bureaucracy. In Chisinau, Marina Vozian's telephone resourcefulness and Vitale Eremia's speedy and detailed emails saved my behind. I'm in eternal debt to Tanya Tsurcan whose tenacity, wit and flirting skills got me into, and more importantly out of, Transdniestr. In Suceava, Ciprian Slemcho rescued me before I could seriously consider pushing my car off a bridge and Tatiana Hostiuc's vast knowledge of Bucovina and careful detail contributed mightily to the Moldova

---

THE LONELY PLANET STORY

The story begins with a classic travel adventure: Tony and Maureen Wheeler's 1972 journey across Europe and Asia to Australia. There was no useful information about the overland trail then, so Tony and Maureen published the first Lonely Planet guidebook to meet a growing need.

From a kitchen table, Lonely Planet has grown to become the largest independent travel publisher in the world, with offices in Melbourne (Australia), Oakland (USA) and London (UK). Today Lonely Planet guidebooks cover the globe. There is an ever-growing list of books and information in a variety of media. Some things haven't changed. The main aim is still to make it possible for adventurous travellers to get out there – to explore and better understand the world.

At Lonely Planet we believe travellers can make a positive contribution to the countries they visit – if they respect their host communities and spend their money wisely. Every year 5% of company profit is donated to charities around the world.

chapter. The lovely Daniela at Info Litoral Tourist Information Centre in Mamaia gave me hours of her time (and incessant follow-up emails) as we discussed the entire Black Sea coast. Thanks to Katie Mardis in Minneapolis for moral support, ad hoc fact checking and pertinent highlights from *People* magazine. In London, I'm indebted to Fiona Buchan and Will Gourlay for holding my hand though my first LP assignment and pacifying various nervous breakdowns triggered by ceaseless car trouble, snow storm delays and bureaucratic impasses. Finally, special thanks to Robert Reid whose advice and cool confidence provided balance to the chaos and snowballing exhaustion that engulfed us.

OUR READERS

Many thanks to the travellers who used the last edition and wrote to us with helpful hints, useful advice and interesting anecdotes:

A Cujba Adriana, Arnon Arbel, Bev & Joe Atiyah, Arne Augedal, **B** Bruce Bachman, Emily Bengels, Andrew Bennett, Miles Benson, Henrik Berlin, Julia Boff, Agnes Boonstra, Kendal Bradley, Nicolae Braguta, Jean Brasille, Katie Brown, Jolanda Brunt, Heather Bull, **C** Donna Callan, Sara Caplain, Tony Chamberlain, Paula Cipolla, Sebastian Comsa, Edward Congdon, Lucy Cooper, Chiriac Corin, Matthew D'Arcy, Sylvain de Crecy, **D** David del Rocco, Herman & Laurens den Dulk, Mario Desiderio, Aldo Diethelm, Justin Dodge, Bill Dost, **E** Christer Ericsson, **F** Lars Floter, Paul Flowers, Thomas Folkerts, Lucian Fratila, Rebecca Friedman, Addie Fryeweaver, **G** Marius Gafen, Andre Gagnon, Tom Gallagher, John Garrick, Gabi Geist, Natasha George, Marco Germani, Ferdinando Giammichele, Peter Goltermann, Peter Grapne, Caroline Grogan, Raoul Gunning, **H** Craig Haig-Prothero, Johan Hallberg, Graham Harman, Tineke Heek, Tracey Henriksen, Don Hindle, Ruth & Tony Housden, Tracey Hughes, **J** John Jackson, George Johnston, Benedikte Jørgensen, **K** Mary Kaschak, David Keyes, Brigitte Kindler, Peter Knorr, Jan Kotuc, Natalia Kudimova, **L** Tanja Laier, Karl-Heinz Laschke, Heike Lichtenthaler, Marilyn Lim, Sarah Lister, Michelle Little, Choi-Bing Liu, Marc Lobmann, Andrea Luca, **M** Vladimir Macarov, Nick Mahieu, Scott Malyon, Paolo Mari, Adam Marius, Marius Marius, Fab Marsani, Michael Mates, Matt McCaw, Charlotte Medeiros, John Miles, Peter Moore, Stephen Morris, Valentina Moshe, Kate Murray, **N** Stephen Nelson, Diana Neuner, Michel & Miranda Noordman, **O** Paul Offermanns, Alexandra Ohlenschlaeger, Elisabeth & Gunthard Orglmeister, Matt Osiecki, Lenneke Oudkerk, Jeroen Overduin, **P** Rolf Palmberg, Tudor Pantelimonescu, Robert Patterson, Maarten Pieterson, Andrei Popa, **Q** Nick Quantock, **R** Andrea Racz, Marlene Radolf, Dee Randolph, Robert Redpath, Anja Remmits, Astrid Richter, Heather Roberts, Julian Ross, Sergiu Rudeanu, Romana Rusa, **S** Constantin Salagor, John Slevin, Wendy Smith, Fenellia Smyth, Patricia Spark, Roland Sprenger, Nicholas Stoian, Ethan Stone, Jonathan Strauss, Roberto Suarez, Matthew Swadener, Edwin Sypolt, **T** Ronnie Tamosiunas, Melanie Taylor, Jo Terrell, Bartek Tomalik, Francesca Toniolo, Janne Tornberg, **U** Rahel Uster, **V** Jan-Willem van der Rijt, Johan van Uffelen, Doina Visinescu, Vicky Vladic, **W** Jan Wasserman, David Weightman, Joshua Welbaum, Dean Whitmore, Caroline Williams, Hywel Williams, Isobel Wilson, **Y** Daniel Yang, Kin Yip, **Z** Sarah Zarrow

SEND US YOUR FEEDBACK

We love to hear from travellers – your comments keep us on our toes and help make our books better. Our well-travelled team reads every word on what you loved or loathed about this book. Although we cannot reply individually to postal submissions, we always guarantee that your feedback goes straight to the appropriate authors, in time for the next edition. Each person who sends us information is thanked in the next edition – and the most useful submissions are rewarded with a free book.

To send us your updates – and find out about Lonely Planet events, newsletters and travel news – visit our award-winning website: **www.lonelyplanet.com/contact**.

Note: we may edit, reproduce and incorporate your comments in Lonely Planet products such as guidebooks, websites and digital products, so let us know if you don't want your comments reproduced or your name acknowledged. For a copy of our privacy policy visit www.lonelyplanet.com/privacy.

Index

INDEX

000 Map pages
000 Photograph pages

INDEX

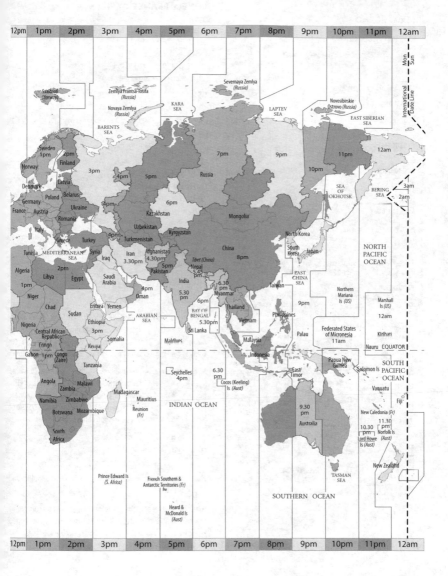

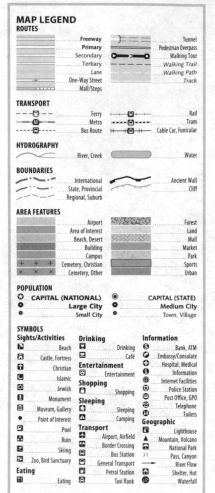

MAP LEGEND
ROUTES
Freeway	Tunnel
Primary	Pedestrian Overpass
Secondary	Walking Tour
Tertiary	Walking Trail
Lane	Walking Path
One-Way Street	Track
Mall/Steps	

TRANSPORT
Ferry	Rail
Metro	Tram
Bus Route	Cable Car, Funicular

HYDROGRAPHY
River, Creek	Water

BOUNDARIES
International	Ancient Wall
State, Provincial	Cliff
Regional, Suburb	

AREA FEATURES
Airport	Forest
Area of Interest	Land
Beach, Desert	Mall
Building	Market
Campus	Park
Cemetery, Christian	Sports
Cemetery, Other	Urban

POPULATION
◉ CAPITAL (NATIONAL)	◉ CAPITAL (STATE)
● Large City	● Medium City
● Small City	● Town, Village

SYMBOLS
Sights/Activities
Beach	
Castle, Fortress	
Christian	
Islamic	
Jewish	
Monument	
Museum, Gallery	
Point of Interest	
Pool	
Ruin	
Skiing	
Zoo, Bird Sanctuary	

Eating
Eating	

Drinking
Drinking	
Café	

Entertainment
Entertainment	

Shopping
Shopping	

Sleeping
Sleeping	
Camping	

Transport
Airport, Airfield	
Border Crossing	
Bus Station	
General Transport	
Petrol Station	
Taxi Rank	

Information
Bank, ATM	
Embassy/Consulate	
Hospital, Medical	
Information	
Internet Facilities	
Police Station	
Post Office, GPO	
Telephone	
Toilets	

Geographic
Lighthouse	
Mountain, Volcano	
National Park	
Pass, Canyon	
River Flow	
Shelter, Hut	
Waterfall	

LONELY PLANET OFFICES

Australia
Head Office
Locked Bag 1, Footscray, Victoria 3011
☎ 03 8379 8000, fax 03 8379 8111
talk2us@lonelyplanet.com.au

USA
150 Linden St, Oakland, CA 94607
☎ 510 893 8555, toll free 800 275 8555
fax 510 893 8572
info@lonelyplanet.com

UK
72–82 Rosebery Ave,
Clerkenwell, London EC1R 4RW
☎ 020 7841 9000, fax 020 7841 9001
go@lonelyplanet.co.uk

Published by Lonely Planet Publications Pty Ltd
ABN 36 005 607 983

© Lonely Planet Publications Pty Ltd 2007

© photographers as indicated 2007

Cover photograph: Hungarian ethnic Csango blind violin player and stepson playing gardon in Ghimes, Transylvania, Nick Haslam/ Alamy. Many of the images in this guide are available for licensing from Lonely Planet Images: www.lonely planetimages.com.

All rights reserved. No part of this publication may be copied, stored in a retrieval system, or transmitted in any form by any means, electronic, mechanical, recording or otherwise, except brief extracts for the purpose of review, and no part of this publication may be sold or hired, without the written permission of the publisher.

Printed by Hang Tai Printing Co. Ltd
Printed in China

Lonely Planet and the Lonely Planet logo are trademarks of Lonely Planet and are registered in the US Patent and Trademark Office and in other countries.

Lonely Planet does not allow its name or logo to be appropriated by commercial establishments, such as retailers, restaurants or hotels. Please let us know of any misuses: www.lonelyplanet.com/ip.

Although the authors and Lonely Planet have taken all reasonable care in preparing this book, we make no warranty about the accuracy or completeness of its content and, to the maximum extent permitted, disclaim all liability arising from its use.